The Girls
We Leave
Behind

JEROME BEATTY, JR.

The Girls
We Leave
Behind:

A TERRIBLY SCIENTIFIC
STUDY OF AMERICAN
WOMEN AT HOME

Drawings by Tomi Ungerer

DOUBLEDAY & COMPANY, INC.
GARDEN CITY, NEW YORK

Library of Congress Catalog Card Number 63–16623
Copyright © 1963 by Jerome Beatty, Jr.

TABLE OF CONTENTS

The Girls
We Leave
Behind

I

Enter, Analyzing

As a result of a paper published several years ago in the now-defunct *Southern Literary Messenger,* I was offered a grant by a well-endowed, non-profitable foundation to elaborate on my subject. The article had shown that, in pilot studies conducted in the home of the author, married women now exercise a deleterious effect on our society, delaying the march toward more perfect democracy as well as hindering progress toward improving intrafamily relations.

The United States of America Institute for Applied Research* asked me to carry this theme through in a full-length study, despite obstacles that would have discouraged a more timid outfit. One, for example, was that I had originally limited myself to white, American, Protestant females for the first paper. This had aroused a bitter controversy among the readers of the magazine, which was published in Charlottesville, Virginia. Actually, in the scientific sense, it was not a true controversy at all: all the attackers were on one side. The editor of the *Southern Literary Messenger* then assigned another investigator to do a new study, which absolved those villains I had defined and which, had it run, would have proved that non-white, non-Protestant women of foreign origin were at fault.

Unfortunately the publication was a quarterly. Before the second survey could be printed, the presses were smashed by persons unknown and the editor had escaped back to Bridgeport, Connecticut, his hometown.

A second unusual feature of my paper was its attempts to link the ups and downs of such economic yardsticks as Gross National Product, recessions, and freight car loadings, to a twenty-eight-day cycle. This struck closer to home than prudence called for, perhaps; the female readers of *Messenger* canceled *en masse*.

In spite of or maybe because of the violent reaction in *SLM,* the USAIAR offered me the task of delving deeper into the matter. I did so, reporting back a year later with a six-thousand-page analysis, *Modern Married Women and Their Good and Bad Influence on American Men and Children and*

---

* Not, despite the name, an official government organization, nor is it connected with the U. S. Testing Co.

2

Institutions. Generally speaking, it bears out the conclusions of the original account in the Charlottesville publication: this generation of females has extended its suzerainty to all corners of the capitalist world.

It has been done by gradual encroachment, beginning in the area where we are the weakest: the home. In this, the seventh decade of the twentieth century, the American custom is for the man to abdicate for hours and days, even weeks, his traditional authority as head of the house. At first, this catapults the woman into direct contact with duties quite beyond her capabilities—child care, homemaking, charge accounts, etc. She soon masters them by a peculiar process.

Shrewdly and intuitively the young mother fashions stopgaps. These have become established over the years as basic foundations of our society. The absence of a man throughout the entire day, much of the evening, and often for a weekend, too, offers a woman unlimited opportunities to improvise. *Improvisations,* then, become S.O.P. Psychiatrists, pediatricians, lovelorn editors, teachers, religious leaders, and other amateurs are called on or in. The question that occurs most often in our sample: "What went wrong?"

What goes wrong is simply enough explained: the husbands and fathers disappear every day and leave the women in charge.

Here are some of the permanent components of modern village life that began as temporary expedients:
1. Having the children buy their lunch in the drugstore.
2. Fixing a broken bra strap with a safety pin.
3. Rye on the rocks before noon.
4. Cashing checks at the dry cleaner's.

3

5. Letting the husband make his own way home from railroad station.
6. Rinsing garbage scraps down the kitchen drain.
7. Buying a birthday cake.
8. Skipping through a book or setting it aside without finishing it.
9. Lying to and cheating husbands and baby-sitters.
10. Driving the car with four pounds of air in the tires.

Here is one of the few human situations where the exception has turned solidly into the rule. The hit-or-miss practices of suburban life have become accepted. They are so familiar that we no longer question them. There was a time, of course, when more reasonable and sensible philosophies were expected.

The reader may wonder how with limited resources I am able to put in a nutshell, and with such discernment, the deceptions used by the other sex. It must be remembered that a year or more study lies behind these revelations. It began with a scientific-type session in the Red Carnation Bar & Grill on New York's Avenue of the Americas where I interviewed many members of the male sex, certainly the most reliable source of factual information on the subject. These men, commuters, were immediately alert to the possibilities inherent in my project.

"I'm sure glad you came to me," said Jack Q. Flanagan, of Mount Kisco, New York. "A lot of researchers would be inclined to question the wives themselves about their habits, and that would be misleading. Naturally they're not going to condemn themselves for the public prints. Another thing— women simply cannot see themselves objectively.

"For example, our wives actually believe they are efficient and domestic, when the exact opposite is the case. Your theory that they are malevolent is perfectly sound. The more you get into it, the more you'll see. I think I'll have another."

While Flanagan was getting the waiter, I scribbled fast to get down all the facts he had offered.

"You want to know what Evie is doing?" he asked, looking at his watch. "She's brewing coffee. Has to have a pot on the stove all day long. She's constantly washing, cleaning, and refilling the percolator. You know why she percolates it? *Because she can't make decent instant coffee!* Something goes wrong every time. It's either boiling the water, spooning out the powder or stirring it that defeats her. She just doesn't have a green thumb, I guess."

Flanagan's was just one of the many case histories that were volunteered as I stayed on in the Red Carnation and word got around. I supplied the drinks and the men supplied the data. The bartender, a bachelor, seemed immensely pleased; every so often a round was on the house. As the research sessions wore on, a great schism manifested itself. There was little disagreement on the Theory of Female Malevolence but there was some doubt as to whether the trait was innocent or deliberate.

"My wife wants to sabotage the whole human race," an otherwise placid husband stated candidly. That was one school of thought. The other is that the wife does not realize what she is doing. There was considerable evidence on both sides.

A model husband, a man of the second persuasion, offered testimony. He had gone home one Friday evening looking forward to a quiet weekend. At the door his wife met him and threw into his arms a wet copy of the previous Sunday's New York *Times*. His knees buckled as he tried to hold the huge soggy mass while she shouted at him: "You march right down to the news store and return this. Tell them if they think they're going to charge me for it they're crazy!"

5

She wouldn't let him into the house.

"You see," he explained to me, "on Sunday the delivery boy had placed the paper on the front porch. Well, we never use the front porch. When the paper hadn't come by noon Denise was hopping mad. She called the stationers and bawled them out, canceling our subscription. They insisted the paper had been delivered. I had to go out and buy a *Times* somewhere else. Then on Friday someone used the front porch for the first time and found the Sunday paper— five days old. I had to carry it back to the news store. They wanted to know why we never use the front porch. It was embarrassing."

This subject, like many others, took great satisfaction in the knowledge that he is fulfilling a function, that his wife respects him enough to pass her antagonisms along to him. It makes him feel wanted, he said, when his wife uses him to avoid humiliation for herself. There was a further incident which illustrates this.

Denise, the wife, rushed out of the house one Saturday morning, late for an engagement at the beauty parlor, and jumped into the car. "It was resting peacefully in the garage where it should have been," said her mate. "She let the starter groan, over and over; she choked it so that the smell of gas permeated the neighborhood; she fussed, fiddled, and cursed; the engine wouldn't catch."

Just at this moment her husband blissfully rounded the corner, wheeling a barrow of topsoil and thinking, as he said, that all was right with the world. Denise leaped from the car, ran out into the driveway, and intercepted him with an irascible cry:

"Oh, Jim, for goodness' sake—why did you park the car here of all places? Now it won't start!"

This took place in a little town overlooking Long Island

Sound. Jim felt rewarded, he reported, that it was a Saturday, so that he could be there to handle the crisis. On a weekday, she would have phoned him at the office to bawl him out.

Day after day, case histories like this piled up at the Red Carnation. Seldom if ever has one segment of the population had an opportunity to reveal so much about another. When I explained the helpful nature of my project, the men were eager to tell their innermost and most dearly held secrets, if it was in the cause of science. Eventually, I knew, I would have to do some fieldwork and track down suburban wives in their lairs, where they alternately growled and purred at each other, prowling back and forth on jungle errands of erratic or erotic description.

At this stage, however, I preferred to remain in the metropolis and, to continue the metaphor, interview the great white hunters. This preparation was essential for the safari.

Certainly one of the most useful sources I encountered was Dr. Scotford K. K———.* Dr. K——— conducts a profitable business in New York. He is a psychiatrist, ministering exclusively to men in the "communications field." That is, he specializes in the problems that beset advertising executives, magazine editors, television producers, and the like. What's more, he limits his practice to commuters—those Philip Nolans who shuttle back and forth between home and office without ever making the scene at either one. Dr. K———, a busy man, opens his office early in the morning for the patients who come directly from Grand Central Station. Late in the evening his couch is still warm.

For professional reasons, of course, Dr. K——— remained circumspect, giving out only the names and addresses of the

* I cannot use his full name.

people he described, but carefully avoiding any discussion of how many appointments he has per day, how many pay cash, and how much he charges.

"A doctor must be discreet," he explained. "The Internal Revenue Service, you know."

Speaking off the record, Dr. K—— said that the twentieth-century American housewife has made a shambles of family life. Almost every case he handles boils down to similar causes. Once it was the Moms; now it is the Wives.

"They're out there right now," he said, pointing in the direction of Westchester County, "carrying on machinations that warp the very marrow of the bones of man."

This was putting it very strongly, I thought. Interviewing Dr. K——'s patients, I began to see what he meant.

"I was a rewrite man on a Boston paper," one young chap volunteered, staring into his dry martini. "We were out on the sidewalk in front of the house and we had an argument. I thought the fight was over, because my wife leaned on my arm to keep her balance as she bent over and took off a shoe. She straightened up, looked at me a moment, and then swung. I put up my arm to fend off the blow and the heel caught me right on the elbow. I yelled 'Ouch! Ouch!' and the fight was over.

"The next day my arm was swollen and sore. She had dented a vital funny bone or something. For four days I couldn't do any work. Hit a typewriter with one finger of the left hand? A rewrite man? Impossible. Well, I was like Herb Score after he got that baseball in the eye. I couldn't even type again very good. I had to quit the job and come to New York. What gets me is her leaning on me for support while she takes off her shoe to conk me."

The wife's influence on the male's career is something that

looms large in his mind. Most have heard the saying, "Behind every successful man is a —— wife." But he is not sure what the adjective is. It couldn't be "nagging" or "spendthrift" or words on that level. It must be that every successful man owes a lot to his "co-operative" wife or his "rich" wife or his "charming" wife. But there is no way to be certain. The survey found evidence of this enigma everywhere, one that haunts American white-collar workers: exactly what kind of wife do you have to have behind you to be successful?

There is available, however, significant material on the kind of wife one need *not* have behind one in the interests of one's career. Dr. Scotford K. K—— opened his files to me to clarify this. The raw data can be shown by the following table:

Who is responsible for your present career status?	Wife	I Am	Don't Know
ASKED OF: Men with income Over $25,000 yearly	2.1 %	47.8 %	50.1 %
Men with income Less Than $5000 annually	95.6 %	0 %	4.4 %

The woman not only influences the salary scale, but the success or failure pattern as well.

Arnold M——, whose work as a magazine editor required him to bring work home every night, told me of the obstacles he was forced to overcome at home in his rise to the pinnacle of success in the field. His wife deeply resented the fact that he showed up each evening with two or three manila envelopes stuffed with manuscripts, notes, correspondence, and

9

other important papers. As he had to do his work on the dining room table, he would quickly gulp his dinner, shove the dishes aside, and dump the contents of the envelopes out.

"She was unfair about this," he said. "When we had people for dinner, she wanted me to forget my homework. She'd hide the manila envelopes. Once I found them, after hours of searching, under the corner of the rug in the spare bedroom. One night I sat at the table working, typing out some notes on the portable, while the guests were in the kitchen helping Nancy with the dishes. I was going along fine when suddenly she stalked in, picked up the typewriter, and threw it across the room. Naturally, it was smashed. Well, I couldn't do any more work that night. In fact, I never took work home again. Nancy, incidentally, had to fix the portable out of the food money."

Six months later Arnold's job vanished into thin air along with his magazine, *Collier's*. He has never said so in so many words, but he is inclined to connect it with his failure to carry work home at night.

My research sessions at the Red Carnation Bar & Grill lasted for some weeks. Upon completion, I took stock of the information I had garnered. Several points were obvious:

One, a well-known conclusion, was that the mainstream of American life flows in what is known as the suburbs. There our people love, live, laugh, and cry. Especially cry.

Another, less remarked, is that this area is a vast wasteland insofar as the male population is concerned. Males do much of their loving, living, and laughing in the cities. Only an appreciable portion of their crying takes place at home.

Again, what is known is that men are well informed regarding the circumstances that prevail when they are at home. Their comprehension of the motives and behavior of their women is uncanny, precise, objective. However, they are away from the home so much that a plateau of ignorance exists

10

on which they seldom tread. This is the daily life of the women they leave behind.

To continue my studies, then, I started to make field trips into the interior. At this point, this study will on occasion adopt another tone. I found it more useful to pass as a writer, living and working in suburbia, than as a man of science. If, at times, a certain note of informality creeps in, even of something less than proper methodology, this should be taken for the guise that it is.

II

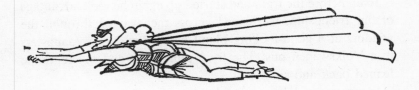

The Space-Age Spouse

"May I share this?" a voice said.

I was sitting next to a window aboard one of those trains that rattles through the jerkwater towns of Connecticut and Westchester County each morning, picking up a strange collection of men and leaving them off at Grand Central. I don't ride these trains much, but I knew well that—except for the rude ones in the bridge car—according to the Commuter Code, you always ask the person at the window if you can sit on the other half of his seat.

The gambit, a mere six or seven years ago, was "Is this seat taken?" Now one finds a growing percentage of young fellows using "Share this?" because of its U nature. "This seat taken?" is mostly confined to Norwalk, New Rochelle, and places like that.

When I heard "Share this?" I knew that we were probably near Darien. I nodded and mumbled and a fellow with thin lapels and a fat stomach sat down, partially on the tail of my jacket, pulling me over to one side. He apologized, gave a little leap into the air, and I deftly snapped my coat out from under. Thus we became buddies for the entire trip to New York.

Even before the train had started up again he took advantage of our friendship. He leaned across me, waving through the window at a good-looking blond woman and two youngsters in a Volkswagen bus. The train pulled out and my seatmate leaned back and smiled.

"Once again I leave all I hold near and dear. Car, checkbook, liquor supply, white shirts. I got no complaints."

"And you owe it all to the mother of your children," I said, getting into the spirit of the occasion.

"I sure do," he agreed with emphasis. "She's in Akron living with her parents and working in the library. This was my second wife you saw." He jerked a thumb toward the rear.

In a burst of candor, the fellow then unfolded the most amazing tale of country life I had ever heard.

"I got out of the Navy in 1946," went the confession. "I went back to Yale, got my degree, and married a Vassar girl whose father was a stockbroker living in Greenwich. Everybody had expected it. Big wedding. Ten years later we had those two kids, the house, and I was working my tail off

14

for my father-in-law. Only one trouble—I never saw my wife or the kids. They weren't up in the morning, and at night the children were in bed and the wife had already had a couple of martinis by the time I got home. Let's face it, we just didn't get along at all.

"She never got my breakfast, and dinner was usually Franco-American something-or-other. She couldn't cope with the kitchen. There was an ironing lady and a cleaning lady and a baby-sitter for a couple of days of the week. I know that because I paid for them. When I tried to telephone her during the day, the phone was either busy or she was out. Plenty of times I walked home or bummed a ride from the station because she wasn't there to meet me. Even after we got a station car, half the time she wouldn't let me have it because her own buggy was in the repair shop, usually the result of her having driven it with the hand brake on for a day or two, or else for having parked it on a grade with the hand brake *off!*"

As our train glided through such communities as Port Chester, Rye, Larchmont, my newfound companion described a long list of indignities and sufferings to which he had been heir. It was to his credit that he refrained from placing the entire blame for his misery upon the woman herself. He felt that perhaps the system was as much at fault as she was. Nevertheless, his magnanimity was not sufficient to hide the real culprit.

"By 1957," he went on, "our account was overdrawn most of the time. It was impossible to know this except when the notices came from the bank. The check stubs were so mixed up and wrong we had long past given up doing any adding or subtracting. I think the last straw was when both the children were held back in school one year. I then realized the horrible truth—you cannot run a home and a family if you are going to be around only on weekends. Most men leave this huge responsibility in the hands of a woman who is utterly incapable of it. It is a tragic error.

"Do you appreciate the fact that American husbands entrust everything to a wife who has been chosen on irrelevant grounds? You're a callow youth. You see this female across a crowded room. Zing! go the strings of your heart. A few years later that slip of a girl carries the key to every compartment of your life, from the deep freeze to the safe deposit box. It's incredible."

This perceptive chap had, of course, stumbled onto a great discovery. The institution of marriage, in the latter half of the twentieth century, is different from what it was a generation ago. Once there was a custom known as courtship. A system of checks and balances kept boy and girl in suspended animation until protocol had been complied with. After the ceremony, then, a husband had a feeling that wisdom had been exercised by someone, even if not himself, and that the match was a proper one.

In addition, there were mothers-in-law, maids, kindly family doctors, aunts and other busybodies who kept looking in on the married couple, who, as often as not, lived with or near their families. A man did not frivolously dump the responsibility for his whole existence into the lap of his wife— he dumped it into the hands of the community of relatives and friends, so to speak.

I reflected on the crafty manner in which women have insinuated themselves into our lives, as my companion continued his story.

"Yes," he mused, "I imagine my existence was typical in this respect. Our love ripened into companionship, our companionship into mutual respect. Nothing is deadlier for a happy marriage than mutual respect. Fortunately the Anglo-

American system of law has made it possible for numerous husbands to salvage their domestic lives by a drastic but sure method—divorce.

"I shall spare you the ugly details except to point out that when the chips are down in a legal action of this sort, a woman's true colors are exposed. Threatened with the loss of her powers, she flagrantly misuses her bargaining strength. My spouse was reluctant to relinquish such hard-earned rights as having been named beneficiary of a will and a life insurance policy. She wrung from me costly concessions: money from the past, money from the future, and the children four months of the year. It was a one-sided arrangement, but if it leads to domestic tranquillity, it bespeaks well of the institution of unmarriage. It also indicates the sacrifices a man is willing to make to regain his freedom."

Only a couple that had mutual respect for each other could come to an agreement of this kind, it was obvious. Unfortunately, three-fourths of the marriages in the United States fail to be dissolved this way. Most of them go on until the demise of one of the partners (usually the male). Studies have shown that the average housewife is eminently satisfied with her hold upon the family unit. More lenient divorce laws, combined with stricter regulation of marriage requirements, would do much to alleviate the deteriorating picture.

As Dr. Fabio Grobart, Resident Psychiatrist of the Flamingo University Marriage Center, put it:

"If American women were more reluctant to get married, and more willing to get divorced, there would be more happy people than there are."

Although I interviewed Dr. Grobart long after my encounter on the train, it was remarkable how both men had arrived at essentially the same conclusions, one by scientific method and the other by intuition. Dr. Grobart told me:

"An analysis of the criticism of the divorce explosion in the United States reveals that most of it is inspired by women. Studies show that the rate would be higher if the wife were more co-operative."

In the chart below, for example, one can easily see the trend. These statistics show what is holding back the breakup of more marriages.

Divorces Unconsummated because of Non-co-operation by:	1910	1930	1960
Male Spouse	11 %	8 %	3.9 %
Female Spouse	.9 %	44 %	67 %

These reports from the famed Flamingo U. Marriage Center show better than mere words how many marriages are deliberately prolonged by willful obstinacy of the female partner. They show why three out of four marital unions are denied relief in the divorce courts.

Frustrated and confused, a man who finds himself tied down this way devotes himself to a career or a hobby. He picks these carefully, making sure that neither is suitable for his wife's participation. Sad to relate, the American male seems willing to abdicate his traditional fief to a presentee landlord, taking refuge in outside activities. An outstanding example of this escapism is the commuter. Despite his complaints about traveling to and from work, he finds the life ideal. The morning train carries him up and out of the routine at home, putting light years between him and "Alcatraz." He eventually becomes utterly satisfied with a setup where he can have a couple of days a week at home and the other five out of sight and out of mind.

All of which could seem difficult to accept but this is proven by the sight of desperate commuters trying to reach work in cases when there is a storm, a strike, a delay. Do they sit back and use it as an excuse to stay home? No, they go to extremes to get to work, often arriving at the office earlier than usual. At the end of a working day, a man is always striving for the opportunity to prolong it, to catch a later train home than normal, while giving the impression he's rushing for it. (This takes practice.)

The wise gentlemen who talked to me on the New Haven Railroad train was fortunate enough to (1) see the issue and (2) face it squarely.

"It was apparent," he explained, "that I had not chosen my life's mate with enough care. She had developed into a typical suburban housewife and mother—an opprobrious species in my estimation, given to lassitude, neglect, and egoism. There was an easy answer: find the right person for the job.

"After the split, of course, my father-in-law fired me. I quickly lined up a job for more money with a research outfit that used IBM machines for everything. It then dawned on me how modern methods could be applied to solving my problem. Most men exercise more wisdom each time they study a menu than they did when they chose their wives. Nowadays, with aptitude tests, psychiatric examinations, motivation research, IQs, color preference charts—with all these available there is no reason why a fellow can't come to the right decision, just as in buying a car or making any other investment."

Briefly, what happened was that the guy deliberately searched for a wife and mother who would be efficient, lovable, honest, and old-fashioned. He found this good-looking young thing that he had waved farewell to from the train.

"She gets my breakfast every morning," he beamed proudly. But I had already surmised it. He breathed hickory-smoked bacon on me for an hour.

Although that happily divorced commuter seemed to offer a lesson for men in the same position, it became apparent as I looked into it that the most rewarding and useful study would be that of married men and women who cling together. But first I had to ascertain just what it has done to our nation to allow wives so much freedom. Briefly, the upshot has been not only to create imperfect circumstances at home, but to affect the health of the country as a whole.

A careful look at the Statistical and Historical Yearbook of the United States shows this.

Taking 1920 as the most likely date from which to start (because of the advent of woman's suffrage at that time), we find a most amazing situation: *the increasing incidence of such grim aspects of our times as juvenile delinquency, automobile theft, murder, suicide, arson, mental breakdown, and political thievery is in direct proportion to the increasing license and emancipation afforded females.*

Without going into the actual numbers, let it merely be noted that in the past forty years there has been a startling growth in the percentages of women lawyers, women policemen, women judges, women doctors, women teachers, women psychiatrists, women politicians, and women realtors.

During those very same years, our prison population has tripled.

On the other hand, there are no female locomotive engineers. And train travel is the safest form of transportation.

Thus it goes, page after page of statistics that bear out

the conclusion drawn by isolated husbands as well as by scientists in their spotless, well-appointed laboratories. To prove the theory, I have plotted on the charts in Figures I and II a small sampling of the results obtained by matching (1) female freedom with (2) growth in non-allied but associated fields.

For instance, we took the number of joint banking accounts in which husband and wife were co-owners, and then laid this alongside the crime statistics on felonies. The similarity was striking, as can be seen, in the table following.

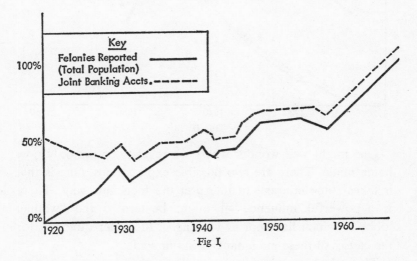

Fig I

Merely at random, I chose the reports of how many new psychiatric clinics were being built over the last forty years. *The percentage of these clinics compared to all hospitals was remarkably close to the percentage of women voters in the population as a whole.* I made a similar comparison of room mothers and incidence of small business failures. The chart shows the shocking truth.

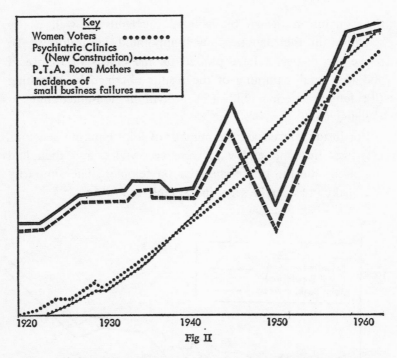

Key

Women Voters ●●●●●●●●
Psychiatric Clinics
(New Construction) ⊶⊶⊶⊶
P.T.A. Room Mothers ▬▬▬▬
Incidence of
small business failures ▬ ▬ ▬ ▬

| 1920 | 1930 | 1940 | 1950 | 1960 |

Fig II

One might well wonder why such revelations are only now being made. There are two possible explanations. One is that it takes some courage to interpret the facts this way. There is a powerful influence—it might be termed the "woman lobby"—which has kept us looking in the other direction for the causes of these malignancies in our society.

The other explanation is startling: the American house-wife and mother has been caught up in the rapid developments of the space age. She used to change gradually from one generation to another. The way our mothers lived and carried on in the late Thirties and early Forties has become a source of amusement if not serious study. The way young women emerged from World War II and re-formed family battle lines is well known.

22

What is not generally noted, however, is that the past ten years have wrought more new scenes and new characters than the fifty years before. Community life in the 1960s is as different from 1950 as it is from 1910. The suburban wives of this era have absolutely nothing to do with, nothing to learn from, nothing to recall of their counterparts of earlier times. They are in complete charge of the world from the day they appear. And they must take the blame for it.

The wave of young marrieds landing on the beaches is poles apart, in behavioristic terms, from the Old Guard, the ones who had their first babies right after World War II and infiltrated the suburbs when they (the suburbs) were a lot more rural than they are now. The newcomers have leveled the woodlands and mobbed the classroom, the store, and the hairdresser.

The awareness of and the resentment at being pushed aside by promising rookies is expressed in the words of one observer who said:

"The little creatures suddenly show up, all equipped with a ranch house, a husband, a baby, a station wagon, a big dog, a helluva lot of ideas, and unlimited energy. When I was her age London still hadn't been rebuilt, my husband's uniform still fitted him, and no one had ever heard of the Diners' Club. What's more, I spent all my time raising children and taking care of the house."

(That last remark, of course, was merely a reflex. All women believe they do nothing but care for the children and the house. This particular woman has always had domestic help of one kind or another.)

In the same town with her resides a girl in her twenties who took her four-year-old son to see *La Dolce Vita*. She explained that since the film was in a foreign language he would not be subjected to any dirty words that he could

comprehend. However, she did want him to see what deca-
dent Italian living was like.

Her husband's reaction, when he heard what she had done,
was par for the Space-Age Spouse. He accepted it. What
else could he do?

"I can't really blame her," he said. "I'm gone most of the
time. She's in charge. What can I expect? I walk out and
leave her behind each day."

III

Salvaging One's Marriage for Fun and Profit

Not long after I has begun field trips into Suburbia, Bill Rasdale requested another conference. I remembered Bill well. At the Red Carnation interviews he had recounted one of the most harrowing tales of female arrogance.

On the previous New Year's Eve the Rasdales attended a festive party at a friend's place. The evening was ending when a pretty thing who had come unchaperoned re-entered to announce that she couldn't get her car started. It was cold and snowy outside. Betty Rasdale thereupon shoved her husband out into the middle of the room and shouted:

"Bill'll take ya home. Go ahead, Bill."

Bill dragged himself out to his own car and drove the young lady to her house. She got out, thanked him, and went inside. As he started turning around in the driveway he skidded off a small bridge and into a little stream that borders the property. It was 3 AM. There was nothing to do but mush back to the party. When he told Betty, she hit the ceiling. They had to walk home. She let him have it:

"Irene lives two blocks away. *She* gets a ride and I have to tramp a mile through this slush."

"It was your idea for me to drive her. I didn't want to," Bill protested.

"You jumped at the chance and you know it!" she retorted with what Bill decided was feminine logic.

Now Bill Rasdale was asking for a summit meeting. And rather than the RCB&G, he wanted to take me to the Hotel Algonquin. He must have some marvelous new material for me, I thought. I was wrong. He was a disturbed person who needed help.

Bill is—I should say "was" for he now lives in California— a commuter's commuter. He had been chosen, for example, as the representative on the 8:37 to take up a collection for the rear-end trainman whose lanterns had been stolen.* That he was willing and able to sit down and have three drinks in the middle of a weekday afternoon shows the stuff of which he is made, the kind of leadership that sets a course for others to follow.

I had no idea what he had in mind. The proposal was bizarre, and he had the sense to break it to me gently. It was brazen enough: he wanted me to check up on his wife and find out how come she was away from the house a lot during the day and wouldn't tell Bill where. Once she had shouted at him that she was attending an exercise class and it was none of his business.

"I want to believe her, but I can't," he blubbered. (This during the third drink.) The reason she needed no exercise was something we both knew. "I can only conclude that she is involved in some peccadillo."

This kind of language, it came out, resulted from his having read a book, *Adultery on the East Coast*.* His suspicions of his wife's behavior became more corrosive after skimming a paperback by Evan Hunter. He told me all this at the Algonquin that day. My notes have the dialogue word for word. Here are pertinent excerpts:

* Quite a few regular passengers would not contribute, suggesting that the gin-rummy player who stole the lanterns should pay for them. .
* Little Blue Books, Boston, 1890.

BILL: You got time for a quick one, haven't you? (*Strains neck looking for waiter. Bangs bell with palm of hand.*) Where the hell is the waiter? (*Leans elbows on table. Rubs both hands over eyes.*)

ME: What's the matter with you? Job got you down?

BILL: I don't know. Partly that, I guess. Mostly it's this problem at home. Like today, I was going home early but I phoned and no one was there to meet me, so I've got to wait for the 5:12.

ME: Home early? I thought commuters always telephoned and said they'd be home later. I didn't know anyone ever went home early. (*Waiter arrives. Stands apathetically and silent.*)

BILL: Martini all right for you? Two martinis on the rocks. With lemon peel! (*Exit waiter.*) I heard that, about the commuting. Just because you don't ride the trains is no reason to get funny. If you want to know, what's eating me is that whenever I call home Betty's never there. Well—I don't mean *never*—but lots of times. (*In confiding manner.*) She's always at that exercise class.

ME: Exercise class? She's built like Tina Louise right now. What does she have in mind?

BILL: Well, she says she wants the Jackie Kennedy look.

ME: They'll have to operate.

(*Waiter arrives with drinks. Throws down paper napkins, stirrers, popcorn, glasses, check.*)

BILL: (*Gulping.*) Say, do you know of any exercise class that meets so often—for wives out there? You've been nosing around in the suburbs. What do you hear?

ME: Nothing, except the once-a-week sodality at the Nugatory River Country Club. They wear leotards and take beach towels with them, the floor's so dirty. But that's for the ones who just had a baby.

BILL: (*Fingering moustache. Finishing most of drink.*)

Last week I tried to find out from Betty where she might be during the afternoons and she became touchy. *I'm* the one who should have been touchy. After all, I'd been trying to reach her for a couple of hours. Want another drink?

ME: Okay.

(*Bill bangs bell, twirls index finger over glasses when waiter looks in our direction.*)

BILL: So she yelled at me. It isn't as though I want her to hang around home all day waiting for my phone call, but I should think she'd be expecting some word as to what train I'll be on. (*Waiter serves drinks.*)

ME: Why not take the same train every day?

BILL: Impossible. Always a meeting. Boss lives in town. Apartment. *He* don't have to catch train. Gets home in ten minutes. (*Rasdale's speech pattern when he's drinking is interesting. His speech becomes clipped, rather than slurred like other people's.*) Fathead calls meetings at 4:30! That's when most commuters start thinking about leaving. Straighten out the desk. Avoid answering the phone so's not to get involved in something. Go to men's room. Wonder about sneaking out ten minutes early and grabbing the 4:59. So if the nut gets us together about 4:30 or 4:45, I quick have my girl get through to Betty, tell her I'll be on the 6:02, can't make the 5:23. So she's not home. Three days in the past week I'm standing at the station bumming rides home. Once in the rain.

ME: All these figures confuse me. You mean she didn't even come back down to get you after you weren't on the early train?

BILL: Don't you get it? I have to call each day to say *what* train I'll be on. I'd sure like to hear where that exercise class meets.

ME: I wouldn't know.

BILL: (*Whining.*) It's got me so frustrated, that's all. I'm so nervous I've stopped taking Ramona to lunch.

ME: Who's Ramona?

BILL: That's my secretary. Ramona Pappagallo. She's nineteen. Dumb as they come. . . . (*After a silence.*) Now, here's what I was thinking. You're wandering around out there getting material about women, aren't you? How about a little private-eye job? Tail her for me.

ME: (*Choking.*) What! I never heard—! Rasdale, you're crazy! I'm not getting involved in anything like that. How many of those drinks have you had? Listen, I'm getting out of here. (*Standing.*)

BILL: Oh, you writers make me sick. (*Disgusted.*) You never want to do anything that sounds like *work*. No wonder you don't know a good story when you see it.

Although I never agreed to Bill's plan, his criticism touched me in a sensitive spot. If Betty Rasdale was conducting a clandestine love affair at teatime, and if I was worth my salt as a researcher, I owed it to myself to look into it. After all, the destruction of the contemporary American family by its women was a primary theme of the investigation. Here, as Bill pointed out, might be a good "story."

It was, therefore, not entirely an accident that my forays into the suburbs often led me to cruise past the Rasdale house in the late afternoon. Sure enough, I was rewarded one day by the sight of Betty hightailing it out of the driveway and down the road at the wheel of her aging convertible. I sped after her. She ignored a stop sign and took off in the direction of the next town. After a few miles we crossed the line, where these huge proud words stand high: "You Are Now Entering the Hatband City of Southern Connecticut!"

Thanks to traffic, I was able to keep up with my quarry,

right up to the point where she parked in the shopping center in the middle of the business district. When she got out of the car wearing sneakers and slacks and with no lipstick and with her hair a mess, and when she skipped across the street and into the YMCA, I envisioned a most uninteresting sort of "peccadillo."

It was then four o'clock in the afternoon. I parked, put a nickel in the meter, went across to the Y, and, without much difficulty, found Betty in the basement. She was there with five other females. They were playing Ping-Pong.

Some rendezvous! According to the bulletin board, three times a week, from four to five, they give lessons. As I stood there, contemplating the results of my detective work, Betty spied me and came over, looking concerned.

"Hey, what are you doing here?"

"Nothing. Looking for the blood bank. What are *you* doing here?" I pointed. Half the females were standing at one end of their tables while the other half were on their knees trying to poke balls out from under couches and chairs. One girl was trying to remove a dent from her Ping-Pong ball by heating it on the radiator. Betty glanced at them, turned back to me and told me a tender story, first swearing me to secrecy.

It was a case of saving her marriage. Bill, table tennis champion of Pi Omicron Omega three years in a row when he was at college, had set up a table in his house the year before the incidents I am describing. Betty, who had majored in domestic science at Wellesley, thought paddles were for making butterballs. Bill hadn't the patience to teach her the game. He associated only with Ping-Pong hotshots.

Many Saturday nights, she told me, some of the guests would be sitting around in the living room while Bill would be downstairs, and you could hear the ball going plop-kerplop-kerplop-kerplop-ker, as he monopolized the Ping-Pong players. Usually it was doubles, but one night the town's bachelor came along with an exchange student from Sweden. Ingrid was eighteen years old and a sort of Miss Universe type. She grabbed a paddle and skunked the Pi Omicron Omega champion at his own game.

He was delighted as well as undaunted, Betty explained. From then on, it seemed to her, it was Ingrid and Bill at the net almost all the time. There were pathetic interludes when, to be a good sport, Ingrid took on Betty. Bill fidgeted and smirked on the sidelines during the slaughter.

Then Betty heard about the YMCA course and signed up. She was there at least three times a week afternoons. That's why Bill couldn't get her on the phone at times. During the rest of the day she could often be found in the basement of her own home practicing serves and kill shots, the cleaning lady standing with eyes closed at the other end of the court holding a paddle, as a kind of dummy target for Betty's twisting and slashing fore- and backhands. A few more months of intensive practice, she felt, would see the greatest upset in suburban Ping-Pong annals. She was planning it as a surprise for Bill.

This story has no known ending, for the Rasdales moved to the West Coast. I never told him what I had found out.

The Rasdale Case was a revelation to me. It opened up a whole new original field for examination: the *wife's* point of view. I had collected voluminous files based on the factual data supplied by the men. They were, of course, in an excellent position to observe what the young mothers of today are up to. Now it occurred to me that—as in the Rasdale Case—the stories might well have other angles than the 180-degrees carefully drawn by the fellows at the Red Carnation, on the trains, at the cocktail parties I had begun to attend, etc.

I vowed to pay as much attention as I could to the female conception of things without prejudicing the original conclusions already arrived at. As it turned out, from then on I obtained all my information from the girls themselves—the matriarchs of the suburbs. It was lots more fun.

IV

The Ironic Curtain

Running across lessons in table tennis where I had hoped for a wife's lessons in love brought me up short. How many more times would the male version of what's happening Meanwhile-Back-at-the-Ranch-House turn out to be a warped one? Or merely a different one? Then which would be the correct one?

Could it be possible, I pondered, that a sympathetic eye

could be cast in the direction of the distaff? Were some of my lively interviews at the Red Carnation going to wither under probing? This seemed unlikely, since the witnesses had sworn—to a man—that they were objective.

Nevertheless, in the interests of science, I continued to go out to our control group: the women, the pale spirochetes of the suburbs, multiplying and devouring each other in the agar jelly.

One of my first encounters was with a young wife named Ginger Burrell. She was on her way to the beach, pushing a stroller with some small human being in it. Mrs. Burrell was wearing her bathing suit, which she kept hitching up here and pulling down there.

"I heard what you were up to," she admonished. "I suppose Gil told you a story about how I made him miss the plane to Phoenix. That's one of his favorites."

He had. It was a vivid account of how his wife had barely gotten him to Idlewild on time. In the rush she had forgotten his briefcase, necessitating a re-scheduling of the trip. Gilbert Burrell referred to it as a classic example of female incompetence.

"Yes," I replied. "But I wouldn't worry about it. It can happen to the best of us."

This seemed to infuriate her.

"Would you like to know what really happened?" she shouted, her brown eyes flashing. "I was *hectic* all that morning, trying to get Gil ready for the drive to the airport. He fooled around *interminably*. He even decided to oil his .22 before he *packed*. Can you *imagine?* He has just absolutely *no* sense of time. *Finally* we got going. By speeding I reached the airport in time, and with relief watched him go through the gate."

"What about the briefcase?"

"Oh, we had the briefcase with us, all right. But, I tell you, I'm not infallible. It just so happens that in the confusion I neglected to take Gil's hand and curl his fingers around the handle of his briefcase. So he walks onto the plane without it. What kind of businessman is this, anyway?"

I pushed the stroller for a few minutes while Ginger Burrell calmed down and continued her account. She was halfway home on the parkway, not having waited for the takeoff, when a taxi came alongside. Her husband was leaning from the window and flagging her down. Both vehicles pulled over.

"You forgot my briefcase," he said as he ran up. There it was in the back seat.

"*I* forgot *your* briefcase!" Ginger echoed in disgust. Then, to her complete amazement, he jumped into the front seat.

"Let's go," Gil said.

"*Let's go?*" she screamed, squirming around and looking back. "Where the hell is the taxi?"

Gil had dismissed the cab, which returned empty to its stand at the airport. Ginger had to turn around and drive Gil and his briefcase ten miles back over the same route, to catch the next plane. His itinerary was off all along the line.

She and I walked silently toward the beach for a while. Then she asked, "Did he mention the time I made him cut the grass?"

"No."

"I guess there wasn't a decent angle for him to exploit. But why don't I tell you about it and you can sort of put it down in your notes."

It happened last spring. One Saturday, after she had been after him all day to mow the lawn, Mrs. B. finally realized that he just wasn't going to do it. As they dressed to go out to dinner, she remarked crankily:

"I don't ask you to do much around here. You'd think you

could cut the grass once in a while. You'll go sailing tomorrow, which means it'll be another week before you—"

"Aw, pipe down," Gil grumbled.

As usual, Ginger was ready before her husband. She sat
in the car waiting, shouting every so often, "Hurry up! We're
late!" Finally she heard a familiar noise, coming closer and
closer. It sounded like a put-put. Around the corner came
Gil, dressed for the party—light blue Rogers Peet washable
jacket, white shirt, regimental tie, charcoal gray Bermuda
shorts, knee-length socks, black loafers. He steered the
power mower before him. Back and forth he went for half
an hour. Ginger Burrell sat there, bemused. When he was
finished, Gilbert Burrell had to take another shower and put
on a clean shirt and socks. Then he sat down and spent ten
minutes scraping grass out of his shoes and cuffs.

Gosh, I was miserable when Ginger concluded this story,
because the fact was that Gil *had* mentioned it to me, but
I'd hate to tell you how different his version was.

After a few more experiences like the one with Mrs. Burrell, it became apparent that the writer had a *Rashomon*
on his hands: as many different explanations of the same
event as there were witnesses to it. Every time I spoke to a
housewife whose husband I had already interviewed, she
brought up the same incidents as he had—but with an alternate interpretation.

Not only was there this confusion of propaganda and truth

about known matters, but there was a tremendous lack of information about unknown ones, unwitnessed events. That is, each man and wife was sure he or she knew what the other was up to all day long, during the exact hours when they seldom made any sort of contact whatsoever. An ironic curtain of ignorance hangs between the working male and his stay-at-home spouse regarding the daytime activities of each.

Yet not once did a husband fail to snap out an answer when I asked him what his wife was doing back home at this particular moment.

"She's at Bloomingdale's in Stamford," stated Jim Van Dorn, assuredly.

"How do I know? She's always there, taking clothes back."

Later checking proved him to be wrong. Anne Van Dorn remembered clearly that she had not been to Bloomingdale's that day. In fact, the reason she remembered it so well was that it was the day she had not been to Bloomingdale's.

"You'll notice where Jim was when he told you about me," she said sarcastically. "In a bar and grill somewhere."

"Yeah, I'll tell ya where Jane is," Bert Disley had replied to the question. "At the percolator, that's where."

"Well, really!" Jane Disley huffed a few weeks afterward. "If I can't have a cup of coffee once in a while. . . . Do you want to know what's he doing right now? He's eating lunch, and he'll still be eating lunch two hours from now."

That is when I began asking the ladies a similar question about their husbands. Lunch seemed to loom strongly in all the replies. As far as I could see, the wifely notion is that a man goes to the office to get ready for lunch. He then eats lunch and returns to the office to get ready for the trip home. Mrs. Van Dorn even volunteered a list of Lunch Remarks that her husband makes over a period of a week or ten days.

"Today I had lunch with . . ."

"I ate lunch at Maria's today. . . ."

"Oh, gee, I had the same thing for lunch. . . ."

"I'm not very hungry—had a big lunch. . . ."

"Had a heckuva time getting a cab back from lunch, got wet. . . ."

"Had to have lunch with Ken Brown today. He's getting divorced. . . ."

"Say, honey, next time you're in town for lunch go to La Belle Bouche. Boy, they have the best. . . ."

"Lunch! Lunch! *Lunch!* God, won't he ever stop talking about lunch?" Anne Van D. groaned. "Is that all he does all day? *'Next time you're in town, honey . . .'* Fat chance I'll get in town. And if I'm there for lunch there'll be so many martini-drinking executives at La Belle Bouche I'll never get a table. You walk into one of *their* luncheon spots with a girl friend and they all glare at you as if you were trying to desegregate the Mississippi legislature. Besides, do I have a charge account at every high-priced eatery in the city? Lend me his credit cards and maybe I will get to La Belle Bouche. Until then I'm afraid it's Schrafft's and the 99-cent Special or The Bird Cage, no tip."

For Ellen G—— the lengthy lunch hour has an annoying corollary: it does not diminish Harold G——'s appetite at dinner time.

"He doesn't work all day," she said. "He eats all day! Catches the 8:37 every morning, so he can be at his desk before the ten o'clock coffee break. I've heard that he jumps off at Stamford for milk and a Danish while the train pauses there. Home on the 5:31 every evening, and with three hours for lunch at La Fonda yet! You figure it out. How long does that give him for desk work?

"So I claim he should have a peanut butter sandwich and a cup of tea for supper, but he wants the works. Like Baked

Grapefruit with Cherry, for dessert. And if there is no saucer under the plate the grapefruit's in, then the whole deal's off —tilt, house collects all bets—I lose!"

She slapped her forehead, closed her eyes, leaned back and groaned while I admired her little conceit, in which Mrs. G—— apparently implied that her domestic life was a giant pinball machine—she the sucker and Harold G—— the croupier, I guess.

A very young woman who goes by her middle name— Sheldon—because her parents wanted a boy named Robert, disappointedly christened her Roberta, and called her Bert for nineteen years—that young woman said that she was not particularly upset about her husband's lunch hour because he eats in the company cafeteria and there is absolutely nothing worth bringing home from that encounter. However, Sheldon confided, she would like to know what happens in the afternoon between closing and the time of his arrival at the front door.

"Whenever he calls and says he'll be late, I just *know* he's not giving the real reason. He usually has a 'meeting' or he was 'delayed when someone failed to keep an appointment,' he tells me. So he's tired and wants to have a drink with the boys on the way to the station. Why doesn't he admit it? Well, we're moving to a suburb fairly far out pretty soon and they have trains with bartenders on them, I understand. Then he can do his elbow-bending on the way home and be on time for dinner for a change."

The little catch in Sheldon's voice when she uttered the quaint phrases "have a drink with the boys" and "elbow-bending" made it clear what her unspoken fears were. She felt sure that her newlywed was still fiddling around with some of his old girl friends, or perhaps dowsing for new ones. The illogic of this theory did not occur to her. He *was* working hard at the office, of course, seeking a raise, promotion, or some recognition. As these rewards come his way over the years, the dowsing might really begin in earnest. Then she will say, "I told you so." Then she will find herself in the big-time competition (where, subconsciously, she may long to be) against opponents such as other women and the lunch hour.

Most females are suspicious, envious, and resentful of their husbands for disappearing into the stimulating environment of the city while they knit up the raveled sleeve of care in a prosaic little community. They rattle dishes noisily, deliberately smoke too much and drink more coffee, shout at children, shop—all in a bewildered, jealous frame of mind that they can't really explain. All they see is this man, dressed to the nines, deserting every morning.

The younger they are, the worse it is. After the private, self-adulatory period of courtship and the extravagance of a honeymoon (physically and financially), a bride has to share her new possession with the "job" or "office" somewhere. It galls. The curtain begins its descent. Wives start their plotting, their revenge, which continues forever.

Whether marital harmony would be promoted by better understanding of a couple's respective daily routines, I did not determine. There is not much evidence that it would. Men show little curiosity about family life, and most women seem to treasure their resentment of their husband's daily defection. The ones I talked to attributed their misconceptions to the fact that "he never talks to me about the office," or some such explanation. This phenomenon is much remarked in other studies. It can be taken as an exaggeration, for the office, as well as the family events of the day, do get discussed. But the *way* they are discussed is probably ineffective. When either party tries to reconstruct a reasonable picture of what the other is up to, he or she goes haywire. These comparisons of case histories—His and Hers—prove this.

I concluded that the proper study of woman is not man. His prejudices might be of interest some other time, but I was supposed to be examining hers. It also became obvious that a woman is principally adept at talking about two topics: herself and other females. Perhaps adept is not so correct as "willing." At times she will disguise certain facts, but usually by the end of the session she has uncovered them. Most often she will reveal everything, and the latitude of the interview is not controlled by her circumspectness but by the interviewer's nerve. How far does he want to go?

Housewives seem to be in perpetual confession. To determine the hidden secrets of their hearts, to locate the wellsprings of their lives, one merely has to ask, and one is told. Their husbands, naturally, never acquire this information, for they seldom request it.

V

Perpetual Confession and Agonizing Self-Appraisal

"Before I married Kenneth I was on a vacation in Maine with my parents and I met a boy who was waiting on table at the inn. We dated a few times. He took me sailing in Penobscot Bay. One day we ran aground near Swan's Island and were stuck there until the tide came in, which must have been about midnight. We got back terribly late. They'd been looking for us all over. My mother and father were very upset."

"Well, did—did anything happen?" I asked, blushing.

"Yes. We returned home early that year."

"No. I mean, out in the boat at night. Anything that should get them upset?" I stammered, sick with apprehension.

"Sure, what d'you think? Also, the centerboard got damaged."

I gripped my pencil too tightly.

"Why do you remember this incident so vividly?"

"It was the last time I ever had any fun," she replied. "Kenneth never runs aground."

Modern girls who go in for perpetual confession disrupt the physiological detachment a writer expects of himself when amassing firsthand information. Where I found it fairly simple to take note of the yarns spun for me by the male commuters I encountered, for I knew they were usually dissembling, I was often shaken by the frankness of their spouses. A woman finds it difficult to fictionalize. A man lies about his job, his money, his drinking—or in whatever field it is that new events occur continually. A woman has to fall back on the same old facts, and what's more, on her own introspection, for material. And there's a dearth of it, too; she uses it up very fast.

The agonizing self-appraisal is a characteristic of the modern female. Just as she is unable to pass a mirror or a store window without looking sideways at her legs or her rear end (inside, the proprietor believes she is studying the displays), and just as she is always tugging at her skirt or pushing a strand of hair back, and just as she is usually thinking, "How do I look?" when someone is talking to her—so the female never ceases staring at the more figurative reflections she casts.

"Who am I?"

"Why am I here?"

"Am I happy?"

"Whither?"

That the questions go unanswered is beside the point. The soul-searching is its own end. In the numerous meetings I had with tormented housewives I always left them in better mind than I found them. Although I never could bring myself to use such an expression as "Get it off your chest," particularly to someone I knew only slightly, perhaps my presence as a scientific reporter lent a sort of Spockian-Freudian air to the proceedings. They unburdened themselves.

One young woman resorted to the mails. She wrote from Elgin, Illinois, about how she had *sat down and thought it all out.*

Oh, those tragic words! If only she could have been warned to avoid thinking things out. But it was too late. Her confession plunged on:

Suddenly I was thirty years old. I asked myself, "Is this it? Is this all there is to life? Taking care of three youngsters and having them run me?"

There go the questions again. I couldn't answer those any more than I could the others. The trouble with confessing women is that they all begin to sound alike after a while.

One did have a solution for her woes. "During the day when he's out of the house," she murmured, "there is an overpowering consciousness of being alone, and a desire to find out what you are and why. Since I moved to the country I have sought the answers. One reads, one philosophizes, and one concludes. There's one book that does the most for someone like me. It gives one the inner strength to carry on, to find out what one is doing on this earth, and those matters are constantly in the thoughts of a wife and mother, I assure you."

"Ah, yes," I intoned, "one reads the Scriptures and one—"

"No, no," she interrupted me, impatiently. "Anne Lindbergh. *A Gift from the Sea.*"

Two insights were produced from this conversation. One is that the Lindbergh book has done more than the Nineteenth Amendment to stir up females. In it the author walks on the beach, picks up shells, and reflects upon the plight of members of her sex.

The second is that the young homemakers of the Sixties are burdened with a serious handicap that most of their mothers did not have: education. The streets and the supermarkets of the suburbs are teeming with girls who have gone to college and, in many cases, who have gone so far as to have been graduated. There are the women who are reading book reviews, book jackets, and even the books themselves. These are the ones who contemplate their navels when their husbands should be doing it for them.

A college girl is so aware of her relationship to the world at large that she makes a restive housewife. She is always cogitating; this inevitably leads to trouble. From this we can postulate an important thesis: the most effective barrier between a woman and a happy domesticity is her brain. Nothing makes a husband more uncomfortable than the possibility that his wife will burst into a discussion of a play, an opera, or a Geneva conference. Nothing upsets the placid ruttiness of life in the country more than a girl whose mind is functioning. She is a poor marriage risk.

One father realized this too late. He told me that he had given his daughter a higher education to improve her chances, so that she would be taken seriously.

"Women are ridiculous," he barked. "My wife is ridiculous.

My daughter is ridiculous. But I thought that by supplying her with a degree she would not be laughed at. I was mistaken."

The girl's four years were spent fruitfully at Sarah Lawrence. Then she married a fellow who had attended the University of New Mexico, where he learned very little except how to behave at a blanket party in the desert. This led to occasions where each considered the other ridiculous. The father's peace of mind has been considerably shattered, as has the marriage.

"*She* should have gone to New Mexico," the old man says, "and *he* to Sarah Lawrence."

When I interviewed her, I carefully refrained from asking the daughter about her marriage. However, she soon volunteered the information. Like other men, I had very poor marks at school. I am the first to be unnerved by a brainy member of the opposite sex. A feeling of inferiority usually causes me to resort to continual lighting, re-lighting, filling and tamping my pipe. This is the best cover-up I know. However, since I do not smoke at other times, there is always a lot of coughing, and hawking and general upset, which on occasion has interfered with the interview.

This time I had no tobacco with me. Therefore, I wrote down everything she said and nodded sympathetically. I have not been able to unscramble my notes since. I haven't the slightest idea what the Sarah Lawrence girl was talking about. She quoted Herman Melville, and I also see a scribble that is underlined: *"Lear was right."* This is all very remarkable when you realize that she was discussing her husband. But for what it is worth, I set down here what must be a significant statement of hers, indicating what the New Mexico blanket major has had to put up with.

"The more brains a woman has the tougher it is for her,"

she burbled. "A young woman spends her time chasing a young man. Having caught him and married him, the intelligent girl is now free, and bored enough, to dabble in intellectualism and relax the emotional tension. This means among other things that she tries to identify rationally with the man she goes to bed with. Well, this is not easy when you're without any source of mental stimulation in sight."

(She looked at me strangely.)

Now, what kind of talk is that? Plainly enough, it's the voluble talk of the Bright Young Housewife of the Souring Sixties. Like any smart person coming upon an old ritual, she observes suburbia with care and figures out what's wrong with it and how she will change it. Nevertheless, at some point along the line, there is the transition to the Period of Resignation: "This is my lot and I'm stuck with it."

I found one who was about to fall over that edge: Laureen, 27, B.A., modern and a mother.

"There's something about this life that has frustrated me," she mused in her Westport kitchen. "Dick and I had so much in common when we were at the University of Illinois together. We surprised each other with the wonder of life and the new knowledge that came to us daily. That was true during the early part of our marriage, too, but then the baby came. Now my day amounts to nothing. I get up, dress, get breakfast, take Dick to the train, come home, have coffee, read the paper alone, try to get the child involved in some inner-directed activity, lunch, take a nap, pick up a bit, and soon it's train time. Then dinner and that's the day.

"I'm panicky. The relationship is gone. I feel irritated when Dick comes home and I have nothing to talk to him about, really. I feel that I have failed, somehow."

Laureen was exhibiting the symptoms of agonizing self appraisal. For her age, she was surprisingly accurate in her

50

adherence to the customary syndrome. She had described her life as a housewife in a way that left her open to accusations of competence. Yet she saw herself as a failure.

One girl I caught in the advanced stages of resignation offered a good example of how female intellects, like lobsters dropped in boiling water, twitch courageously against their environment but finally give in to it. She is Monica Pulver, who had been studying anthropology and had made field trips to different parts of the world such as Mexico, South America, and Greece. She met George, a writer for trade journals, at a Democratic Party rally in Chicago.

"Yes, I'm going to try it," were the bizarre words she used when telling a friend about how she had fallen in love with George. "You two are so happy out here. I think it'll be fun, country life and all that."

So she and George bought a house in a Chicago suburb. It was filled with spears, shields, ebony heads, and a Zuñi fetish. Soon it was also filled with the cries of a boy child, and the paraphernalia that goes with that. In less than two years Monica Pulver had moved from potsherd to potty. It was not a graceful transition, she admits now. The baby made her extremely nervous, mainly because she could never get him out of her lap—or her mind, what with neighbors telephoning and coming around to talk about children and not much else. Even Monica's friend—the one who was "so happy out here"—began to look dull and monsterish.

As for George, he had his own ideas of who was interesting, and it was usually civil engineers and their families. No one wanted to talk intelligently to Monica. She re-enrolled at the university and started after a Ph.D. She became involved in the social life of her fellow students. The little suburban home became a fascinating place, so much so that the neighbors couldn't get in. There were Egyptologists and

Sepik River experts for Monica to consort with, and George had his trade editors and writers to be entertained.

The one who wasn't entertained was the baby boy. He was cared for by a combination of relatives, teen-age sitters and George, who worked at home. He had a diaper rash and one night burned his arm on a hot radiator. But the story has a pleasant ending.

"Mother Nature won out," Monica told me. "One day I thought the boy was starting to stutter. That did it. I quit school and came home for good, where I belong. Now I teach Sunday School and we're having another baby."

The striking thing about the perpetual confession and agonizing self-appraisal of wives, both young and old, is their lack of hypocrisy. They are utterly sincere in their desire to purge themselves and thereby achieve Nirvana. Of course, it is a fruitless ambition. Even if a woman found The Answer one day, something would come up that night and the next morning she would be puzzled again. My advice would be for her to understand that she and all others like her tread common ground. She is not isolated in her foxhole; on the contrary, there are myriads of others like her. If they all stuck their heads above the ground at the same time they would see how unalone they are.

Nevertheless, soul-searching is a necessary adjunct of her existence, and to save the busy housewife a lot of time the following test has been devised by a Dr. Hoyle. The advantage of it is that the correct answers keep changing as time goes on. (This phenomenon is known as dynamism.) The purpose of the test is to permit the subject to examine her position *vis-à-vis* her family, her community, her world, without the painful experience of rehashing old incidents to deduce the secret of life. This test, when taken—as it should be—along with one or more friends, acts as a soporific.

THE PERPETUAL CONFESSION AND AGONIZING
SELF-APPRAISAL TEST

Rules: In the company of one or more friends of the same sex, answer each statement True or False without consulting with the others taking the same test. When all participants have finished, determine upon which answers there is disagreement. These are the departments in which you are weakest. Analyze each other's reasons for answering as you did. Repeat the test at six-month intervals and with different partners. It will be seen that no answers remain constant, and that the discussion of each helps to clarify the matter.

1. I am working harder than housewives did in the past.   T   F
2. My friends are taking it easier than anyone could possibly imagine.   T   F
3. A woman is endowed with some special magic.   T   F
4. I find fault with myself when I shouldn't.   T   F
5. A woman should never correct her husband.   T   F
6. I could be an excellent cook if I had the time.   T   F
7. I make a better mother than several people I could name.   T   F
8. My husband's work is interfering with our marital happiness.   T   F
9. I am probably going to get cancer of the breast.   T   F
10. After I'm gone, they'll wish they hadn't spoken to me that way.   T   F

Where does this leave us in our study of the American housewife? Can we make use of her verbal extravagances to discover what it is that ails her? Can we pin her down to some basic matter, rather than flying along with her through clouds of generalities?

These are the questions I put to myself as I listened to confession after confession. Fortunately the answers were positive. Her happy propensity for telling everything gave me the opportunity to steer the dialogues into specific fields. Every day, I found, she was tilting at the same windmills; she was saddling the same bronco over and over again. A definite pattern was emerging that made it possible to see what was eating her.

The ugliest sore of suburban suffering is rubbed raw and re-opened thrice daily: at mealtimes. In the next chapter we shall see its horrors inherent in that hated chore, common to the maternal instincts of the species, feeding the faces of the family.

VI

Three Square Snacks a Day

What's the Latin for "avoid, avert, avail"? It should be blazoned on the culinary coat of arms of the American wife. In a good-natured, resigned, lackadaisical way she applies herself to mealtimes with those imperatives in mind. In other words, there are three ways of coping with the monster that threatens three times daily:

One way is merely to sidestep it. As we shall see, breakfast is a typical example.

A second is to turn it aside. The threat of lunchtime is put down by this method.

Third, she finds some tangential offshoot, some red herring, some substitute, some expedient. The dinner specter is often appeased this way.

A research team from the Rocky Mountain School of Nutrition completed a shattering survey in 1961. Curiously, their findings have received little publicity. They revealed, among many startling statistics concerning the nation's eating habits, that the average housewife prepares 17.4 meals per week for her family. Since in a seven-day period one would expect at least 21 meals (minus one here and there because of being invited out or eating at a public restaurant) the figure is shocking. To maintain an *average* of 17.4 a huge number of women have to be serving a lot fewer than that.

I am not as jolted by these figures as you might expect, for I know how the average housewife keeps the meal ratio low: she simply avoids at least one a day, as per her coat of arms. A friendly female relative asked me to spend a day in her home to observe her food preparation procedures. "Come about 11:30," she suggested.

"About *when?*" I squinted. "I'm interested in breakfast, too, you know."

"Breakfast?" Her jaw dropped in disbelief.

Women stopped getting breakfast long ago. There was a time when the menfolk did a couple of hours' work before sitting down to a groaning board at about 10 AM to put away a thousand calories. In those days there seemed some sense and urgency to the meal.

Today the brief moments between awakening and blast-off in the American family are hardly enough to allow for lengthy fueling operations. The romance of the breakfast meal is gone, except in several outlying districts where they hold incongruously to outmoded customs.

Fern McClure sat in her tiny Morris County (N.J.) breakfast nook and growled, "Why should I fill their bellies with food they are going to digest elsewhere?"

Her reasonable attitude seems to be fairly prevalent. A good many of her ilk, when I spoke of "the first meal of the day," were confused. Some thought I referred to lunch, and a few were unable to distinguish between the terms "meal" and "snack." The principal stumbling block in performing a proper breakfast ritual is the inconvenient hour called for. Most wives see no point in arising earlier than absolutely necessary.

"Most women stay in the sack as long as they possibly can," one Joann corroborated, speaking for all. "And preparing some small meal for your husband is not worth getting up for. It's the damned school schedule that does it. That's what drives us out. I have a bus that leaves at the ungodly hour of ten minutes to eight. Last year it was *seven*-thirty. Can you imagine? Of course, many's the time I've been so utterly exhausted that I shouted instructions from bed while the kids got themselves ready for school. But that seldom works out. They forget their homework or their lunch money or something."

I was chatting with another girl about her matinal habits and she said, "I feign slumber."

"You what?"

"I *feign slumber*," she repeated carefully.

Apparently a lot of them, when they hear their husbands stirring and getting dressed, lie very still, hoping that if they are quiet he will disappear. Eventually he does.

I knew there was dry rot in the timbers of the breakfast tradition as far back as my interviews at the Red Carnation

Bar & Grill. In a controlled sample, 98.7 percent of the respondents declared that they had had breakfast that morning. When asked for a description of it, they failed miserably. Many of them, it developed, were speaking of the chicory-laden coffee and cardboard "Danish pastry" they had obtained at one stage of their regular routine, *after* leaving home. A few had been able to find juice, instant coffee or toast here and there in their own kitchens. Most were extremely antagonistic to the idea of those cold cereals that come in boxes, and none of my sample—skimpy it may have been—knew anything about bacon, eggs, pancakes, or anything grand. Not a one had sat down to a delightfully-laid glass-top table in a cozy little dining alcove, while his spouse, charmingly attired in frilly negligee, poised behind him with a silver coffeepot, inquiring, "More coffee, dear?"

Getting him out of the habit of breaking fast early is one of a modern wife's first accomplishments. He is seldom in a position to call for a showdown, and he soon settles into alternatives. Usually it is to satisfy his hunger when he reaches his place of employment. In numerous cases the fellow cannot wait that long and he merely makes his own skimpy meal at home.

The automatic percolator has been a boon to the coffee-loving commuter. *He* can get it ready the night before. I found one home where it is plugged into the self-starting radio in the bedroom. The whole works goes off at once: coffee and alarm. He shaves (electrically) and then comes back in and pours a cup for his wife as well as for himself. She complained to me that the worst feature of this was carrying the pot down to the kitchen and cleaning it every day.

This plaint is fairly normal compared to another I came across rather early one morning. It was ten minutes before eight on a weekday. I wandered into the drugstore to pick up a paper and a young matron was sitting on a stool at the soda fountain. This fountain is generally crowded almost all morning with women buying their own breakfast. This one, however, was having a piece of coffee cake and a Coca-Cola. I soon found out why.

She cannot stand the smell of coffee. It seems her mother used to drink seventeen cups a day. Her daughter had an unhappy upbringing and she now associates neurotic childhood experiences with the odor of coffee. This girl's husband *loves* coffee, but he is never allowed to drink it in the home. He gets up and prepares his own breakfast—minus coffee—then she dresses and runs him down to the station. On the way back she stops in for Coke and pastry. That's how she gets her caffeine every day.

So many husbands have been brainwashed into neglect of that first meal that they are apt sometimes to engage in freakish practices. One Darien adman dissolves a gelatin tablet of high nutritional values in a glass of warm water and then proceeds to work on a "full" stomach. Another eats a peanut butter sandwich and a glass of skim milk. His car pool has practically broken up, due to each member's mad scramble to keep from sitting next to a recently eaten peanut butter sandwich at that hour of the day.

If breakfast is a case of avoiding, then lunch is when the housewife averts. She simply turns aside the repast, if possible. The most popular method is to have the children take their lunches to school. Sadly enough, there is a probem here: one must prepare these lunches before they leave the house in the morning. Some mothers are able to do this. Others cannot, and they provide their offspring with money and permission to walk down to the drugstore and eat there during luncheon recess. On days when the cleaning or ironing ladies are at work, they are drafted to make lunch for the children who come home. The woman of the house takes that day off, as a rule. As children grow older, they attend schools where there are lunch programs.

I cannot leave lunch without reporting a Long Island story, which has not been traced to its source but which everybody says is true. One loving mother became disenchanted with her task, as day after day her moppets complained about what she put in their lunch pails—the eggs were boiled too long or the anchovies were too big—the ham must be imported and the cheese mustn't be too tough. The woman sighed one day and thought about how the only member of the group who seemed satisfied with his meals was the dog. Frivolously she made sandwiches of dog food, adding a dash of lemon juice and some sliced radishes. That afternoon the kids came home without a complaint; in fact, one of them praised mom for the swell sandwich, when she solicited an opinion.

Lunch is a pipsqueak repast, a sporadic unpredictable custom that is not only frustrating in its demands but inconvenient. It kills the day, popping up annoyingly like a commercial in the middle of a television show. Like breakfast, it can be dealt with on the spur of the moment, avoided or averted by minor ploys of one sort or another. But dinner is a different story. Here the enemy forces—members of the family, sometimes reinforced by guests—concentrate their fire. It takes a major defensive maneuver for the suburban slavey to win out. That's why I say dinner is where she "avails" and takes advantage of every possible ruse.

Happily I was able on a certain occasion to piece together a fine example of such conflict. By a lucky combination of on-the-spot reportage and later investigative follow-up, I am able to reconstruct what happened in a *typical* household, where the aim of one adult was to stay home for dinner, and the aim of the other, not to enter the kitchen.

Actually, it was Morris County's Fern McClure who was involved in this contretemps with her husband Rob. As she dropped him off at the station in the morning she mentioned casually that she would be attending a tea party in honor of Carol Kronchmeyer's mother. The story unfolds.

Rob, opening his dispatch case on his knees, preparatory to doing some office work as he rides to town, is unable to concentrate. Another crisis looms. He deduces:

1. Carol's mother is visiting.
2. Therefore, drinks will be served at the tea party, because Carol's mother is a souse. (She starts with rum in the tea, then switches to martinis out in the open.)
3. Therefore, the tea party will go on until the first commuter train arrives from the city: 5:52 PM.
4. Carol's mother constitutes a built-in baby-sitter, and neither she nor Carol (nor Fern) will want to do any cooking after meeting their large quota of spiked tea.
5. Ergo, Carol will want to go out to dinner. (Her mother will see the kids to bed, then pass out for dinner.) She will have to have another couple along because Milton Kronchmeyer, her husband, cannot stand eating dinner alone with his wife.
6. Conclusion, reached by Rob McClure: I do not want to go out to dinner with Carol and Milton. Countermeasures are in order.

McClure is not a successful businessman by chance. He has applied his executive skill to the problem and brainstormed a solution. When he hops off the train that night he feels sure he has the situation well in hand. He also has in hand two cardboard boxes containing mouth-warming delights purchased at a retail bakeshop in the city: a truly delicious lemon meringue pie and fresh-out-of-the-oven seeded rolls. He carries the boxes gingerly by the string and as he drags himself toward the car where Fern waits, he lets his shoulders slump. Before she can move over he falls into the seat next to her.

"You drive, honey, I'm exhausted." It is the Home-Sweet-Home gambit. *"God,* what a day! Can't wait to get home and relax. Hope we're having something good for dinner."

Fern's heart skips a beat. "The clever son-of-a-bitch," she says to herself before she can prevent the epithet from registering on her brain lobes. Aloud, she says, "You poor thing. Give me a kiss." She pretends not to have heard the dinner reference. There is silence as each plans the next parry. Fern drives toward home and suddenly blurts out, "Darling, I've got the most *wonderful* idea!"

Rob is too smart for her. He tosses in the Bakeshop Pass Play, interrupting. "Say!" he fairly shouts. "Here's a surprise for you and the kids. No, we won't open it now. We'll save it!" He keeps up the chatter until they get to the garage and he can jump out of the car, leaving Fern at the wheel, speechless. But only for a moment. When she follows him into the house she does not even wind up before putting one over the outside corner. "Rob," she yells, "Carol-and-Milton-taking-us-out-Clam-Shack-dinner-tonight!"

This is a desperate move on her part. It commits the Kronchmeyers to picking up the check. Of course, she and Carol have made no such agreement. But under the circumstances, Fern feels, Carol will see that it was the only way out. Carol will just have to sell it to Milton somehow, perhaps by cornering him and claiming, "We owe the McClures and we just have to pay them back some way. . . ."

Fern's gamble almost pays off. It stuns Rob. He has to stall for time, which fortunately is available to him as the youngsters come charging toward him. "Whadja bring me, Daddy?" He hands them the packages from the bakery, fumbling at the string while his mind works, precision-like, on his next step. Fern, sensing that she has her tormenter on the ropes, swings again.

"There isn't a *thing* in the house to eat, honey," she remarks.

This gives Rob the new opening he is waiting for. He recalls a similar difficulty years before and decides to try the maneuver he used then: the Oriental Encirclement. This requires that children be present, too, so the stage is set. He straightens up and cries out, with an expansive sweep of his arms:

"*I* know what we can do. I'll drive down to the Chink's, see, and bring back some of that yummy sweet and sour pork, shlimp flied lice, pepper steak, egg foo yong—"

"Oh, boy, Daddy, Chinese food, Chinese food!" The kids jump up and down with joy; the noise level is near-pandemonious.

Fern knows when she is licked. She goes to the phone to call Carol

Much later, when she told me much of the details I have recounted here, she admitted, "I didn't care whether I went out. I just didn't want to have to do any work in the kitchen. It was better this way. I didn't have to find a sitter. Carol Kronchmeyer didn't mind. She went out anyhow."

When Rob gave me his version of the incident, he concluded with the observation that seeded rolls and lemon meringue pie do not go very well with Chinese food.

VII

Through the Cooking Class

"Hear those noises?" a petulant dame asked me one afternoon as I poked about her establishment for the secrets of homesteading. Listening and detecting quite a few sounds, I nodded assent. "Those are hunger pangs," she explained. "They start popping every day right about this time."

She rushed to the cabinets and brought down boxes and bags and bottles—potato chips, fritos, Triscuits, Seven-Ups, etc.—and laid them all out strategically as though she were Rommel booby-trapping Normandy beaches. Pretty soon a phalanx of raggle-taggle gypsies appeared through the doors and fell upon the goodies.

It was nearly five o'clock. "I sure hope it spoils their appetites," their mother told me in disgust.

She is as good an example as any of the way her kind deals with impending repasts. She can putter around the house for hours and still blot from her mind any constructive thoughts about dinner. Her cookbooks and file boxes are all there, with jammed-up tear sheets from the domestic science pages of the home magazines, but few and far between are the occasions when she makes use of them. Reading those chatty recipes and licking lips at the full-color photos of family banquets is a favorite pastime. As she gets hungry, a homemaker's imagination runs riot at these stories, carefully put together by men and women editors who eat most of their meals out.

But when the chips are down, when mere appetite is replaced by the mental image of a gluttonous husband and fussy, finicky children, when the pains of hunger are indistinguishable from the incipient ulcer pains caused by the antagonisms of family life—then flights of culinary fancy crash to earth and simplicity is the keynote. Hamburgers fried in their own fat, home-heated baked beans, TV dinners— that's the speed.

Oh, there are exceptions. There are women who will cook but hate menu-planning. I made sure to follow up the lead given me by a producer of commercials for television, Aaron Stookey. He had praised his wife's cooking, and I investigated eagerly. Rita Stookey admitted that the preparation of meals in her household had been hit or miss until she heard about something known as chicken baked in wine. She discovered that her children would eat chicken seven times a week. Crazy about it.

"Aaron, of course, dislikes chicken," she said. "But look here." She opened a door and showed me a shelf filled with wine bottles. "He loves wine."

So she bakes chicken in a casserole, feeds the kids, and then pours a bottle of red wine over what's left. Aaron gobbles the shreds of poultry to get at the wine. He eats it with a spoon. If possible, she delays serving it until he has had a couple of martinis.

"Now, naturally, I couldn't keep that up forever, much as I wanted to. Aaron was getting suspicious. So I began experimenting. I mean, you won't find anything about this in any cookbook I've ever seen. The idea of disguising things. I learned that pot roast would go over big that way, too. After the boys are through, in goes the burgundy and Aaron will eat. And you know what?" Her eyes brightened with self-satisfaction. "Believe it or not, once I used bourbon instead of wine, and he ate corned beef. And he *hates* corned beef!"

Rita Stookey's experiments have known no bounds. She disregarded all traditions and tried everything. Once she discovered that her kids were so crazy about mayonnaise that they would eat spinach if it were so flavored. This led to more and more applications until now she adds mayonnaise to practically all green vegetables. (Aaron's vegetables, of course, are merely thrown in the main dish with the liquor.)

Involuntarily, at the end of the interview, I wrote the word "Tums" in the margin.

If there is any fallacy abroad concerning the cooking skill of today's young women, it's not that they are exceptionally talented. Nobody I questioned, not even the girls themselves, claimed that American women were being underrated. Most were willing to confess inadequacies in the kitchen.

They just don't care very much. Today, quite unlike times of yore, a man doesn't give a thought to a girl's cooking ability when he marries her. American standards are such that domestic science runs way down the list behind important attributes such as a bride's hair, figure, money, sex appeal, parentage, and that sort of thing. Much attention is given to sexual compatibility, or at least sexual attraction. A husband, therefore, who has laid so much emphasis on what he will find in bed has no right to be disappointed at anything he finds on the table.

There has been so much attention given to the sexual aspects of matrimony that no studies have been made on a more serious problem: the woman's frigidity in other parts of the house. She is more afraid of what will happen in the kitchen than in the boudoir. At least she knows her way around in bed. College has helped prepare her.

Today's kitchens, on the other hand, reflect the housewife's lack of interest in cooking. They are small and sometimes are not even separate rooms. Dining rooms once had all but disappeared from the architectural consciousness. Nothing jars a modern girl so much as a glimpse at one of those old-fashioned homes. She stands before a huge fireplace with hooks and kettles all about and hears the guide say, "And this was the kitchen."

"My God," she thinks, "it has tables, chairs, cradles, butter churns, and *it's the largest room in the house*. What gives? That poor woman must have spent her life here. Work, work, work."

It is only natural that the mid-twentieth-century pioneer would be attracted to the opposite pole: breakfast "nook" and dining "area," for instance. The ideal kitchen is one in which the occupant can stand in one spot and reach everything, including telephone, radio, cigarettes, aspirin, and cooking sherry. De-emphasize the dirty work; that's the builder's motto. The garage and playroom are each large enough to take the place of the old-fashioned kitchen, and they do. Why bother to cook, when you can drink or drive? The progression, in a couple of generations, has been from Galley Slave to Instant Escoffier.

A girl named Kitty Parnell, who has been married six years, knows no more about cooking than what she learned the first few months of her marriage—and she doesn't intend to know more.

"I learned to cook after we were married," she said with pride. "You see, we always had servants at home. I never even went into the kitchen at Tuxedo Park. I understood there were twelve basic meals in the suburbs. I started with the easiest: ham steak. I served ham steak three times a week, until one night Hank said, 'I don't like ham steak that much.' I schooled myself in the variations, and now our basic menus consist of hamburgers, spaghetti, hot dogs, and meat loaf. Oh, once in a while I find something in a magazine, like chicken tropicale." She poked a cigarette into a holder. "That's fried chicken in oranges and peaches, you know."

(I wrote down "Alka-Seltzer.")

Days of reckoning come along when a woman has to entertain to pay back invitations she accepted with alacrity some weeks or months before. Her first thought is a barbecue, which means she can toss a salad and make frozen French fries, leaving the rest to her caveman with his apron, lighter fluid, and charcoal. Most of the time the weather, season, or occasion doesn't lend itself to such goldbricking, and an indoor meal is necessary. She usually relies on her favorite dish: a casserole, a roast, a curry, ham steak. These can be tasty; usually they are adequate. Often they are ruined.

I had heard that the Moroni Youngs were excellent hosts

and it was with eager anticipation that I accepted an invitation to dinner there, traveling all the way out to the country to do so. I first noted that Mr. Young was a teetotaler, but that he tended bar. Either out of revenge or ignorance, his theory was to keep the glasses full. He used no measure; he just poured things out of bottles.

Mrs. Moroni Young kept staggering into the kitchen and out again, whispering to him, "The roast isn't ready; give 'em another round."

By 9:30 she decided to remove the roast from the oven. In the interests of science I went in to watch, and I stayed to help. In taking the pan from the oven, she dropped the dinner on the floor. When we got around to eating it, everyone was so pie-eyed they didn't realize it was practically black, it was so well-done. A few guests said, "I like mine rare." It was a rare occasion, at least.

I was not surprised, some months later, when Mrs. Roy Swift had a similar experience. I concluded that it was rather a commonplace for women to spill the entree. In this case it was a casserole with chunks of ham, macaroni, and other ingredients. Once again I was observing, when the rack slipped—onto the floor. She scraped it up and put it back into the big iron dish. She seemed to be put out at me, for some reason, but I didn't feel very guilty, inasmuch as she described how in another crisis the rack had slipped in the other direction and the food had slipped *into* the oven.

Roy later told me that he keeps his asbestos gloves in the kitchen, rather than out with the rest of the barbecue equipment, because "I'm always rescuing that damned casserole dish."

I thought that if she'd get the rack in place properly this wouldn't happen again, but I didn't say anything.

There are many tricks for sidestepping the heavy responsibility of a dinner party. They range all the way from the extravagance of hiring caterers to the dessert-and-coffee ploy. In the latter, guests are invited to one's house with all the hospitality one can muster, but for dessert and coffee! Men would just as soon eat dinner at home before going out for the final course, but their wives insist on being taken to a restaurant so they can have the full advantage of a night out. When the check comes, it usually includes the cost of dessert and coffee, whether taken or not. This leads to sarcastic talk, and when all the lucky people arrive at the party they are ordinarily in a terrible mood.

But the hostess considers that she has discharged an obligation.

Another instance of "Avoid, avert, avail!" came to my attention in a small town near Cleveland. A young woman invited a lot of friends to her house for dinner to meet some visitors from Texas. Then a week before the party the surprised guests received postcards detailing what they were supposed to do: bring a tossed salad for fourteen; bring chairs; bring a casserole; bring your own liquor, etc. All the hostess provided was after-dinner coffee, and the guests took their dirty crockery back home, so there was a minimum of dishwashing.

"We were sandbagged," commented my informant. "And now she thinks *I* owe *her*."

What the hostess showed, I say, was remarkable ingenuity in coping with the horrors of SPCA. Those initials stand for the four distasteful features of mealtimes: Shopping, Preparing, Cleaning Up—

Wait a minute. I can't pretend I invented the catchy idea myself. My favorite suburban spy gave it to me. I went along with her on the first three. She paused dramatically so that I'd ask, as she wanted, what the A was for.

"Arguing," she replied with a display of emotion. "After a party is over and they've all gone home, there is always an argument. He objects to my talking too much, or to having invited So-and-So, or God knows what. SPCA. Put that down." She pointed to my notebook.

"A–arguing—it takes two," I jotted down. I never reveal my notes to research subjects.

Today the housewife regards as degrading the chores that once were her *raison d'être*. This is really an attitude that hides her utter inability to accept them, much less enjoy them. The notion that a woman should *like* housework is so outlandish that—well, it looks ridiculous in black and white, doesn't it? That's how far we've come from the original concept of domesticity. The SPCA viewpoint shows how the resistance has spread. Once it would have been just cleaning up that rankled. Then they broadened the area of complaint so that preparing was included. Next, postprandial heated discussions were linked to the annoyances of getting meals. Now shopping itself, the basic task of gathering the food, is objected to. And there are no vegetable gardens, no fishmongers roaming the streets, no baking from scratch—there is no work at all to buying groceries.* "So what's eating the girls, anyway?" asked one lean and hungry husband.

Though I gumshoed my way through many a food emporium, I found no answer, unless it was the revelation that the modern shopper for victuals is apparently untrained in what used to be fundamental: planning a menu and making a list.

* A backyard in Westchester County, New York, contains four peach trees. The owner has sprayed them year after year. They are so laden with fruit he must prop up the branches. The peaches are perfect and delicious. Once he ate peaches at the table and guessed they were not his. His wife had bought them at the store. He asked why not off the trees. She replied, "Oh, they're all the way up there [the tree is only twelve feet high] . . . it's so much trouble."

This method has been replaced by Supermarket Assault. I witnessed over and over again the spectacle of women inching their way up and down the aisles, engaged in what the gleeful retailers, wholesalers, manufacturers, and advertisers call "impulse buying." I prefer to call it mere *surrender*. The formula for Supermarket Assault:

$$A+B+C\times D= \$62 \text{ weekly}$$

A. *Amount of food purchased is determined by size of the cart.*

B. *If possible, have child walk so more items can be removed from shelves and placed in cart.* Corollary: If he knocks over display, ignore him. Sub-corollary: Let him open and eat whatever he grabs first.

C. *When possible, take husband shopping.* He chooses luxuries you would ordinarily skip for lack of money. He carries wallet.

D. *Buy two of everything.*

The Supermarket Assault is the greatest affront to the philosophy of moderation in all things that was ever invented. The go-carts now have hooks, permitting a customer to hitch them in trains. What this will lead to, even the visonary forward-looking investigator cannot imagine.

From this display of overconsumption I looked into an entirely different approach to shopping: the Local Grocery Foray. Here, unplanned raids are made on cans, bottles, and boxes, which are spirited back to camp. There are numerous reasons why a housewife prefers this costly system. One might have something to do with the size of her family; another might be that she doesn't wish to be seen in the supermarket wearing conspicuous heels, stockings, dress, and earrings. Another and the most likely reason to avoid the big store is simply the lack of cash.

One late afternoon I spoke with a person in her early thirties who said her name was Bunny. She was racing through a small grocery store in straight lines. The pace was quite the opposite from that of the supermarket. Her system, she explained, was to operate as close to the deadline as she could.

"I shop every day," she testified. "Usually I don't know until about five what I'm going to have. Oh, sure, I plan ahead sometimes. Why, sometimes I smell something good at some friend's house and I swear I'm going right home and prepare a nice meal for the family. But, my goodness, so many things come up that before I know it it's 5:30 and there is just barely time to rush down here before they close and grab a few cans off the shelves and go home and heat them up."

Her eyes misted over as she reminisced.

"I remember when we lived in the little old house on Strawberry Hill. I kept saying, 'Oh, Bill, if I just had a freezer, I'd stock up on all sorts of goodies and we'd have the swellest meals.' Well, we moved here, got a big fridge with a freezing compartment, and for the first few weeks it was filled with frozen delicacies. That was five years ago. Now it is always empty, except for ice cubes and frost."

Bunny hastened away, seizing a Sun Yat-sen Egg Foo Yung Chicken TV Dinner.

I spent a morning at another neighborhood store and it was an experience. There an animated social group functioned. The females stood around and talked and shifted from one leg to another for what seemed hours. The butcher and the other clerks were virtually idle. Every so often a wing would peel off, load up with supplies, and all appear at the little check-out counter at once. Or five women would suddenly meet at the meat counter and all want the eye of the butcher at the same time. Then a new social group would form, made up of the newcomers to the store.

The most shocking event occurred at 11:30. I was sitting on a case of soap, dozing fitfully, when there was a scream. "Heavens! It's out in fifteen minutes!"

With that there was the maddest scramble one could imagine. "Hurry up, Art," someone said. That wasn't too surprising, but the reaction of Art, the proprietor, was. He began cursing terribly.

"You goddamn women!" he shouted. "You been standing there an hour and now you all want to be checked out at one time! What the hell do you—"

The women loved every minute of it. I found out later they would not *dream* of shopping anywhere else.

And what was out that cleared the place out? School.

VIII

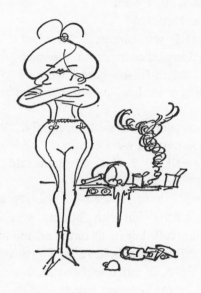

Umbilical Cord with Princess Extensions

Early one bright day I took hold of my note-book and began making contacts with six interviewees who had promised to aid in my project. Their names were Liz, Jane, Rose, Gammy, Joan, and Georgia. It was 8:55 AM and I started at the top of the list. I dialed Liz.

The line was busy. I dialed Jane. Busy. I dialed Rose. I dialed Gammy. The line was busy. The line was busy. I dialed Joan. BUSY. I dialed Georgia. *The line was busy.*

It was now 9:05. I began random dialing. Soon my finger hurt and I switched to using the pencil end. Busy. Busy. Busy. Busy. Back and forth I went.

I dialed Jane. Not busy!

NO ANSWER!! It was almost 9:15 when I ran out to the car and sped down the street to the nearest house of the six. I was admitted to Rose's home, where I found her standing in the kitchen in her quilted robe stirring a glass of Metrecal.

"Oh, there you are," she said cheerfully. "Why didn't you call and let me know you were coming?"

"You—the—well—" I choked, then told her what had happened.

"What phone? I haven't been—" she replied defensively. "Oh, I did have a little chat with Gammy, yes."

The incredible truth began to dawn on me at that moment, but I was too stubborn to believe it. Thirty minutes later, at approximately 9:45, I ran into Jane in the drugstore where she was seated at the counter having coffee—the rim of the cup was laden with lipstick—and on the stool beside her was her five-year-old, finishing up a milk shake. When she vaguely recalled a telephone conversation with Liz earlier, the pieces began to fall together.

A later check with Joan and Georgia clinched it. When I had tried to reach just any one of those six, *they had all been talking to one another.* Whether they had been hanging up and dialing back and forth, or whether each of the three pairs had hung on just to each other, could not be determined. I did learn that when Jane had finished with Liz she tried the other four and got nothing but busy signals. So she broke off and went to the drugstore. This helped to disintegrate the network, and eventually the girls stopped talking.

The discouraging news was that Liz, when Jane broke off,

tried to reach me. Naturally, to use her language, she got "a busy."

"You were doing a lot of yakking," she chided when she told me about it.

This experience taught me that of all the great inventions that are continually credited with setting the housewife "free" from her "drudgery"—automatic dishwasher, Waring Blendor, ice-cube freezer, electric pancake-turner, things like that —Alexander Graham Bell's is the most effective. It is not only an outstanding piece of machinery, but it has a psychological value. There is something about cradling that smooth instrument in her hand that appeals to a female. There is a quickening of the pulse at the thrilling possibilities it offers, like moments at the theater before the curtain goes up. The lifeblood of the community flows through the phone.

On looking into phonophilia, I learned how much a part of her life the Bell System is to a woman (*see* Fig. III). It is (1) an important stimulus to get her moving in the morning. There may be (2) a brief flurry of curt messages back and forth at about 7:30 AM. These are usually for the purpose of confirming and correcting car pool assignments of the day— school, depot, etc. As foggy as she is at that hour, the wife realizes that these ragged edges cannot be left for later smoothing. Thus she exhibits a brief period of marvelous clarity, then falls back into a sort of lethargy until the husband and children go toward the horizon.

Then she tries to remove all obstacles in time for (3) the nine o'clock telephonics. The air becomes filled with the sounds of dials whirring, instruments ringing, voices babbling, plans being consummated, and gossip being disseminated. It is at about this time that the majority of schemes are hatched which result in daily peregrinations of the female sex.

This brings us, if we skip over (4), (5), (6), (7), (8), and so on, to the (23) emergency call to the expensive-delicatessen-but-they-deliver at 5:45 for a few forgotten items, optionals like butter, sugar, salt. The phone is largely inactive after 7 PM, unless there are teen-age children in the home. Most evenings are given over to the wife's mild urgings—for her husband to tell her what happened today because she never gets to talk to anyone during the day.

Ruth Baldwin summed it up this way. "I cannot explain to anyone what goes on here; it's just mad, that's all. Getting Jack and the children off. They're gone by 8:55 at the latest, and it's a moment of collapse. I feel as though I've done a day's work already. Maybe I've thrown a few clothes into the washer, put away a few dishes, but probably not. Most of the time I just head for the coffeepot and the telephone. I have to call somebody."

Ruth Baldwin is the Baron Richtofen of the Bell System. After all these years, she is still supreme on the phone in her district. She has been awarded the Distinguished Dialing Cross for telephoning above and beyond the call of duty. On the occasion for which she was commended, she was sick in bed with some virus or other and the doctor was there at the time, examining her. (His advice was for her to save her life by remaining in bed, advice which was subsequently ignored, resulting in a case of pleurisy.)

The physician went to his bag to find something and to replace his stethoscope. There was the sound of a bell. When he turned back to the patient, she was gone. In the other room he could hear her voice.

"Oh, Ann, for God's sake, I'm glad you called. I've been trying to get you all morning."

The doctor eventually got her back into bed and then managed to squeeze in two calls of his own, one to the pharmacy and the other to his office, before leaving. Ruth hurried to call Ann back the moment he had gone.

You will be interested to know that on another day Ruth earned the Extension Cluster, given in lieu of a second DDC. It was for bravery practically unheard of in her town. She called a friend at about 7:15 one morning and the husband answered. Instead of quietly hanging up and pretending it was the wrong number (which is what most frightened women do at that hour if a man's voice comes over the wire), she asked to speak to the lady of the house.

"She's getting ready to drive me to the station. Can't she call you back later?"

"No," said Ruth firmly, "it'll only take a minute. Let me speak to her."

They say the man missed his train.

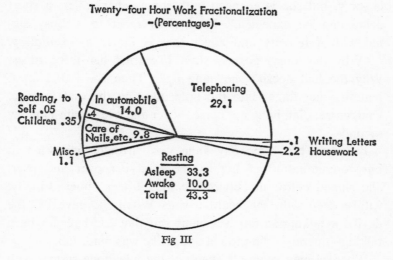

Twenty-four Hour Work Fractionalization
-(Percentages)-

Reading, to Self .05 Children .35

In automobile 14.0 .4

Telephoning 29.1

Care of Nails, etc. 9.8

.1 Writing Letters
2.2 Housework

Misc. 1.1

Resting
Asleep   33.3
Awake   10.0
Total   43.3

Fig III

HOUSEWIFE'S DAILY CHORE RATING AND TIME
UTILIZATION—1962
(*Based on Fragg-Niblingen Samplings, Cook County, Illinois, and Barnstable County, Massachusetts.*)

In 1961 and 1962, Dr. Herman Niblingen and his wife, Winnifred Fragg Niblingen, surveyed the areas indicated in an attempt to determine how close the work habits and routines of today's U.S. housewives are to those of 1890. The two sociologists observed and questioned 1009 women. I am privileged to show the chart above, which comes from a portion of the survey; when the Niblingens complete the second part of their task—analyzing housewives of 1890*— the entire report will be put before the public.

The world is at your fingertips with the modern telephone; but if a busy signal occurs, you might as well be marooned in the Galápagos Islands. And this has an effect on today's talkative female quite the opposite from what one would hope. Instead of the buzzing suggesting that "The party is sorry, but she is engaged with some other caller; a short delay can be expected," housewives react to a busy signal with a ferocity and anger that is far from exemplary.

"Why the lousy, gossipy slob! I've tried her three times. Why the hell doesn't she hang up?" Then she'll dial *hard*, jamming her finger into the hole, twisting the dial in rage. Dial, curse, dial, hang up, curse—over and over again in a few seconds.

I've seen this. One day Jane was virtually overcome in burgeoning hatred of Liz as she tried her over and over. She sipped coffee in between, calling fifteen times. Finally, with a deep sigh, she heard a ring. When she gave Liz the devil for talking so much it came out that Liz had not been talking—merely trying to get Jane. *She* was mad, too.

Whereas men generally speak of the telephone system with contempt, women offer it their respect. The phone seems to impart significance to words that pass through it. Ordinary superficialities can sound like profundities when concentrated

* They are scarce.

in a tiny space next to one's eardrum. Furthermore, the phone gives a woman a simple means of acquiring some importance; by dialing, she can capture an audience for her very own, another whole human being—more than she could do if she were on the spot in person. In an attempt not to lose that audience, she will combine garrulousness, gossip, and flattery. Housewives, in the grip of phonophilia, are the worst offenders when it comes to that phoney courage that lets you say over the copper wires things you would *never* say to someone's face.

And a third reason for their love of the instrument is their utter dependency upon it. It is the only way that a woman can make sure of her plans, that she can see to it that she is not stuck in her house all day with nothing to do, no place to go. It is both escape and excuse.

Their admiration for this instrument is extreme, then. Like a god, it beckons and they must respond. The worst sin, to a woman's mind, is the unanswered ring. I have heard them say, more than once, "I'm tired of being a slave to it; I'm going to let it ring." Everyone agrees to go along, but when the acid test comes—by gum! There isn't a woman on earth who doesn't break down and run obscenely toward the machine after the seventh ring.

A terrible case of abasing one's self to the idol occurred once within my sight and hearing. A woman drove into her driveway; as she stopped the car she could hear the Western Electric bell doing its duty inside her empty house. She leaped from the vehicle and charged straight across the shrubbery to the front door. Her legs got scratched.

The front door was locked! Her bag containing the key was on the seat of the car. She yelled, "——!" and tore around the corner, through the back door. I heard furniture being knocked aside. I entered to find the poor girl standing with the dead instrument in hand, muttering imprecations. They'd hung up just as she got there.

On the other hand, this very same housewife showed me, on another occasion, how she could temporarily undo the fetters that bound her. For the phone, in some cases, enslaves the unwilling. I was in her house observing, in my most professional way, while she was engaged in a serious conversation (telephonic, of course) with a friend. The subject was: How many days after the spots go away can you send the child back to school? Dr. Spock said one thing, the local doctor said two days later, but she was looking for just the slightest encouragement to cheat a day or two and send him back early.

The kid looked well enough; at that very moment he was breaking a soup plate with his bare hands. He had been in the house for upward of ten days, it seemed, and the mother was close to a breakdown. She was hoping someone would tell her, "Sure, it's all right. Send him back tomorrow." But the answer on the other end of the phone was discouraging.

My attention strayed for only a minute, and the phone had disappeared, as had the housewife. I heard voices in the back room. I found her standing there, rigid and incommunicado before the television screen watching "Today." I traced the telephone wire under a door and found the instrument hidden in an overcoat pocket in the hall closet. I jumped as it started to buzz. When I shut the door the sound was completely muffled. Back in the TV room, the lady was unaware of what she was missing. She was still standing there, watching an author interview. ("No," the author was saying, "I wrote it for money.") The housewife was holding a half-unfolded ironing board. She never finished unfolding it while I was there.

Studies at the crack Matrimonial Trouble Center of Finger Lakes University had made it obvious that the reason so many American marriages are floundering and more than a few foundering is *lack of communication*. What I found out about the telephone situation in the United States tends to confirm this. While it is quite possible for wives to communicate with other wives, it is very difficult for husbands to reach their own spouses.

In my own examinations at the Red Carnation Bar & Grill I found at least thirteen men—Bill Rasdale will be remembered as one of these—who spoke despairingly of their attempts to communicate with home during the day. The chart below sums up the matter.

	No Answer	Busy Signal	Hung Up on me	TOTAL
Reason for lack of communication	5	7	1	13

One New York businessman told me how he had arrived at a solution for getting in contact with his busy Pelham, New York, wife. It came to him once after he had tried during the entire morning from his office in the city and found the line busy. About noon he got a call through but, sure enough, there was no answer. So he sent a telegram, asking her to call him, and went to lunch.

He heard nothing during the afternoon; every time he called there was no answer. Just before leaving for home he took drastic measures. He engaged an answering service. When he arrived at the house his wife was standing in the living room with her hat on, reading the telegram.

"Oh, dear," she said, "this came too late for me to do anything."

"It's all right," he assured her. "Sit down, I want to explain something to you."

He told her about the answering service and how it works. Now at regular intervals during her crowded day she contacts the operator and asks, "Any calls?"

Almost always the reply is, "Yes, your husband wants you. He's at this-or-that number."

This can be whenever she returns to the house, or during a session at the bowling alleys, or while she's dummy at a bridge game. Once, she remembers, she was barreling down the Thruway after spending most of the day up-county. Suddenly she pulled over at a toll station, dodged into the public booth at the side of the road, and checked in. Fortunately, there was nothing for her that time. But, as the operator monitors all calls to her home, her friends and relatives are always leaving their numbers and when she checks in she may find a dozen messages. She always attends first to the one from the guy who's paying for the answering service, however.

He told me, "It costs me $12.50 a month and it's worth a million bucks."

If any aspect of this procedure seems illogical or *irrational*, the reader has not been paying attention. An answering service is impractical and unnecessary, it might be said. The woman could simply call her husband's office during the day to see if he wanted to talk. But he works in a small office and frequently *his* line is busy. This way she always gets an answer, even when the service says, "No, Mrs. W——, there are no messages."

Those evenings she tells her husband that no one ever calls her.

IX

Alcoholics Obvious

An indelible stain upon their escutcheon is the memory that our own darling females are mainly responsible for pushing through the Eighteenth Amendment to the Constitution—Prohibition. Deep in their unconscious lies this guilt feeling that here was a boo-boo on a national—nay, international—scale for which they have found no excuse. Even today it is the female sex that supplies us still with the diehards who rail against John Barleycorn.

I am happy to report that most American women are doing their utmost to tip the scales back to the other extreme. Having dabbled in Prohibition and seen its shortcomings, they—or their daughters and granddaughters, I should say—are now seriously engaged in another noble experiment—Intemperance. In other words, they are taking the responsibility lying down. It's a staggering thought.

Charging the American housewife with drunkenness is a much too popular and familiar theme now for me to bother to repeat it. They say that alcohol is a substitute for happiness, or else a tragically misguided attempt to find it, and so forth. I sometimes suspect that desperate sociologists, editors, and writers are deliberately confusing mere love of liquor with alcoholism, because it is a story line that appeals to women. You know: "Am I an alcoholic?" "Is my husband to blame?" Etc.

No, I can truthfully say that I ran across but one real alcoholic in my travels. She appeared at a kindergarten show at 11 AM, loaded. Later a fund-raiser told me the woman's little boy had stopped her on the street and said, "Don't go to our house; my mother always sleeps late."

Furthermore, as we well know, alcoholics consume comparatively small amounts of booze. They conk out early and shirk their duty. It is the steady drinkers who put their minds to it who help bring the national average up. And who but a housewife and mother has the time available for this? Rather than leading to alcoholism, the constant daytime tippling in which she indulges becomes a useful and reliable cinder block in the foundation of life. It has little to do with a search for happiness; it is more of a time-killer and a problem-solver.

In another respect her drinking is different. Liquor is simply one feature of the liquid day. The other major ones are coffee and tea. I mentioned a few pages back that the telephone was used to arrange extracurricular activities, to start something or to find out what someone else has started. The first order of the day is to pin down a coffee klatch. If there isn't one in sight, organize one. Early in the morning, coffee is served at such a function. As time goes on, alcohol edges onto the scene. Afternoon tea is, as suggested, often the setting for a tea party, but eventually the cocktails and highballs appear. As far as I can make out, the borderline is a hazy one and the emphasis shifts back and forth, with the non-alcoholic drinks gradually losing out as the day wears on (*see* Fig. IV).

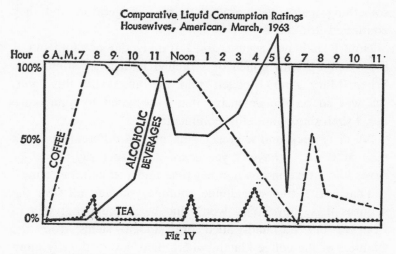

Comparative Liquid Consumption Ratings
Housewives, American, March, 1963

Fig IV

A man's coffee-tea-booze chart would show an entirely different pattern. But Figure IV illustrates vividly the unique feature about a woman's drinking: she doesn't need alcohol for purposes of tongue-loosening and conviviality. This state comes with any of the beverages. The intermingling of the three principal liquids shows that. The reasons that liquor comes into prominence are mainly (1) one gets tired of tea and coffee after a while, and (2) the clash by night (when husband and children come home) is more easily approached on a snootful.

When does it all begin? Well, I saw Mary Ann Blodgett's automobile parked in front of Nina Rasmussen's at 7:30 AM. On her way home from depositing her spouse at the early train she had paused at Nina's—whose husband had also departed for work—to share a pot of coffee. She was still there at 10:45. She then hastened home to see if the children had gotten themselves off to school properly (as she had instructed by telephone from Nina's) and to pick up a tray of ice cubes. Mary Ann then returned to Nina's, where apparently something had gone wrong with the refrigerator, and they continued drinking.

Now I shall not accuse, for I frankly did not find out if they kept up with coffee or switched to heavier stimulants. When Mary Ann Blodgett told me about all this later, she was so on the defensive that I hesitated to antagonize her. I shall simply note this comment:

"A dirty sock and a greasy sink are no different at 3 PM than at 8 AM. I haven't yet heard a dustrag say, 'Now or never.' So I take my own sweet time and you can quote me."

That is the kind of caffeine courage you find all over the suburbs these days. You won't find her talking that way in front of her husband. Such braggadocio stems from the stimulus of the coffee klatch, where there are ordinarily more than just two people present. *Antemeridian* gadding about is so popular that attendance may run as high as eight or ten. The klatch may start at any time after nine. Almost always it is an unplanned affair, hastily organized at 9 AM on the telephonic launch pad. From the evidence I have been able to gather, the klatchers sit around and bolster each other's confidence with attitudes like Mary Ann Blodgett's, exhibited above.

One lady I asked gave this account:

"What do you do? You just sit and yak. The idea of the coffee klatch is to drop over and have a quick one on the way back from the station or after school starts. That sounds harmless, but you just sit and yak, about doctors, clothes, schools, teachers, hair. But instead of a quick cup you are apt to find yourself there until 11:30."

The coffee klatch cycle becomes so universal, she told me, that women find themselves "owing" other women, becoming indebted for a coffee session just as though it were a dinner party.

Naturally the question arose in my mind as to how a woman could do any housework if she attended these matinees regularly. The best answer was given to me by one whose frankness was engendered by my promise never to reveal her name.*

"We don't have enough to do, if you ask me," she declared. "When the day starts, and if there aren't any babies around at the time—women with small babies lead a different life in the morning, they're busy every second for hours—we get involved in a series of unimportant errands and visits and talkfests. Sure, I used to do everything around the house, but when I found other wives doing less housework than me and having more fun, I got a cleaning woman. Then I got an ironer—an ironing lady, I mean. Now I don't want to do anything. I straighten up a bit, make the beds, and cook—the nights we don't go out for supper. That's it. So the first thing in the morning, I'm gone, out of the house like a shot. My

* She's Mildred Lafollette, 2134 East North Second Street, Shaker Heights, Ohio. Frank Lafollette is an old friend of mine and he deserves to know the truth, regardless of any vows of secrecy.

time is so occupied that at the end of the day I can't see that I had a spare moment, but when I ask myself what did I *do,* I find I didn't do *anything.* Now don't you dare tell Frank I said this!"

Having killed a good portion of the morning in the haphazard manner suggested by the descriptions above, the girls are faced with lunch. As noted on Figure IV, the alcoholic beverage consumption takes a big jump here. It will also be seen that coffee comes close to holding its own. That's because of an influx of a large group of sherry drinkers. Women who would not feel comfortable starting on hard liquor at 11:30 AM are quite willing to take sherry.

This is where they begin to take seriously their desire to erase the Eighteenth Amendment stigma. Pre-luncheon and luncheon drinks are quite prevalent in the villages. Sherry seems always to be the testing ground that leads to bigger things. For instance, I found in a town near New York City a group that called themselves the Sherry Club. The idea was to get together at about 11 AM Tuesdays and Thursdays for an eye-opener before lunch. Pretty soon some of the girls began taking their sherry in water glasses, and later someone added ice to hers. It was easy to take the next step: a scoop of real liquor instead of sherry. As of this writing, the Sherry Club is devoted to dry martinis and whiskey on the rocks and has added Wednesday to its meeting schedule. After breaking up for lunch, the members usually reconvene for an afternoon of bridge, gossiping, and a few more drinks to stave off Same-Day Hangover.

The Sherry Club is the only one of its kind I encountered, a group deliberately organized for the purpose of drinking in the morning. My own feeling is that they exhibit less hypocrisy than those who pretend to gather for coffee and slide into cocktails before lunch. A Sherry Clubber put it this way, and I admire her for it:

"What's all this talk about when is it time for drinking? That sun-over-the-yardarm baloney. It's time for a drink if you're ready for it, that's all. *Is the sun over the bedpost?* How's that for a rule, huh?"

The coffee-klatchers, on the other hand, are self-righteous about their position. I know for a fact that a good many of these sessions hang on until a hostess, without a trace of embarrassment, says "How about a little something before you go?" But getting any one of them to admit the truth is virtually impossible. She denies it completely, or else treats your one bit of evidence as a rarity that will never recur. This is a marked exception to the well-known symptoms of perpetual confession and agonizing self-appraisal, dissected in Chapter V, *q.v.*

It isn't that a housewife and mother particularly wants to hide her tippling; it's only that she has little excuse for turning the coffee meeting into a cocktail party. She doesn't want to have to try to explain it. On the other hand, the minute there is any *reason* given for breaking open the liquor locker, there are no misgivings. The luncheon party is a popular way of providing the justification. Here, in the words of a participant, is the history of one of these, which I call the Luncheon for Each Other:

"We started a group, just a friendly little thing to get away from the kids and talk to someone for a change. The idea was to take turns providing a glass of sherry and a light lunch. It was fun. The first few times around, sherry was served. Then someone offered martinis, and the next week the hostess whose turn it was had to do the same. It was hard stuff from then on. I can remember some afternoons at 5 PM trying to drive home and weaving all over the road. I wasn't the only one. It was pure logic. If we were going to get plastered, let's do it quicker with gin. That went on until we moved East."

For those who haven't formed a regular sorority, there is the Luncheon for Somebody. Usually it is for one of the girl's mothers who is visiting. Sometimes it is given at the country club, sometimes at the home of the hostess. Sherry is always offered as the pre-luncheon aperitif; hard liquor is usually requested and served. The guest of honor sometimes gets a chance to meet all the other guests, often not. It matters little, anyway. This luncheon is but one of many that will be given while she is in town staying with her daughter, and she will see the same faces over and over, eventually hearing the names of all of them at least once.

One girl told me that the Luncheon for Somebody has become a farce, and she intends to prove it by hiring some old female fruitcake to come to town, pretending it's her aunt from California, and get the two of them invited to a slew of parties. I don't know whether she has done it yet. I saw her the other day meeting a fat lady at the train, but it could have been her real mother or cleaning woman.

The Luncheon for Somebody is often rough on the Somebody, mainly because she is expected to keep up with the local boozehounds. This is not easy, when she has to wait an hour and a half for food. One of them told in my presence of a terrifying experience she underwent in New Canaan, Connecticut. She arrived on time and someone put a dry martini in her hand. Not accustomed to drinking at noon, she nevertheless wanted to be polite, so she sipped it carefully.

An hour later she was still sipping a martini, but, as she now suspects, the original must have been replaced at least once. She was very hungry and pleased when the food was finally served. Before sitting down, however, she made a trip to the ladies' room. It was there that she found out how tipsy she was. When she tried to get up, she fell forward headfirst into the stall shower. Because of her condition and her position inside the shower, she was unable to get out. As she crouched there, helpless, on her elbows and knees, there came a rattling and knocking on the locked bathroom door.

"I'll be right out," she called. But, her voice being muffled by the enclosure in which she was imprisoned, the words were unintelligible to the knocker. The next thing she knew, there was a crowd gathered outside the door, some wanting to use the facilities, others wanting to rescue the guest of honor. With a superhuman effort, she backed out of the shower, regained composure, and opened the door. She told no one what had happened; she forced her way through the knot of spectators and went to her seat at the head of the table.

The rest of the afternoon went without incident. But the next morning she had two huge black eyes from striking her nose on the shower wall. She wore a pair of dark glasses to the rest of the affairs in her honor, and always ate a sandwich before going.

In addition to the Luncheon for Each Other and the Luncheon for Somebody, there is another series of daytime bibulous conclaves: the Luncheon-Bridge, the Tea-Bridge, and the Bridge-Bridge. The excuse for each of these is that bridge will be played. Let's take them briefly one at a time and in the words of participants.

Luncheon-Bridge. "Sally is having a luncheon for Ann and her mother, who will be here another week. But we don't play. We have a drink or two, eat a big lunch, sit at the bridge table and fall asleep—practically. As you well know, I can't play the game, anyway. I know spades from hearts, that's true, and I'm great at doubling. That's about all, but I keep getting invited to bridge parites. No one cares, even when I renege."

Tea-Bridge. "The tradition has always been to have tea served, but also to be prepared at the bar. One summer the Tea-Bridge was given on the terrace of the club, in the hot sun. When the hostess, pouring, asked the first girl, "One lump or two?" she replied, "Whiskey sour." The idea was catching, and all eight of us ordered drinks. It was fatal; we couldn't keep our heads up."

Bridge-Bridge. "We meet after lunch, taking turns at each others' homes. We usually start out with Cokes, but as the evening draws nigh we get into Scotch. The meeting breaks up at 5 sharp."

As for the kind of game that is played at these matches, the most interesting description comes from another young woman:

"You deal, you look at your hand, bid, and start talking. We play three hours sometimes and don't finish the second rubber. Sometimes there is a real fanatic present and she gets furious. But usually the hostess will see to it that no one is invited who can play bridge very well. The idea is to get good talkers, not good bridge players."*

Far be it from me to make false accusations against the housewives of the Sixties. I merely report what I discover, and I find little emphasis on abstinence as I poke about the country on weekdays. One of my most memorable interviews was with a homebody in lower Westchester County. I called upon her at 1 PM. She had not eaten lunch yet, but she was seated there alone, in the middle of a huge vodka martini, drinking from a mint julep mug. She forced one upon me. I could not finish it, but I had enough to put me to sleep a cou-

---

* For what is said at these gatherings, see Appendix.

ple of hours later. That woman's approach is the Luncheon for Nobody.

Suburban imbibers show little reluctance to cover up. They were quite willing to tell as much as they could about the drinking habits of their sex. One of them simply said, "I drink, that's all. I like it."

Another was frank enough to claim that alcohol was good for her. She said that being drunk had saved her life. Here's how it happened, in her own words:

"One day Andy and Rip were out of town. Doris came over here in the afternoon and started on martinis with me. We felt that feeling that wives always deny feeling: husbands away; they may hate it and be working like hell, but it always appears to us they're having a helluva good time, merely because they are away, and we're stuck here.

"I staggered back to Doris' house for dinner. She had some people in, and Dusty Rhodes (a bachelor) was there for me. It was election time and we argued about block voting. Dusty got so mad he finally shouted:

" 'Don't serve me dinner; I'm leaving!'

"We calmed him down and persuaded him to stay. We were all tight. I bet Jerry Laird on the details of an old Katie Hepburn movie plot. He won. Twenty-five dollars. Rip paid him the next week in the Princeton Club squash court.

"Where was I? Oh, yes, I got home and I was so intoxicated I just fell onto the bed, half-asleep. This is where the lifesaving part comes in. My electric blanket was making a funny buzzing noise. I got up at 4 AM and investigated because I couldn't get to sleep anyway. I wandered around the house and couldn't get any lights to turn on.

"The fact was the garage was on fire, right by the fuse box. That dope Rip had put a 150-watt bulb in the cat's sleeping quarters instead of the 60-watter called for. The fire department came.

"Moral: I sleep like a log when I'm sober. If I'd been sober I wouldn't have heard the blanket buzzing and I wouldn't be here to tell you this story and neither would my house."

X

Profiles in Damage

Let's get one thing straight right at the outset. I am not here to pick on women automobile drivers. In the first place, they are subjected to much more ridicule and abuse than they could possibly deserve. In the second place, it is such a boring theme—crazy women at the wheel of monstrous vehicles, causing if not directly involved in numerous accidents—who wants to hear all these tired truisms again?

On the other hand, I am not coming to their defense. Just

let me state the facts as I found them and see if you don't notice certain myths being dispelled.

The statistics that purport to show that female drivers are contributing more than their share to the traffic mess are compiled by men and machines in statistical cubicles. My own research was done on the scene. Now wouldn't you prefer a direct report rather than dry figures? All right. In my travels around the suburbs looking for data, I saw but one automobile accident. No one was hurt. A small truck, driven by a man, came out of a side street, stopped at a stop sign, looked to see if anyone was coming, and while he was looking a woman ran into him.

It is true that the truck had nosed out into the main street a little bit too far. The lady cried, "I had the right of way!" The man cried, "I stopped at the stop sign!"

It was a perfect accident from the standpoint of affixing blame. You just take your choice.

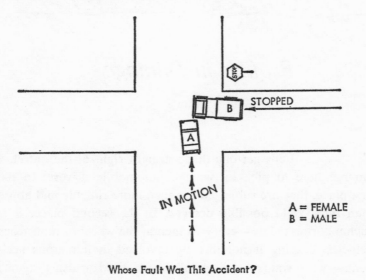

Whose Fault Was This Accident?

Fig V

Of course, one small accident is insufficient evidence of anything in itself (except the likelihood that if a car hits you while you are stopped, it is apt to be aimed by a woman). But in the interests of compiling information on driver *attitudes* in suburbia, I took this one accident and made the following opinion survey:

I asked forty-four persons: who was to blame for the crash? For twenty-two of them I labeled the vehicles Car A and Car B, without mentioning sex. For the others I labeled them Woman Driver and Truck Driver. There were eleven men and eleven women in each group. Here is what they said:

Group I (Not Knowing Sex of Drivers)			
	Car A to Blame	*Car B to Blame*	*Undecided*	*Total*
Men	4	7	0	11
Women	3	3	5	11
Group II (Knowing)			
	Woman Driver's Fault	*Truck Driver's*	*Undecided*	*Total*
Men	10	0	1	11
Women	1	10	0	11

For those of you who cannot read charts, what this means is that the people who knew the sex of the drivers had no trouble at all in making up their minds. In Group II, incidentally, the undecided male is married to a lady truck-driver. The woman who pinned the blame on her own sex lives near the scene of the accident and always drives right through the stop sign herself. But those are atypical facts.

This study shows more about human nature than it does

about automobile drivers. My own reaction was quite different from that of anyone else. I wanted to know where the lady was going when she had the mishap. On a subsequent occasion I was able to ask. She was on a very important mission. She was rushing her son's galoshes down to school. He had forgotten to take them and she didn't want him out in the slushy play yard at recess without them.

"I had the right of way, remember!" she called from the front stoop as I departed.

She thought I was going to crucify her, but I'm not. I'm going to point out that the rapid delivery of overshoes is one of the vital missions a housewife performs day after day in her automobile. She looks upon the vehicle as she does her washing machine, for instance: she hopes it doesn't break down and if it causes her too much trouble her husband will have to get a new one. She is in and out of the car all day, backing and filling, speeding here and speeding there. Neither rain nor snow nor rules of the road shall stay them from the swift completion of their appointed rounds.

The car offers them mobility and escape—exactly what they need in other words, to cope with brittle suburban life. They press on the accelerator and steer—the car, unlike life, responds. Sometimes they are alone, but usually they are carting a maniacal mob in what is known as a car pool. Every time a child broadens his outlook, his mother has to join or start another car pool. Schools (regular, nursery, and Sunday), swimming, Brownies, ballet, railroad station, horseback riding—these are but a few of the demands for a low-cost, localized taxi service. They go on all day long, all week long. Is it any wonder, then, that a woman asks only for the right of way and a tankful of gas? Is it any wonder, then, that driving is a means to an end, without importance, calling for minimum concentration? Is it any wonder that a woman driver's mind is miles away?

We can have nothing but understanding for the girl named Florence, for example. Hurrying across town after delivering a child to afternoon kindergarten session, she paused momentarily at a friend's house on an errand—she had to leave off a small remnant of gossip. She left the car in the driveway and ran inside. When she came out, the engine would not start, and she couldn't imagine why.

We now know what had happened. When Florence dashed into the friend's house, she had left the motor running. When she rushed back out—*an hour later*—the tank was empty!

Another incident I noted took place when a woman backed her car out of the driveway with the two rear car doors open. She realized this first when there was a crunching sound as they caught on trees and stones. They were so sprung out of shape she couldn't shut the doors, so, resourcefully, she tied them with a clothesline, and went on her way—to the railroad station. As it was reported to me afterward, her husband had to be tied inside the car. This was the third time in eight months that he was faced with a major repair bill for collisions before the car had left the driveway.

Sally, a former high school English teacher, drove around East Orange, New Jersey, with the hand brake on. The ensuing smell convinced her that the car needed oil and she stopped at a service station. After the reaction there, she got out of the habit of using the hand brake at all, whereupon the inevitable finally took place: the car rolled backward in her own driveway and smashed into a tree. To hide this damage from her husband, she kept the car backed into the garage for quite some time. He found out about it when, at a party, some wise guy said,

"Hey, unnerstand a tree trunk rolled uphill and rammed Sally's car. Haw! Haw!"

That's when I found out about it, too. Later she gave me her side of the story—about how it is better to leave the brake off at all times than to drive around with it on once in a while—and I saw that once again a "woman driver" story turned out to have a reasonable explanation which actually reflected credit on her rather than shame.

An even better example of automotive doublethink is Mary Nestor. Her husband Ben had taken the Austin to the railroad station and she was left with the Thunderbird. When she trotted out for the first errand of the day, she stepped on the starter and heard a strange clicking noise. Eventually the serviceman showed up and reported that the battery was dead. When Mary heard that she would need a new one at $31.75, she uttered a shriek.

"I don't have one with me now, ma'am," the fellow said, "but I'll just get you going with my own starter and you can follow me down to the garage and I'll fix you up in no time."

He crossed two cables and got the Thunderbird going.

"Don't let her stall, now," he warned, and drove away in his truck, Mary tagging along behind.

She began thinking: if the car is running now, why should I bother with a new battery? I'll just keep it from stalling. So she peeled off at a side street and shot off on her daily driving chores. She kept the Thunderbird going all day long, stopping at least once for sixteen gallons of gas. A good deal of the time the machine was just sitting in the driveway at home idling. When Ben got home that night she was so excited.

"Oh, darling," she gushed, "I've saved thirty-one dollars

and seventy-five cents." She told him all about it. "And all we have to do is keep the engine running."

He looked at her, trying to appreciate what he desperately hoped was merely a sense of humor.

Another time when a housewife showed enviable ingenuity occurred on a Thursday, I was told, when Mrs. N. O. Walker, a member of a three-car family in Darien, went to New York City. She missed the train she first tried for, so she sped down the line to Stamford, parked there, and caught a local. When she boarded the evening train for home she forgot this, taking an express, which raced through Stamford without slowing down. Undaunted, she alighted at Darien and after a search found the vehicle her husband had used to reach the depot that morning. She jumped in it and drove home.

She immediately telephoned Mr. Walker's office to tell him to take a train to Stamford and come home in her car. It was 5:30 PM and he had already left. No one has ever heard the full story of how he got down from his regular train in Darien and spent an hour looking for his station car, trying to recall exactly where he had parked it. They say he ultimately reported the theft to the police and took a taxi home. They say that when he found out the truth he did not appreciate his wife's theory that if he had only worked a little later, she would have saved a lot of trouble for everybody concerned.

Most women think the solution to all their car troubles is to own more cars. One told me seriously that a family just has to have four cars to get along comfortably. Here is her logic. It is impressive. What is even more impressive, they own four cars.

    1.   A *station wagon,* for carrying bikes, sand, spars, etc. No man can live in the country without one.

Also, this is just the right vehicle for the maid to do errands in.

2. A *sedan,* a clean, impressive one such as a Mercedes, if possible with the foreign license plate still attached, for going to parties and places where you are to be seen getting in and out.

3. A small *sports car,* for quick dashes to the drugstore, or for last-minute shopping, for situations where parking and maneuvering around in traffic are problems. This is also useful for a couple going out to a restaurant for dinner. It comes in handy, too, when a husband and wife can't agree on the proper time to arrive at or leave a party; they can go separately, one in the sedan and one in the sports car.

   A sports car is also needed when one of the children borrows the sedan.

   A sedan is needed when one of the children borrows the sports car.

4. A *jalopy.* This is for going to the station every day. The way to show off in a good many high-status towns is to drive to the train in the oldest car you can get. This indicates you are so rich and highly placed that you needn't worry about appearances; it's simply reverse-snobbism.

From what this four-car housewife tells me, her family is quite pleased with the arrangement. Everything runs smoothly, with a few exceptions. When there is band practice at high school and their son cannot get his French horn on board the bus, he is allowed to drive the jalopy. His father has to take the sports car to the station that day, unless it's raining, when he drives the station wagon. If one of the cars is being repaired, there is often a snag in the plans. But my female subject has already seen the solution.

"We are going to have to pick up another cheap car," the lady told me.

This is the kind of thinking that deserves credit. Women refuse to be dominated by their automobiles the way men are. I think there is an essential honesty in their attitude. Men are apt to see the car as an extension of their own personality, and to hope for some security and inflation of ego from the way the car looks and behaves. A woman is just the opposite: the car owes her complete allegiance; it must do her bidding at all times. That's why women drive the way they do, seemingly ignorant of such obstacles as holes in the road, curbstones, white lines, traffic to the rear, gas gauges, and so forth.

Actually, she expects the vehicle she is driving to worry about all that. At the maximum, she will steer it. The rest is up to the car. This is a sincere way of looking at automobiles which even Detroit recognizes. Advertising campaigns seldom stress anything as unimportant as the engine; instead, they just show pictures of the car *moving,* the wheels going around as they are supposed to, and the paint job nice and shiny.

Women, of course, are key figures in the purchase picture. Which reminds me of the time when the Brian Merrimans, after months of discussion at home, decided to get rid of the old station wagon and buy a new convertible. The choice narrowed down to a beautiful, yellow Lark. When Merriman showed up at the dealer's for "finalizing," he naturally took his wife along. There were some negotiations, and he considered himself rather sharp as he squeezed an added $150 out of the salesman on the trade-in.

"Play it cool," Merriman whispered to his wife as the man

drove up to give them a decision-making spin in the Lark. "He's offering us more than I thought he would for the wagon."

They climbed into the car and took off, the salesman at the wheel. During a lull while waiting for a light to change, Mrs. Merriman asked:

"Do these convertibles leak much?"

Certainly *not,* the salesman insisted. It was as if he had never heard of a leak.

"That's good," she replied as her husband began to shrink in horror, "every time it rains the water comes through the windshield of our station wagon in sheets."

XI

Sex Rears Its Lovely Head

An unattractive man grabbed the wrist of a young wife, not his own, at a late party in the country and pulled her toward the staircase.

"Come on," he whispered. "I go for redheads, you know."

"Why you must be *mad*," the pretty thing cried indignantly, wriggling free.

When she later told her friends, she declared, "Imagine, go upstairs with that funny-looking so-and-so?"

This true incident calls for several observations, which may clarify the situation in the Sexy Sixties. One is that a female has no compunction about repeating such stories, whether they concern her or others. Also, the apparent reason for declining the invitation was that the chap is ugly. Furthermore, there is that false indignation, which actually hides the fact that her ego was flattered. Finally, there is the hint that under certain circumstances she just might "go upstairs" with someone sometime.

Her experience typifies the utter confusion in the female mind about sex. She'd like to think that it is a simple matter, but it really is complicated. She wants to preserve her image of herself, however unreal. At the same time she has the uneasy feeling that somewhere along the line she has been missing out on a monumental love experience. It will be beautiful. It will prove to the world that she is not just an animal, not just a concubine. Will it come with a man grabbing her at the foot of the staircase? Probably not, for reasons I'll get into later on.

There are these conflicting conceptions that dog the young woman of our time. For her own satisfaction she wants to be as attractive as possible to as many men as possible. Yet when it leads to something serious, she has to deny it. Her quandary is not lessened by her belief that every other female is getting a better sex deal than she is, and that the countryside is a miasma of adultery and perversion. Thus she is under great pressure to prove herself sexually. Usually she feels she has failed in this respect.

The housewife is the victim of a paradox. She is rendered fairly ordinary when placed alongside the tremendous barrage of sex-dream stuff that whips our society from books, magazines, movies—from all sides. She is supposed to join in this emphasis on physical love and beauty; she is supposed to further it by being part of it. Yet she can't take part in it, can't go on the make. *She* can't grab a *man* at the foot of the stairs, much as she'd like to, to answer a few questions of her own. But it's okay for her husband to grab someone, because that's the American Way.

Incongruities also arise from the fact that a very wiggly line has been drawn to dictate how a woman is supposed to act in regard to sex. Nowadays there are no basic rules that can be argued, and from which a girl can draw conclusions. It used to be easy. For example, some twenty years ago there was a huge controversy over whether a girl should go to bed with the man she loved before he went overseas, perhaps never to return. Now that sounds like a joke. No one would even bother to bring up such a discussion.

Today a lot of wives look back upon their sex experiences before marriage as their happy ones. There was a feeling of wantonness that can seldom be carried over to this side of the wedding ceremony. Half the husbands even claim their wives don't believe in postmarital sexual relations. What happens is that at some point in a girl's life she finds out that making love is not something for its own sake, but it is *important*. It has to take its place on the agenda with fights over money, having a baby, losing a job, becoming jealous, and so forth. The emancipated marriage counselors on radio, television, in books and in magazines report frankly on such matters as "climax" and "impotence." A woman learns she is subject to sexual incompatibility. (No marriage worth its salt can afford to be without a little sexual incompatibility. All marital troubles stem from it.)

In a pseudoscientific bestseller about how people are trapped in the suburbs, the authors wrote of a frustrated wife:

"She had never felt so aroused sexually before. She wanted

111

to experiment with new techniques and positions she had heard and read of, some of which were unusual. . . ."

This is the kind of phony hot stuff that starts a wife worrying about whether she's doing her part, bed-wise. There is nothing more in the book just mentioned about what the new positions might be, so the most a female reader can do is turn to Kinsey, for example, for further edification.

A Westchester County mother, thirty-six years of age, told me that she had learned more from *The Carpetbaggers* than from any other source. The novel appears to be a collection of lurid and informative anecdotes. The lady's eyes brightened as she told me of the plethora of love scenes: "There are things in there you never even *heard* of."

One of the best-known matrimonial psychologists, a university professor, often writes of "poor sexual adjustment." He once tried to help with this tidbit:

"The measure of compatibility is not the frequency of relations nor the wife's ability to achieve climax; the only standard is whether husband and wife are both getting from the relationship what they want and need."

This gobbledygook comes from a family magazine, believe it or not, and it scared hell out of at least four million housewives. It is exciting to read stuff that skirts pornography as that statement does, but what is worse is that such a statement rather than helping adds fuel to an inner fire that already consumes the wife: the fear that she is not supplying her family with enough carnality. All this over-emphasis makes her extremely nervous about it, particularly since she seldom has any way of making comparisons. She can quickly determine if her cooking is lousy or if there is dust on the chiffonier, but her sexual quotient is a complete mystery to her.

In view of the ignorance, myths, hearsay, exaggerations,

and misconceptions that prevail, it's no surprise that many women engage in extramarital activities. They do it for various reasons, several of which I shall list here:

1. *For educational purposes.* Sometimes the enigma of sex looms so large that a woman wants to try for a few answers. Having an affair with another man might be instructive.

2. *To test her popularity.* Today's housewife is insecure. Most of her time is spent in trying to overcome her feeling of inadequacy. A desperate competition with other women keeps her on edge. A love affair with a man who pays attention to her makes her feel one-up on her friends.

3. *For a gain in prestige.* This explains why the adulteress must divulge her infidelity to at least one other person. As word gets around, she is viewed as something a little special. Others talk about her.

4. *To explore the unknown.* She dreams of finding herself at a quiet bar where a handsome swain picks her up. Living it up from one gay moment to the next, with tears sandwiched in between, she would be mysterious. There would be laughter at his charming wit and compliments. Gypsy violin, popping cork, and so on. That's the fantasy, and most women would like to try for it. Another venture into the unknown is to find out if she is "good in bed." She has heard so much about it that her sense of inadequacy runneth over.

5. *For fun.* Some girls like to have love affairs.

How do I know all about this? Well, you go around with a clipboard, ball-point pen, white coat, and big spectacles and people will tell you *anything*. On this very subject one wife informed me that an extramarital involvement was a good influence on her marriage. The theory is that it brings the couple closer together. It stirs up a greater mutual appreciation between husband and wife as well as indoctrinating the less apt lovemaker in new techniques. Some philanderer must have developed this hypothesis, but the woman who told me believed it thoroughly.

For the purposes of this treatise I was especially interested in the daytime seduction rate. A controlling factor is that there are not many males around. A commuter town on a weekday is a most lopsided seraglio. One Bucks County woman told me that she had been hearing tales about the milkman and the iceman for years but never could put her finger on anything definite until "next door."

By next door she meant that one morning she glanced out her window in time to see the grocery boy opening the neighbor's garage door—from the inside. From then on, there seemed to be a delivery almost every day.

In an eastern shore town a much more fascinating affair unfolded a few years ago. It, too, involved a local character —a lobsterman. The lady was a Canadian who retained her loyalty to the Crown. Living on the water's edge, she would haul up the Union Jack when the coast was clear. The lobsterman, tending his traps on Long Island Sound, would then chug in. You couldn't keep a routine like that secret; everybody in the cove knew what was up.

Her husband didn't catch on, however, until one Fourth of July he found the foreign flag and ran it up the staff as a gag. His rival soon appeared at the terrace door. In the crisis, he cleverly blurted out:

"Lobsters for sale."

Hubby's suspicions were aroused. (For one thing, the lobsterman, although red himself, was without lobsters.) A breakup eventually resulted, with the not-surprising aftermath: now that the woman was free, the lobsterman was scared to death of her. At times she would jerk the flag up and down like a distress signal, while he remained out on the water tending to his traps. The couple soon parted.

How many married women are fooling around is a figure that need not be determined exactly. Enough so that there are many stories being repeated. I heard many that sounded alike. Referring briefly to the unusual ones is all that is necessary here. One adman made his connections while he was commuting. He lives way out in Fairfield County, an area that seems to bear the brunt of so much miserable propaganda. He should have been driving to Norwalk for the train every morning. Instead, he would swing onto the turnpike and race several stops down the line to a little riverside depot where he would park and entrain for the city.

In the afternoon he would get off there and drive a few blocks to where his doxy awaited him with gin and blandishments. When he'd had his fill, he would speed home on the turnpike—before her husband, a habitually late, tired worker, arrived home.

The shortage of trysting places is also a controlling factor in the seduction rate. It led to a peculiar arrangement between a couple who dallied briefly. She made an auto tour of the mid-West, where, she told her husband, she wanted to visit her old hometown and the graveyards where her ancestors were buried. She actually spent most of the ten days in one motel or another near Detroit with a guy who lived not a block away from her home in Connecticut. He flew out and back a couple of times; his wife thought he was on a business trip.

There is a happy ending. They saw enough of each other and now they are merely friends.

Once an architect from New Jersey walked into a Boston

hostelry's dining room for breakfast and found a friend and another friend's missus sharing a table. "For God's sake, don't mention this back home," they begged him. "They wouldn't understand."

He promised he would not, but the fact that you see it here shows how well he kept that vow. Of course, he told but one person: his wife.

One of the most amazing developments recently is the custom of separate vacations. The reason for this practice is said to be that the marital ties are strengthened by permitting the couple to get away from constant proximity, to let each forget the annoying habits of the other, and to return with a newborn appreciation and love. Emancipated marriage counselors call for this tactic on occasion.

Let's face it, class, the real fun and purpose of separate vacations is that each party is freed of guilt feelings. All obstacles are removed for a carefree week or two of unmitigated lechery, he or she having palmed him or herself off as single on the cruise, at the resort hotel, the ski lodge, or on the beach. It is surprising how many ladies have gone for this gimmick. Husbands do not object, I imagine, if they can enjoy similar privileges. A flagrant example was the couple who went on a windjammer cruise to Catalina. When it was over, the skipper's wife and the male passenger disembarked for shore duty, while the schooner put out to sea again with the second man's wife in the captain's bunk. When she got home she told her amazed friends that the gay sea dog claimed to have been to bed with fifteen hundred women. Despite his rank, the skipper seems a perfect second mate.

In the East there is a young matron who takes a ten-day cruise every winter on a liner. She comes back so refreshed and remains so delightful for the rest of the year that her husband would not think of putting a stop to the custom.

Once, in a moment of magnanimity, she suggested that he come along. He nipped that silly notion in the bud and it never came up again.

No better example of the value of extramarital affairs can be given than Helen. She found herself separated from her husband after nine years of marriage. Living alone, she began to frolic in her newfound freedom, finding enjoyment in making love that was not hers previously. She became so confident that on one occasion too complicated to describe in detail, she seduced her former husband! Later she became pregnant. She confronted him with her condition. The pleasant outcome is that the couple are back together again and living happily ever after.

This is a personal observation in an otherwise impersonal and objective study, but you've got to hand it to young people nowadays. When you see them making accommodations for each other and battling to bring some measure of meaning to their marriages—as I've described—you just know deep down inside that our way of life will triumph.

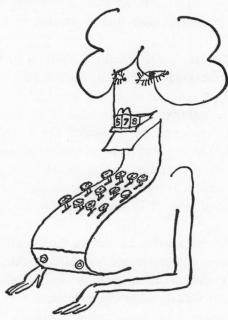

What Good Little Girls Are Made Of

At some point in her dreary existence, once or many times, "a chick gets propositioned," said a Denver (Cherry Hills) matron.

Before marriage, it is expected, and she deals with it on what can be called pragmatic grounds. After marriage, when she is installed in a home on Bayberry Lane in Moondale Acres, a different philosophy applies. It takes into consideration all the taboos and frustrations mentioned in the previous chapter. As we have seen, in some cases this leads to the courageous experimentation that is known as new frontier philandering.

Mostly, however, wives remain faithful to their own husbands. I am speaking in general. Specifically, figures show that of any ten given spouses at any given time, nine of them are resisting temptation. But—and this is an important thing to remember—although the statistics are fairly static, the wives are not. The population is exploding, as we well know, and to keep up that ratio of one to ten, new adulteresses must keep coming along. Generally, though, one stumbles across nine good women in the search for one of the other kind.

This is quite remarkable in view of the American girl's attitude. Put plainly, there is not one who wouldn't go to bed with another man if the circumstances were propitious.

For each individual, these circumstances vary, but if the right combination and permutation occurred, her answer would be yes. Almost always the answer is no, but the vital reality is that whenever a woman receives an offer of illicit sexual intercourse, *she always considers it*. Her desire for extramarital research is tempered by the considerable restraint of what we shall call the Ten Points of Purity. These are a series of rationalizations, justifications, taboos, and honest judgments which serve to preserve her morality for the time being.

A woman does not sit down and reflect on the matter, for she has already gone over it in her head many times. Therefore, when she is tempted, faster than an electronic calculator go the Ten Points through her head—working on the material already stored there—and the cards come out with the right answer. Here are the data that the machine feeds on:

1. "I don't want to get caught." There are numerous sex-starved females who never get beyond this. Their principal reason for avoiding adultery is that they just don't want to be the topic of conversation, either with their husbands or among their friends.

2. "He'll tell his buddies. They'll laugh about it in a bar somewhere." She hates to think that men-are-interested-in-only-one-thing.

3. "He wants me just for my body and not because of the stimulating conversation we've been having." Stargazer that she is, she hopes she'll be taken to bed because she is intelligent.

4. "Am I still that sexy? How reassuring. But am I? Or is this guy just hot?" She wonders why her husband doesn't feel this way about her.

5. "How many others have fallen for this line?" Her ego is at stake here.

6. "Shall I play difficult?" An expression of moral indignation is called for at some stage of the game.

7. "He won't respect me afterward." A prescient babe knows her dignity will be hurt when, in the bleak aftermath of lovemaking, he gets up and walks away from his little guinea pig.

8. "Is he really serious about this?" If she goes along, and he chickens out, she will be humiliated; it will appear that *he* rejected *her* advances.

9. "Where shall we go?" Just being practical.

10. "Is he prepared? Am I?" Romantic lust is one thing, but there is always a performance to consider, and there is always tomorrow.

A lot of girls will deny these points because they tick off so rapidly they sometimes don't realize it. But that's the kind of dope that is fed into her processing machine; there is seldom any card reading "Is it wrong?" or "Will I achieve climax?"—which religious leaders and psychological experts are so fond of mentioning. These queries, if made at all, would be framed in the past tense. As a rule, the Ten Points of Purity are sufficient to bog down the most fiery flirtation. Like the arrester gear on the deck of an aircraft carrier, to use a military metaphor, the chances are that one of the cables will catch her tail before she goes over the side.

That's what happened in the case of the redhead at the banister, referred to a few pages back. Just exactly which Point brought her down we shall not know, but she reacted. Her disengagement came in the form of one of the well-turned phrases that women use to report the result of the lightning calculator: "Why you must be *mad!*" Another is, "What do you think this is, anyway?"

Sometimes the rejection must be more subtle, and "Not here" is a very useful gambit. Many girls employ the flattering turndown and say, "You're very attractive, but . . ." This is well received by most chaps. As she matures and becomes more clever, the virtuous female handles these situations with skill and humor. One told me that she accepts every proposal as a joke, grabbing the man's arm and whispering eagerly:

"I'm ready. Let's go!"

She claims this cuts through a lot of red tape; she has scared off so many rakes this way that nothing has ever happened to her.

In a little summer resort town in New England the town bachelor had his hopes dashed—or at least postponed—in a most prosaic fashion. After a game of tennis the fellow found himself driving toward her home a young woman who had been his doubles partner. He held a can of beer in one hand and steered his top-down sports car with the other. The hair on her brow was damp with perspiration. Her arms were bare and her legs were smooth and beautiful. He letched for her and murmured meaningful compliments to leeward as they breezed along.

"Your game has improved since last year. . . . You're the prettiest partner I've ever had—on the court or anyplace else for that matter. . . . Why not stop at my place for a drink and some singles? Ha, Ha. You know, love–thirty and all that?" He is reported to have chuckled at his approach.

She was not surprised at his suggestion, especially since he had been hinting around like this all through July and half of August, without success. Whir! The tape went through the lightning calculator, giving her the formula with the speed and accuracy that only female automation can offer.

"I haven't time." She looked at her watch. "The children will be home any minute, and besides I don't have a sitter." Then she uttered the remark that became a classic after she told her best friend. "How about a rain check?"

A year later I tried to follow up this story, but all sources of information had dried up. No one was talking. This led me to conclude that her IBM machine had finally granted permission. Or she had run out of cards.

Occasionally I was lucky enough to trace the course of a romp to the actual Purity Point that stymied it. One wench described how, in the midst of a heavy necking session with another's spouse, she received an invitation to go the limit. But it was qualified this way: "Too bad this isn't New York City. No one would ever know. But this is a small town and I'm a family man."

Her mental slot machine clicked and whirled. Three lemons came up. "Yeah," she quickly responded. "And I'm a family woman. In fact, I can hear them calling."

Nothing illustrates the efficacy of the lightning calculator as much as its failure. It can break down under a strain, as it did in the case of a blond beauty we'll call Terry. On a holiday at a ski lodge high in the Andes, her husband fractured his ankle. They had been there four days. She refused to go home and he found himself confined to the bar.

"I was skiing for two," Terry recalls.

She met two South American college fellows on the slopes who ultimately told her they were experimenting to discover whether they could sleep out in that weather at that altitude. After a good deal of horseplay, one of the boys eventually moved inside, keeping the husband company at the bar. Terry and the other young man experimented in sleeping bags on the heights.

"He told me," she says now, "that you can't conceive above the timber line. It changed the whole complexion of my vacation."

At sea level this Terry is as proper as they come, but put her morality in a mix with an Andean ski lodge, the disabled husband, the handsome Latin American *hombres,* the crisp weather, the broad expanse of the mountains, and so on, and my next major discovery becomes clear: Purity Points are irrelevant in exotic settings.

I have the utmost faith in the lightning calculator as a safeguard of family life. But I ran into a most interesting phenomenon, a species of females who make little or no use of it. They are the unattached ones. Each village has a few divorcées who, keeping house and children after the split, try bravely to carry on in their familiar surroundings on one leg, as it were. Although these girls may by nature and temperament be quite different from each other, they tend to congregate. They have that one thing in common: no husband. They have a second quality in common, a fierce devotion to sexual propriety.

There are exceptions. I have noted one in Helen, the separated one who finally got back to her own spouse. There was at least another: a little boy told me he slept in the playroom "when Uncle Ted comes to visit." (Both these girls are now happily remarried, which may prove something.)

But unattached women are terribly anxious to protect their reputations. There are several reasons for this. One is that they are smart enough to know that their future chances depend on it. Another, society automatically looks upon them as fun-loving wanton types, and simply in a defensive mood they want to dispel that myth. A girl on her own has already had her share of jolts out of life; she needn't ask for another by being promiscuous. To retain community respect and status she must be good. I'm not saying these women are prim and proper in the distasteful sense of the words, but merely that they are careful, and that their so-called freedom, instead of offering them license, offers restrictions.

It isn't easy, as one young woman—Alexandra—found out. After her divorce she remained in her Philadelphia suburban home. She began going with a widower, dating so regularly that her friends began gossiping about their sleeping together. "When is Dick going to make her an honest woman?" they kept asking each other.

One day the girl said to a friend, "You know, the first thing after Dick and I get married, I'm going to have a baby."

The lid was off. Everyone assumed she was pregnant and preparing them for a quick conception after the ceremony. Dick and Alexandra eloped and, sure enough, she soon gave out the news. When the baby came, everybody in town counted backward on their fingers and got *seven months*. You see? they all said to each other. They were elated that they had been in on some debauchery. Alexandra's private love life was then considered to be in the public domain and it was alluded to frequently until, two and a half years later, an event occurred that shut people up: she had another seven-month baby! Then someone recalled a fact that had been ignored in the earlier excitement. Alexandra's ten-year-old boy by her first marriage had also been premature.

The woman who told me this tale was disgusted with the whole business. "People should be glad when a divorcée gets a boy friend," she said, "and instead of having erotic dreams about it, just take it for granted it's a normal relationship."

A single girl described her situation this way: "You get a feeling after a divorce that you are not going to tell anyone what to do and you don't want anyone telling you what to do. There is a heightened feeling about privacy and personal affairs. I know I'm on the spot, living here in a town of families with husbands and fathers. People think I have men tossing pebbles at my window every night, I'm sure. Married women think this is just the place for their clandestine meetings, and I've had a few run-ins with them. How can I stop them? If I say anything, they burst out laughing and say, 'Oh, come off it, will you?'"

The folklore calls for a divorcée to lead a lascivious existence; it is hard for her to live it down. Deedie Cartright found this out when she was one of the sponsors of a block party and square dance for the benefit of the church located nearby. In the afternoon the pastor was visiting the houses along the street to thank the inhabitants who had sponsored the event.

He was standing at Deedie's front door, telling her how thoughtful and generous she had been, when in popped one of Deedie's married friends hoping she could snag a drink or two before heading for the depot to pick up her husband. When she laid eyes on the handsome young clergyman—whom she had never seen before and who was attired in mufti—she thought he was cute.

"Well-ll-l-l, what have we here?" she trilled. "Where'd Deedie find *you,* hey? Come on in and split a martini."

The poor man finally got away, white-faced.

Deedie's pal was running true to form. She is typical of the women who, stymied by the protection of the Ten Purity Points, indulge in fantasies. Those who followed Alexandra's case so closely were not shocked at what they assumed was happening; they just wanted to have daydreams in which Dick was their secret lover. Deedie and her ilk are supposed to be making whoopee night and day and a lot of frustrated married ladies can't get it off their minds. The fact is that women talk about sex half the time, and the other half they are thinking about it.* This is without a doubt a steam-releasing device that does a lot toward making monogamy easier to take.

Another species of female must be mentioned here. She is the one who has had her illicit experience and lived to tell about it. I ran into a few of these in my underground travels collecting this priceless information, and I found them to have the zeal of missionaries. They feel it their patriotic duty to denigrate the idea of affairs for housewives. This, obviously, assuages guilt feelings; it also lets them get the floor more often.

Their angle is that extramarital love sequences are always

---

* A Darien, Connecticut, wife and mother ran into a man she hadn't seen for a few weeks. "Oh," she gulped, her face lighting up, "I had the most *divine,* sexy dream about you the other night and I was so *mad* when I woke up because I couldn't remember a *thing* about it. Now the whole thing comes back to me."

tempered with the ludicrous. Nothing ever works out the way it does in movies and books. Something silly comes along. As one graduate said:

"You have to be a real professional and work at it to carry on a successful affair. There are people who think, 'Oh, this is going to be nice. Just this once and it'll be terrific all the way.' But they are always disillusioned."

As proof she reported the case of a twenty-three-year-old wife who found poison ivy while out in the bush on an illicit errand to find love. Seven hundred and fifty miles from that ivy, another talkative missus offered a similar point of view. "Love is a comic thing," she asserted. "That's why news of affairs gets around. We hear about the funny stuff, and that's why it is so damned hard for a woman to be serious all the time about it. It's nothing like Boyer or Grant. The position for intercourse is a ridiculous one to begin with. You're in the midst of it and you start to laugh. He gets mad. Or else he goes impotent. That happens all the time in adultery, you know. You're all ready and he can't make the grade. Or you're in bed and a dog comes in and wants to be petted. Or you get a leg cramp. That's the worst. In fact, I think it's miraculous that human beings can reproduce at all."

Another practical young woman admitted that lovemaking is a precarious adventure when performed extramaritally. "My worst problem is hiccups." She blushed. "I'm always getting them. That's why I am sold on matrimony; you can get the hiccups during sexual intercourse and it doesn't really matter."

A Cook County charmer gave me her thinking on the subject. "Carrying on outside the pale is simply too nerve-racking. I advise wives to forget it. The problem of getting out of the house at the right time is too difficult. I think it's like owning a sailboat. You wait for the right season, the right day, the right weather, the right tide. Then you need a place to go and someone to go with. It's too much trouble waiting for all that to come together."

Most women are in love with their own husbands, and if romance seems to fade, they could follow the advice of Angela del Rio Cruncher, who found her *norteamericano* spouse losing interest. She remade herself. She slowly lost a few pounds here and there, avoiding the customary bleating about "the diet" which so many men find objectionable. Then she struck while the iron was hot. Mr. Cruncher was gone on a four-day convention in Miami and when he returned he found her stretched out on the couch, having had her hair cut and dyed blond. She wore clinging black toreador pants, high heels, a low-cut blouse. She puffed on a cigarette at the end of a long holder. She looked like a high-priced call girl.

"My God, Angela, what have you done?" the thunderstruck Cruncher cried, dropping his suitcase on the floor.

Telling her breathless acquaintances about this later, the pleased Mrs. Cruncher declared, "He wouldn't leave me alone for *two weeks*." There was more to it than that. She confided to a slightly smaller circle of friends that she had begun to engage in some of the sex practices that she had been brought up in Brazil to think sinful and wrong.

That's the kind of affair even the marriage counselors can hardly object to.

XIII

If Anything Can Go Wrong, It Will

It was one of those warm, foggy New England evenings. I sat on a terrace in the country, facing a slim damsel and engaging her in superficial conversation. There was the hum of engines in the distance as an airplane flew into earshot. Suddenly I lost contact with my companion, whose huge, sad, brown eyes had rolled upward and fixed themselves like radar on the hidden craft. They moved slowly across the overcast, as though piercing it, following the sound.

"She thinks it's going to crash," I told myself.

It didn't, and she soon continued telling me about a horse she had bought for the children which had turned up lame. I refrained from questioning her about her concentration on the plane, for I concluded she must be expecting some loved one to arrive by air, and was thus concerned over the bad weather.

Subsequently I learned I was mistaken.

"She didn't know who was on that airplane," I was told by her family doctor. "It's just that she expects the worst from every situation, and a plane crash would fit in with her philosophy. If she stared at an airplane long enough, it *would* crash. And I suppose she was bitching about that lame horse, wasn't she? Well, you know something? She bought that horse because she *wanted* a lame horse."

This was my first encounter with what seems to be a sort of natural law of the temperate zone. This has now come to be known as Beatty's Law. It is divided into two parts; together they explain to my own satisfaction one of the mysteries of female existence—why do so many women get into so many jams? The two parts of the law are (1) The Theory of the Induced Predicament, and (2) The Doctrine of Universal Retaliation.

Scientific evidence can often be analyzed so that one or the other of the two can be applied. But just as often the dividing line is vague and both applications can be made. Today's women subscribe to these hypotheses and are subject to them. Quick as they are to take credit for innumerable intangible and cosmic powers such as "intuition," they would not deny that some omnipotent force governs their environment and their relationship to it. On the contrary, they welcome an occult explanation for mundane eventualities.

The Induced Predicament. The lame horse is a good illustration. So much has been said about it that I really could not pin down the truth. The girl says the horse went lame; others say she deliberately or unconsciously—depending on their degree of sarcasm—purchased the animal because of its defect. According to my theory, it doesn't matter because *by buying the horse she made it lame.* In other words, she is one of those housewives who bring things upon themselves. The Theory of the Induced Predicament (abbreviated to TIP) is traced to some inherent attribute in the female organism, once ignorantly known as witchcraft.

Universal Retaliation. Here the influential forces can be found in the macrocosm, a kind of Somebody-Up-There-Doesn't-Like-Me idea. The doctrine is simple enough: God is Male; unknowingly He inflicts more punishment on the female sex. He can't help following man's impulse for revenge. As a result, a woman finds that the more she tries to do right, the more goes wrong.

Here's a case from Delaware. Winter was approaching. To surprise her husband, a Wilmington wife ordered some firewood, looking forward to cozy evenings at the hearth. When the truck arrived, the driver asked, "Where do you want it?" She replied, "Oh, just dump it in the driveway." As she heard the rumbling and the crash, she remembered that the car was in the garage. Now the car was sealed in, as it were. The Doctrine of Universal Retaliation (DUR, for short) was in operation. She couldn't drive to the station.

She paid off the wood man and tried again. She hired the boy next door to move the wood into the shed. When she brought her husband home that night she said, "I've a wonderful surprise for you." She led him to the shed, opened the doors, and a huge swarm of flying creatures emerged. "Termites!" he screamed. "What the hell kind of surprise is that?"

Once again DUR had struck down a well-meaning housewife.

As it turned out, they were probably just flying ants. But every piece of wood was sprayed thoroughly with chemical, just to make sure. Each time a log burned that winter, its peculiar redolence reminded him of termites and her of the immutable doctrine.

The tendency would be for women to blame everything on universal retaliation, if it were not for one other consideration. It is very important for a wife's piece of mind to undergo adverse events. It gives her a certain status in the community. But if she could only blame these troubles on some outside force, she would not be unique. That's where the idea of the induced predicament comes in; this permits a woman to claim that she and Fate are working together. Her mishaps are different, because she is.

Certainly this applies to Heather Finch. Her boy, being an aviation nut, littered his room with airplane models. One day, trying to straighten things up, Heather screwed eyelets into the ceiling and suspended the little planes by thread. When Andy Finch saw the result, he liked it. It showed off his aircraft to good advantage.

The day I came along I found Heather kneeling on the floor moaning, "Oh, what's Andy going to say?" Several of the planes had crashed to the ground, and the way she was carrying on there might have been real pilots in them. It was several months after she had first put the planes up; the hot-air heat had taken its toll and the threads were drying out and breaking in the low humidity. Each day another plane crashed, and each day she had to tie it back up with dental floss, which she hoped wouldn't dry out.

"If hot air makes thread break," she asked with eyes glistening from incipient tears, "how come their clothes don't fall apart?"

Knowing the Theory of the Induced Predicament as well as I do, I thought it best for her not to dwell upon this. I left, holding my seams together as best I could.

The Finch case was unusual. Ordinarily the girls have to cope with more prosaic enemies such as Venetian blinds, small closets, water pressure, broken Thermos bottles and so on and so forth. One dame I know was honing a blade with the electric knife sharpener and she just sawed right through the wire, blowing a fuse and almost electrocuting herself. Each has a recent traumatic experience like this to report, to show how civilization tramples over her. Grace Krim has what she calls Black Tuesday, the first day in a period of long reverses that the family thinks of as the time the bed fell on Mother.

It has nothing to do with a bed, really. Here's how it started, in Grace's own words:

"Well, Betty, the cleaning woman, was here. That is, she's a former cleaning woman I've taught to iron. Now she irons everything—socks, bras, washcloths—she gets paid by the hour. When I catch her I tell her to get started on the shirts and slips, but by then she claims she's too tired.

"I've had her fifteen years. Everybody says they can't keep a cleaning woman; I can't *give* mine away. I've said to her, 'Betty, you're too old to go on like this.' She looks at me strangely, because she is about five years younger than I am. I just can't get rid of her.

"Black Tuesday was the day she broke the heat regulator knob off the oven. The repairman said he'd be right up and he came two weeks later. That's when he put on the new knob and now the regulator is off a hundred degrees, but I'm not sure which way. It's always a surprise when something comes out baked right.

"The next thing that happened on Black Tuesday was the

dishwasher filled up with water and stopped. It wouldn't drain or go or anything. Yes, one thing—you could open the door and look down at the dirty dishes."

In the next few days the washing machine and the dryer quit, each time with Betty in charge. The Krim family had to postpone a vacation, because there were so many repairmen coming and going that Grace had to be in the house for about a month. She sees all this as DUR while Mr. Krim insists it is TIP. Betty says nothing.

A Higher Authority must be responsible for the troubles that came one day to a socialite we'll call Mrs. Von Tasselberg. Her pride and joy was a huge sign with the family cognomen on it. A man in a Nantucket shipyard had painted it to look like the name of a ship. It was a pretty big sign, too, for it had thirteen letters on it. He got forty dollars for the job.

The sign arrived in time for a tea party Mrs. Von Tasselberg was giving, so she herself carried it down to the road, finding a location where the guests could gaze upon this clever nameplate as they drove in the driveway. She wedged it into the typical New England stone fence that surrounds the property. You couldn't miss it: VON TASSELBERG, with a gilt edge around it.

She returned to the house where the man from the liquor store finished unloading supplies for the tea party.

"Well, good-bye, Mrs. Von Tasselberg," he called out as he backed his delivery car out of the driveway. "If you need anything just give me a ring."

He was still waving in friendly fashion when his vehicle crashed into the protruding sign and with it, now, the stone fence. There was a rumble as a section gave way, having been loosened by the leverage action of the car pressing against one end of the Nantucket man's handiwork. Boulders fell into the driveway. When the liquor store man tried to pull forward, there was a screeching. A fender was jammed tight against a rear tire; he couldn't budge. Guests had to pick their way around the rocks and the immobilized car. The sign read: BERG. The VON TASSEL part was on the ground.

"Why me?" she asked as she told me this story.

There is no rhyme or reason for DUR. Like gravity, it just *is*, that's all.

Mrs. Von Tasselberg's case falls under the Doctrine of Universal Retaliation because she was unwilling to have any of the blame attributed to her. This is in contrast to the case of Alfreda Starkey of Pelham, New York, which comes under the Theory of the Induced Predicament and which shows rather well the fine line between the two rules.

Motivated by the common female desire to improve one's husband, she blurted out one time, "Howard, why don't you have a hobby?" Howard Starkey's hobbies had always been eating and drinking. She was therefore all the more surprised when he took Howard, Junior, to the motorboat show, There, unknown to her, they ordered a do-it-yourself dinghy kit. In one convenient box came all the supplies and parts needed to put together an eight-foot rowboat.

"Well, Freddy," he boasted with a slight edge in his voice, calling his wife by the nickname she despised, "the kid and I got a hobby today." When she inquired as to its nature he merely chuckled. "You'll see."

Alfreda was not at home on Saturday when the delivery was made. When she showed up she was not half so surprised at the nature and size of the project as she was at the place Howard Senior and Junior had chosen to lay the keel. It was February and the garage had been "too cold"; they tried the basement but the floor wasn't "level enough" and there was not "Nearly enough light." So the kit was being assembled in the dining room! The drop-leaf table was shoved over to one side and already one could note a fine film of sawdust forming here and there, as the boys sandpapered.

That boat remained in the Starkey dining room for weeks. If there was a murmur of protest, Howard would say it was his hobby. A gang from the office came out for a big party March 11, and the boat had to be moved outside. The next day it was back in the house. By spring it was finished, and the dining room became a dining room again.*

I'm sure you'll agree that this was an induced predicament.

I would be less than honest if I did not admit here that there is a fiery controversy raging in the sociologists' world over these two theories I have dealt with briefly above. It reminds one of the question, "How many angels can dance on the head of a pin?" The battle is over whether or not the two—DUR and TIP—are not really one and the same. A good many reputable scientists—Mona and Harley Tragg of the Semalina Survey Center, for instance—claim they are.

The Doctors Tragg have shown in their own comprehensive study, too profound to go into here, that American women are unable to differentiate between universal retaliation and induced predicaments. On the other hand, the famous Radcliffe studies at Cambridge, with which we are so familiar, tend to indicate that *all* female contretemps are induced; no outside influence ever intervenes.

There is nothing more confusing to laymen or damaging to science than to have scientists hurling brickbats at each other. What the Traggs say about the Cambridge people is virtually unprintable, and vice versa. It isn't easy for me to try to apply their findings to my own subjective research,

* Oh, no! You didn't really believe this would end up with them unable to get the finished dinghy out through the door, did you?

when they are constantly running each other down. That's why, for one example, I have not been able to fit the Stolen Chain Caper into either of the two categories covered by Beatty's Law.

This title covers a series of mishaps that took place between January 4 and 14, 1962, in a small town near (again) Darien, Connecticut. One snowy afternoon a Mrs. L—— had chains put on her Buick station wagon and drove it home from the service station. The next morning Mr. L—— went out and found that someone had made off with the chains from the right rear wheel. Mr. L. went to the office and his wife called the constable. He investigated and found that the day before, when she picked up the car at the garage, she had driven it away before the men had put the chains on both wheels.

A few days after this she called the same constable and declared, "There's a crime wave in this town. First the chains and now the mailbox."

Ignoring her false conclusion about the chains, he asked for more information. She reported a stolen rural mailbox from her property. He solved this case by digging in the drift at the side of the road and finding that the snowplow had apparently knocked over the box and buried it.

On the final day of the period in question, Mrs. L. approached the refrigerator to start a peanut butter and jelly sandwich. She grabbed the handle and an electric shock of enough voltage coursed through her to throw her to the floor. Stunned, she dragged herself across the floor away from the frightening appliance. She reached up and grasped the edge of the counter to pull herself to her feet. Another jolt hit her. The whole kitchen was short circuited.

She crawled out to the phone and gingerly dialed the electrician. The first thing he told her to do was to put shoes on her bare feet. He soon came and fixed the trouble, a complication arising out of "strip wiring," a new world of convenience Mrs. L—— had seen described in *Better Lawns and Mortgages*, her favorite magazine.

I have sent a full description of Mrs. L——'s case to the Traggs and to the Radcliffe folks, asking them if she is subject to the Theory of Induced Predicaments, the Doctrine of Universal Retaliation, either, both, or neither. At the time of publication of this book, I had not received any replies.

XIV

What Makes Mammy Run

My year in the hinterland was drawing to a close. As I went over my notes I found two conflicting themes. First, the evidence was statistically strong that the treatise— *Modern Married Women and Their Good and Bad Influence on American Men and Children and Institutions*—would be concerned mostly with the bad. My own personal attitude, however, had changed so that I now exhibited a subjective sympathetic reaction to the plight of American females.

In other words, I was beginning to feel sorry for them. It must be understood that today's young homemaker takes a helluva beating. There is no gradual increase of responsibility that gives her time to prepare defenses as she goes along. The game is played in one inning nowdays. In a jiffy she finds herself—at age twenty? twenty-two?—in charge of a complex apparatus know as the family. She is involved in *every phase* of it, from her husband's insecurity on the job to her own fear of fallout; cooking a roast is no more, nor less, important than joining a committee to argue over the widening of Highland Avenue.

I don't think there's any doubt that an American housewife in the 1960s makes ten times as many actual family decisions as her husband. And she may have to start before she is old enough to vote!

Another thing—there is no longer a simple goal to keep in mind. Once she knew her job: get meals, care for the house and children, provide husband with comfort. That sounds anachronistic today. A woman's mission—daily or lifetime— is so complicated, fluid, undefined, and unaccomplished that she can't identify it.

All this pressure is apt to get a woman down. Some of them adapt one of Newton's laws to the situation: *every action has a reaction, so why start any action?* Others take a different view: *leap quickly from one incipient crisis to another, before anything can really come to a head.* A third philosophy is summed up in a motto Mrs. Al Bruno gave me: *Planning Ahead Leads to Trouble—Plan Backward Instead.*

The reason I mention Mrs. Bruno as one of those who deserves sympathy is because of what happens at her house every morning. She, being an Old World type, prepares a fine big breakfast for her family. They have fruit, bacon and eggs, pancakes, and the like. Al and the kids all sit at the table and partake; she remains in the kitchen. She is such a terrible grouch in the morning that for the good of the cause she stays away, eating her own breakfast standing up at the counter. I just feel sorry for her, that's all. Her penchant for planning backward comes from having to prepare lunch for Al. He runs a boatyard and takes a pail with him each day.

For eleven years he has had the same thing: two cheese sandwiches, two cookies, and coffee. Once in a while she will sneak in a piece of fruit, but when she cleans out the pail at night, it's still there. If she dared another kind of sandwich— it would be *Divorce, American style.* And he likes cheese sandwiches so much that when he is home on Sunday he orders them for lunch.

My heart went out to a person named Maureen, too. I encountered her in a supermarket where she was grumbling audibly. She stood out from the others because she was armed with a most unusual weapon: a shopping list. No other shoppers in sight held a shopping list; they just charged at the walls and pulled cans down *ad lib.* Maureen's problem was that she dealt with the most finicky family this side of the Kremlin. She told me awful stories, one concerning the orange juice imbroglio.

She pointed to the go-cart; in it were fresh oranges as well as canned frozen orange juice. In an ill-advised maneuver she had once suggested to husband Stan that the health of the group would be improved if they drank fresh instead of frozen.

"Great!" he cried.

Maureen began squeezing fruit each morning. But wait a minute! There are three boys in the family and they won't touch it. They've been raised on the canned stuff and—to them—*that's* orange juice. Stan won't go back to the artificial stuff, so each day she both squeezes and uncans, defrosts, and stirs.

Oh, she's tried all sorts of tricks. She has sneaked fresh stuff into the boys' glasses, but they know better. Once she tried to fool Stan by leaving some orange skins on the counter, and pouring him a glass of the reconstituted frozen stuff out of the pitcher, used for the squeezed juice. No luck.

"Once you give ground like this, you're sunk," Maureen impressed on me. She then described a sort of turning point, the time when Stan brought home a magazine article about cholesterol and the diet.

"I can just feel my arteries choking up," he complained. "Maureen, you've got to protect your loved ones from an untimely demise."

Ever since then Stan has been off a few foods—eggs, cheese, milk, bacon, pork, and other hubby-killing materials. He has steak, lamb chops, hamburger, and similar delights three meals a day, including the first one. Maureen is up at 6:20 starting these special meals. And he wants little touches like parsley garnishments or broiled tomato slices, too. Stan's arteries have stopped choking up, but Maureen hasn't.

The exasperations and frustrations of ministering to the family's appetites are probably number one on the suffer parade of most women. I have already discussed the female attitude toward food in another chapter and I don't wish to go into it here beyond pointing out that her genuine dislike of kitchen chores might well have come from the ever-growing intransigence and non-appreciation on the part of her audience. I was in one happy home at lunchtime when two youngsters marched in from school and went directly to the stove. They looked into the pot and wrinkled their noses.

The girl cried, "Oh, no!" and ran upstairs.

The boy pointed and said, "I ain't gonna eat that," and kept on going toward the other exit. The mother recovered her balance by this time, sidestepped and blocked his path. As they collided she asked wearily:

"You what?"

"I ain't—"

"You *aren't*—"

"Okay, I aren't gonna eat that soup."

"But it's homemade soup."

"I know. That's the worst kind."

For many a woman, life is a series of baffling reverses like this. No wonder she hates and loves her family at one and the same time. What I said a few lines above about her being inextricably involved in everything applies here. Where once she could apply mere soothing words and a dispensation of mother love, now she has to be an executive.

One day I found the mother of a third-grader in tears. Her child was attending a class where team-teaching was practiced. Sometimes this is called the Rockefeller Plan, because it's his money that's behind it. The main idea is to keep the mothers busy. This one described it to me:

"He came home yesterday and said he needed an Irish poem. We went through all the books and couldn't find a thing. The other day it was two shirt cardboards, but we don't go to that laundry any more. Then it was Saran Wrap and muffin tins. One morning he took the only two tablespoons we have in the house. They needed them to stir up the finger paints. Next week I have to have two shoe boxes—not one, but two, plus an egg box and some stringable macaroni. Then they need nylon thread and a blunt needle. By the time I got to the handicraft shop, they were out. 'What's all this rush on thread and blunt needles?' the man asked me.

"I don't know what I'm going to do about the Irish assignment. They need hats and white aprons, too. They're going to walk through the school on St. Patrick's Day singing Gaelic. In two weeks the mothers have to help in the tombstone assignment. We're going to lead the students around town reading all the historical grave markers and memorial plaques."

She rubbed her fingertips hard back and forth across her temples. Then she cursed lightly.

Young readers will not remember it, but there was a time when children got up in the morning, walked out of the house, and went to school. In the afternoon they came home, threw their things down, got a slice of bread with butter and jam, and ran out of the house until dusk or later. Mother's contact with school affairs was brief and remote. In the 1960s, however, she often feels as though she were *in charge* of them, and she usually feels guilty and inadequate about the way they are going. Enough has been said elsewhere about the agonies and humiliations of the Parent-Teacher Associations. I'm talking about the Chinese Torture System, where each day a little drop falls from the teacher or the principal onto the mother's forehead. Soon she is raving.

Ann Jones, a young woman with three children in a Long Island elementary school, gave me her formula for coping with it. She has made it a rule never to go inside the school building. This way she avoids any conversations with teachers or principal, and it also means she won't join in meetings or tea parties. Her practice stems from a long parade of painful events, coming to a head with a small scene.

The principal telephoned her to come down to the office one day; her child had caused a disturbance in the classroom. When she arrived, she was told that it was a mistake; they had meant to call another Jones. Ann was standing there pressing her lips together the way she does when she is mad, when a teacher walked in pushing two third-grade girls before her.

"I am worried about them," she said. "Look at the red spots." There had been a few measles cases around town.

As friends of the ROWAYTON PTA — we are offering you the opportunity of participating in our benefit T-SHIRT – SWEAT SHIRT SALE. All items are available without an imprint of "Rowayton School" so we hope that all our friends, neighbors and alumni will stock up for spring and summer wear. Samples may be seen at Rowayton School.

The profits will buy special equipment for our children and school, such as safety patrol raincoats and basketball uniforms.

For any information or orders — contact your neighbor —

Name _____

Address _____

Phone _____

ORDER BLANK

	School name		Children's sizes								Adult's sizes								Total	
	Yes	No	6	8	10	12	14	16	No.	Amt.	Yes	No	S	M	L	No.	Amt.			
T – SHIRTS Children's $1.25 Adult's 1.35																					
SWEAT SHIRTS Children's $2.00 Adult's 2.25																					
HOODED SWEAT SHIRTS NAVY ONLY Children's $3.00 Adult's 3.50																					
BASEBALL CAP $1.25			XXS 6¼	XS 6½	S 6¼	M 7	L 7½														
CREW CAP $1.25				XS 6½	S 6¼	M 7	L 7½														

NAME _____ TEACHER _____

CHECK $ _____

CASH $ _____

Fig VI

Actual document distributed to parents in one community.
(Reprinted Without Permission.)

But the principal's secretary looked at the girls and said, "Oh, they're all right. Measles are blotchy. That's not measles."

Ann said, "Why of course that's measles. Little red spots. And a fever, too." With that she felt the foreheads of the children.

The secretary felt their foreheads. The teacher did the same. One of the kids felt her own forehead. The principal came out of his office and felt both foreheads at the same time.

"I know they have measles," Ann insisted.

So the parents were called. Neither had a car. The principal turned to Ann and said, "Would you mind driving them home, Mrs. Jones?"

As Ann was delivering her, the second child burst out furiously, "I don't want to go home! If it hadn't been for you I'd still be in class!"

Staying away from school is not as effective as it was before the day of the copying machine. Now every school has several gadgets that have taken the place of mimeograph machines. The new devices can turn out myriads of notices, instructions, schedules, and pleas that are sent home daily in the hands of the students. They have been so conditioned now that they thrust these pieces of paper upon the mothers until some sort of acknowledgment is made. The purple-printed ultimatums are scattered all over the house. I reproduce one here which was distributed throughout a community *after* the semester had started. In other words, after women had brought all their children's fall clothes, this notice arrived:

To Parents of 4th, 5th, and 6th Grade Girls:
In our new physical education program we will have tumbling and exercises with our new equipment. This

sort of lesson will make it necessary for the girls to be appropriately dressed. Our schedule is so tight that it does not permit time for the girls to change before and after their phys ed lesson.

I'm sure that we all agree that our girls look much nicer in a dress or skirt while at school, so those girls who go home for lunch may wear a dress in the morning and change at noon. Those who must stay at school for lunch have the following alternatives to consider, listed in recommended order (girls who go home for lunch should consider these, also):

1. Wear shorts under skirt (skirt to be taken off just before gym time and put on right after).

2. Wear Bermuda shorts with regular school blouse or sweater.

3. In cold weather—tights under skirt or slacks. Sneakers must be worn for phys ed.

In order not to let down the high standard of dress demonstrated by the children of our school, let's rule out the wearing of blue jeans. If you have any questions, please feel free to call the school.

Obviously this message was written by a bachelor who can no longer think straight.

Tyranny is not confined to school days. A grown woman had to cancel all her weekend activities. She told a friend, "We can't do anything this weekend. We have to do Rosalie's homework. We have to collect rocks, identify them, and get a speech ready to go with them."

I can't help but feel the utmost sympathy for the American housewife who gets caught up in the eddy—she can't break away from it and yet she can't go under; just around and around along with everyone else. Oh, there are moments when somebody's top blows and there are plenty of cases of strong-willed girls who break the pattern. In the next chapters, I am going to describe a few of them from various parts of the nation. In fact, I can tell of one right here, now that we are on this school nonsense.

In one town the flow of messages from the authorities is supplemented by the classwork folders. In these folders go page after page of daily accomplishments by the pupils. It all ends up at home, like everything else. One annoyed mother found that the marks were often wrong. That is, her child was getting a "Correct" when there was a mistake. This mother then began correcting the teacher's corrections and sending them back. She acquired a red pencil just for this purpose. It lasted about two weeks. The teacher told the principal who telephoned the mother and asked her to stop. Nonetheless, the mother was so pleased at being one up on the school.

Yes, I must admit a shiver of patriotic fervor went through me as I ran across each example of a resourceful female who had said, "The hell with it," and had refused to take her lot lying down. Despite the overwhelming proof that American women are a bunch of nitwits, there is much heartening evidence that sprinkled in the ranks are enough brave types to keep us ahead of the enemy domestic-wise, if not shotput-wise.

XV

Square Pegs in Square Holes

"If you want a crazy, mixed-up dame, go see Livia. Don't tell her I said so, but there's one with real problems. She's hiding them deep down inside, but maybe you can get her to talk."

Those were the approximate words of an informer who tipped me off to Livia, the thirty-year-old who never complained about anything—doctor, husband, child, hair. So I went to see her. If she's unhappy, she just doesn't realize it. Livia savors the role of housewife and mother. If there's anything deep down inside it's her love for the whole domestic shebang. Her acquaintances, not hearing any carping from Livia's direction, assume she is just taking it all like the brave little soldier she is.

On the contrary, she is cut out for it. She said:

"I get great satisfaction from this. I love my home and I'm always working for it. My friends have a compulsion to get the minimum chores over with and that's the end of it. My own theory is to get a cleaning woman to do the housekeeping dirty work—which I dislike—and for me to concentrate on the extras, on what I like to do. I like to paint and paper and make curtains. I don't even mind ironing. It's restful, like smoking a cigarette must be for others.

"I don't feel oppressed by the house and the work that goes with it. Women always seem so dissatisfied and I can't imagine why. The home is a wonderful outlet for creative urges. I even get satisfaction out of balancing the budget. Women are afraid to be by themselves. Not me. I don't even play the radio during the day, and television is completely out. My mission? Entertaining and good living is my mission. It's exciting."

It must be brought out here that Livia attended school in Switzerland, lived in Hong Kong for a few years, and once drove to Alaska on the Alcan Highway. Now that she's married to a commercial artist, I guess homemaking is just another adventure to her. But whatever the reason, there she is, living proof that drudgery can be beautiful.

Not many girls get a chance to trod the Canadian muskeg, building up an immunity like Livia's. All the more reason to admire those who are sprung from Prosaic Junior College with slight promise and somehow rise to great domestic heights when the occasion calls for it. There are women who have the situation well in hand; they are almost at the point where they can control it. They seem to have progressed beyond the trite conjuring up of "intuition" and to have substituted a certain resourcefulness instead. Whether it comes from a love of the home, as in Livia's case, or from other causes, I can't say. (I found plenty of wives who were on the ball for a simple reason: their husbands were incompetent and the survival instinct is strong in the female of the species. That's my explanation for a strange sight I often witnessed: in some families the woman does all the driving. The man sits there and is chauffeured. Ninety percent of the time in suburbia, men take the wheel, for prestige, but this ten percent is where she has usurped the throne, apparently for security.)

The best example of a Take Charge Girl is the one who sold the house and bought another without consulting her husband. He came home from New York one night and his wife, Helen, said:

"We've got a new house, Nick."

"Oh, really?" he replied. "Where is it?"

The other case I ran across was that of Christina and Nils. She sold the house right out from under their feet, but three months before they could get title to the new place. So she had to pile the baby and the dog into the car every day and go searching for a rental. She finally found one, and one day she picked up Nils at the station and drove home there instead of to the old place. It was the first time he'd seen it.

"You mean you rented the house without even showing it to him?" I asked Christina.

"Well, I had Sweetie Pie with me," she answered. Sweetie Pie is a Great Dane that weighs—oh, about one hundred and fifty pounds. The neighbors call him The Abominable Snowman after tracing his huge pawprints through their gardens. "The landlady said she'd take Sweetie Pie so I knew she'd take Nils."

It's damned peculiar, but there are housewives who can't boil water without burning it who can wheel and deal in real estate transactions that would give Zeckendorf an attack of humility. Don't ask me to explain it. It merely fits in with the phenomenon of the square pegs in the square holes. And there is something about buying and selling houses that fits some female hands like a glove.

A chap who now heads up a publishing firm in New York moved from California a few years ago. His wife came East to look around Connecticut for a place to live. When they had finally settled down the real estate agent offered her a job. "I'd feel safer with you on my side of the fence," he said flatteringly.*

A guy on the way to the top wanted to move out of his modest little salt box and head for Fairfield County, Connecticut. He listed his place with the agencies; for four weeks nothing happened. One day his wife grabbed a pencil and roughed out an ad for the real estate section of The New York *Times*. "Executive's home . . ." it began.

They got thirty-nine responses in one weekend and six firm offers. They sold the wreck—water in the basement and all —for $21,000. From this success stemmed a whole series of "Executive's home" classifieds in the papers. You can still see them occasionally. They even report that a farmer disposed of an outbuilding this way, listing it as an executive's barn.

* Sometimes, though, the drive of these high-pressure girls backfires, as in the case of a Greater Boston fireball. She made $17,000 in fees the first year of her career in real estate! As the dough rolled in she and her husband began living on a more lavish scale: horsey set, travel, deb parties for daughter, etc. The next year the bottom fell out of the market and she has never come close to that first year's velvet. They can't retrench—status, you know—and they are hopelessly in debt and in need of full-time psychiatry. However, there is one possibility: they're thinking of selling their house.

For those males who get the nervous shakes at the thought of trying to drive a bargain of any dimension, the aplomb of these assured women is heartwarming. Here's what happened in a fine residential suburb recently. An agent was invited by a Mrs. Brown to drop by and inspect her house, which would be put on the market. When the agent got there, the street was jammed with cars. Mrs. Brown had asked every dealer within phoning distance. After the party was well under way—everyone having looked the place over and having had coffee or a cocktail—Mrs. Brown announced that she wanted $55,000 for the house and would do business with the highest bidder.

Even the most ordinary and unaggressive women are capable of astonishing inventiveness. I was fortunate enough to witness another one of these remarkable ladies in action. When Sam Miller got himself a job in Phoenix, he went out there to take over the new position before selling his place in Rye. There was a school year in the East for the kids to finish up and besides Ann, his wife, thought she could strike a better bargain without having him around underfoot giving her poor advice. Once he was gone she put the house on the market. I stopped in one morning when she was showing it.

Someone had telephoned that they would arrive about 10:30 AM for a look-through. Ann and her daughter Connie bustled about fluffing up pillows and trying to close a few doors that always stick in the spring. At precisely 10:30, it being Saturday, the buzzer rang and Ann rushed to the side kitchen door. There stood a ten-year-old with dirty face and hands.

"Chris around?"

No, Ann said in disgust, Chris was not around and she she didn't *want* him around, either. She shut the door and came back to the living room, standing there and looking about.

She picked up a baseball mitt from the coffee table. Just then a gong, rather than a buzzer, sounded. She stiffened and screeched:

"Oh, my God, they're coming in the front door!"

She ran from the room. She soon marched back leading a man, a woman, and a boy. She was still holding the baseball glove. She had slipped it on her left hand and was punching it with her fist. I thought this showed great presence of mind.

"You'll have to excuse the mess," Ann said in keeping with tradition. Of course, the place was as neat as a Dutch parlor on Sunday. But behind the party came Rumpelmayer, the Miller dachshund. I remembered that Ann had predicted that the animal would get into the house. "Viewers always let her in, and she expects it," Ann had said. The danger was that Rumpelmayer, at the age of eight years, was not housebroken. Deftly fielding the questions thrown at her by the man and woman, and patting the glove, Ann showed the visitors through the downstairs. "Yes, the hi-fi is built in, and I'm afraid it goes with the house whether you want to listen to it or not." She giggled.

Then she showed them the mud room. "This is where the children hang their messy clothes and take off their wet socks and muddy boots before they are allowed into the house proper."

I knew that the Miller children always ran through the living room in their muddy things to get to the mud room, but I didn't say anything.

"And here is the two-car garage with room for bicycles," she continued. "Right now, you see, the cars are parked in the driveway because the boat is in this half and the dog's kennel had to be put over there while we reseeded that section of the lawn, and . . ."

They all trooped back into the main part of the house. She immediately noticed that Rumpelmayer had wet the rug. As Ann had already thrown the wall-to-wall living room carpet into the deal, she quickly moved over and stood on the dark spot.

"Now I can show you the upstairs," she announced. "What's that noise?" She glanced at the ceiling. Everyone was silent. A sloshing could be heard. "Oh, no! Connie's taking a bath. Of all the— Well, you won't be able to see the upstairs bathroom. Come on."

They went single file up the stairs and tramped around. Pretty soon the whole gang was back downstairs and Ann was pointing out at the rear yard. She showed them the sliding doors, explaining how the screens and windows were interchangeable.

"Oh, I love a screen porch," the lady exclaimed. "What about schools? Are they good?"

"Oh, sure," Ann replied emphatically.

"I'm flunking out," said Chris, who had joined the caravan.

"Can the children walk to school?"

"Oh, yes. They go right through this backyard and through there"—she indicated the back of Andersons' yard—"and down the street to the school. It's all right to go that way. The whole neighborhood does it."

The man looked worried. "You mean *everybody* walks to school through your yard?"

"Well, a *few* children do," Ann backtracked.

The couple wandered around a few more minutes with their son. Suddenly she turned to Ann and asked, "Which way are the prevailing winds?"

This was the acid test. Obviously a trick question thrown in as an exercise in gamesmanship, it was a woman-to-woman confrontation that only they themselves can understand.

How Ann handled it would establish her superiority or her incompetence. I needn't have worried; she had been through tougher tests. "From the west," she replied immediately, without batting an eye. The woman looked satisfied and the man admiring. They left by the kitchen door. Ann walked steadily to the sideboard, took out a bottle of Scotch, poured us a drink. She looked at me. "Which way *are* the prevailing winds?" I told her she had guessed right. I learned later that with subsequent customers she always added, "And the prevailing winds, of course, are from the west."

Ann Miller sold her house. She got a lawyer and made all the arrangements. Sam flew East for the closing, signing where they told him. Ann persuaded him to drive one of the cars back, solving another problem. When school closed, she called the movers, packed up and went to Phoenix. There she found Sam huddled in a rented room. She organized everything and finally found a house with air conditioning and a swimming pool. She pointed her finger again and Sam signed.

Sure, you'll say, these real estate gambits are vivid, all right. They go some way toward documenting the theory that there are women with inner strength and self-confidence. But, you ask, how about the intramural domestic riddles? How do these so-called smart girls handle the tough ones that come up a dozen times a day right at home?

Well, they handle them. There are women who do not fold up in the face of adversity; there are women who think fast on their feet.

The Case of the Threatening Epidemic

Problem: Doris Lumpkin and her husband are planning a cruise to Nassau. Suddenly there is a mumps scare in town. If any of her three youngsters get mumps, all will eventually catch the disease and the sitter won't come and the trip will have to be called off.

Solution: She quick gets mumps shots from local M.D. Then day after day she drags the children from one contagious household to another—including four calls on perfect strangers—infecting them. Happy ending: within a month all three had recovered from a mild attack of the disease. Cruise goes on as planned.

The Case of the Generous Mother

Problem: It is summer. Mrs. M. is sending her John to Wyoming to visit a ranch owned by relatives. They are taking John's friend David, too. Each must have two pairs of sturdy dungarees. David's mother cannot afford to buy them. How to get two pairs of dungarees for David without making her pay for them? Cannot purchase them for her because of possible hurt feelings.

Solution: Mrs. M—— buys two pairs of dungarees, puts them through her own washing machine, then gives them to David's mother saying they are an old pair of John's that don't fit him.

The Case of the Hot Plates

Problem: Newlyweds. Arthur, having been a bachelor for ten adult years, insists Mary do dishes immediately after each meal. One evening, five minutes before he is due to return home, she washes the day's accumulation of dishes, silver, etc. Then she fears he will feel them (as he has done before) to see if they are warm from recent washing.

Solution: Place hot plates and silver in refrigerator for a few moments.

The Case of the Ill-Timed Delivery

Problem: Pregnant wife has appointment at trusty haircutter's for one week before doctor's predicted birth of baby. Two weeks before appointment, labor pains. She can't go to hospital with hair looking like this.

Solution: She makes phone calls in this order: to Jimmy, the trusty haircutter. "You've just got to squeeze me in this morning. It's an emergency!" (2) To her mother. (3) To her doctor. Mother rushes over, packs suitcase, drives daughter straight to Jimmy's. He trims her suitably for a stay in the maternity ward, while she squirms at recurrent labor pain. Mother pops in saying, "Hurry!" Jimmy finishes and mother gets pregnant daughter to hospital in time for delivery. Her hair is hardly mussed.

The Sweet Smell of Success

Problem: This time a Wilton, Connecticut, woman returns from driving her man to the station and finds a skunk in the kitchen.

Solution: She goes immediately for tranquilizers. Instead of taking one herself, she dissolves several in warm milk, putting a saucer down for the intruder. An hour or so later the animal is sleeping peacefully on the floor. She scoops it up with a shovel and replaces it in its natural surroundings where it awakes, the happiest skunk in the suburbs.

The Case of the Reluctant Carpenter

Problem: Upon moving into a new house, husband reneges on pre-purchase promises to do-it-himself; put on screen doors, build a playroom, paint the porch floor, make valances, construct bookshelves, and install doorbell. His running excuse: how can he be a handyman when he doesn't even have a workbench or any tools?

Solution: Wife hires a carpenter, not to attend to the unfinished tasks about the house, but to build a workbench. He stocks it with tools, brushes, sandpaper, paints, lumber, nails, the works. The tab comes to two hundred and ten dollars. (As of this writing, the toilet-paper holders have not yet been put in place.)

XVI

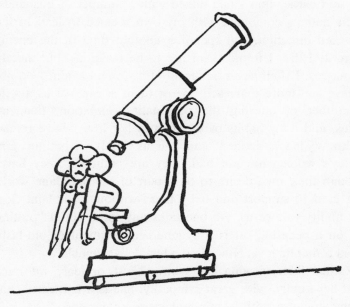

Exit, Bitching

When I first went out into the country I was prepared to prove that the girls of the unurban frontier were more or less representatives of the devil, with a few exceptions. The typical male attitude toward the other sex is contempt veiled by a superficial show of emotion, or it is fear hidden by a display of superiority. He says with a sneer, "Aw, that's a woman for ya," and then he goes to a bar and watches a prizefight to prove he's a man. Naturally this attitude is part and parcel of the theory that women are really evil.

I said earlier that I had talked with a number of husbands. Their notions combined with my own seemed to lead in the expected direction. But spending all that time in the enemy camp as I did, I found them not to be insidious, but merely innocuous. I shall never be afraid of a woman again. I do not believe any more that each one of them is capable as a wife or mother of altering the personality, ambition, financial status, and daily habits of the man in her life. I have reread Philip Wylie's indictment and it is as timely as bathtub gin. Today's women are not bad; they are pathetic. They have, through their own desire to be a part of the mundane world that used to support and baby them without complaint, lost any ability to awe us. No one talks any more about "putting her on a pedestal." It is a bygone accouterment of old-fashioned romantic love. Nowadays a female is a female.

Rather than viewing her with disgust or fear, we must treat her kindly, with great sympathy. She is a frustrated, unhappy creature with a minimal sense of humor. What she thought would be a pleasure—homemaking—has become an inferno to escape. Labor-saving devices and ready-made foods have done away with most of the satisfaction that used to come from the knowledge that there were tasks that only she could perform for her loving family. The climax of her existence comes somewhere around the middle of the wedding ceremony. From then on it's all downhill, a steady letdown, sporadically relieved by the occasional appearance of a baby. Caring for small children is an interesting job, diminishing in appeal as the child grows older. Girls gradually start hating their mothers, and growing boys simply ignore them. Thus a mother reaps what she sows and winds up as nothing more than a chauffeur.

A woman puts up a brave front, though. Relying on the traditional mysterious "intuition" is only one ploy, and an ancient one. The newest angle is that the twentieth-century girl is "free," that she has the vote, can get a job, can earn her own living, can seek a divorce, can have an affair, can be the boss of the family, can treat her husband like a little boy, can be indulgent, helpful, firm and yet unyielding. The truth is, of course, that she has in the 1960s merely been transferred to a larger cell, but she is still incarcerated. The propaganda has been spread without surcease that she is emancipated. Who started this I do not know. Who really believes it? She wants to, and perhaps she does. But she is not prepared to argue the point very persuasively.

When a woman understood the boundaries of her responsibilities, she was less confused. Now, in her so-called emancipated state she spends most of her new free time trying to find out what's wrong. From the strictly practical considerations of what's-the-best-girdle-for-me to the other extreme—"Oh, I feel like such an idiot. I'm going to start reading books, and the editorials, too"—she is constantly probing, probing, plumbing, plumbing, hoping to learn why and where she is inadequate and miserable.

If she can afford it, she may end up at a psychiatrist's feet. One who tried that confessed to me that she had been advised to "identify with my husband when he comes home with his problems. I should create an empathy."

Then she screeched at me. "Identify? Empathy? I've identified so many problems in the past seven years that I could open an office myself. I feel that it's about time he started solving a few of mine instead of saving his own and bringing them home at night. I'd like to go on first some night for a change. I'd put on a good show."

For each visit to an analyst, there are five thousand letters written to the lovelorn columns in the papers, or to the radio and television advice-dispensers. The saddest feature is that one can read or hear, between the lines of these edited appeals, a cry for help. The responses, naturally, have to be along non-controversial, unoriginal, Puritanical lines.

Just for fun, I show you a typical anguished call for The Secret, and the expert's reply. In this case the expert was a woman, too, adding evidence to the theory that when two or more females come in the door, humor flies out the window.

"Dear Dr. B——," was the query, "I am 28 years old and have been married two years to a man of my own age. We have a young baby. The trouble is that our marriage is breaking up, I'm afraid. My husband stays out late at night and when he comes home and I ask him where he's been he says it is none of my business. I have gone on strike now; I am not speaking to him. I guess the thing that bothers him most is that I am jealous of his freedom." —ANXIOUS.

"Dear Anxious," was the lady doctor's straight-faced reply, "you are not jealous of his freedom but of his immaturity. This man has never grown up, if he stays out late at night. He doesn't understand the pact of marriage. Now the thing to do is to give up the non-speaking program; that will solve nothing. Instead, you must bring out the maturity in him. You must tell him that marriage is an agreement, and would he mind sitting down and writing down the rules of behavior, the rules of conduct for marriage, as he sees them. Then you should do the same. You two can discuss these rules and he will soon begin to understand the requirement of marriage."

The picture comes to mind. One time she corrals this impossible fellow, when he's around, and when the baby's not screaming or being fed. She gives him a pencil and paper and says, here, write down the rules of marriage as you see them. "Whadaya, some kinda nut?" he will sneer. She will insist. He will finally grab the paper and scribble: "A man should be left alone—should have a night out with the boys—shoont hafta do dishes—answer no questions—"

The conflict is between a man who sees matrimony in the old terms and a woman who doesn't. The advice was unrealistic but safe. In any case, the exchange reveals, I believe, the anomalous position of the new split-level girls. My own advice to ANXIOUS would have been to start pressing for a house, a car, new furniture—go out and run up some bills if necessary. In other words, enmesh the guy in the Sixties trap where he belongs. Then he would find himself tied down, and she would have the freedom she thinks should be hers.

Puzzled housewives who have no money for psychiatrists or no faith in letters fall back on the plethora of pontification that comes in the magazines and books day after day. All about married love, how not to give your husband a heart attack, how to live with an alcoholic, how to make yourself attractive again—every conceivable kind of hot tip flows from the busy quills of the experts. For example, one of them recently presented a list of ten signs of "trouble ahead" for his women readers to look for and to correct:

Poor communication, poor sexual adjustment, lack of companionship, inability to compromise, lack of co-operation, selfishness, criticism or nagging, neglect or indifference, escapist behavior, and involvement with another.

I discussed these with a jumpy housewife. When she was told that these were situations that could lead to the termination of a marriage, she grabbed the paper from my hands, pointed at the list and sarcastically cried, "Oh, I'll try this one first, and then this, and—"

Obviously the ten signs of crumbling homelife are merely ten descriptive terms to be applied to a typical American marriage. That kind of talk is utterly useless for the bewildered bride. She just wants to know why her husband isn't nicer to her and why she doesn't feel contented. No one will tell her.

I even found ladies who were listening to astrologers, palmists, and mediums. One advantage there is that the spiel is infinitely more interesting and exciting than what Dr. Grump writes in his column. Women have great faith in the future, as they have in the distorted memories of the dim past. (It's the present that bothers them.) So they love to hear what's going to happen because it is bound to be better than what is happening. I tested the strength of their beliefs by asking at least a dozen women what they had wished for when they blew out the candles on their most recent birthday cake: not one would tell me. They obviously were still waiting for whatever millennium they had conjured up.

When you get right down to it, there isn't any reliable and convenient method for a woman to find out what's eating her. The best she can do is kick around her annoyances with her friends. Misery loves company and it is reassuring to hear that others have their sorrows too. As one might expect from what one hears about the frictions between spouses, there has to be a scapegoat, and so *she* picks *him*. I collected quite a lot of material from women who wanted to describe the hard lines of their existence. In every sample there was something about the husband's intransigence, indolence, or lack of understanding. (These cases can be found in the Appendix for those who wish to delve further into the matter.)

In view of all this, I call for a program for the rehabilitation of the American housewife. First, a commission must be appointed to study her; the members must be bachelors and spinsters. Second, we must set up clinics to help her solve her *non-sexual* problems. Third, we must repeal the Nineteenth Amendment to the Constitution; she gave up all her female prerogatives to gain the one advantage of voting, which doesn't really do anything for her. Fourth, a massive educational campaign must be instituted to convince people that a girl is not an utter failure if she doesn't get married.

In other words, modern woman has progressed too far too fast. She is not yet ready for the space age, and like a diver with the bends, we must rush her into the decompression chamber, giving her a chance to adjust to this era a bit more slowly. It is apparent from what I found in my year in the villages of our nation that American girls are not suited for the role that has been assigned them. This is shocking, all right, but for a real jolt take a look at the young teen-age chicks who are coming up.

Bibliography and Suggested Further Reading for Those Studying American Female Behavior

Advice and Dissent
The Compleat Wrangler
The Decline and Fall of My Third Wife
Generation of Diapers
Mein Cramp
My Wife in Court
The Organized Man

Appendix A

Messages, Remarks, and Other Forms of
Communications Intercepted, though Not
Necessarily Translated, and Taken at
Random from the Author's Notes

One cat to another: "Say, Marge, when did you get out of
college? We're having a little bet."

Man has run out of gas on the parkway. As he trudges down
the road in search of service station, his wife calls after him:
"Don't forget to look for a place that gives stamps!"

Child to parent: "I hate you! I want to go and live with Gwendolyn's mother!"

"And there I was, sitting with that awful fairy, telling me about Haiti, wrist limp, flicking his shoulders. I was so embarrassed. What should I have done?"
"Why, put your hand on his knee, spit, tell a dirty joke. . . ."

A woman encountered her psychiatrist out in public. She introduced her husband to him, saying, "Doctor, here's one of the men I've been telling you about."

Parent to child (with catch in throat): "Some day you'll be sorry you spoke to me that way."

"Pauline, what are *you* doing back in the States?" asked a local girl of a recent returnee from Mexico.
"Frankly, I came to spend fifty-two dollars on the ——— Rejuvenation Plan."
"Wonderful! When do you start?"
"Start? I've already been!"

Wife to husband: "I suppose you'll turn into quite a gay blade after I'm gone."

A wife was dressing her kiddies for school. Her husband waited outside impatiently, tooting the horn as was his custom to hurry them up. "Dear," his wife calls, "you dress the children and I'll come out and honk the horn."

"We can't possibly use our basement for a bomb shelter. That's where the cat goes to the bathroom."

If the way to a man's heart is through his stomach, the key to a woman's innermost secrets is in another direction. There is an incantation that seems to cast a spell, like a truth serum. It is in the form of a rhetorical question:

"What have you done to your hair? It looks wonderful."

Appendix B

Further Studies from My Casebook
(Cf. Chapter XVII)

ERICA: "What do you do all day?" If I hear him say that once more I'll murder him. How can I describe it? I get in and out of the car all day. If I told him I was tired from getting in and out of the car all day he'd laugh in my face. I say to him at night, "You're lucky. You can put your feet up and I have to go out and get dinner." He says, "Well, what did you do all day?" He comes in the kitchen and stands there, peeking at the top of the refrigerator. "Hey, look at the dust up here." I blow my top. He's six feet two inches. I've lived here five years and I've never even *seen* the top of the refrigerator, much less dust it.

FLORENCE: Bill leaves me messages, day after day: *Shovel the snow away from the fuel tank inlet.* I've uncovered the whole house. I can't find it. I finally phone the oil company. Bill accuses me of being stupid.

JEAN: We lived in an apartment. One day there was a story in the paper about a crime that took place in our town: an intruder had rung the bell, pushed his way into an apartment similar to ours, and raped the lady of the house. Hugh read this and said, "Gosh, that worries me. The same thing could happen to you. I'll get a chain lock for the door, so you can see who's outside without opening it all the way." Loyal guy, he came home that night with the lock. It was prompt action on his part, because usually he talks about something for a long time before getting it done. I felt flattered that his fears for my safety had made him act so quickly.

"I am really worried about intruders," he repeated as he opened the box, held it up against the doorjamb and showed me how the chain worked. We talked about it that night. To make a long story short, the chain lock remained on the foyer table for quite a long time. Finally during a cleaning it got put in the drawer. Every so often I'd ask, "When are you going to put that chain lock on?" and he'd reply, "Gosh, do it right now," but on his way to the screwdriver, something would sidetrack him.

Three months later I installed the chain lock myself. When he came home that night it was hooked and he couldn't get in. When I released it, slowly, he was surprised but happy. "Gosh, I'm glad that chain lock is up," he said. "I've been really worried about these intruders." He wasn't being funny, though today he claims he said it as a joke.

CARLA: On my last—and I mean it was my fourth, counting miscarriages—I said, "I want a private room this time. It's the last chance I'll have." And I got it. Pure luxury. Private shower and a big room. One floor nurse assigned to me alone. I could have visitors whenever I wanted. Telephone. Boy, that was really living. The next thing I knew, a couple of years later, I was pregnant again. I said, "How about the private room deal again?" He blew up. "That's why you got pregnant again! I thought we agreed Sara was to be the last." Back to semiprivate I went.

CATHY: I'm in the hospital. I've had a female operation, and I've spent four days there. Ollie is getting the kids off to school, then catching the train, and then coming home a little early to get supper for them. There is a cleaning woman during the day who watches for the younger children when they return from schol. Well, I have a telephone and one morning I ring up to see if everything is all right. I know right away from the way he answers that Ollie is upstairs in the bedroom and a little questioning makes it clear that he is still in the bedroom and more questioning makes it clear that he is still in bed! It is 8:30 AM and there are four kids to feed, dress, and get off to school, two of them leaving long before 8:30.

How the hell did he do it? Here's how: he missed the train that day. It wasn't until later, when I returned home, that I discovered that he had come downstairs and put breakfast on the table and then gone back up to bed. What kind of breakfast? He had put out pretzels and milk and they loved it. They spoke about it to me.

When I was ready to come home, incidentally, I asked the hospital to call a cab, but they said the doctor had decreed no cab, only a private car. So I phoned the house at 8 AM that morning and he was still in bed, as I might have expected. "You've got to come and get me," I said. He yelled bloody murder. "God, Cathy, I've got a job to do, to pay for this operation of yours, you know. I've got to get to work." I yelled back at him, "You're in bed now, and if I hadn't telephoned you'd still be asleep. How can you get to work that way?" He came for me, grumbling all the way. When I got home I expected some attention, but the whole bunch of them acted as though I'd been on a vacation. They put the pressure on. "Get this place cleaned up, will ya?" Ollie said, pointing to the mess, and it really was a mess, with me gone four days, and no one to tell the cleaning woman what to do, and the boys yelling for pretzels and milk.*

PHYLLIS: We were involved in the Junior League Teen-age Benefit affair and Audrey—she's talented, you know—wrote a musical play pitched to the kids and we were going to put this on and raise some dough. I was picked as stage manager. Ernie hates to have me go out at night, but after some special pleading he give in and said okay. There were the usual night rehearsals and of course they lasted until all hours. Wives were coming home at 1 AM night after night, and the husbands were getting upset, especially Ernie. The strain was beginning to tell. One night he was late getting home. I put the kids into bed and after they had fallen asleep I went to rehearsal. While I was gone Glen got sick and threw up. Ernie came home to this, and I wasn't there. He was wild. He'd had a few drinks. He stamped into the club and shouted at me in front of everybody, making a terrible scene, castigating the whole benefit, which made mothers neglect their children who were throwing up at home and so forth. He grabbed me by the arm and dragged me out of the hall. Naturally I had to resign, and the next day Ruth took over. Two days later Ernie bought me a mink coat, which shows how he felt about *that* rampage.

SANDRA: The only thing I do to my hair is to have it cut. Once in a while I try something different, but it never seems to work out. I once went to Maurice and it cost a fortune. Well, one day I bought some tint at the drugstore and I started working on myself that afternoon, hoping to cover

* In the office that day his secretary asked him, "How is your wife?" Ollie replied, "Grouchy as hell." The secretary answered, "Then she must be recovering all right; they get grouchy when they're getting better."

179

some of the gray. In the middle of it I panicked and screamed for Violet, the cleaning lady. She came running and helped me finish. The result was a sort of two-tone job, something old and something new. I asked Hal that night if he noticed anything. He looked me up and down and said, "No, what?" I was glad it wasn't noticeable and I told him so. For years I had complained that he never noticed anything about me. That night we had people in for dinner. During a lull in the conversation Hal piped up, "How d'ya like Sandy's hair? She dyed it today."

NANCY: Dave said to me once, when I shouted for the children, "Your voice is so shrill. It goes right through my head. There's nothing worse than a shrill woman." He clapped his hands over his ears in mock pain. Now I go out and softly call, "Children, dinner's ready." And no one comes.

Appendix C

TAPE-RECORDED SCENE

Scene: A Living Room. Bell rings.

SHE: Who the hell can that be? (*Opens door.*) Oh, my God, it's Mr. Andrew about the upholstery. Hello, Mr. Andrew.

HE: Hello.

SHE: Now, here's the chair, and there's the couch. Your father did this one. Are you going to tie up the springs, too?

HE: (*Nodding.*) Do you want a foam rubber back?

SHE: Lord, no, I can't afford it. [She has just been telling a vistor about her forthcoming two-week Christmas vacation in Mexico.] Now, tell me, how many yards will we need, with the flounce?

HE: (*Calculating.*) Six and a half yards.

SHE: My God, at ten ninety-five a yard! (*Looking at couch and poking same.*) This seat needs some more down, I suppose.

HE:	Yes.
SHE:	How much?—at seven-fifty a pound, I suppose.
HE:	Seven-ten a pound.
SHE:	It'd be cheaper to buy the geese and pluck them yourself. Then you'd eat the meat and have the feathers.
HE:	We use half and half.
SHE:	Half and half what? Half duck feathers and half goose?
HE:	Half goose feathers and half goose down. You can't stuff with duck feathers.
SHE:	Why not?
HE:	They smell. On a humid day your whole house would smell like a barnyard.
SHE:	(*Musing.*) Maybe that's why those Southern homes always smell that way. Say, Mr. Andrew, does it kill the goose to pluck the feathers? Could you take a few from each goose and then let him go and pick some more from him another time?
HE:	I really don't know.
SHE:	Does it hurt when they pull the down out?
HE:	I don't know. I never went that far back.
SHE:	What do you mean?
HE:	I mean all I know is that it comes in a bag.
SHE:	(*Looking at the couch again.*) Would a pound do anything?
HE:	(*Smiling.*) Not a thing.
SHE:	Two pounds?
HE:	Two pounds you're apt to notice it.
SHE:	Put in two pounds.
HE:	Might as well not put any in as not enough.
SHE:	Okay, I'll go to two and a half pounds. No more.
HE:	Of course, we air it out and sometimes that helps.

You see, it gets packed over the years and when we air it out, well, it sometimes puffs it up some. We'll do that and see how it comes out.

SHE: *One* pound, then! (*Aside.*) Don't ever have your chairs upholstered. It costs a fortune. I hate slip covers. They come loose, and when a fellow sits in the chair he goes sliding down on the floor with the slip covers coming along with him. (*To Mr. Andrew.*) Now, let me know how much for the material and the labor.

HE: That's what I'm going to figure. (*After much measuring.*) The chair, upholstered, with kick pleat, sixty-two fifty.

SHE: Yes, that's what you said before.

HE: No, I said sixty-seven fifty. And the couch, retied, labor, upholstered, and all, a hundred and twenty-five.

SHE: When will you have it done.

HE: (*Hesitates.*) Before Christmas, I hope. Depends on the material.

SHE: And a pound of feathers.

CURTAIN

Production Operating

Decisions in the Total

Business Strategy

ARCH R. DOOLEY, *Associate Professor of Business Administration*

ROBERT E. McGARRAH, *formerly Associate Professor of Business Administration*

JAMES L. McKENNEY, *Assistant Professor of Business Administration*

RICHARD S. ROSENBLOOM, *Assistant Professor of Business Administration*

C. WICKHAM SKINNER, *Associate Professor of Business Administration*

PHILIP H. THURSTON, *Associate Professor of Business Administration*

Harvard University Graduate School of Business Administration

CASEBOOKS IN PRODUCTION MANAGEMENT

Production Operating

Decisions in the Total

Business Strategy

John Wiley & Sons, Inc., New York · London · Sydney

Except where specifically attributed to other sources, all cases in this volume are copyrighted by the President and Fellows of Harvard College and are used by express permission. In certain instances the name of the company has been disguised. Also, in various cases, certain dates, quantitative data, and the identity of some individuals, locations, organizations, and products have been disguised. Disguises so employed leave unaltered the salient characteristics of the problems which confronted the management of the firm. Case material of the Harvard Graduate School of Business Administration is prepared as a basis for class discussion. Cases are not designed to present illustrations of either effective or ineffective handling of administrative problems.

To Franklin Erton Folts

Foreword

This book is part of a series composed of materials employed in the required Production course in the MBA Program of the Harvard Graduate School of Business Administration. In the main, these materials consist of case studies describing authentic production-management problems that have arisen in specific firms. Each case places the student in the role of the manager responsible for solving the problem described.

When studied and then used as a basis for classroom discussion, these materials can make five major contributions to a student's educational preparation for a management career:

• an understanding of the principal facets of the total process involved in the production of manufactured goods, and of the numerous, interrelated activities that occur within that process;

• an appreciation of the extent to which a variety of feasible choices are likely to be present at each stage of the production process, the multiplicity of decisions that therefore are demanded of production management, and the varied—and often conflicting—considerations that can be germane to such decisions;

• an insight into the interactions existing between the production decisions of a given company, the activities in other sectors of the same business, the practices of other concerns in that industry, and forces affecting the entire economy;

• a comprehension therefore of the specific factors that make skill in the art of production management a prime competitive advantage for the individual company and a crucially important asset for the nation;

• an opportunity to make a beginning toward the development of such skill.

The series has been divided into five independent, but complementary, volumes. This is in recognition of the considerable variations existing among schools of business administration and of engineering in regard to the teaching of production management. These variations extend to the specific topics to be covered, the emphasis to be given to each, the pedagogic methods employed, and the allocation among various faculty departments of teaching responsibilities for these topics. The division of series materials is designed, therefore, to offer considerable latitude to the individual instructor in selecting a mix and sequence of materials, depth of coverage, and degree of reliance on case studies, that parallel his specific objectives in one or more courses. Three of the volumes—those dealing, respectively, with the topics of wage administration, operations planning and control, and the introduction of new products, processes, and facilities—should be of particular interest to instructors who wish to employ case studies to supplement texts in courses dealing exclusively with these subjects.

The topical emphasis of each volume of the series is indicated in its subtitle, and is described in the volume preface. Each volume can be employed independently of, or in conjunction with, others in the series. The volume subtitled *Basic Problems, Concepts, and Techniques* provides a broad introductory background to the field. The value of each of the other volumes in the series will be enhanced if the student has an understanding of production management which is equivalent, in coverage and depth, to that provided in the series' introductory volume. It is not essential, however, that case studies be employed in developing this background.

The series also assumes that other courses, taken previously or concurrently, will have equipped the student with a working knowledge of accounting principles and of basic concepts of statistics. It is not assumed, however, that the student will have a background in higher mathematics, managerial economics, or engineering. As is true of the actual practice of production management, however, the cases in this series provide numerous opportunities for persons who are knowledgeable in any of these disciplines to employ their skills advantageously. This is true also of persons who are skilled in the behavioral sciences. Indeed, we see as one of the unique educational assets inherent in case materials the opportunities they represent for testing generalized concepts and techniques in specific situations, and for gaining practice in the adaptations that such applications may demand.

Certain characteristics are common to all volumes and reflect the basic premises underlying the series.

The most basic of these characteristics is that throughout the series the primary focus is upon management activities—the decision making, planning, and implementing that must underlie effective utilization of the manpower, money, materials, facilities, information, knowledge, and time which constitute the productive resources of any company. This emphasis reflects our conviction that the challenges confronting production management represent the most effective pedagogic vehicle for developing the student's understanding of the production process and of the managerial skills demanded by that process.

The management decisions called for by the cases in the series are principally at the operating level. This is consistent with the educational objectives for which the series is designed. In the context of numerous case situations, however, the discerning student repeatedly will observe the relationship between policy guidelines and operating decisions, and see evidences of the numerous ways in which the nature of specific operating problems may demonstrate the need for revisions in, additions to, or clarifications of, existing policies.

A second characteristic that is common to all volumes of the series is that the case materials do not attempt to present single-dimensioned abstractions of reality. Instead, as in the world of production management, the problems dealt with are commonly characterized by a mix of technological, economic, and human considerations. In numerous instances, analysis will indicate that certain of these elements are sharply in conflict. Use of such materials reflects our conviction that continuing exposure to realistic portrayals of the multidimensioned complexities of production problems is the most effective pedagogic device for developing student insights into the true character of the challenges confronting production management. Indeed, in our judgment, this is the only way to portray accurately what we view as the distinctive dimension of production management: its continuing responsibility not only for detecting and evaluating the technological, economic, and human considerations that relate to a specific situation, but also for dealing with the intensely complex amalgam that is created when, as so frequently happens, all three types of considerations converge and comingle. It is in responding to this complex that production management renders its unique contribution to the business enterprise.

A related characteristic that is shared by all volumes of the series is that in most case situations the student must base his analysis not on perfect information, but rather on an array of facts and judgments, not all of which are invariably consistent with the others, and some of which may represent only indirect evidence relative to the problem at issue. Furthermore, as in the practice of production management, information that would undeniably reduce, or eliminate, uncertainties inherent in the problem sometimes will be lacking.

This characteristic is rooted in two considerations. First, it is an accurate portrayal of reality. The world of production management is not often a world of perfect information. Nor can it be. Time pressures, cost considerations, the multiple activities involved in the production process and the complex interrelations existing among those activities, and the sheer unavailability of certain types of information repeatedly create situations in which production management has no alternative but to employ judgment to buttress imperfect knowledge. In this context it is important to stress that except for rare instances the case studies employed in the series provide the student with no less information than that the company personnel employed in dealing with the problem described. Not infrequently, information actually has been made available in more precise and documented form than that utilized by company personnel.

The second consideration, closely related to the first, is that this realistic portrayal of the information which in fact was brought to bear on specific production situations provides what we consider to be an important opportunity for enhancing the learning opportunity afforded the student. It underscores the fact that information is an asset, that its lack can entail risk, but that its availability often demands tangible efforts which, in turn, can entail costs measured in terms both of money and time. The student therefore is provided repeated opportunities to deal—in terms of a specific situation—not with the theoretical question of whether additional information would be helpful, but rather with the managerial questions of whether additional information could in fact be obtained and, if so, whether the costs of obtaining it would be justified.

Relatedly, we are convinced that an authentic portrayal of the degree and quality of the information available in specific production situations provides valuable opportunities for the student to gain further insights into the applicability of techniques of formal analysis which presuppose the availability of certain types of data, to assess the contributions such techniques can render, and to recognize the steps and costs that may be required before they can be employed in a specific situation.

An additional consideration that is common to all the volumes is the effort to create an environment in which the student will discern the purposefulness of the knowledge that he is required to master. In the aggregate, the materials in each volume provide an extensive inventory of information regarding practices, concepts, and techniques that are unique to the functions of production management. They also provide various insights into the characteristics of the manufacturing processes employed in a number of industries. In the main, such knowledge is conveyed as part of the information relating to specific case situations. Wherever it has seemed pedagogically useful to do so, however, such material has been incorporated into reference notes or readings.

But whatever the form in which it is presented, the flow of information in each volume is ordered in such a way that, with reflection on the previous experiences to which the volume has exposed him, the student will be able to perceive the purposefulness of new knowledge as it is made available to him, and to discern how its mastery and judicious use will increase his effectiveness in dealing with production management problems. The materials in each volume are arranged so as also to provide repeated opportunities for the student to test and to strengthen his command of knowledge previously acquired by utilizing it in ensuing case situations.

In summary, the materials in this series are designed to develop the student's understanding of and competence in the functions of production management by confronting him with many decision-making responsibilities for dealing with the challenges that those functions represent.

Preface

This volume integrates the various elements of the "Casebooks in Production Management" series. Its focus rests on both the interaction of production management with the operating strategy of the individual company and its contribution to that strategy. This focus is achieved through case studies of specific operating problems which, because of their importance, ramifications, or both, cannot be solved effectively through the efforts of only one phase of a company's production endeavors, nor even through the aggregate activities of the complete production process. These problems transect boundary lines. They demand solutions in which production considerations are related to and involved in the total operating program of the company. To permit a focus of this kind, each of the case studies in this volume contains not only detailed descriptions of the company's production practices and requirements, but also other business and background data pertinent to the total operating conditions under examination.

The character and the level of the problems portrayed render significant educational contributions to the student who, through study of the other volumes in this series, or exposure to comparable educational materials, or actual business experience, has acquired a basic familiarity with the major facets and techniques of the production process as well as the functions and responsibilities of production management. By placing himself in the role of the production manager who is obliged to respond effectively to the problems posed by these cases, the student strengthens his mastery of production management skills and reinforces his previously acquired insights. He thus gains experience in the vitally important managerial art of blending individual responses to various facets of a problem into a cohesive solution to the total problem.

The sequence of the cases in this volume emphasizes two major operating responsibilities of production management. Part 1 considers the continuing responsibility for assessing the over-all effectiveness of existing production practices against the ever-changing background of the business environment in order to determine and implement the action requirements of the present or the future. The total impact of the cases in this section of the volume should impart a realization that the challenges confronting production management are not confined to situations of urgent crisis. They also exist in the responsibility for maintaining a satisfactory status quo based on subjective standards of attainable production efficiency and analysis of probable future developments and needs.

Part 2 of the volume features cases portraying immediate operating problems which impede the effectiveness of existing production operations and jeopardize production commitments and goals. The focus is upon production management's responsibility for discerning the causes of such problems and providing effective remedies.

The final section of this volume, Part 3, provides a brief insight into foreign production operations. If the instructor elects to do so, the cases in this section can be employed merely as further opportunities for the student to test his analytical and decision-making skills in production management situations that are challenging in their own right. These cases further enjoy the pedagogic asset of an unfamiliar and, hence, more than routinely interesting setting.

If desired, however, these foreign production management problems can be employed to achieve still broader educational objectives. For students whose career interests lie in overseas business operations, these cases provide opportunities for developing valuable insights into the distinctive managerial challenges that may arise in a foreign setting. Similarly, they offer concrete examples of the continuing managerial responsibility for determining the extent to which familiar domestic concepts and techniques of production management can be employed —with or without adaptation—in a foreign setting. Moreover, the unique operating environment in these foreign cases can provide a basis for thoughtful analysis of the extent to which, in either a domestic or a foreign setting, production management decisions can be shaped primarily by the technological requirements of the manufacturing process, as well as the extent to which they must reflect the total environment of the production operation.

Throughout the volume, the organization and presentation of the cases place on the student the primary responsibility for diagnosing the critical aspects of the problems confronting each company, for differentiating symptoms from causes, and for identifying among a diverse array of information the data most germane to the management decisions demanded. As in the actual practice of production management, the student cannot rely on artificial "illuminating beacons," such as chapter headings, amplifying footnotes, or similar devices, to identify the major thrust of the problems confronting the company, or to indicate the concepts or techniques that would prove most helpful in dealing with the particular situation. Nor can he assume that some infallible force has sifted all available information to spare him the burden of differentiating the relevant from the irrelevant. Instead, these are judgments that the student must make himself from his analysis of the specifics of the case situation confronting him.

The abundance of detailed information provided in each of the case studies permits this volume to be used with particular effectiveness as a basis for extensive action-planning. Indeed, the rigors of classroom discussion can be counted on to provide some painful but rewarding educational experiences for any student who assumes that he has fulfilled the operating responsibilities of production management merely by identifying a general response to a case situation without detailing the specific steps required, and the costs, risks, and difficulties incurred in achieving this response. Instead, in their entirety, the cases in this volume repeatedly document the urgent need for identification and assessment of the actions required to implement a given solution to a specific operating problem; these action requirements are always important and sometimes represent a critical factor in determining the suitability of the response. To no less an extent, the cases provide opportunities for the student to condition himself to deal with the frequently encountered situations in which production management must choose between a highly desirable solution that would be administratively difficult to attain, and a less satisfactory response posing fewer administrative difficulties, uncertainties, and risks.

Although the case studies in this volume were designed for use in the more advanced stages of an introductory production management course at the professional school level, they have been employed usefully for other purposes as well. These include educational programs designed to intensify the discernment and broaden the administrative insight of management personnel whose business experiences have provided them with considerable expertise on certain specialized aspects of the production process, but have not included opportunities for a systematic exploration of the ways that these individual activities relate to each other and to the total operating strategy of a company.

Cambridge, Massachusetts   THE AUTHORS
December, 1963

Acknowledgments

A ny volume that relies primarily on case studies of authentic business situations owes a major debt of gratitude to those companies and individuals whose cooperation has made such materials available. The authors of this series acknowledge this indebtedness without reservation. Our deep appreciation to the numerous production management personnel who have given so generously of their time and advice to assure that the cases in this series present accurate, realistic accounts of production problems they encountered is heightened by our awareness of the continuing challenges and time pressures which characterize the day-to-day business responsibilities of these individuals.

The authors wish also to express their sincere appreciation to former Dean Stanley F. Teele and former Associate Dean Russell H. Hassler of the Harvard Business School. They encouraged the initial decision to prepare this series for publication and helped provide the time and research assistance required in developing a substantial portion of the materials included in it. Similarly, we acknowledge with gratitude the support and encouragement of Harvard Business School Dean George P. Baker and Associate Dean George F. F. Lombard during the latter stages of the preparation of the series.

In addition to the members of the series' author group, various of our present or former colleagues on the Faculty of the Harvard Business School contributed directly to the development of certain materials in this volume. Franklin E. Folts supervised the preparation of materials comprising a portion of one of the cases. A. Zaleznik assisted him in this work. Richard Robinson furnished information supplementing the field research into one of the case situations. Frederick R. Garrity and Donald R. Riehl, while serving as members of the School's case research staff, were responsible, wholly or partly, for the research underlying several cases and played active roles in developing these data into case materials. Valuable assistance in the preparation of manuscripts was rendered by Carol Kassabian, Bea Siegel, and Nancy Hayes of the Harvard Business School secretarial staff. We similarly are indebted to the School's Division of Audio-Visual Education which, under its Director, George W. Gibson, assisted in the preparation of exhibit materials.

We wish also to express appreciation to Keio University, Tokyo, Japan, for permission to include its copyright case, Osaka Sharin Seizo K.K., which was prepared by Ichiro Kataoka of the Keio Business School Faculty and Stanley S. Miller of the Faculty of the Harvard Business School.

Cambridge, Massachusetts   A. R. D.
December, 1963.   R. E. M.
                                                   J. L. M.
                                                   R. S. R.
                                                   C. W. S.
                                                   P. H. T.

Contents

PART 1. OVER–ALL ASSESSMENT AND

DETERMINATION OF ACTION REQUIREMENTS

Dominion Engineering Works, Ltd.

Several years ago, when describing his company to members of an executive development course at McGill University, Mr. H. G. Welsford, President and Managing Director of Dominion Engineering Works, Ltd. (D.E.W.), of Montreal, Canada, said in part:

My company's business is to market and design industrial machinery of our own manufacture. We are by far the largest company in the nonelectric machinery industry in Canada.

[D.E.W.] was organized in 1920. . . . Dominion Bridge Company was the majority shareholder and it presently holds about 62 per cent of the capital stock.[1] Less than 3 per cent of its shareholders are resident outside of Canada. It is a wholly Canadian venture.

To give you some idea of the size of the operation, we are employing in our offices and shops about 2,700 people.

There are five main Product Divisions[2] each carrying on a distinctly different kind of machinery business. These are:

An Hydraulic Machinery Division whose products consist principally of hydraulic turbines for hydro-electric power development and certain types of associated equipment such as pumps and valves.

A Paper Machinery Division whose products consist essentially of paper-making machines for the production of newsprint and other classes of paper and board.

A Diesel Engine Division whose products include diesel engines for railway locomotives, oil pipelines, and other industrial purposes; marine power plants; and gas engine compressor units for gas pipeline transmission.

---

[1] Mr. Welsford had been the chief executive officer of Dominion Engineering Works for 30 years when, in 1956, he assumed the additional duties of President of the Dominion Bridge Company, the largest Canadian firm of its type. Dominion Bridge's sales typically ran about three times those of D.E.W.

[2] In 1958 a sixth product group—the Roll Division—was given divisional status. This newly organized unit manufactured chilled iron rolls, steel rolls, and shear knives. The rolls were used by mills which processed such products as grain, plastics, and steel.

3

EXHIBIT 1 DOMINION ENGINEERING WORKS, LTD.

(all dollars in 1,000's)

	1958	1957	1956	1955	1954	1953
Sales	$33,723	$35,874	$31,846	$28,435	$26,524	$28,473
Gross Earnings from Operations	2,147	4,198	4,503	4,657	5,402	5,495
Transfer from Operating and Inventory Reserves	635	—	—	—	—	—
Revenue from Investments	16	70	72	79	67	93
Profit on Sale of Bonds and Equipment	(6)	40	(7)	41	34	10
	$ 2,792	$ 4,308	$ 4,568	$ 4,777	$ 5,503	$ 5,598
Deduct:						
Executive Remuneration	$ 148	$ 161	$ 164	$ 160	$ 129	$ 126
Directors' Fees	24	24	23	14	16	17
Legal Fees	8	11	6	5	12	3
Research and Development	581	518	395	267	354	239
Provision for Depreciation and Replacement of Plant, Machinery, and Equipment	1,338	1,470	1,260	1,082	1,089	1,095
	2,099	2,184	1,848	1,528	1,600	1,480
Net Earnings before Income Taxes	693	2,124	2,720	3,249	3,903	4,118
Less: Income Taxes	3	889	1,119	1,493	2,125	2,211
Profit for the Year	$ 690*	$ 1,235	$ 1,601	$ 1,756	$ 1,778	$ 1,907

* Including transfer from reserves.

Source: Annual Reports of the Company.

A Power Crane and Shovel Division whose products consist of convertible power cranes and shovels, both rubber and crawler mounted.

An Industrial Machinery Division whose products include rolling-mill machinery, hydraulic presses, and rubber and plastics mill machinery, all of these including the largest and heaviest types used in this country. . . .

There is a single manufacturing organization which is responsible for manufacturing all the products of all the Product Divisions. . . . The reason we have one manufacturing organization instead of a separate one for each Product Division is mainly a matter of economics. No single Division has a large enough market in Canada to support the very large and expensive special facilities necessary to manufacture its products as efficiently as some of its competitors in a large domestic market such as the United States. But by pooling the products of all of the Divisions there is enough in common in the facilities they require to enable us to support manufacturing facilities which quite reasonably approach the efficiency of larger competitors.

Data relative to the size and profitability of the company during the years immediately preceding Mr. Welsford's remarks are shown in Exhibits 1 and 2. In the same address, Mr. Welsford also commented on the sector of Canadian industry in which D.E.W. operated, saying:

In the United States the machinery industry, not including electrical machinery, is the second largest employer of labor among all the manufacturing industries in that country. The largest employer of labor is the transportation equipment manufacturing industry which makes equipment for road, rail, water, and air transport. The electrical machinery manufacturing industry is in eighth place as an employer of labor.

In Canada the position is somewhat different. Transportation equipment is first as it is in the United States; electrical equipment is sixth instead of eighth, and the manufacture of nonelectrical machinery is only in ninth place as an employer of labor.

This difference in the relative position of the nonelectrical machinery industry in these two countries is due to a national economic policy in Canada which has favored low tariff rates for a wide range of industrial machinery, while the same policy has not been followed with regard to transportation equipment or to electrical machinery. Customs administrative practices, particularly with regard to class or kind rulings and protection against dumping, have made it very easy for foreigners to compete for business in the Canadian market for machinery.

The small size of the Canadian market in relation to the United States is, of course, also a factor, but this factor affects nearly all manufacturing industries in Canada.

MARKETING CHARACTERISTICS

As of 1959 all but one of Dominion Engineering's six product Divisions faced severe competition from within or outside Canada, some

EXHIBIT 2 DOMINION ENGINEERING WORKS, LTD.

(all dollars in 1,000's)

	1958	1957	1956	1955	1954	1953
ASSETS						
Current Assets						
Cash	$ 92	$ 379	$ 828	$ 1,168	$ 1,132	$ 508
Call Loan	7	7	90	600	1,392	500
Government Bonds	2	1,299	2,769	2,777	2,735	3,200
Refunds Due by Taxing Authorities	452	—	—	—	—	—
Accounts Receivable less Reserve	3,633	5,597	5,273	3,949	4,852	3,851
Deposits on Tenders	39	48	47	39	39	39
Work-in-Progress and Manufactured Stock at Standard Cost, Raw Materials and Supplies at Lower of Cost or Market, less Reserve	18,155	24,644	21,351	14,904	17,557	18,688
Balance of Employees' Canada Savings Bonds Subscriptions	—	—	272	225	220	244
Prepaid Tax, Insurance, and Expense	326	187	182	164	154	175
Total	$22,706	$32,161	$30,812	$23,826	$28,081	$27,205
Less: Bills to and Collections from Customers	10,464	13,524	12,487	8,914	13,773	13,597
Total	$12,242	$18,637	$18,325	$14,912	$14,308	$13,608
Fixed Assets*						
Real Estate, Plant, Machinery, and Equipment at Cost, less Amounts Written Off	23,324	21,654	19,353	18,071	16,448	15,652
Less: Reserve for Depreciation	—	—	—	10,425	9,505	8,604
	—	—	—	$ 7,646	$ 6,943	$ 7,048
Total Assets	$35,566	$40,291	$37,678	$22,558	$21,251	$20,656

LIABILITIES

Current Liabilities						
Bank Overdraft	—	$ 2,492	—	—	—	—
Accounts Payable, Accrued Charges, and Operating Reserves	$ 4,154	6,943	$ 8,390	$ 5,719	$ 4,941	$ 5,324
Estimated Amount Due to Taxing Authorities in Canada	35	582	772	787	1,389	1,562
Total	$ 4,189	$10,017	$ 9,162	$ 6,506	$ 6,330	$ 6,886
Reserve for Contingencies	250	250	250	250	250	250
Reserve for Depreciation and Replacement of Fixed Assets	14,055	12,886	11,614	—	—	—
Capital Stock:						
625,000 Shares of an Authorized Issue of 1,000,000 No Par Value Shares	2,900	2,900	2,900	2,900	2,900	2,900
Capital Surplus	426	426	426	426	426	426
Balance as per Statement†	13,746	13,812	13,326	12,476	11,345	10,194
Total Liabilities	$35,566	$40,291	$37,678	$22,558	$21,251	$20,656

* In prior years, provisions for depreciation of plant, machinery, and equipment, as shown in the statement of earnings, have been determined in accordance with the capital cost allowance regulations of the Income Tax Division of the Department of National Revenue.

In 1956, the provision for depreciation and replacement shown in the statement of earnings has been determined on the basis of the life expectancy of the various classes of fixed assets and estimated replacement costs in dollars of current value. Capital cost allowances claimed for federal income tax purposes for the year 1956 are in excess of the provisions for depreciation and replacement shown in the statement of earnings. Therefore, income tax for the year is $102,357 less than if only the latter provisions were claimed.

In future years the provisions for depreciation and replacement in the company's accounts may exceed the capital cost allowances deductible for income tax purposes, in which event income taxes would increase in relation to earnings if tax rates remain unchanged.

† Not included here.

Source: Annual Reports of the Company.

from both. The exception was the Roll Division which then represented the sole Canadian source of chilled iron rolls.

D.E.W. did not reveal specific sales figures for its individual Divisions. Certain general facts, however, were available. With the exception of the recently organized Roll Division—virtually a single-handed development of the former foundry manager who was subsequently promoted to officer rank when the Division was established —annual sales of each of the other five Divisions were usually within roughly $2 million of each other. The largest dollar volume usually came from sales of paper machinery and diesel units. Sales of the Hydraulic, Industrial, and Power Crane and Shovel Divisions generally were about equal, while the Roll Division's sales usually were considerably smaller. Exhibit 3 shows representative examples of each Division's products.

Typical prices, or price ranges, of the products manufactured by the various Divisions were:

Paper mill	$2,000,000
Hydraulic turbine	$250,000 to $1,000,000
Rolling mill	$1,500,000
Rolls	$700 to $25,000
Power crane or shovel	$20,000 to $100,000
Diesel engine	$30,000 to $100,000

These figures do not reflect the inclusion in the total sales for each Division—and particularly the heavy machinery group[3]—of replacement parts, equipment rebuilding, and the design and construction of a single portion of a machine, such as a head box for a paper mill.

Products of the Paper, Hydraulic, Industrial, and Roll Divisions were sold direct to the consumer, as were diesels for industrial applications. Railroad diesels were sold through the Montreal Locomotive Company, Ltd. Power cranes and shovels, sold direct prior to March, 1958, currently were marketed through distributors. This change reflected the Division's desire to reach more customers in the construction and earth-moving industries whose business previously had been sought somewhat less intensively than that of industrial customers, many of whom also bought other D.E.W. equipment.

Certain changes in the relative contributions of the various Divisions

---

[3] The Paper Machinery, Hydraulic Machinery, Industrial Machinery, and Roll Divisions constitute the "heavy machinery group." The Diesel and the Power Crane and Shovel Divisions are referred to collectively as the "standard products group."

EXHIBIT 3A · DOMINION ENGINEERING WORKS

ANTI-FRICTION-BEARING CALENDAR ROLLS

EXHIBIT 3B DOMINION ENGINEERING WORKS

A DOMINION FINE PAPER MACHINE

EXHIBIT 3C DOMINION ENGINEERING WORKS

A PARTIALLY ASSEMBLED 2,000-HP GAS ENGINE

EXHIBIT 3D DOMINION ENGINEERING WORKS

A 120,000-HP KAPLAN TURBINE RUNNER

EXHIBIT 3E DOMINION ENGINEERING WORKS

THREE SIZES OF IMPULSE TURBINE RUNNERS

EXHIBIT 3F DOMINION ENGINEERING WORKS

PARTIALLY ASSEMBLED BALL AND ROD MILLS USED IN THE MINING INDUSTRY

EXHIBIT 3G Dominion Engineering works

A DOMINION ENGINEERING POWER SHOVEL (CAPACITY: 2½ CUBIC YARDS)

to company-wide sales seemed probable in the years ahead. For example, the railroad industry's recent rapid rate of conversion to diesel equipment already had contracted the market for original diesel equipment and suggested a long-term demand for little more than replacement parts in the future. As a basis for comparison, one D.E.W. official cited the experience of a United States manufacturer who reportedly had sold only about 300 new locomotives in 1958, compared to some 1,200 in 1953.

The Power Crane and Shovel Division had seen its former exclusive position compromised by the entry of five additional Canadian manufacturers into the market between 1953 and 1958. Increasing competition also was being encountered from exports of these products to Canada by non-Canadian manufacturers.

Offsetting the possible decline of sales trends in these several lines was the anticipated growth in sales of the gear products (speed-reduction units) in the Industrial Division's product line. Although the market for these components was now serviced by a number of other foreign and domestic companies, D.E.W.'s marketing staff expressed confidence that the company could nonetheless make further inroads in this field. These predictions seemed reinforced by a recent steady increase in gear products sales. As a result, D.E.W.'s management team was considering the possibility of establishing a separate Gear Products Division.

PLANT FACILITIES AND OPERATIONS[4]

D.E.W. maintains one of the most complete industrial plants of its kind in Canada. A general layout of the plant site is shown in Exhibit 4. Various representative photographs of the manufacturing areas are shown in Exhibit 5.

The facilities include a pattern shop for fabricating complex wood patterns and core boxes. From these, the company's foundry prepares intricate sand molds used in casting the numerous and, in many instances, huge iron, brass, or steel workpieces required by the various product lines.

D.E.W.'s machine shops contain a great variety of conventional metal-working machine tools and equipment necessary for close tolerance metal fabricating. There is also an impressive array of special

---

[4] As of 1959.

EXHIBIT 5A DOMINION ENGINEERING WORKS

A PORTION OF THE IRON FOUNDRY

A large sand pattern is being prepared in the foreground.

EXHIBIT 5B DOMINION ENGINEERING WORKS

STEEL CAST USED IN CASTING BLADES FOR A LARGE HYDRAULIC TURBINE

EXHIBIT 5C DOMINION ENGINEERING WORKS

POURING A LARGE STEEL CASTING

EXHIBIT 5D DOMINION ENGINEERING WORKS

CLOSE-UP VIEW OF CASTING POURING

EXHIBIT 5E DOMINION ENGINEERING WORKS

A PORTION OF ONE OF DOMINION ENGINEERING'S TWO MACHINE SHOPS

In the center of the photograph, a stay ring for a 180,000-HP hydraulic turbine is being machined on a 52-foot vertical boring mill.

EXHIBIT 5F   DOMINION ENGINEERING WORKS

MACHINING A SPHERICAL VALVE ON A 52-FOOT BORING MILL

EXHIBIT 5G   DOMINION ENGINEERING WORKS

MACHINING A RUNNER FOR A 105,000-HP TURBINE ON AN 18-FOOT VERTICAL
BORING MILL

EXHIBIT 5H DOMINION ENGINEERING WORKS

A DRYER ROLL FOR A PAPER MACHINE BEING TURNED ON A LARGE ENGINE LATHE

EXHIBIT 5I DOMINION ENGINEERING WORKS

CUTTING A 20-FOOT DIAMETER, 14-INCH FACE GEAR ON A HYDRAULIC
ELECTRIC GEAR GENERATOR. OPERATOR IS TO THE LEFT.

17

EXHIBIT 5J DOMINION ENGINEERING WORKS

A PORTION OF THE CONTRACT STORES AREA

Fabricated parts and purchased components are inventoried temporarily
while awaiting final assembly.

EXHIBIT 5K DOMINION ENGINEERING WORKS

ASSEMBLING THE DRIVE FOR A ROLLING MILL

EXHIBIT 5L DOMINION ENGINEERING WORKS

A PORTION OF THE ASSEMBLY FLOOR

The parts shown will be assembled into a small gear dryer drive for a paper (newsprint) manufacturing machine.

purpose machinery. Exhibit 6 lists the total groups into which shop machinery and equipment were classified, and, where available, the type and number of units within each group. Exhibit 7 shows the D.E.W. product Divisions which normally require a portion of the manufacturing capacity of the various Tool Groups.

Certain of the machine tools operated by D.E.W. are the only ones of their kind in Canada. The company's manufacturing personnel were especially proud, for example, of a large gear-cutting machine of D.E.W.'s own design and manufacture, which can process gear blanks up to 21 feet in diameter and is capable of cutting full herringbone gear teeth without a center slot.

Within the company, unique special tools such as this, as well as other particularly expensive or "one-of-a-kind" facilities, are termed "key tools" and are classified into one of 18 Key Tools Groups (Exhibit 8). Inclusion in this classification indicates that it is difficult —in some cases even impossible—to subcontract the type of processes performed by these particular units. When scheduling work into the machine shops, D.E.W.'s planners give particular attention to the Key Tool Groups. This practice reflects not only the inherent

EXHIBIT 6   DOMINION ENGINEERING WORKS, LTD.

MACHINE TOOL GROUPS*

Tool Group†	Description	Number of Tools‡
1–18	Key Tool Groups	§
19	Tube Roll Lathes (7' x 51')	8
20–21	Radial and Horizontal Drills	5
22–23	Turret Lathes	—
24	Large Engine Lathes	5
25	Medium Engine Lathes	15
26	Small Engine Lathes	—
27	Small Planers	5
28	Shapers and Slotters	7
29	Grinders	—
30–31	Small Milling Machines	3
32	Chilled Roll Lathes	5
33–34	Horizontal Boring Mills	13
35	Special Dryer Lathes	3
36	Cut-off and Centering Machines	—
37	Miscellaneous Small Machines	5
38–39–40	Vertical Boring Mills	20
41–42	Gear-Cutting Machines	26
46	Cutter Grinders	45
47	Toolroom Machines	24
48	"Standard Products" Machine Tools (These tools are located in Shop 23 and consist of items which, if classified, would fall in Tool Groups 20 through 42)	92
50	Fitters' Tools	—

* Data provided by the Manager of Machine Shops.

† There are no Groups 15, 43, 44, 45, and 49.

‡ Tools in Groups 1 through 42 are found either in Shop 1 or in Shop 17. For Groups 22, 23, 26, 29, 36, and 50, the exact number of tools is not compiled.

§ See also Exhibit 8.

EXHIBIT 7 DOMINION ENGINEERING WORKS, LTD.

The following schedule indicates which Machine Tool Groups were normally utilized in manufacturing the various products of the six Divisions, plus gear products.

	Products						
	Paper Machinery	Hydraulic Machinery	Industrial Machinery	Rolls	Power Cranes and Shovels	Diesel Engines	Gear Products
		1	1				
		2	2				
			3				3
	4						
M	5	5	5	5			
A	6	6	6	6	6	6	
C	7		7	7	7	7	7
H	8	8	8				
I	9		9	9	9	9	9
N	10	10	10		10		
E		11	11				
					12	12	
T	13						
O	14	14	14		14	14	
O	16	16	16			16	
L				17			
	18	18	18	18		18	
G				19			
R	20–21	20–21	20–21	20–21	20–21		20–21
O	22–23	22–23	22–23	22–23	22–23		22–23
U	24	24	24	24			24
P	25	25	25	25			25
S	26	26	26	26			26
	27		27				
U	28	28	28				28
T	29	29	29				29
I	30–31	30–31	30–31	30–31			30–31
L				32			
I	33–34	33–34	33–34	33–34	33–34		33–34
Z	35						
E	36	36	36	36	36	36	36
D	37	37	37	37	37	37	37
	38–39–40	38–39–40	38–39–40		38–39–40	38–39–40	38–39–40
	41–42	41–42	41–42	41–42	41–42	41–42	41–42

(Groups 46 and 47 are tool room machines)

					48	48	

EXHIBIT 8   DOMINION ENGINEERING WORKS, LTD.

PARTICULARS AND SPECIFICATIONS FOR KEY MACHINE TOOLS

(Groups 1 to 18 Inclusive)

Group No.	Description	Working Ranges		
		Swing	Vertical Travel (Tool post)	Max. Height (under rail)
1	Large Boring Mills Three Machines (1-B-65; 1-B-11; 1-B-62)	25'-0" – 42'-0"	7'-0" – 18'-0"	
2	Large Boring Mill One Machine (2-B-12)	18'-2"	6'-0"	13'-1"
3	Gear Cutter One Machine (3-C-15)	Max. Dia. 21'-0"	Face 60"	
4	Multispindle Horizontal Drill One Machine (4-D-32) 90 Spindles 2¼" Center Used only for Drilling Suction Couch Rolls and Suction Press Rolls			
5	Large Grinders Three Machines (5-G-1, 5-G-40, 5-G-60)	Range of Work Pieces: Length 20'-0" – 27'-6"	Diameter 32" – 72"	

	Horiz. Travel	Forward Travel	Vertical Travel
6 — Large Horizontal Milling Machine Two Machines (6-M-17, 6-M-38)	20'-0"– 22'-0"	20"– 72"	96"
7 — Large Horizontal Milling Machine Three Machines (7-M-20, 7-M-70) (48-M-662) All 4-Head Mills	20'-0"	72"	84"
8 — Large Horizontal Milling Machine Two Machines (8-M-21, 8-M-71)	25'-0"	47"	144"
9 — Large Horizontal Milling Machine One Machine (9-M-27) A 4-Head Mill	14'-0"	72"	72"
10 — Large Horizontal Milling Machine Two Machines (10-M-35, 10-M-69)	26'-0" (10-M-35) 4'-0" (10-M-69)	108" 20'-0"	120" 8'-0"
11 — Multispindle Horizontal Drill One Machine (11-D-87) 15 Spindles			

EXHIBIT 8 (*Continued*) DOMINION ENGINEERING WORKS, LTD.

PARTICULARS AND SPECIFICATIONS FOR KEY MACHINE TOOLS

(Groups 1 to 18 Inclusive)

Group No.	Description	Working Ranges		
		Horiz. Travel	Forward Travel	Vertical Travel
12	Hardening Machine One Machine (12-1H-1)			
13	Multispindle Drill One Machine 110 Spindles			
14	Large 4-Head Mill One Machine (14-M-65)			
		Length of Table	Width of Table	
16	Large Planers Two Machines (16-P-20, 16-P-28)	27'-4" – 30'-0"	4'-6" – 7'-0"	
17	Large Planer One Machine (17-P-24)	24'-6"	5'-0"	
18	Roll Grinder One Machine (18-G-162)	Capacity: 44" dia. x 18'-4" long		

importance of the Key Tools facilities, but also the fact that under customary volume levels, sufficient excess capacity is available in most other types of equipment to absorb normal scheduling inaccuracies.

Detailed layouts of Shops #1 and #23, the machine shops, are shown in Exhibits 9 and 10. Representative examples of some of the types of production orders customarily processed in these shops are shown in Exhibits 11 and 12.

EXHIBIT 11 PRODUCTION ORDER

Pattern Shop November 10	Foundry January 7	Machine Shop #1 April 30	Delivery June 20
Contract 302-317	Bill 1	Line 2	Order Date February 6	Quantity 1

Drawing ME-51536 ME-51537	Material & H.T. S55 S.C.	Pattern M-53741

Description
Estimated Rough Weight 167,000 lbs. New Pattern
Mill Housing (Spindle Drive Side) (C-22660)

Operation No.*	Operation	Unit Time (hours)	Tool Group (or Dept.)
5	Mark Off Mach. Lines	—	(163)
10	Weld Machine Pads (if necessary)	—	(162)
15	Mill Bottom Sides and Top	100.0	14M
20	Mill Joint Faces	40.0	8M
25	Drill Joint Face	10.0	20D
30	Assemble Caps	40.0	(161)
35	Mill Bore and Face Assembled	700.0	8M
40	Mark Off	—	(163)
45	Drill and Tap	50.0	20D
50	Drill and Tap	35.0	20HD
55	Chip	30.0	(168)
60	Grind	10.0	(168)
65	Deburr and Drill Ream and Tap	50.0	(161)
70	Weld Necessary Plates and Plugs	—	(162)
75	Inspect	—	(MS)

* On the original operation sheet prepared for a given job, operation numbers were assigned in increments of 5. This permitted subsequent revisions and additions while keeping renumbering of operations to a minimum.

EXHIBIT 12   MASTER PRODUCTION ORDER

	Description	
List 31W 71433-1		Cylinder Block Weldment
Cylinder Block Machining		(MTL DSL for Weldment)

Pattern	Drawing
	31-AA-71472

Operation No.	Operation	Set-up Time (minutes)	Unit Time (minutes)	Tool Group*	Machine No.
5	Mark Off		300.0		
10	Plane		3600.0	27	P-27
15	Mill	104.0	490.0	48 (7)	M-662
20	Bore	104.0	198.0	48 (7)	M-662
25	Drill	83.0	296.0	48 (20)	D-131
30	Drill	100.0	565.0	48 (20)	D-131
35	Bore		840.0	48 (33)	HB-73
37	Drill	80.0	160.0	48 (20)	D-131
41	Drill	85.0	440.0	48 (20)	D-131
43	Drill	85.0	1450.0	48 (20)	D-131
45	Mill	240.0	250.0	48 (7)	M-662
47	Fitters		180.0		
48	Mill	60.0	180.0	48 (7)	M-662
50	Assemble		540.0		
55	Bore and Face		600.0	48 (33)	HB-73
60	Inspect				
65	Wash and Degrease		120.0		
70	Bench		510.0		
75	Paint		60.0		
80	Fitters		360.0		
85	To Stores				

Tags	Requisition	Raw Matl. Card	Pro'd Orders	Heat Treat
Cast. Order	Envelope	Cost Card	Follow-up Card	Load. Card

* Although all "Standard Products" machine tools were assigned to group #48, the specific types of machines (as categorized in Exhibit 6) have been added in parenthesis by the case writer.

Exemplar Bookbinding Company

Mr. Walter Dix, manager and sole owner of the Exemplar Book-binding Company, was evaluating the results of his firm's operations during the six and one-half months since he had purchased it, and, as a prelude to developing plans for the future, was assessing the strengths and weaknesses in Exemplar's current situation. Profit and loss statements for the period in question, and the most recent balance sheet, are shown in Exhibits 1 and 2.

COMPANY BACKGROUND

The Exemplar Bookbinding Company is a "library bindery," serving educational, business, professional, and private libraries by rebinding worn or damaged books and by binding magazines, newspapers, and other types of periodicals into volumes for permanent retention. Nearly all the company's manufacturing operations are performed on customer-owned articles, with Exemplar being fully liable for the care of these items while they are in its custody. Many of the books and periodicals processed by the company are difficult, in some instances impossible, to replace if lost or damaged.

The company is located in a large metropolitan area which also is served by three other library binderies. Approximately 15 additional firms of this type, many of them quite small, are located within a radius of 250 miles. Transportation considerations, however, usually restrict binderies to operations in their immediate locality. Selected statistics on the industry from the most recent U.S. Census are shown in Exhibit 3.[1] In contrast to the industry average,

---

[1] Figures in this paragraph and those in Exhibit 3 relate only to companies that perform binding operations on materials printed by firms other than themselves. They do not include binding operations performed by publishers, or by specialized bindery concerns, on newly published volumes.

EXHIBIT 1 EXEMPLAR BOOKBINDING COMPANY

PROFIT AND LOSS STATEMENTS

(To Nearest Dollar)

	April 17–May 31	June	July	August	September	October
Sales	$21,106	$15,734	$17,448	$13,253	$9,908	$15,211
Cost of Goods Sold	16,275	11,531	12,567	12,733	8,913	12,459
Gross Income	4,831	4,203	4,881	520	995	2,751
Selling and Administrative Expenses:						
Salary and Wages	522	617	608	576	826	799
Travel	29	11	1	—	1	—
Subscriptions	3	5	11	5	—	46
Donations	—	—	—	—	—	46
Telephone/Telegraph	60	45	50	34	52	68
Professional Services	1,166	—	—	66	—	275
Sales Promotion	70	30	50	50	—	—
Depreciation—General	6	6	6	6	6	6
Entertainment	—	—	—	—	—	—
Miscellaneous	40	177	95	188	3,833	34
Freight Out	—	18	—	23	—	—
Postage	—	134	107	56	111	—
Taxes	—	2	—	9	1,164	584
Total	$ 1,896	$ 1,046	$ 928	$ 1,015	$5,993	$ 1,812
Net Income before Income Taxes	$ 2,935	$ 3,158	$ 3,952	$ (495)	$(4,998)	$ 940

Source: Company records.

EXHIBIT 2 EXEMPLAR BOOKBINDING COMPANY

BALANCE SHEET, JULY 31

ASSETS			LIABILITIES		
Current Assets			Current Liabilities		
Cash		$ 5,482.18	Notes Payable		$ 3,975.00
Accounts Receivable (less			Accounts Payable		2,608.49
Reserve for Bad Debts)		13,724.28	Accrued Liabilities		
Inventory—Raw Materials		6,091.32	Payroll		1,549.39
Inventory—Work in Process		3,223.37	Payroll Taxes		1,486.94
Prepaid Expenses		1,698.06	Other		1,000.00
Total		$30,219.21	Total		$10,619.82
Fixed Assets	$14,017.00		Long-Term Note		
Less Depreciation	551.10		Payable		11,925.00
		13,465.90	Net Worth		21,140.29
TOTAL		$43,685.11	TOTAL		$43,685.11

Source: Company records.

Exemplar's product mix usually includes very little "edition binding" or "mechanical binding." In regard to the latter operation, Exemplar's plant is equipped to perform only power-stapling operations.

Over the several years before Mr. Dix's acquisition of the firm, Exemplar's sales had averaged about $130,000 annually. Around 80 per cent of this volume was usually obtained from a large university located in the community. This institution's collection of books and periodicals was among the largest in the world, currently numbering in excess of six million items. The university had relied upon Exemplar for all its binding requirements for many years. Over this period, Exemplar management personnel had developed cordial relationships with the university's business officers, the personnel in charge of the central library, and most of the librarians in the more than 50 specialized book collections maintained by various schools and departments of the university.

The balance of Exemplar's business was obtained from a variety of sources. These included a number of smaller universities and colleges in the area; local business concerns, particularly those engaged in research activities; professional people, especially doctors and lawyers; private libraries maintained by scientific or cultural societies; and private collectors of books. The local public library, however,

EXHIBIT 3 EXEMPLAR BOOKBINDING COMPANY

THE BOOKBINDING INDUSTRY

General Statistics

	1939	1947	1951	1954	1955	1956
Value Added $ × 10⁶	33.4	90.2	67.3	84.7	94.5	104.4
Employees $ × 10³	N.A.	22.2	16.3	17.2	18.1	19.7
Value of Shipments $ × 10⁶	44.6	116.0	85.0	119.9	N.A.	N.A.
Number of Firms	620	686	N.A.	730	N.A.	N.A.
Payroll $ × 10⁶	N.A.	57.5	51.1	59.0	N.A.	72.1
Cost of Materials $ × 10⁶	11.2	25.7	17.7	27.2	N.A.	N.A.

1954 Data	1–4	5–9	10– 19	20– 49	50– 99	100– 249	250– 499	500– 999	1,000
Number of Establishments	274	124	137	127	38	21	6	2	1
Average Value Added $ × 000	13.2	38.8	71.0	150	350	710	1,600	4,813	N.A.

(column group header: Number of Employees)

National Averages for the Industry in 1954

Average Value of Shipments per Company	$154,000
Average Number of Employees	23.5
Average Hourly Wages	$ 1.65
Capital Expenditures	$ 5,010 per year

Product Mix Based on Value of Shipments for Industry:

Edition Binding—Hard Board*	40%
Pamphlet Binding	28
Library Binding	14
Mechanical Binding†	7
Miscellaneous	11
	100%

* *i.e.* The binding of specially printed volumes, published in small quantities, usually at the expense of the author.

† *i.e.* The use of brads, staples, plastic or metal spiral devices to bind the pages of a volume.

Source: *U.S. Census of Manufactures*, 1954 and 1956.

had long operated a bindery department servicing its own needs. Local agencies of the state government similarly were served by a state-owned bindery.

The original owner of Exemplar had a number of other local business interests. He therefore had never devoted more than modest personal attention to the bindery, and eleven years earlier had retained Mr. Dix as Bindery Manager, giving him an almost entirely free hand in running the company. Mr. Dix, then in his late 20's, had just earned a Master's degree in business administration, and through his family was reasonably familiar with bookbinding operations. His starting salary with the bindery was roughly equal to the average earnings reported by other graduates of the program Mr. Dix had just completed.

Over the next four years, Mr. Dix increased Exemplar's annual sales from about $50,000 to $126,000. He also accomplished certain production economies through methods and process improvements, and through increased mechanization of a few phases of the firm's operations. The average unit cost of a typical hardcover binding, for example, was reduced from $3.35 to $2.65 during this period.

After four years Mr. Dix negotiated an arrangement whereby the bindery's owner permitted him to accept an administrative position with another employer in the same city, while continuing to serve as Bindery Manager on a part-time basis. While this plan was in effect, Exemplar's sales volume and production efficiency continued to improve, although at a more modest rate than in the four years immediately preceding.

This arrangement was terminated three and a half years later by Mr. Dix's acceptance of a responsible position with a nationally known industrial-design consulting organization in another state. After Mr. Dix's resignation, the bindery owner was unsuccessful in obtaining the services of anyone whom he considered a satisfactory manager. The owner therefore assumed these functions himself, devoting to Exemplar whatever time he could spare from his other business commitments.

MR. DIX'S PURCHASE OF COMPANY

Three years later, while visiting the city, Mr. Dix was told by one of the bindery's employees that the owner was considering selling the company in order to devote more time to his other business interests. Mr. Dix therefore arranged an appointment with the owner who verified the employee's information. Mr. Dix stated that he would like to consider submitting an offer.

For the next five months, while conducting exploratory negotiations with the owner, Mr. Dix weighed the advisability of acquiring the company. Finally, in April of the current year, an agreement was reached under which Mr. Dix acquired full title to the firm, its equipment, raw materials, and work-in-process inventory for $25,900.

During the early negotiations Mr. Dix and the owner had substantial differences of opinion regarding the valuation of Exemplar's manufacturing equipment. A consultant retained by the owner had argued that Mr. Dix should purchase these items at their estimated replacement cost. Since much of the equipment was old, Mr. Dix maintained that replacement value was too intangible a concept to be utilized in reaching a purchase price, and contended that the attempt of the consultant to do so had yielded an unreasonably high figure. After much discussion, agreement was reached upon an equipment valuation of $13,495. This was substantially lower than the figure originally proposed by the consultant, but closely approximated depreciated book value of the items in question. Little difficulty was experienced in agreeing upon a value of $7,818 for raw material, and $4,587 for work in process. No valuation was placed on the company name or on the good will attached to it.

Under the purchase agreement, Mr. Dix paid $5,000 in cash on April 15, and gave the original owner a mortgage note for $20,900 secured by the assets of the company. Mr. Dix was to pay an additional $5,000 the following July 15th, leaving a noninterest-bearing mortgage balance of $15,900 which was to be paid in twelve consecutive, quarterly installments of $1,325 starting the following October 15th.

Mr. Dix had entered into the negotiations with a cash position of $15,300, representing almost all of his personal savings. In the event of an extreme emergency, Mr. Dix believed that he could probably rely upon his family, or upon a small group of friends, for modest additional funds. It was his firm intention, however, to avoid such a necessity.

Mr. Dix's decision to purchase the company was based upon a variety of considerations. In his judgment, ownership of Exemplar offered an unusually attractive opportunity to satisfy his long-standing ambition to be in business for himself. It represented an industry, and a firm, with which he was already familiar. He was satisfied that the company was basically sound, its workforce thoroughly competent. While it did not represent "big business" in any glamorous sense, Mr. Dix was certain that Exemplar possessed significant profit potential. Although its past earnings had been only modest, Mr. Dix was confident that imaginative, full-time management could expand them appreciably. The likelihood of such expansion seemed reinforced by the numerous indications of a growing, nationwide emphasis upon education and research, and by the forecasts of rapid —even explosive—increases in college enrollments over the next decade. Mr. Dix reasoned that such developments clearly would intensify demand for bindery services. On the basis of these and related considerations, Mr. Dix had finally concluded that the long-term financial rewards he could achieve as owner of Exemplar would probably equal —and indeed might well surpass—those attainable as a salaried employee of a large corporation.

Before reaching a final decision, Mr. Dix also scheduled appointments with various officers and library personnel of the large local university to discuss future demands for bindery services. The general reaction he obtained appeared to be that although no firm commitment could be made, there seemed no reason to believe that the university's long-standing association with Exemplar would be altered merely because of a change in the bindery's ownership. On the contrary, most of the university's personnel expressed the opinion that if Exemplar's services and prices remained satisfactory, their institution would probably continue to treat it as the major source of bindery services. A number of the persons with whom he discussed these matters had known Mr. Dix during his earlier service as bindery manager. Many of these individuals informally expressed pleasure at the possibility that Mr. Dix might be rejoining the firm as its owner.

Prior to the purchase Mr. Dix also held discussions with representatives of a number of companies supplying the bindery industry. Their views seemed to him to verify his conviction that future prospects for library binderies were bright. They also confirmed his impression that many firms in the industry were small, family-owned concerns. Mr. Dix believed that organizations of this type often went out of existence upon the death or retirement of the original owners. He concluded that the industry therefore might become less competitive in the years ahead.

OPERATING CHANGES INTRODUCED SUBSEQUENT TO PURCHASE

Labor Relations

One of the first decisions confronting Mr. Dix after acquiring the bindery involved negotiation of a new labor contract.

At the time of purchase, Mr. Dix had made an informal commitment to the former owner to retain for at least 60 days all employees who wished to continue with the company. A notice to this effect was circulated among the workforce shortly before the purchase was completed. On the day following the change in ownership Mr. Dix was pleased to see that all personnel reported to work as usual. About half of these were persons whom he himself had hired during his former management of the company. The 20 employees were equally divided between men and women. Their average age was about 40, and their average length of service with Exemplar was approximately eight years.

From his previous association with the firm Mr. Dix knew that in common with most of the industry, Exemplar often had experienced a high turnover among less skilled female employees. In recent years, however, the company had encountered almost no losses among the more experienced women employees, and none among its male personnel, all of whom were highly skilled. Mr. Dix believed that such labor stability was an asset of considerable significance, since it was virtually impossible to hire experienced bookbinders in the local market and since several years were normally required before an unskilled trainee became proficient in many phases of the work.

Under the former owner, Exemplar's hourly personnel had been organized as a local of a nationwide craft union. The contract, however, was not phrased in such a way as to be binding upon a new owner. After consultation with his attorney, Mr. Dix elected to consider the former agreement invalid. Notice of this decision was included in his initial announcement offering continued employment, at prevailing pay rates, to the entire workforce.

On the second day after acquiring the firm, Mr. Dix was approached by a committee representing a substantial majority of the employees. They advised him of their desire to form an independent company union and to organize the bindery on a union-shop basis. Mr. Dix agreed to negotiate on these topics.

Within a week, with the assistance of attorneys representing both parties, a one-year contract was signed in which the company recognized the new bargaining unit. The working conditions, benefits, job classifications, and wage levels agreed upon were almost identical with those contained in the former contract. Mr. Dix believed that the wage rates specified in both the former and the new contracts were about 10 per cent below those paid locally by large union shops performing highly mechanized, mass-production binding of large lots of identical new volumes, but met or exceeded those paid by comparable small library binderies in the area. The new contract did not provide retirement-pension benefits or group life insurance. Mr. Dix hoped, however, that it might some day prove possible for Exemplar to afford such benefits.

During the first several days of his ownership of the company, officials in the district office of the former union made repeated but unsuccessful efforts to see Mr. Dix. After the new contract was negotiated with the independent union, however, the representatives of the national union made no further efforts to approach him; nor did they challenge the jurisdiction of the new bargaining unit. One male employee who had been active in the former local, however, did voice strong objections to the formation of the independent union. Although becoming a dues-paying member of the new organization, he remained persistently outspoken in his criticism of its activities. After about a month, Mr. Dix discharged the employee for his lack of cooperation. This move had the energetic support of the officers of the new union, several of whom had stated to Mr. Dix that "unless he [the 'trouble-maker'] goes, we go!"

Aside from this episode, it seemed to Mr. Dix that employee relations had proceeded satisfactorily. Beginning in late summer he had held informal monthly meetings with the union officers. These sessions were conducted at the plant after the end of the regular shift. In Mr. Dix's judgment the tone of these meetings had been exceptionally cordial, and he was particularly pleased that the union representatives had enthusiastically presented a number of suggestions for improving operations. It had been possible to implement most of these proposals promptly, and with apparently good results.

Discussions of more formal company-union matters also seemed to Mr. Dix to be carried out in a spirit of constructive cordiality. After Exemplar had moved to its new quarters, to be subsequently discussed, some employees had frequently expressed the view that the company had not yet regained the operative effectiveness it had enjoyed in the former location. Mr. Dix believed that the employees were correct in this conclusion, and saw no evidence that they offered this observation in a disgruntled or hostile manner. On the contrary, he believed that their remarks reflected their genuine concern for Exemplar's productivity and profitability.

Plant Relocation

Another major operating change occurring since Mr. Dix's acquisition of the firm was its transfer to a new location. Terms of the purchase contract had stipulated that Exemplar must be moved from its existing site no later than December 31 of the current year in order to free the building for other business activities of the former owner. Shortly after the purchase was executed, therefore, Mr. Dix had begun to look for a suitable new location.

After surveying a number of alternative sites, by midsummer Mr.

Dix's interest had become centered upon an old but well-built, currently unoccupied, four-story building several blocks distant from the present location. He was satisfied that with several thousand dollars' worth of improvements these quarters would be quite suitable for the bindery's operations. He also was convinced that the location was excellent in that it was within a few miles' radius of most of the company's regular customers, including the university. Mr. Dix was concerned, however, by the fact that it would be necessary to lease the building in its entirety, even though its 16,500 square feet of space represented almost four times the area available in the quarters now occupied. Although convinced that the present location did not provide enough space for maximum production efficiency, Mr. Dix still doubted that an ideal layout of equipment would require more than half the building under consideration.

After further study, Mr. Dix concluded that it probably would be possible to negotiate subleases for at least some of the excess space. After assuring himself that terms of the lease would permit subletting, he entered into a five-year commitment for the building. The lease terms called for payments of $950 per month, with a provision for subsequent adjustments to reflect any changes in the property taxes paid by the owner. The lease contained no formal renewal clause. The owner had assured Mr. Dix, however, that he would be allowed to extend it if he desired.

Exemplar's equipment, raw materials, and work-in-process inventory were moved to the new location over the Labor Day weekend. Most of the transfer was executed by the company's own personnel using a rented truck. Movement and installation of the heavier pieces of equipment, however, required the services of a commercial rigging firm. With the aid of the production superintendent and the advice of some of the employees, Mr. Dix developed a layout which employed only the second and third floors for bindery operations. Such an arrangement, in Mr. Dix's judgment, maximized the chances of negotiating a favorable sublease for the excess space available in the building.

The two weeks following the relocation were largely devoted to establishing the company in its new setting. Extensive cleaning and refurbishing of the building were required. It was also necessary to construct partitions to form offices. Accomplishment of these tasks created conditions which made it exceptionally difficult to carry out normal bindery operations. Mr. Dix, anticipating that this might be the case, had allowed roughly half the workforce to take this period as vacation time. This allowed him to keep the remaining personnel busily engaged either in bindery work or, more frequently, in activities relating to improvements in the new quarters.

The cost of the move and the physical improvements to the building amounted to roughly $5,000. To help finance this, Mr. Dix successfully negotiated with a local bank for an unsecured loan of $4,500 at an interest rate of 6 per cent. Although the note was callable at any time, the bank officials had assured Mr. Dix that the balance outstanding could be repaid at his convenience. By the end of October, Mr. Dix had reduced the principal by $1,500 from Exemplar's sales income.

Shortly after the move, Mr. Dix sublet the first floor of the building to a nearby publishing firm for use as storage area. The agreement was to run for three months and called for monthly payments of $200. The publishing house had indicated that it might wish to continue this arrangement, on a month-to-month basis, after the first of the year. Mr. Dix knew, however, that the firm was constructing new facilities on the outskirts of the city and was certain that its sublease arrangement with Exemplar was only temporary. Except for a small area used to store miscellaneous equipment not currently needed by the bindery, the fourth floor stood vacant.

OPERATING PRACTICES

Customer Requirements—Their Impact upon
Manufacturing Operations

Customers' orders received by Exemplar vary in size from a single publication to many hundreds. Most orders, however, contain somewhere between 70 and 100 books, or several hundred periodicals,[2] or a roughly equivalent mixture of both. The individual items included in an order usually embrace a wide range of physical characteristics, with the publications differing as to page size, thickness, the type of paper on which they are printed, and their general state of repair. Exhibit 4 shows the width and length dimensions of the individual items included in the orders received in a fairly typical day.

These physical dissimilarities usually are compounded by differences in the covering materials, and in the variety of title stamping, which

---

[2] A number of consecutive issues of a periodical, arranged in sequence, are usually combined into a single, bound volume. The number of issues per volume vary from periodical to periodical, depending on the thickness of a typical issue. The majority of the periodical binding performed by Exemplar is about equally divided between volumes containing six issues and volumes containing twelve.

EXHIBIT 4 EXEMPLAR BOOKBINDING COMPANY

WIDTH AND LENGTH DIMENSIONS OF ITEMS CONTAINED IN
FOUR REPRESENTATIVE ORDERS RECEIVED SEPTEMBER 5

Dimensions of Item	Number of Items in Order #			
	1	2	3	4
4½″ x 7½″				1
4½″ x 17½″			1	
5″ x 6½″				4
5″ x 7″				7
5″ x 7¾″				2
5¼″ x 8″			1	
5½″ x 7½″				5
5½″ x 8″				6
5½″ x 8¾″				4
6″ x 8½″			2	
6″ x 9″		125		
6″ x 9½″		75		
6″ x 10″			2	
6½″ x 9½″		25		
6½″ x 10″			3	
7″ x 10″		25	4	22
7½″ x 10″			3	
7½″ x 10½″	24			
7¾″ x 10½″	24			
8″ x 10½″				78
8″ x 11″	104	75		
8½″ x 11″		125	7	
9½″ x 13″				6
10″ x 13¾″				1
Total	152	450	23	136

NOTE: Each of the orders included books, pamphlets, and periodicals. In
the case of the latter, a customer might request that as many as 12
consecutive issues of a single periodical be bound into a single volume.
Mr. Dix believed that the nature of the binding processes made
variations in the width and length of the items being bound far more
significant than variations in their thickness.

Source: Survey by Harvard Business School researcher.

customers wish to have employed for the cover of each book. Some customers (including the university which is the company's largest account) have selected a single, standard grade and color of covering material, and a single form of title stamping, for all routine orders. Even in these cases, however, the variations in the size and condition of the diverse items included in any single order still pose significant production problems.

As a result of the lack of standardization in the physical characteristics of the items to be processed, Exemplar production personnel have always considered it virtually impossible to schedule long production runs. Instead, each order is scheduled into production as a self-contained unit, with every individual item receiving whatever treatment its size, its other physical characteristics, and the customer's instructions require. The company also makes relatively little use of the numerous types of mechanized equipment that are available in the industry. Mr. Dix believes that Exemplar's heavy reliance upon hand operations is typical of the practices of most library binderies. Highly mechanized operations are, he judges, generally confined to binderies that specialize in the manufacture of new books and are thus able to process large quantities of identical volumes.

Further complexities in Exemplar's production processes arise from the fact that customers often desire that the binding of a particular volume conform exactly to those of volumes that the company bound months, or even years, earlier. This is particularly true in the case of periodicals, since customers usually wish each successive volume to be identical with those previously bound, so that the complete series will be of uniform appearance. To achieve such conformity requires not only the use of the same grade and color of covering material, and variety of title stamping, but also steps to assure that titles are positioned on the cover in exactly the same way on each volume. To assure these desired characteristics in its finished products, Exemplar maintains files of production and design data on over 10,000 items that the company has previously bound for various customers and that seem likely, by their nature, to require duplication in the future.

The operating procedures of most libraries require that various clerical operations be performed before an item can be temporarily withdrawn from circulation and sent to a bindery for processing. In order to smooth out their own clerical work load, therefore, most libraries that regularly employ Exemplar's services send in orders of roughly equal size about once each month. Although this practice minimizes seasonal variations in Exemplar's volume, it accentuates the varied product mix in process at any time.

In the past, most of the company's customers have seemed satisfied with four to six weeks' delivery on routine orders. Mr. Dix believes that only one or two of his local competitors are able to render such service. By contrast, up until shortly before he took over the company, Exemplar had usually been able to make delivery in slightly less than four weeks.

On roughly 10 per cent of the items received for processing, Exemplar is asked to provide "rush-order" service, with delivery in a few days or "at the earliest possible date." Such requests usually arise in the case of publications for which demand is particularly heavy, making the library anxious not to have them out of circulation for any significant length of time. Rush orders can also arise when an unforeseen demand for an item occurs after it has been dispatched to the bindery for routine processing. In some such cases the library will request that the item be singled out for rush-order processing, or that it be withdrawn from the order and returned to the library unbound.

If necessary, an order of average size can be pushed through the plant in several working days; in an extreme emergency, a single item can be processed in one day. Any such rush order requires substantial disruption of previous shop plans, however, and entails a lowering of production efficiency. It has been Exemplar's long-standing policy, nonetheless, to make every effort to honor all such requests from regular customers, and to do so without additional charges.

Most orders arrive at the bindery accompanied by two copies of a customer packaging list describing the various items included and giving instructions regarding the binding and the delivery desired. The volumes usually are transported to the bindery in large wooden boxes that are retained by Exemplar and used subsequently in the delivery of finished products.

Sales Efforts, Sales Volume, and Production Backlog

In the past, Exemplar's sales efforts had received only modest emphasis, except during the period of Mr. Dix's previous full-time management. Many of the company's regular customers, such as university libraries, are organizations whose annual budgets include a definite allocation for binding services. Once this figure has been established for a given year it is rarely increased. By the same token, it is unusual for the personnel involved not to spend all of the funds that have been allocated to them.

These factors had led Exemplar's former owner to conclude that the demand for the company's services was relatively inelastic at any given moment, and probably would be largely unresponsive to any selling efforts. During his ownership of the company, therefore, its sales activities had usually been concentrated on maintaining close ties with established customers in the hope that they would call upon Exemplar for whatever bindery services they were in a position to afford. In recent years, with so much of his interest channeled along other lines, the former owner had usually not even responded to inquiries received from potential new accounts which approached the company.

Mr. Dix was confident that more intensive sales efforts would yield impressive results. He was certain, for example, that numerous manufacturing and engineering concerns were making increased use of technical journals. He believed that in many instances such organizations were not binding these publications for permanent retention simply because no one had attempted to convince them of the advantages of such a practice.

In the face of the personal time pressures he had encountered since purchasing Exemplar, Mr. Dix had not yet been able to devote any major portion of his time to sales activities. Notwithstanding this fact, since April, orders from established customers had continued at least at their normal rates, and in some instances had even increased in volume. At the same time, even in the absence of any intensive sales efforts, a substantial number of orders had also been received from new customers. Many of these were companies or institutions whose business had been declined by the former owner of the bindery who, as previously noted, had not felt that he had time to devote to any expansion of Exemplar's operations.

As a result of these new orders, Exemplar's production backlog had risen noticeably since Mr. Dix's purchase of the firm. Since incoming orders were not checked until they were started into production, and were not priced until the production operations had been completed, it had not been possible to evaluate the exact dimensions of this increase. By visual inspection, however, Mr. Dix estimated that the backlog of items waiting to be processed was perhaps 50 per cent larger than that previously considered normal by the company. Exemplar's accountant also expressed the opinion that the amount of work in process had perhaps tripled since Mr. Dix's acquisition of the firm.

In view of the unexpectedly favorable sales picture, Mr. Dix was now frequently finding it necessary to quote delivery times of 12 weeks to both old and new customers. Thus far, there had been no indications of serious customer dissatisfaction with these conditions. Mr. Dix believed that this response was at least in part attributable to

Exemplar's exceptionally high quality standards, a consideration to which he believed most customers attached major significance.

Production Processes and Controls

Exemplar's manufacturing operations were under the direct supervision of the Production Manager, Angelo Dichio. Mr. Dichio, who was in his mid-forties, had been with the company in a supervisory capacity for about ten years and was skilled in all phases of bindery work. In addition to serving as Production Manager he would, from time to time, actually engage in direct-labor operations to fill in for employees who were absent, or to help break production bottlenecks. Mr. Dix also took an active interest in all phases of the factory's activities and spent a considerable portion of his time on the floor of the plant in direct supervisory contact with the operating personnel.

Layouts of the manufacturing areas are shown in Exhibits 5 and 6.

EXHIBIT 5   EXEMPLAR BOOKBINDING COMPANY

FLOOR PLAN (INCLUDING LOCATION OF MACHINERY AND EMPLOYEE WORK AREAS)

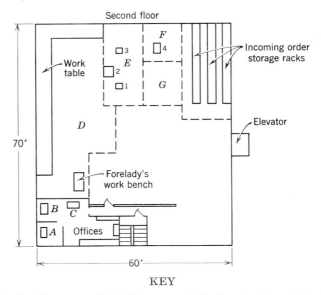

KEY

A, *B*, and *C*, Office area; *D*, Pulling area (including hand-sewing); *E*, Shear, saw, and press area; *F*, Machine sewing area; *G*, Inspection and write-up area; *1*, Power saw (used to cut slots in items requiring hand-sewing); *2*, National shear; *3*, Hand press; *4*, Oversewing machine.

EXHIBIT 6 Exemplar Bookbinding Company

FLOOR PLAN (INCLUDING LOCATION OF MACHINERY AND EMPLOYEE WORK AREAS)

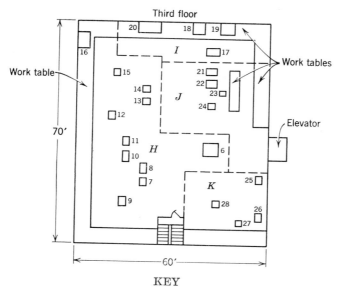

KEY

H, Forwarding area; *I*, Stamping area; *J*, Casing-in (cover-attaching) area; *K*, Pamphlet section; *6*, Seybold shear; *7, 8*, Backing benches; *9, 10, 11*, Hand shear (for cutting harboard covers); *12*, Skiver (used to bevel edges of leather); *13, 14*, Hand presses (floor type); *15*, Gluing machine; *16*, Turn-in machine; *17*, Ludlow typecasting machine; *18, 19*, Kensol stamping machine; *20*, Type storage cabinets; *21, 22*, Hydraulic presses (floor-type); *23, 24*, Hand presses; *25, 26*, Wire stitching (stapling) machines; *27*, Gluing machine; *28*, Hand press.

PRODUCTION PROCESSES. Publications received for binding are stored on racks located in the second-floor work areas (Figure A) until the entire order in which they are included is scheduled into production. At that time, the forelady in charge of second-floor manufacturing activities removes the order from the rack and transports it to her workbench by hand truck. There she checks each item against the list that the customer included with the order. If any irregularities are discovered, or if the customer's specifications are not clear, the forelady confers with Mr. Dix or Mr. Dichio. If necessary, one of these men then consults the customer regarding the matter.

While executing this preliminary check of an order, the forelady also carefully examines each item to ascertain what production processes it will require. One of the most important objectives of this preliminary

FIGURE A. Incoming order storage area.

inspection is to determine whether a publication will need machine- or hand-sewing operations. The former process is quicker and more economical, and when used properly gives excellent results. If, however, the paper on which a publication is printed is particularly "soft" or "brittle," or if the printing extends too near the edges of the pages, a quality binding job can be achieved only by employing hand sewing. Differentiation between publications that can be satisfactorily sewn by machine and those that cannot is a matter of judgment requiring considerable skill and experience in binding operations. Mr. Dix believed that Mrs. McDuffy, the second-floor forelady, who had been with the company for almost 30 years, was the only member of the second-floor staff fully qualified to make this decision.

After completing this initial checking and inspecting of each volume, Mrs. McDuffy marks an identifying number lightly in pencil on its first page. This indicates the customer order in which this volume is included and the "item number," in that order, that has been assigned to this particular publication. After thus marking each item, Mrs.

McDuffy moves the entire lot of publications on a hand truck to the workbench of one of the five "pulling operators." In making this work assignment, Mrs. McDuffy takes into account not only the goal of achieving an equal distribution of workload, but also the fact that the more complex orders require the services of the more experienced pullers.

Although considerable variations occur, depending on the physical condition of the items in an order, Mrs. McDuffy believes that she usually devotes about 60 per cent of each day to these initial inspection and routing functions. The remainder of her time is spent instructing and assisting the pullers, inspecting their work as well as that of the "oversewing operator," to be described subsequently, conferring with Mr. Dix and Mr. Dichio, and in related duties. If an order contains extremely difficult items, Mrs. McDuffy sometimes sets these aside and then personally performs the necessary pulling operations on them.

The responsibilty of a pulling operator includes the removal of the old binding from each volume. This is accomplished by pulling off the cover, clipping the threads or, in the case of periodicals, removing the staples, and scraping off the paste that previously held the volume together (Figure B). These operations reduce the volume to

FIGURE B. Pulling operator at work. Production Manager is in background.

a set of loose pages. The pulling operators are then responsible for seeing that these pages are arranged in the proper numerical order and, where appropriate, that they are mended and cleaned. In the case of periodicals, most customers also require that all full-page advertisements be removed from volumes being bound. In such instances, the pulling operators are responsible for the page removal. This requires extreme care to assure that nonadvertising material is not unintentionally included in the pages being eliminated.

For planning and estimating, Mrs. McDuffy has employed a rule of thumb that, on the average, these initial pulling operations should require about 15 to 20 minutes of an operator's time per volume. The process is entirely manual. Over the years, Exemplar has tested numerous mechanical devices to assist in the pulling operations, but without achieving satisfactory results. The work is tedious and often involves coping with volumes that are soiled and covered with dust.

Mrs. McDuffy believes that it usually takes about a year before a new employee learns to perform routine pulling operations without considerable supervision. To acquire enough experience to handle independently all of the great variety of work that might be encountered requires perhaps another two years. Upon two different occasions after purchasing the company, Mr. Dix hired a new employee to be trained as a pulling operator. Each of the women quit within a few days, complaining that the work was hard, dirty, and boring.

After the pulling operations, all of the volumes in the order are routed to a large power shear located on the second floor. Operation of the shear trims the back (binding edge) of each volume, creating a smooth, even surface for the subsequent sewing operation. The shear operator then applies a light coat of glue to the freshly cut edge to hold the pages of the volume temporarily in place. According to Mr. Dichio, the trimming and gluing require an average of about one-half minute per volume. Responsibility for these steps is not assigned to any single individual. Instead, whichever of the forwarding operators— men regularly located on the third floor of the plant—can most conveniently be spared from his third-floor work is temporarily diverted to this job whenever the need arises.

After trimming and gluing, the entire order is next routed to the sewing operation. If Mrs. McDuffy has determined that hand sewing is required on any of the volumes, these are routed to one of the more experienced pullers. Hand sewing (Figure C) involves anywhere from one-quarter to one and one-half hours per volume, depending on the thickness of the publication.

Volumes to be machine sewn are moved by hand truck to the over-

Figure C. Hand-sewing operation.

sewing machine, which also is located on the second floor. The over-sewing operation is progressive. The operator separates the pages of each volume into sections of about one-eighth inch thickness which then are clamped into the oversewing machine individually (Figure D). The machine punches holes along the left-hand edge of the section, and stitches the pages together with high-grade, flax thread. By adding subsequent sections, the whole volume is assembled and sewn, including heavy-paper "end pages" positioned at the front and back of the book. Mrs. McDuffy has estimated that the machine sewing typically requires two to three minutes per volume, depending on its thickness. Changes in the length of the pages being sewn require about a three-minute adjustment on the machine. Thread breakage rarely occurs and seldom involves more than 20 minutes downtime, usually less.

After all second-floor operations have been completed on an order, each volume is inspected by Mrs. McDuffy. The entire order then

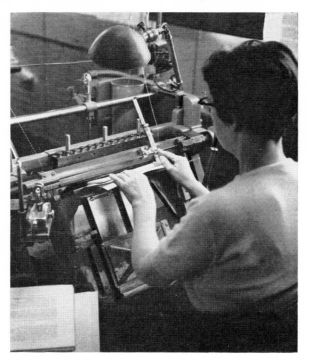

FIGURE D.   Oversewing machine operation.

remains on a hand truck or a workbench on the second floor until moved (usually by the third-floor foreman) via elevator to the third floor for the remainder of the binding operations.

The third-floor activities are supervised by a working foreman, Philip Wardell, who himself is a skilled "forwarder." His duties include the assignment of individual workers to specific jobs, and ringing the time-bell for breaks, lunches, and quitting time. He estimates that these functions account for approximately 25 per cent of his working day.

The remainder of Mr. Wardell's time is spent as the operator of a large Seybold shear to which all orders are routed as the initial third-floor operation. The Seybold, although larger in size, is similar in design and in operation to the shear employed on the second floor. To operate the shear (Figure E), Mr. Wardell inserts each sewn volume into the Seybold and successively trims the three unsewn edges, leaving each with a clean, even surface. Such trimming demands painstaking care to avoid cutting away any printed matter. On the average, Mr.

Wardell believes that about a minute and a half is required to trim each volume, including the time taken to inspect the volume to ascertain the amount of paper that can safely be removed.

The assigning of all third-floor trimming operations to Mr. Wardell was an innovation introduced by Mr. Dix shortly after the company moved to its new location.   Previously, each of the "forwarders," operators whose functions will be explained subsequently, had been responsible for trimming any order assigned to him.   Under the new arrangements, after Mr. Wardell trims all of the volumes in an order, he piles them on any one of the numerous benches or hand trucks adjacent to the shear until one of the five forwarders in the department can be assigned to the order.

It is the responsibility of a forwarder to perform all of the remaining operations required to produce the components of a bound volume for each item in the customer order assigned to him.   These operations include "rounding," "backing," and "cover making."

FIGURE E.   Third-floor trimming operation.

"Rounding" is performed manually through the use of a broad-nosed hammer, and is a preliminary step to the "backing operation" described in the paragraph immediately following. To round a volume, the sewn and trimmed packet of pages is placed lengthwise on a table. By light taps of the hammer, the forwarder shapes the bound edge of the volume into a convex curve along its entire length (Figure F). This forms a slightly concave cross section on the book's opposite (outer) edge. Approximately four volumes can be rounded per minute.

The ensuing operation, "backing," is performed on either of the company's two backing machines, each of which cost about $1,500 when new. The purpose of backing is to "bend" the sewn pages at a depth of roughly one-sixteenth of an inch along the entire length of the sewn edge. This "fans" outward the sewn edge of each page. This fanning, together with the contour obtained through the rounding operation, permits the pages of a volume to turn easily after it has been bound.

FIGURE F. Rounding operation. Packets in stack on the left have been rounded; those on the right are awaiting the rounding operation.

Figure G. Backing operation. Roller is in contact with rounded, sewn edge of volume. Operator will now guide roller back and forth in arc across sewn edge until entire sewn surface is smoothly curved.

To accomplish this backing, the forwarder places a "rounded" packet of pages lengthwise in the vise on a backing machine, with the sewn edge up and roughly one inch above the vise jaws. The forwarder then pumps six to eight times on a hand-operated hydraulic device to tighten the vise jaws securely. He next pounds the sewn edge with a hammer until the desired degree of fanning is obtained. By turning a hand wheel the forwarder then brings the machine's heavy metal roller into contact with the sewn edge, and manually guides the roller in an arc across the edge until its entire surface is smoothly curved (Figure G). Mr. Dichio has estimated that the entire sequence of backing operations, including workpiece set-up, release, and machine adjustment, requires on the average about three minutes per volume.

The next step in the forwarding operation consists of making a cover for each volume in the order. This requires cutting to size two or three pieces of heavy cardboard, using a hand-operated shear, and cutting with scissors one piece of whatever covering material the customer has specified on the job sheet accompanying the order. In most cases, the covering material is special book cloth impregnated with a starch or plastic filler. The cut cloth is passed through the rollers of a machine which coats a thin, even layer of glue across its entire inner surface. The cloth is then placed flat on a workbench, glue-laden side up. The pieces of cardboard then are carefully positioned on the cloth so as to leave a border of cloth around the outer edge of the boards, and to provide for the thickness of the packet of pages which, at a later point of the process, will be bound with this cover (Figure H). This positioning is done by sight and requires considerable skill, since the glue forms an almost instantaneous bond between the cardboard and the cloth, preventing any major repositioning after the original contact has been made.

After any excess cloth has been cut away, the remaining edges of the cloth are turned in over the cardboard to form a tight cover. The cloth is then pressed down firmly to remove any air bubbles. The

FIGURE H. Cover-making process (one stage only). Pieces of cardboard are being positioned on glue-laden piece of cover fabric. Fold-in machine operation is visible in background.

folding and pressing operations can be done by hand, using a small paddlelike instrument. Usually, however, these operations are performed by a "turn-in" machine which is operated by a girl who assists all five of the forwarders. Since this function normally occupies only about one-third of her time, this girl also works in Exemplar's pamphlet department. After completing each cover, the forwarder writes the item and order number in pencil on the upper left-hand corner of the inner surface of cardboard.

A forwarder usually cuts cloth and boards for a number of volumes in an order at one time, processes these into covers, then cuts another pile of boards and cloth pieces, and so on. On the average, the cutting of the cover fabric requires about one-half minute per volume, and the cutting of the cardboard pieces one-eighth of a minute each. Mr. Dichio estimates that when assisted by the girl operating the turn-in machine, and using cloth and boards already cut to size, a forwarder can produce about 80 covers per hour. If the helper is not available, the forwarder's output drops to about 40 covers per hour.

From time to time Mr. Dichio and Mr. Wardell inspect items in process in the forwarding department. Mr. Dichio also usually spot-checks each order after all forwarding operations have been completed.

The sewn packets of pages of the items in the order then wait on one of the numerous benches or hand trucks located at random throughout the third-floor work areas, while all of the covers are sent to the stamping department to have titles affixed.

As the first phase of the stamping operation, one of the typesetters, working from both the job number on each cover and the information on the master job sheet, selects from one of the drawers in a storage cabinet the individual piece of metal type required for each letter in the title. These pieces of type are placed in proper sequence in a "chase" which holds them securely in position. The type and chase are given to one of the stampers, who heats them on a small burner until he judges them to be at the proper temperature for the material used for the cover. He then immediately places the chase and heated type in one of two Kensol stamping machines, the second of which had been added to the department about three months after Mr. Dix bought the company. The Kensol machines were designed to hold in proper alignment a book cover, a sheet of gold leaf, and a chase of type. Operation of the machine brings the heated type against the gold leaf and the cover, permanently transferring the gold onto the cover material in the form of the letters of the title (Figure I).

At the time of Mr. Dix's purchase, the Stamping Department consisted of two women, who functioned as typesetters, and two male

Figure I. Kensole stamping machine operation. Book cover is mounted on table of machine; chase filled with type (indicated by wooden handle) is also in position for stamping.

stampers. In addition to setting up the type for each title and placing it in the chase, the two typesetters were responsible for dismantling the type and returning it to the proper drawer of the storage cabinet after the stamping had been completed. On the average these operations— assembly and disassembly—took about four minutes per volume.

The heating of the letters in the chases and the operation of the Kensol machines were performed by two stampers. Mr. Dichio estimated that when a stamper was not required to wait for either the chase or the cover, the total stamping operation required on the average about three minutes per volume. The stampers also did hand lettering on those few volumes requiring it, and performed touch-up lettering when necessary—as, for example, when a single letter in the title did not emerge clearly from the Kensol operation.

As one of his first sizeable investments in new equipment, Mr. Dix had purchased a $5,100 Ludlow type caster (Figure J) and accessories for use in the stamping department. The order had been placed in September, and called for a 15 per cent down payment with the balance payable to the vendor in monthly payments over the next three years, at interest of 4½ per cent.

With the Ludlow it became unnecessary to set type by hand, except in the case of a few special volumes requiring other than conventional lettering in their titles. Instead, the Ludlow operator would select type molds for each letter, insert all of the molds for one line of type into the machine, and automatically cast the entire line in the form of a single lead slug. All of the lines necessary for a title could then be passed to an assistant, who would lock them into a chase to be handed to the stamper for heating and use in the Kensol machine. After use, each slug could be remelted and the lead utilized in manufacturing subsequent slugs. Since each slug of type would be individually cast and used only once, Mr. Dix was confident that the Ludlow would assure the company excellent quality on all its stampings. Recently some difficulty had been experienced in obtaining good impressions with the old hand-set type which, through use, had developed worn edges.

The Ludlow had been delivered to Exemplar only a few days before and was just now being placed in operation. Unable to locate an experienced Ludlow operator, Mr. Dix had decided to train one of his

FIGURE J. Ludlow type-casting machine.

typesetters in its use, and to make the other typesetter her assistant. In both instances, the women would continue at their former wage rates. The local Ludlow sales representative had agreed to assist in the training and had expressed confidence that no more than four weeks would be required to bring the two women to reasonable levels of proficiency.

Mr. Dix hoped that the Ludlow would reduce operating costs and increase capacity. He was confident, however, that the new unit's contribution to quality improvement would in itself fully justify its purchase. With two Kensol machines in operation, he was also convinced that the Ludlow could be kept reasonably loaded with work. For the time being, at least, Mr. Dix planned to retain Exemplar's entire supply of old hand-set type, saleable at perhaps a few hundred dollars, even though it was not required in the Ludlow operation.

The last remaining step of the binding operation consists of attaching the stamped cover to the corresponding packet of sewn pages. This is known as "casing-in" and is performed by an "assistant finisher." The physical joining is accomplished by gluing the outside surfaces of the end papers, that is, the top and bottom pages of the sewn packet, and securing them to the cover of the volume (Figure K). Careful checking by the assistant finisher is necessary to assure that the identifying

FIGURE K. Casing-in operation. Note large press containing cased-in volumes behind worker.

number on the sewn pages corresponds with the number on the cover itself, thus avoiding misbound volumes. After the cover has been attached, the book is placed under pressure in a large press for at least three hours to allow the glue to set firmly. Mr. Dichio believes that it is usually possible to perform these total casing-in operations at the average rate of about 20 volumes per hour, including loading and unloading of the presses.

Within both Exemplar and the bookbinding industry, forwarders and stampers are regarded as very highly skilled craftsmen. It is generally believed that to become competent in either operation requires a training period of at least four years. An even longer period is required to become skilled in the binding of leather volumes. Stamping in particular is considered an art. In order to assure a successful transfer of the gold leaf, the type has to be heated to "exactly the right temperature," and this differs for each of the numerous varieties of covering material. If the type is too hot, the cover will burn and have to be replaced. On the other hand, if it is not hot enough, there will be an imperfect bond between the cover and the gold, causing the gold to flake off after a short period of time.

PAMPHLET SECTION. Exemplar also operates a pamphlet section on the third floor. Here pamphlets, reprints, monographs, and other periodicals that normally see only limited use are bound in relatively inexpensive materials, usually cardboard covered with heavy paper. The cover is attached with heavy staples instead of sewing, and the entire manufacturing process is quite simple in comparison to hard-cover binding. Exemplar normally employs two people in the pamphlet department. This staff is augmented from time to time by other third-floor personnel who are temporarily out of regular work. Customers usually do not expect prompt delivery on pamphlet binding and Mr. Dix believes that this work can, in large measure, be scheduled at company convenience.

During a recent summer, Mr. Dix hired four university students to work exclusively on pamphlets.[3] Mr. Dichio had shown the young men how to perform the required operations and then had allowed them considerable latitude in working out their own system of work scheduling. Both he and Mr. Dix were pleasantly surprised at the quantity of work the team succeeded in producing. Before leaving the company to return to school, the four men had reduced the average unit cost of a pamphlet binding from 35 to 27 cents.

---

[3] In view of the temporary nature of this assignment, the union waived membership requirements for the young men.

QUALITY CONTROL. In addition to the several formal inspections cited previously, various additional informal inspections are made by Mrs. McDuffy, Mr. Wardell, and Mr. Dichio during all stages of the production process. Mr. Dix also makes a final inspection of each item before it is delivered[4] to the customer, his normal practice being to examine each day's work before he leaves the plant that evening. Defects are only rarely encountered. Although formal records have not been kept, Mr. Dix judges that the reject rate rarely exceeds 1 per cent of the items processed. When errors are detected, however, Mr. Dix invariably has them repaired, even when this means repeating the entire binding process.

LABOR PRODUCTIVITY. Mr. Dix was convinced that in general worker productivity in Exemplar was good. Although most of the operators never appeared to be working at an intense pace, Mr. Dix believed that their speed was consistent with the highly skilled work they were doing, and the quality results demanded. The most recent available summary of company output, for the period April 17 through July 31, appears in Exhibit 7. Exhibit 8 shows what Mr. Dix believes is a reasonably representative example of average direct-labor performance on a variety of orders. Exhibit 9 shows a roster of wages and salary levels. Exhibit 10 shows a monthly breakdown of costs of goods sold and manufacturing expenses.

PRODUCTION CONTROL. While performing her initial check of an order being routed into production, Mrs. McDuffy assigns an identifying number to the entire order and to each volume in it, writing them lightly in pencil on the first page of each volume. Then she fills out, in duplicate, a job sheet covering the entire order, showing the identifying numbers assigned, and giving any necessary details regarding the cover materials and variety of title stamping required on each item. One copy of this job sheet, together with one copy of the list prepared by the customer, stays with the order throughout the entire production process. The duplicate copies of the job sheet and of the customer's list are sent to the office where they are logged and filed by the accountant. A separate slip of paper identifying the entire order is also kept with the order until it has passed through the sewing operation. After the volume is sewn, the second-floor inspector/write-up clerk adds the identifying number, together with the processing instructions, in pencil on the front end paper. The same identifying number, obtained from the job sheet, is also entered in pencil

---

[4] Delivery is generally by commercial trucks. Sometimes, however, Mr. Dix delivers small rush orders in his own car.

EXHIBIT 7 EXEMPLAR BOOKBINDING COMPANY

VOLUMES PROCESSED* APRIL 17–JULY 31

	Periodicals†	Monographs and Rebinds †‡	Pamphlets	Theses†	Leather-Bound Volumes	Stamp Title Only	Mechanical Binding (Staple)
April§	668	700	2,943	86	0	32	0
May	2,201	704	608	396	69	154	928
June	1,949	1,362	4,060	76	139	36	0
July	2,459	808	6,259	29	21	217	0

* Excludes minor, miscellaneous work including repairs, orders for slip cases, and similar processes.
† Cloth-covered, hard-board bindings.
‡ Includes "Edition Binding."
§ Less than full month operation.

EXHIBIT 8 Exemplar Bookbinding Company

REPRESENTATIVE SAMPLE OF DIRECT-LABOR TIMES ON ORDERS BY OPERATIONS*

Operation	BOOKS								PERIODICALS								Work Included in Operation
	Number of Volumes in Order								Number of Volumes in Order								
	67	77	78	79	77	112	91	135	120	95	84	85	88	84	89	105	
	Minutes per Volume (Average)																
Pull	8.0	8.6	9.3	8.9	2.5	4.2	7.9	3.3	28.7	13.3	16.2	15.8	21.6	27.4	22.0	14.0	Remove old binding, clean binding edge, sort, collate
Trim	0.4	0.8	0.9	0.1	0.7	0.8	0.1	0.9	—	0.8	1.5	1.1	0.8	1.1	0.6	1.6	Trim, glue, separate sections
Saw	0.6	—	—	0.5	0.1	—	1.2	0.1	—	—	—	—	0.2	0.1	0.6	0.4	Saw slots for hand sewing
Machine Sew	3.5	3.5	3.5	2.5	3.3	3.2	2.6	3.1	5.5	5.1	5.0	5.5	4.4	2.1	4.2	5.9	Self-explanatory
Hand Sew	1.3	1.6	1.0	0.3	0.5	0.4	1.6	0.5	0.8	2.8	1.5	1.4	1.2	2.0	1.7	3.1	Self-explanatory
Check and Write Up	1.7	1.8	1.3	1.7	2.6	2.5	2.6	3.9	1.7	1.6	1.7	1.8	2.0	1.5	1.9	2.3	Check sewing and write on end paper information
Forward	12.7	14.3	11.7	12.0	11.7	11.2	10.3	10.0	12.0	11.6	12.0	13.2	14.0	11.5	14.2	14.3	Round, back, make covers
Set Type	2.3	5.9	6.4	6.5	7.8	2.7	5.7	2.4	1.0	3.7	2.9	3.4	2.2	3.6	3.0	5.7	Self-explanatory
Machine Stamp	6.4	6.7	—	5.9	6.2	4.2	5.5	5.5	4.5	0.7	5.9	5.5	6.5	3.9	4.0	1.6	Kensol machine operation
Hand Lettering	8.2	—	6.2	—	—	5.0	—	3.5	0.3	4.7	2.6	3.6	0.6	4.3	3.7	2.7	Self-explanatory
Assistant Finish	2.9	2.9	2.9	2.3	4.0	2.2	2.0	3.2	3.4	2.7	3.3	3.5	3.2	3.7	3.4	2.9	Casing-in
Inspect	0.5	0.4	1.5	0.8	0.8	0.5	0.7	0.5	0.3	0.5	0.4	0.4	0.4	0.6	0.4	0.4	Self-explanatory

* Derived by dividing total time shown on employee's time card on a specific order by the number of books in the order.

NOTE: Times for third-floor trimming operations not available.

EXHIBIT 9 Exemplar Bookbinding Company

PERSONNEL ROSTER WITH WAGE AND SALARY LEVELS

Position	Usual Work Area (see Exhibits 5 and 6†)	Hourly Wage or Monthly Salary
Owner-Manager (M)	A	Withdrawals
Accountant (F)	B	$410.00
Production Manager (M)	Entire Plant	$500.00
Secretary (F)*	C	$ 1.50
1 Forelady (F)	D	$ 2.00
5 Pullers (F)	D	$1.26–$1.53
1 Oversewing-Machine Operator (F)	F + K	$ 1.64
1 Apprentice Machine Operator (F)	F	$ 1.37
1 Inspector/Write-Up Clerk (F)	G	$ 1.53
1 Working Foreman (Seybold Operator) (M)	H	$ 2.57
5 Forwarders (M)	H	$1.96–$2.43
1 Fold-In Machine Operator (also Pamphlet Work) (F)	H + K	$ 1.31
2 Typesetters (F)	I	$1.26–$1.53
2 Stampers (M)	I	$ 2.43
1 Assistant Finisher (M)	J	$ 2.10
1 Pamphlet Worker (M)	K	$ 1.67

(M) Male   (F) Female

---

* With company's concurrence, often works less than 40 hours per week.

† Pages 42 and 43.

---

by the forwarder on the cardboard backing of each cover he makes.

Mr. Dix believes that this system has worked reasonably well. Individual items occasionally have been misplaced in the shop, however, and sometimes have remained lost for varying periods of time.

No other production-control techniques are now in use. For a short time Mr. Dix posted data to a large board to show the status of each job in the plant. This system was discarded after a brief trial because of the considerable time required to keep the postings up to date.

The scheduling of an order into each of the various process stages is handled informally. Mr. Dix, Mr. Dichio, Mrs. McDuffy, and Mr. Wardell all check frequently on the orders ahead of each stage of the

EXHIBIT 10 Exemplar Bookbinding Company

COST OF GOODS SOLD

(To Nearest Dollar)

	April 17–May 30	June	July	August	September	October
Sales	$21,106	$15,734	$17,448	$13,253	$9,908	$15,211
Cost of Goods Sold						
Raw Materials	3,002	2,117	1,009	1,818	1,144	1,668
(less) Sale of Gold Waste	141	—	—	83	—	28
(less) Discounts Taken	4	17	32	17	—	—
Net Raw Materials	2,857	2,100	977	1,716	1,144	1,640
Direct Labor	10,341	7,183	8,060	6,159	4,625	7,278
Manufacturing Expenses						
Unabsorbed Supervision	335	121	317	422	494	491
Apprentice Training	142	119	74	160	201	264
Vacation/Holiday/Sick Pay	473	13	373	23	461	100
Supplies	47	317	230	248	293	472
Payroll Taxes	583	380	450	384	410	484
Depreciation	140	205	187	187	187	187
Insurance	282	114	132	132	132	132
Rental (net)	880	600	1,350	600	—	750
Utilities	—	—	—	—	32	130
Repair/Maintenance—Labor	7	4	38	5	31	2
Repair/Maintenance—Materials	—	2	—	1	—	—
Trucking	187	259	243	1,795	324	356
Freight	—	19	7	273	8	—
Miscellaneous	—	95	131	628	573	180
Total Actual Manufacturing Expenses	3,077	2,247	3,531	4,857	3,144	3,542
TOTAL COST OF GOODS SOLD	$16,275	$11,531	$12,567	$12,733	$8,913	$12,459
GROSS INCOME	$ 4,831	$ 4,203	$ 4,881	$ 520	$ 995	$ 2,751

Source: Company records.

process, and on the delivery dates that have been requested by customers. On the basis of this knowledge, individual decisions are made regarding order sequence each time an operator is free to take on a new assignment.

COSTING AND PRICING. Most work performed by Exemplar is priced on a cost-plus basis. From previous dealings with the company, regular customers are able to judge the approximate charges involved in any work and thus can usually determine whether their budget will permit a particular order to be placed.

As the initial step in calculating the cost of an order, each operator turns in a daily time card showing the various orders on which he has worked, the operations performed, and the amount of time spent on each. The company's accountant uses this information to make daily postings in a "job book" showing the cumulative direct-labor hours spent on each individual order.[5]

When all the operations on an order have been completed, the hours spent on each operation are multiplied by the hourly rate of the operators involved. An amount equal to 50 per cent of the total labor charges is then added to cover manufacturing overhead. Next are added the charges for raw materials and supplies. Usually these are based on a standard charge of 45 cents for each volume in the order. In the event that the materials used are sufficiently unusual to make the standard charge inappropriate, Mr. Dix uses his own judgment in determining the cost figures to employ. In the case of expensive leather bindings, the actual quantity of the leather employed is shown and costed on the job order. These various cost items then are totaled, and an amount equal to 18 per cent of their sum is added to cover other expenses and profit. The customer is billed for the grand total.

If all of the operator time cards accumulated on an order calling for the rebinding of 74 books showed that total labor hours spent on

---

[5] The foreman and forelady also fill out time cards to cover any portion of their time actually chargeable to a specific customer order. Whenever the Production Manager, Mr. Dichio, personally performs a manufacturing operation in the absence of a regular hourly employee, the time he spends is also charged to the job in question at the rate of either $2.43 per hour, or $1.53 per hour, depending on whether he does work normally assigned to a male employee or to a female employee. For internal-control purposes, in the monthly cost summaries the total amount of time spent by supervisory personnel on direct production work is charged under the category of "Direct Labor." The difference between these charges and the total salary and wage payments actually made to the supervisors is included as a "Manufacturing Expense" item, under the category of "Unabsorbed Supervision."

this work represent $104.30 in wages, the customer would be billed $223.90, computed as follows:

Direct labor	$104.30
Manufacturing overhead (50% of direct labor)	52.15
Raw materials and supplies (at 45¢/volume)	33.30
Subtotal	$189.75
Expenses and profit (18% of subtotal)	34.15
Total billed to customer	$223.90

As a check upon the system, Mr. Dix usually divides the total billing figure by the number of volumes in the order to establish an average unit price. In the case of the above order, for example, the unit price per book is $3.03. If this unit price is substantially higher, or lower, than the customer is accustomed to being charged for generally comparable work, Mr. Dix usually will adjust the total to bring it in line with the customary figure. He believes that such adjustments are appropriate, since substantial deviations from historic cost patterns are usually attributable to errors which operators make in recording data on their daily time cards. This can happen, for example, when an operator accidentally switches order cards, recording under one particular job the direct-labor hours actually spent on another order.

During the past several months, some of Exemplar's customers have begun to request price lists or to ask for quotations in advance of orders. The company also received an invitation to bid on a large order for a local U.S. Air Force installation which desired to have a collection of technical publications bound. Mr. Dix believed that requests of this type might increase in number, particularly if Exemplar were to make a concerted effort to expand by attracting new customers.

With these facts in mind, Mr. Dix was evaluating the strengths and weaknesses of the company's position to determine the action plan he should follow in the months ahead.

Morrisville Hardware Company

In early October, Eric Dudley, Owner-President, and Albert Foster, Executive Vice President, of the Morrisville Hardware Company met to discuss possible operating goals which the company might set for itself for the year ahead. In a recent series of meetings, the two men had assessed the results of company operations since Mr. Dudley's purchase of the business four years earlier when it had been in extremely poor financial position.

As their October meeting drew to a close, Mr. Dudley said:

Al, we've clearly come a long way, particularly since you took over as Executive Vice President. Our number-one target has been to keep the company alive and get its operations out of the red. It looks as if this is just about achieved. We've every right to be proud of these results, but the one thing we cannot afford is to ease up on the pressure now. The operating phase that we are now entering is likely to be just as tough—and may in fact even place higher demands on us as managers—than the period we've just finished. Up to now it hasn't been much of a problem to decide where to direct our efforts, or what aspects of our operations to single out for improvements. Everything was a problem; almost every phase of the company needed strengthening. The real question in the past hasn't been 'What to do?' but rather 'How to find time enough to do it?'

It's going to be different in the months ahead. The most urgent operating problems have now been solved; the wide-open gaps in operating efficiency have been plugged. What we now have to do is to begin smoking out the less obvious things—and we both know that there are a lot of them—that stand between us and some really decent earnings. We've already had ample indications from the banks that until Morrisville does earn some respectable profits it's unlikely to get financing for any significant long-range plans or improvements.

I don't want to leave profits to chance, or to whatever forward momentum we may have as a result of the crash-program to salvage the company from the mess it was in four years ago. Instead, I want us to make immediate profit improvement a specific target, one we strike out for with everything we've got.

65

What I therefore would like you to do now, Al, is to review our present situation in its entirety, its strengths and weaknesses. On the basis of your conclusions, I'd like you to propose a detailed operating plan for the next 12 months, describing the precise steps we should take to improve profits during that period. As soon as you're ready, I'd like your recommendation.

OPERATING CONDITIONS

Morrisville's Product-Line and the Market Served

The Morrisville Hardware Company manufactures a wide variety of hardware for mounting, balancing, actuating, locking, and weather-stripping residential windows. Its product line includes items specifically applicable to each of the principal types of windows in residential construction. These include double-hung, awning, panel, casement, and horizontal-sliding varieties.

With sales currently totaling approximately $1,500,000 annually,[1] and with a product line of 15 major types of apparatus, Morrisville's management believes that its firm is one of the largest in the industry. Few of the 35 or so competing companies have comparably wide product lines. Most specialize instead on only a few items. Furthermore, somewhat less than half of its competitors follow Morrisville's practice of distributing on a nationwide basis.

Residential window hardware differs substantially from that used in industrial construction. Industrial window units usually are made of aluminum or steel, and are generally larger and heavier than the typical wooden residential window installations. Both classes of windows require distinctive types of hardware equipment, and are served by entirely different channels of distribution. In view of these differences, Morrisville always had concentrated its efforts solely in the residential field. Insofar as its management could determine, no window hardware manufacturer was attempting to serve both markets.

The potential market for residential window hardware depends largely on the number of residential housing starts in any given period. As a rough guide, Morrisville sales personnel assume on the basis of construction statistics that the average new residential unit has 14 windows, each of which requires about one dollar's worth of window hardware at the manufacturer's selling price.

According to U.S. Government estimates, annual housing starts on new, permanent, one-family dwellings in nonfarm areas for the six years prior to the Dudley-Foster conversation had varied from a low

---

[1] Budgeted figure for the current fiscal year.

of approximately 873,000 units to a high of roughly 1,200,000 units. The over-all six-year average was slightly more than 1,000,000 units per year. On the basis of industry reports, Morrisville's sales department believed that double-hung window units were used in about 60 per cent of all new homes, with the remainder divided roughly on an equal basis among the various other window types.

Sales volume varies from season to season, reflecting the changing pattern of housing construction. During the peak period, the summer months, sales had been averaging about $150,000 per month. In the winter, volume dropped to around $100,000 monthly. Exhibit 1 shows recent Morrisville sales by product for selected periods.

Manufacturers of residential window hardware sell to three major types of customers: *jobbers,* who typically stock the product-lines of several different manufacturers; *unit manufacturers,* who produce complete window units, usually bearing a brand name, which they sell to contractors for installation; and *retail lumber yards.* Morrisville officials believed that jobbers usually account for about 80 per cent of the market, with the other two types of accounts equally sharing the remainder. Morrisville's own pattern of sales normally conformed closely to that of the industry.

Competition, particularly in price, generally is intense and had been unusually severe during the latter half of the current year. Prices of competing manufacturers seldom differ by more than a few cents per unit on comparable items. In the opinion of both Mr. Foster and Mr. Dudley, these conditions would continue for the foreseeable future.

Mr. Foster estimated at the time of his talk with Mr. Dudley that the entire industry consisted of perhaps 2,500 potential accounts. Morrisville's active customer list currently numbered about 250 firms throughout the country. A few of these generated sales of as much as $100,000 each per year, but the majority of the accounts were considerably smaller. Morrisville's Sales Department maintained no summaries of accounts by size of orders.

The company paid its 12 sales representatives on an 8½ per cent commission basis. In addition, Morrisville provided each man with an automobile and paid all registration and maintenance expenses on it. Mr. Foster believed that sales representatives of the caliber the company desired should expect to earn at least $1,000 per month on the average, and thus would have to generate sales of at least $150,000 per year. During the most recent fiscal year of operations only three of the company salesmen had exceeded the $150,000 sales mark; two had sales between $100,000 and $135,000; the others each had achieved

EXHIBIT 1   MORRISVILLE HARDWARE COMPANY

UNIT PRICE AND DISTRIBUTION OF SALES BY PRODUCTS

Product	Representative Unit* Price	12 Months Ending November 30 2nd Prior Year	12 Months Ending November 30 1st Prior Year	10 Months Ending September 30 Current Year
Sash Pulleys	—	$ 11,620	$ 5,615	$ 1,166
Undetectable Window Balance	$1.44 (box of 4)†	557,128	386,273	252,341
Tape and Cable Clock Spring Balances	.42	93,539	88,060	12,020
Cabinet Flat Hinges		108,386	6,390	85,697
Actuating Mechanisms†	3.00	207,162	146,871	229,173
Tight-Seal	2.76	32,150	157,414	65,438
Weatherstrip‡	.02	52,180	57,273	929
Crank Actuator	1.90	36,888	37,939	70,438
Crank Actuator	1.90		30,185	30,160
22″ Friction Hinge	.90		28,540	30,160
Cabinet Locks and Latches	1.47	14,879	8,192	436,407
Double-Hung Hardware Unit†	2.76		213,783	34,699
Special Slider	.90		400	41,652
Push Bars		—	—	17,632
Job Shop (contract press work)	.90	—	—	11,970
32″ Friction Hinge		—	—	1,424
Miscellaneous	—			
		$1,113,932	$1,166,935	$1,299,008

* Most products were available in a variety of sizes. The unit price shown for each item is for hardware that could be used with what the company believed to be "an average sized" window in each of the various window types. In the case of double-hung windows, for example, the unit prices pertain to hardware used with the familiar 24″ x 24″ window. Remaining inventories of products which had been dropped from the line were sold on a negotiated price basis.

† Special prices are available for bulk pack and truck load lots.

‡ Price quoted is average price per foot.

NOTE: Sales summaries were maintained on a December 1–November 30 year to facilitate comparison with records of previous years which had been maintained on this basis.

Source: Company records.

sales of less than $100,000. On the average, the sales representatives had been with Morrisville for two and a half years, and the most recently hired salesman had a year and a half's service.

Morrisville's Present Manufacturing Facilities and Production Practices

Morrisville's manufacturing operations are located in a 55-year-old, two-story building on the outskirts of a midwestern city with a population of approximately a quarter of a million. The ground floor of the plant, which is about 26,500 square feet, is used primarily for parts fabrication. Its equipment includes an electroplating unit, 36 punch presses of various sizes, five rolling mills, one slitting machine, one spiral tube roll-forming machine, four screw machines, two spring-winding machines, and six drill presses. The ground floor also houses the tool and die shop, the maintenance shop, the Research and Development Department, the cafeteria, and the spring-flocking room. Arrangement of these various facilities is shown in Exhibit 2.

The machines in the Parts Fabrication Department permit Morrisville to perform all the heavy cutting, shaping, and forming work required to produce metal parts of window hardware. The punch presses shape small steel or aluminum parts with a single stroke of the press head. The slitting machine, using adjustable circular blades, cuts rolls of steel or aluminum sheeting into strips of desired widths. Rolling mills then form the strips into various contours, or into weather-stripping. The spiral tube forming machine twists narrow strips of cold rolled steel into the straight, hollow, spiral tubes required in one of the company's products. Automatic screw machines turn identical small parts from bar stock at high rates of speed. The spring winder converts steel wire into tightly coiled tension springs that are needed in large quantities in the manufacture of sash balances. The flocking equipment, located in an enclosed room on the first floor, sprays the springs with a liquid adhesive and then coats them with a fine, wool-like fiber. This serves to muffle the vibration sounds generated by the extension or contraction of the tension balance springs as the window to which they are attached is opened or closed.

Morrisville's Tool and Die Shop is equipped with numerous varieties and sizes of milling machines, shapers, lathes, drill presses, and grinders, and is manned by experienced machinists. The shop constructs almost all of the tools, dies, and fixtures required for the company's operations and also does experimental work for the Product Development Department.

The second floor, shown in Exhibit 3, contains about 26,000 square

EXHIBIT 2 Morrisville Hardware Company

GROUND FLOOR

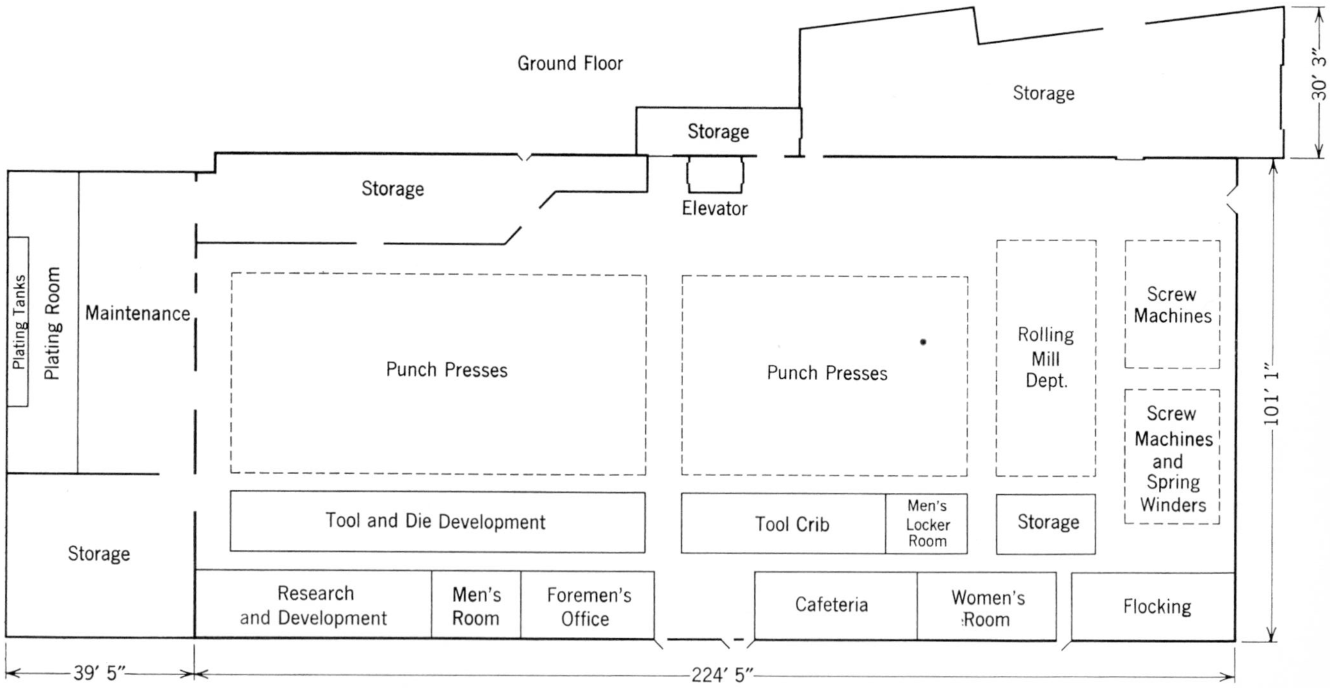

Ground Floor

Storage

Storage

Elevator

Storage

Storage

Punch Presses

Punch Presses

Tool and Die Development

Research and Development

Men's Room

Foremen's Office

Tool Crib

Men's Locker Room

Cafeteria

Women's Room

Rolling Mill Dept.

Storage

Screw Machines

Screw Machines and Spring Winders

Flocking

Maintenance

Plating Room

Plating Tanks

Storage

30' 3"

101' 1"

224' 5"

39' 5"

EXHIBIT 3 MORRISVILLE HARDWARE COMPANY

SECOND FLOOR

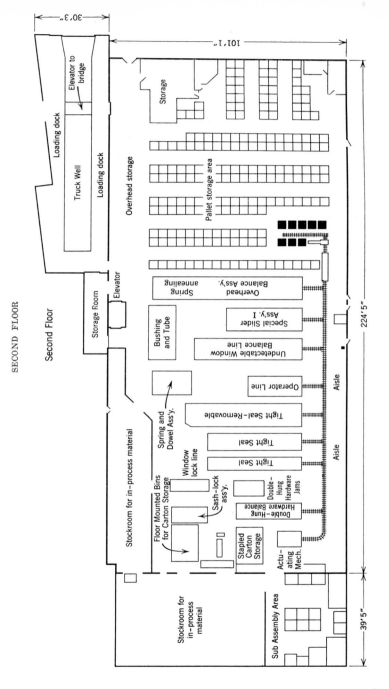

feet and accommodates all assembly work as well as the less heavy forming operations required for parts fabrication. It also provides storage space for finished goods and parts inventories. The latter are stored in a 40' x 64' room, located in the west end of the factory. As parts are needed for assembly they are moved from the storage room by lift trucks and brought to the appropriate assembly area. Each of these areas is serviced by a conveyor belt which carries completed items to the end of the assembly tables where they are inspected, lubricated if necessary, and placed in open shipping cartons. The cartons are fed by a gravity-roller conveyor to the Shipping Department where their contents are checked visually. The cartons are then closed, either by use of a power stapler or, in the case of heavy items, by the use of metal straps. After closing the cartons, the Shipping Department personnel place them on wooden pallets and move them to a storage area in the east end of the room. When customers' orders are received the cartons are moved to the shipping dock. Although a railroad siding lies adjacent to the plant, all outgoing shipments are made by truck, as are all but a small fraction of incoming shipments of materials and supplies.

Photographs of several representative shop areas are shown in Exhibits 4, 5, and 6.

Production operations were currently on a one-shift basis with the exception of the rolling mills and the spring-winding machine which were being operated on two shifts. Morrisville's Tool Room, however, was constructing a second spring-winding machine which it expected to complete by mid-November. The company also had on order a 20-stand mill which would increase the Rolling Mill Department's output by 15 to 20 per cent. Delivery had been promised by January 15 of the coming year. With these equipment additions, Mr. Foster believed that the entire plant could be placed on a single shift. A space problem would arise, however, with the arrival of the new rolling mill, the dimensions of which were approximately 5 x 15 feet. Production personnel believed that to achieve maximum efficiency in the utilization of the new mill, it would be necessary to rearrange the entire Slitting and Rolling Mill Department.

For the past several months the screw machines had been used only rarely, and the Punch Press Department and the Plating Room had operated at only about 50 per cent capacity, notwithstanding Morrisville's efforts to obtain subcontract work to keep these facilities more fully loaded. Since the first of the year, however, gross billings for subcontracts had totaled only about $18,000. Mr. Foster believed that this reflected, in large part, the influence of a business recession in the

EXHIBIT 4   MORRISVILLE HARDWARE COMPANY

PLATING ROOM AREA

EXHIBIT 5   MORRISVILLE HARDWARE COMPANY

ASSEMBLY AREA

EXHIBIT 6 MORRISVILLE HARDWARE COMPANY

FINISHED GOODS STORAGE AREA

area. In his opinion most potential local sources of work of this type were experiencing sales declines and were thus able to handle their own requirements without the help of subcontractors.

Morrisville at the moment employed about 100 people, administered by the organization shown in Exhibit 7. Roughly two-thirds of the employees were engaged in production operations. Of these, about half were women who ran punch presses, assisted on the rolling mills, operated the spring-flocking equipment, and did most of the assembly work. Male production workers operated the heavy punch presses, the slitting machine, and the spring-winding machine, and performed the heavy operations on the rolling mills. Of the 29 persons in the office and sales staff, seven were women employed as secretaries, receptionists, or bookkeepers. None of the personnel was unionized. In Mr. Foster's opinion, employee morale was reasonably good, and he detected no particular signs of bitterness among the workforce over the six-month strike that had occurred four years earlier (to be discussed subsequently).

Morrisville's production workers now averaged $1.75 per hour on an incentive piecework system. This compared favorably with earnings levels in similar companies in the area. Piece rates were set by a

EXHIBIT 7 MORRISVILLE HARDWARE COMPANY

ORGANIZATION CHART

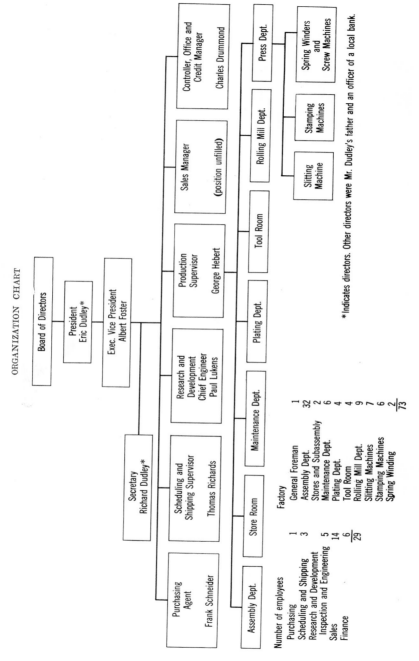

Board of Directors

President
Eric Dudley*

Exec. Vice President
Albert Foster

Secretary
Richard Dudley*

Purchasing
Agent

Frank Schneider

Research and
Development
Chief Engineer
Paul Lukens

Production
Supervisor

George Hebert

Sales Manager

(position unfilled)

Controller, Office and
Credit Manager

Charles Drummond

Scheduling and
Shipping Supervisor

Thomas Richards

Assembly Dept.

Store Room

Maintenance Dept.

Plating Dept.

Tool Room

Rolling Mill Dept.

Press Dept.

Slitting
Machine

Stamping
Machines

Spring Winders
and
Screw Machines

Number of employees

Purchasing   1
Scheduling and Shipping   3
Research and Development
Inspection and Engineering   5
Sales   14
Finance   6
                                        ——
                                        29

Factory

General Foreman   1
Assembly Dept.   32
Stores and Subassembly   2
Maintenance Dept.   6
Plating Dept.   4
Tool Room   4
Rolling Mill Dept.   9
Slitting Machines   7
Stamping Machines   6
Spring Winding   2
                                        ——
                                        73

*Indicates directors. Other directors were Mr. Dudley's father and an officer of a local bank.

member of the Engineering, Research, and Development Department after he had standardized and time-studied the jobs. Mr. Foster believed that the company's standards were "tight," and that labor productivity was good.

The same employee who set time standards also served as cost clerk, keeping cost records on work in process and finished goods inventories. Before any job order was released into the shop for production, he determined the physical amount and cost of all the raw materials to be required. For most items in the line, materials costs ran somewhere between 50 and 60 per cent of total cost of goods sold. As the order progressed through the production operations, the cost clerk also accumulated the direct labor costs charged to the order. This required him to extract data from the daily time cards filled out by the production employees. As workers shifted from one job to another, they were required to ring "out" and "in" on the time clock, entering on their cards the number of the job they were about to begin. To calculate the cost of each job, the clerk totaled the raw material and direct labor costs, and then added standard burden charges, computed at a rate of 165 per cent of direct labor costs.

Supervisory Incentive Plan

Under a plan developed by Mr. Foster during the previous summer, the four supervisors whose duties he believed had a particularly direct influence on gross factory profits now participated in an incentive system which permitted them to supplement their basic salaries. The Production Supervisor, and the Director of the combined Engineering, Research, and Development Department, each received a salary supplement of one-third of 1 per cent of gross factory profit[2] calculated monthly; the Purchasing Agent and the Shipping/Scheduling Supervisor each received a supplement of one-sixth of 1 per cent of the monthly gross factory profit. Mr. Foster believed it was too early to evaluate the full effect of this incentive. He thought, however, that he had detected evidence that the supervisors were now striving more aggressively for efficiency in factory operations.

Mr. Foster considered all four men, who ranged in age from the mid-thirties to late forties, reasonably competent in their jobs. They seemed to him to be hard-working and cooperative, although none of them displayed what he regarded as more than routine amounts of imagination and resourcefulness in responding to new problems.

---

[2] Net sales less cost of goods sold.

Control Techniques

During the preceding year, Mr. Foster had introduced several internal control techniques which he thought provided management with helpful information. These were:

Daily Production Sheets, which shop foremen posted in several readily accessible places throughout the plant. At the close of each shift, machine operators and assembly crews entered on these sheets the number of parts, or completed items, each had produced that day. By scanning these daily sheets, Mr. Foster and the Production Supervisor kept informed on production rates throughout the shop.

A daily *Summary Sheet,* which was prepared by the Production Supervisor. It showed the number of workers assigned, the total man hours, the number of pieces completed, the unit price, and the total labor cost of all items put through final assembly during the day just ended.

A *Weekly Direct Labor Cost Summary* by Production Departments (Exhibit 8) which was prepared by the Accounting Department for submission to Mr. Foster.

Weekly Sales Reports, which sales representatives were required to submit each Friday showing their selling activities during the week just ending. Using this information, the Sales Department maintained a current record on each customer and potential customer.

BACKGROUND TO MR. FOSTER'S ASSIGNMENT

As he approached the assignment just given him by Mr. Dudley, Mr. Foster was convinced that in determining the best course of action for the period immediately ahead, he would have to take into account the turbulent period through which Morrisville recently had passed. Mr. Foster had been with the company for less than two years, and had been Executive Vice President for only the past eight months. His original job, assumed in January of the previous year, had been that of Sales Manager. Four months later, Mr. Dudley had promoted him to the newly created position of Vice President in charge of Sales. With his subsequent promotion to Executive Vice President, Mr. Foster had assumed complete operating responsibility for the company.

During this entire period, as in a number of the preceding years, Morrisville had experienced serious operating losses. On the basis of his observations while in charge of the company's Sales Department, Mr. Foster had assumed the post of Executive Vice President with the

EXHIBIT 8   MORRISVILLE HARDWARE COMPANY

ANALYSIS OF DIRECT LABOR BY DEPARTMENTS

Week*		Total	Monthly Total	Assembly	Screw Machine and Wire Coiling	Press Room	Rolling	Slitting	Plating	Flocking
March	8	$3,113.43		$2,099.55	$223.00	$425.31	$193.67	$ 57.75	$114.15	
	15	3,044.76		1,901.54	300.33	431.11	331.97	68.69	6.12	
	22	3,004.62		1,723.53	332.66	205.51	366.07	47.25	29.60	
	29	3,108.18	$12,270.99	1,824.19	221.23	539.51	286.69	97.71	136.79	
April	5	3,056.34		1,827.75	253.81	573.66	287.17	46.25	70.70	
	12	3,201.32		2,073.65	217.41	415.11	339.48	66.94	88.73	
	19	3,058.84		1,974.09	234.44	397.03	355.44	69.13	28.71	
	26	3,169.42	12,485.92	2,228.14	161.80	350.27	331.21	0	98.00	
May	3	2,928.70		2,144.81	215.97	252.89	242.43	63.00	9.60	
	10	2,587.04		1,622.04	262.86	286.43	353.58	62.13	0	
	17	2,988.57		1,910.62	246.20	271.33	309.53	69.13	181.76	
	24	3,177.31		2,090.81	156.40	403.72	351.97	70.54	103.87	
	31	2,953.25	14,634.87	2,035.97	157.06	260.67	376.39	0	37.85	$ 85.31
June	7	3,085.89		2,095.71	139.05	209.17	433.40	0	0	208.56
	14	3,170.48		2,026.71	119.88	156.36	479.08	33.26	113.13	241.86
	21	3,768.55		2,264.44	124.13	342.99	544.11	158.96	82.47	251.45
	28	3,649.84	13,654.76	2,512.42	125.24	297.72	380.14	139.29	0	195.03

July 5	3,346.81		2,130.83	144.15	295.66	369.10	154.29	148.62	104.16
Vacation									
19	3,624.34		2,243.68	84.40	279.61	516.46	157.95	158.27	183.97
26	3,672.15	10,643.30	2,110.36	345.20	244.47	322.58	306.07	59.46	284.01
August 2	4,034.79		2,372.33	257.54	284.24	412.36	131.63	212.56	346.13
9	3,781.90		2,329.47	297.62	222.92	360.98	130.00	35.04	405.85
16	3,759.37		2,156.53	309.00	262.85	445.39	104.63	59.21	421.76
23	3,894.87		2,185.93	294.58	334.76	455.51	113.33	110.00	400.76
30	4,089.81	19,560.74	2,362.93	273.28	425.27	467.09	83.02	74.87	403.35
September 6	3,794.19		2,009.51	254.56	568.59	439.36	131.55	55.00	335.62
13	3,852.09		2,063.84	219.53	487.25	495.25	115.84	113.79	356.56
20	3,718.58		2,082.94	154.64	472.09	527.73	102.01	83.02	296.15
27	4,099.76	15,464.62	2,235.63	363.56	483.50	432.38	154.03	67.64	363.02
October 4	4,276.46		2,102.86	308.74	569.06	638.94	157.89	77.74	269.43
11	4,281.55		2,248.27	169.17	643.83	771.64	148.63	55.00	245.00
18	4,262.73		2,126.97	302.62	599.80	654.24	142.67	92.67	343.76

* All current year.

conviction that drastic and immediate improvements were required in Morrisville's product line, customer service, management personnel, and in its entire factory operations, particularly in the area of cost control. He knew that each of these problems had roots deep in the past history of the company.

The First Six Decades of Morrisville Hardware

The company had been founded in 1898 to manufacture sash pulleys and balances. In both these products Morrisville originally enjoyed an extremely advantageous patent position. On the basis of this, company operations had been highly profitable from its founding until the period following the Second World War. During this entire time the firm was run by the founder and his family as a closely held private corporation.

In the postwar period, Morrisville began to experience major declines in sales volume and profits. These were caused primarily by rapid changes in home construction techniques which had rendered obsolete most of the items in the company's line. In an effort to remedy the situation, over the next several years the company, now under the control of heirs of the founder, introduced a number of hurriedly designed new window hardware items. Most of these met with severe competition, and several contained serious design flaws which caused operational malfunction and breakage. As a result, the company's sales and profit position had continued to deteriorate.

Realizing that Morrisville was in serious trouble and in need of major changes, and with no members of the family particularly anxious to assume personal leadership in the situation, approximately four years ago the owners decided to sell the company.

Mr. Dudley's Acquisition

Mr. Dudley, the owner of a manufacturing concern in another area of the state, learned of this decision and started negotiating with the family for possible purchase of the firm. Five other potential purchasers also expressed interest in the company at about the same time. In late November, shortly before the close of Morrisville's fiscal year, Mr. Dudley extended an offer of $250,000 for the name and all other assets of the firm, except the plant itself, which he proposed to lease under a five-year contract calling for monthly payments of $1,500. He also agreed to assume the company's outstanding liabilities of about $196,000. Mr. Dudley's offer was quickly accepted, thus permitting the present owners to take advantage of a loss on the sale in the current tax year.

Mr. Dudley had raised the purchase funds by drawing on his own resources, as well as those of a small group of associates and a few members of his family. Three of these individuals then joined him on Morrisville's newly constituted board of directors. The other directors, however, tended to leave the company decisions almost entirely in Mr. Dudley's hands.

Although he had visited Morrisville's plant and examined company records, Mr. Dudley had not made any exhaustive study of its facilities or operations at the time of its purchase. From even this brief exposure, however, he had seen what he believed to be clear evidence that the company was suffering from high labor costs, a poor product line, and a weak supervisory organization.

At the time, Morrisville's production workers were represented by a local affiliate of a strong national industrial union. At various times in the past Morrisville had performed contract stamping and plating work for major corporations in the industry in which this union was dominant and, on the basis of this association, had been singled out for a successful organizing campaign some 12 years earlier. Morrisville's production workers therefore currently were being paid on a straight hourly basis with rates pegged at the level of wages paid by several major unionized employers in the city, but well above those paid by most hardware manufacturers.

At the time of Mr. Dudley's purchase, Morrisville's product line had consisted of: sash pulleys; cabinet latches and hinges; tape and cable clock spring sash balances; dual sash balances for double-hung windows; cam window latch; "Undetectable Window Balance" (a trade-name item); and actuating mechanism for awning and casement windows. Of these, only the Undetectable Window Balance and the actuating mechanism were selling well. Conventional pulleys and balances for double-hung windows, although formerly the major items in the company's line, largely had been displaced in home construction by new types of hardware. The remaining items in the line were products similar to those manufactured by numerous firms in the industry and therefore subject to extreme price competition which Morrisville was unable to meet without selling at or, in some cases, below cost.

Shortly after acquiring the firm Mr. Dudley also had become aware that serious friction existed among certain of the key personnel, particularly the Chief Engineer and his assistant. Their mutual antagonism was, in fact, a subject of plantwide conversation. There also was ill will discernible between the Scheduling and Production Supervisors. Mr. Dudley believed that these several areas of hostility resulted not only from personality clashes, but also from differences in interpretations of individual responsibilities and company goals.

Mr. Dudley's Early Actions

THE STRIKE. It was apparent to Mr. Dudley that radical steps had to be taken before the company could return to its former profitable state. As one of his first moves, therefore, he announced to the workforce that on the advice of counsel he did not consider the existing labor contract binding upon the new management. The union immediately called a strike which lasted for six months and received vigorous support of other organized labor groups in the community. Although there was no violence, repeated threats were directed against management, and considerable quantities of literature were distributed bitterly denouncing the company and singling out Mr. Dudley for extremely personalized criticism. During the latter stages of the strike, strikers several times stopped and detained Morrisville's truck on the road, although they did no damage to it.

During this period Morrisville abandoned all efforts to continue factory production. The company did remain in operation, however, meeting what sales requirements it could out of inventory. Finally, in June of the following year, the strike was terminated and efforts by the union to force recognition were discontinued.

CHANGES IN PERSONNEL AND PRACTICES. While the strike was in progress Mr. Dudley made a careful evaluation of the company's manpower requirements. He concluded that the organization had been seriously overstaffed in the past and that many of its present supervisory and management personnel had little potential. As a start toward improvements, the President and the Controller were dismissed from their positions and replaced, respectively, by Mr. Dudley and by one of the former Controller's assistants. Furthermore, when the strike ended, only about half of the former staff of production workers—those believed to have the greatest skill—were asked to return to work.

As soon as the company resumed operations after the strike, Mr. Dudley introduced a system of piece-rate incentives. As rapidly as possible, a clerk in the Engineering, Research, and Design Department conducted time studies and established standards for all types of production jobs. Little opposition was shown by the work force.

NEW PRODUCT DEVELOPMENT. Even while the strike was still in progress, Morrisville dropped four poor-selling items from its product line and undertook a crash-program of new product development, attempting again to give the company a complete line of window hardware. Some of the development work on a majority of the new products had been undertaken earlier by the former management of the company on request from window manufacturers who wanted specially designed hardware for their window installations. In several such instances the window manufacturers later had abandoned the projects, leaving the development costs to be absorbed by Morrisville. The former owners, therefore, had decided not to undertake any further development work for others, but to devote the efforts of Morrisville's Engineering, Research, and Development Department[3] solely to the company's own projects.

The roster of the new products added to the Morrisville line during the months following Mr. Dudley's purchase of the firm was as follows:

Product	Number of Months Elapsing Between Mr. Dudley's Purchase of Company and Introduction of Item into Product Line
"Pushbar X" (for awning windows)	3
Guidehook (for awning windows)	5
Sash lock (for double-hung windows)	7
"Tight-Seal" line (vertical window hardware)	9
22" friction hinge (for awning and casement windows)	10
32" friction hinge (as above)	11
Pinlock (for awning windows)	11
Crank actuator (for awning windows)	16
Slider (for removable horizontal windows)	17
New type double-hung hardware unit	20

Out-of-pocket development costs of these new products totaled approximately $100,000. None of the items were new to the industry. Instead, each represented Morrisville's own version of items currently enjoying consumer acceptance. In keeping with the industry's practice, Morrisville attempted to obtain patents on all of its new products, even though this usually offered little real protection. Successful new products developed by any manufacturer almost invariably were

---

[3] This department consisted of the Chief Engineer, an assistant engineer, a time study and cost control clerk, a draftsman, and an experimental machinist.

duplicated in a short period of time by new competing items which had been designed to circumvent the patents while still providing the same general product features.

With these additions to the Morrisville product line, Mr. Foster was convinced that the company was again in a position to meet, in a fully competitive manner, every conventional need for residential window hardware.

THE SEARCH FOR MANAGEMENT LEADERSHIP.   For the first six months after purchasing Morrisville, Mr. Dudley divided his time between it and his other manufacturing enterprise located in a town of 7,000 persons 65 miles away. Mr. Dudley finally concluded that by serving each company as President on a half-time basis he was unable to do justice to either firm. He therefore started looking for a man to assume full responsibility for the Morrisville operation. After a half-year's search he hired an executive from a large manufacturing company which supplied aircraft and automobile manufacturers with parts and assemblies.

Even with the new General Manager devoting full time to the Morrisville activities, conditions failed to improve significantly. Sales did not increase, and numerous production problems relating to cost and to quality control remained acute. About six months later Mr. Dudley began looking for a replacement for the company's Sales Manager, believing that the company needed particular strengthening in this area. After listing the opening with various placement offices and advertising in trade journals, Mr. Dudley was introduced to Albert Foster, then 42 years of age. For the past seven years Mr. Foster had been General Manager of a large integrated lumber mill in another section of the country, having complete responsibility for both sales and manufacturing operations. Mr. Foster had terminated his association with this firm shortly after the death of the late owner when the heirs introduced a number of policy and personnel changes with which he was not in accord.

After preliminary discussions had convinced both men that their association might be mutually advantageous, Mr. Foster accepted Mr. Dudley's offer of the position of Sales Manager of the Morrisville company and began work immediately. The former Sales Manager had left the firm several months earlier, accepting a similar position with a noncompeting organization.

Mr. Foster's entry into the company coincided with still further changes in the management organization. Two weeks prior to his arrival, Mr. Dudley, with the active support of his new General Manager, had discharged the company's Production Supervisor, and had appointed a shop foreman as his successor. Roughly a month later—and less than two weeks after Mr. Foster's arrival—the Chief Engineer resigned after having unsuccessfully attempted to persuade Mr. Dudley to appoint him operating head of the company. He was replaced by the man who had been serving as his assistant. Although the new Chief Engineer did not have an engineering degree, Mr. Dudley believed that he was competent and well-versed in window hardware technology by virtue of his ten years' experience with the company.

Within three weeks after Mr. Foster assumed his new position, he was confronted with a crisis in the Sales Department. This occurred during his first meeting with the entire sales force, all of whom had traveled from their respective areas to New York City to attend a builders' hardware show. At the New York conference the salesmen voiced to Mr. Foster their complete dissatisfaction with the company's products and service, and flatly threatened to resign en masse unless "the factory problems are straightened out within the next 30 days." The array of complaints they presented included such episodes as products being shipped to customers without having been lubricated, moving parts being fitted so tightly they could not be operated, and delivery promises being violated almost continuously. Mr. Foster assured them that their grievances would receive his immediate attention.

During the weeks that followed, Mr. Foster spent most of his time in the field, visiting the sales representatives and obtaining a firsthand impression of the problems they cited. On the basis of his findings he became convinced that the salesmen generally were able and hardworking, and that their complaints in most respects were valid. The real problems of the company, he concluded, were concentrated in its factory operations. The time spent in the field also led Mr. Foster to conclude that the existing sales districts had been designated inequitably and needed to be realigned. He also formed the opinion that sales representatives needed more detailed information regarding Morrisville's products. At that time the company had no catalogues and its salesmen had not even been supplied with a complete set of sample products to show customers.

As one of the first phases of his efforts to rebuild the morale of the sales organization, Mr. Foster developed a catalogue of the company's product line and provided each sales representative with a supply for distribution to customers. Next he re-zoned the 11 existing sales territories and formed a twelfth one. The new sales territories were arranged to contain approximately the same number of active accounts, representing a reasonable territorial potential of $150,000 annual sales. Mr. Foster also introduced a new policy whereby the sales representatives were expected to call on each active account at least once every six weeks.

Armed with the information he had gathered in the field, Mr. Foster also discussed the problems of poor product quality and delivery service with the Production and Scheduling Supervisors, and made a point of personally investigating factory conditions. There he found what he considered to be numerous evidences of poor manufacturing practices and inept production management. He discovered, for example, that regularly items were packed and shipped without final inspection. Furthermore, products were being scheduled into production only as orders were received. As a result, production lots usually were small and numerous, and shipments often were made four to six weeks after an order had been received, even though customers usually were quoted two weeks' delivery by company salesmen. Despite Mr. Foster's efforts to work with the Production and Scheduling Supervisors in seeking ways to correct these conditions, only modest improvements were made.

About four months after Mr. Foster joined the firm, Mr. Dudley dismissed the General Manager, and turned management responsibilities over to a three-man committee composed of the Sales Manager (Mr. Foster), the Production Supervisor, and the Controller. Under this arrangement, Mr. Foster continued to press for broad improvements in manufacturing. His proposals included an urgent plea to take steps to assure that shipments would be made within seven days after the receipt of an order. To accomplish this he strongly advocated a policy of producing for stock and establishing minimum-maximum inventory levels for each item in the line. He also demanded the institution of sufficient inspection to guarantee that faulty products would not be shipped to customers. Only in this latter area was Mr. Foster able to get his proposals promptly implemented. He did observe, however, that the Production Supervisor seemed to give more intensive personal effort to the activities in the plant, and that orders did receive somewhat prompter processing than in the past. As a rule, nonetheless, deliveries still took considerably longer than seven days.

The sales representatives seemed satisfied with the new Sales Manager's efforts and with the improvements that were forthcoming. Their morale appeared to improve rapidly, and only one of the salesmen made good the threat to leave the company. This occurred several months after Mr. Foster's arrival and was caused by his refusal to agree to the salesman's demand for permission to carry an auxiliary line of products. Mr. Foster remained unyielding in his insistence that all salesmen handle Morrisville products exclusively.

Mr. Foster's Promotion to Executive Vice President

As the months passed, Mr. Dudley grew increasingly impressed with the ability and drive shown by Mr. Foster, and with his apparent grasp of problems relating to both production and sales. In January of the current year, therefore, he asked Mr. Foster to assume complete control of company operations with the newly created title of Executive Vice President. Under this arrangement, Mr. Foster continued to head the Sales Department, but now also assumed responsibility for all other activities. With Mr. Foster's promotion, the Controller and the Production Supervisor who had served with him on the general management committee were now accountable only for their specific functional areas, and the committee itself was disbanded. Mr. Foster believed that the other two men both seemed somewhat relieved at being allowed to resume their more specialized and less demanding responsibilities.

Now in a position to move aggressively in treatment of the manufacturing problems, Mr. Foster immediately launched a sweeping program to decrease costs. As one of the initial phases of his campaign, he turned his attention to the company's use of subcontractors.

For the past several years Morrisville had subcontracted annually anywhere from $100,000 to $200,000 worth of work which the production personnel believed could not be manufactured satisfactorily within the company. This included the winding and flocking of springs, straightening and cutting to length of aluminum rods, and the manufacture of hinges and handles. On such items Morrisville usually furnished the raw materials required, and the subcontracting company furnished the labor and machinery.

The largest dollar amount of subcontracting was for the winding and flocking of the high-grade steel wire springs which were needed in double-hung windows.[4] At present volume levels, Morrisville usually required about 100,000 springs per month on the average, and was paying an average price of about $89 per thousand for them.

The special technical problem involved in straightening rods stemmed from the fact that the one-eighth-inch diameter aluminum wire from

---

[4] As noted previously, the flocking operation coated the wound springs with fine wool-like fibers which muffled the humming sounds caused by vibration of the springs when they expanded or contracted.

which they were made was purchased in coil form and, as a result, had a tendency to curl. Morrisville's Engineering Department repeatedly stressed, however, the vital importance of rod straightness to assure the proper functioning of the item in which the rod was used. The company always had believed that the services of a subcontractor were necessary to assure this characteristic. In addition to straightening and cutting the rods, the subcontractor also performed a simple forming operation which bent a hook in one end of the rod. This was done on a punch press at high speed. For this straightening, cutting, and forming, the subcontractor was charging Morrisville 15 cents per rod for about 5,000 rods per month.

The hinge work which always had been subcontracted consisted of the manufacture of long, piano-type hinges used on panel windows. The operation was essentially a punch press job, with Morrisville requiring 4,000 to 5,000 hinges each month at a cost of about five cents apiece.

The subcontracted handles never had developed into a high-volume item. Consequently this was the least costly of all the subcontracted work, rarely amounting to more than $100 per month. Detailed breakdowns of the subcontractor's charges for both the hinge and handle work were not available.

Mr. Foster was convinced that the subcontracted work represented needless expenses since Morrisville had ample plant space and labor, and, except for a few installations, adequate equipment for the work. He reasoned, too, that recalling the subcontracted work would help absorb Morrisville's overhead charges. Even though some new equipment would be required, and even though subcontractors' prices appeared to be less than Morrisville's own cost estimates for the work in question, including standard overhead charges, Mr. Foster concluded that all outside subcontracting should be stopped as soon as practicable, and launched a program to achieve this.

The tooling and equipment required to permit Morrisville to eliminate use of subcontractors cost approximately $10,000, with the major expenditure of $8,500 going for the automatic sprayers and conveyors needed for the flocking operation. The die required for the rod-straightening operation and the mechanical adaptations on available machinery for the hinge and handle jobs cost approximately $1,500. As a result of these efforts, within ten months after Mr. Foster's promotion to his new post, all subcontracting by Morrisville had ceased. Mr. Foster reported to Mr. Dudley that the company had detected no unexpected technological difficulties in the new work, and that the entire undertaking had proven satisfactory.

The second step in Mr. Foster's program of cost reduction entailed his decision to discontinue advertising in magazines and in builders and hardware journals. Henceforth he planned to rely exclusively on direct mailings to jobbers, unit manufacturers, and retail lumberyards. Morrisville's advertising expenses had varied in the past from period to period, but had averaged roughly 1 per cent of net sales. Mr. Foster's program also included closing a storage warehouse maintained on the east coast, and the revamping of the company's telephone facilities by removing the switchboard and substituting a single telephone line with several extensions.

Mr. Foster had made no detailed analysis, but estimated that to date his cost reduction efforts had saved the company about $100,000. Approximately $58,000 of this total had been saved by the recall of subcontract work, $30,000 by reductions in the number of salaried and hourly waged personnel, and about $5,000 each as a result of the new telephone system and the warehouse closing.

After assuming the Executive Vice Presidency Mr. Foster also had made changes in Morrisville's purchasing procedures. Certain raw materials needed in large quantities, such as sheet aluminum, now were purchased under three-month "blanket orders" rather than on an "as needed" basis. Changes were made also in procuring boxing and packaging materials for finished goods. Formerly the company had purchased preformed corrugated boxes in many different sizes and shapes. Now Morrisville ordered blank, prescored sheets of boxboard, 27 x 97 inches in size, which could be cut to any length needed for the product to be packed. By folding the boxboard along a predetermined combination of scored lines, cartons of different cross-sectional shapes could be formed. The flat, prescored sheets were less expensive than ready-made boxes and were easier to handle and store.

To help achieve his long-standing objective of shipping from the factory within seven days of receiving an order, Mr. Foster had attempted to move in the direction of establishing minimum-maximum inventories of finished goods. To determine specific levels for each of the products in the Morrisville line, he had made a sales forecast for each item for the following year and then had broken down the yearly total into estimated monthly figures based upon previous experience. In general he then had set one-month average sales requirements as the minimum inventory level for any item, and two months as the maximum.

Having decided on the range of finished goods inventories levels desired, Mr. Foster attempted insofar as possible to increase the size of each production order going through the plant so as to achieve the inventory goals and also reduce set-up and changeover time. The actual scheduling was performed by the Scheduling Supervisor who served also as the Supervisor of Shipping and Receiving. In determining the work to order into production, the scheduler made frequent visual inspections of the stocks of finished goods and component parts, relying on his experience to tell him when the newly established minimum inventory limits were being approached. He also employed the written records of raw materials inventory. These were kept on a perpetual basis.

In order to implement the proposed new inventory policies, Mr. Foster had attempted to borrow the additional funds this would entail. This proved to be exceptionally difficult. Morrisville's application for a working capital loan to be secured by finished goods inventory had been refused not only by the bank which had long serviced the company, but also by another local bank which had been aggressively seeking new business in the community. Officials of both institutions explained that Morrisville would have to show a far more favorable earnings position before they could consider making funds

EXHIBIT 9   MORRISVILLE HARDWARE COMPANY

INCOME STATEMENTS

	Fiscal Year Ending October 31, Prior Year	Percentage	Eight Months Ending June 30, Current Year	Percentage
Net Sales	$1,218,650	100.0	$911,635	100.0
Cost of Sales	963,541	79.1	709,205	77.8
Gross Profit	$ 255,109	20.9	$202,430	22.2
Selling Expenses	199,549	16.4	136,588	15.0
Gross Profit less Selling Expenses	$ 55,560	4.5	$ 65,842	7.2
Administrative Expenses	94,833	7.7	60,195	6.6
Profit on Operations	$ (39,273)	(3.2)	$ 5,647	.6
Other Income	2,717	.2	2,514	.3
Total	$ (36,556)	(3.0)	$ 8,161	.9
Other Expense	29,079	2.4	19,284	2.1
Net Profit	$ (65,635)	(5.4)	$(11,123)	(1.2)

NOTE: Operations during the fiscal year ending October 31 included direct labor costs of $129,700 (rounded). During the eight months ending June 30 of the current year, direct labor costs were $93,600.

Source: Company records.

available to it. Mr. Foster received the distinct impression that the officers of both banks believed Morrisville's chances of survival still were highly questionable.

With a bank loan apparently unavailable, Mr. Foster decided that the only means through which inventories could be expanded toward the desired levels was to stretch Morrisville's accounts payable to the limit. This he proceeded to do, meeting bills only at the last possible moment.

Net sales for the first eight months of the current fiscal year[5] totaled approximately $912,000. The earnings statement for the period showed a net loss of about $11,000. Mr. Foster was confident, however, that the break-even point would be reached during the current month (October) and that the company actually might show some slight profit for the entire year, as opposed to its $65,000 loss on operations for the prior fiscal year. The most recent comparative earnings statements and balance sheets are shown in Exhibits 9 and 10. The most recent analysis of manufacturing expense is shown in Exhibit 11.

It was against this background that Mr. Foster approached the assignment given him by Mr. Dudley.

---

[5] The company's books were maintained on a November 1–October 31 fiscal year. Sales summaries were kept, however, on a December 1–November 30 year to facilitate comparison with sales records of previous years which had been maintained on this basis.

EXHIBIT 10   MORRISVILLE HARDWARE COMPANY

BALANCE SHEETS

	October 31, Prior Year	June 30, Current Year
ASSETS		
Current		
Cash	$ 20,710	$ 22,732
Accounts Receivable	162,273	215,801
Inventories	387,479	401,539
Prepayments	36,597	33,870
Total Current Assets	$ 607,059	$ 673,942
Other Assets		
Notes Receivable	2,774	2,774
Cash Surrender Value, Officer's Life Insurance	6,412	9,297
Total Other Assets	$ 9,186	$ 12,071
Fixed Assets (net)	390,494	400,059
Total Assets	$1,006,839	$1,086,072
LIABILITIES		
Current		
Notes Payable—Bank	$ 153,000	$ 156,000
Notes Payable—Officers	42,998	41,997
Contracts Payable	12,830	—
Accounts Payable	171,550	214,711
Taxes Payable	4,332	4,609
Accruals	15,517	25,016
Reserves	2,253	5,580
Total Current Liabilities	$ 402,479	$ 447,893
Fixed Liabilities		
Notes Payable—Bank	87,000	63,000
Notes Payable—Officers, Stock-holders, and Others	382,995	451,937
Total Fixed Assets	$ 469,995	$ 514,937
Net Worth		
Capital Stock	200,000	200,000
Earned Surplus	(65,635)	(76,758)
Total Net Worth	$ 134,365	$ 123,242
Total Liabilities and Net Worth	$1,006,839	$1,086,072

Source: Company records.

EXHIBIT 11 MORRISVILLE HARDWARE COMPANY

MANUFACTURING EXPENSE

($ in thousands)

	Fiscal Year Ending October 31, Prior Year	8 Months Ending June 30, Current Year
Depreciation and Amortization	$ 34.0	$ 32.4
Die Expense	3.4	.7
Supervisory Labor	38.1	—
Indirect Labor	97.8	90.7
Heat, Light, Power, and Water	13.9	11.8
Social Security Taxes	6.2	3.9
State Unemployment Tax	11.2	7.2
Federal Unemployment Tax	.6	.5
Repairs—Machinery and Equipment	1.2	.9
Repairs—Building	.2	—
Factory Supplies	20.2	11.6
Insurance	5.3	3.4
Rent	18.0	12.0
Truck Expense	1.1	.4
Property Taxes	15.1	12.9
First Aid Supplies and Expenses	.1	—
Vacation and Holiday Pay	8.4	2.5
Workmen's Compensation Insurance	2.2	.9
Employee Welfare Fund	1.6	.5
Hospital and Life Insurance Benefits	9.9	6.4
Machine Rental	5.3	4.1
Storage Rental	4.7	2.2
Employee Business Travel	.7	—
Pre-employment Physical Examinations	.1	—
Unclassified	.3	.4
	$299.4	$205.8
(less) Labor and Expenses Capitalized	—	15.6
Total	$299.4	$190.4

Source: Company records.

The NPK Fertilizer Company

The NPK Fertilizer Company is one of the larger fertilizer manufacturers serving several of the nation's principal agricultural regions. When founded more than a half century ago, the firm had been a small, one-plant operation. Currently, however, NPK operates eight plants, located in five different communities scattered over two states, and is a wholly owned subsidiary of a large, highly diversified manufacturing company. Under this corporate arrangement, NPK's management retains considerable operating autonomy and has to obtain approval from the parent corporation only on basic policy decisions, or on capital expenditures in excess of $250,000 for a single, nonrecurring project.

NPK's manufacturing installations include a superphosphate[1] plant at Hilltown, a large industrial city located near the center of the state in which NPK has its corporate headquarters. The Hilltown plant supplies superphosphate to NPK's four fertilizer mixing plants located in the home state.[2] Two of these latter installations, located in the communities of Yorkton and Newton, had been purchased as going concerns during the present year and are being operated as independent subsidiaries, manufacturing and distributing fertilizers under their own brand names. The locations, manufacturing capacities, and sales for the current sales year[3] in NPK's home-state mixing plants, as well as those of its principal competitors in this market area, are shown in Exhibit 1.

---

[1] An important raw material required in the manufacture of fertilizers.

[2] NPK also operates another large superphosphate plant and two additional mixing plants in another state. These units serve a different marketing area and their operations are not involved in the issues posed by this case.

[3] That is, the 12-month period between July 1 of one year and June 30 of the next.

EXHIBIT 1* THE NPK FERTILIZER COMPANY

CAPACITY AND ESTIMATED SALES OF NPK'S AND
COMPETITORS' MIXING PLANTS, HOME STATE
12 Months Ending June 30, Current Year

	Capacity† (Tons)	Sales (Tons)
NPK Fertilizer Company—Mixing Plants		
Hilltown‡	56,000	55,800
Newton	20,000	21,200
Yorkton	37,000	40,100
Midvale	50,000	45,400
NPK Total	163,000	162,500
Competing Plants		
The Agri-Industrial Co.		
Lincoln	50,000	50,000
Waterton	16,000	12,000
Midvale	60,000	40,000
State Plant Food Inc.		
Daleport	20,000	14,000
Crown Chemicals Co.		
Stanley	16,000	14,000
Center States Cooperatives		
Lincoln	5,000	5,000
Peoria	20,000	20,000
Singer Brothers		
Elrose	16,000	15,000
Graham Fertilizer Co.		
Port Rumford	7,000	6,000
Bradshaw Fertilizer and Chemical Co.		
Bradshaw	3,000	3,000
Tardy Company		
Lincoln	18,000	14,000
Ajax Fertilizer Co.		
Athens	6,000	5,000
Rainbow Fertilizer Co.		
Trout Center	4,000	4,000
Competing Plant Total	241,000	202,000
INDUSTRY TOTAL	404,000	364,500
Industry Excess Capacity	39,500	

* All names and locations are disguised.

† Based on twice the plant's storage capacity. (See Supplement A for an explanation of a plant's ability to sell in excess of its nominal capacity.)

‡ Also the site of an NPK superphosphate plant.

MARKET CHARACTERISTICS, HOME-STATE SALES AREA

The ultimate customers for fertilizer products in the home-state market area fall into two general categories: growers of cash crops, and "mixed crop" farmers. Cash crops are products raised for immediate sale, such as wheat, tobacco, corn, soybeans, potatoes, and fruit. Mixed farming, by contrast, consists of crops, such as grass and alfalfa, which are grown to nourish dairy and beef cattle. Cash crop farming generally involves more "intensive" use of farm acreage than mixed farming, that is, more intensive efforts to obtain maximum yields per given unit of land. To a considerable extent, the market area served by NPK can be divided into geographic zones corresponding to these two customer categories, that is, regions which are given over predominantly to cash crop farming, and others in which mixed farming dominates.

Both cash crop and mixed farming customers serviced by direct shipments from NPK's factories or warehouse fall into three broad groups: (1) Direct Sales Customers—that is, large growers who purchase solely for their own farming use; (2) Farmer-Dealers—that is, farmers who not only purchase for their own requirements but also sell fertilizer to neighboring farmers; and (3) Distributors, such as agricultural merchants, feed mills, cooperatives, and food processing companies. The food processors usually distribute fertilizer to growers whose fruits or vegetables they have contracted to purchase during a given season. This practice provides an answer to the perennial problem of credit for smaller farmers; the processor underwrites the cost of the fertilizer needed by the farmer, later deducting it from the price due the grower on delivery of his crop to the processing plant. NPK's sales from its factories or company warehouse for mixed crop usage also involves a fourth customer category—independent livestock truckers—whose functions are described in another portion of the case.

On the average, for both cash and mixed crop customers, annual NPK home-state sales have been distributed as follows:

Type of Account	Percentage of Total NPK Home-State Volume	Sales Range in Tons per Customer per Year	
		Cash Crop	Mixed Farm
Direct Sales Customers (Large Growers)	23%	15 or more	15 or less
Farmer-Dealers	27	15 to 1,000	15 to 300
Merchants, Feed Mills, Co-Ops, Processors, Independent Live-stock Truckers	50	50 to 4,000	50 to 500

NPK'S COMPETITIVE SALES POSITION IN HOME-STATE MARKETING AREA

NPK's product line was extensive. At any given moment it included most of the different recognized grades of fertilizers that were appropriate for use with each of the major crops grown in the area. During the current selling year, approximately 95 per cent of NPK's sales have been concentrated in the grades and products shown on the wholesale price list (Exhibit 2). Marked variations in volume exist between products, however.

NPK's estimated share of the home-state total fertilizer market and production capacity has been declining in recent years, as reflected in the following figures:

Sales District	Average NPK Market Share Past 5 Years	NPK Market Share for Year Ending June 30		
		Prior Year	Current Year	Next Year (Est.)
Hilltown and Midvale	33%	29%	28%	26%
Yorkton* and Newton*	20	18	17	14
Total share of market	53	47	45	40
NPK share of industry's total productive capacity (estimated)	48	46	40	39

---

* Plant purchased as a going concern during the current year.

Industrywide sales in the market area served by NPK's four home-state plants have increased by an estimated 73 per cent during the past decade. In the last two years, however, sales have stayed at a

EXHIBIT 2 THE NPK FERTILIZER COMPANY

PRICE LIST, CURRENT YEAR

Midvale, Home State
January 6th

TO OUR FERTILIZER DEALERS:

Reproduced below are prices, terms, and conditions of sales covering NPK fertilizers, effective 5th January. This supersedes all previous Price Lists.

BRAND	Your Cost per Ton F.O.B. Nearest NPK Plant	BRAND	Your Cost per Ton F.O.B. Nearest NPK Plant
0-20-10	$52.63	4-24-20	$73.10
0-20-20	57.67	5-10-13	46.60
0-12-20	43.27	6-12-12	51.50
2-12-10	40.03	Triple Ten	61.40
2-12-20	46.96	5-10-5	56.00
2-16-6	43.00	Ammonium Sulfate	63.20
2-18-9	52.40	Muriate of Potash 60%	53.30
3-18-15	55.10	Sulfate of Potash	65.00
4-12-10	44.80	Nitrate of Soda	71.30
4-24-12	68.60	20% Superphosphate	34.90
		Triple Superphosphate	78.50

You will note that two new analyses have been added to our Compound Fertilizer List. There has been no price increase over the former list, but two brands have been reduced in price.

PRICE: Subject to change without notice. Goods will be invoiced at prices in effect on date of shipment.

TERMS: On shipments to approved accounts up to 31st March, Net 30 Days, 1st April. After that date, Net 30 Days.

EARLY DELIVERY DISCOUNT:
$2.00 per ton up to and including 31st January.
$1.25 per ton up to and including 28th February.

CASH DISCOUNT:
(1) A Cash Discount of 2% will be allowed for payment by 28th February of goods shipped to that date.
(2) A Cash Discount of 2% will be allowed for prepayment by 28th February of goods shipped after that date.

relatively stable level. In the judgment of NPK's sales officials this leveling-off of the demand rate probably would continue through at least the current and next sales years. On the other hand, fertilizer manufacturing capacity in the area has more than doubled during the past ten years and it is an established fact that still further expansion is being contemplated for the near future by several of the NPK company's competitors. NPK officials believe that this continuing "race for capacity" reflects the industry's confidence—shared by NPK management—that the area's long-term prospects for the fertilizer industry are favorable. This has prompted the determination of many firms to increase capacity so as to hold, or to expand, their relative share of a growing market.

The combined impact of the current excess of manufacturing capacity, and the serious seasonality and transportation problems, to be discussed subsequently, create intense sales competition. As a result certain marginal fertilizer manufacturers often resort to price cutting. This is particularly true of the operators of small "dry-mix" factories[4] who usually attempt to sell only in a limited geographic area, purchase all of their raw materials, and whose operations therefore involve modest investment and low overhead.[5] If, during a given sales year, the weather is especially uncertain, or if it appears that either of the two planting seasons will be unusually short, such operators often slash their prices drastically in the hope of unloading their inventories. Furthermore, over the past decade, as NPK and the other larger producers reached out from their traditional markets to sell their increasing productive capacity, they frequently infringed on markets formerly served primarily by the small local operators. The latter then often retaliated by price cutting.

THE SEASONALITY FACTOR

Fertilizer sales in the area served by NPK home-state plants are subject to one minor and one major seasonal sales peak each year. The minor peak, usually accounting for 10 to 15 per cent of NPK's annual volume, takes place in August or September, and is associated with the planting of the winter wheat crop. The major sales period usually occurs in late April or May, when roughly 85 to 90 per cent of the year's fertilizer is used by consumers.

The timing of usage by the ultimate customer differs somewhat from

---

[4] See Supplement A.

[5] See Supplement A.

the timing of factory shipments, however, since most fertilizer manufacturers, including NPK, offer discounts designed to encourage customers to accept factory shipments several months in advance of the start of the peak selling season. In recent years such "early commitment sales" have been averaging about 15 per cent of NPK's total annual sales. Company officials believe it unlikely, however, that the volume of such early orders can be appreciably increased. Impediments include the limited amount of storage space which most customers have available, the fact that many customers find it difficult to finance the carrying of an inventory of fertilizer for the additional period involved, and the ever present risk that powdered fertilizer, in either bagged or bulk form, will cake in storage.

THE PROBLEM OF CAKING

The caking problem is a particularly vexing one perpetually confronting fertilizer manufacturers, distributors, and farmers alike. Changes in the moisture content of the surrounding atmosphere, or of the temperature, can cause powdered fertilizer to cake into a solid mass.[6] In most instances there is not time for the farmer to return the caked material to the manufacturer or to the distributor for replacement. This is because the ideal timing of the spreading of fertilizer is dictated by weather conditions over which the farmer has no control, and about which he usually has little more than a day or two of advance notice. To correct the caking condition by manual or mechanical crushing of the caked mass necessitates extra time and labor for the farmer. Furthermore, if the recrushing is not effectively done, it can prevent the uniform distribution of a fertilizer in the field. If the distribution is irregular, some plants may be injured by an excessive application of the fertilizer, while others may be insufficiently fertilized to produce effective results.

Investigating and responding to customer complaints of caked fertilizer is one of the important functions of the NPK sales force. If a complaint is found to be valid, the company pays the farmer for the cost incurred in recrushing the fertilizer, or for the cost of repairing any damage to the farmer's spreader caused by oversized lumps in the compound. If the farmer is unable to spread the

---

[6] Such caking does not affect the nutrient characteristics of a fertilizer; recrushing of the caked mass again renders the fertilizer fully satisfactory for use. If re-exposed to adverse atmospheric or temperature conditions, however, the recrushed fertilizer again solidifies.

fertilizer at all because of its caked condition, he is refunded the full purchase price upon returning the material to the company.

CUSTOMER DELIVERY

One of the continuing problems in the physical distribution of fertilizer to customers involves the highway load limitations which frequently are enforced during the spring thaws. In the NPK home-state region the soil usually freezes to a considerable depth during the winter months. After thawing begins in the spring the soil softens, providing poor support for highways. If heavy loads are hauled continually over the roadways during such a period, the road surfaces will crack and rupture. For this reason, many county governments enforce a "half-load" limitation on all commercial trucking over county roads during the thawing period, which frequently includes the entire month of March. During this period, unpaved secondary roads often become so muddy that truck deliveries to individual farms are delayed.

Since early seeding usually begins around the middle of March, and since roughly 95 per cent of shipments to farmers are made by truck, delivery delays caused by highway conditions frequently have an important effect on fertilizer sales for a given season. A farmer who has completed any appreciable amount of his seeding before receipt of a fertilizer order usually refuses to accept delivery since the fertilizer is no longer of any use to him during the current season.

NPK SALES FORCE AND SOIL CHEMISTS

In total, the NPK sales force in the home-state area, including that of the two subsidiary firms, numbers 32 men. All are paid a straight salary. Most salesmen service all accounts in their territories, rather than specializing in only one type of customer. Many of the firm's sales personnel are graduates of agricultural colleges and a number possess actual farming experience.

In addition to its salesmen the NPK sales organization maintains a laboratory and a two-man staff of soil chemists at its sales offices in Lincoln and Newton, and small test facilities at Midvale and York-ton. These technical experts work with the sales personnel, providing advisory services, soil analysis, and other data which the salesmen then relay to customers. The chemists sometimes also work directly with large farm operators, many of whom base their fertilization plans on the results of soil tests performed for them by the NPK laboratories. In the opinion of NPK management, the company's technical staff and facilities are superior to those of any competitive operations in the home-state area.

During the late winter and the spring, NPK salesmen usually are busy making calls on customers and booking orders. During the other months of the year the salesmen concentrate on reorganizing their distribution outlets, attempting to find replacements for any farmer-dealers and merchants who have proven ineffective, and also endeavoring to expand the company's distribution channels. NPK sales officials, in common, they believe, with the rest of the industry, find that continuing attention is required to assure that distributors put forth an effective sales effort. Some of the distributors have vigorously resisted attempts to persuade them to handle a single manufacturer's fertilizers exclusively and to promote them aggressively. Instead, they apparently have preferred to stock the products of a number of competing fertilizer manufacturers, thus placing themselves in a position where their own sales efforts are limited to the passive act of filling orders for whatever product a retail customer happens to choose.

PRODUCTION AND WAREHOUSING FACILITIES

All four NPK mixing plants in the home-state area manufacture extensive lines of "dry-mix" fertilizers through use of the batch process.[7] The specific product mix of each plant is determined by the nature of the adjacent market areas. Distances between the four plants range from approximately 30 to 150 miles. The Hilltown plant is centrally located in an area in which farming is concentrated principally on mixed crops. It is also the NPK plant nearest to the livestock area. The Newton and Yorkton plants are both located in the mixed crop farming area, but near the areas that concentrate on tobacco farming. The Midvale plant is located in the center of the cash crop area.

Most of the company's production is shipped in 80-pound bags, 25 bags to the ton, by rail or commercial trucking. A small portion of the output of the Midvale plant, however, is shipped to customers in bulk via commercial truckers. The volume of such bulk shipments

---

[7] For a description of batch production process and other facts relating to the technology of fertilizer manufacturing, see Supplement A. It is not unusual for a fertilizer mixing plant to produce varying quantities of a dozen or more different types of fertilizer formulations during a given sales year.

has increased gradually over the past several years, and has amounted to approximately **3,000** tons of the Midvale plant's sales volume during the current sales year. The company's pricing structure currently provides savings of approximately $3.50 per ton (F.O.B.) to customers who accepted bulk rather than bagged deliveries.

In addition to the storage space provided by its four mixing plants, NPK also maintains a 650-ton capacity storage warehouse at Lincoln, a community centrally located in the home state's livestock producing areas and the site of a number of slaughterhouses and meat-packing plants. At current sales levels the Lincoln warehouse handles about 5,000 tons of NPK products each year from January through March, and another 13,000 tons during April and May.[8]

For the remaining seven months of the year, activity at the Lincoln warehouse slackens. During the peak period, however, operations at the Lincoln warehouse usually are conducted around-the-clock, with the warehouse often becoming little more than an interchange point as the bagged fertilizer from the mixing plants is transferred directly from incoming railroad box cars to waiting trucks. A majority of the latter are owned by livestock truckers who function as independent fertilizer dealers during the height of the selling season. In this capacity, such truckers transport NPK products on their outbound trips to the livestock producing area, selling the fertilizer to local farmers en route, usually charging only a sufficient premium above wholesale prices to cover the cost of the outbound trip. The truckers then load up with livestock for the return trip to the various meat-packing plants at Lincoln.

NPK management personnel recognize that certain operating disadvantages are associated with the fever-pitch of activity existing at the Lincoln warehouse during the peak season. They realize that these inefficiencies could be alleviated in some respects if company storage facilities were enlarged. The present Lincoln site provides suitable space for expansion, and study has indicated that at current price levels, construction of additional warehouse space would run about $10 per cubic yard. Company officials are convinced that space requirements can be estimated with reasonable accuracy by use of a rule of thumb calling for one cubic yard of warehouse area for each 1,750 pounds of fertilizer to be stored. Management has not yet reached a decision, however, regarding the amount of additional ware-

---

[8] A major share of the volume handled by the warehouse consists of fertilizer produced at the Hilltown mixing plant some 40 miles away, this being the nearest NPK plant to Lincoln.

house space that could be utilized effectively at Lincoln, or whether the advantages to be gained would justify the investment required.

FACTORY MANPOWER UTILIZATION AND EMPLOYMENT PRACTICES

In view of the seasonal variations in sales, the NPK company often finds it necessary to vary the size of the workforce in each of its four mixing plants, and at the Lincoln warehouse. The range of fluctuations during recent years, for example, had been as follows:

	Number of Employees	
	Spring Peak	*Summer Low*
Hilltown mixing plant	106	44
Midvale mixing plant	62	15
Yorkton mixing plant	69	41
Newton mixing plant	17	7
Lincoln warehouse	25	4

Workforce variations of this sort are common in the industry, and NPK officials are convinced that their company's problems in this regard are no more serious than those encountered by other fertilizer manufacturers in the area. Moreover, NPK management believes that the impact of seasonal layoffs is tempered by the fact that many of its employees own small farms and are able—and in some instances seemingly even prefer—to work their land during those periods in which they are not employed at NPK. Another mitigating factor is the fact that during the period of peak activity it usually is possible for NPK employees to work more than eight hours a day. Total annual earnings from NPK employment, therefore, usually are somewhat higher than would be suggested by considering only the number of weeks an employee actually is on the payroll.

Roughly 75 to 80 per cent of the factory jobs required by NPK's manufacturing processes involve only moderate skill, and a new employee can gain reasonable proficiency in these assignments in a week or less. Furthermore, in a majority of instances, experienced NPK employees laid off during the periods of low production again report for work during the company's peak production months. Although no formal seniority provisions are in force, NPK's normal practice is not to recruit any new employees until it has recalled all laid-off personnel who desire to resume work.

Factory wages are averaging about $1.55 per hour. NPK officials are convinced that this compares favorably with the wages of all other major fertilizer manufacturers in the area, and is substantially above the rates paid by most of the small "dry-mix plants."[9] None of the NPK plants are unionized, and management has seen no indications that any particular interest in organizing exists among its workforce.

PURCHASING PRACTICES

NPK's principal purchase requirements include such materials as phosphate rock, anhydrous ammonia, various nitrogen sources and potassium ingredients, and sulfuric acid. In common with most other firms in the industry, the company negotiates with major chemical suppliers for the purchase of raw material requirements for all four mixing plants on a "contract year basis." This usually has entailed entering into a binding purchase contract with a supplier in July of each year, the agreement calling for a specific amount of material to be purchased during the next 12 months at a stated price, with a prescribed schedule of deliveries to each plant for each month of that period.

In the main, suppliers have been extremely reliable both as to quality and delivery. To accomplish an upward revision in the quantities called for in a contract normally would require about one month's advance notice to the supplier, and could entail a different price on the additional quantities to be purchased. At any given moment raw material prices quoted by major suppliers tend to be fairly comparable. The prevailing price level of most materials often varies from year to year, however, and such variations not infrequently lead to fluctuations of as much as $2 per ton—either upward or downward—in total average manufacturing costs[10] of fertilizer from one selling season to the next.

Supplement A. Technology of the Fertilizer Industry[1]

AGRICULTURAL CHEMISTRY

All plant life obtains from the soil certain vital food elements that nourish it. Scientific research has proven conclusively that insufficient

---

[9] See Supplement A.

[10] For purposes of analysis you may assume that NPK's gross profit before taxes typically averages about 10 per cent of sales.

[1] This Supplement is based on information supplied by NPK personnel whose active, major role in the preparation of this material is gratefully acknowledged.

quantities of any one of a number of specific nutrient elements in the soil can be a limiting factor in crop production. The process of plant growth, however, results in a gradual depletion of these essential soil nutrients. If these are not replaced, the land bcomes barren. Replenishment of soil nutrients by various natural means, such as the decay of organic matter and the decomposition of rocks and minerals, is often too slow a process to meet fully the needs of modern agricultural activities characterized by intensive cultivation of high-yielding crops. However, by adding chemical fertilizers to the soil, in a form suitable for utilization by plants, depleted nutritive elements can be restored.

The nutrient elements most commonly found to be deficient in soils are nitrogen, phosphorus, and potassium. Chemical compounds providing these elements are therefore the chief ingredients of commercial fertilizers and are called the "primary" plant food elements to distinguish them from various less critical but desirable nutrient elements.

The nitrogen, phosphorus, and potassium content of fertilizers may be supplied by a wide array of alternative chemical raw materials. Selection from among these for use in commercial fertilizers is essentially a function of price and availability, with the former including the important element of transportation costs from the supplier's plant. A complicating factor in selecting a combination of raw materials arises from the fact that certain nitrogen materials are not compatible in all proportions with every phosphorus and potash source. Similarly, certain phosphorus ingredients cannot be combined successfully with various potash components, and so on.

Traditionally, the industry classifies different strengths of commercial fertilizer by their content of nitrogen (N), of phosphorus pentoxide (P_2O_5), and of potassium oxide (K_2O). Such content is expressed in terms of "units," a "unit" of plant food being 20 pounds or 1 per cent of a ton. A fertilizer designated "4-8-4," for example, is one that contains per ton four units, or 80 pounds, of N; eight units, or 160 pounds, of P_2O_5; and four units, or 80 pounds, of K_2O. The elements in question actually are not usually supplied in the form of nitrogen, phosphorus pentoxide, or potassium oxide. Instead, more complex chemical combinations often are employed as raw materials in the production of fertilizers. The $N-P_2O_5-K_2O$ nomenclature has nonetheless provided a convenient and uniform device for identifying and comparing different grades of fertilizers.

FERTILIZER MANUFACTURE

Fertilizer manufacturing plants are classified according to type of operation and equipment, as follows:

COMPLETE PLANTS. These are production units which manufacture their own supply of a caustic—usually sulfuric acid—grind their own supply of rock phosphate, and then mix these ingredients together. Through the processes of acidulation, the acid and the rock phosphate form superphosphate, an important fertilizer component. To this are added ingredients to compound mixed fertilizers in whatever grades are desired.

SUPERPHOSPHATE AND MIXING PLANTS. This type of plant purchases its acid requirements from outside producers and then either processes, or purchases, ground rock phosphate with which to produce a superphosphate. This is mixed with other ingredients to compound mixed grades of fertilizers.

DRY MIXING PLANTS. This type of installation has only mixing equipment. Accordingly, it buys all the materials it needs for compounding mixed fertilizer in whatever grades are desired.

THE COMPOUNDING OF MIXED PRODUCTS

Compounding mixed fertilizers requires a thorough blending of carefully selected materials in specially designed rotary mixers to obtain a predetermined formula. Research activities at agricultural experimental stations, usually government-sponsored, in each area or region customarily result in certain recommended ratios of plant nutrients for the various major crops grown in the region serviced by the station. The fertilizer industry then blends raw materials to satisfy these requirements. Selection of the specific chemical ingredients to be employed as raw materials usually reflects the recommendations of agronomists, the preference of local farmers, and the experience and economic analyses of manufacturers. It is not unusual for as many as 40 different types of recognized fertilizer formulations to be prescribed for different types of agricultural needs in a given area.

A fertilizer manufacturer may employ eight or more different ingredients in the production of a "three component" or "complete" fertilizer, that is, one supplying nitrogen, phosphorus, and potassium.[2] Hence,

---

[2] Combinations of raw materials may also be varied to produce either a distinctly acid-forming, or alkali-forming, product while still yielding the same

it is essential that the compounding be accurate and the mixing thorough in order to secure as perfect a mixture as possible. The analysis—that is, the physical and chemical composition—of the resulting product is guaranteed by the fertilizer manufacturer and the guarantee usually is subject to regular checks by a government agricultural control authority.

Under the "dry-mix" process, the mixing usually is done in batches of one, two, or three tons, depending on the capacity and equipment of the plant. Any purchased materials required are bought on specification from chemical suppliers in accordance with well-formulated industry standards. For example, sulfate of ammonia can be purchased on a "guaranteed 20.5 per cent nitrogen" basis. To ascertain how many pounds of each raw material will be needed, the number of pounds of each of the nutrient elements required is divided by the percentage of that element known to be present in the particular raw materials being utilized. Depending on the materials used, it is usually necessary also to add some specific amount of "filler," such as sand, which is agriculturally inert, or dolomitic limestone, to bring the weight of the batch up to the required tonnage.

The compounding process can be classified into one of two broad alternative categories, "dry-mix" or "ammoniated," depending on the raw materials employed.

THE DRY-MIXING COMPOUNDING PROCESS[3]

In the dry-mix compounding process, carefully calculated and controlled quantities of superphosphate and all other necessary raw materials, in dry form, after having each been ground through a sizing screen, are placed in large batch mixers and mixed for a period of from one to two minutes.[4] As previously noted, eight or more separate raw materials may be employed. After mixing, the resulting compounds have to "cure"; that is, the chemical reactions between the various ingredients have to be allowed to reach a state of equilibrium. These chemical reactions are accompanied by the generation of heat,

---

plant food ratio. This is important in that certain plants require an acidic soil, while others thrive in an alkaline (base) environment.

[3] The process employed in NPK's four mixing plants in the home state.

[4] Unless two successive batches being compounded in a given mixer involve the use of chemically incompatible elements, rarely more than 15 or 20 minutes is required to clean the mixer between batches. More often, no cleaning is necessary.

the amount of heat and the speed of the reactions being interrelated. To retain the heat created by chemical reaction, dry-mix fertilizer is put into metal or wood storage bins immediately after the mixing process and left there throughout the curing process, that is, until there is no further drop in the temperature of the mass.[5] This usually requires from one to two months.

SACKING OPERATIONS

Both "dry" and "ammoniated" fertilizer components eventually solidify into a hard mass while curing. They can be left in this hardened state indefinitely. Prior to shipping, the mass is extracted from the bins with heavy tractor shovels which dig and carry approximately one ton at a time. The tractors discharge their loads to high speed "sacking units" where the hardened fertilizer is crushed to powdered form, screened, and immediately packed in 80-pound bags.[6] This entire crushing, screening, and sacking process is performed at an output rate well in excess of a bag per minute.

Because of the threat of the fertilizer again caking into a solid mass after it is bagged, the general industry practice is to schedule the crushing, screening, and sacking operation for the last possible moment before actual shipment from the factory. To facilitate this in the face of severe selling peaks, most plants maintain a number of high speed sacking units. It is not uncommon for activities to be so scheduled that filled bags move directly from the sacking unit to waiting trucks or railroad cars to be shipped almost immediately. As a result of this practice, only a modest percentage of the finished goods inventory of most dry-mix manufacturers is composed of sacked fertilizer.

PLANT CAPACITY

The common industry practice is to express fertilizer plant capacity in terms of storage bin capacity available. Separate bins have to be used for each grade manufactured since different formulations cannot be mixed. Furthermore, batches of the same formulation in varying stages of cure normally are not mixed since such a procedure is likely

---

[5] To speed up the curing reaction, certain chemicals often are added to the compound for the express purpose of raising the temperature of the mass.

[6] As previously noted, a small percentage of NPK shipments from the Midvale plant are made in bulk.

to induce a new chemical reaction within the combined batches. These factors, coupled with the seasonality of sales, cause storage capacity to have an important influence on the turnover rates of both sales and production, and, therefore, on plant capacity.

In the area in which NPK competes, most plants operate on a one-shift basis during the late summer, the entire fall, and the early winter months, filling bins in anticipation of the coming selling season. Shortly after early shipments begin in January, the typical mixing plant moves to two-shift operations. Then, at the height of the selling season in March and early April, the plant goes to three shifts, operating around-the-clock with the objective of refilling its storage bins as quickly as possible after they are emptied, thus allowing time for curing and grinding of the maximum possible volume before the peak selling season ends. In some firms, the mixing plant is then shut down entirely during the early and middle summer months, except for the activities of maintenance crews.

This operating cycle permits most plants to fill and empty their bins about twice annually. Thus, a plant's manufacturing capacity usually is assumed to be about twice its storage capacity.

Unsurpassed Lumber Corporation

Lawrence Bunn, who was nearing the close of his third year as General Manager of the Unsurpassed Lumber Corporation, recently had decided to make an intensive re-evaluation of the firm's manufacturing operations.

The company, headquartered in the small southern community of Logantown, was, and for many years had been, a profitable operation. Mr. Bunn's decision to review its manufacturing operations therefore did not reflect any urgent operational crisis, nor did it grow out of a particular problem area. Instead it emanated from Mr. Bunn's belief that a variety of factors made this an appropriate time to reassess the organization's manufacturing facilities and practices, in terms both of current requirements and of changes that might be anticipated for the future.

For example, Mr. Bunn knew that it had been over 30 years since any significant innovations had been made in the facilities, methods, or procedures employed in the planing mill, the last stage of the lumber manufacturing process and the point at which final finish and dimensions were imparted to the lumber. Although the mill's equipment still operated satisfactorily and without major downtime for repairs, Mr. Bunn was convinced there would be merit in reassessing the long-standing pattern of operations.

Similarly, Mr. Bunn was convinced that there was a more than routine possibility that the geographic area in which the company operated would experience substantial upward pressures on wage rates in the years ahead. Were this to happen, it seemed likely that competitive price pressures would prompt the firm to place greater emphasis on labor-saving devices than had been true in the past.

Mr. Bunn's decision also reflected his awareness of the frequent suggestions from numerous lumber industry sources that mills needed to become increasingly concerned with the efficiency of both manufacturing and merchandising activities. For example, he had saved and recently re-read an article summarizing the views expressed several years previously by various lumber executives attending an annual meeting of the Western Pine Association.

The article had noted, in part:

> . . . the lumber industry has been experiencing a period of sharp readjustment. It has been a difficult and unsatisfactory time for most lumbermen. Such a situation should, and does, result in more attention to costs of production, to product quality, and to merchandising methods. It is a dividend from our reverses. . . .
>
> Two basic factors in the loss of lumber markets are poor quality and failure to meet changing market requirements both in the form of our product and in practices such as packaging, branding, and grade marking. The battle in this vital area is at the mills. . . .[1]

In the case of his own firm, Mr. Bunn believed that any meaningful assessment of the latter of the "two basic factors" cited in the article should include careful reflection upon the company's recent experiences with "unitized lumber," a process in which individual pieces of lumber were stacked and strapped together into large packs for shipment from the mill, rather than being shipped as loose, separate pieces. Unsurpassed had introduced the unitized approach experimentally about ten years before at the specific request of a few customers. To permit the extra processing steps required for unitizing, the mill had instituted certain new production procedures at that time, and had installed some additional shipping facilities. These moves had been made hurriedly, without major study, on the assumption that unitizing operations probably would be used only temporarily, on a low volume, experimental basis.

Customer responses to the unitized approach proved considerably more enthusiastic than the company originally had anticipated, however, and over the next eight years grew until they accounted for roughly 25 per cent of the mill's total shipments. At that time (two years ago) the mill had expanded the unitizing facilities to increase capacity. Since then, unitized shipments had risen to almost 50 per cent of the mill's total volume, and now were nearing a point at which unitizing capacity would again be taxed severely. Mr. Bunn believed that if it again became necessary to expand facilities for unitized shipments, the company might be well advised to give careful considera-

---

[1] *The Lumberman,* May 1958, pp. 39–40. Reproduced by permission of the publisher.

tion to the possibility of introducing substantial changes in its manufacturing or shipping processes, or both, rather than merely making a
third "piece-meal" response to the unitized requirements. He suspected
that similar opportunity—perhaps even a necessity—for substantial
changes in manufacturing facilities and practices also might arise if
Unsurpassed at some future time were to adopt any of the still more
complex new techniques of lumber packaging which some of the
industry's spokesmen now were vigorously advocating.

With these thoughts in mind, Mr. Bunn began his analysis of current
manufacturing practices.

GENERAL BACKGROUND

Unsurpassed Lumber Corporation was located on the outskirts of
the community of Logantown, on a 15-acre tract adjacent to the Dixie
River, and normally provided employment for around 250 of the
town's 5,000 residents.

In addition to the Logantown lumber mill, the company also owned
160,000 acres of "tree farms" (woodlands which were planted, thinned,
and harvested scientifically on a perpetual basis). These were located
within roughly a 50-mile radius of the mill.

About 60 per cent of the timber cut in the company's woodlands
was consumed by Unsurpassed's lumber operations, satisfying the
majority[2] of its requirements. The remaining 40 per cent was sold as
pulpwood to several paper manufacturers.

The Logantown lumber mill represented a significant component
of the lumber industry. For example, its production volume of 36.4
million board[3] feet placed it fifteenth out of the approximately 250
southeastern mills in terms of lumber produced during the most recent
calendar year.

THE LUMBER INDUSTRY

Lumbering, one of America's oldest and largest industries, is a
complex activity embracing the growing, harvesting, transporting,
processing, and marketing of wood. The industry is comprised of

---

[2] The lumber mill's small requirements of cypress, as well as virtually all of
the hardwood required for flooring, were purchased from outside sources.

[3] BF or BMF; the standard unit of measure in the industry; one board foot
equals 1″ x 12″ x 12″. All quantities of lumber in this case are expressed in
terms of board feet unless specifically stated otherwise.

numerous sawmills, lumber wholesalers, retailers, and transportation systems, and is characterized by intense competition in each of these sectors. According to generally accepted estimates there are about 20,000 sawmills scattered throughout the United States. Many of these are located far from markets, and their output is distributed largely through the industry's approximately 4,000 lumber wholesalers who, in total, usually handle about 75 per cent of all lumber processed. Reliance on wholesalers is prevalent among mills located in the western states. Retail lumber dealers—about 26,000 in number, roughly 60 per cent of whom are located in towns of less than 5,000 population—form the largest single link in the distribution channels. Trade associations, representing the three principal elements of the industry, that is, manufacturers, wholesalers, and retailers, assist in developing and maintaining industry standards.

Since the turn of the century, national lumber consumption has experienced only a modest growth rate in absolute terms, and a substantial decline on a per capita basis. This has been in sharp contrast to sales of certain other types of building materials, such as wallboard, plasterboard, glass, brick, cement, and various metal products, which have experienced dramatic rates of growth during this period. In addition, the traditional lumber dealer of the past, to a considerable extent, has transformed himself into a "builders' supply dealer," selling not only lumber but also many of the competitive materials that have made such marked inroads into the building materials market.

Many persons in the lumber industry believe that an important factor contributing to the rapid growth of many of these competing products is the fact that their design and packaging have made them easier to handle and store than lumber. In order to meet this challenge, various elements in the lumber industry currently were studying possible methods of revamping the techniques used in lumber packaging and merchandising. One theory which was gaining some support held that lumber should be packaged, handled, and shipped not in separate pieces, but in "standard packs," each pack containing a fixed number of board feet and having the same over-all exterior dimensions, regardless of the number and dimensions of the individual pieces comprising it. Several mills apparently had met with initial success in experimental efforts along these lines. Insofar as Mr. Bunn could ascertain, however, all such efforts thus far had been confined to the larger sizes of lumber, such as "structural" and "dimension,"[4] which were usually sold in standard lengths and in sufficient order quantities

---

[4] See Glossary, Supplement A.

(usually boxcar loads of a single width, thickness, and length) to make feasible the use of standard packs.

In the case of high-quality "finish" and "common"[5] lumber, however, as well as paneling, molding, flooring, and siding—items representing the vast majority of Unsurpassed's sales—the operations required in their manufacture included frequent trimming to eliminate defects present in the rough lumber. Such trimming invariably resulted in considerable variations in the length of finished pieces. To avoid becoming overstocked with shorter lengths which inevitably are produced in the manufacturing operations and yet which customers, if given a free choice, would regard as less desirable, mills usually sell many types of items "random length" in two-foot increments within a length range of 6 to 16 feet. Except for "structural" and "dimension" lumber, and for certain types of flooring, which by common industry practice is sold to length, most lumber manufacturers refuse to allow customers even to specify the length desired on those few items[6] that most mills actually bundle by length in the last phase of the manufacturing processes.

The practice of selling certain types of lumber only random length also is reinforced by the fact that such items are demanded in a great variety of grades, widths, thicknesses, and "workings."[7] This variation reflects the numerous end-uses that can be made of such lumber. It is therefore not uncommon for a single carload or truckload order shipped from a mill to incorporate a great diversity of items. The feeling of most mills always has been that they can respond to this complex demand—and to the intense production and inventory problems it entails—only by adhering to the long-established practice of selling random length. Mr. Bunn had seen no indications that any mills yet had overcome the numerous difficulties involved in assembling items of this type into packages of standard dimensions.

THE DIVISION'S PRODUCT LINE

In industry terminology (Supplement A), the Logantown mill produces "yard lumber" in "select" and "common" grades. Almost all production is to order rather than for inventory. About 95 per cent of the division's volume is "dressed" or "worked" in lengths of from 6 to

---

[5] See Glossary, Supplement A.

[6] These are usually items less than six inches in width which many mills normally bundle by length, six pieces to the bundle.

[7] See Glossary, Supplement A.

EXHIBIT 1   UNSURPASSED

MANUFACTURING

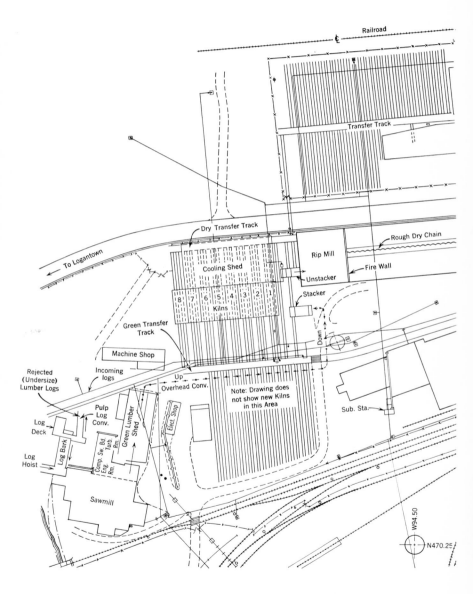

LUMBER CORPORATION

FACILITIES

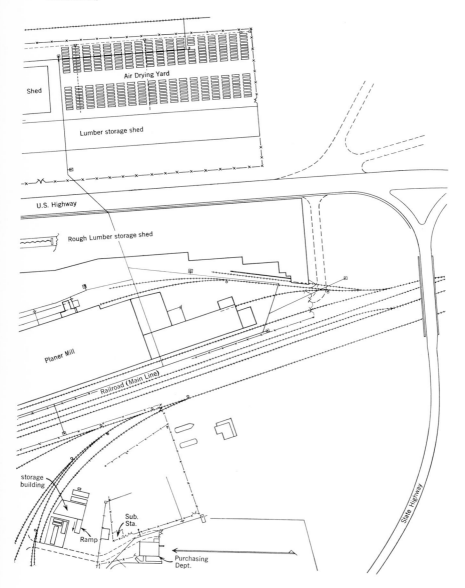

16 feet.   On occasion, the mill also produces small quantities of "structural" or "dimension" lumber.   However, the major market for this latter type of lumber, which by industry practice was sold in standard lengths of 12 to 36 feet, was for larger lengths than those usually produced by the Logantown mill.   Trees of the size required to produce these longer lengths grew mostly in western forests, rather than in southern pine woodlands such as those maintained by Unsurpassed.   Mills located in the western states therefore generally dominated this sector of the market.

In keeping with the general industry practice, Unsurpassed sold most of the items in its regular product line, except plain-end pine flooring, random length only.

MANUFACTURING FACILITIES AND PERSONNEL

The layout of the company's manufacturing facilities are shown in Exhibit 1.   Its organization chart for line activities is presented in Exhibit 2.   In addition, the company was provided with a typical range of staff services, including a Personnel Department, an Engineering Group, and a Data-Processing Section which was equipped with punch-card equipment.

The lumber mill, which was currently operating on a five-day week, consisted of the sawmill, drying kilns, rip mills, and loading and shipping facilities.   For the past two and one-half years all operations except the planing and flooring mills, loading, and shipping had been on a two-shift-per-day schedule.[8]

Approximately 265 employees currently were employed in the mill under a union contract.   Mr. Bunn believed that labor relations were "good"; there had never been a strike in the 80-year history of the operation.   The wage rates of various lumber mill jobs and the complement of the several sections of the plant are shown in Exhibit 3.

PRODUCTION PROCESSES

Woodlands Operations

Trees, harvested under the supervision of trained forestry technicians, are cut in the field and sorted for use as pulpwood or lumber. The largest, straightest trees, showing the fewest deformities, are

---

[8] A third planer-matcher in the planing mill had recently been placed back in service on a one-shift basis to permit increased output.

EXHIBIT 2 Unsurpassed Lumber Corporation

partial organization chart, line operators

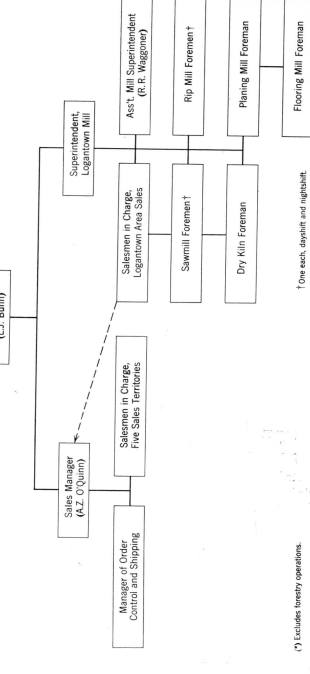

General Manager
(L.J. Bunn)

Sales Manager
(A.Z. O'Quinn)

Manager of Order
Control and Shipping

Salesmen in Charge,
Five Sales Territories

Superintendent,
Logantown Mill

Ass't. Mill Superintendent
(R.R. Waggoner)

Salesmen in Charge,
Logantown Area Sales

Rip Mill Foremen †

Sawmill Foremen †

Planing Mill Foreman

Dry Kiln Foreman

Flooring Mill Foreman

† One each, dayshift and nightshift.

(*) Excludes forestry operations.

119

EXHIBIT 3 UNSURPASSED LUMBER CORPORATION

WORKFORCE AND WAGE RATES, LOGANTOWN MILL

Area or Department	Personnel Required at Current Volume	Representative Job Classifications and Hourly Wage Rates	
Saw Mill	78*	Sawyer	$2.77
		Head Saw Filer	2.77
		Saw Filer	2.66
		Gang Sawyer	1.72
		Sawyer Learner	1.49
		Clean-Up Man	1.37
Rip Mill	54*	Grader	$2.04
		Trimmer	1.42
		Feeder	1.37
		Unstacker	1.37
		Trim Saw Helper	1.37
Planing Mill	56	Head Machine Setter	$2.19
		Machine Setter	2.04
and		Inspector (Grader)	2.04
		Tally Man	1.49
Flooring Mill	30	Feeder	1.40
		Outman	1.34
		Tie Man	1.31
Dry Kiln	26*	General Laborers	$1.25 to $1.31
Lumber Yard	17*	Lift Truck Driver	$1.37
Miscellaneous	4 to 10	Carrier Driver	1.42

* Two-shift operations.

selected for manufacturing into lumber. While still in the field the felled trees are sawed insofar as possible into logs slightly longer than 16 feet,[9] and then are transported to the sawmill by truck.

The Sawmill

At the sawmill the logs are cut into boards by skilled sawyers. Relying solely on judgment and experience, the sawyers work the logs through a complex array of band, gang, rip, and circular saws to yield boards of the greatest possible length and width.

---

[9] Sixteen feet is the maximum standard length for Unsurpassed lumber. Logs are cut oversize, however, to permit a full 16-foot board to emerge after trimming operations in the mill.

As the boards leave the sawmill, each is trimmed to the longest possible standard length, from 6 to 16 feet, in two-foot increments (6 feet, 8 feet, 10 feet, etc.). The trimmed boards then are stacked on small, railroad-like flat cars. When loaded, a car is moved into the kiln (ovens) where the lumber is "seasoned" (dried) at controlled humidity and temperature for three days.

The Rip Mill

Following the drying operation the cars containing the stacked lumber are moved to storage sheds to wait their turns in the rip mill and grading shed, facilities that are laid out as shown in Exhibit 4.[10] Here the rough boards are unstacked automatically and dumped lengthwise on a chain conveyor. They then are moved by the conveyor past three graders who mark symbols in crayon on each board to indicate its grade, and the manner in which it is to be resawed (that is, ripped lengthwise into narrower strips, or trimmed, or both) to eliminate defects and to create the standard width and grades which are used for rough inventory. Boards not requiring ripping or trimming are merely graded.

After being marked by the graders, the boards move to the "off-men" (designated as A and B on Exhibit 4) who pull off those boards marked for ripping and send them to the rip sawyers (designated C and D on Exhibit 4). After the ripping operation the boards move back onto the main conveyor where they join those boards that do not require ripping. The boards then pass lengthwise under the trim saw station. A turn man (E) turns each board so the trim sawyer, located in a pulpit (F) above the conveyor, can read the black crayon notations by which the graders have indicated the type of trimming required. The trim saw consists of nine circular saw blades on movable arms. These are mounted vertically, two feet apart, beneath the conveyor. The sawyer actuates or lifts the appropriate saw blade or blades to trim the board according to the graders' markings.

The Grading Shed

From the trimming operation the boards move at a speed of 30 feet per minute along a 260-foot conveyor known as the "rough-dry chain." Stationed at intervals on either side of the chain are 11 "pullers," men

[10] The waiting time can be as much as three days, depending on the volume of lumber ahead of the cars coming out of the kiln. The company's normal practice is to move lumber into the rip mill in the same sequence in which it emerges from the kiln.

EXHIBIT 4   UNSURPASSED

RIP MILL AND

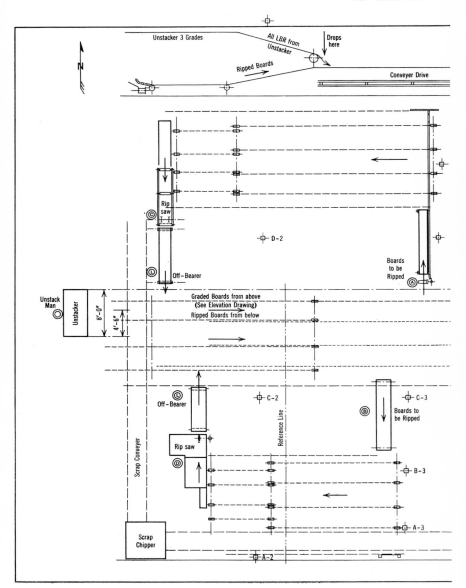

Lumber Corporation

Grading Shed

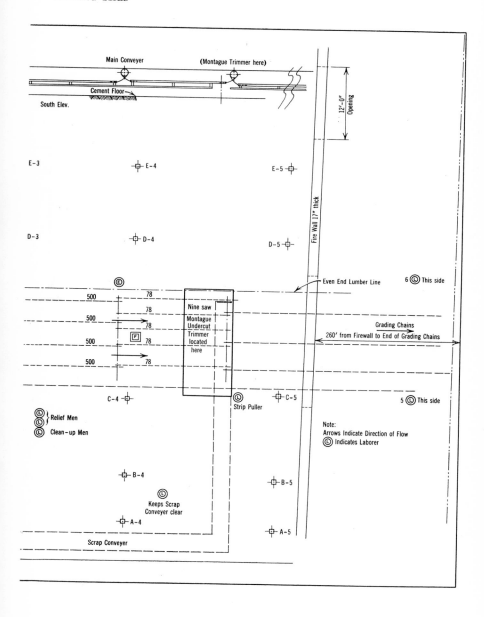

who pull the pieces of rough lumber off the conveyor and arrange them into different stacks or "sorts." Each sort contains lumber of the same thickness, width, and "grade group," although in random length.

The "pullers" determine the grade of each board by noting the grade mark that the rip mill graders previously have placed on each piece. Since the grading of rough lumber is merely a preliminary step in the total grading process, and is at best a difficult task, it is not expected that its results will be 100 per cent accurate. The Logantown mill, like many in the industry, sorts rough lumber only into "groups of grades," such as "Grade C and better"; "#2 and better"; and so on. Within each of these grade groupings, rough lumber is sorted by thickness and width. When a "sort" reaches dimensions roughly 4 feet wide, 4 feet high, and 16 feet long, it is picked up by a straddle truck and moved to the rough inventory storage sheds where it is stacked with similar sorts.

A second, more exacting grading into each of the individual grades offered for sale is made by specially trained inspectors during planing mill operations.[11] Although these inspectors are Unsurpassed employees, they have to be certified by the Southern Pine Inspection Bureau (SPIB), and their grading skills periodically are rechecked by Bureau examiners. On the average, the company has found that graded rough lumber usually generates about 70 per cent "on-grade" finished lumber, and 30 per cent "off-grade," that is, lumber that actually proves to be some grade other than that which the rough graders had classified it originally. It therefore always is necessary to start a greater quantity of rough lumber into production than the amount of finished lumber actually desired.

Unsurpassed's manufacturing, pricing, and selling of lumber are based on the following grades:[12] "B and better," "C," "D," "#2 and better," and "#3." Disregarding the lumber cut for use as pulpwood rather than for lumber, company experience over a number of years has demonstrated that about three quarters of an average cut of timber is usable lumber, and one quarter is composed of nonusable stumpage, limbs, bark, trimmings, sawdust, and so forth. Among small lumber mills, this waste factor could run as high as 75 per cent. Of the usable lumber, Unsurpassed's experience had been that about 78 per cent usually would be in grades #1 and below, and 22 per cent in grades D and better.

---

[11] Sometimes referred to as "remanufacture."

[12] Unsurpassed did not separate out and price grades A, #1 or #4.

Remanufacture

Ninety per cent of the finished lumber produced at the Logantown operation is processed in the planing mill. The remaining 10 per cent comes from the flooring mill which produces "end-matched"[13] products of oak and pine. End-matched flooring in lengths of eight feet or less is a standard item produced for sale from inventory. Since flooring products are manufactured by a separate process, involving many distinctive problems and the use of specialized equipment, Mr. Bunn had decided not to include the flooring mill in his current study of the company's manufacturing operation.

The planing mill produces four basic products: molding, plain-end pine flooring, dressed lumber, and worked lumber. The layout of the mill is shown in Exhibit 5.

MOLDING OPERATIONS. At the west end of the planing mill are located three molding machines, only two of which are currently in operating condition. These two machines produce molding for both inside and outside use, ranging from the simplest "quarter-round" pieces to intricate, decorative designs for interior trim.

Molding usually accounted for less than five per cent of the planing mill's production. The company was equipped, nonetheless, to produce almost all of the more than 250 types of molding which are standard items in the industry. In keeping with general industry practices, Unsurpassed molding is sold by the lineal foot, rather than by board foot, and is manufactured for and sold from inventory. Due to its fragile nature and low volume, Mr. Bunn did not consider packaging practical for this product and knew of no one in the industry who currently was considering this possibility seriously.

PLANER-MATCHER OPERATIONS. The bulk of the production in the planing mill, consisting of the manufacture of plain-end pine flooring, dressed lumber, and worked lumber, was processed by the three planer-matchers, each of which could be used in the manufacture of any of these items.

Rough lumber is fed through the planer-matchers at speeds of from 100 to 350 lineal feet per minute, depending on the size of the board and the complexity of the working. On the average, the planer-matchers were operated at about 275 lineal feet per minute. Exhibit 6

---

[13] "End-matched" flooring is differentiated from plain-end flooring in that the ends, as well as sides, are machined "tongue and groove." Plain-end flooring is processed in the planing mill.

EXHIBIT 5   UNSURPASSED

PLANER

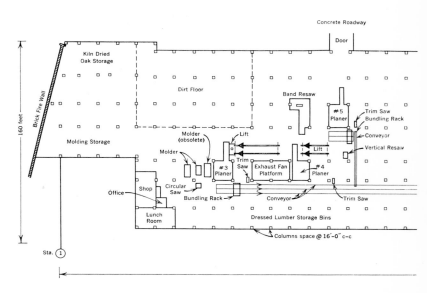

shows some typical operating times for each machine in terms of the number of pieces (random length) per minute discharged onto the conveyor. A specific employee was responsible for setting-up and operating each of the machines. A set-up required from 15 to 40 minutes, and, on the average, each machine was "down" about three hours per day for set-up changes. The general nature of the planer-matcher operation, and of the similarities and differences between the three machines available, may be characterized as follows:

#3 Machine. Operation of the #3 planer-matcher required 11 men: a machine setter, a machine feeder, two graders, two tie-men, an inspector, a trim sawyer, an "out-man," and two pullers.[14]   In addition, a tally-man was assigned to keep an output count on each machine.

Producing an order for 5,000 BFM of grade "C" or better finished

---

[14] The arrangement, work force, and operating features of each of the planer-matchers is somewhat different, although the general production processes are essentially the same.

Lumber Corporation

MILL

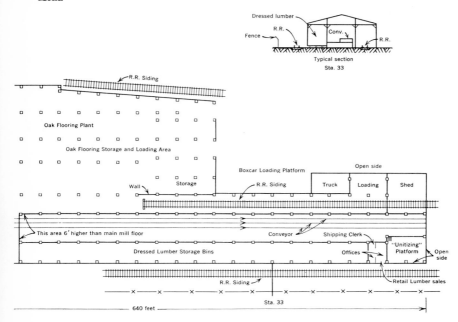

plain-end pine flooring on planer-matcher #3, for example, would involve the following sequence of operations. (Note: By industry practice, this order for plain-end pine flooring would be manufactured in widths of six inches or less, and would be bundled by length and grade, six pieces to the bundle.)

A straddle truck would move to machine #3 a load of rough lumber which, in the prior operations, had been graded "C and better" and had been sorted into the appropriate width and thickness. In keeping with the company's over-all experience pattern, it would probably later be determined that only about 70 per cent of this rough lumber was actually grade "C and better," and that of this, perhaps 20 per cent would actually be grade "B and better." Since each finished grade was tallied and priced separately,[15] the question of yield by grade was of considerable importance.

The straddle truck would deposit the load of rough lumber on an automatic unloading device located behind the #3 planer-matcher.

---

[15] Except, as indicated earlier, grades "A," #1, and #4.

EXHIBIT 6   UNSURPASSED LUMBER CORPORATION

TYPICAL CONVEYOR SPEEDS AND OUTPUT RATES
FOR PLANER-MATCHER OPERATIONS ON STANDARD ITEMS

Planer Mill Main Conveyor Speed: 49 feet per minute
Planer-Matcher #5 Conveyor Speed: 48 feet per minute

Planer-Matcher #	Item being Produced	Machine Speed (lineal feet per minute)	Output in Pieces per Minute
3	1″ x 4″ strip 4DS*	300	28
4	1″ x 12″ boards 4DS	200	16
5	1″ x 2″ boards 4DS (produced by splitting 1″ x 4″ rough lumber into two pieces by incorporating a saw blade into the set-up of the planer-matcher. Splitting and dressing occur simultaneously.)	200	42

* *i.e.* "Dressed" on all 4 sides.

By use of a tilting arrangement, a workman known as a "feeder" would cause each successive layer of rough lumber to slide down onto the machine table. He would then hand-feed the boards, one at a time, into the machine's intake rollers. With the machine in operation the lumber was then fed lengthwise out on the main conveyor (see Exhibit 5). Most of the boards coming out of the machine were from 6 to 16 feet in length, in increments of 2 feet. Defects in the wood, however, occasionally caused the boards to crack or break during this stage of the process, resulting in an "off-length" piece.

As the boards moved along the main conveyor, each would be lifted off the graders, examined, and then placed with the other pieces of the same grade and length in a specific compartment in the sorting rack located over the conveyor. When six pieces in a given grade and length had been obtained, the graders, standing on opposite sides of the sorting rack, would hand the entire stack, that is, all six pieces, to the tie-men who tied it with twine. The inspector then would stamp the top board on the stack to show the grade involved, in this case either "B and Btr" (that is, B and better), or "C."

Off-length pieces and "below grade" lumber (pieces that had been misjudged in rough grading) were left on the conveyor which then carried them to the trim sawyer. It was his job to try to upgrade the pieces by trimming them,[16] or by removing ends of sections containing knotholes, splits, cracks, or other damaged material. The reworked pieces were then handed back to the graders for sorting.

Even after the trimming operation a substantial quantity of off-grade lumber usually still remained. This would be placed on the main conveyor and carried along to the "out-man," also known as the "off-grader." He would pull each piece off the conveyor, ascertain its grade, and place it, by grade, into one of the finished goods storage bins adjacent to his work area. Eventually such pieces would be included in an outgoing shipment of lumber of the grade in question.

After being stamped, each on-grade bundle of flooring was placed back on the 300-foot main conveyor and carried at 49 feet per minute to whatever point, determined by the location of the truck or boxcar, the loading operation was to be performed. En route, each bundle would pass the tally-man who made a written notation of its length and grade to provide information for billing, and ascertained when the required quantity (in this case, 5,000 BF) had been loaded. Two pullers would remove the bundles from the conveyor and manually load them in the boxcar or truck.[17] If there were no abnormal operating conditions, the total manufacturing cycle time on this particular order, exclusive of shipping, would be about three quarters of an hour.

#4 Machine. Operations of the #4 planer-matcher differed from those of #3 in several respects. Since it was not equipped with an over-conveyor platform and bundling racks, the two tie-men were replaced by two additional pullers who worked at the boxcar or truck to assist in loading the separate pieces. In addition, no graders were assigned to the #4 machine. Instead, an inspector was stationed at the point where the boards dropped on the main conveyor. After turning and examining each board, he placed crayon markings on it, thus providing instructions to the out-man, the trim sawyer, and stamp-man. Boards which were marked as "off-grade" were pulled off the conveyor by the out-man and placed in storage bins. Boards which were marked for further sawing were sent along to the trim sawyer. Boards which were marked as acceptable were stamped by

---

[16] The trim sawyer endeavors to salvage the longest lengths possible, in increments of two feet, down to the minimum allowable length of six feet.

[17] "Unitized" shipments require different treatment, to be described subsequently.

the stamp-man according to the notation of the inspector. The tally-ing and trimming operations were performed in a manner similar to that employed in the operations on the #3 machine.

#5 Machine. The #5 machine was equipped with an over-conveyor platform and bundling racks, and also had its own short "transit" con-veyor located about 50 feet in back of the main conveyor. Unlike the #3 and #4 machines, however, the #5 unit had no tilting device. An assistant feeder therefore was required to hand boards up to the feeder. An inspector was assigned to this machine, as with the #4 machine, and was responsible for marking each board with trimming and grading instructions. The graders sorted the pieces according to the inspector's crayoned notations, and the stamp-man marked the bundles accordingly. Bundles were then placed on a transit conveyor which carried them to the main conveyor for tallying and loading. Two pullers worked at the machine as tie-men.

PRODUCTION FOR STOCK. In the event that any of the planer-matchers was producing for stock[18] rather than for a specific customer order, the pullers loaded the pieces or bundles in bins located adjacent to the conveyor on the side of the building opposite the railroad siding. Finished inventory for stock also was generated by any over-runs which occurred when a machine produced more of a given item than was required for a specific customer order. Such over-runs also were loaded into the bins along the conveyor.

Photographs of various phases of the manufacturing process are shown in Supplement B.

ORDER SCHEDULING

Incoming orders are received and processed by personnel in the company's Sales Department and copies are routed to the Assistant Mill Superintendent, the Planing Mill Foreman, and the Manager of Order Control and Shipping. The Assistant Mill Superintendent, Richard Waggoner, was responsible for production scheduling and shipping, and worked closely with the sales staff and the shipping personnel in coordinating these activities.

For planning purposes, an estimate of the physical inventory of rough lumber on hand and on order, by grade, width, and thickness, was prepared once a week by one of Mr. Waggoner's assistants and

---

[18] About 5 per cent of production is for stock, usually in the form of plain-end pine flooring.

recorded on a "Stock and Order Report."[19] Against each specific inventory item shown on the Report, the assistant also noted the total board feet of rough lumber already committed for existing orders that had not yet been started into production.

Orders received for items for which the existing rough inventory was inadequate were held until sufficient rough lumber of the proper size and grade could be processed. Normally, however, the existing inventory permitted prompt scheduling of the planing-mill operations required to process any customer order. Most orders therefore were shipped within two weeks of receipt, and one week delivery often was accomplished.

After noting total current sales requirements, including rush orders, that had to be satisfied, Mr. Waggoner each week compiled a list of orders to be shipped the following week. Then, using a separate sheet of paper for each of that week's working days, he listed the specific customer orders, by customer and by Unsurpassed order number, that were to be produced each day. In developing these "Daily Work Sheets," Mr. Waggoner took into account the method of shipment specified by the customer, in order to assure that the mix of truck and freight carloading activities required during any given day would be consistent with the loading facilities available. He also noted on the Daily Work Sheet the type of workings required for each order, the total number of board feet in thousands, the planer-matcher on which each order was to be run, and its sequence in relation to other orders scheduled for the same machine on the same day.

Mr. Waggoner also prepared a week in advance a daily "House Memo" for each of the three planer-matchers. On each memo he showed the orders the machine was to process that day, the type and quantity of the items comprising each of these orders, and the grade and quantity of rough inventory that would be required. Mr. Waggoner retained the original of each House Memo and sent copies to the straddle truck driver, the appropriate machine setter, and the Shipping Department.

In order to permit loading operations on three different orders to occur simultaneously off the one main conveyor, and also in an effort to avoid overloading the pullers, Mr. Waggoner usually scheduled each planer-matcher to work on a separate order. Also, almost without exception, all items called for in a specific customer order were run through a planer-matcher before the machine would be shifted to

---

[19] The Stock and Order Report includes only those rough items ordered into production frequently enough to warrant recording.

EXHIBIT 7   UNSURPASSED LUMBER CORPORATION

PLANER-MATCHER MACHINE LOADINGS FOR A REPRESENTATIVE FIVE-DAY PERIOD

Day	PLANER-MATCHER #3 # of BF	Size	Grade	Patt'n*	PLANER-MATCHER #4 # of BF	Size	Grade	Patt'n	PLANER-MATCHER #5 # of BF	Size	Grade	Patt'n
Monday	4,000	1 x 4	C and Btr.	EV1S	7,500	1 x 8	C and Btr.	E and CB	15,000	1 x 6	3	D–M
	1,000	1 x 6	C and Btr.	116	1,000	1 x 3	2	R.Cyp.	10,500	1 x 6	2	E and CB
	1,500	1 x 7	2	D–M	750	1 x 6	C and Btr.	½ x 6 SE	1,500	1 x 5	2	D–M
	22,000	1 x 3	B and Btr.	D4S	1,000	1 x 8	C and Btr.	D4S	2,500	1 x 8	2	D4S
					1,500	1 x 6	D	P105	14,000	1 x 5	3	D4S
					5,500	1 x 8	D	P105				
					6,000	1 x 8	2	P105				
					6,000	1 x 10	2	PWK				
Tuesday	2,000	1 x 3	2	D4S	15,000	1 x 6	3	D–M	7,000	1 x 5	2	D–M
	2,000	1 x 4	2	D4S	13,000	1 x 7	2	E and CB	5,000	1 x 5	2	D–M
	15,000	1 x 6	2	D–M	1,500	1 x 10	2	S.L.	7,000	1 x 6	2	D–M
					13,000	1 x 8	2	S.L.	15,000	1 x 5	2	EV1S
					5,000	2 x 3	2	D4S				
Wednesday	30,000	1 x 4	B and Btr.	D4S	325	1¼ x 6	C and Btr.	½ x 6 SE	10,000	1 x 6	2	P105
					2,500	1 x 7	2	D4S	5,000	1 x 5	2	R.Cyp.
					2,500	2 x 4	2	D–M	12,000	1 x 7	2	E and CB
					10,000	1 x 8	2	D4S	5,000	1 x 7	2	E and CB
					30,000	1 x 5½	2	D–M	8,000	1 x 8	2	E and CB
Thursday	15,000	1 x 5	2	D–M	3,000	1¼ x 6	C and Btr.	DCM	5,000	1 x 5	2	DCM
	15,000	1 x 4	2	FLG	5,000	1¼ x 8	2	D4S and RSN	6,000	1 x 7	2	E and CV
					1,500	1 x 12	2	D4S	6,000	1 x 7	2	E and CV
					1,500	1 x 8	2	D4S	5,000	1 x 7	2	EV
					2,000	1 x 6	2	D4S	3,000	1 x 5	2	D–M
					2,000	1¼ x 12	C and Btr.	D4S	5,000	1 x 10	2	D–M
					1,000	¾ x 10	2	N1E	10,000	1 x 8	2	D4S
					9,000	1 x 6	C and Btr.	E and CB				D4S
					3,000	1 x 8	2	E and CB				
					25,000	1 x 7	C and Btr.	DCM				
					2,000	2 x 8	2	D4S				
					1,600	2 x 8	2	D4S				
Friday	10,000	1 x 5	2	D–M	12,000	1 x 6	2	E and CB	5,000	1 x 5	2	EV
	6,000	1 x 6	2	D–M	15,000	1 x 6	2	E and CB	2,000	1 x 7	2	EV
	7,000	1 x 8	2 CYP	D4S	22,000	1 x 8	2	D4S	5,000	1 x 5	2	D–M
	1,000	1 x 3	1	D4S					7,000	1 x 12	C and Btr.	D–M
		1 x 2		D4S					3,000	1 x 5	2	D4S
									1,000	1 x 12	2	D4S
									18,000	1 x 6	2	E and CB

* Pattern, or dressing, or working required.

another order. Furthermore, to avoid confusing the pullers and tally men assigned to each of the planer-matchers, Mr. Waggoner attempted to schedule work so that no two planer-matchers were processing identical types of products at the same time. Exhibit 7 contains a summary of machine loadings for five reasonably typical working days.

In making his work assignments, Mr. Waggoner also endeavored to consider the relative effectiveness of each of the machines in terms of particular types of orders. Past experience had convinced him, for example, that the 11 man team assigned to Planer-Matcher #3 made it the most effective unit for processing plain-end pine flooring. Similarly, he believed that Machine #5 was the most effective unit for producing items, other than flooring, that required bundling six inches and less in width. Similarly, he attempted to assign Machine #4 to orders calling for large quantities of wide board. Although Mr. Waggoner made every effort to take such considerations into account when scheduling, the mix of incoming orders sometimes required him to make less than ideal machine assignments.

SHIPPING—PREPARATION OF UNITIZED LUMBER

Total shipments from the mill during the past two calendar years had been approximately 31½ and 36½ million board feet, respectively. Indications were that the current year would at least equal and might well surpass the previous year's volume. Currently about one-third of the mill's output was transported by enclosed railroad freight car. These were usually 40 feet long and 8 feet wide, with 6-foot wide door openings. Trucks used for the remaining two-thirds of the shipments included customers' vehicles, commercial trucking facilities, and Unsurpassed's own equipment.[20] These units represented a wide range of freight capacities. On the average, however, a truck shipment contained about 15,000 BF, as opposed to the 25,000 BF average for railcar shipments.

While virtually all rail car shipments were hand loaded,[21] about

---

[20] These include four 15,000 BFM capacity flat-bed trailers, two tractors for the trailers, and one 7,000 BFM capacity truck.

[21] On an experimental basis, Unsurpassed recently had been making about two unitized shipments per month utilizing a new type of wide-door railway freight car being tested by the railroad serving the mill. The new width door permitted the use of fork-lift trucks in loading lumber into the car.

two-thirds of the lumber currently being shipped by truck was "uni-tized" and thus could be loaded by fork-lift truck. Such units were prepared for shipment at the end of the main conveyor. Instead of pulling individual boards directly into a truck, the pullers took the individual pieces of random length lumber off the conveyor and assembled them into a stack on a concrete platform. When a stack reached a "standard" dimension roughly $3\frac{1}{2}$ feet high and 4 feet wide,[22] the entire "package" was strapped tightly with steel bands. The unit was then moved over rollers to the end of the platform and loaded onto the truck with a fork-lift.

On the average, each unitized unit contained approximately 1,800 board feet. This figure varied substantially from item to item, how-ever, because of the "dead-air pockets" created in each unit as pieces of random length lumber were stacked together. Depending on the variety of items specified in a customer's order, a unit also might consist of more than one type, or grade, of lumber.

Unsurpassed officials believed that "unitizing" offered a number of significant advantages to customers. For example, when unitized ship-ments were employed, a shipment arriving from the mill could be unloaded quickly with a fork-lift, thus holding to a minimum the delay of the truck. Furthermore, if the customers' yardmen were occupied elsewhere when the delivery arrived, the strapped units could be quickly and conveniently stacked on the ground until the personnel were free to place it in bins. Notwithstanding the advantages which Unsurpassed personnel believed were inherent in unitized lumber, the company's policy thus far had been to employ it only upon specific customer request.

Although no detailed records had been kept, company officials estimated that the steel strap required in the unitizing process cost about $1 per thousand board feet shipped. This was exclusive of the cost of the additional time spent by the pullers in assembling the lumber into stacks and strapping them to form units instead of loading individual pieces directly into the truck. As a rule, it took somewhere between four and five hours to load a conventional boxcar, two and one-half to three hours to load a truck with a nonunitized shipment, and about 30 minutes to prepare and load a unitized truck shipment. The latter operation, however, required the services of a fork-lift operator to assist the pullers. To date, Unsurpassed was charging

---

[22] The over-all length of the stack was, of course, 16 feet, i.e., the maximum length of the random length pieces of lumber comprising it.

the same price for items, regardless of whether they were shipped in unitized form, or via conventional methods.

All rail shipments were governed by strict governmental regulations which included requirements that loads be secured before transit. In the case of lumber, this involved certain "make ready" operations, such as placing lengths of steel strap in the rail car before the lumber was loaded into it. After the loading was completed, these straps were brought over the lumber, tightened, and clamped to prevent the load from shifting while in transit. These pre- and post-loading operations took approximately 20 minutes per car in addition to the time (cited above) required for the actual loading.

Since trucks did not normally encounter violent shocks in transit, and the driver usually had occasion to check his load frequently, the amount of "make-ready" time for loading trucks was negligible. In addition, the driver himself usually was anxious to assume personal responsibility for securing the load once it was in position in his vehicle.

SALES

Five salesmen under the direction of a general sales manager represented Unsurpassed in the sales areas indicated on the organization sheet in Exhibit 2. These men, who sold direct to retail lumber dealers and industrial concerns, accounted for about 90 to 95 per cent of the company's sales. In New England and certain other areas not covered by its own sales force, Unsurpassed relied on wholesalers, or on agents. The latter type of distributor maintained no lumber inventory; instead he placed sales with the company on a 5 per cent commission basis.

To take advantage of freight and truck rates, which were based on weight as well as volume and distance, virtually all customers ordered in carload or truckload lots. As previously noted, however, such orders were not necessarily composed of only one item or one type of lumber. On the contrary, most orders comprised at least two items, and many were so-called "hash" orders calling for eight or ten different items.

Unsurpassed had approximately 500 active accounts. The sales manager, Arnold O'Quinn, considered most of these as very stable, many of them being customers the company had dealt with for 25 years or more. Mr. O'Quinn believed that product quality, service, and honesty were the essential ingredients in good sales relations, and that most customers were willing to pay a "reasonable" premium for these attributes. Although the lumber business was highly competitive and subject to marked price fluctuations, there was usually an appreciable range between the high and low prices that a customer could find quoted for each type and grade of lumber at any given moment. The spread usually ran from two to four dollars per thousand board feet. By building sound customer relationships and avoiding certain market areas which were predominantly price-oriented, Unsurpassed had always been successful in selling on the top side of the range. On an over-all basis, recent sales income had been averaging about $105 per thousand board feet.

Lumber manufactured from southern pine competed directly with lumber produced by western mills from such trees as western pine, Douglas fir, hemlock, birch, and spruce. Whereas the western mills shipped a wide variety of lumber items into the eastern market, few eastern mills shipped to the west, largely because of the freight rate structure.

The western mills which competed in the eastern market usually worked through wholesalers or through wholesale distribution yards. During the past several years the wholesale distribution yards had increased in importance in the larger metropolitan areas, serving as collecting points for carload shipments of lumber from the mills. These they warehoused and then made up into small mixed or "hash" orders for retail lumberyards on short notice, but at a price usually about 20 per cent above F.O.B. mill prices.

Mr. O'Quinn believed that over the long run such distribution yards probably represented a potential competitive threat for Unsurpassed, although at present their operations had not seriously affected company sales. He believed that retail dealers were most likely to turn to wholesale distribution yards, rather than buy direct from a mill, in a declining market in order to avoid the expense and risk of buying and warehousing carload and truckload shipments.

Mr. O'Quinn was convinced that one of Unsurpassed's most significant long-term competitive advantages lay in its ability to dress or work lumber to almost any standard molding pattern. Only about 40 or 50 of the 250 or so major southern pine mills operated their own molders and not all of these had the attachments and cutting wheels necessary to permit their planer-matchers to produce the full range of patterns. The other mills were equipped merely to dress lumber to a limited number of the most prevalent designs and therefore produced only the smaller (12 to 24 feet) lengths of dimension and boards. Many small mills actually limited their activities to the production of rough green lumber, which they sold to larger mills which were equipped to perform the drying and remanufacturing operations.

Mr. Bunn believed that Unsurpassed enjoyed another important competitive asset in the fact that it was one of the few mills engaged in the manufacture of flooring. This permitted it to divert to the flooring mill some of the shorter pieces of lumber obtained in the processing of rough inventory. Mr. Bunn was confident that as a result of such diversions, Unsurpassed's shipments of random length items contained significantly fewer short pieces than was true of the industry in general. The company also had as customers several crate manufacturers who actually desired short pieces of lumber. By diverting to such firms a portion of the shorter pieces produced by the mill, Unsurpassed was able to increase still further the average length of items sold random length to its other accounts.

The company's production and sales records were based on total board feet produced and sold per month. No records were kept showing total sales of specific items. Exhibit 8 shows, however, a breakdown, by item and grade, of production during a reasonably typical five-week period of the current year. During this period, 201 truckloads and 69 carloads were shipped.

Supplement A. Unsurpassed Lumber Corporation

GLOSSARY OF INDUSTRY TERMINOLOGY*

A. TIMBERS:

Lumber that is five inches or more in its least dimension; known also as beams, stringers, posts, caps, girders, purlins, sills, etc.

B. STRUCTURAL LUMBER:

Lumber that is two inches or more in thickness and width, and is varyingly stress-rated for use when specific working stresses are required.

C. DIMENSION:

Lumber that is two inches to (but not including) five inches thick and two inches or more in width; classified also as framing, joists, planks, rafters, studs, small timbers, etc.

---

* Source: 1963 Grading Rules (Handbook) for Southern Pine Lumber, published by the Southern Pine Inspection Bureau. Reproduced by express permission.

D. BOARDS:
   Lumber that is less than two inches in nominal thickness and one inch or more in width; if less than six inches wide, also classified as strips.

E. FACTORY and SHOP LUMBER:
   Lumber that is produced or selected primarily for industrial uses or remanufacturing purposes.

F. YARD LUMBER:
   Grades (P), sizes, and workings (K) of lumber that are intended for ordinary construction and general building purposes; these are divided into select lumber (G) and common lumber (H).

G. SELECT LUMBER:
   Lumber of good appearance and finishing qualities (O), and identified by grade names (in order of decreasing quality) of B and Btr., C, C and Btr., and D.

H. COMMON LUMBER:
   Lumber suitable for general construction and utility purposes and identified by grade names (in order of decreasing quality) No. 1, No. 2, No. 3, and No. 4. Common lumber, as a group, ranks just below Select lumber.

I. ROUGH LUMBER:
   Lumber that has not been dressed (J) but which has been sawed, edged, and trimmed at least to the extent of showing saw marks in the wood on the four longitudinal surfaces of each piece for its over-all length.

J. DRESSED LUMBER:
   Lumber that has been planed or dressed by a planing machine on one side (S1S),[1] two sides (S2S), one edge (S1E),[2] two edges (S2E), or a combination of sides and edges (S1S1E, S1S2E, S2S1E or S4S).[3]

K. WORKED LUMBER:[4]
   Lumber that in addition to being dressed has been matched (L), shiplapped (M), or patterned (N).

---

[1] S1S: surfaced-one-side, sometimes written D1S: dressed-one-side.

[2] S1E: surfaced-one-edge.

[3] S1S1E: surfaced-one-side and one edge, etc.

[4] Excerpts from Section I, 1963 Grading Rules—Southern Pine Inspection Bureau.

L. MATCHED LUMBER:

Lumber that has been worked with a tongue on one side of each piece, and a groove on the opposite edge, to provide a "T and G joint" by fitting two pieces together. When *end-matched*, the tongues and grooves are worked in the ends also.

M. SHIPLAPPED LUMBER:

Lumber that has been worked or rabbeted on both edges of each piece to provide a lapped joint by fitting two pieces together.

N. PATTERN LUMBER:

Lumber that has been worked to a shaped or molded form in *addition* to being dressed, matched, or shiplapped, or *any combination* of these workings.

O. FINISH:

Lumber of a sufficiently high quality to be adaptable for natural finishes or stains. Usually "B and Better" is specified, but occasionally C and Btr., and even D grades are suitable for economical finish. The term "finish" is sometimes used interchangeably with "select lumber" (G).

P. GRADING:

The designation given to southern pine lumber to identify the various levels of quality for segregating, pricing and selling. The grade ranges in order of decreasing quality: B and Btr., C, D, No. 1, No. 2, No. 3 and No. 4. In actual practice, most mills actually segregate, inventory, price, and sell the following grade classifications: B and Btr. (which includes A); C; D; #1; #2; #3.

The grading of lumber cannot be considered an exact science because it is based on a visual inspection of each piece and on the judgment of the grader, but the provisions of these rules are sufficiently explicit to establish 5 per cent below grade as a reasonable variation in judgment between inspectors and graders.

In judging the quality of lumber to establish its grade, the following represent some of the factors taken into account: surface checks, knots, holes, pitch (sap), stain (discoloring), warp, decay, and splits.

Supplement B. Unsurpassed Lumber Corporation

REPRESENTATIVE PHOTOGRAPHS
OF MANUFACTURING OPERATIONS

FIGURE 1. Early stages of operations in the Rip Mill and Grading Shed. The three graders are visible in the left background; an off-man is in the center foreground. The conveyor is moving the rough lumber toward you.

FIGURE 2. Trim saw operation in the Rip Mill. The off-men are visible in the right and left foreground; the turn-man is in the left background; the trim sawyer (his back toward you) is in the pulpit in the center background. The conveyor is moving the lumber away from you.

FIGURE 3. Close-up view of trim saw operation in the Rip Mill. The nine vertically mounted circular saw blades are mounted beneath the conveyor. The six circular blade-like objects visible in the photo are blade guards.

FIGURE 4. The rough-dry chain in the Rip Mill. Pullers and sorts are visible to the right and left of the conveyor.

FIGURE 5. Feeding rough lumber into the intake rollers on planer-matcher number 3 in the Planing Mill.

142

FIGURE 6. Bundling plain-end pine flooring in the Planing Mill.

FIGURE 7. Plain-end pine flooring bundling operation (as shown in Figure 6) viewed from opposite direction. Note storage bins to the right. Main conveyor in the background.

FIGURE 8. Main conveyor, Planing Mill. Note grader in foreground.

FIGURE 9. Loading railroad boxcars with dressed lumber from Planing Mill main conveyor. Note tally-man in background.

FIGURE 10.   Unitizing platform.

U.S. Shirt Company

Executives of the U.S. Shirt Company were evaluating the company's manufacturing facilities to determine whether the existing types and mix of processes in the various sewing plants adequately met the criteria of economy and flexibility. The study had been prompted by a recommendation recently advanced by a company industrial engineer that all of the firm's sewing plants not already employing the "unit-system" of production should be converted to this process as soon as possible.

BACKGROUND: COMPANY HISTORY AND PRODUCT LINE

In the 1880's an immigrant and his wife started manufacturing men's shirts in a loft in New York City. Although the business always faced severe competition, it grew slowly and steadily, eventually becoming the vast U.S. Shirt Company. Currently, the firm operates 23 plants in four states and sells on a nationwide basis. Its product line includes dress shirts, sport shirts, pajamas, and jackets.

Fourteen million men's dress shirts, the most important item in the company's line, had been produced during the previous calendar year. This required the purchase of almost 40 million yards of piece goods and corresponding quantities of supporting items. For example, 800,000 gross of buttons had been used in the previous year's operations.

The company sold its line of popular-priced shirts, usually retailing at $3.95, to the trade through the Prince-Wear Shirt Company, one of its four sales subsidiaries. Its quality-priced line of shirts, generally retailing at $4.50 or higher, were sold through another sales subsidiary, the Style-Master Shirt Company. A third subsidiary,

146

the Hi-Style Company, sold its medium-priced line of shirts which customarily retailed at $2.95. All three subsidiaries maintained their own sales forces to call on independent retail outlets throughout the country, and employed national advertising. The fourth subsidiary, the J. P. Jamison and Sons Company, usually sold over half of the company's output. Its customers consisted of the jobbing trade, large and small chain stores, mail order houses, and foreign customers. Jamison sales were solely in medium- and popular-priced lines.

All the company's shirts were known throughout the trade for their excellent quality. Price lines differed according to the quality of the piece goods and the buttons used, and the number of stitches per inch employed in the sewing process. Each sales subsidiary featured a line of shirts composed of several styles. White broadcloth, white oxford, solid colors, and narrow striped materials were staple styles which were in demand season after season. In addition, each line included "novelty," or "fancy," styles which were changed frequently.

Each style was manufactured in several models which differed as to cut. The main difference in models was the collar, which might be soft or fused, high or low, long point or short point, with or without stays, button-down or non-button down, and so on. The popularity of some models changed from year to year, but certain models were always in demand.

Retail sales of dress shirts were subject to three seasonal peaks: Christmas, Easter, and Father's Day. Salesmen offered the Christmas line to the trade starting in May, sales of the Easter lines began in September, and Father's Day lines were first offered in January. Each season's line consisted of staples and of nonstaples designed and produced especially for that one season. There was some carry-over of nonstaples from one season to the next, but, in general, the popularity of a nonstaple was short-lived. Occasionally, however, a nonstaple item would "catch fire" with the retail public and temporarily generate a peak demand on the shirt manufacturer until its popularity waned.

Five of U.S. Shirt's 23 plants made dress shirts exclusively. The weekly capacity of these plants varied from 1,200 dozen to 6,500 dozen; the smallest plant employed 120 sewing operators, the largest 550. All work was allotted to these plants by company headquarters in New York City; there sales estimates were converted into production requirements, production schedules were made up, and sewing orders (tickets) were prepared and forwarded to the plants. The sewing tickets supplied all the information a plant required to produce the desired quantity of each style and model, usually with a standard mix of collar sizes ranging from 13½ to 17, and a standard mix of three specified sleeve lengths, 33, 34, and 35 inches, for each collar size. Materials cut to these specifications, as well as the necessary thread, buttons, linings, and related items, were also supplied to each plant as a result of shipping orders originated by the New York office. In assigning work to the plants, the New York personnel gave careful attention to models, types of material, length of runs, delivery requirements, and plant loads.

Approximately 25 cloth parts are required for a dress shirt (Supplement A).[1] The work of a sewing factory consists of stitching these pieces together, making buttonholes, and sewing on buttons. In the company's plants the sewing together of the parts required to form a shirt has been broken down into numerous short, simple operations (Supplement A),[2] an operation ordinarily consisting of sewing a single seam. Each sewing-machine operator, normally a woman employee, specializes in a single operation and thus, over time, becomes very proficient in performing her highly specialized task.

Any change introduced into the operation—including changes in the size or shape of a piece, the length of a seam, or the type or weight of the cloth being sewn—almost always instantly reduces a worker's output. As she gradually gains experience with a new, or changed, operation, the operator's output slowly increases until she performs at a high degree of proficiency. For example, a change from a white broadcloth to a white oxford cloth requires the operator to become accustomed to handling the heavier oxford cloth and adjusting to the slower rate at which the heavier material has to be fed into the sewing machine. A change from white cloth shirts to a print also results in reduced output until the operator becomes accustomed to positioning the various shirt parts in such a way that the stripes, or designs, match up on the finished shirt. On the other hand, a change from printed cloth to white usually does not adversely affect worker output, since the new work requires no matching of parts. Changes from a print cloth to a woven madras similarly involve no added positioning efforts since in a woven madras the pattern is woven in the cloth through use of different colored threads.

---

[1] See p. 159 (Figure 1).

[2] See pp. 158–162.

MANUFACTURING PROCESSES CURRENTLY EMPLOYED

Three distinct forms of process organization currently were in use in the various U.S. Shirt plants. Each process was the result of detailed engineering studies and of experience. In the early days, the shirt manufacturing industry operated on what was known as the "bundle system" in which individual bundles of cut shirt parts[3] were delivered to small contractors who performed the stitching operations. Under this system, operators performed several stitching operations on the shirt parts in the bundle; the sewn parts would then be rebundled and the bundle delivered to a storage point until another operator was ready to take it and perform all, or part, of the additional stitching operations required to complete the shirts. Under this system the worker had to be able to perform any of the stitching operations, and many times was required to sew a complete shirt. Work floor layouts under the bundle system typically had no relationship to the sequence in which the operations were performed.

Progressive Bundle System

One of the three manufacturing processes now employed by U.S. Shirt, the *progressive bundle system,* was an outgrowth of the old bundle system. Under this process (Exhibit 1), work was divided so that an operator performed only a single stitching operation. The basic unit of work was still the bundle, but the workers were assigned to specific work stations which were located in such a way as to conform to the required sequence of stitching operations. Each bundle of parts was then passed from one operator to another in proper sequence.

The progressive bundle system currently was employed in only one of the company's manufacturing facilities, Plant 4, which employed 120 operators and had a stated capacity of 1,300 dozen shirts per week.

Line System

Roughly a decade ago, a second type of manufacturing process, the *line system* of production (Exhibit 2), had been introduced in the company's Plant 1 in a bid to increase worker output.

---

[3] To insure high quality each of the individual items in a stack of parts had to be kept in the same sequence in which they had been cut so that all of the parts comprising a single shirt would come from the same "ply" of cloth.

EXHIBIT 1 U.S. SHIRT COMPANY

PROGRESSIVE BUNDLE SYSTEM

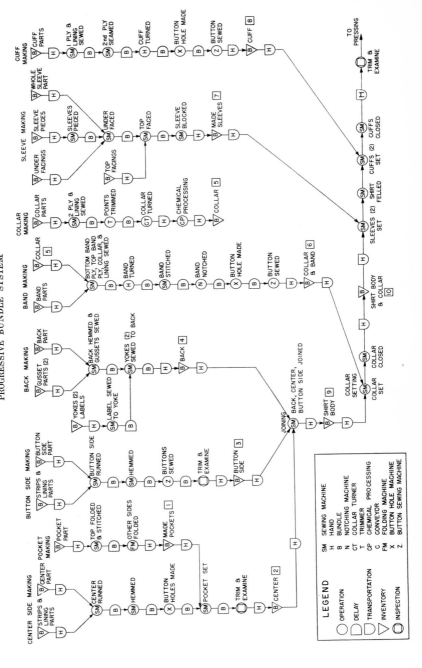

EXHIBIT 2 U.S. SHIRT COMPANY

LINE SYSTEM

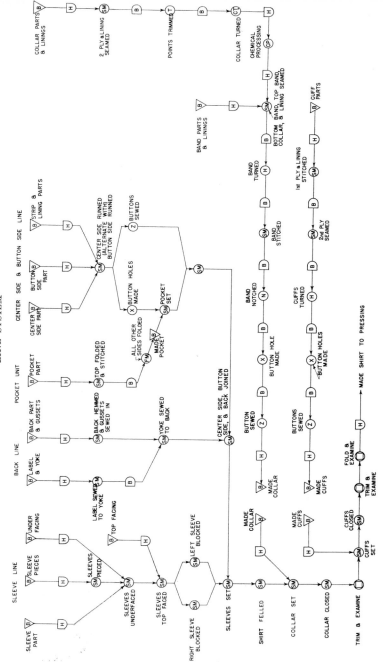

EXHIBIT 3 U.S. SHIRT COMPANY

UNIT SYSTEM

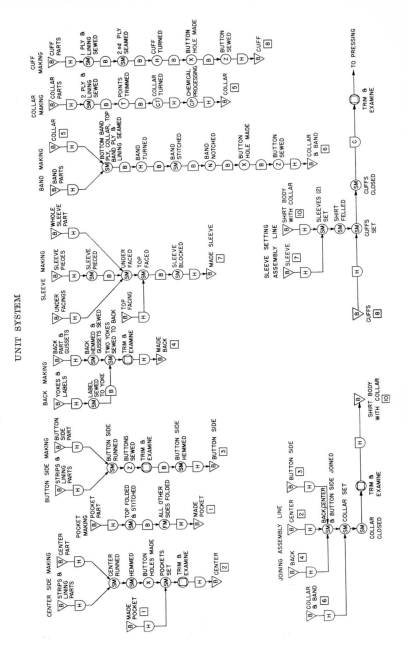

Unit System

Following a period of experience with the line system, company engineers developed a third manufacturing process, the *unit system* (Exhibit 3), and installed it in Plant 2 which previously had been operating on the progressive bundle system. Introduction of the unit system in Plant 2 quickly resulted in a 25 per cent reduction in direct labor sewing costs per dozen shirts. Over the ensuing years, two more facilities (Plants 3 and 5) were converted from the progressive bundle process to the unit system.

COMPARATIVE OPERATING RESULTS

As one phase of their study, company officials decided to make a comparative evaluation of the operating results typically achieved by the various plants. Such a comparison, they reasoned, might serve to highlight significant differences among the three different manufacturing processes employed and thus help determine whether changes in the current mix of processes would be advisable. With the help of the managers of the five plants and of the central scheduling group in the New York headquarters, they decided to study the period from January through March of the current year which, it was believed,

EXHIBIT 4 U.S. SHIRT COMPANY

SUMMARY OF SEWING TICKETS

Plant #1 (Line System)

Date Issued	Cloth	Collar	Brand	Model	Doz.	Work Started	Work Completed
1/10	White Broadcloth	Fused	Chain Store	Z	27	1/17	*
1/13	White Broadcloth	Fused	Chain Store	Z	199	1/31	2/17
1/28	White Broadcloth	Fused	Chain Store	Z	1019	2/4	2/21
1/14	White Broadcloth	Fused	Chain Store	Z	965	2/14	*
1/31	White Broadcloth	Fused	Chain Store	Z	379	2/14	*
1/6	Oxford White	Soft Bi Angle	Prince-Wear	Palm Spring	320	2/7	*
1/8	Oxford White	TT Soft	P.J.S.	TT Soft	350	2/14	*
1/28	End on End Broadcloth	Fused	Chain Store	Z	1004	2/21	2/28
1/30	White Broadcloth	Fused	P.J.S.	Z	369	3/7	*

* Information not available.

EXHIBIT 5   U.S. Shirt Company

SUMMARY OF SEWING TICKETS

Plant #2 (Unit System)

Date Issued	Cloth	Collar	Brand	Model	Doz.	Work Started	Work Completed
1/3	White Broadcloth	Fused	Chain Store	Z	1696	2/1	2/7
1/3	Woven	Fused	Chain Store	Z	137	1/30	2/5
1/3	Woven	Fused	Chain Store	Z	402	1/31	2/5
1/7	Prints	Fused	Hi-Style	Everfirm	1061	2/5	2/12
1/2	Prints	Fused	Hi-Style	Z	546	2/6	2/17
1/2	Prints	Fused	Hi-Style	Z	437	2/10	2/13
1/10	Prints	Fused	Hi-Style	Z	247	2/14	2/24
1/8	Prints	Fused	Prince-Wear	Z	1314	2/10	2/19
1/14	Prints	Fused	Prince-Wear	Z	815	2/12	2/19
1/10	Prints	Fused	Hi-Style	V	306	2/17	2/19
1/13	Prints	Lined	P.J.S.	F	771	2/13	2/19
1/6	White Broadcloth	Fused	Export	Z	557	2/14	2/26
1/14	End on End	Fused	Chain Store	Z	1763	2/7	2/17

could be considered reasonably typical of the volume and type of orders sent to, and of the operating conditions existing within, the various plants. Data relating to operations for this period for Plants 1 through 5, respectively, are shown as Exhibits 4 through 8.

EXHIBIT 6   U.S. Shirt Company

SUMMARY OF SEWING TICKETS

Plant #3 (Unit System)

Date Issued	Cloth	Collar	Brand	Model	Doz.	Work Started	Work Completed
1/7	Woven	Fused	Chain Store	Z	2021	1/28	2/4
1/16	Woven	Fused	Chain Store	Z	407	2/5	2/14
1/8	Solid Color	Fused	Chain Store	Z	342	1/30	2/10
1/8	White Broadcloth	Fused	Chain Store	Z	306	1/30	2/10
1/14	Print	Fused	Chain Store	Z	2026	1/30	2/11
1/10	Print	Fused	Chain Store	Z	546	1/30	2/6
1/10	Print	Fused	Chain Store	Z	1354	2/4	2/11
1/9	Print	Fused	Prince-Wear	Z	675	2/5	2/18
1/10	Print	Fused	Prince-Wear	Z	558	2/5	2/14
1/14	Print	Fused	Prince-Wear	Z	540	2/6	2/13
1/13	Print	Fused	Prince-Wear	Z	1081	2/11	2/17
1/14	Print	Fused	Chain Store	Z	847	2/11	2/20
1/8	White Broadcloth	Fused	Chain Store	Z	1631	2/3	2/14

EXHIBIT 7   U.S. SHIRT COMPANY

SUMMARY OF SEWING TICKETS

Plant #4 (Progressive Bundle System)

Date Issued	Cloth	Collar	Brand	Model	Doz.	Work Started	Work Completed
1/3	Woven Madras	Fused	Chain Store	Z	205	2/7	*
1/13	Prints	Lined	P.J.S.	F	401	2/14	2/21
1/13	Prints	Fused	Chain Store	Z	690	2/14	*
1/3	Solid Colors	Fused	Chain Store	Z	357	2/21	2/28
1/14	Woven Madras	Soft Calif.	Prince-Wear	V Cal	461	2/21	2/28
1/17	Prints	Lined	P.J.S.	F	479	2/28	3/7
1/29	Skip Dent White	Fused	Chain Store	Z	499	2/28	3/7
1/20	Preshrunk Chambray	Soft	Prince-Wear	V Cal	213	3/7	*
2/6	Preshrunk Prints	Fused	Hi-Style	Boys' Z	354	3/14	3/21

* Information not available.

Exhibit 9 shows a summary of the average number of employees in each of the plants, the plants' stated output capacity, their weekly output in hundreds of dozens of shirts, their weekly production in dozens of shirts per man hour, and the "index of loss on minimum" (ILM), during the operating period chosen for the survey. The ILM provided a measure of the extent to which workers' piece-rate earnings failed to equal their guaranteed minimum earnings. The index

EXHIBIT 8   U.S. SHIRT COMPANY

SUMMARY OF SEWING TICKETS

Plant #5 (Unit System)

Date Issued	Cloth	Collar	Brand	Model	Doz.	Work Started	Work Completed
1/2	Preshrunk	Del Monte Bi Angle Stay	Hi-Style	Del Monte	677	2/3	2/12
1/16	White Broadcloth	H.S. Fused	Chain Store	Everfirm	1081	2/10	2/21
1/15	White Broadcloth	H.S. Fused	Chain Store	N-1	150	2/20	3/3
1/16	White Oxford	Soft Flat	Chain Store	N-S	1042	2/24	3/7
1/7	White Oxford	Del Monte Bi Angle Stay	Hi-Style	Del Monte	192	2/24	3/12
1/31	White Broadcloth	Prep	Hi-Style	Prep	50	3/11	3/14

EXHIBIT 9   U.S.

OPERATING

Plants

	Average No. Operators	Stated Capacity	Week of January						
			3	10	17	24	31	7	
PLANT #1	145	1800 Doz.							
Output in hundreds of dozens			13	15	17	18	18	17	
Output in dozens per man hour			.313	.283	.324	.324	.314	.300	
Index of loss on minimum									3.4
PLANT #2	440	5000 Doz.							
Output in hundreds of dozens			41	52.5	51	50	48	50	
Output in dozens per man hour			.327	.337	.321	.330	.312	.334	
Index of loss on minimum									3.8
PLANT #3	550	6500 Doz.							
Output in hundreds of dozens			50	53	59	64	61	65	
Output in dozens per man hour			.321	.313	.316	.325	.316	.341	
Index of loss on minimum									2.7
PLANT #4	120	1300 Doz.							
Output in hundreds of dozens			8.5	11	12	10	11	10.5	
Output in dozens per man hour			.280	.296	.317	.277	.293	.271	
Index of loss on minimum									5.6
PLANT #5	120	1200 Doz.							
Output in hundreds of dozens			9	11.6	12	11	11	11	
Output in dozens per man hour			.250	.260	.268	.256	.264	.256	
Index of loss on minimum									5.6

NOTE:

"Index of loss on minimum" figures are given as percentages. The index of loss figure 3.4 actually is 3.4%; 3.7 is 3.7%; 2.7 is 2.7%; and so on. An explanation of the calculation of these index figures is given below.

was computed by dividing piece-rate earnings expressed in dollars into the sum of money that had to be paid to operators whose piece-rate earnings were less than their base-rate to bring their take-home pay up to the guaranteed minimum. For example, an operator whose base rate was $1.30 per hour and whose piece-rate earnings for 168 hours of work during a month amounted to only $212.14, would receive an extra $6.26 (168 hours x $1.30 = $218.40; $218.40 — $212.14 = $6.26) to bring her earnings up to the guaranteed minimum. The resulting index of loss would be 2.9 per cent ($6.26 ÷ $212.14).

SHIRT COMPANY

STATISTICS

1–5

	Week of February			Week of March				
	14	21	28	7	14	21	28	Average for Period
	18	16	16	15	17	16	16	16.31
	.307	.295	.286	.284	.286	.286		.300
	3.7	2.7	1.1	1.8	2.9	2.2		2.54
	47	50.5	50	44.5	46	43.5	42.5	47.42
	.332	.341	.370	.319	.326	.313		.330
	2.5	2.7	2.7	2.9	3.2	3.3		3.01
	68	67	48	57	63	59	65	59.92
	.349	.348	.289	.324	.352	.328		.327
	2.2	2.3	3.1	2.6	1.9	2.5		2.47
	11	8.6	10	9	11	12	12	10.51
	.291	.276	.279	.296	.299	.313		.291
	4.7	6.5	4.6	3.5	2.2	2.1		4.17
	10	10	11	11	10	10	10	10.58
	.232	.253	.247	.248	.227	.224		.249
	6.3	6.7	8.1	6.2	7.1	5.7		6.53

Supplement A. U.S. Shirt Company

DRESS SHIRT MANUFACTURING PROCESS STAGES

The manufacture of men's dress shirts is comprised of three main processes: cutting, sewing, and pressing.

Raw Materials

On the average, the manufacture of a man's dress shirt consumes about 2½ square yards of fabric, a portion of which actually will be lost as scrap, that is, tiny pieces that cannot be used. The cloth employed usually is purchased in 36-inch wide rolls. A typical shirting material—cotton broadcloth—36 inches wide and of suitable quality for U.S. Shirt's popular price "Prince-Wear" line currently sold for about 36 cents a yard in commercial quantities. Cloth could be obtained from any of a number of domestic or foreign sources. Procurement leadtime, from order to receipt of goods, ran anywhere from 60 to 180 days. Although both higher- and lower-priced fabrics were employed in the "Style-Master" and "Hi-Style" lines, respectively, officials believed the $.36 per yard figure was a representative companywide average.

Cutting

In the cutting process, the parts (Figure 1) that make up a shirt are cut from the piece goods. As many as 240 layers of cloth are spread on a table 90 to 180 feet long. A sheet of paper with the part patterns drawn on it is placed on top of the cloth and becomes the guide for the cutter who runs some form of cutting tool—often a power-driven knife—over the tracings on the paper to cut the parts. Small parts sometimes are cut with dies on power presses. An alternative process is "short-knife cutting," in which the cutters use hand knives instead of power knives for cutting. After the parts are numbered and tied into bundles, they are delivered to the sewing room (or, in the case of the U.S. Shirt Company, to a separate sewing plant) for stitching.

Sewing

In the sewing process the shirt parts are stitched together. In U.S. Shirt plants the sewing had been broken down into very short stitching operations, each worker performing and becoming very adept at only one operation.

The various operations in sewing a shirt are as follows:

Collar Making

1. Two plies of cloth and a lining are seamed together with the inside out. (.05537)[1]
2. The collar points are trimmed to remove excess material. (.01242)
3. The collar is turned right side out. (.01882)

---

[1] Figures in parenthesis are hours typically required by an "average" U.S. Shirt Company operator to perform the operations on one dozen shirts.

U.S. Shirt Company

Figure 1

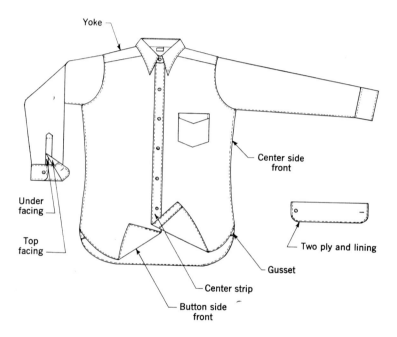

4. The finished collars are sent for special chemical processing. (Required on "fused" collars only.)

Banding

1. The bottom band ply, the collar, the top band ply, and the lining are sewed together. (.08648)
2. The band is turned right side out and stitched on the outside. (.01957 and .02285)
3. Notching—the band is marked to guide the operator in setting the collar and band on to the yoke. (.02025)

4. The buttonhole is made on a semiautomatic machine.[2]   (.01280)

5. The button is sewed to the band.[3]   (.01153)

Cuff Making

1. The first ply of material and the lining are folded and sewed. (.03555)

2. The second ply is seamed to the first ply.   (.04077)

3. The cuff is turned right side out.   (.03878)

4. The buttonhole is made on a semiautomatic machine.   (.02246)

5. The button is sewed on a semiautomatic machine.   (.02133)

Pocket Making

1. The top of the pocket piece is folded and stitched down.   (Two operations—.01348 and .02462)

2. The pocket is folded on all other sides on a semiautomatic folding machine.   (.01348)

Backs

1. The back is hemmed and two triangular bits of cloth called gussets are sewed on the sides of the shirt tail to give extra fullness. (.03657)

2. The label is sewed on the inside of the yoke.   (.03657)

3. The inside and outside yokes are sewed to the backs.   (.03657 for each yoke)

Center Side (One front half)

1. The center side is hemmed.   (.03855)

2. The center strips (one ply of fabric and the lining) are sewed to the center side—Runned.   (.03855)

3. The buttonholes are made on a semiautomatic machine.   (.07710)

4. The pocket is set on the center side and is stitched in place. (.07710)

Button Side (The other front half)

1. The button side is hemmed.   (.02509)

2. The lining is sewed to the button side—Runned.   (.02509)

3. The buttons are sewed on using a semiautomatic machine.   (.05020)

---

[2] The operator feeds the work; the machine automatically cuts and sews the buttonhole.

[3] The operator feeds the button and work; the machine automatically sews the button to the band, taking the proper number of stitches.

Sleeve Making

1. The sleeves are pieced. About 50 per cent of the sleeves are cut in two pieces so that maximum economy in cloth utilization is attained. The two separate pieces are sewed together (pieced) and then treated as any other sleeve. (.05333)
2. The sleeve is underfaced—a narrow piece of cloth lining is sewed to the button side of the sleeve opening. (.05333)
3. The sleeve is topfaced—a wider piece of cloth and a lining strip (facing) is sewed to the buttonhole side of the sleeve opening. (.05333)
4. The sleeve is blocked—the sleeve is stitched where the underfacing and the topfacing meet. (.05333)

Joining

1. A completed back, a button side, a center side, and the yoke are stitched together. (.07529)

Collar Setting

1. The collar band with the collar attached is sewed to the front and yokes. (.10000)

Collar Closing

1. The band is closed by stitching along the front and yokes. (.10000)

Sleeve Setting

1. The right sleeve and the left sleeve are attached to the body of the shirt by stitching around the shoulder and armpit. (.10322)

Felling

1. The shirt is closed by stitching up the inside of each sleeve to the armpit and then stitching down each side, thereby closing each front to the back of the shirt. (.10322)

Cuff Setting

1. The finished cuffs are stitched to the sleeves. (.10000)

Cuff Closing

1. The cuffs that were set on the sleeves in the preceding operation are closed and pleated if called for. (.10000)

Trimming and Inspecting

1. All loose threads are trimmed from the shirt. The shirt is examined for misweaves, faulty stitching, etc. (.09411) and (.04706)

All U.S. Shirt sewing operations are performed on single-needle, lockstitch machines except sleeve setting and felling. These operations are performed on double-needle, chainstitch machines which give extra strength to the garment.

Pressing

After the shirts are sewed and inspected, they are pressed and boxed for shipment. Three types of pressing are commonly used in the shirt industry: hand pressing, conveyor pressing, and buck pressing. In hand pressing, one operator presses a shirt completely, using a hand iron. In conveyor pressing, the operation is broken down into five steps so that each operator performs only one part of the pressing operation as the shirt passes from one operator to another on a timed conveyor belt. In buck pressing, a large machine, similar to a tailor's steam press, is used to press the entire body of the shirt in one operation. In both conveyor and buck pressing, shirt collars are pressed on a machine that is similar to a tailor's press, but smaller in size.

Labor Costs

Wages paid to U.S. Shirt Company operators varied from plant to plant. Currently, however, the companywide average base rate for sewing-machine operators was $1.35 per hour, with take home pay on piece rates averaging $1.58.

A rule of thumb frequently employed in the industry was that direct labor operations—that is, cutting, sewing, and pressing—usually accounted for about seven-eighths of the labor cost of a shirt, the remaining one-eighth being composed of indirect labor such as janitorial service, materials handling, and so on. Sewing was by far the largest element of direct labor, usually about 75 per cent of the total.

Effect of Manufacturing Quality Upon Price

As a rough approximation, it can be assumed that any shirt that has to be sold as a "second" because of some unrepairable defect incurred in its manufacture will probably bring only about 50 per cent of the price obtained from a first-quality shirt of the same type. If the defect is a major one, it may make the shirt unsalable, even at a reduced price.

Fixed Assets

It is common for many shirt manufacturers, particularly small and medium-sized firms, to rely heavily on leased or rented manufacturing equipment and facilities, thus reducing the capital investment required. It is not unusual for the depreciated investment in the fixed assets owned by a small shirt manufacturer to be equivalent to as little as 1 per cent of the firm's annual sales volume.

Sunshine Builders, Inc.

In the five years since its founding, Sunshine Builders, Inc., had become one of Florida's largest builders of residential housing. In the opinion of the company's management, major credit for this success was attributable to customer-oriented service and guarantee policies which, in combination with good construction, reasonable prices, and on-time completions, had earned the firm an excellent reputation.

The founders of the company, Charles and Arthur Root, came to Florida six years earlier at the ages of 28 and 26, respectively, having spent the preceding five years as owners of a retail furniture business in Chicago. Charles Root had majored in economics at college and Arthur Root in chemical engineering. Although their furniture business had been moderately successful, both brothers eventually had concluded that the potential margin of profit was becoming increasingly narrow and that the personal time and effort required was disproportionate to the return attainable. They therefore had decided to sell their furniture store and move to Florida, a state which they believed offered rapid growth and attractive business opportunities.

The Root brothers spent their first several months in Florida becoming familiar with a metropolitan area with a population of nearly 500,000 within a ten-mile radius. During this period, realizing that land was appreciating in value, the Roots purchased eight lots for speculation. Shortly thereafter, with the encouragement of their father, who had some experience in building, they decided to erect houses on the lots, subcontracting the construction work to local contractors.

Within a few weeks after completion, all eight houses had been sold at a profit. Since this initial housing venture proved successful, population growth and industrial activity in the area were accelerating, and land was relatively inexpensive, the Root brothers became convinced that the home construction business in Florida offered excellent prospects. They therefore founded Sunshine Builders, Inc. Five years later, commenting on the company's early days of operations, Arthur Root stated, "We realized at the outset—just as we realize today—that five principles represent the key to success for our firm:

1. Sunshine houses must be completely liveable.
2. They must have 'eye-appeal.'
3. As builders we must have a reputation for honesty, skill, and 'on-time' completions.
4. We must offer exceptional value.
5. Our houses must be properly promoted.

Below-par performance in regard to any one of these areas would hurt us badly. Our task is to do a top-flight job in all five."

OPERATIONS DURING THE FIRST FOUR YEARS

The first major move of the newly formed company was to erect a model home which displayed the type of building it was prepared to construct on customers' lots. Orders were quickly received for 40 units which Sunshine arranged to have constructed by local building contractors. Under terms of the purchase agreement with the company, a customer made an initial downpayment of 15 per cent of the purchase price and then made regular progress payments as the construction proceeded toward completion. With these arrangements the Roots were required to invest relatively little of their own capital. During the next two years, they were hard pressed to build enough houses to meet the sales demand.

During this period Charles Root found that his greatest business interest lay in land development. He therefore formed a separate firm, Root Land Development Corporation, for this purpose, while Arthur, as President of Sunshine Builders, concentrated on home construction.[1] Each brother devoted nearly all of his time to his own field of operations, assisting the other only as requested, or when major policy issues had to be decided. Later, a third corporation, Root Associates, was established to handle sales for Sunshine Builders, with Arthur serving as President. Cooperative selling arrangements also were established with local real estate firms.

---

[1] Their father took no active part in the management of either firm.

The activities of all three organizations expanded steadily during the next four years. During this period management operations at all three firms, although hectic and requiring consistently long hours on the part of both brothers, had been simple in concept. With few exceptions the land on which Sunshine Builders constructed homes was already owned by the customer as a result of purchase from either the Root Land Development Corporation, or some other source. All construction work was performed by various local subcontractors who, by mutual consent, concentrated most of their efforts on work for Sunshine Builders.

During the early period of operations, Arthur Root was assisted in the construction phase of the operations by Herbert Playford. Mr. Playford, who was in his mid-twenties, had known the Root brothers in Chicago and had moved to Florida at their request only a few months after Sunshine Builders was founded. Mr. Playford had a high school education and prior to joining Sunshine had worked successively as a shipping clerk, a neon glass blower, and in his father's junk business. On arrival in Florida, Mr. Playford was taken by Arthur Root to see 13 home sites which were then in various stages of construction. He then was given immediate responsibility for their completion with the instruction, "Build them." In carrying out this assignment Mr. Playford acted as superintendent, working with and through the various contractors in scheduling, coordinating, and supervising the various construction activities.

As the business grew, four additional superintendents were hired at salaries that were equal to, or slightly above, the earnings that a top construction tradesman could expect in the local area. After about a year Mr. Playford was "moved into the office" to serve as expediter and coordinator of the four superintendents, and also given responsibility for the mounting volume of paper work associated with the firm's construction activities. One of his contributions in this new capacity had been to set up the systems of scheduling and cost control to be described subsequently.

Mr. Playford's handling of many of the daily "home-office" details relating to construction left Arthur Root free to concentrate more time on sales work, purchasing, and managing the company's finances. A few months later, a younger brother, Daniel Root, 25, who had been pursuing graduate studies in history, also was taken into the firm to assist Arthur.

After spending about two years with the company, Mr. Playford resigned to establish his own construction firm, Meadowlark Builders. He was aided in this move by a substantial investment which the

Root brothers made in the new concern. Meadowlark was successful from the start, building approximately 200 low-cost homes during the next 24 months. At the close of this period, however, Arthur Root persuaded Mr. Playford to return to Sunshine as Treasurer, Assistant Secretary, and Manager of Production and Service, and the Meadowlark operation was discontinued.

By now, Daniel Root, who had become Vice President and Secretary of Sunshine Builders, had assumed full responsibility for sales, broker relations, customer relations, advertising, and the developing and merchandising of new models. Arthur Root, as Sunshine's President, handled all financing and purchasing. Charles Root continued to devote his time principally to the Root Land Development Corporation.

Sunshine's construction work, under Mr. Playford, now required eight subcontractors, who were responsible for the following functions:

Plumbing	Plastering
Electrical work	Carpentry
Painting	Heating
Masonry	Cleaning

Each subcontractor submitted a weekly bill to Sunshine for the wages he had paid to his crews, plus an 8 per cent override for use of equipment. Except for the masonry crew, the subcontractors' employees were not unionized, but the wages received approximated the general community average for the craft in question. The subcontractor's own time was also charged to Sunshine at an hourly rate approximately 15 per cent above that earned by the highest paid man in the crew. Material was purchased and supplied by the subcontractor at cost. Each one hired and fired as he felt necessary, but Sunshine Builders had the right to approve any wage increases. Arthur Root and Herbert Playford made it a practice to question the subcontractors on jobs on which their costs appeared out of line with previous experience. To furnish this information, total costs of each subcontractor were tabulated for each job.

The subcontractors each employed an appropriate number of crews, whose activities were scheduled by the four Sunshine superintendents. Each superintendent was responsible for all Sunshine Builders' homes under construction in the geographic territory assigned to him— roughly one-fourth of the seven-mile radial area which embraced the bulk of Sunshine's activity.

By the latter part of Sunshine's fourth year of operation Arthur Root had become increasingly concerned about the effectiveness of this arrangement. In discussions with his brothers and Mr. Playford, he advanced the following observations and criticisms of existing practices:

1. The four superintendents spent most of their time competing against each other for subcontractors' crews to work on the houses in their respective territories. It could be argued, in fact, that the superintendents functioned merely as "high-grade expediters," and made little or no effort to coordinate company-wide crew requirements.
2. Seven[2] of the subcontractors were netting $11,000 to $12,000 per year from their association with Sunshine. Actually, however, they were acting more in the capacity of foremen than of independent contractors. Foremen could be hired at a far lower cost.
3. The subcontractors were not buying new labor-saving equipment but tended instead to "run old equipment into the ground."

Arthur Root's net conclusions were that it should be possible to centralize controls and scheduling, and thus eliminate conflicts, delays, and the need for superintendents. After considerable discussion of these matters, a unanimous management decision was reached the previous November to absorb the subcontractors' organizations into the Sunshine firm by employing the previous subcontractors as Sunshine foremen, and placing their labor crews on the Sunshine payroll.

During the month following this decision, Arthur Root and Herbert Playford held individual meetings with the various subcontractors to explain the proposed changes. Each was offered employment as a foreman at a salary reflecting his experience and ability. The proposal also included Sunshine's offer to negotiate a fair purchase price for each subcontractor's equipment.

In spite of the fact that the salaries offered were 10 to 25 per cent below their recent annual earnings (the masonry subcontractor, for example, previously had been making about $12,000 and now was offered $9,250), each of the subcontractors accepted the Sunshine proposal. Arthur Root reasoned that this response reflected the fact that the salaries offered were actually higher than the earnings the men could reasonably expect to achieve if they ended their association with Sunshine. He suspected also that the men realized that their previous arrangement with the firm had been "a gravy train that had to stop sometime." He also believed that most of the subcontractors

---

[2] The eighth, the cleaning subcontractor, had been receiving approximately $5,000 per year.

actually were glad to be relieved of the paper work entailed in the payroll and other responsibilities required of them as independent contractors. Under the new arrangements the former subcontractors, in their new capacity as salaried foremen, were to continue to hire and fire crews, as necessary. The foremen also were promised possible year-end bonuses, dependent on Sunshine's annual profit.

On January 1, having reached agreement with all of the former subcontractors, Sunshine management shifted to the new method of operation and dismissed the four superintendents.[3] An additional eight construction workers, who had been in the employ of certain of the former subcontractors but engaged on other projects, were hired, thus bringing Sunshine's new construction crew to 124 men.

OPERATIONS DURING THE CURRENT YEAR

Initial Reactions to the New Organization

After the organizational change was completed, the Sunshine payroll numbered 161 persons (Exhibit 1). The distribution of employees among the various functions is indicated by the number shown in parentheses after each descriptive title. With the exception of the cleaning crew, which employed only unskilled general labor, the employees of each construction crew were divided fairly equally between skilled tradesmen and helpers.

Both Arthur Root and Herbert Playford felt enthusiastic about results achieved during the first few months under the new organization. They said that there now seemed to be "a closer, more direct line of communication between the office and the crews." Mr. Playford remarked that fewer mistakes were being made, and Mr. Root believed that the foremen appeared to be taking a broader point of view, demonstrated, for example, by their now keeping the office better informed regarding the progress of each job.

Planning and Control Techniques

The basic approaches to planning and controlling production were essentially those that Mr. Playford had established during the initial year of operation. The dispatching office had "production boards" mounted on two of its walls. These provided the nucleus of production information. While no formal scheduling was attempted, the

---

[3] Three of the former superintendents subsequently took positions as tradesmen on the various Sunshine crews.

EXHIBIT 1   SUNSHINE BUILDERS, INC.

ORGANIZATION AS OF MAY 1, CURRENT YEAR

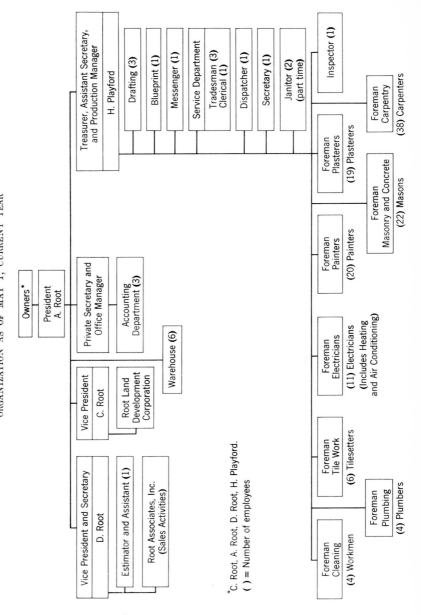

*C. Root, A. Root, D. Root, H. Playford.

( ) = Number of employees

"boards" aided the dispatcher in keeping up-to-date regarding the status of each job. The boards themselves consisted of wall-board material on which was tacked blueprint paper divided into two-inch grids. Across the top, along the horizontal scale, were headings for the owner's name, the address where the house was to be built, the model number of the house, and the 65 individual steps, operations, or phases of the construction work required. These are described in Exhibit 2. The houses were then listed vertically, with new homes being added at the bottom as orders were received, as shown below:

JOBS			CONSTRUCTION STEPS							
		M O D E L	1 SIGN CLEAR LOT	2	3	4	5	6	7	. . .
OWNER	LOCATION		DELIVER	POWER	STAKE	DIG	POUR	ORDER		. . .
E. K. Williams	14 Coral St.	69								
D. W. Onan	262 Beach Rd.	14								
A. T. Bovril	60 Hacienda	190L								

The company's dispatcher, Mabel Roark, age 35, was responsible for issuing work assignments to the foremen and for keeping the wall charts posted with current information. Although each of the foremen knew, of course, the specific operations, material, and equipment required for each of the construction steps his crews had to perform, they all relied on Miss Roark to instruct them regarding the exact house, and the step, or steps, that should be undertaken next. After relaying these instructions to the foreman, Miss Roark would make note of this assignment by initialing the appropriate box on the wall chart, and writing in the date by which the foreman had promised completion of the work. Later, when the foreman reported that the particular steps had, in fact, been completed, Miss Roark would record this fact by adding the notation "O.K." to the box.

Miss Roark also employed the following colored-pin code system to call attention to a particular box on the wall chart:

Pin Color	Status Indicated
Black	"On order."
Red	"Did not arrive, or get completed, as promised."
White	"Crew is there, on the job."
Yellow	"Need to call foreman."
Blue	"Have a question for the foreman when he calls."

Since a considerable proportion of the purchasers of Sunshine homes were new residents in the community, with many moving details to schedule, Arthur Root and his associates were convinced that any delays in house completions would be the source of extreme personal inconvenience and thus significantly jeopardize customer relations. He and Mr. Playford were convinced that the wall chart helped identify potential delayed completions while there was still time to remedy the situation.

Since the most recently contracted houses were added at the bottom of the chart, and the construction steps were listed in sequence from left to right, the completed steps indicated by the boxes containing Miss Roark's "O.K." formed a slightly irregular diagonal line on the chart, slanting downwards from right to left. Thus, any house on which construction had fallen behind schedule showed up as an "indent" to the left of the diagonal line of the "O.K." boxes. A quick visual check of the chart promptly identified "trouble-spots." Mr. Playford took pride in the fact that during the past 12 months Sunshine had completed the typical house in roughly 80 to 85 calendar days, a figure well under the 100 calendar days specified in the Sunshine construction contracts with purchasers.

In addition to assigning the work to the foremen and maintaining the production boards, Miss Roark served as a communication and recording center for all reports and instructions. She employed the company's two-way radio system under which each foreman, Mr. Playford, and the warehouse supervisor had a two-way unit in his car or truck. The system had been installed the previous year on a lease basis calling for a monthly rental of $375.

Miss Roark usually talked with each foreman by radio at least three times each day. In a typical conversation the masonry foreman might call in and tell her that the footings his crew had been constructing at the Kelly house were now completed, but that the iron work for the Kent job had not arrived and that Mr. and Mrs. Kent had visited the construction site that morning and asked for a change in the dimensions of their back patio from 12 x 15 feet to 12 x 20 feet. He might ask where Miss Roark wanted his crew to work the next day and also request her to check whether the Larsen house was to have a front planter and whether the plumbers had finished work at the O'Leary house thus permitting the masonry crews to lay the slab.

During a typical day's operation, Miss Roark independently made innumerable decisions regarding operations and jobs to be done next, receiving little or no aid from Mr. Playford, whose office was next door. Mr. Playford checked the wall charts once or twice a week, but usually did not participate in the hour by hour job of scheduling the crews.

To prevent delays and idle crews, Miss Roark had to have a clear understanding of the various construction operations required and the relationship among them. It was essential, for example, for her to know that the electricians could not "rough-in" until the studs were up, that the heating work could be done while the carpenters were trimming, that the electricians and plumbers had to work either ahead of, or behind, the painters on certain operations, but could work simultaneously with them on other jobs, and so forth. Miss Roark said, "I still make some mistakes, but I've learned a lot about house building during this past year."

In scheduling the crews, Miss Roark employed the "time and crew requirements guides" shown in Exhibit 2. These had been prepared by Mr. Playford and Miss Roark out of their combined experience regarding how many men were required, and how much time was necessary, for the completion of each construction step. They had learned, for example, that it was reasonable to expect a crew of four carpenters, working at an ordinary pace, to "frame-up" an average house (Exhibit 2, Step #20) in five days.

Purchasing and Warehousing

Miss Roark's purchasing function was confined to ordering specific items from vendors previously selected by Arthur Root. Arthur Root handled all major negotiations with suppliers, including questions of prices, delivery, and payment terms. This work occupied a significant portion of his time. He regularly "shopped" for better values in windows, fixtures, lumber, appliances, and similar items, and had effected considerable standardization of purchased items.

Late in the previous year Sunshine had leased a 6,000 square-foot warehouse, thus making it possible to stock required items and to realize discounts on quantity purchases. In advocating this move, Arthur Root had predicted that once Sunshine was in a position to accept deliveries in quantities equivalent to about four months' requirements it would be possible—on an over-all basis—to realize annual savings of perhaps 4 per cent on items representing roughly 75 per cent of Sunshine's dollar purchase requirements. The statistics of the leading trade journals showed that, on a national basis, construction material costs had been rising at an average rate of about 2 per cent annually

EXHIBIT 2 SUNSHINE BUILDERS, INC.

STEPS OF THE CONSTRUCTION JOB AS USED ON THE COMPANY'S PRODUCTION

Step Number	Operation Required	Explanation	Crew
1	Sign posted, lot cleared		Masonry
2	Deliver stakes, material and steel		Warehouse
3	Power pole and water meter in	Done by utilities	Power Co.
4	Stake out		Masonry
5	Dig footing	Footings only 12″–18″ below the surface	
6	Pour footing		Masonry
7	Order sliding glass doors		(Mabel)
8	Lay foundation	Set reinforcing steel and pour concrete	Masonry
9	Fill foundation	Fill and pack dirt within foundation for slab	Subcontracted
10	Tie-in foundation	Plumbing for water and sewer connections	Plumbing
11	Plumbing rough-in	Set plumbing for slab	Plumbing
12	Grade slab		Masonry
13	Pour slab		Masonry
14	Strip for terrazzo	Place strips for sills or sliding doors	Subcontracted
15	Pour terrazzo		Subcontracted
16	Deliver blocks, steel, sills		Vendor and Warehouse
17	Lay block walls		Masonry
18	Form and pour lintels		Masonry
19	First grind, terrazzo		Subcontracted
20	Carpenter's frame	Frame up interior wall studs and roof	Carpenters
21	Order cabinets		(Mabel)
22	Dry-in	First layer of lumber on the roof	Carpenters
23	Flue and/or duct work		Masonry
24	Set tub		Subcontracted
25	Electrical rough-in	Place most of electrical wiring	Electricians
26	Prime cornice	Paint under overhang of roof	Painters
27	Order lath		(Mabel)
28	Lath		Plaster
29	Order vanity		(Mabel)
30	Ceiling heat	Electrical radiant heating usually used	Electricians
31	Roof complete	Pitch and gravel built up roof	Subcontracted
32	Scratch for tile	Preparation for tiling	Plaster
33	Brown coat plaster and stucco	First coat	Plaster
34	Second grind, terrazzo		Subcontracted
35	Iron work	Any decorative iron work	Carpenters
36	Tile walls	Bathrooms and sometimes kitchen areas	Tile
37	Plaster and stucco complete		Plaster
38	Glaze	Install window glass	Subcontracted
39	Install sliding glass doors		Subcontracted
40	Insulation		Subcontracted
41	Clean and rough grade lot	Remove debris and grade	Subcontracted
42	Front stoop		Masonry
43	Form outside concrete		Masonry
44	Pour outside concrete		Masonry
45	Outside gravel or asphalt		Subcontracted
46	Order trim material	Moldings, door frames, etc.	(Mabel)
47	Carpenter's trim		Carpenters
48	Glaze jalousie doors		Subcontracted
49	Install cabinets		Subcontracted
50	Septic tank		Plumbers
51	Plumber's trim	Final plumbing work	Plumbers
52	Heating	Install and (or) complete heating system	Electricians
53	Paint		Painters
54	Install operators and deliver screens	Window mechanisms	Carpenters
55	Electrical trim	Install lamps, outlet plates, etc.	Electricians
56	Polish terrazzo		Subcontracted
57	Clean windows and interior		Cleaning
58	Grass		Subcontracted
59	Install screens		Carpenters
60	Painters complete, inspect		Painters
61	Wallpaper and mirror		Painters
62	Plumbing inspection	By city inspector	
63	Electrical inspection	By city inspector	
64	Permanent electrical connection	By power company	Power Company
65	Production inspection		Co. Inspector

* SC (subcontracted). At the present time the average house required approximately $2,500 of subcontracted work.

BOARDS   MANPOWER AND TIME ESTIMATES FOR DISPATCHER

Norm. Crew No. Men	Man-days of Work	Elapsed Time Allowed (days)	Remarks
1	1	1	In typical subdivision lot already cleared
—	—	—	
{3	{3	{2	{Includes a day for checking by foreman
2	1	½	
—	—	—	
2	1	½	
SC*		1	
2	{5	—	Done during No. 11
3		2½	Includes a day for city inspection
2	2	2	Includes a day for city inspection
3	1½	1½	Includes a day after pouring for slab to set
SC	—	1	
SC	—	1½	Includes a day for terrazzo to set
—	—	—	
5	10	2	
2	1	½	Must be inspected
SC	—	2	
4	20	5	
4	1	—	
2	4	2	Included in time allowance for #20
SC	—	½	Done during framing
2	4	2	Done during framing
2	1	½	Done during framing (after studs in)
—	—	1	
4	4	1	One day necessary for framing and elec. inspection
—	—		
2	2	{2	
SC	—		
2	3		
4	4	2	
SC	—	½	Includes a day for drying
2	1	½	
4	6	1½	
4	4	1	
SC	—	1	Need two-day notice
SC	—	1	
SC	—	1	Does not interfere with any other work
SC	—	1	
2	1	½	Usually done while framing
2	2	1	
2	2	1	Need good weather
SC	—	2	
—	—	—	
5	20	4	
SC	—	½	
SC	—	1	
2	2	1	Done by vendor during trim operation
2	2	1	
3	6	2	Done while carpenters are trimming
4	16	4	Must be alone in house
1	½	½	Now done before glazing
3	3	1	
SC	—	2	Must be alone in house
2	2	1	
SC	—	1	
1	½	½	
5	15	3	
2	2	1	Includes final inspection and adjustments
—	—	1	City inspection
—	—	1	City inspection
—	—	1	
1	1	1	Note also inspection at step No. 60

over the past four years.[4] This fact seemed to Mr. Root to give added significance to the purchase economies the warehouse would permit. He and his associates became convinced that Sunshine could benefit also from being able to control delivery of materials to individual housing sites.

Administrative procedures developed after the start of warehouse operations required the various foremen to submit orders direct to the warehouse for all items required by their crews, with the exception of staking-out material which Miss Roark ordered. The warehouse truck would deliver the items to the appropriate building site. If the work being done by the crew involved a standard operation, the quantity of each of the materials delivered was predetermined on a basis of 110 per cent of estimated actual need. If the work being done was nonstandard in response to a customer request, the material delivered was 110 per cent of the amount that the Sunshine estimator had included in costing the work involved. In Mr. Playford's judgment, this oversupply actually was economical in the long run, for it avoided the loss of labor time otherwise spent by construction crews in "picking and hunting" for materials. Excess material left after the completion of a job was returned to the warehouse and restored to the inventory.

Operation of the warehouse (receiving, storing, and delivery) required six employees. One of these, however, was a truck driver who had been required previously. The net increase in the Sunshine workforce created by the warehouse actually was only five persons.

Pricing

Sunshine houses were priced by estimating "construction costs"[5] and adding 5 per cent for "expenses" and 15 per cent for selling costs and profit. The estimating was performed by Daniel Root's assistant, an employee who had some architectural training and who spent a large portion of his time supplying customers with price quotations on construction changes they wished to make in standard plans.

Sunshine had found that the construction costs associated with a given model tended to rise slightly as improvements of a minor nature gradually were introduced into the design or specifications. Thus far

---

[4] The same sources indicated that during this period, construction labor costs had been increasing at an annual average rate of roughly 4 per cent.

[5] The average house constructed by Sunshine included approximately $2,500 of subcontracting.

EXHIBIT 3   SUNSHINE BUILDERS, INC.

SALES PROMOTIONAL MATERIAL FOR A TWO-BEDROOM MODEL

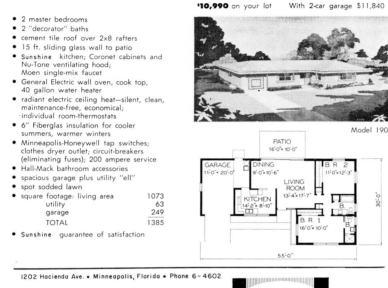

'10,990 on your lot   With 2-car garage $11,840

- 2 master bedrooms
- 2 "decorator" baths
- cement tile roof over 2x8 rafters
- 15 ft. sliding glass wall to patio
- Sunshine kitchen; Coronet cabinets and Nu-Tone ventilating hood; Moen single-mix faucet
- General Electric wall oven, cook top, 40 gallon water heater
- radiant electric ceiling heat—silent, clean, maintenance-free, economical; ·individual room-thermostats
- 6" Fiberglas insulation for cooler summers, warmer winters
- Minneapolis-Honeywell tap switches; clothes dryer outlet; circuit-breakers (eliminating fuses); 200 ampere service
- Hall-Mack bathroom accessories
- spacious garage plus utility "ell"
- spot sodded lawn
- square footage: living area   1073
  - utility   63
  - garage   249
  - TOTAL   1385
- Sunshine guarantee of satisfaction

Model 190

1202 Hacienda Ave. • Minneapolis, Florida • Phone 6–4602

it's a ⟨SUNSHINE⟩ **home**

Model Home on Poinsettia Rd. — 2 Miles South of Key Drive

in its history, however, Sunshine never had increased the price originally quoted for a model.   In this context, Arthur Root and Herbert Playford agreed with Daniel Root that Sunshine's prices could not be increased if the firm was to remain competitive.   Brochures describing the least costly, and the most expensive, models in Sunshine's line are shown in Exhibits 3 and 4.

Customer Change Orders and Post Construction Repairs

Sunshine encouraged customers of standard model homes to make any nonstructural changes they desired.   In commenting on this practice, Mr. Daniel Root noted, "Different models are featured in each Sunshine subdivision, thus providing a considerable range of choice for the buyer.   This fact, coupled with the changes which Sunshine offers to make in its standard models at a nominal price, permits customers to acquire a home which offers considerable in-

EXHIBIT 4   Sunshine Builders, Inc.

SALES PROMOTIONAL MATERIAL FOR A THREE-BEDROOM MODEL

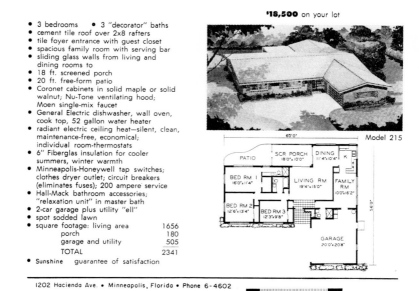

$18,500 on your lot

- 3 bedrooms   • 3 "decorator" baths
- cement tile roof over 2x8 rafters
- tile foyer entrance with guest closet
- spacious family room with serving bar
- sliding glass walls from living and dining rooms to
- 18 ft. screened porch
- 20 ft. free-form patio
- Coronet cabinets in solid maple or solid walnut; Nu-Tone ventilating hood; Moen single-mix faucet
- General Electric dishwasher, wall oven, cook top, 52 gallon water heater
- radiant electric ceiling heat—silent, clean, maintenance-free, economical; individual room-thermostats
- 6" Fiberglas insulation for cooler summers, winter warmth
- Minneapolis-Honeywell tap switches; clothes dryer outlet; circuit breakers (eliminates fuses); 200 ampere service
- Hall-Mack bathroom accessories; "relaxation unit" in master bath
- 2-car garage plus utility "ell"
- spot sodded lawn
- square footage: living area   1656
  - porch   180
  - garage and utility   505
  - TOTAL   2341
- Sunshine   guarantee of satisfaction

Model 215

1202 Hacienda Ave. • Minneapolis, Florida • Phone 6-4602

it's a SUNSHINE home

dividuality, and yet is still moderately priced." The nature and quantity of the exceptions and additions a customer might specify in a typical purchase contract are indicated by Exhibit 5.

Once the basic purchase contract was executed, Miss Roark and the foreman were given copies of the basic house plan, plus the blueprints for any construction changes specified. From these documents Miss Roark prepared a "customer detail sheet" listing the original construction requirements, plus any additional requirements arising from changes negotiated subsequent to the initial contract. Any of these postcontract changes were priced by Sunshine's estimator and summarized in a "Customer Request for Extra Work" form which was signed by the customer. The original of this document was sent to the office to be used for billing purposes, with copies going to the customer, the foreman of the work crew whose services would be required, and to Miss Roark.

Before actual construction could begin on a specific house, from two to three weeks were required to complete the 25 preliminary steps

EXHIBIT 5 SUNSHINE BUILDERS, INC.

EXCERPT FROM BUILDING AGREEMENT WITH CUSTOMER

THIRD: All details of material and construction will be identical with those used in the model home located at

    ... Lot #4, Belle Lake Subdivision ... with the following exceptions:

1. Model 190L.		$10,990
2. Place wrought iron shutters, with oak leaf design on kitchen windows, front bedroom windows, and left side bedroom window. Retain stucco decoration.		90
3. Substitute screen patio with terrazzo floor at house level, full foundation, 1 waterproof electric outlet, light fixture centered over sliding glass doors. Floor area 16' x 10'. Roof to extend 2' past floor area with screening to be canted toward floor. Roof to be aluminum with styrofoam insulation.		740
4. Install glass shower door in bath #2.		50
5. Substitute American Standard Bildor castiron tub for present steel tub.		n/c
6. Erect tile wainscot in bath #2 to 3'8'' height.		145
7. Install air-conditioning aperture centered under front windows to bedroom #1, with 220V outlet on separate circuit for same.		28
8. Install tile backsplash above base cabinets in kitchen.		50
9. Install gutter and downspout over front entrance, left side of bedroom wing, kitchen and garage.		50
10. Eliminate Walltex in baths #1 and #2.		
11. Install bookshelves between living room and dinette in lieu of present planter and wrought iron. Shelves to be placed at 42'', 54'', and 74'' height.		n/c
12. Raise 1'' x 4'' pressure treated drapery hanger above sliding glass doors in living room to ceiling height.		n/c
		$12,143

shown on the Start Chart (items 1 through 25 on Exhibit 6). Mr. Playford personally performed all of these preproduction activities.

    Considerable emphasis was placed on customer satisfaction after the house was completed. Sunshine's policy was that during the first year following completion of a house, the company's service department would repair, without charge, any item that the customer considered unsatisfactory. Within the Sunshine organization such jobs were referred to as "punch work," that is, work that was to be "punched out, without delay." The biggest single form of punch work

EXHIBIT 6   SUNSHINE BUILDERS, INC.

START CHART

CUSTOMER'S NAME:	BROKER:
ADDRESS:	LEGAL DESCRIPTION:
PHONE:	

1. Contract signed or on file ☐
2. Detail Sheet #1 received ☐
3. Plans ordered ☐
4. Survey ordered ☐
5. Detail Sheet #2 received (if there is more than 48-hr. lag between #3 and #5 report to A.R.) ☐
6. Plans returned ☐
7. Plans inspected (if there is more than a 24-hr. lag between #6 and #9 report to A.R.) ☐
8. Plans returned for correction ☐
9. Corrected plans returned ☐
10. Plans inspected for correction ☐
11. Plans sent to ☐
12. Plans received from ☐
13. Building permit applied for ☐

14. Plans and letter to customer (Air Mail Special Delivery with enclosed return envelope) ☐
15. Send loan plans ☐
16. Submit plans for subdivision approval (special messenger) ☐
17. Subdivision approval received ☐
18. Survey received ☐
19. Notify supervisor and production to check lot for clearing and for errors in lot line ☐
20. Customer's approval ☐
21. Notify accounting of loan approval and of who holds the loan ☐
22. Construction loan ☐
23. Add name to production chart ☐
24. Building permit picked up ☐
25. Water meter permit picked up ☐

involved repairs to ceiling cracks. In pricing a house, about 2 per cent of the expected retail price was included in construction cost as an estimate of punch work requirements.

Some Explanatory Remarks by Mr. Playford

In commenting about present practices in the construction phase of the business Mr. Playford made the following observations:

1. Two employees have been added to Sunshine's drafting staff since the first of the year to eliminate the subcontracting of drafting work. We find it necessary to have separate plans for every house because of the large number of construction changes requested by the typical customer.

2. Under our new organizational structure, responsibility for the different phases of construction is divided as follows:

Operation Number[6]	Supervisor or Foreman Responsible
1– 2	Mr. Playford
3	Electrical
4	Carpenter
5–10	Mason
11	Plumber
12–18	Mason
19–23	Carpenter
24	Plumber
25	Electrician
26–30	Plasterer
31	Carpenter
32–34	Plasterer
35	Carpenter
36–37	Plasterer
38–49	Carpenter
50–51	Plumber
55–55	Electrician
56–65	Inspector

3. In my judgment, low-cost construction is achieved when jobs are performed in a conventional manner. Cost savings are accomplished by making operations fast and smooth. In recent years Sunshine has reduced the time required for building the average home by two weeks. Eventually we should be able to cut this by still another week or two. I made a study at Meadowlark which showed that a home comparable to Sunshine's $15,000 models could be built in 52 calendar days if everything worked out well. The methods our men use for each step in every house—the block work, slab, framing, electrical work, plastering—are pretty much standardized. Our crews use only the most common tools and equipment, such as power saws and cement mixers.

By and large "prefabbing" does not pay unless the customer is not permitted to make any changes in the house he buys. If Sunshine adopted such a policy we would lose sales. Also, the size of our line argues against our relying on prefabbing. For instance, prefabbed roof trusses, which many construction firms use, are more expensive than "on site" construction for Sunshine because we have so many models.

A few years back I visited Classentown, New Jersey,[7] to see if I could pick up any helpful ideas on construction economies. I discovered that the Classentown people permitted customers to make no construction changes whatever. Also, by building houses block by block they were able to employ more precutting and standardizing than would be possible for Sunshine since our houses are usually not adjacent.

One way we can—and do—save time is to encourage "productivity-consciousness" on the part of our supervisors. Our masonry foreman has learned, for example, that a mason will lay blocks faster if his helper keeps

---

[6] See Exhibit 2.

[7] A major low-cost housing development which had attracted international publicity for its mass-production construction methods.

a supply piled-up ahead of him. But over-all, conventional methods of building—well executed—are our surest path to construction economy.

4. Our foremen hire and lay off workers as needed. They usually already know, or hear about, good craftsmen whom we might want to add to our workforce. Many of the men they hire are their friends, or have been recommended by friends. Crews work a five-day week, nine hours a day. The crew members tend to work in two-man teams, a journeyman and a helper. They also tend to specialize. For instance, a typical carpenter crew will consist of certain men whom the foreman always assigns to construct door-jambs and window frames, others for rafter cutting, others for cornices, others for general framing, and a saw specialist.

Our current wage structure is: helpers, $1.25 to $1.75 per hour; masons, $2.75; plumbers, $3.00; electricians, $2.25; painters, $2.40. We offer our construction crews no systematic job progression, no guarantee of security, and no benefits other than those required by law, that is, social security, and the like, which add up to about 8 per cent over hourly rates. But Sunshine has never had to make any major layoffs, and we have darn good crews.

5. Up until this January, Arthur Root used the six charts on my office wall to control costs. These charts, which I originally introduced, showed the dollar-per-square-foot cost for each phase of work for each house. They were designed to reveal any over-all trends, and also to pinpoint any house where costs were out of line. No trends ever appeared, however.

We have now discontinued use of the charts. They simply required too much work. Instead, about once a month we spot-check costs by studying several completed jobs quite closely and calculating the total cost per square foot on various operations, such as electrical, plumbing, and the like. Every three months I make a still more detailed check on a dozen houses randomly selected. Also, on a day-to-day basis, I, of course, control material costs by authorizing the amount delivered to each house. Arthur keeps check on supply sources.

If any costs begin to appear out of line, I talk to the foreman involved. For example, I recently noted that tile costs had increased around 15 to 20 per cent. Upon investigation I found a number of sources of trouble. The foreman was driving 20 miles for supplies every day; I showed him how to order in advance and to stock more in our warehouse. He had also guaranteed his crew 10 hours of pay regardless of the actual time worked. And some of his crew were driving to our warehouse to pick up material instead of getting material delivered. We corrected each of these problems.

In summary, I am confident that as long as I'm out watching, and the crews are working, and Miss Roark keeps things moving, Sunshine's costs will be O.K.

6. I suspect that we are still too lax in our attitude toward delays. I want more flow and speed, better customer relationships, lower work in process. I am getting out in the field more now that I've got things set-up better in the office here, and I am keeping my eyes open for jobs where no action is taking place. Miss Roark gets along fine with the foremen and they like her. But she is not firm enough with them, or with outsiders. She can learn to do her job even better.

7. Since our crews work a nine-hour day, this means that if on a given morning a crew starts a job that really requires only eight hours of work,

the workmen will probably actually spend the full nine-hour day on it. But this practice works in the other direction, too. Ten-hour jobs are often pushed through in nine hours to make it unnecessary for the crew to return to that particular site for only an hour's work the following morning. Our instructions to foremen are to let a crew work up to one hour of overtime if this will permit them to complete a job in a given day.

Current Volume of Operations

As of May 1st, Sunshine's production boards listed 42 houses "in process." Comparable figures for the start of operations six months, and one month, earlier had been 35 and 36 houses, respectively. The 42 units now under construction were divided among 12 different models, as follows:

Number of Units of a Model Under Construction	Number of Models
7 to 9	1
3 to 6	5
2 or less	6

None of the 12 models in Sunshine's current product line had fewer than one unit in process. The most popular model had nine.

The six-unit increase in houses-in-process over the previous month's totals reflected an influx of orders which had begun in late March and continued throughout April. In response to the increased sales, Mr. Playford gradually had increased the number of houses started into production each week from the level of three, during the first week of April, to six in the last week of April. From all indications sales prospects for the balance of the year were excellent and Mr. Playford expected to be able to continue starting five to six houses into construction each week. He said, however, that he liked to make any such change on a gradual basis in order to maintain a smooth flow of work for all crews. "The rate of starts," he said, "paces the whole operation."

Operating statements for the first four months of the current year, and for the three full preceding years are shown in Exhibit 7.

EXHIBIT 7   SUNSHINE BUILDERS, INC.

OPERATING RESULTS

(Expressed as % of Sales)

| | Current Year minus | | | 1st 4 Months |
	3	2	1	Current Yr.
Sales*	100.00%	100.00%	100.00%	100.00%
Construction Costs†	85.20	86.60	83.33	84.80
Gross Profit	14.80%	13.40%	16.67%	15.20%
Expenses				
Sales Expense	5.00	5.00	5.00	5.00
Salaries and Wages‡	3.15	3.85	5.23	5.20
Sales Promotion and Advertising	0.63	0.27	0.78	1.38
Depreciation	0.10	0.21	0.40	0.61
First-Year House Maintenance ("Punch Work")	0.13	0.45	0.38	0.37
Auto and Aircraft Expense	—	0.17	0.33	0.33
Office Expenses	0.37	0.18	0.18	0.32
Radio Expenses	—	—	0.10	0.19
Production Office§	0.37	—	0.16	0.70
Equipment Rental	—	—	—	0.36
Maintenance of Model Homes	0.07	0.10	—	0.02
Maintenance of Trucks, Tools, and Equipment	—	—	—	0.66
Legal and Accounting	—	0.04	0.16	0.04
Taxes and Licenses	0.46	0.15	0.13	0.69
Travel and Entertainment	0.10	0.08	0.20	0.34
Telephone and Postage	0.08	0.09	0.10	0.14
Warehouse Expense	—	—	—	0.81
Insurance	0.19	0.10	0.09	0.23
Christmas Gifts to Employees	0.19	0.07	0.09	0.12
Plans and Designs	—	0.10	0.08	0.12
Discounts and Collection Fees on Mortgages	—	—	0.04	0.46
Rent	0.10	0.10	0.08	0.21
Miscellaneous	0.08	0.11	0.05	0.11
Total Expenses	11.02%	11.07%	13.58%	18.41%
Operating Profit ( ) = loss	3.78	2.33	3.09	(3.21)
Number of Houses Built	124	134	151	52
Average Selling Price	$13,500	$14,250	$15,000	$15,250
Average Number of Construction Workers	94‖	114‖	113‖	124

  * Based on completed houses. A "sale" was made only when a house was completed.

  † Construction costs include direct labor, material, subcontracting cost, and the salaries and wages of foremen, superintendents, warehousemen, draftsmen, blueprint operators, messengers, and the Service Department, plus fringe benefits for those salaries and wages included.

  ‡ Includes all other salaries and wages not included under "construction costs."

  § General purpose production requirements, such as blueprint paper, steel tapes, forms, office supplies, small hand tools.

  ‖ Subcontractors' crews.

The Whirlpool Corporation (I)

The Whirlpool Corporation is one of the nation's largest producers of major appliances for the home. In early 1959 the firm employed approximately 13,800 people and operated the following production facilities. Recent sales and profit figures are shown in Exhibit 1.

Plant Location	Products
Clyde, Ohio	Automatic washers and wringer-washers
Evansville, Indiana	Air conditioners, dehumidifiers, refrigerators, upright freezers
Hamilton, Ohio	Built-in ranges, freestanding ranges
Marion, Ohio	Automatic dryers
St. Joseph, Michigan	Automatic washers, combination washer-dryers
St. Paul, Minnesota	Chest-type freezers, dishwashers, food-waste disposers, ice cube makers, vacuum cleaners

A substantial portion of Whirlpool's output was marketed through exclusive distributorships which sold to retail outlets under the brand name RCA-Whirlpool. The RCA firm supplied these same retailers with various lines of radios, TV sets, hi-fi equipment, electric fans, and similar items, thus providing a complete line of home appliances.

Extensive national and local advertising programs were used to promote RCA-Whirlpool products. This practice reflected the general belief in the industry that appliance advertising could be an important factor influencing sales between competitors.

Sales of major appliances were somewhat seasonal. Factory shipments of washers and dryers, for example, generally tended to be heaviest in the third quarter. Similarly, a pattern of about 21 per cent–

EXHIBIT 1 THE WHIRLPOOL CORPORATION (I)

SALES AND PROFIT DATA

	Net Sales	Net Income
1958	$404,628,433	$10,178,597
1957	402,322,212	10,591,570
1956	390,976,925	14,217,895
1955	319,268,545	15,069,167
1954	298,714,654	15,833,884
1953	284,086,637	10,053,294
1952	227,329,089	9,184,941

NOTE: Data includes sales and earnings of Seeger Refrigerator Company previous to merger in 1955, and Birtman Electric Company previous to merger in 1957.

Source: Moody's Industrials.

23 per cent–29 per cent–27 per cent, from the first through the fourth quarter, was considered a fairly normal distribution of factory shipments of home laundry units.

THE ST. JOSEPH DIVISION

In 1955, the St. Joseph, Michigan plant was organized as a Division of Whirlpool under the direction of the General Manager, Lee Johns. In this capacity Mr. Johns was responsible for product development, engineering, and production functions, and for the profits of the Division. Responsibility for sales of the Division's products rested, however, with the corporate Sales Department headquartered in nearby Benton Harbor, Michigan. The Division's Director of Engineering worked closely with corporate-level sales and merchandising personnel to develop new models on a continuous but irregularly timed basis. Typically, new models of most major appliances were introduced annually. Competition and customer's demands for new features, sizes, and styles not infrequently made it necessary, however, to develop new products and place them in production under severe time pressures between annual model changeovers.

Organization of the St. Joseph Division's top echelon of management is shown on Exhibit 2. Late in May, 1959, the division employed 1,848 persons. This total reflected a layoff of 119 employees on May 1 in an effort to balance sales and production.

EXHIBIT 2 THE WHIRLPOOL CORPORATION (I)

ST. JOSEPH DIVISION

General Manager's Staff (Names disguised)

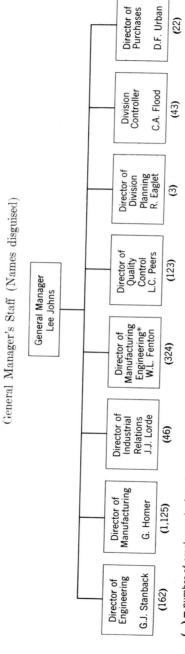

( ) = number of employees in department.

*Includes maintenance, die and fixture repair, and tool room.

The total plant complex then represented approximately 878,000 square feet of working area. A functional layout of the various buildings is shown in Exhibit 3. Almost all phases of manufacturing operations throughout the entire plant were linked by conveyors.[1] Altogether there were 76 conveyors, individually ranging from 112 to 5,510 feet in length, and in total adding up to a length of nearly 14 miles. Twenty-six of these conveyors were used at least partially for storage purposes, utilizing overhead areas in Buildings 1, 3, 5, and 6. (The upper levels of Buildings 2 and 4 were occupied by an additional floor.)

As of May, 1959, Mr. Johns had been with the Whirlpool company for four years, having previously had a background of successful production experience in the aircraft industry. During his first two years with Whirlpool he had been General Manager of the Marion, Ohio Division. In February, 1957, he had been promoted to the post of General Manager of the somewhat larger St. Joseph Division.

EXPERIENCE WITH COMBINATION WASHER-DRYER UNITS

To Mr. Johns, the company's experience to date with the manufacture of combination washer-dryer units was fairly representative of the problems and challenges of the major appliance industry. The design and engineering stages of the company's combination unit dated back to 1954, and the first models had been in production for several months by the time Mr. Johns assumed managerial responsibility at St. Joseph in early 1957. When the design work on the combination was first undertaken, the corporate Research and Development staff was responsible for the design function for all new products and models. Beginning in 1956, however, activity at the corporate level had been confined to research activity, with design responsibility for new products assigned to the Engineering Departments of the various Divisions. Thus, the original design work on the combination unit had been performed in 1954 and 1955 by the corporate R and D Department, and then transferred to the St. Joseph Division in January of 1956.

At that time, certain of Whirlpool's competitors had been selling combination washer-dryers for several years. As soon as it assumed design responsibility, therefore, the St. Joseph staff immediately launched the production engineering stage of the development process

---

[1] In many instances, conveyors extended between buildings.

EXHIBIT 3   THE WHIRLPOOL CORPORATION (I)

ST. JOSEPH DIVISION

Plant Layout (Simplified and not to exact scale)

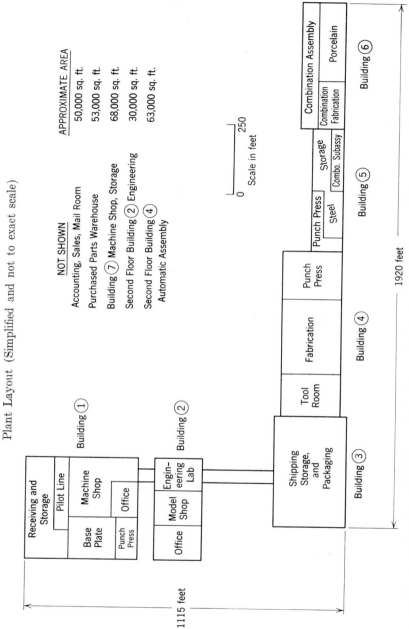

NOT SHOWN

	APPROXIMATE AREA
Accounting, Sales, Mail Room	50,000 sq. ft.
Purchased Parts Warehouse	53,000 sq. ft.
Building ⑦ Machine Shop, Storage	68,000 sq. ft.
Second Floor Building ② Engineering	30,000 sq. ft.
Second Floor Building ④	63,000 sq. ft.
Automatic Assembly	

on the new unit. This entailed the verifying of tolerances, checking for "producibility," making various design changes for cost reduction, working out the manufacturing and assembly processes, designing and ordering necessary tooling, working with vendors in arranging the procurement of purchased components, and closely co-ordinating the entire manufacturing process during the early weeks of production. The first Whirlpool combinations came off the newly established production line in October, 1956.

Decision regarding the amount of tooling and assembly capacity to provide for the new units had been difficult. Combination washer-dryers had first been introduced in the industry in late 1952 by a major competitor. During 1953 and 1954 this firm had promoted the new product vigorously with advertising and publicity. Various other competitors joined the field during 1955 and 1956, and the industry-wide sales of combination units grew considerably.

During these years, however, the performance and reliability of many washer-dryer combinations compared unfavorably with those of individual automatic washers and dryers. Service-calls on the units produced by one manufacturer reportedly averaged around four per unit per year, for example, and there were indications that certain of the other brands were faring but little better. Two companies experienced such service problems that they recalled all of the units they had sold. One of these firms replaced the recalled units with separate washer and dryer units. The other company came out with a new combination model, but apparently continued to encounter troubles with quality and dependability.

Throughout the industry, service problems on combination units seemed particularly pronounced in regard to leaks, excessive noise, malfunctions of timers, pumps, solenoid valves, clutches, and gears, and difficulties in controlling the drying-cycle temperatures. The consuming public also apparently did not respond favorably to the low capacities (usually about 10-pound maximum), the high rate of hot water consumption (typically 70 gallons per cycle), the bulky size (about 40 to 50 per cent greater than the typical automatic washer), and the lengthy time-cycle (about two hours) provided by units which were priced at roughly $500 retail. There was also some evidence that many retailers and repairmen alike were aggressively promoting the sale of individual washer and dryer units, rather than risking customer displeasure over the faulty performance of a combination. Furthermore, the gross profit margin to the retailer on the sale of a separate washer and a separate dryer often worked out to be significantly above that realized on a sale of a combination unit.

The industrywide sales history of combination units at the time Whirlpool faced tooling decisions regarding its own line of combinations was as follows:

Year	Combination Units Sold
1952	1,746
1953	50,815
1954	41,706
1955	76,330

To Whirlpool sales personnel, the combination market appeared to offer great potential. The poor performance of many competitive units suggested to them that there was an excellent opportunity for a company with a sound product to capture a large portion of the market. The total sales growth to date in the industry further encouraged them to believe that once combination units achieved a satisfactory quality reputation, their total sales volume might increase dramatically.

On the basis of the assurances of the corporate R & D staff that Whirlpool had indeed benefited from its slower, more cautious approach to the design of a combination unit and that it now possessed a satisfactory model, the Sales Department authorized the St. Joseph Division to provide tooling for a piece-part and component rate of 1,000 units per day, and an assembly capacity of 400 units per shift. In the words of one executive, these decisions were supported by the belief that "were sales requirements to grow quickly past 800 units per day,[2] it would be relatively easier to expand assembly capacity than to tool the additional component capacity. Thus the capacity decision [provided] insurance against the possibility that volume would grow quickly. At the beginning of the program this was considered very likely." This capacity decision was used by the Division's Manufacturing Engineering and Industrial Engineering Departments, as well as the factory operating group, in planning production of the new unit.

The combination's design embodied significant new approaches in comparison with those employed in the individual washer units then being produced by the company. Instead of employing the tank and agitator washing principle, for example, the combination unit was designed to tumble clothes in a revolving basket and wash them with a nozzle-directed stream of hot water. This allowed the subsequent drying cycle to take place in the same tumbling basket. Entirely new controls, valves, timers, drives, and tanks were necessary to accomplish

---

[2] That is, the assembly capacity of two-shift operations.

this new approach. Since the combination unit was about 50 per cent larger than the typical automatic washer, completely new assembly-line set-ups were also required, as well as new presses and welding rigs to form and weld the more massive cabinet and frame.

Determining the location of manufacturing facilities for the new model also posed a difficult set of decisions for management. At the time this question arose, a new plant was being built at Marion for the production of dryers, and the Clyde and St. Joseph plants were running at, or near, their capacity levels on washer manufacture. The company's other plants were producing substantially different types of products (freezers, dishwashers, refrigerators) and therefore were not seriously considered as a location for the combination unit. After careful study it was decided to assign production responsibility for the combination to the St. Joseph plant since the nearby corporate R and D group would be available for immediate support in the event technical difficulties were encountered in manufacturing this complex product. Since St. Joseph already was operating at full capacity on automatic washer production (and would continue to produce those units), additional space would have to be provided at the plant to accommodate production of the combination.

Another factor complicated the space and facility problem, namely, the porcelain (enameling) requirements. At the time, part of the porcelain and enameling operations needed by the St. Joseph plant was obtained from the company's Clyde plant, and the balance was sub-contracted to firms in the Chicago area. It was known, however, that the new line of combination units would require more porcelain on the interior parts and on the cabinet than were needed by the typical automatic washer. Furthermore, the combination parts to be enameled were heavier and bulkier than those of an automatic washer, and to ship these items to and from the enameling operation would be prohibitively expensive. It was concluded therefore that Whirlpool itself should construct a porcelain facility at St. Joseph to provide sufficient capacity for 500 combinations per shift, plus full support for the automatic washer requirements.

Since the St. Joseph plant already had an extensive conveyor system, company officials decided to minimize the need for physical rearrange-ments by building 90,000 square feet of new space for the combination unit and the porcelain facilities at the end of the long line of buildings already in existence. It was recognized that this proposed arrangement was not ideal, but Division officials were confident that substantial improvements could be made at a later date if they were warranted by shifts in product mix. It was originally assumed, therefore, that a major rearrangement of plant facilities would probably be undertaken in several years if, as forecast, sales of the combination units increased rapidly, and sales of the automatics declined as a consequence.

Work on the new building, Building 6, was started in late 1955 and completed in 1956, at a cost of approximately $1 million. Of the 90,000 square feet provided, 33,000 square feet was set up for the combination assembly line, 13,000 square feet for certain subassembly operations, and 44,000 square feet for the porcelain facility. The latter consisted of: (a) a milling area with large batch mills for preparing the frit;[3] (b) a series of pickling tanks where the metal to be coated was dipped and cleaned while being transported on a conveyor system; (c) spray booths where the parts were automatically sprayed with the frit solution as they passed; (d) touch-up spray booths where workers could spray manually any small areas that the automatic sprayer missed; (e) ovens for baking the frit into a porcelain finish. Two passes through the spraying operations and the baking ovens were required, thus building-up two layers on the metal. Colors could be introduced into the frit, providing the new pastel shades that were increasingly popular in the appliance market. Mix, consistency, thickness of spray, and oven temperatures had to be controlled accurately to assure top-quality results.

In addition to the porcelain equipment, which cost approximately $1.1 million, six new 200-300 ton presses to produce the new large cabinets also were purchased, at an average unit price of $65,000. Other special-purpose tools required for the combination unit, including jigs, dies, fixtures, and inspection equipment, required additional investment in excess of $3 million.

Although the combination represented many new engineering approaches, and embodied very few parts which were not of a completely new design, the actual manufacturing processes required were fairly comparable to those already employed in manufacturing automatic washers. Exhibit 4 lists the various major parts and subassemblies of the combination, in the order of their final assembly. The stampings that were needed were produced in the punch press area of Buildings 4 and 5. Welding operations were performed in the "Combination Fabrication" area in Building 6. Subassembly work, such as that needed on the pump, thermostat bracket assembly, and blower assembly, was accomplished in the "Combination Subassembly" area in Building 5. The new final assembly area for combination units in Building 6 consisted of a series of platform-type conveyors arranged in a U-shape. Units

---

[3] That is, the glazing compound.

EXHIBIT 4 THE WHIRLPOOL CORPORATION (I)

PARTS AND ASSEMBLIES USED IN COMBINATION WASHER-DRYER UNIT
SHOWN IN ORDER OF FINAL ASSEMBLY

Part/Assembly	Source
Cylinder	Stamping-welded—Porcelain
Tank	Stamping-welded—Porcelain
Air Duct Cover	Stamping-welded—Porcelain
Lint Tube Assembly	Stamping-welded—Porcelain
Cover and Shield Assembly	Stamping-welded—Porcelain
Shield and Heater Support	Stamping-welded—Porcelain
Heater Box, Inner Baffle	Stamping-welded—Porcelain
Heater Box Cover	Stamping-welded—Porcelain
Flue Assembly	Stamping-welded—Porcelain
Combustion Chamber Assembly	Stamping-welded—Porcelain
Top	Stamping-welded—Porcelain (or Paint)
Console	Stamping-welded—Porcelain (or Paint)
Inspection Door	Stamping-welded—Porcelain (or Paint)
Side Panel	Stamping—Porcelain (or Paint)
Outer Door	Stamping—Porcelain (or Paint)
Front Panel	Stamping—Porcelain (or Paint)
Inner Door	Stamping—Porcelain (or Paint)
Base Plate Assembly	Stamping—Weld—Paint
Leveling Link	Stamping—Paint
Pylon	Stamping—Weld—Paint
Blower Assembly	Purchase Blower, Die-Casting, Assemble with Stampings
Motor and Pump Assembly	Purchase Motor, Assemble Pump from Subcontracted Parts
Motor Bracket	Stamping—Paint
Upper Back Panel	Stamping—Paint
Lower Back Panel	Stamping—Paint
Rear Upper Panel Cover	Stamping—Paint
Plate and Control Mounting Bracket	Stamping—Paint
Hood and Handle Assembly	Stamping—Paint
Control Shelf	Stamping—Paint
Terminal Cover	Stamping
Gas Burner Assembly	Purchase Components and Assemble
Thermostat Bracket and Baseplate	Stamp and Assemble
Combustion Chamber Housing	Stamp and Assemble
Timer	Purchase

(Pulleys, belts, hoses—all purchased items—are not included.)

were assembled to the point of operability and given complete tests. Following this the side panels, tops, consoles, and access doors were added. After a functional check, acceptable units were placed in prefabricated crates, which were transported to Building 3 and stored until shipped. Units that failed to pass inspection were set on a repair line which could hold 30 units. Especially skilled workers made the necessary changes and repairs, and the units were then sent back to the inspection line for a recheck.

LABOR COSTS AND WAGE ADMINISTRATION

Prior to the start-up of operations on the combination line in 1956, the company made a detailed study of labor costs in the St. Joseph–Benton Harbor area. The survey revealed that the average take-home earnings, $2.60 per hour, paid by the Division in 1955, were approximately 45 cents per hour higher than wages paid for comparable jobs in the Chicago area,[4] as well as in other Whirlpool plants. Furthermore, wages earned by Division personnel had risen considerably faster than the BLS cost of living index during recent years, as reflected in the following data:

Year	St. Joseph Plant Average Hourly Wage Earned	BLS Cost of Living Index (1947–1949 = 100)	Negotiated Increases During Year
1950	$1.72	103	$0.065 per hour
1951	2.05	110	0.070
1952	2.25	113	0.050
1953	2.40	113	0.050
1954	2.55	114	0.000
1955	2.60	115	0.050

Most of the Division's factory workers had been on an incentive plan for many years. The Division management felt that pressures for production since the Second World War, together with the consistent efforts of strong unions[5] which had gone on strike in 1945, 1950, and 1955, had resulted in a gradual deterioration and loosening of production standards in the Division. It was also the Division management's belief that since the war some foremen had relied too heavily on the incentive plan to assure reasonable production output, instead of

---

[4] Approximately 70 miles to the west.

[5] United Electrical Workers during the period 1942–1955, and the International Association of Machinists since 1955.

maintaining close supervision. In this regard, both the Director of Industrial Relations and the Manager of Industrial Engineering stated their conviction that the typical work pace maintained by Division personnel was not steady, and that there was no workable concept of "normal" output or effort. Many workers apparently were making their rates "by working harder earlier in the day than late in the shift."

Grievances were legion. Almost every new rate or change of rate was challenged, as were most changes relating to methods of production, assembly lines, tools, conveyors, or machines. In the judgment of many persons, the climate of relations between the union and the company seemed to be worsening year by year. The evidence that average pay was so much higher than that prevailing in the surrounding industrial area, and that incentive standards gradually had deteriorated until neither employees nor supervisors had a firm base from which to negotiate, had become matters of serious concern to Division management.

Against this background, at the time the porcelain, painting, and combination unit facilities were established in the newly completed Building 6, management proposed that employees in these new Departments be compensated on an entirely new wage system through which jobs would be evaluated and paid on a daywork hourly rate. Under this proposal, new job grades and rates would be established on a basis that would assure that take-home pay would approximate the earnings for comparable work in other parts of the factory. To Division officials this proposal seemed eminently fair: since the new combination, porcelain, and paint operations would not be operating at full efficiency for many months, newly hired employees assigned to this work could probably earn little more than the $1.20 per hour base rate under the existing plan. Furthermore, if the continuous strife and wrangling over incentive rates could be halted without a cut in actual take-home pay, it seemed obvious that both the employees and the company would benefit. The union apparently concurred, and a special agreement was negotiated covering Building 6 only, to become effective in the new facilities when they were placed in operation late in 1956.

The combination line thus became a test area for the entire plant insofar as new wage administration techniques were concerned. In the judgment of Division management, the initial results seemed favorable in terms of an improved climate of relationships. Management personnel stated that under the new system there proved to be no more serious arguments over rates; foremen devoted more time to supervision; industrial engineers felt freer to develop improvements;

a steadier, longer day was worked; and apparently there was no drop in work pace. This latter point, of course, was difficult to measure, but seemed to be borne out by a series of ratio-delay[6] studies performed by the Industrial Engineering Department.

The successful operation on this new wage payment plan in Building 6 encouraged the company and the union to negotiate a new contract in 1957 whereby the entire plant was converted to a system of job evaluation under which daywork pay ranges were established for each evaluated job. This contract was signed in August, 1957, and became effective for the balance of the plant on January 2, 1958.

Under the new arrangement, the Industrial Engineering Department continued to set standards on various jobs, and on entire lines, for the purpose of management controls. These standards were developed from time-study data which reflected the previous concept of "normal" used with the former incentive system. Daily and weekly reports of performance by Departments were made, with a rating of 100 per cent being equivalent to the average work pace maintained over an entire eight-hour shift under the former incentive plan. On this basis, the over-all performance of the plant fell to about 90 per cent when the new system was first placed in effect early in January, 1958, and then quickly climbed to 95 per cent. Since that time, the rating gradually inched upwards until by spring of 1959 it was running at 96 to 97 per cent. Plant officials felt that during the 16-month experience with the new plan, the total hours actually worked had been increasing (approaching eight hours per day per employee), but that the work pace had dropped slightly.

SCHEDULE CHANGES ON THE
COMBINATION UNITS

During this same 16-months, many changes were introduced in the combination line, permitting reductions in costs under production schedules which varied considerably. Morale, nonetheless, had seemed to be conspicuously high throughout Building 6 ever since its opening.

The changing production schedules reflected the result of continued disappointing sales of combination units throughout the entire industry. Total industry sales subsequent to 1955 had been as follows:

---

[6] A technique by which a trained observer passes predetermined work stations at random intervals, recording and rating what is occurring at the time of each observation. The data compiled by this sampling procedure is then processed to provide over-all evaluations of productivity, and to ascertain the proportion of time spent in different types of activity.

Year	Industry-Wide Sales of Combination Units
1956	104,000
1957	179,000
1958	164,000

While these results represented substantial gains over 1955, they were, nevertheless, equivalent to only a small fraction of the volume attained on industry-wide sales of separate automatic washers and dryers.

For Whirlpool, the continuing cool response of the customers to combination units was a major problem. Service records on its product seemed to confirm its belief that Whirlpool had a more reliable unit than ever previously offered in the industry. Whirlpool personnel also were convinced that the capacity of their machine was actually 25 per cent greater than competing models rated at 10 pounds per load, and that the low water consumption and new spray-tumble washing system featured in the Whirlpool units should have definite sales appeal. Their unit had, in fact, almost immediately gained what Division officials felt was a remarkable percentage of the combination market, and had improved this share still further in 1958. Nevertheless, in terms of the tooling and facility capacities available, Whirlpool officials considered the sales results on the combination disturbingly low. An index of daily combination production rates for the Division, averaged by month, is shown in Exhibit 5.

The frequent schedule changes authorized on combination unit manufacturing throughout 1957 and 1958 adversely affected cost results, particularly in regard to tooling charges. In accordance with the company's normal practice, the combination had been priced to absorb a given dollar amount of tooling per unit, with the tooling investment being reduced with each unit sold. Because sales proved lower than anticipated, however, the unabsorbed tooling balance carried on the books at the end of 1958 represented a significant portion of the original tooling expenditure. Under the company's regular procedures of writing off special-purpose tooling on a two-year basis, the entire balance of unamortized tooling, therefore, was charged off against Division profits for 1958.

The amount charged against 1958 profits both from unamortized tooling and other new development costs was substantial in proportion to total corporate profits. The Chairman of the Board, Elisha Gray II, and the President, Robert Brooker, stated in the Whirlpool Corporation's Annual Report for 1958 that "during a period of growth and development of new products and markets, there are always substantial

EXHIBIT 5   THE WHIRLPOOL CORPORATION (I)

INDEX OF COMBINATION UNIT PRODUCTION, ST. JOSEPH DIVISION
(November 1958 = 100)

Year	Month	Production	Year	Month	Production
1956	October	6	1958	January	75
	November	26		February	85
	December	56		March	116
1957	January	78		April	122
	February	112		May	122
	March	126		June	90
	April	130		July	72
	May	112		August	66
	June	83		September	66
	July	88		October	63
	August	80		November	100
	September	86		December	123
	October	57	1959	January	115
	November	59		February	124
	December	71		March	124
				April	115
				May	80*

* Scheduled rate as of May 1, 1959.

'make ready' costs. While we hesitate to state that these changes are totally nonrecurring, we do expect that next year they may be reduced by as much as eight to ten million dollars." The combination unit tooling write-off alone amounted to a significant portion of the total expenses. After-the-fact estimates by some Division officials regarding the amount that might have been saved had the tooling for the combination unit been based on a more accurate sales forecast, ran in excess of $1 million.

Even more serious in the judgment of Division personnel was the fact that the organization of the entire factory had been influenced by the expectations held for the combination unit. The conveyor lines and assembly areas devoted to the combination unit had been equipped to produce a much higher volume than now actually was required, and therefore were tying up a great deal more space than necessary. Had the combination unit grown in volume as expected, long-range plans for major layout improvements would have been incorporated. For example, it had been planned to move combination production into

Building 4, and to place base plate assembly, then in Building 1, closer to the automatic assembly lines. Under the existing arrangement, this assembly, containing the agitator, gears, base, motor, pump, and wiring harness for the automatic washer, was transferred by conveyor from Building 1 to Building 4 over 3,800 feet of conveyor. The extra inventory carried on the conveyor was considerable. Under existing circumstances, however, long-range plans for improving such situations through physical rearrangements had to be postponed to permit re-examination in the light of actual sales results.

The May 1, 1959, schedule reduction on combination units also had been accompanied by a 15 per cent reduction in schedules on automatic washers. This reflected the fact that factory inventories of completed washers had increased appreciably since the beginning of the year. The production schedules on automatics had varied from an index of 100 in January, 1958, to 174 in October, 1958, and had dropped to 124 on May 1, 1959. Total factory inventories on automatics had ranged from an index of 100 in January, 1958, to 22 in December, 1958. Mr. Johns therefore believed that the changes in the schedule for combination units were not significantly more severe than the variations recently experienced on the automatics, aside from the fact that the automatics, unlike the combination, had not been overtooled in terms of capacity.

ORGANIZATIONAL CHANGES

During the two years since Mr. Johns had joined the Division, he had taken a number of steps to improve operations, to develop more efficient production, and to enhance design capabilities. Beyond the immediate profit potential of these changes, Mr. Johns felt that certain of these improvements also might increase the Division's ability to adapt more flexibly to changes in products and to variations in volume.

Major changes, for example, had been made in the production control area starting in early 1958. Dissatisfaction with the present system, particularly in regard to what he considered excessive inventories, lost parts, and materials, and a great deal of expediting of short parts, led Mr. Johns to appoint a one-man committee to develop recommendations for a Production Control Section. Until that time, the Division had been served by a small Planning Section which performed certain basic scheduling functions and reported to a Production Service Department. There had been, however, no production control group as such. Instead, the system had functioned as follows:

1. The Planning Section received sales forecast data from, and maintained liaison with, the Sales Department.
2. Based on the Sales Department forecasts, the Planning Section developed an assembly schedule, and also placed requisitions with Purchasing for purchased parts and raw materials.
3. Machine shop fabrication and subassembly foremen received the assembly schedule, and then scheduled their own parts-production to meet the specified assembly requirements.
4. Assembly lines were scheduled and coordinated by the assembly foreman, using the assembly schedule. Expediting, if needed, was performed by expediters who reported to the Production Service Department.

In June of 1958, the "one-man committee" submitted a report to the Director of Manufacturing and the General Manager (Exhibit 6). As a result of this presentation, and after further discussions, Mr. Johns authorized the establishment of a Production Control Department to report to the Director of Manufacturing. The revised system, which was in operation by January 1, 1959, resulted in the general allocation of functions as illustrated by the production control organization chart (Exhibit 7). The new organization relieved the foremen of all scheduling and expediting efforts, and allowed them to concentrate on supervision, a function which Mr. Johns believed had been neglected previously.

The present Manager of Manufacturing, George Homer, age 55, previously had served 11 months as Superintendent of all St. Joseph assembly operations. Prior to that, he had been Superintendent of the combination assembly area for five months and, before that, Superintendent of the punch press department for six years.

Mr. Homer stated that he felt the new production control organization established the previous January already had resulted in a number of improvements. He particularly cited four areas: (1) his organization now knew of problems affecting production in advance, rather than after "they hit"; (2) productivity was increasing because the foremen were "running their jobs instead of chasing parts"; (3) purchased parts were arriving now in time to receive inspection checks instead of having to go straight to assembly; (4) his staff group was good, it kept him up-to-date, and checked on special problems, such as "why the factory had spent such and such an amount of dollars for overtime in the first quarter."

To improve the total operation further, Mr. Johns recently had promoted Richard Eaglet to the job of Director of Division Planning,

202

EXHIBIT 6   THE WHIRLPOOL CORPORATION (I)

PRODUCTION CONTROL PRESENTATION OUTLINE

June 1958

*The Basic Deficiencies of Our Present Production Control System
are as Follows:*

1. The various responsibilities and functions of the production control activity
   are scattered throughout the Division's organization causing:
   a. Reduced coordination between the segments except during periods of
      emergency.
   b. A lack of coordinated direction of effort.
2. A lack of *organized* production control within the manufacturing areas
   causing:
   a. The foreman to devote an excessive amount of his time providing a rudi-
      mentary production and materials control service.
   b. Imbalances in inventory—too high on some versus too low on others.
   c. An unnecessary exposure to possible high obsolescent losses.
   d. Uneconomic machine loading and excessive machine set-up charges.
3. A lack of *organized* coordination and control within the assembly departments causing:
   a. Absorption of the foreman's time as in *2a* above.
   b. Mistiming of line changeover activities.
   c. Overlooking important changeover steps.
   d. Failure of material to arrive.
4. Our present inability to control, in an accurate, current, and usable manner,
   the inventory's level, its flow, and physical location, causing:
   a. Inaccuracies in the perpetual inventory level.
   b. Loss of various segments of the inventory.
   c. Shortages caused by the above reasons.
   d. Knowledge of a shortage only after it is actually experienced.

What We Want Our Production Control System to Do:

1. Increase assembly line flexibility.
   a. Provide greater potential speed of response to sales requirements changes
      than our assembly plant facilities actually allow.
   b. Provide the ability to control accurately the assembly of a greater
      variety of product models than sales actually desires or requests—
      recognizing that the assembly plant facilities actually determine the
      maximum degree of flexibility possible.
2. Establish an integrated, centrally directed, production control function.
   a. Increase coordination between the various production control groups.
   b. Provide positive, central control over all production control functions
      and their direction of development.
3. Reduce to a realistic minimum assembly line and manufacturing production
   losses and changes caused by:
   a. Improper and (or) inadequate flow of materials into the producing area.
   b. Nonavailability of materials due to a lack of forward planning, coordina-
      tion of activities, location control, or supplier-monitoring and follow-up.
   c. Material received unusable because of improper quality.

d. Production supervisors too busy with production control activities to devote adequate attention to the management of their departments.

e. Machine downtime caused by excessive, uneconomic, and unjustified machine set-up and changeover time resulting from inadequate production control within the area.

4. To automate as much of the production control paper work as possible.

Steps Believed Necessary to Obtain Objectives:

1. Collecting all the scattered segments of the production control function into an integrated, homogeneous group.

   a. Unification will consolidate all present:

     (1) Production planning and scheduling activities.

     (2) Purchased parts and raw materials, internal and external ordering, follow-up, and expediting groups.

     (3) Materials handling and storage groups.

     (4) Parts listing groups.

   b. Unification will also include:

     (1) Those production control functions presently performed by the foreman.

     (2) Expansion of several activities presently underdeveloped, such as manufacturing production control.

2. Educate and inform all affected persons as to objectives of the production control functions, its responsibilities and reasons for existing; how its various systems operate; what services it is expected to perform, and its effects upon each person's job.

3. Improve and expand the planning, scheduling, dispatching, and progress inspection activities within the various manufacturing areas, and between these areas and the assembly plant.

4. Increase control and coordination over and between all production activities of the Division's assembly and manufacturing departments.

5. Develop and improve our control over the inventory's level so that our perpetual inventory information is accurate, current, and useful.

6. Increase control over all material and its flow into, through, and out of the Division, and in each production department within the Division.

7. Develop and integrate a materials-progress monitoring program.

an outgrowth of the former Planning Department. Mr. Eaglet came to his new post from production control and quality control jobs in other Whirlpool Divisions. The basic functions of the new Division Planning Department were to serve as liaison between the factory and sales, to develop over-all schedules, and to coordinate the introduction of new models. Exhibit 8 is Mr. Eaglet's written description of his job, as presented to Mr. Johns and his staff in January, 1959.

Further changes in the organization had been made in early 1958, when a new Director of Engineering, James Stanback, and a new Director of Manufacturing Engineering, William Fenton, were appointed. Mr. Stanback had served with another Whirlpool Division

EXHIBIT 7 THE WHIRLPOOL CORPORATION (I)

ST. JOSEPH DIVISION

Production Control Organization

```
                    ┌──────────────────┐
                    │ Director of      │
                    │ Manufacturing    │
                    └────────┬─────────┘
                             │
                    ┌────────┴─────────┐
                    │ Production Control│
                    │ Manager          │
                    └────────┬─────────┘
          ┌──────────┬───────┴───────┬──────────┐
          │          │               │          │
┌─────────┴──┐ ┌─────┴──────┐ ┌──────┴──────┐ ┌─┴────────────┐
│Preproduction│ │Assembly    │ │Manufacturing│ │Materials     │
│Control      │ │Production  │ │Production   │ │Inventory and │
│Supervisor   │ │Control     │ │Control      │ │Control       │
│             │ │Supervisor  │ │Supervisor   │ │Supervisor    │
└─────┬───────┘ └─────┬──────┘ └──────┬──────┘ └──────┬───────┘
      │               │               │               │
┌─────┴───────┐ ┌─────┴──────┐ ┌──────┴──────┐ ┌──────┴───────┐
│New Model and│ │Assembly and│ │Manufacturing│ │Shipping      │
│Special      │ │Subassembly │ │Scheduling   │ │              │
│Projects     │ │Scheduling  │ │             │ │              │
└─────────────┘ └────────────┘ └─────────────┘ └──────────────┘
┌─────────────┐ ┌────────────┐ ┌─────────────┐ ┌──────────────┐
│Engineering  │ │Purchased   │ │Raw Material │ │Receiving     │
│Records      │ │Parts       │ │and Farm-out │ │and Stores    │
│             │ │Ordering and│ │Ordering and │ │              │
│             │ │Follow-up   │ │Follow-up    │ │              │
└─────────────┘ └────────────┘ └─────────────┘ └──────────────┘
┌─────────────┐ ┌────────────┐ ┌─────────────┐ ┌──────────────┐
│Engineering  │ │Assembly    │ │Manufacturing│ │Central       │
│Change       │ │Dispatching │ │Dispatching  │ │Inventory     │
│             │ │            │ │             │ │Control       │
└─────────────┘ └────────────┘ └─────────────┘ └──────────────┘
```

EXHIBIT 8 THE WHIRLPOOL CORPORATION (I)

ST. JOSEPH DIVISION

Responsibilities and Functions, Director of Planning

As directed by the General Manager, assume full responsibility for co-ordination of the activities of the various Divisions and Departments concerned to obtain the proper product and project schedules consistent with the attainment of optimum company profits.

Product Scheduling Functions

1. Exercise full responsibility as Division sales contact with Whirlpool, International Sales, Corporate Planning, and other divisions.
   a. Coordinate in the establishment of new schedules and the changing of existing schedules.
   b. Establish schedule and product forecasts, both short and long range, to enable the Division to plan properly the profitable use of assets, organization, and personnel.
   c. Review sales forecasts with other Division policy members.
   d. Direct scheduling activities for automatics and combinations at St. Joseph and Clyde.
2. Exercise full responsibilities toward the attainment of the following scheduling objectives:
   a. Give sales product required.
   b. Obtain optimum profit.
   c. Levelize manpower.
   d. Minimize inventory.
   e. Obtain flexibility of model mix.
   f. Plan for future requirements.
3. Assume responsibility for coordination of Division activities on all major expansion and reduction programs.
4. Develop procedures and policies required to establish scheduling functions and responsibilities outlined above.

Project Scheduling Functions

1. Exercise full responsibility for establishing and coordinating major Divisional project programs.
   a. Establish Division plan for any new project.
   b. Keep policy members informed on all phases of new programs.
   c. Direct activities of personnel assigned to the detailed fulfillment of project scheduling activities.
2. Assume responsibility for representing the Division position to the Sales Department in the development of new merchandise programs.
   a. Attend or be represented at merchandise development meetings which consider timing of programs.
   b. Coordinate activities and programs between Division and Sales.
3. Assume responsibility for coordinating the new merchandise program timing with St. Joseph, Marion, and Clyde.
   a. Keep planning at Marion and Clyde informed on new programs.
   b. Initiate schedules for new product programs and coordinate with Clyde and Marion.

    c. Obtain product requirements on automatics, combinations, and dryers and review with proper Departments.

    d. Coordinate program requirements of Clyde and Marion and review with those Departments concerned.

    e. Supply product quantity and timing information and follow up all Departments concerned to be certain objectives are attained.

4. Develop required policies and procedures required to attain project objectives.

General Functions

1. Provide information to all policy members regarding future trends which may have an effect on the product and work of our Division.
2. Assume responsibility for field service programs as required, particularly in matters which require the coordination of several Departments.
3. Coordinate Division's activity with sales in matters other than schedules or projects, such as competitive analysis programs.
4. Assume responsibility for contact with Market Research.
    a. Keep Policy Group informed as to market penetration, competitive activity, product acceptance, business forecasts, and other related matters which concern the Division.
5. Coordinate Division's product planning activities.
    a. Coordinate information required from Staff Departments.
    b. Develop Division program for discussion with those concerned, taking into account over-all profit objectives.
    c. Report results of meetings to those concerned.
    d. Establish program and follow up completion of same.
6. Direct Division activities in other programs, depending on the discretion of the General Manager.
7. Assist in any way possible the attainment of product quality consistent with the objectives of maintaining or increasing our company's share of the market and obtaining an optimum return on investment.
8. Review status of Division schedules and programs with General Manager and staff regularly.
9. Participate as a member of General Manager's staff in developing Division profit planning program and goals.
10. Carry out special assignments and studies as directed by General Manager.
11. Inform General Manager of the progress made against assigned responsibilities.
12. Assume responsibility and act as Division contact for mobilization planning.

for one year prior to this promotion, and before that had seven years' experience with a competitor. Mr. Fenton had held several responsible jobs in the auto industry. Mr. Fenton's job was a newly created one in the Division. Prior to his appointment in March, 1958, industrial engineering, plant engineering, tools, and operations had been separate staff functions, reporting to the Director of Manufacturing. Mr.

Fenton's new position combined these responsibilities into a single Department.

Mr. Fenton was particularly hopeful that his new Department could help the Division to do a better job in long-range factory planning. Since the various plant buildings had been erected separately and at different times, and because, as he phrased it, "conveyors are almost as expensive to move as to install," Mr. Fenton was convinced that the Division did not have an ideal plant layout or arrangement of facilities. With a better coordination of plans for new products and with improved market forecasts, Mr. Fenton was confident, however, that more efficient production could be achieved. In this regard, Mr. Fenton observed, "The combination line was placed 'out back' on a temporary basis to get it started. This required very expensive supporting conveyor and assembly conveyor systems, both for the automatics and for the combination. We expected eventually to move the combination line to Building 4. Maybe you could argue that we have a preconception that the only way to do anything is on a conveyor."

In May, 1959, Mr. Fenton and his Department were developing a five-year plan relating to items to be produced in the St. Joseph Division and to the way plant facilities could best be laid out during this period. In an effort to adjust for schedule shifts, several further matters also were being studied seriously. These included a review of make-or-buy and subcontracting decisions, both on a long- and short-range basis. Typically, in the industry, anywhere from 40 to 65 per cent of total factory costs were spent on purchased components, subcontracted parts, and raw materials.

Mr. Johns believed in periodic and critical reappraisals of all such decisions. He recognized that all of the topics now under study were difficult, complicated issues. He was convinced that it was nonetheless essential for the Division promptly to consider various possible changes in existing practices.

PART 2. RESPONSES TO

SPECIFIC PROBLEMS

The Whirlpool Corporation (II)[1]

On Friday, May 1, 1959, *The Daily Whirl,* a house organ published each working day for the employees of the St. Joseph Division of The Whirlpool Corporation, carried the following lead article:[2]

EXPLAIN SCHEDULE REDUCTION

Yesterday, Lee Johns[3] and George Homer[4] visited several departments to explain the current schedule reduction and the efforts that were made to prevent it. Believing that those who were laid off should have a complete explanation of the situation, superintendents followed this up with similar meetings with the people affected by the reduction.

The discussions dealt with five major points:

1. They explained that our original schedule had to be set last October, based on what we hoped to sell and the amount we could carry in inventory. An attempt was made to set a steady level of production, and this was maintained at considerable effort through April.

2. When combination and automatic sales slowed down, every effort was made to prevent a layoff by maintaining the schedules. Mr. Johns explained that meetings were held with Bud Gray,[5] Bob Brooker,[6] John Hurley,[7] and Bob Upton[7] to help find ways to stimulate sales, but the results of these efforts won't be seen immediately.

3. And while the Sales Department is redoubling its efforts . . . results will not be visible for several months. Automatic Washer schedules will probably continue at their present rate.

---

[1] For background information regarding the company and its St. Joseph Division, see The Whirlpool Corporation (I).

[2] Excerpts only.

[3] General Manager of the Division.

[4] Director of Manufacturing.

[5] Board Chairman.

[6] President.

[7] Sales executive.

4. Despite the schedule reduction, Mr. Johns pointed out that the Combination is still a very important product in our future. Competition is making it even more important, so all our efforts will have to be increased to establish an effective program.

5. As we reported in an earlier article, schedules have been maintained above last year's levels—about 10 per cent—despite the reduction. Employment is also up about 10 per cent over a year ago, showing that large gains have been made toward reducing this seasonal problem.

Mr. Johns said that all employees, including those on layoff, would be informed of any substantial change in schedules.

MR. JOHNS' VIEW OF SUCH PROBLEMS

Virtually all facets of plant activity were affected by schedule changes of the type and magnitude taking place. As Mr. Johns, the Division General Manager, reviewed the situation, the May 1 reduction and the resulting layoff of 119 employees seemed to him to typify some of the problems of managing a plant in the consumer hard goods industry. Not only were sales often erratic (Exhibit 1) and difficult to forecast accurately, but also the high rate of production volume for which the plant was geared, and the significant unit costs involved, combined to create considerable capital risk if the company produced for inventory during periods of low sales. These inventory hazards were reinforced by the fact that the major appliance industry was characterized by intense competition, not only in terms of price, but also in terms of product obsolescence created by frequent model changeovers and design improvements.

From experience Mr. Johns knew that the Division's manufacturing costs would rise and its profits would decline as volume was cut. This reflected the influence of the substantial fixed costs represented by tools and production facilities. The plant's heavy reliance on a conveyor system and other types of high-volume production equipment also contributed to a lack of flexibility. Once a decision had been reached to introduce a family of new models, manufacturing facilities, tooling, assembly lines, and in-process storage capacity usually were planned and completed as rapidly as possible in order to gain a competitive advantage. If events proved the forecast of volume requirements to be seriously in error, Mr. Johns felt that operating management was left with a substantially rigid set of variables and only a few choices.

Actually, a lengthy time-period was required to develop new or modified products and to change buildings and facilities. These tasks were complicated by the fact that a portion of the previous tooling

EXHIBIT 1 THE WHIRLPOOL CORPORATION (II)

U.S. APPLIANCE SALES IN THOUSANDS OF UNITS 1949-1958

Year	Ranges	Refrigerators	Ironers	Washing Machines		Washer-Dryer Combinations	Dryers
				Automatic and Semi-Automatic	Wringer and Spinner		
1949	1,056	4,450	307	928	2,137	—	106
1950	1,830	6,200	409	1,646	2,626	—	318
1951	1,400	4,075	284	1,589	1,795	—	492
1952	1,060	3,570	211	1,684	1,582	2	635
1953	1,250	3,650	160	2,071	1,521	51	737
1954	1,350	3,600	90	2,401	1,209	42	941
1955	1,600	4,200	87	3,123	1,268	76	1,397
1956	1,585	3,700	64	3,314	1,228	104	1,523
1957	1,365	3,350	44	2,814	977	179	1,294
1958	1,335	3,050	35	2,744	948	164	1,211
Forecast 1958	1,390	3,487	N.A.	3,048	866	N.A.	N.A.
Forecast 1959	1,375	3,270	N.A.	2,760	800	N.A.	N.A.
Av. Retail Price 1958	$266	$320	$215	$280	$155	$485	$226

Source: *Electrical Merchandising*, January 1959, Statistical and Marketing Issue. Reproduced by permission.

and plant set-up costs probably would have to be written off. Since the St. Joseph–Benton Harbor metropolitan area was relatively small, with a population of approximately 35,000, and since there were only two other large employers in the vicinity, employees laid off during such periods of adjustment usually could be rehired when volume again increased. But such layoffs and subsequent recalls, as well as the job shifts throughout the plant during a change in output level, were expensive in terms both of reduced productivity and a higher unemployment payroll tax rate.

POSSIBLE RESPONSES TO THE CURRENT SITUATION

In the face of the disappointing sales achieved on the combination washer-dryer, Mr. Johns and his staff had been considering various product changes which might now be made. James Stanback, the Division's Director of Engineering, said that he believed two major factors had contributed to the poor industrywide experience on the combination units. "First," he said, "the product the industry is offering can be improved." Citing technical difficulties encountered by certain competitors which he believed had harmed the general reputation of combination units, Mr. Stanback concluded that on an industrywide basis the technical and engineering work on this type of product had been perhaps too hasty. In this respect he believed that, in general, Engineering Departments throughout the industry had been understaffed. He also was convinced that in contrast to the achievements in such products as electronics, there may have been a failure to realize that there were challenges and problems in the home laundry area that went beyond purely technical considerations— designs not only must be technically adequate but satisfactory also from the economic and marketing viewpoint.

Mr. Stanback's second major criticism of present industrywide practice was that the combination units were priced too high. "The combination unit of the future," Mr. Stanback said, "must be lower priced, more compact, have a total cycle of less than one hour, use less hot water, and be completely reliable mechanically." In support of this view he noted that a major competitor had just brought onto the market a new combination featuring a "fast spin" operation that would reduce the time of the drying cycle. The spin rate of 500 rpm was much faster than that of Whirlpool's current model (200 rpm), permitting a reduction of about 20 minutes in cycle time.

In Mr. Stanback's opinion, however, the competing unit was still bulky, slow, and high priced.

On the basis of studies of the current situation, Whrlpool officials had become convinced that several courses of action were open to them in bringing an improved combination unit to the market. Essentially the choice lay between: (a) making various improvements in the Division's present model, but retaining essentially "the same basic package"; or (b) bringing out a completely new model, embodying far more radical product developments.

The latter type of undertaking usually required about two years from the initial engineering work to the start of regular production on the assembly line. This 24-month cycle typically would be divided along the following lines:

Month Numbers	Engineering Section Responsible	Functions Performed
1 through 7	Advance Development	Determine basic technical concepts and approaches.
8 through 13	Special Products	Determine the specific design of each part; build and test prototypes.
14 through 15	Combination Engineering	Determine marketing and styling features including design "aesthetics"; establish liaison with Manufacturing.
16 through 24	Manufacturing Engineering	Decisions on process tooling, assembly layout; start pilot-line operations.

To maintain security on an important new product development, negotiations with suppliers of parts and with materials vendors normally were undertaken only at the last possible moment. Ordinarily the Division's own Engineering Department did much of the actual designing of the new components required, releasing detailed drawings to vendors only perhaps two to nine months before the parts were needed, depending on the complexity of the component.

Recent discussions between representatives of the corporate sales department and members of Mr. Johns' staff resulted in an estimate that certain significant improvements in the Division's present combination model could be introduced within approximately seven months. A substantially longer time would be required if it were decided instead to perfect a totally new model which was now in the prototype stage. A market forecast of the sales which might be achieved by each of these alternatives was pertinent to a choice between them. By 1959 a Market Research Group had been developed in the company to provide sales forecasts that were considerably more thorough, and based on more sophisticated techniques, than those employed when decisions had been made regarding tooling for the original combination unit. Development and tooling costs under each of the alternatives were also important factors to be considered, but Division personnel were confident that these could be estimated with a high degree of accuracy.

Mr. Johns realized that he now was confronted by problems similar to those his predecessor had faced in 1954–1955 when important and far-reaching manufacturing decisions, involving major commitments, had been made regarding the present combination unit.

Gravehardt Printing Company

By October, T. H. Richards, owner and President of the Gravehardt Printing Company, had become seriously concerned about the future of his firm, a job printing shop in a large eastern city. Notwithstanding numerous steps he had taken to strengthen the company since purchasing it about two years before, its operating losses had reached alarming levels. Mr. Richards was therefore attempting to determine what steps to take next.

At the time he acquired the firm, Mr. Richards assumed that since it had been highly profitable in the past, he could devote his initial few months as owner primarily to the task of familiarizing himself with the company and the industry. This was not the case, however, for during his first three weeks as President the following events occurred:

1. Almost immediately he began receiving complaints from both customers and salesmen of poor quality printing. Several of the callers threatened to take their business elsewhere unless Mr. Richards promptly reversed what one of them termed "Gravehardt's three-year trend of steadily deteriorating quality."

2. A number of Gravehardt's major customers, mainly manufacturers of capital goods, began to feel the effects of a business recession. Although there was no immediate decline in the number of orders received, several firms advised Mr. Richards that it was possible that their printing requirements would be curtailed substantially in the months ahead.

3. Mr. Richards' salesmen asked him to raise their present 7½ per cent commission on sales to 10 per cent, a figure that they contended was generally employed in the industry.

4. The shop employees also demanded raises, presenting Mr. Richards with evidence that their wages were at least 20 per cent below the local community rate for jobs of their type.

5. Mr. Richards received a letter from the owner of the building occupied by the company, giving him six weeks to vacate the premises which would then be demolished to permit construction of a new freeway. Mr. Richards had known of this impending highway project before buying the company, but all concerned had assured him that it would be unnecessary to relocate for at least six months.

It also became increasingly clear to Mr. Richards that in two different respects, age was a serious threat to his newly acquired firm. Six of its key personnel—the three salesmen, the shop superintendent, the cost estimator, and the chief layout man—were over 60 years of age, the latter three actually over 65. Furthermore, the printing equipment was antiquated, a fact underscored by the large amount and frequency of press "downtime" for repairs.

After less than a month as owner, therefore, Mr. Richards became acutely aware that he and his company faced serious and urgent problems. He realized that the profitable past record of the firm had caused him to overassess the strength of the organization and the soundness of its assets. Recognizing that these errors in judgment

EXHIBIT 1   GRAVEHARDT PRINTING COMPANY

PROFIT AND LOSS STATEMENT

(Dollars in thousands)

	1/1 to 12/31		1/1 to 9/30	
	2nd Prior Calendar Year	Prior Calendar Year	Prior Calendar Year	Current Calendar Year
Sales	$398	$366	$265	$251
Materials and Services	153	136	101	99
Labor	103	115	81	88
Factory Overhead	25	35	27	26
Total Cost of Goods Sold	281	286	209	213
Sales and Administration Expenses	104	107	79	74
Other Income	57	57	45	19
Other Expenses*	23	29	18	15
Net Profit	47	1	4	(32)

* Interest, life insurance premiums, sales discounts allowed for prompt payment.

Source: Company records.

EXHIBIT 2   GRAVEHARDT PRINTING COMPANY

PROFIT AND LOSS STATEMENT

September, Current Year

Net Sales			$27,493
Materials and Services			
Paper	$ 2,818		
Ink	401		
Engravings	1,185		
Electrotypes	4		
Miscellaneous	992		
Ruling and Bindings	1,620		
Art Work	188		
Total	$ 7,208		
plus Beginning Inventory	11,766		
	$18,974		
(less) Ending Inventory	7,559		
Materials and Services Used		$11,415	
Labor			
Composition	$ 2,220		
Presses	3,527		
Schedule-Layout Man	493		
Shipping Clerk	337		
Shop Supervisors	1,147		
	$ 7,724		
plus Beginning Inventory	1,982		
	$ 9,706		
(less) Ending Inventory	1,278		
Labor Used		8,428	
Overhead			
Rent	$ 766		
Light and Power	173		
Shipping	(3)		
Repairs to Presses	76		
Depreciation	475		
Supplies and Expenses	242		
Insurance	90		
Taxes	174		
Equipment Rented	106		
Workmen's Compensation	67		
General	223		
Total Overhead		2,389	
Total Cost of Goods Sold		$22,232	
Gross Profit			$ 5,261

EXHIBIT 2 *(Continued)* GRAVEHARDT PRINTING COMPANY

PROFIT AND LOSS STATEMENT

September, Current Year

Sales and Administrative Expense			
Sales Salaries and Commissions (including Advertising Commissions)	$ 3,328		
Sales and Officers' Expenses	257		
Auto Expenses	46		
Auto Depreciation	183		
Depreciation, Office Equipment and Leasehold Improvements	209		
Office Salaries	3,055		
Office Supplies	(12)		
Telephone and Telegraph	207		
Legal and Professional Fees	100		
Insurance	35		
Workmen's Compensation	10		
Taxes	41		
General	227		
		$ 7,686	
Profit (Loss) before Taxes and Other Income and Expenses			($ 2,425)
Other Income			
Publishing Advertising Commissions	$ 1,465		
Discounts Taken	8		
Total Other Income	$ 1,473		
Other Expenses			
Discounts Allowed on Purchases	493		
Life Insurance Premiums	65		
Interest	295		
Total Other Expenses	$ 853		
Other Income less Other Expenses			$ 620
Net Profit (Loss) before Taxes			($ 1,805)

Source: Company records.

were now beyond recall, Mr. Richards resolved to overcome them. For almost two years, therefore, on essentially an "around-the-clock" basis, he had been engaged in an intensive campaign to improve the quality of the company's printing, its personnel, and its equipment, tasks made all the more difficult by the effects of the recession. As he now approached his second anniversary as owner, Mr. Richards acknowledged to himself that although the various changes he had

EXHIBIT 3 GRAVEHARDT PRINTING COMPANY

SELECTED BALANCE SHEETS

(Dollars in thousands)

| | ASSETS | | | | | |
| | Prior Year | | | Current Year | | |
	Jan. 31	June 30	Dec. 31	March 31	June 30	Aug. 31
Cash	$ 12	$ 19	$ 7	$ 4	$ 1	$ 1
Accounts Receivable	36	55	50	47	37	31
Inventory	24	22	19	10	15	14
Cash Value, Life Insurance	15	15	15	16	16	16
Prepayments	3	2	3	4	2	3
Securities	30	0	0	0	0	0
Total Current Assets	120	113	94	81	71	65
Machinery, Equipment, Leasehold Improvements	46	73	71	75	73	72
Total Assets	166	186	165	156	144	137
	LIABILITIES					
Accounts Payable	$ 27	$ 27	$ 26	$ 25	$ 25	$ 31
Notes Payable Due within One Year	18	24	12	21	22	18
Notes Payable Secured by Life Insurance Policies	14	14	14	14	14	14
Accruals	11	11	20	13	13	6
Total Current Liabilities	70	76	72	73	74	69
Notes Payable	32	39	24	23	21	24
Accounts Payable to Officer	5	4	5	4	4	4
Accrued Advance Billing	0	0	0	1	0	0
Capital Stock	50	50	50	50	50	50
Earned Surplus	9	17	14	5	(5)	(10)
Total Liabilities	166	186	165	156	144	137

Source: Company records.

introduced undoubtedly had strengthened the firm, its problems remained acute. (See Exhibits **1**, **2**, and **3**.)

BACKGROUND TO PURCHASE

The Company

The Gravehardt company was founded almost a half century ago. Over the years it acquired an excellent community reputation for low-volume, high-quality printing, such as full-color sales brochures, catalogues, advertising reprints, and direct mail pieces. Exceptional quality was an important factor in only a relatively small percentage of the total printing market, but it was in this niche that the Gravehardt company had competed successfully and profitably for nearly five decades.

The firm's principal customers were manufacturing establishments in the community—a highly industrialized center of roughly 600,000 persons. At the time of Mr. Richards' purchase, the company had four local competitors for high-quality, low-volume printing. Each of these firms was roughly comparable to Gravehardt in size. About a dozen larger printing establishments with high-volume production equipment also competed for the local market. Although on large orders these concerns could underprice the Gravehardt company and its four principal competitors, they could not compete successfully with them on small runs of complex, high-quality work. There were an additional 60 or so small and medium-sized letterpress printing shops in the community, as well as approximately 100 sources of off-set printing. These latter companies generally did not cater to the quality market, tending instead to compete on the basis of price. During a typical year a number of small, new printing establishments entered the market, and there was an appreciable number of printing shop failures, particularly among the smaller firms. This tended to keep the printing business highly competitive, especially in terms of price.

Although Mr. Gravehardt, the founder of the company, never had expanded its workforce beyond 40 employees, he had gradually amassed a personal fortune estimated at approximately $1 million almost entirely from company operations. Since he had no relatives interested in entering the business when he decided to retire at the age of 74, Mr. Gravehardt placed the firm on the market.

When considering the purchase of the Gravehardt company, Mr. Richards had made a hurried study of industry statistics. From these he ascertained that among the nation's job printers in general, net profit after taxes recently had been averaging roughly 3.5 per cent of sales. His study indicated that in a recent year, among firms which were comparable to Gravehardt in size, and which confined their activities to letterpress operations, average performance ratios had been as follows:

Net Sales		100 %
Materials and Purchased Services	34.6%	
Labor	30.7	
Plant Overhead	11.1	
Total Cost of Goods Sold		76.4
Print Shop Profit		23.6
Selling and Administrative Expense		18.9
Profit before Taxes		4.7%

The fact that for many years Gravehardt's operating results had been considerably better than these figures strengthened Mr. Richards' growing belief that the company was unusually sound. He also gained the impression that the high-quality sector of the printing market usually did not experience pronounced seasonal fluctuations in sales demand.

Mr. Richards' Background

Mr. Richards was 36 years old when he purchased the firm. After graduating from high school he had entered college, later interrupting his studies to serve in the Army Medical Corps during the Second World War. Following release from the service he returned to college, working evenings as a technician and supervisor in several hospital laboratories while completing an undergraduate major in Philosophy. Upon graduation he took a salaried position as a salesman for a major pharmaceutical house, selling antibiotics and other medicines to doctors and druggists. He supplemented his income during this period by selling supplies to medical laboratories, he and an acquaintance having established a small distributorship to serve this market.

Three years later Mr. Richards severed his tie with the pharmaceutical concern and the laboratory supply house, and took a position with a publishing company in the same community, selling medical textbooks on commission to doctors, libraries, and hospitals. With this change, Mr. Richards' earnings almost immediately doubled to an annual rate of approximately $14,000. In addition to representing the publishing firm, he also formed his own book distributorship through which he sold the books of various other publishers, operating from his home by phone and personal calls.

During this period Mr. Richards became attracted to the idea of buying a small manufacturing business. For the next several years, therefore, he investigated a number of possibilities. Finally, through his lawyer, he learned of the availability of the Gravehardt company. After investigation, he negotiated its purchase, receiving advice on the price and other aspects of the transaction from his banker and from the lawyer who originally had called the firm to his attention. On the basis of Gravehardt's past earnings, present assets, and future sales prospects, Mr. Richards was confident that his successful offer of $250,000 for the firm (including its cash assets of $157,000) represented a most favorable investment, even allowing for the additional costs that would arise in the next half year in connection with the plant relocation. Under the terms of the purchase agreement, Mr. Gravehardt, at his own request, was retained on the company payroll as a consultant at a monthly salary of $500. This arrangement continued until Mr. Gravehardt's death about a year later. During this interval, he offered few suggestions to Mr. Richards, and showed only casual interest in the company's operations.

To finance the purchase and to obtain adequate working capital, Mr. Richards borrowed $50,000 from a local bank, using as security $96,000 (book value) of common stock he owned, through inheritance, in a privately held manufacturing company. Repayment was to be at the rate of $3,000 per year. These funds were supplemented by an additional loan from the same bank of $36,000, secured by assets of the Gravehardt company and repayable at $12,000 per year. An additional $14,000 was borrowed from the same bank, secured by a life-insurance policy on the life of two of Gravehardt's key personnel, and repayable on demand. The balance of the purchase price was met from the cash assets present in the Gravehardt company at the time of the purchase. Mr. Richards felt that in a crisis situation, he could probably borrow an additional $15,000 or so from family sources.

MR. RICHARDS' RESPONSE TO EARLY CRISES

New Equipment and Quarters

After being notified that the company had to move from its present building in six weeks, Mr. Richards began to consider the advantages that would be achieved if certain new presses could be acquired coincident with the relocation, thus avoiding the cost of moving almost obsolete units which would have to be replaced in the near future. He had become convinced that the poor operating condition of some of the equipment accounted for many of the quality difficulties Gravehardt was encountering, particularly in color printing.

GRAVEHARDT PRINTING COMPANY **225**

To equip himself to evaluate such matters, Mr. Richards embarked on a crash program to strengthen his knowledge of printing equipment. Over the next several weeks he visited printers in other cities, read a number of books on printing technology, consulted with equipment salesmen, and, accompanied by plant supervisory personnel, made several trips to observe different types of presses in operation. Mr. Richards also endeavored to learn what he could about offset printing to determine whether it might be advisable at some future date for Gravehardt to enter this field, one which apparently was becoming an increasingly important sector of the printing industry.

On the basis of these investigations, Mr. Richards and his associates decided that with the move to new quarters, the company would retire four old letterpresses, replacing them with two newly acquired cylinder presses. One of these would be purchased new for $15,300; the other would be a manufacturer's floor model priced at $14,200. Both presses would be delivered to the new plant shortly before the relocation, and the four old presses would be sold as junk prior to the move. Mr. Richards estimated that these arrangements would save several thousand dollars in moving costs.

While he was reaching decisions regarding the purchase of new presses, Mr. Richards also actively pursued the question of new quarters for the plant. A survey of the metropolitan area uncovered a number of suitable locations. Mr. Richards finally selected 9,000 square feet on the first floor, and 2,000 square feet on the fifth floor, of a downtown building several blocks from the present site. Construction of considerable numbers of partitions and additions to available electrical circuits were needed to adapt this space to the company's needs. In Mr. Richards' judgment, however, these considerations were more than offset by the fact that the new setting—adjacent to a park, a museum, and a university club—assured the company a location in keeping with its tradition of highest quality printing. The rental on the new facilities was $9,000 per year, on a five-year lease. This was the same amount paid for Gravehardt's old quarters, which contained about 20 per cent more space.

In spite of many difficulties and problems, the move to the new location was completed on schedule, with but modest loss of production. This was due in large part to the fact that the two new presses had been installed in the new quarters before the move and put into operation prior to the shutdown of operations at the former location.

The cost of preparing the new facilities and completing the move represented a significant cash outflow.

Leasehold Improvement
General Contracting $9,235
Electrical Work   8,874
Painting   1,901
                                                      $20,010
Moving Expenses   4,383
                Total $24,393

After the move was completed, Mr. Richards continued his analyses of the company's equipment. Continuing to augment his knowledge of printing equipment and technology, he attended several trade association training courses and made numerous trips to new printing installations. The following spring Mr. Richards purchased the following additional items, which were delivered in June.

1 Platen Press $3,850
1 "Make-up Gauge" (A device for squaring-up a set of
   type and assuring that the type will not work up out
   of the chase.)   1,000

None of the new equipment which Mr. Richards had purchased required new skills on the part of the workforce. The shop, therefore, was quickly able to achieve what Mr. Richards considered good operating results from the new units. The salesmen repeatedly told Mr. Richards that the quality of the shop output was better than they had ever known it to be. Shop personnel seemed similarly enthusiastic. Employees in the composing room and press room, for example, initially had not been particularly impressed at the decision to acquire the make-up gauge. After a year's use, however, senior employees assured Mr. Richards that "this was the best investment the company had ever made."

Organizational Changes

Several months after the relocation, having become convinced that the workforce was now reasonably settled in the new quarters and in the use of the new presses, Mr. Richards' next step was to replace the plant superintendent, who was then in his seventies. Mr. Richards had seen repeated indications that the information supplied by the superintendent regarding deliveries and quality often was inadequate and sometimes simply incorrect. He appeared to Mr. Richards also to be lax in supervising the workforce, spending most of his time revising schedules and pacifying salesmen when deliveries were late. Mr.

Richards also was critical of him for allowing shop equipment to deteriorate through poor maintenance. On the other hand, he had been with the company for many years, and Mr. Richards was reluctant to discharge him outright. Therefore, he moved him into the office to perform minor administrative duties and to serve as a liaison man for one key customer whose purchasing agent was one of his closest friends. Under this arrangement, the superintendent's salary remained at its former level of $500 per month.

To replace him, Mr. Richards promoted Robert Brinker, age 48. Mr. Brinker had been with the company for 30 years and Mr. Richards believed that everyone acknowledged that he was the most skilled employee in the composing room. Since Mr. Brinker's experience had been confined primarily to this one phase of the business, Mr. Richards thought that as superintendent he would require particular assistance in the supervision of the Press Department. Mr. Richards therefore created the new position of press foreman to which he appointed Robert Gregory, age 38, a man who he believed was recognized by his associates as the best pressman in the plant. Mr. Brinker and Mr. Gregory were younger and less experienced than several Gravehardt employees, but Mr. Richards had seen numerous indications that both men had leadership potential. This fact, plus the unquestioned technical competence possessed by both of them, convinced Mr. Richards that they would prove effective in their new responsibilities.

Shortly after promoting Mr. Brinker and Mr. Gregory, Mr. Richards moved the former assistant superintendent, age 65, into the office and placed him in charge of scheduling. To Mr. Richards he seemed excitable and temperamentally ill-suited for the continuing pressure of supervising responsibilities in the shop. Mr. Richards hoped that in this new position, the former assistant superintendent would schedule shop operations in such a way as to decrease press downtime. In addition, he would continue to be responsible for the layout and design of printing jobs, functions he had performed for many years.

Decision Regarding Offset Printing

Mr. Richards' next area of concerted study related to the possibility of diversifying into offset printing. The offset process differs from letterpress printing in that it does not require the use of type. Instead, printing is accomplished by the use of an etched aluminum plate which usually is prepared by a photo process. A sample page of the material to be printed is first produced, either through use of type composed in the usual manner and run off on a proof press, or through use of a varityper, a typewriter-like device which automatically spaces letters to create an even margin on the right hand side of each page. A photographic negative of the sample page is then made, and placed on top of a light-sensitive aluminum plate. Exposing the plate to light results in the transferring of an exact image of the page to the plate. The plate surface is then chemically etched, its nonexposed areas—that is, the areas that would not generate any printed impression—being partially eaten away by this process. The exposed areas therefore stand out in relief from the rest of the surface, and the plate is ready for the press.

In the printing operation, the etched plate is mounted on an offset press and its surface alternately dampened with water and coated with a greasy ink. The plate's raised area absorbs the ink, while the balance of the surface absorbs water and repels the ink. The inked portion of the plate, representing the image to be produced, is then transferred to a rubber roller, and the roller, in turn, transfers the image to the paper being printed.

The chief advantage of offset printing is that its "make ready operations" require only 10 to 30 minutes, in contrast to the one to seven hours required to prepare work for conventional letterpress printing. Furthermore, where photographs or drawings are to be printed, offset plates are cheaper than the engravings, cuts, or both, required in letterpress. Finally, the running speed of an offset press usually is 40 to 60 per cent faster than letterpress.

Disadvantages of offset are that the process is more complex than letterpress, requiring precise control of chemical and physical variables to achieve good quality. Also, offset plates have a limited life, and the paper and ink required are more expensive than those used in the letterpress operation. Letterpress is therefore usually cheaper on long production runs where only a few "halftones"—that is, engravings, pictures, cuts, and so on—are required.

Mr. Richards' analysis of industry data indicated that offset's share of the national market had roughly doubled in the past 20 years and currently accounted for perhaps one-third of all printing revenues. In its own market area, Gravehardt recently had seen increasing evidences that it was now competing not only with other letterpress firms, but also with offset printers. Mr. Richards had concluded, therefore, that his company's competitive position would be strengthened if it acquired offset facilities. He also had seen indications in trade literature that many letterpress firms were currently adding offset equipment, and that more than a few offset printers were diversifying into letterpress operations.

In January of the current year, after much study, Mr. Richards purchased a used offset press for $6,750, and also hired Robert Jenner, an experienced salesman of offset printing. In discussions with Mr. Richards, Mr. Jenner had stated that he had been selling approximately $100,000 worth of offset printing annually for his present employer, and had every confidence that he could do the same, or better, for Gravehardt.

Since its operation differed from those of the company's other presses, none of Gravehardt's employees were able to operate the new offset unit. Mr. Richards therefore hired an experienced offset operator. The new employee proved disappointing, however, turning out work of only marginal quality at what Mr. Richards believed was an unreasonably slow pace. After several months the operator was discharged. Mr. Richards then selected one of the company's press helpers to become an offset trainee, arranging for him to attend trade school at night for instruction. The trainee seemed to learn quickly and was now operating the offset press with reasonably satisfactory results, although still somewhat below the pace and quality levels Mr. Richards was confident of obtaining eventually.

While investigating the advisability of acquiring offset facilities, as well as during his earlier study of printing equipment, Mr. Richards had seen numerous indications that printing, although an ancient craft, was undergoing a period of rapid technological progress. Numerous new techniques, either already in existence or apparently in their final stages of development, seemed to hold promise of far-reaching changes for the industry. These included such innovations as phototypesetting, a technique for preparing negatives for offset plates; fast magnesium etching, a process reducing from hours to minutes the time required to prepare engraved plates; and numerous new techniques in the field of color printing.

OPERATING PRACTICES AND PROCEDURES CURRENTLY IN EFFECT

Production Facilities and Personnel

Gravehardt's major manufacturing facilities consisted of the items listed in Exhibit 4, arranged into the layout shown in Exhibit 5. The company's employee roster numbered 30 people divided among the job categories and wage brackets cited in Exhibit 6. In March of the prior year most shop personnel had received a wage increase averaging five cents an hour for the compositors, and ten cents an hour for the pressmen. The specific wages paid to each man were negotiated on an individual basis rather than being premised upon any formal

EXHIBIT 4 GRAVEHARDT PRINTING COMPANY

MAJOR PLANT EQUIPMENT

COMPOSING			Key*
	2	Lanston Monotype Keyboards	1
	5	Lanston Monotype Casting Machines	2
	4	Composing Benches and Type Drawers	3
	1	Vandercook Make-Up Gauge	4
	4	Stones	5
	1	Proof Press	6
	—	File Racks (for storing set-up type)	7
PRESS AREA			
	1	Brandtjan & Kluge Platen Job Press	8
	1	Chandler & Price Platen Job Press	9
	1	Original Heidelberg Platen Job Press	10
	2	Miehle Vertical Cylinder Presses	11
	2	Original Heidelberg Horizontal Cylinder Presses	12
	2	Kelly C Horizontal Cylinder Presses	13
	2	Miehle Horizontal Cylinder Presses	14
	1	Harris Offset Press	15
	1	Seybold Cutter	16
	1	Baumfolder Folding Machine	17
OFFICE AREA			
	—	Dark Room, Camera, Developing Equipment	18
	1	Productrol Board	19

* See Exhibit 5 for location.

wage schedule. As a result of these increases, Mr. Richards was satisfied that Gravehardt's wage structure and pattern of fringe benefits were now roughly in line with the union scale in the local area.

No union attempts to organize the plant had ever occurred, and Superintendent Brinker was confident that no significant interest in unionism existed among the workforce. However, several of the employees were known to be "good union men," who regularly paid dues to the International Typographical Union.

In general, Mr. Richards and the key supervisory personnel believed that employee relations were satisfactory. Morale seemed good, and the men appeared cooperative and hard working. Turnover was not a major problem, the average length of Gravehardt service among the shop employees being roughly 15 years. Whenever recruiting was

EXHIBIT 5 GRAVEHARDT COMPANY

PLANT LAYOUT

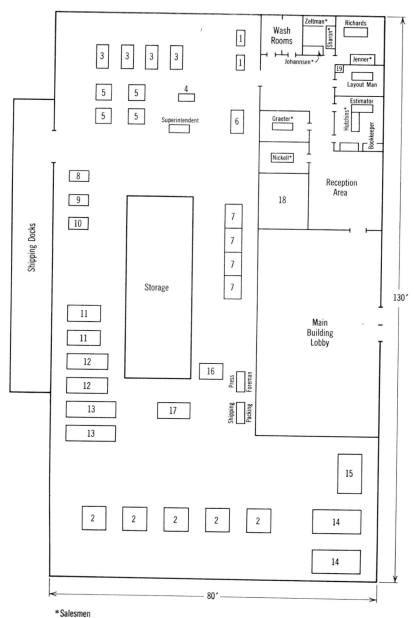

*Salesmen

EXHIBIT 6 GRAVEHARDT PRINTING COMPANY

PERSONNEL AS OF OCTOBER 1, CURRENT YEAR

NAME	TITLE OR FUNCTION	SALARY OR WAGE
T. H. Richards	President	$15,000 per year
Robert Jenner	Sales Manager	Commission Basis
Richard Hutson	Miscellaneous Office and Sales Duties	$300 per month
August Moog	Layout Man	$2.85 per hour
Herbert Pogue	Estimator	$425 per month
George Graeter	Salesman	Commission Basis
Donald Johannsen	Salesman	$300 per month
Albert Nickell	Salesman	Commission Basis
Walter Sharon	Salesman	Commission Basis
Howard Zeltman	Salesman	$300 per month
Herta Balchen	Bookkeeper	$375 per month
Jane Bradley	Stenographer (Part Time)	$40 per week

NAME	TITLE	DUTIES	COMPENSATION (Hourly unless specified otherwise)
Robert Brinker	Superintendent	Shop Supervision	$700 per month
Robert Gregory	Foreman	Press Foreman	$550 per month
Minnie Allen	Keyboard Operator	Lanston Monotype and Binding	$2.50
Fred Alms	Castor	Lanston Castors	$1.85
W. Hivers	Compositor	Composing	$2.30
M. Jerndt	Compositor	Composing	$2.55
C. Wentsel	File Man	Maintain Orderly Storage of Pages of Type	$1.60
L. Berkeley	Stone Man	Lock-Up	$2.00
C. Bell	Pressman	Can Run Presses 8, 9, 10, 13	$2.00
W. Divita	Pressman	Can Run Presses 12, 13, 14	$2.40
B. Oster	Pressman	Can Run Presses 11, 13	$2.30
T. Smith	Pressman	Can Run Presses 11, 13	$2.55
A. Zaile	Pressman	Can Run Presses 11, 12, 13	$2.50
G. Fischer	Pressman (Part Time)	Can Run Press 14	$2.40
M. Lumpp	Press Helper	Can Run Presses 11, 14, 15	$2.05
N. Straub	Press Helper	Can Run Presses 13, 14	$2.05
C. Earle	Cutter	Seybold Cutter	$2.40
G. Hancher	Shipping Clerk	Shipping—Sweeper	$1.60

necessary, experienced printing personnel were usually in fairly plentiful supply in the local labor market. Several experiences had convinced Mr. Richards, however, that care had to be exercised in recruiting new men in order to maintain the exceptionally high quality standards required by Gravehardt.

Production Processes

When a salesman turned over an order or a request for a price quotation to the shop personnel it was usually in the form of a sketch of the work, or the exact copy of text to be printed, accompanied by a specification sheet (Exhibit 7) which the salesman was supposed to fill

EXHIBIT 7 GRAVEHARDT COMPANY

SPECIFICATION SHEET

SPECIFICATION SHEET

Is this an Order or do you want Quotation? *Quote*

Buyer *Mr. William Koster* Date *10/8/*

For.. Address..

DESCRIPTION

Quantity and Description *2000 Catalogues – 8½ x 11 (blue on covers) 4 sides*
24 pages plus covers

No. Pages—Inside.. Cover..

STOCK

Inside Stock *#80 Warrens Brilliant Gloss*
Cover Stock *Beckett Double Thick Cover*

PRINTING

Proof to..

Ink—Inside *Black* Ink—Cover *Dark Green*

SERVICE

Copy..Layout..To be charged for if not used..

Itemize as separate charge..Absorb work charges..To be charged in cost of printing..

Electros..Halftones..Designs..Photographing..

Remarks..

BINDING

Cut..Fold..Wire Stitch..Punch..Perforate..

Rule..Round Corner *✓*..Number..Die Out..Crimp..

Gather..Pad..Page..Letter..By..

Punch & Plastic Bind GBC-22 Hole

REMARKS

Plates #118°° Schultz-Gosiger

Estimate Wanted..Signed..

Delivery.. Quoted..Open..
Form 34 1M 5-58

out in complete detail. In practice, the "spec sheets" submitted by the salesmen often lacked certain detailed information, either because these matters had not yet been determined, or because of carelessness. If not remedied, such omissions could create subsequent delays in preparing the final layout of the job, or in the printing operations themselves.

The sketch and specification sheet were given to Lloyd Pogue, the estimator. Mr. Pogue was 85 years old and had more than a half-century of experience in the printing industry. Mr. Richards believed, notwithstanding his age, that Mr. Pogue provided the company with an invaluable fund of knowledge regarding printing, and was impressed by the energy and keenness of judgment which Mr. Pogue displayed.

On about 25 per cent of the jobs brought in by salesmen, price quotations were required before the order was confirmed. To be competitive, Gravehardt usually had to respond to these requests no more than a day or two after they were received. The price quotations were prepared by Mr. Pogue on the basis of his estimates of the cost of the paper, engravings, and other materials to be used, and the labor time that would be required on the various press operations. Mr. Pogue believed that paper costs represented the most difficult phase of the estimating process because they depended not merely on the number of copies to be run, but also on the variety of paper requested by the customer, the ink, colors, and type to be used, the over-all appearance desired, and the size requirement, which related, in turn, to the capacity of press on which the job would have to be run.

The quotations submitted to the customers included both the price and the promised delivery date, the latter being determined by Mr. Pogue in conjunction with the shop superintendent. Usually little or no negotiation regarding price was carried on between the customer and the company once the quotation was made, except when job specifications were changed. Mr. Pogue regularly checked all of his estimates against the costs actually incurred, discussing with Superintendent Brinker any major variations.

Once an order became firm, Mr. Pogue used the specification sheet to identify any special paper and ink that would have to be ordered. About 45 per cent of the company's orders required a standard ink, and one of two types of paper in a 25 x 38 inch size. Gravehardt therefore regularly purchased a three-month supply, at a cost of about $4,000, of 38 x 50 inch sheets of these particular papers to obtain quantity discounts. Two paper suppliers were patronized to avoid overdependence on any one source. The balance of the paper was bought by Mr. Pogue as required, usually with one-day delivery. Mr. Pogue believed that no advantage was gained by "shopping" between suppliers, since the prices of similar grades of paper almost always were identical.

Purchases of any engravings required for a job always were negotiated by the salesmen who had obtained the order. This practice reflected the belief that the salesman had the best knowledge of the specific requirements of a job. Each of the Gravehardt salesmen tended to rely on a different engraving firm. Mr. Pogue observed, however, that the rates charged by the several engravers for comparable work were usually almost identical. The quality of the engravings had a major influence on the appearance of the printed item, and also was an important factor influencing make-ready time on the presses.

After Mr. Pogue completed his preproduction activities, he turned the job—in the form of two copies of the specification sheet and the sketch—over to Superintendent Brinker. After examining the order, Mr. Brinker gave one copy of the specifications to Press Foreman Gregory to use for planning, and as the basis for ordering supplies of standard ink, paper, or both in the event the inventories of either of these items was depleted. The other copy of the specification sheet and the sketch were given to the layout man.

The layout man was responsible for preparing the job for the shop. To do this he made a new sketch, that is, a "layout sheet," showing the exact spacing, layout, and type required and including specific instructions in the form of notes. Any errors or omissions in the information included at this stage of the process usually resulted in later delays and press down-time in the shop. Conversely, the preparation of accurate, thorough specifications and instructions contributed to a smooth, efficient flow of production operations. The layout man's duties also included ordering any other necessary items or materials, such as electrotypes or special type, and filling out a job card listing the due date promised, the various operations needed, the scheduled completion date for each, and a column for entering the actual completion date.

This job card was placed in one of the pockets of a scheduling board which provided a column of space opposite each listed operation (Exhibit 8). Use of a piece of string stretched to the appropriate column position and held in place by a peg, provided a quick, visual impression of the status of an order. When he had completed all of these steps, the layout man returned the copy of the specification sheet and the detailed layout sheet to the superintendent.

Each day the layout man checked the status of the 50 or so orders

EXHIBIT 8 GRAVEHARDT PRINTING COMPANY

Operations or Departments	
1. Layout	9. Proof Returned O.K.
2. Artwork	10. Alterations
3. Paper	11. Electros
4. Ink	12. Lockup and Ready for Press
5. Engravings	13. Running
6. Machine Composition	14. Printing Finished
7. Hand Composition—Makeup	15. Bindery
8. Proof Out	16. Delivered and Billed

which were typically in process in the shop, stamped the date on the appropriate line of the card when each production step was completed, expedited any engraving, plates, or other purchased materials that were impeding production, and kept the salesmen informed on any delay which threatened delivery promises. He regularly had discussions with the superintendent, advising him when various new jobs would be ready for the shop, and ascertaining the progress of jobs already in process.

Production Processes

On a typical order requiring letterpress operations, the superintendent started the job into production by giving the layout and specification sheets to the operator of the monotype machines. The ensuing steps were:

STEP 1—MONOTYPE OPERATION. A monotype machine, which resembles an oversized typewriter, was used to prepare a punched tape in which the holes were located in such a way as to correspond to the letters in the copy to be printed. The punched tape was used to operate the mechanical type-casting machine (Step 2 of the process). About five minutes were required to set up the monotype, and tapes for an ordinary page could then be run off in about 10 minutes. The monotype operator spent about 50 per cent of her time on monotype work, and the balance in binding operations and in clerical duties. Gravehardt's two monotypes were 22 years old, but were in good operating condition. Superintendent Brinker, who was himself a highly skilled monotype operator, believed that at least three years were required for an operator to become reasonably proficient. After the tapes had been punched, the monotype operator returned the layout sketch and specifications sheets to the superintendent, and gave the spools of punched tapes to the operator of the type-casting machines.

STEP 2—TYPE-CASTING. Type-casting machines functioned on somewhat the same principle as a player-piano. Spools of punched tape prepared by the monotype operator were mounted on the machine and, as the machine was operated, air escaping through the holes in the tape activated the positioning of a matrix die, causing a single letter of type to be cast in metal.

All five of Gravehardt's type-casting machines were over 20 years old, but functioned satisfactorily. About 15 minutes were needed to set up a machine and mount spools. Thereafter, the operation was essentially automatic. Only a short training period was required for a new employee to learn to operate a machine, and an operator often ran two units simultaneously. To set up a machine, however, or to service or repair it, or to replace its complex mechanical linkages, in Superintendent Brinker's judgment, required three to five years of experience. Only one of Gravehardt's present employees, a man 63 years old, had these qualifications.

As each letter was cast, it was assembled automatically into properly spaced and dimensioned lines of type, conforming to the original copy from which the tape had been prepared. These lines of type were discharged into a flat box, known as a "galley." When each galley was filled, the type-caster carried it, as well as the specification sheet, to the composing room for the next operation.

STEP 3—COMPOSING. Two compositors handled the job of composing, that is, the task of assembling the lines of type into a page. Using the galley of type from the type-casting operation, the compositor formed the page, using a combination of type, spacers, and fillers, plus any engravings or cuts of pictures, trade-marks, or drawings. Composing was a painstaking process since the specification sheet and layout had to be followed in minute detail. Assembly of the type for an 8 x 11½ inch page typically required about an hour of a compositor's time.

Work to be printed in more than one color necessitated setting up a separate page for each color. A three-color illustrated sales brochure recently printed for a piano manufacturer, for example, required that the type for the text material, plus a cut of certain of the piano keys, and a cut of the lines in the background, be set up as one page to be printed with black ink; a cut of the piano itself was set up as a second page to be printed in brown ink; certain letters and features to be printed in red ink, were set up as a third page. When the job was printed, each of the three page set-ups was run in sequence over each piece of paper, creating, as an end result, the multicolored images desired. Blends and shades of colors were accomplished by "mixing" dots of individual colors, all the dots of one color being placed on one galley set-up, those of another color on a second set-up, and so on.

Exact spacing and alignment—that is, the "register"—of each set-up was essential in color printing. Even the slightest alignment error would cause an overlap of colors, seriously decreasing the quality and appearance of the job, and sometimes ruining it completely.

STEP 4—MAKE-READY UNIT. Each page of type needed to be exactly square, and firmly compact, without any looseness or "give." When a compositor had completed assembling a page he tied it with a string to hold it together temporarily, and carried the galley by hand to the "Make-Ready" unit. This is a jig that squares-up the type and measures the amount of movement that occurs as the type is squeezed together from the ends and sides, as it would be in the subsequent printing operations. If the unit indicated that the page had not been squared, or that it had too much "give," the compositor added or removed spacers until the Make-Ready circuit showed that the set-up was satisfactory.

STEP 5—PROOF PRINTING. The compositor next slid the type onto a temporary galley set-up, locked it in place, mounted the galley in a hand-controlled "proof press," which he then operated to print a sample page, or "proof." The compositor carefully examined the proof, making any necessary changes and running more proofs if necessary. When satisfied that the proof was in all respects correct, he submitted it to the superintendent, together with the specification and layout sheets.

STEPS 6–7—INTRAPLANT CHECKING AND PROOFREADING. Superintendent Brinker checked the proof in a general way, and if he noted no obvious flaws, sent it to the layout man for detailed proofreading. Proofreading had to be performed with great care to assure that no errors were present in the copy. Mr. Richards believed that the layout man did a thorough job, and perhaps even had a tendency to be overly meticulous, as attested by his sending about 75 per cent of the jobs back to the shop for some form of correction or alteration. Sometimes the corrections specified were minor—even debatable—changes in spacing which he believed would improve the appearance of the work. Mr. Brinker viewed such rework as the price that inevitably had to be paid in achieving high quality printing.

STEP 8—CUSTOMER APPROVAL OF PROOFS. When the layout man became satisfied that the proof, or proofs, for a given job were in order, he returned them to Superintendent Brinker, who in turn gave them to the salesman for transmission to the customer. Obtaining the customer's approval on proofs usually delayed the job several days, but was considered essential in insuring complete customer satisfaction with the end-product, thus avoiding misunderstandings and possible reprinting. The salesmen themselves were not required to inspect the proof before submitting it to the customer, but in practice they did so, and if they felt changes were required, the shop invariably complied. The same was true of corrections requested by the customer.

STEP 9—FINAL INTRACOMPANY CHECKING OF PROOFS. When the customer approved and returned the proof, the salesman gave it to the superintendent who sent it to the layout man for a final check. If he judged it ready for printing, the proof was returned to the superintendent.

STEP 10—LOCKUP. The superintendent then authorized the start of the final printing operations on a job, and had the galley pages delivered to the "stone man" for "lockup" operations. This process consisted of placing the type on a large flat metal surface, known as a "stone," and carefully locking it into a chase under pressure. Different sized chases were required by the different presses. The larger presses would hold a chase permitting either four or eight pages to be printed simultaneously. The lockup required about 15 minutes for a four-page chase. Mr. Gregory, the press foreman, instructed the stone man regarding the specific press to be used for each job.

STEP 11—PRINTING. The chases were then delivered to the designated press and installed by the pressman. After the job had been set up the operator ran off proofs and gave them to the press foreman to check. If he found them satisfactory the foreman authorized the start of the production run. Throughout the run, the copies coming off the press were continuously examined by the pressman. The foreman also checked from time to time. If either of them was dissatisfied with results, the presses would be stopped and adjustments made.

After the necessary number of copies had been run, usually with some extras as a safeguard against poor copies that may have been created by flaws in the paper, they were bundled and carried to the side of the shop for transportation to customers. If the order was small, it usually was delivered by the salesman himself. Larger orders were sent by a commercial delivery service.

Production Supervision

As noted above, the specifications, layouts, and proofs on each job going through the shop repeatedly passed through the hands of the superintendent. Mr. Brinker believed that this practice was vitally important in assuring both quality and productivity, and permitting him to keep track of the status of each job. As he saw it, scheduling work, keeping people busy, and getting jobs out on time were actually his most important responsibilities. Except for a notebook containing one copy of every job order in process, Mr. Brinker maintained no reports or records, and received none from the Accounting Department. Instead, by using the information in the job-orders notebook to plan his assignments to the compositors and to the press foreman, by seeing the work at frequent stages of the process, and by spending much time on the floor of the plant, Mr. Brinker prided himself on always knowing what jobs were being worked on by each man and each machine.

Shop personnel were expected to report either to the superintendent, or to the foreman, when they ran out of work. If no other assignment was available, a pressman often was told to act as a helper to another pressman who was running a job. In such cases, the time of the pressman would be charged to the job itself, and the time of the helper would be charged to "idle time." Mr. Brinker recently had begun also to have temporarily unassigned workers sort and disassemble Gravehardt's considerable accumulation of old type which no longer was required for reruns. Mr. Brinker estimated that there were about 15,000 pounds of such type waiting to be reviewed and scrapped. The metal could be sold at 12 cents per pound and Mr. Brinker believed that a man could process one ton in about 40 hours.

Mr. Brinker believed that he was a more demanding superintendent than his predecessor. In his judgment, the former superintendent had not required the men to work as hard or keep as busy. Even so, he believed that most of the employees actually had been somewhat afraid of his predecessor. On balance, Mr. Brinker was confident that the shop was now turning out more work with fewer people and less overtime than ever before. He believed, and often mentioned to Mr. Richards, that he was accomplishing these improved results by shifting men constantly to meet deadlines, and by keeping many jobs running simultaneously.

Mr. Richards acknowledged that the time pressures confronting the shop superintendent were considerable. If all phases of the work went smoothly, most jobs could be handled in one to two weeks. Customers often postponed important decisions concerning various aspects of an order until the last minute, however, and these delays, plus the apparently inevitable array of changes and corrections, created an almost unending stream of problems for the superintendent to solve. These pressures were intensified still further by the tendency of everyone—customers, salesmen, even Mr. Richards—to press the superintendent for delivery priorities.

Scheduling of Presses

The decision regarding which press to assign to a particular job was made by the press foreman, Mr. Gregory. Mr. Brinker and Mr. Richards were convinced that this was one of the truly crucial determinants of shop efficiency since the press on which a job was run had a direct influence on the quality obtained, the press time required, the shop's ability to meet due dates, and the cost of the order. Mr. Gregory based his scheduling decision on such considerations as present press load, quality standards, the availability of qualified operators, the paper to be used, the estimated set-up and running time, and similar variables. He, along with Superintendent Brinker, made every effort to keep presses fully loaded.

The various presses available, and the operating capabilities of each, are shown in Exhibit 9.

Labor Controls

Each direct labor operator filled out a daily labor time sheet, accounting for his entire day by six-minute intervals. The job number and the type of work were indicated on the time sheet, the latter by use of one of the 30 account numbers that had been established for classifying shop operations. The sheets covering the prior day's operations were collected by Superintendent Brinker each morning and sent to the office.

Mrs. Herta Balchen, the bookkeeper, used the time sheets to post labor charges on the individual cost sheets maintained for each job. For many years she also had prepared two monthly reports for the President, one summarizing machine usage and the other giving a breakdown of labor time charges. In the face of an increased personal workload growing out of reductions in clerical help, Mrs. Balchen had not prepared these reports for the past five months. It was her intention to bring them up to date as soon as possible, however. The latest reports available, covering April of the current year, are shown in Exhibits 10 and 11.

Mrs. Balchen listed on a summary sheet the various costs accumulated for each order, and when the job was ready to be billed,

EXHIBIT 9 GRAVEHARDT PRINTING COMPANY

DESCRIPTIONS OF THE PRINTING PRESSES

Press No.*	Type	Age of Unit in Years	Maximum Size Paper	Make Ready Minutes||	Capacity Impressions/Hr.	Remarks
8	Job-Platen†	28	9″ x 12″	45	3,500	Automatic Feed
9	Job-Platen†	17	9″ x 12″	20	1,000	Hand Fed
10	Job-Platen†	1	9″ x 12″	30	5,000	Automatic Feed
11A	Vertical cylinder‡	10	14″ x 20″	30–120	4,000	Two Pages/Impression
11B	Vertical cylinder‡	7	14″ x 20″	30–120	4,000	Two Pages/Impression
12A	Horizontal cylinder§	1	21″ x 28″	60–120	3,800	Four Pages/Impression
12B	Horizontal cylinder§	1	21″ x 28″	60–120	3,900	Four Pages/Impression
13A	Horizontal cylinder§	12	18″ x 24″	60–120	4,000	Four Pages/Impression
13B	Horizontal cylinder§	21	18″ x 24″	60–120	4,000	Eight Pages, Requires Two Operators
14A	Horizontal cylinder§	45	40″ x 52″	420	700	Make Ready Excludes Plate Making: 15 Minutes
14B	Horizontal cylinder§	45	40″ x 52″	420	700	
15	Offset	8	23″ x 35″	10–20	6,000	

* See Exhibit 5 for plant location.

† The three job presses were used for short runs and specialty work, for they printed but one sheet at a time. The printing action resulted from movement of both the chase and the press bed, bringing them into contact with each other. The chase was inked by contact with the platen, a flat surface covered with a smooth layer of ink rolled on by rollers as part of the cycle. The chase moved up and down to match the circumferential speed of the roller.

‡ On these presses the paper was held on a cylinder and rolled over the chase. These presses were very accurate for color work.

§ The paper was held on a cylindrical roller; the bed of the press holding the chase moved horizontally back and forth as the roller rolled over it. The print was inked between impressions by other smaller rollers. Presses No. 12 were best from the standpoint of quality.

|| Set-up time was a major factor in costs. During the set-up (or make ready) the operator had to (1) load the machine with the proper ink, (2) adjust the ink flow to obtain proper coverage, (3) load the paper, (4) adjust the automatic feed, (5) position the chase on the bed of the press to obtain proper register, (6) adjust printing pressures to obtain clear copy, (7) shim up with tissue paper under any part of the chase where letters or pictures appeared faint, (8) set the speed of the press for the highest output commensurate with good quality, (9) adjust the gas flames which the printed sheets passed over for drying the ink, (10) adjust the position and flow of a spray mechanism that sprayed a fine coating of powder between each printed sheet to prevent one sheet inking another when stacked.

These adjustments, with many variations, depending on the paper, humidity, ink viscosity, colors, and type set-up, were precise in nature and required considerable skill and experience. As the press ran, the operator constantly examined the printed sheets and made minute adjustments. The skill of the pressman determined to a significant degree the length of the set-up, the quality of the product, and the length of time the run required.

EXHIBIT 10 GRAVEHARDT PRINTING COMPANY

PRESS USAGE REPORT

(Times in hours)

Press No.	Set-up	Hours Run	April Nonchargeable*	Idle†
8	1.1	0.6	0.4	173.9
9	1.5	5.2	0.6	168.7
10	24.9	44.8	18.3	88.0
11A	34.4	39.3	11.1	91.2
11B	28.9	32.6	15.3	99.2
12A	61.7	42.7	19.8	54.0
12B	55.2	39.4	21.4	60.0
13A	42.3	66.2	13.1	54.4
13B	49.5	79.0	10.4	37.0
14A	7.6	9.9	9.8	153.7
14B	6.7	12.8	45.1	111.4
15	12.0	15.5	37.0	111.5
12A‡	19.7	34.8	6.0	115.5
12B‡	18.4	41.2	6.2	110.2

* Machine in use but time not chargeable to customer.

† Based on one complete shift (or two complete shifts if used on second shift).

‡ Second-shift operations.

NOTE: Mr. Richards believed that a useful rule-of-thumb was that even with careful scheduling, the mix of incoming orders would cause, on the average, about 20 per cent idle press time per shift and that only somewhere between 65 and 80 per cent of the remaining press time could be charged to customers.

Source: Company records.

EXHIBIT 11   GRAVEHARDT PRINTING COMPANY

LABOR ANALYSIS REPORT

April

Group	Chargeable	Nonchargeable	Total
Compositors	$1,149	$1,326	$ 2,475
Cutters	252	202	454
Pressmen	2,328	1,998	4,326
	$3,729	$3,526	$ 7,255
Shop Supervisory (base rate plus overtime)			1,448
File Man, Sweeper, Shipping Clerk, Layout Man			1,366
Total Labor Payroll			$10,069

BREAKDOWN OF NONCHARGEABLE HOURS

Compositors
Distribution Type	552.6 hours
Faulty Type	2.0
Sorting	80.9
	635.5 hours
Cutter—Idle	84.0 hours

Pressmen
Idle	672.1 hours
Waiting for O.K.	68.3
General Wash-Up	44.8
Repairing Press	24.4
Faulty Make-Up	12.8
Waiting for Stock	7.8
Repairing Plates	6.9
Changing Rollers	6.6
Loading Automatic Feed	5.9
Waiting for Ink	4.8
Faulty Composing	12.5
Waiting for Form	2.2
Wrong Plate	1.1
Total	870.2 hours

Source: Company records.

calculated the total charges for Mr. Richards' approval. Her calculations on a representative bill were as follows:

Materials and Services	$60.00[1]
Plus 20% (Gravehardt's Standard Processing Charge)	12.00
Total	$72.00

Machine and Labor Time

Hours	Operation	Rate	Amount
10.6	12A Press	$11 per hour	$116.60
6.0	Composition	9 per hour	54.00
0.5	Trimming	9 per hour	4.50
		Total	$175.10
Total Materials and Shop Expense			247.10
Plus 10% profit			24.71
Total			$271.81

Mr. Richards checked the billing calculations against any price quotation the customer had received. Generally, the original estimates proved fairly close to the proposed billing and no problem was posed. If, however, the actual cost was considerably in excess of the quoted price, Mr. Richards discussed the matter with the salesman. To preserve good will, the final decision in such cases usually was to bill the customer the original quotation. This same procedure generally was followed in the rare cases in which actual costs came out substantially below the quote.

The billing rates used in charging for press time and direct labor were: Presses 8, 9, and 10—$5 per hour; Presses 11A and 11B—$6 per hour; Presses 12A and 12B—$11 per hour; Presses 13A and 13B—$8 per hour; Presses 14A and 14B—$15 per hour; Offset Press—$12 per hour; Composition—$9 per hour; Trimming—$9 per hour. These billing rates had been recommended to Gravehardt by the Graphic Arts Trade Association on the basis of a lengthy plant inspection conducted the previous year. This association employed a permanent staff to perform this type of service upon request. For the typical job, Gravehardt's total charge usually averaged about $9 per chargeable hour.

---

[1] This figure was obtained from stock requisition tickets and invoices of purchased materials charged to the job.

Selling Activities

Salesmen played a particularly important function in the quality printing market. For example, Gravehardt salesmen were responsible for working out the specifics of the order with the customer, and for designing and laying out the copy. These duties reflected the fact that in the past many of Gravehardt's customers did not have an art staff or advertising agency, apparently preferring instead to work with an experienced and competent printing salesman to develop the material desired.

Mr. Richards was convinced that a feeling of confidence on the part of customers concerning the skill and judgment of the salesmen was uniquely important in the printing industry since the final product could not be seen until it was completed. In this sense Mr. Richards had been impressed with the close relationship that apparently existed between Gravehardt's three older salesmen and many of their customers. As a result of the intimate knowledge of a customer's operations, gained through years of association, Gravehardt's salesmen often actually were the source of new sales promotional ideas and programs adopted by the customers, resulting in printing orders for Gravehardt.

Acquiring a new customer, according to the salesmen, usually required persistent efforts over a period of years, until the customer gained confidence in the salesman and his company. Winning over a customer from a competitor usually could be expedited only if the customer became dissatisfied with the price, quality, or service provided by his current source of printing.

Gravehardt's sales force consisted of Walter Sharon, age 67; George Graeter, age 58 (currently the leading salesman), and Albert Nickell, age 57, all of whom were now paid the 10 per cent commission common in the industry. Except for a few minor house accounts, these three men accounted for all incoming orders. Mr. Richards occasionally accompanied salesmen when they called on key customers, but did virtually no selling himself.

Since acquiring the firm, Mr. Richards had been concerned over the age of his sales force. Clearly each of the men could be counted on for only a few more years of service at most. Further, since all three men had been accustomed to earning anywhere from $8,000 to $25,000 annually for many years through sales to the same few customers, Mr. Richards suspected that they now had little incentive to seek new business.[2] No major new accounts had been added to Gravehardt's list in

---

[2] Mr. Richards had been told that Mr. Gravehardt actually had discouraged

over three years, and accounts that were lost to competitors usually were not regained. Mr. Sharon, for example, had lost a major account two years earlier, and since that time had allowed his total sales to decrease considerably, although he still exceeded Mr. Nickell in total billings. Mr. Nickell seemed to Mr. Richards to lack the personal approach of the other two men, and ranked a poor third in sales for the current year. Notwithstanding his reservations about them, Mr. Richards was confident that all three men knew the printing business thoroughly, and were capable of laying out and supervising imaginative and effective printing.

In January, concern over the future contribution of the present sales force led Mr. Richards to hire Robert Jenner, age 50, as an additional member of the sales organization. As noted earlier, Mr. Richards was particularly enthusiastic about Mr. Jenner's prior experience in selling offset printing. Knowledge of this newer process seemed particularly desirable since the three older salesmen were unfamiliar with offset and seemed reluctant to move aggressively to promote this new phase of Gravehardt's operation. Mr. Richards had persuaded Mr. Jenner to leave a competitor by offering him a drawing account of $9,600 a year against commissions, a figure somewhat higher than his previous earnings, and by giving him the title of Sales Manager. Since space was limited in the company, Mr. Jenner had been given a desk in Mr. Richards' office.

Mr. Jenner's performance during his first six months with Gravehardt proved disappointing. He brought in only modest amounts of sales, and gave the appearance of lacking energy and drive. He offered little explanation for the lack of orders other than general comments concerning the business recession and the fact that one of his prime contacts, a large manufacturer, had a temporary dearth of defense contracts. Mr. Jenner made no effort to act as Sales Manager and largely was ignored by the three older Gravehardt salesmen. The one large sale he had made since joining the firm had called for such crash program delivery, and was processed in such a disorganized manner, that both Gravehardt and the customers were disturbed over the quality of the work. This, coupled with the considerable overtime costs that were incurred, made the job an unsatisfactory experience for all involved. The customer had loudly stated his dissatisfaction, but continued to allow Gravehardt occasionally to bid on additional jobs.

---

salesmen from soliciting new accounts, urging them to concentrate instead on a few key customers.

In August Mr. Richards had discontinued Mr. Jenner's draw against commissions and placed him instead on the customary straight 10 per cent commission. Mr. Jenner's sales performance did not improve noticeably immediately following this change. Mr. Richards was reluctant to discharge Mr. Jenner, however, because of his verified record of sales for his former employer, and because he apparently did have entries with a major potential customer. Furthermore, during the past several weeks, Mr. Jenner appeared to be putting forth somewhat greater effort and was working on several sales possibilities which appeared promising to Mr. Richards.

During the past summer, Mr. Richards also had hired three additional men in a further effort to strengthen the sales force. To avoid any resentment on the part of the three original Gravehardt salesmen, Mr. Richards made it clear that the new employees were to call only on prospective accounts.

The three new employees were paid on a straight salary basis, with the understanding that when their sales were large enough to yield more than present salaries, they would be switched to a commission basis. One of the new men, Howard Zeltman, age 37, had considerable experience in selling graphic arts work, especially offset printing, and also had some prior knowledge of letterpress work. Mr. Richards gave him a monthly salary of $300 for half-time work until he could arrange to terminate other commitments in a noncompeting field, and promised that his salary would be reviewed as soon as Mr. Zeltman shifted to a full-time basis. The other two new salesmen were Donald Johannsen, age 31, who had been a teacher of graphic arts in another city, and Richard Hutson, age 25, who for several years had been selling decals. Both men were given salaries of $300 per month, on a full-time basis. All three had come to Mr. Richards' attention through friends or business associates.

By mid fall, Mr. Richards was impressed with the efforts and personalities of the new employees. Mr. Zeltman seemed to be particularly well-poised, and, although he had yet to obtain a sale, had been calling on potential big accounts and seemed optimistic that one or more of these would be the source of an appreciable order in the near future. Mr. Johannsen had concentrated on calls to small companies and already had brought in a number of modest orders. None of these new accounts appeared to offer possibilities of substantial business, but Mr. Richards was nonetheless encouraged by Mr. Johannsen's demonstration of sales ability, and was hopeful that eventually he might begin developing more significant accounts.

From the moment he joined Gravehardt, Mr. Hutson showed particular interest in the company's office work and internal procedures. Mr. Richards had therefore authorized him to spend part of his time learning the estimating and layout jobs, believing that he might eventually serve as a replacement for the two elderly men now holding these assignments. Although he continued to do some selling, with modest results, Mr. Hutson was now spending a majority of each day in the office.

Mr. Gravehardt had never required salesmen's reports, and Mr. Richards had been reluctant to ask the three veteran salesmen to begin submitting formal records of their activities. They therefore operated quite independently, maintaining fairly irregular schedules which prevented them from having many opportunities to associate with the new salesmen. The new men, however, conferred informally with Mr. Richards regarding their sales plans, and advised him of results they were experiencing.

The close liaison between the older salesmen and their individual customers had resulted in the Gravehardt company sometimes serving as an advertising agency, as well as printing firm. In such cases, salesmen developed the ads and placed them in media, with the customer being billed the usual 15 per cent advertising commission. This commission was then divided equally between the Gravehardt company and the salesman. To accomplish this, the entire commission paid by the customer was shown on Gravehardt's books as "other income," and the half which was given to the salesmen was then treated as part of Gravehardt's selling and administrative expense. To promote this source of income, the Gravehardt letterhead for years had read, "The Gravehardt Company, Printing & Advertising." None of Gravehardt's printing competitors offered such advertising services.

During the past 18 months, income from advertising commissions had decreased considerably. Mr. Richards and the salesmen both felt that this decline reflected intensified sales efforts by local advertising agencies. Mr. Richards also noted that increasing numbers of printing orders were being placed directly by advertising agencies, rather than by the firms whose products were being advertised. In such cases, the agency usually performed all of the creative work itself, the specifications, the layout, selection of paper, and so on, and asked printing firms to bid competitively on only the production activities associated with the actual printing.

ACTION TAKEN TO IMPROVE OPERATING RESULTS

As Mr. Richards became increasingly concerned over Gravehardt's continuing losses, he had turned to his public accountant and auditor, F. F. Brown, for advice. Mr. Brown's recommendation had been that Gravehardt raise its prices. Mr. Richards felt, however, that any major price increase would probably cause sales to deteriorate further, especially since many of Gravehardt's major customers were seriously feeling the effects of the current recession. Federal Reserve statistics on the first eight months of the year, for example, showed that industrial activity in the area was 21 per cent below that of the previous year. Furthermore, Mr. Richards knew that a significant number of local printers had been forced out of business during the past year and a half, and some of Gravehardt's competitors reportedly had suffered severe financial losses, even after cutting quality levels to compete at lower prices. Notwithstanding his doubts, Mr. Richards did increase to 20 per cent the rate which Gravehardt added to the customer's billings[3] for raw materials and services. Formerly the charge had been 10 per cent.

Mr. Richards also discussed Gravehardt's problems with J. R. Gill, his attorney. Mr. Gill strongly criticized Mr. Richards' earlier decisions to buy new equipment. He was critical also of the more recent move of adding salaried salesmen to the payroll during a period of financial crisis. Mr. Gill suggested no solution to the company's problems, however, other than urging that the three newly hired salesmen be discharged immediately.

Mr. Richards also had sought advice from L. W. Cotter, an officer of the local bank which had helped finance his purchase of the Gravehardt company two years before. The conversations with Mr. Cotter had provided Mr. Richards with no new ideas regarding ways to improve operating results. They did, however, make emphatically clear to him that the bank would not be interested in lending him additional funds at this time.

Since January, in an effort to cut costs and thereby reduce losses, Mr. Richards had executed a series of layoffs which had reduced the workforce by ten persons.

---

[3] See page 245.

Date	Employees Laid Off
March 1	2 Pressmen
April 1	2 Compositors
August 1	1 Miscellaneous shop helper
September 1	1 Clerical worker (office)
	1 Compositor
	2 Pressmen
	1 Miscellaneous shop helper

Notwithstanding these reductions, operating losses had continued, and, in so far as Mr. Richards knew, were being experienced even this very moment.

Defiant Products, Inc. (I)

Management personnel of Defiant Products, Inc., a major manufacturer of heavy industrial equipment, were stressing efforts to reduce the company's indirect manufacturing expenses (IME). As an active participant in the numerous management discussions on the problem, Mr. Douglas Bowman, Director of Manufacturing Administration, was attempting to formulate specific recommendations to present to his immediate superior, Mr. C. F. Goodwell, Manufacturing Vice President.

BACKGROUND

Sales and Cost Patterns—The Present and the Recent Past

The capital goods items produced by Defiant are required in quantity by both industry and the armed forces. In times of war, these products assume major strategic importance. As a result, throughout the Second World War and the Korean engagement, the Defiant company and its competitors had expanded volume to unprecedented levels, with almost all sales being either to the armed forces or to industrial concerns operating under government certificates of necessity.

Subsequent to the Korean War, the industry continued to experience unusually high demand for its products. This reflected the influence of the general industrial expansion taking place in the country, as well as of the pent-up demand of customers in noncritical industries who had been forced to defer re-equipment expenditures because of wartime restrictions. During the post-Korean War period, advances in military technology, coupled with the tense international situation, caused the armed forces also to place orders for Defiant products and those of its competitors at a rate well in excess of previous peacetime periods, although substantially below recent wartime levels.

252

In recent years, as the company responded to the new mix of civilian and military orders,[1] Defiant's management became increasingly concerned by the fact that IME totals consistently were running substantially over budgeted estimates. During the previous calendar year, for example, the excess of actual total IME over budgeted standards reached a postwar high of approximately **18** per cent. As a result, profits have been well below management expectations, notwithstanding the fact that the company was enjoying good sales and was usually operating at, or below, budgeted standards in most of its direct manufacturing costs. Commenting upon the IME problem Mr. Bowman said:

> I'm certain that there is nothing unique about the situation in which we find outselves. Hundreds, perhaps even thousands of manufacturers— probably including all of our domestic competitors—must be in the same boat. But that doesn't make our problems any easier to solve.
>
> During both the Second World War and the Korean action, our number one company target was volume, volume, volume. Cost? It went right out the window as a major consideration. Volume! That was all that counted.
>
> Well, we got the volume. We cranked out units at a rate that I suspect none of us ever had dreamed was possible. We developed new manufacturing techniques and shortcuts surpassing anything the industry had seen. The armed forces awarded us enough "E-Flags" to cover Yankee Stadium.
>
> But, in a sense, the very things that pushed us over the wartime hump are rising up to haunt us now. Half, maybe two-thirds, of the people in our shops—supervisory and hourly people alike—came to us during the war. In terms of turning out goods they're worldbeaters. I would stack them up against anybody. But in terms of running a tight shop, they're babes in the woods. They've never had to pinch pennies before. Cost control is a phrase they simply don't understand. Even those of us who were around before the war have forgotten how to squeeze 100 cents—or better yet, 101 cents—out of every dollar we spend. That's what's behind our problem.
>
> In many respects, the people in our Sales Department have found their way back into today's world. They've had to. Almost all sales in the industry have switched back to the competitive bid basis that prevailed before the war. That goes for government and civilian orders alike. Nowadays, the outfit with the sharpest pencil lands the contract.
>
> We're making out all right in that regard. We're still getting our share of the market, even expanding our prewar position somewhat. This is true even though we have to fight tooth and nail with General Electric, General Motors, Westinghouse, Allis-Chalmers, and similar bluechip U.S. competitors for every order. This is not to mention the British and West Germans who

---

[1] Defiant's sales forecasts for the coming calendar year called for a $62,000,000 volume, to be divided about 30 per cent/70 per cent between armed forces and civilian sales, respectively.

are now again back in the industry in a big way, and enjoying a tremendous advantage over U.S. companies in regard to labor costs.

But the past couple of years have taught us the hard way that landing the order isn't the same as landing the profit. Profit is earned on the floor of the plant. And we simply haven't been doing enough there. Sure, we're still making money. But not as much as we should be making. Its excess IME that's making the difference.

Although management concern over IME had been pronounced for several years and had resulted in numerous efforts to instill increasing cost consciousness at all levels of the Defiant organization, the entire topic recently received added impetus. Sales forecasts for the coming year indicated that Defiant would experience a major volume expansion, with sales reaching an annual level of approximately $100,000,000, a figure only slightly below the peak years experienced during the Second World War. About half of this anticipated increase would result from Defiant's successful bidding on several large government contracts for new products required in connection with major technological innovations in military equipment. The remainder would reflect increased industrial sales.

In terms of existing plant and equipment, and of manpower availability in the local labor market, the prospects of this substantial increase in volume seemed to pose no insuperable challenges for the Defiant organization. Within the management group, however, there was genuine concern that this rapid a build-up of volume might result in still further disintegration of the company's already disturbing performance in the area of IME. Were this to happen, Defiant might find itself in the position of seeing sales soar while profits dived. To assure that this would not happen, the search for ways "to pull in the reins" on IME was being pursued as a major objective of the entire management organization.

PRODUCTION FACILITIES, PERSONNEL, AND SUPERVISORY ORGANIZATION

Defiant Products is located in a large midwestern industrial center where it currently employed approximately 3,000 production employees and operated on a three-shift basis in all but a few operations. About half of these personnel were direct labor employees engaged in machining and assembly activities. Roughly 50 per cent of the direct labor jobs are on piecerate incentives under which workers on the average earn about $2.75 per hour. The rest of the direct labor personnel are paid on straight hourly rates averaging around $2.25. The remaining production workers are engaged in various indirect labor activities for which they are paid straight hourly wages ranging from about $1.50 to $2.25, and averaging around $1.90. All production employees are represented by what management considers to be strong, militant industrial unions.

The principal product in the company's line consists of three related types of extremely large, complex mechanical equipment. An assembled unit usually costs at least several hundred thousand dollars, often weighs in excess of 100 tons, and involves 50,000 or more parts, a majority of which have to be machined within tolerances of a few thousandths of an inch. Machining certain parts to a few ten-thousandths of an inch is not unusual, and some of the specially designed units recently manufactured for the armed forces required that certain critical dimensions be held to tolerances measured in millionths of an inch.

Total manufacturing cycle time for most individual orders runs anywhere from six months to two years, depending on whether special engineering, special tooling, or both, are required. Special order items usually represent only about 10 per cent of Defiant's annual sales volume, but it is not uncommon for just the engineering and design phases on a single special unit to necessitate six or seven months' full-time work by a task force of as many as 20 to 50 of Defiant's engineering specialists and draftsmen.

Because of size, cost, and intricacy, even standard design units are manufactured only to specific customer order. Since there are approximately 60 standard models from which customers may choose, and since customers rarely order more than a single item at a time, it is unusual for more than one unit of any specific product model to be undergoing the same stage of the production process at any given moment. Instead, most units are put through production on an individual basis.

Defiant's shop areas consist of eight major buildings scattered over a 70-acre tract and provide over 2,000,000 square feet of manufacturing floor space. With the exception of the Punch Press, Screw Machine, and Welding Departments, which are arranged functionally and service the requirements of all product lines, each of the three product groups has its own shops and manufacturing facilities. As a result of wartime volume requirements, many of the shops have been arranged to provide a number of the features of a product-line layout. Within a number of the buildings, therefore, manufacturing equipment is located to permit as much of a straight-line, continuous work flow as is consistent with the size of the units being processed, the handling problems, the complexity of certain of the machining, and the frequency of the need to accommodate special orders requiring unique manufacturing operations.

For purposes of supervision, Defiant's manufacturing operations have been divided into three departments, one for each of the three main products. Each department is headed by a production superintendent who reports to the company's Manufacturing Vice President. Successive levels of manufacturing supervision involve, in direct chain of command, 38 general foremen or "functional managers," each of whom is in charge of a "section," and 102 foremen each supervising one of the section "subunits," that is, a specific manufacturing area, or function, during a particular shift.

At present levels of production, the company's Cost Standards Department estimated that total factory costs for all three classes of products should average about 68 per cent of sales, distributed as follows:

	Per Cent of Sales Dollar
Raw Material	31
Direct Labor	10
IME	27
Total Factory Cost	68
Sales and Administrative Expenses, and Profit	32
Total	100

These estimates were based on a number of years of operating experience, and were reinforced by careful and continuing analysis by Defiant's staff of highly-trained cost specialists. Management was convinced, therefore, that the estimates were sound, reflecting high, but attainable, performance expectations. The confidence with which management viewed these cost standards was further enforced by the fact that actual costs of both raw materials and direct labor usually corresponded closely to the budgeted estimates. IME, however, remained stubbornly out of line.

IME ACCOUNTING AND CONTROLS

Under Defiant's accounting practices, 141 different types of activities, occurrences, internal financial transactions, or allocations are classified as indirect manufacturing expenses (Exhibit 1).[2] For control purposes, each of these activities was assigned a six-digit account number. The following 12-digit identification system was then used

---

[2] See pp. 257–258.

EXHIBIT 1 DEFIANT PRODUCTS, INC.

Indirect Manufacturing Expense

General Supervision
Foremen—Salaried
Working Leaders
General Assistants
Inspectors
Materials Release Personnel
Materials Release—Machinery
Planning and Wage Rate Personnel
Factory Methods and Equipment
  Personnel
Production Clerks
Stock Clerks
Shipping Clerks
Receiving Clerks
Dispatchers
Production Followers
Production Form Clerks
Time and Shop Clerks
Purchasing Clerks
All Other Clerical Personnel
Mail Clerks
Movemen and Shippers
Janitors and Sweepers
Riggers and Chainmen
Fork Truck Operators
Make-up Payments
Idle Time
Unassigned Time
Direct Labor Trainees
Instructor of Direct Labor Trainees
Training of Indirect Hourly
  Workers
Training of Salaried Workers
Night Shift Bonus
Shop Vacation and Other Payroll
  Allowances
Salary Applied Vacations and
  Holidays
Death in Family Payments
Continuity of Service Premiums Paid
Social Security Taxes

Stock Bonus Plan
Relief and Loan Plan
Suggestion Award Payments
Workmen's Accident Compensation
Other Employees' Benefits
Standard Tools
Shop Supplies
Office Supplies
Patterns
Special Tools
All Other Helpers and Laborers
Elevator and Crane Operators
Stockkeepers and Helpers
Tool Crib Attendants
Transportation Employees
Dispensary Attendants
Plant Protection—Fire
Plant Protection—Guards
Firemen
Boiler Cleaners
Auxiliary Operators
Turbine Operators
Switchboard Operators
Gas Plant Operators
Other Power Station Attendants
Personnel Service Employees
Packers
Other Factory Service Personnel
Overtime Premiums Paid—
  Direct Labor
Overtime Premiums Paid—
  Indirect Hourly
Overtime Premiums Paid—
  Indirect Salary
Overtime Premiums Paid—
  Maintenance Personnel
Water Supply
Manufacturing Fuel—Purchased
Manufacturing Fuel—Liquidations
Power and Light
Purchased Power

EXHIBIT 1 (*Continued*) DEFIANT PRODUCTS, INC.

Power Station Fuel—Purchased
Maintenance
  Buildings
  Building Appurtenances
  Structures
  General Plant Facilities
  Roads and Sidewalks
  General Service Piping and Wiring
  Railway Tracks and Overhead
    Equipment
  Boilers and Accessories
  Steam Producing Auxiliaries
  Engine and Turbo Generators
  Rolling Stock
  Automotive Equipment and
    Electric Vehicles
  Storage Battery Trucks
  Other Cataloged Equipment
  Miscellaneous Shop Equipment
  Pipings and Fittings
  Calibration of Instruments
  Electrical Equipment
  Oven and Furnaces
Manufacturing Steam Consumed
Compressed Air—Heating Steam
Information Service
Employee Education and Welfare
Memberships and Contributions
Patent Application Expense
Rearrangement and Transfer of
  Equipment
  Normal Only
Taking Inventories
Unassignable Transportation and
  Packing
Laboratory Services
Office Service
Factory and Equipment Development
Telephone

Telegraph
Outside Legal Expense
Traveling and Entertaining
Employee Transfers—Expense and
  Allowance
Losses Due to Errors
Tests
Other Controllable Expense
Rentals—Other
Rentals—Tabulating Equipment
Taxes—Other
Taxes—Property
Insurance
Depreciation
  Plant and Equipment
  Amortization of Plant and
    Equipment
  Amortization of Lease
    Improvements
General Company Assessment
Within Department Assessment
Within Manufacturing Section
  Assessment
Within Subunit Assessment
Works Assessment
Expense Credits
  Fuel and Power Liquidation
  Maintenance and Repair of
    Patterns and Tools
  Other
  Works Assessments
Maintenance—Unusual
Rearrangement—Unusual
Snow Removal
Heating (Steam)
Other—Unusual
Strike Expense
Unusual Development

by the Financial Department to identify each individual expense transaction, actual or imputed, that occurs in any of the manufacturing areas of the company.

Digit	Identifies
1st	Department being charged
2nd and 3rd	Section of the department involved
4th thru 9th	Account number involved (six-digit account number)
10th thru 12th	Specific transaction involved

If account number 314-300 were assigned to IME arising from wage payments to dispatchers, the identifying number "323-314-300-000" would identify the wage payments made during a given accounting period to dispatchers assigned to Section 23 of Department #3.[3]

Departmental and company totals of actual and budgeted expenses, and variances between the two, for each of the 141 IME accounting categories, were prepared monthly by the Financial Department. This monthly summarization of tens of thousands of separate transactions was made possible by the use of extensive punch card tabulating equipment. These tabulating facilities were operated by the Financial Department and used for receivables, payables, and inventory accounting, as well as for the tabulation of IME and other manufacturing data. The IME applications, in total, required on a one-shift basis about 25 per cent of the man and machine hours available in the tabulating section.

The monthly IME results normally were available about ten working days after the close of the month. They then were distributed to the following persons:

C. F. Goodwell, Manufacturing Vice President
D. A. Bowman, Director of Manufacturing Administration
    (in charge of manufacturing systems, standards, methods, procedures, schedules, production control)
E. H. Grace, Director of Manufacturing Engineering
    (in charge of tooling, quality control, materials)
D. C. Marrie, Production Superintendent, Department #1
B. F. Richkemper, Production Superintendent, Department #2
L. L. Menelli, Production Superintendent, Department #3

Shortly after the IME results were available each month, these six men would meet and discuss the departmental and companywide results, noting areas in which performance appeared to be usually good or bad and, when appropriate, discussing remedial action.

---

[3] Individual wage payment transactions actually are not given separate identifying numbers. The final three digits of the identifying number shown in this example would, therefore, be 000.

It was the responsibility of each of the three departmental superintendents to determine the specific causes of any IME categories in which his department's monthly totals seemed seriously out of line. This required that the over-all results reflected in the departmental totals "be tracked down" to the individual subunits responsible.

Very few of the subunits regularly incur all 141 types of IME. Instead, the monthly IME totals for each of the 102 subunits would show changes in only about 40 of the possible IME catgories. The mix of IME items regularly incurred by any one subunit usually differed, however, from that of any other subunit. One subunit for example, might require Fork-Lift Operators but not employ any Working Leaders. Another subunit might have exactly the reverse situation. And so on.

When IME "trouble" categories were noted, the three departmental superintendents generally did not limit follow-up actions merely to calling their subordinates' attention to those expenses where over-all departmental totals seem disturbingly high. Instead, starting with the known fact of his department's totals, each superintendent would attempt to draw on his own "feel" for the situation "on the floor of the plant" to identify the specific subunits most likely to be the source of any excessive expenses incurred. When discussing IME with general foremen and foremen, the production superintendent usually did not stress the variable budget system *per se,* or compare budgeted standards with actual departmental results. The emphasis usually was placed instead on the fact that the superintendent was convinced that a given type of IME was out of line in a particular section or subunit, and that improvements were expected.

DETERMINATION OF BUDGETED IME FIGURES

To determine the budgeted figures for each of the 141 IME categories in each of the three departments, Defiant employed a variable, straight-line IME budget. This system had been introduced into the company almost a quarter of a century ago and focused attention on the relationship between production volume and indirect manufacturing expenses. For purposes of the system it was assumed that IME should vary *directly* with volume changes, the latter being measured in terms of budgeted direct labor costs.

In implementing the system, estimates were made periodically of the various IME items that reasonably should be incurred in each of the three departments when production volume is at both the *upper* and *lower* limits of the most likely range of operations during a given period of time. If, for example,[4] the sales forecasts for a given year suggest that Defiant probably would be operating between 75 and 90 per cent of capacity, estimates are made of the number of dispatchers that would be required in each department at both the high and the low volume level. In the case of Department #3, such estimates might show that seven dispatchers would be required when volume was at 75 per cent of capacity, and nine when volume was at 90 per cent of capacity.

As the next step in the variable budgeting procedure, the increase in the department's monthly expenses for dispatchers as production volume rose from 75 to 90 per cent of capacity is related, in terms of percentage, to the estimated changes in monthly departmental direct labor cost that should result from a comparable change in the volume rate. In the case of the dispatchers in Department #3, for example, if, on the average, a dispatcher earns $2.00 per hour and works 40 hours per week for 4.3 weeks per month, then the monthly cost of Department #3's seven dispatchers at a volume of 75 per cent of capacity would be $2,408 (seven dispatchers x $2.00 per hour x 40 hours/week x 4.3 weeks/month). The monthly cost of the nine dispatchers required if volume rose to 90 per cent of capacity would be, in contrast, $3,096 (nine dispatchers x $2.00/hour x 40 hours/week x 4.3 weeks/month). The increased IME incurred for dispatchers in Department #3 as a result of increasing production volume from 75 per cent to 90 per cent would therefore be $688, that is, $3,096–$2,408.

If Department #3's standard direct labor cost was $279,174 per month at 75 per cent of capacity, and $334,010 at 90 per cent of capacity, increasing that department's capacity from 75 to 90 per cent would result not only in an increase of $688 in IME for dispatchers (as shown in the prior paragraph) but also in an increase of $54,836, that is, $334,010–$279,174, in standard direct labor costs. On the average, therefore—assuming the existence of a straight-line relationship between the two variables—for every one dollar of change in standard direct labor cost occurring in Department #3 between 75 and 90 per cent of capacity, there would be a corresponding change, in the same direction—either upward or downward—of ($688 ÷ $54,836) = $.013 in IME for dispatchers. Stated another way, starting from a base figure of $2,408 per month, IME for dispatchers in Department #3 would be expected to vary directly at a rate of 1.3 per cent of the Department's budgeted direct labor costs in excess of $279,174, at all volume levels between 75 and 90 per cent of capacity. During a month in

---

[4] Illustrative figures only.

which Department #3's volume justified a standard direct labor budget of $306,170, budgeted IME of dispatchers would therefore be $2,408 + .013 ($306,170–$279,174) = $2,759.

In a similar manner, straight-line percentage relationships between standard direct labor costs and standards for each of the 141 individual IME items were calculated periodically for all three departments. These were then used to prepare the budgeted estimates which, on a monthly basis, were compared with actual departmental results.

It was the responsibility of members of the 12-man Manufacturing Administration staff under Mr. Bowman to work closely both with production operating personnel and members of the Finance Department to make sure that the percentage relationships employed were kept current and that they corresponded with the actual volume ranges within which the company was operating. These tasks normally required the equivalent of several months of the full-time services of the Manufacturing Administration Department's staff each year.

It was apparent to the Defiant management that actual expenses incurred for specific IME items do not, in fact, always vary directly with changes in production volume measured in terms of direct labor costs. Within the organization it was not expected, therefore, that individual actual IME results could, or should, always correspond exactly to the budgeted figures. There was a conviction, nonetheless, that the straight-line budget system did shed light on the general efficiency of IME control and did signal the presence of out-of-line situations that required the attention of the departmental supervisors.

CORRECTIVE ACTIONS TO DATE

In commenting upon the corrective actions recently taken by management in an effort to accomplish IME reductions, Mr. Bowman said:

It's been somewhat like trying to move jelly with a hammer; you seem to be making progress in one direction, only to find that it's all oozing back somewhere else. Our monthly departmental IME totals really haven't revealed any major areas of consistent weakness. Instead, there are usually indications of excessive costs in dozens of different areas. But the 'trouble-spots' keep changing. Sure, it would be nice if we could isolate a handful of really weak IME areas and go all out to cure those permanently. But it just isn't this simple or easy a problem.

Defiant Products, Inc. (II)

Douglas Bowman, Director of Manufacturing Administration for the Defiant Corporation, knew that within the managerial and top supervisory echelons of the company there were some persons who believed that the best answer to the IME problem[1] could be found in a "get tough" policy. The reasoning advanced by such individuals usually ran something like this:

Costs and expenses are a function of the acts of people. It's people—and the way they do their jobs—that make or break a company. It's people that lie behind our present problems with excess IME. Too many people just aren't doing a day's work.

What will it take to change the picture? Change in the behavior of people.

How can we get that change? We'll have to get tough. We'll have to make it clear that the honeymoon is over. The company is again having to fight its way through a tough competitive world where any significant internal weakness can ruin us.

Now understand we aren't so naive as to suggest that we can push our personnel relations back to the Dark Ages. We aren't talking about equipping our supervisors with thumb-screws or black snake whips, or anything like that. Nobody would stand for unreasonably harsh or irresponsible acts by the company—our own top management would be as opposed to any such attempt as the unions themselves. Everyone knows it wouldn't work. It would be stupid even to try.

But what we are saying is that in a just and reasonable manner the company has to become more demanding; we have to get better performance from our people. This applies all up and down the line—to management, supervisory, and hourly personnel alike. It's our conviction that getting a fair day's work out of people isn't inconsistent with good personnel relations. If we're wrong in such a belief, Defiant as well as every other company had better toss in the towel right now.

---

[1] For a description of the company and the problems currently encountered regarding IME, see Defiant Products, Inc. (I), pp. 252–262.

By getting tough we mean things like this: the superintendents should really lay down the law to the general foremen. Tell them that our IME performance simply has to improve immediately, or else! Make it clear that management will do everything it can to help, but that the battle to get IME under control has to be fought and won on the floor of the plant. Let the general foremen then pass the same word on to the foremen and so on, right down through the entire organization. Then, *follow through* on it! People who don't deliver get called on the carpet with a demand for explanations and for specific plans to remedy the situation. Over the long pull, really shabby performance would mean dismissal. Again we're not advocating abuse or "chewing-out," although in some instances it might be that this would be the most helpful thing that could happen. And we're not proposing "head-rolling" just for the sake of stirring things up. But whatever it takes, let's get across to everybody involved that we have to plug the loop holes. If anybody can't contribute as a *productive* member of the organization, the company can't use him.

As an organization we ought to be intelligent enough to execute such a program without getting trapped in all of the obvious pitfalls that could conceivably be involved. No one would be dismissed for subpar performance until he had a fair chance to prove himself. And surely we could take steps to guarantee that extenuating circumstances were brought into the open and taken into account.

But when the facts are decisive, let's have guts enough to act. Let's not be ashamed or afraid to exact high, fair standards of performance.

In thinking about this, don't underestimate the power of the grapevine. For once it could work for us. If word got around that the foreman in only one subunit was in serious trouble because of carrying too many dispatchers, or that there had been a housecleaning of excess helpers in Department X, don't think that people in other Departments wouldn't learn of it immediately. Every improvement we made would therefore have a cumulative effect.

In summary, there is no longer any reason to believe that we can just *talk* our way into improved IME performance. If words alone would do it, the IME problem would already be past history. We've pleaded for improvements; we've explained the reasons behind our concern over IME performance a hundred different ways to everybody involved. It hasn't been enough.

So the time has come to back up words with action. It's time to get tough.

Defiant Products, Inc. (III)

Douglas Bowman, Director of Manufacturing Administration for the Defiant Corporation, knew that among his colleagues in the managerial and top supervisory echelons of the company there were some persons who believed that the best answer to the IME problem[1] lay in an all-out drive to bring the motivating forces of incentives into the IME area. Their reasoning and proposals usually ran somewhat along these lines:

IME performance is going to improve only when the people involved put forth the extra effort required to accomplish IME functions more efficiently. What is most likely to motivate people to put forth that "something extra"? It's money.

Oh sure, there are other things that could be relied on. You could try to get the extra effort by moral suasion. You could plead with people, make dramatic statements about loyalty to the good old company, and so forth. Going a step further you could add a dose of fear—stressing the long-term danger to everybody's jobs if Defiant continued to face the competitive handicap implicit in an excessive expense picture. Going further you could try to achieve the desired motivation by threats of immediate dismissal if better results weren't immediately forthcoming.

But human nature being what it is, over the long run none of these approaches, or all of them together, is going to be nearly as effective, with nearly as many people, as the face of George Washington looking out from the front of a crumpled dollar bill.

It's a well established fact that a well-conceived, properly administered incentive program in the direct labor area usually results in improved productivity. Even after these gains are shared fairly with the workers, the net result is an improved cost picture. We've seen this happen in our own company.[2]

---

[1] For a description of the company and the problems currently encountered regarding IME, see Defiant Products, Inc. (I), pp. 252–262.

[2] Roughly half of the approximately 1,500 direct labor jobs in the company

Well let's get the same force working for us in connection with our indirect jobs.

From the very outset we admit that it's different—it's probably tougher—to develop an incentive wage plan for indirect jobs than for direct labor assignments where you can make an exact measurement of output. We admit, too, that there aren't very many companies that have developed an intensive approach toward IME incentives. But heaven help Defiant if we always wait until other companies have made a breakthrough on some problem that's plaguing us.

We think we can lick this one ourselves. We believe that a good portion—maybe all—IME jobs could be paid on some kind of meaningful incentive if we really make such an objective the target for our all-out efforts. Ingenuity, and imagination, and resourcefulness are qualities we think the Defiant organization possesses in fairly decent quantities.

Look at it this way. How many people do we have setting standards for our direct labor incentive program? Usually about 25. Right? What we are suggesting is that if we were to invest anything like the same amount of competent manpower in the task of developing and administering IME incentives, the results might be astounding. In many instances, we'd probably have to come up with something quite different than piece-rates. At least at the start, some of the standards might have to be pretty crude. Maybe some would just have to be set arbitrarily. But the standards would improve as we gained know-how. And even from the outset the figures we develop would at least give you something to measure against. Indirect workers would now have a target to try to beat—and the incentive of knowing that there would be extra money in their pocket if they succeeded. Besides, in the course of setting these standards, who knows how many new approaches in and improvements to specific IME jobs might be uncovered?

Some of the consulting firms contend that the motivation that can be realized from a good incentive plan for direct labor jobs usually results in a productivity increase of around 30 per cent. If an all-out drive for IME incentives got us anything like that much improvement, Defiant's problem would be licked.

And another thing, we believe that with a little imagination ways could be found to bring the motivating influence of incentives to bear not only on hourly workers, but on supervisory personnel as well. An extra dollar is still an extra dollar, no matter where a person sits in the organization chart.

---

currently were paid on a system of piece rate incentives under which workers, on the average, performed at 125% of standard and took home $2.75 per hour.

Defiant Products, Inc. (IV)

Douglas Bowman, Director of Manufacturing Administration, knew that some of his associates in the management group believed that the best answer to the company's IME problem[1] was an intensive effort to strengthen Defiant's control and accounting procedures. In particular, these individuals suggested that the available computer facilities be used to expand drastically the quantity and frequency of the analyses made of IME performance data. This was their tack:

The best way to begin closing in on the IME problem is to pinpoint the actual sources of our difficulties. Our present practices and procedures simply do not do this.

It isn't enough for management to learn once each month the over-all IME results in each of the three departments for the prior month, getting even this information several weeks after the month has ended. Furthermore, we can't afford to continue to rely on comparisons between these actual results and budgeted targets based on the drastically over-simplified assumption that IME expenses should vary directly with volume as measured by budgeted direct labor costs.

Maybe we had to settle for such crudeness in the past, simply because of the staggering volume of clerical work that would have been required to obtain any better information. But it's not necessary now. With the 11-Z-F computer[2] employed in the Finance Department, a whole new world of information flow is open to us if we have the imagination to move into it.

---

[1] For a description of the company and the problems currently encountered regarding IME, see Defiant Products, Inc. (I), pp. 252–262.

[2] Disguised name. The equipment in question was one of the most advanced designs of a major computer manufacturer. The 11-Z-F, for example, was capable of performing several thousand simple addition or subtraction calculations per second. The unit had been installed in the Defiant company the previous spring and was currently being employed for various financial calculations, including preparation of weekly payroll, and for engineering and design computations. These current applications absorbed about 75 per cent of the computer's one-shift capacity.

To be specific, we have discussed this general topic with the computer supervisor. He is confident that it would be well within the capabilities of the 11-Z-F, and the existing workload of his section, to provide us with *weekly* as well as "year to date" breakdowns of actual and budgeted expenses and variances for each of the 141 different IME items in each manufacturing department, each section, and each subunit. In fact, he sees this application as a "natural" for the 11-Z-F. If we would be willing to accept estimates, rather than actual results, in a few IME categories where the company is billed only monthly, the computer-run on results for the week just past could easily be available by no later than Tuesday of the second following week, that is, in seven working days.

In short, through use of the computer it is well within our grasp to switch to new procedures whereby instead of *six* high level executives getting over-all *monthly departmental* IME results *once* each month, well after the month ends, these same people could have far more detailed results available *weekly*, within ten days after the close of the period. Furthermore—and potentially of far greater significance—the same detailed information regarding IME performance in his own specific area of responsibility for the week just passed would be available to *every person* with supervisory responsibility, right down to the subunit foreman level. Therefore, instead of feeding monthly departmental totals only to a few people at the top of the organization, the new computerized system would provide detailed weekly information, broken down to the subunit level, to over 150 vitally affected line supervisors extending right down into the heart of our operation.

Then we would know exactly where IME trouble was arising. No one could plead ignorance of the facts. No supervisor could just "assume" that his unit's IME performance was satisfactory. He'd know. And so would his boss.

But the advantages wouldn't end here. With a computerized control system it would also be feasible for us to break away from the existing variable straight-line budget, and all of the inexactness it involves. Instead, we could adopt a "step level" system. Rather than merely utilizing estimates of IME likely to be involved at the upper and lower limits of the probable range of operations for a given period of time, we could determine what IME should be in each and every subunit of the company at each of a *number of different levels of activity* within the probable range of volume.

For example, if we think the probable range of activity for a year is likely to be not less than 75 or more than 90 per cent of capacity, we now have to limit ourselves to determining what would be reasonable IME in each of the 141 different categories in each department at both volume levels, and then assume that within the 75 to 90 per cent range, each IME item varies directly with budgeted direct labor costs. We know that often this just isn't true. Within certain limits, changes in the volume of operations may require no changes in IME whatsoever. On the other hand, under certain circumstances an increase of only a few percentage points in volume may make it necessary to add a second person to a particular IME function, thereby creating a huge percentage spurt in IME. And so forth.

Previously we had to settle for the inexactness implicit in the straight-line budgeting system simply because it would have been almost impossible to come up with something more accurate. But the computer would change all that. Now we could determine, say, six important "steps" or "levels" that are likely to be generated in each IME item in each subunit as volume fluctuates within some given range. If, for example, a particular subunit actually didn't have to add any dispatchers if volume increased from 75 to 85 per cent, but had to add another full-time dispatcher if volume went above 85 per cent, the system could show this in its budgeted figures for each week. Now it can't. Instead, with its assumption of a straight-line relationship, our present system erroneously shows a big increase in budgeted figures between 75 and 85 per cent, and only a very slight one between 85 and 86 per cent. This kind of distortion simply isn't necessary with a computer.

Sure, you can argue that carrying electronic data processing this far would generate a flood of paper that would drown the organization. There is no denying that it would mean about a hundredfold increase in the IME reports prepared each month. But for the computer that's nothing. And paper's cheap. If having this type of information available permitted us to spot even one major source of excessive IME that we otherwise would have missed, the system probably would pay for itself a dozen times over.

Obviously it will require a good deal of work to set up the computerized system. Preparing the budgeted estimates for six or so different volume levels for each of the IME categories in each subunit unquestionably will be tough. Programming the information for the computer also will take time and effort. On the basis of conversations we've had with personnel in our computer operation, the full time services of three people might be needed for about twelve weeks to program the system and get it debugged.

This is exclusive of the time required for developing the budgeted estimates themselves. It's hard to say exactly how long these budget preparations would take, particularly the first few times we did it. Operating people, right down to the foreman level, clearly would have to play an active part in formulating the estimates. This would take time. And it would require educating some of the supervisors—developing in them a "figure consciousness" that many of them do not now possess. Also, it's likely that ways will have to be found to acquaint shop people with the entire concept of computers and, in more than a few cases, help overcome the scepticism, or fear, that introduction of these more sophisticated techniques may generate. But once we had the system going, we'd really have IME headaches on the run. Learning where IME troubles really lie is better than half the battle. The 11-Z-F can give that knowledge.

Nolder Manufacturing Company—
Electric Motor Division

At 8:30 A.M., Wednesday, August 8th, the managerial personnel of the Electric Motor Division of the Nolder Manufacturing Company gathered for their regular weekly staff meeting. The Division's annual conference between home office officials and the four District Sales Managers had been in session since the previous Monday. The Wednesday meeting offered the Division's production and engineering personnel their first opportunity to learn of sales forecasts for the coming year.

The Electric Motor Division was managed by the organization shown in Exhibit 1. The six key operating personnel, all present at the August 8th meeting, ranged in age from mid-thirties to late forties. Each of the men had been with the Division for a number of years and a close, cordial working relationship existed among them. Harry Austin, the Division Manager, presided at the weekly conferences which usually were conducted with a minimum of formality. As soon as the last of the men entered the room it therefore was not unusual for the Division Sales Manager, Tom Gregory, to begin the session abruptly by enthusiastically announcing that the forecasts of the District Sales Managers regarding sales for the coming calendar year had been exceptionally favorable and indicated that the Division was about to experience a major increase in volume.

The following discussion ensued:

FORBES: Tom, don't you ever get tired of peddling that same old
(Production story? Every year after you salesmen wind up your pep
Manager) session down at the hotel, you come back with reports that orders are going to blast the Division off the map. Then the District men go back home, take a second look,

EXHIBIT 1 NOLDER MANUFACTURING COMPANY

ELECTRIC MOTOR DIVISION

Partial Organization Chart

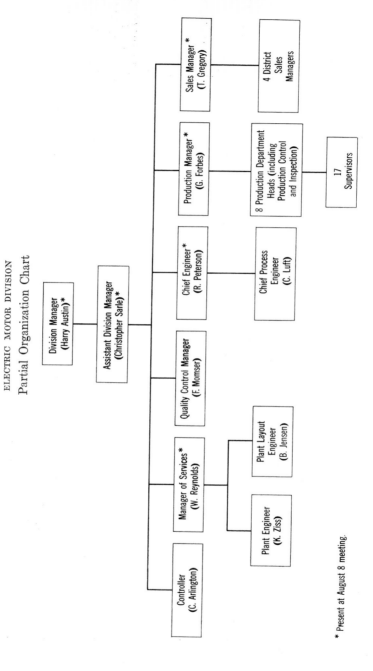

* Present at August 8 meeting.

and start calming down. So what happens? A big nothing. Volume stays right about where it was.

REYNOLDS: *(Manager of Services)* Sure, come off it, Tom. What brand of stuff do you pour at those sales meetings of yours, anyway? How about bringing a bottle along for us working men to sample?

AUSTIN: *(Division Manager)* Don't let them give you a hard time, Tom. We all know it's tough to come up with sales predictions a year in advance. Considering all the uncertainties involved, the forecasts have been good in the past. And they know it.

REYNOLDS: *(Manager of Services)* Sure, Tom. You can't help it if you're a salesman. We like you in spite of it.

AUSTIN: *(Division Manager)* Look, in case anybody's interested, I was with Tom and the District men at last night's meeting. They were in dead earnest about their forecasts. What's more, they had evidence to back them up. Things are just breaking wide open. And we have to face up to it.

SARLE: *(Assistant Division Manager)* How big is "wide open"?

AUSTIN: *(Division Manager)* Give them the story, Tom.

GREGORY: *(Sales Manager)* Well, even trying to be conservative, the forecasts on fractionals and small integral motors show that we need to gear up to ship an average of around 1,200 units per day for the next calendar year, with the mix being around 90 per cent single phase models and 10 per cent three phase.[1]

PETERSON: *(Chief Engineer)* And I suppose it goes without saying that at least three-quarters of this increase will be special orders?

GREGORY: *(Sales Manager)* We wouldn't do that to Engineering, Pete. No, indications are that most of the increase will be in standard models. Pete's people aren't going to be pushed next year any more than they usually are.

PETERSON: *(Chief Engineer)* That's bad enough!

---

[1] For more than two years, shipments of these types of motors had been averaging 900 units per day.

AUSTIN:
(Division Manager)

To give you some idea of how big this thing looks, I personally worked on the District Managers to squeeze out any fat in their forecasts. I reminded them of how manufacturing would be over a barrel if the estimates proved wrong. Not a one of them would budge. Things are just snowballing and we've got to gear up for it.

SARLE:
(Assistant Division Manager)

Is this likely to be a permanent increase in volume—or just a temporary spurt?

AUSTIN:
(Division Manager)

We went into that pretty carefully last night. You can never be 100 per cent sure, but the sales people think that unless we really drop the ball, the Division's volume should continue well above the present level of 900 units per day for the foreseeable future. Not a single district manager seemed to see any major chance of things turning down any time soon. There are a lot of reasons behind the upswing: capital expansion and re-equipment in industry, the do-it-yourself boom in home power tools, good sales on farm implements and kitchen appliances, a lot of things. A number of regular customers are increasing the size of their orders, and new customers are being lined up all the time.

GREGORY:
(Sales Manager)

I think at least part of the story is that we are beginning to get a real pay-off on the size and diversity of our product-line. A number of present and potential customers are in the middle of fairly extensive product redesigns and "face-lifts." As they get into specifics, a lot of them are remembering our sales pitch about offering motors tailored to exact needs, instead of just "a motor."

SARLE:
(Assistant Division Manager)

Well, we've all been hoping this would happen. What about large motors? Are they going up too?

GREGORY:
(Sales Manager)

No. Apparently the big push will be in the smaller integrals and fractionals. It looks as if large motor sales will stay at about their present levels.

AUSTIN:
(Division Manager)

Let's get down to cases. Chris,[2] what'll it take to get Plant #1 up to 1,200 units a day average, and how soon can we be there?

---

[2] Christopher Sarle, Assistant Division Manager.

SARLE:
(Assistant Division Manager)

Well, anyway you look at it, it will be rough and will require some major changes. There's no sense trying to duck this fact. With our present set-up we're at the limit of capacity now; there's no chance of getting the plant's average output above 900 units daily without expanding facilities. I'm talking about space and equipment and manpower—the whole works. The real story on how rough it will be depends mostly on the product-mix. We'll all need some specific figures on that before we can come up with meaningful estimates. Can Sales give us a firm figure —a really firm one, without any fudge factors—of estimated monthly requirements by models for the coming year?

GREGORY:
(Sales Manager)

Sure we can. It'll take a couple of days to summarize the District estimates, that's all.

AUSTIN:
(Division Manager)

Okay. How about it, Chris? If Sales gives us an estimated monthly schedule of specific model requirements in a day or so, when can we have a machine-load figure to show where we'll need extra manufacturing capacity, and how much?

SARLE:
(Assistant Division Manager)

George,[3] that's your department. How long will it take?

FORBES:
(Production Manager)

I hope I remembered to say goodbye to the wife and kids this morning; it doesn't look like I'll get home in the near future. No, seriously, it will be forced draft, but I'll see that my department has the load figured a couple of days after next year's estimated monthly schedule is available. Of course, we'll have to calculate on the basis of current models and processes. If Engineering comes up with many major redesigns or model changes, they could knock my load figures into a cocked-hat.

AUSTIN:
(Division Manager)

How about it? Are there likely to be major design changes in the next year or so? If so, we'd better take them into account now.

PETERSON:
(Chief Engineer)

Well, there are some in the works, as always. It would take a while to determine the ones that are likely to involve significant process changes next year. I doubt if I

---

[3] George Forbes, Production Manager.

can have all of the particulars on these lined up by the time Production wants to start calculating next year's load. It would be safe for Forbes to go ahead, though, using the existing models as the basis for rough preliminary planning. None of the engineering changes presently in sight should throw things so seriously out of line that we couldn't handle them with only the usual headaches. I can get more specific information together in maybe a week or so.

AUSTIN: *(Division Manager)*
Do the best you can, Pete. You know that the more advance notice you can give us, the easier things will be on everybody.

PETERSON: *(Chief Engineer)*
Sure.

AUSTIN: *(Division Manager)*
Look, while we're thinking about machine load, we may as well push our planning beyond the mere question of the additional equipment needed for an average daily production rate of 1,200 units. If there's equipment that should be replaced because of age or inefficiency, this is probably as good a time as any to take this into account.

FORBES: *(Production Manager)*
I was going to ask about that. Chris and I will work together in trying to nail down this aspect of things. Okay, Chris?

SARLE: *(Assistant Division Manager)*
Fine.

AUSTIN: *(Division Manager)*
What about manpower, Chris?   Am I right in thinking that this shouldn't be too much of a problem?

SARLE: *(Assistant Division Manager)*
That would be my hunch. My rough guess is that we can get the average daily rate up to 1,200 units by adding maybe 150 people. That shouldn't be too tough. Personnel currently has a backlog of job applicants, and we turn away good prospects pretty regularly. A lot of applicants come to us with experience,[4] and even those who don't can be trained for any job but inserting[5] in about a

---

[4] The Division's plants were located near an industrial center in which several other large electric motor manufacturers were located.

[5] Training for the inserting operation required approximately six months.

month. I know that my estimate of manpower require- ments may seem low for this big a volume increase, but I think we can hold it to that. What do you think, George?

FORBES: *(Production Manager)* I go along. Not all of the indirect labor jobs will have to increase proportionately, so a 150 man buildup ought to about do it, give or take 10 per cent.

AUSTIN: *(Division Manager)* Okay. What about increased materials consumption at the new volume? How soon can we have the story on that, Bill?[6]

REYNOLDS: *(Manager of Services)* I should be able to have the procurement picture worked out within a day or so after I get the estimated sales re- quirements. We shouldn't have too much trouble, provided we work fast and give suppliers plenty of advance notice.

AUSTIN: *(Division Manager)* What about the increased power load?

REYNOLDS: *(Manager of Services)* The municipal power plant can handle it okay. But look, before we get all wrapped up in details, I want to know just where the devil we're going to put more equipment? For that matter, how can we find room to carry any more raw material or work-in-process? Or anything? The plant's bursting its seams as it is.

SARLE: *(Assistant Division Manager)* Looks like Production will just have to get rid of that excess inventory they like to carry as a cushion against headaches.

PETERSON: *(Chief Engineer)* No—you know what'll happen. We'll all fritz around, and at the last minute somebody will yell, "Engineering doesn't need all the space they've got—*there's* the place to cut." It happens every time.

AUSTIN: *(Division Manager)* Look, I know you're kidding, but before we get too wrapped up thinking about all the problems there'll be in this—and there'll be plenty—let's remember that we've been hoping for a breakthrough like this for a long time. If we don't deliver on this one, we'll probably never get an- other like it. So regardless of what it takes, we'll do it. And we've got damn little time, so we've really got to make tracks.

---

6 William Reynolds, Manager of Services.

GREGORY:
(Sales Manager)

Amen!

AUSTIN:
(Division Manager)

And another thing. We have to remember we're only one of nine Nolder divisions. For all we know, everybody else may also be hitting top management for authorization on things that look just as promising to them as this does to us. We'll have to double check every proposal to make 100 per cent sure that we're right, and, that we can prove our case.

SARLE:
(Assistant Division Manager)

Harry, I've been piecing together all of the different time estimates we've heard this morning. It looks like each of us should have our individual picture in mind by the 17th. So by a week from next Monday we should be able to give you a fairly complete picture on what it will take to get up to the new rate. Then all you'll have to do is sell top-side on the authorization and we'll be on the way.

AUSTIN:
(Division Manager)

Good enough, Chris. I'll expect you to coordinate things and see that we have the whole story as soon as possible. If we come up with a plan that makes sense, I think we can get the money. Our Division's profit picture has been good in the past. If we have facts and figures to justify it, I think management will go along with some expansion. Okay, let's summarize where we stand on this thing. Ruth Anne,[7] please take a memo to all staff members. You people listen and check me on this:

TO ALL STAFF MEMBERS:

This summarizes the promises agreed upon in our staff meeting this date. These are firm commitments and must be met—no alibis accepted.

Tom Gregory: By August 10, a motor schedule forecast by model on an average monthly mix.
George Forbes: By August 14, the machine load requirements for next year, assuming average daily volume of 1,200 units.
Bill Reynolds: By August 20, a complete report on material requirements at 1,200 motors per day.
Pete Peterson: By August 20, the full story on any design

---

[7] Ruth Anne Mader, Mr. Austin's secretary.

changes which may result in new processes affecting next year's machine loads, tooling, or equipment requirements. *Chris Sarle:* By August 20, a complete plan, including investment estimates, for increasing fractional production to 1,200 units per day.

Next week's regular staff meeting is canceled. There will be a meeting in my office at 9 a.m. on Tuesday, August 21, to go over the results of these studies. All staff members will be expected to attend.

Harry Austin
Division Manager

AUSTIN: Does that check with everybody?
*(Division
Manager)*

GROUP: (Sounds of general agreement.)

AUSTIN: Okay, that does it for now. I guess we've all got our work
*(Division cut out for us.
Manager)*

BACKGROUND TO THE ELECTRIC MOTOR DIVISION, NOLDER COMPANY

The Electric Motor Division is located in a small suburb of a midwestern manufacturing center of about 300,000 persons.

The Division's manufacturing activities are divided between two plants. In both, the machine shops and punch press departments currently were operating on a three-shift basis, five days a week. The remaining departments in each plant work a single shift.

Plant #1 produces motors having capacities of from one-fourth to five horsepower, in both single and three-phase models. At the time of the August 8th meeting, the plant employed about 600 workers and 17 line supervisors. Larger motors, with capacities up to 150 horsepower, are manufactured in Plant #2 which then employed roughly 100 workers and four production supervisors. In both operations, about two-thirds of the workforce are engaged in direct labor activity. Of these, about 85 per cent perform machining operations. The remainder are engaged in assembly work. Most activities are paid on a piece-rate incentive system. Machine operators were earning about $2.18 an hour on the average and assembly workers about $1.70. Employees in both plants are represented by an affiliate of a national trade union, and in the opinion of management, company-union dealings are mutually satisfactory. Grievances are rare, and are usually settled quickly and amicably when they occur.

Plant #1 contained about 90,000 square feet of space; Plant #2 had 56,000 square feet. The layout of equipment in both plants permitted an essentially straight line process-flow from one work area to the next. This is illustrated by the simplified floor plan of Plant #1 (Exhibit 2). Transfer between successive operations generally was not conveyorized. Instead it was accomplished manually, or by hand-truck or fork-lift, depending on the size of each workpiece and the number of pieces in the lot.

The Division's principal customers are manufacturers of equipment and appliances utilizing self-contained electric motors. Since motor manufacture is an involved and technical process, many producers of equipment and appliances purchase their motor requirements from suppliers, such as the Nolder company or its competitors, which specialize in motor manufacture. Necessarily, the performance, design, and dimensional characteristics of the motors must meet specific needs of the customer's product. Two competing manufacturers of similarly priced electric water pumps, for example, each might use a one-half horsepower single-phase motor to power their respective units. Differences in their pump design, however, might cause substantial difference in the size, appearance, or construction characteristics of the motor required by each customer.

In an effort to meet the wide range of variations in customer requirements, the Division had more than 2,000 active motor models in its present product line. Not all of these were regularly produced or kept in inventory. The company was prepared, however, to offer each of these models as a standard product.

It is a major responsibility of Division salesmen and sales engineers to assist customers in determining whether any of these standard units satisfy their exact motor requirements. Notwithstanding this extensive range of choice, customers sometimes desire motors whose specifications cannot be met by any of the standard models. In such cases, the customer and the Division negotiate the special design and manufacture of a motor offering the necessary characteristics. Sometimes the differences between special and standard models are slight, involving perhaps only a change in the canopy or in a shaft diameter. On the other hand, some special orders required extensive engineering and special tooling. In a typical year, special orders of all types account for about 15 per cent of the units produced by the Division and a comparable, or even slightly larger, share of its dollar volume.

The Division's slogan is *"The* Motor for *Your* Need." In keeping

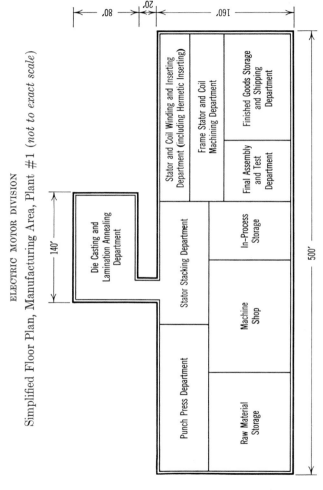

EXHIBIT 2 NOLDER MANUFACTURING COMPANY

ELECTRIC MOTOR DIVISION

Simplified Floor Plan, Manufacturing Area, Plant #1 (*not to exact scale*)

with this, the majority of the motors in its line have, at one time or another, been developed in response to a specific customer requirement. Depending on its size and complexity, and whether or not special engineering or tooling is required, a motor produced by Plant #1 might be priced anywhere from $15 to $150, the average being around $40.

The industry, which is comprised of at least 15 companies—many of them large and well-known concerns—is extremely competitive. Because of their ability to choose among many potential suppliers who vigorously compete for their business, customers are usually in a position to demand shipments on any standard item within 60 days of placing an order. The lead-time for special-order motors usually is longer, but even here, competitive pressures make time a premium.

In common with most of its competitors, the sales efforts of the Nolder company have been built around intensive direct selling. For these purposes, the Sales Department has divided the United States into four sales Districts. In each of these, on the average, five or six sales engineers operate under the supervision of a District Sales Manager. In each District Nolder also maintains a factory branch with a staff of six to eight servicemen and a stock of replacement parts. In addition, 260 authorized factory service representatives are located in principal cities from coast to coast.

The company believed that at the present time it was among the leaders in the industry, and that its profit on sales was above the industry's average which was estimated to be running about 4.5 per cent after taxes. Nolder's officers were convinced, however, that the retention and expansion of their firm's share of the motor market was dependent on its continuing ability to offer excellent quality, reasonable prices, reliable and prompt delivery, and effective service. They believed that an appreciable disadvantage in any of these areas could result quickly in major sales declines.

Because of the great variety of motor models demanded by customers, it is not unusual for both of the Division's plants to produce as many as 350 different types of motors per month. Individual customer orders average about 140 units, but range from a single motor to many thousands of a given type.

The production of electric motors entails a series of complex manufacturing and assembly operations. The equipment required includes high-speed automatic lathes, boring mills, external grinders, roll-forming machines, hydraulic presses, degreasing units, heat-treating ovens, and specially designed automatic coil-winding and wire-inserting machines. In order to assure satisfactory operation of the completed motors with a minimum of friction and vibration, machining operations have to be held to close tolerances, in some cases .0003 of an inch. Care also has to be taken, both in machining and assembly, to assure concentricity of cylindrical surfaces. To accomplish this, many operations—for example, the turning and grinding of shaft diameters— require complex special tooling permitting several diameters to be machined simultaneously in a single workpiece set-up. Careful in-process inspection, as well as final inspection and testing, are standard practice in the Division's shops. On the average, total manufacturing cycle time, from raw stock to finished goods, is ten working days.

For the typical standard motor produced in Plant #1, total manufacturing cost as the managers of the Division attacked their new challenge was as follows:

Raw Materials and Purchased Parts	69%
Direct Labor	10%
Factory Overhead	21%

Since set-up and changeover time requirements for each operation on each model are sizeable, considerable management attention is given to the "motor mix"—that is, the number of different models which are in process in the plant at any given time. Control of the mix was of decisive importance in determining the volume and efficiency of the manufacturing activities in each of the plants. If small lots of many different models were in production simultaneously, that is, if the motor mix were high, the ratio of set-up time to operating time became large, unit costs increased, and the volume of plant output was reduced.

To avoid such conditions, the Division's production staff makes a continuing effort to hold the mix to the lowest possible levels consistent with sales and financial requirements. Since a portion of plant capacity always has to be held in reserve for special orders, many of which involve small lot sizes, particular care is required in planning the production of standard motors that can safely be inventoried. Ideally such models are produced in lot sizes large enough to improve the plant's production efficiency and to assure that customer requirements can be satisfied until the next scheduled run of that particular model, and yet small enough to keep finished goods inventories from becoming an excessive financial burden or risk.

As a result of these efforts, there is great variation in manufacturing lot sizes and in inventory levels maintained for different models of motors and of motor components. In the case of certain standard components common to a number of different motor models, manufacturing operations are carried on almost continuously throughout the year. On the other hand, an estimated year's supply of a highly specialized standard motor having only limited demand might be produced in a single run, and the assembled units kept in finished goods inventory. Between these two extremes, decisions have to be made regarding the manufacture of each of the models in the Division's line. On the average, between 4,000 and 5,000 completed motors are held in finished goods inventory. In terms of selling price, these usually represent about 3 per cent of the Division's total annual sales.

Successful execution of this scheduling and inventory policy depends on the availability of reliable, detailed sales forecasts. If the forecasts for any given model underestimate actual requirements, the Division either has to quote abnormally long delivery dates, with almost certain loss of sales, or has to accept production inefficiencies through the hurried scheduling of a small lot into production. On the other hand, if the forecasts overestimate actual requirements, finished goods inventories are enlarged and the inventory turnover rate slackens, creating pressure on the Division's finances and its available storage space.

The annual sales forecasts of the District Sales Managers are therefore of great importance to the production organization. Even though these preliminary estimates can be only approximations, they are used for advance planning of machine-load and of manpower requirements. Actual production is scheduled monthly on the basis of the most current sales information, but in order to obtain delivery on the necessary purchased parts and raw material, tentative production plans and firm procurement commitments must be made three months in advance.

Under the conditions existing in August of the current year, an average daily output of 900 motors had been established as the production goal for Plant #1. When this average was maintained on a monthly basis, as it had been for the past several years, Nolder officials were confident that the mix was being held to reasonable levels and that satisfactory production efficiency was being achieved in the plant. It was this figure which now had to be raised to 1,200 per day in response to increasing sales pressures. The average daily target figure for the larger motors produced in Plant #2 was 100 motors.

INVESTIGATIONS OF EXPANSION POSSIBILITIES

Immediately following the staff meeting of August 8, it was agreed that each of the key personnel would spend the remainder of the day considering the probable effect of impending volume increase in his own area of activity, advising subordinates of the situation, and taking steps to obtain the data requested at the meeting. On the following morning, Chris Sarle called a conference in his office for preliminary discussion of various means by which the desired increase in volume could be achieved. Present at the meeting were the Manager of Services, the Plant Engineer, the Chief Process Engineer, the Production Manager, the Supervisor of Production Control, and the Plant Layout Engineer.

The discussion lasted the major part of the day. As a starting point, each of the promises made at the prior day's meeting regarding the submission of information was reviewed and specific due dates were re-emphasized. Consideration then was given to a wide range of ideas regarding the expansion. Eventually, major interest centered on two alternatives. One called for physical expansion of Plant #1 through new construction. The additional space would be utilized for the new equipment required to meet the expanded volume of operations and for storage of increased inventory. The Production Manager expressed the belief that the added space also would permit a more advantageous layout of certain existing equipment.

The second alternative entailed the continuation of Plant #1 in its present physical form and dimensions, but called for the installation of an extensive system of conveyors to permit a more effective utilization of the space presently available. It was suggested that with conveyors, sufficient floor space might be freed in the existing plant to provide room for the additional equipment and inventory needed, without having to construct additional plant facilities.

Because the alternatives represented such totally different approaches to the problem, the group meeting on August 9 agreed that a thorough study should be made of both possibilities and the results presented to the Division Manager for his consideration. Since August 20 already had been established as the deadline for the presentation of an expansion plan, it was decided that the same date also should terminate the two-pronged investigation now being undertaken. This involved an even more substantial workload on each of the men than originally had been contemplated. To make sure that all of the individual responsibilities were understood, and that the various deadlines would be met, the results of the August 9 meeting were written up in the form of minutes (Exhibit 3).

During the week and a half which followed, the entire manufacturing staff worked under great pressure to assemble the information for which it was responsible. Faced with various deadlines, most of the men appeared at the plant each morning well in advance of the

EXHIBIT 3   Nolder Manufacturing Company

ELECTRIC MOTOR DIVISION

Extracts of Minutes of Staff Conference of August 9

The following are the responsibilities and dates on which plant information is due. . . . Each date must be met.

1. Machine load figures . . . *due* August 14 from Production Manager.
2. Plant Engineer and Plant Layout Engineer to plan a complete system of conveyors to cover machine shop, punch press department, including scrap removal, stator inserting, rotor and shaft department, and final assembly. All parts for final assembly to be conveyed near ceiling to free floor area below for production. . . . *Date due:* August 17.
3. Plant Engineer to obtain construction costs on plant addition. *Due* August 17.
4. Chief Process Engineer to get cost data on any necessary new machines and equipment. *Due* August 17.

. . . .

8. Plant Layout Engineer to purchase three dimensional layout templates (price not to exceed $1,500) for use in planning.

There will be a daily meeting in the Assistant Division Manager's office at 8 a.m., to report progress. These sessions are not to last over 45 minutes. . . .

normal starting hour of 8 A.M., and continued working until late at night. For most of the production staff, the weekends of August 11 and 12, and August 18 and 19, were full working days.

Of major assistance in meeting the deadlines was the fact that when Plant #1 had been constructed six years before, consideration had been given to the possibility of future expansion. Rough drawings had been made at that time to show possible annexes which might be added. Tentative layout plans also had been prepared showing how much machinery might be arranged in the new space. The equipment in Plant #1, moreover, had been laid out in such a way as to minimize the need for drastic revisions in the event additional space were to be constructed at some later date. Furthermore, even during the initial construction of the plant, some members of the management group had become interested in the possible use of conveyors. Preliminary studies of this possibility had been made at that time and were available as a starting point for the current investigations.

As a result of the intensive efforts of all personnel, a report summarizing both plans for expanding capacity was submitted to the Division Manager on Monday, August 20. This information, together with data relating to the requirements for achieving an output of 1,200 motors per day, was available for consideration at the staff meeting on August 21.

EXHIBIT 4 NOLDER MANUFACTURING COMPANY

ELECTRIC MOTOR DIVISION

Machine Load at Average Daily Rate of 1,200 Units (only extracts of complete report are shown)

Machine	Est. Required Production Time/Day	Est. Set-up Time/Day	Est. Total Hrs. Required	Hrs. Presently Available	Comments
		Standard Hours			
FOR SHAFT PRODUCTION (77 different types)					
Saw and Center	9	4	13	23	O.K.
Sundstrand Automatic	38	12	50	46	1 new req'd.
Grinders	43	9	52	69	O.K.
Mill	17	3	20	46	O.K.
Thread Grinder	22	2	24	23	Put thread roller on Sundstrand
Knurl	6	1	7	23	O.K.
Drill Press	10	2	12	23	O.K.
FOR ROTOR IRON PRODUCTION (80 different types)					
Dennison Die Cast Machine	30	3	33	46	1 new req'd. (for cost reduction)
INT. Die Cast Machine	8	1	9	23	O.K.
FOR JET LAMINATIONS					
(Stator) Minster #100 Press	21	4	25	23	1 new req'd.
(Rotor) Minster #100 Press	21	4	25	23	1 new req'd.

FOR STATOR STOCKING (60 different types)					
Stator Rivet Machine	53	4	57	69	Replace for quality improvement
ANNEALING AND BLUING					
Not applicable					Need new continuous oven; 8,000#/week to be subcontracted
FOR FRAME, STATOR, AND COIL					
Auto Turning Lathe	29	10	39	46	Need stand-by
FOR MAIN FRAME					
Seam Welder	11	6	17	23	Replace existing
Grinder	10	1	11	23	Replace with scarfing machine (cost saving)

FINAL ASSEMBLY DEPARTMENT

Std. hrs. req'd./day   598
12% for Rejection, i.e., 598 ÷ (100% − 12%) = 680
Average Earned Hrs.   10 per worker
680 ÷ 10 = 68 ass'y. personnel
Present   = 56 ass'y. personnel
Need   = 12 at 10 Std. hrs.

(NOTE: Only 62 work stations now available.)

FOR ROTOR AND SHAFT MFG.					
Balancing Machine	36	3	39	46	Replace (Quality)

ESTIMATES OF EXPANSION REQUIREMENTS
AND CHARACTERISTICS OF ALTERNATIVE
EXPANSION PLANS

Expansion Requirements

Extracts of the Production Manager's estimates of machine-load requirements, based on the Sales Manager's monthly forecast of sales for the coming year and on the staff group's decision that the machine shop and punch press departments would continue on a three-shift basis, are shown in Exhibit 4. To provide this capacity and retire certain obsolete units in use, the Production Manager estimated that it would be necessary to acquire the equipment shown in Exhibit 5, which also includes purchase price and delivery information. Since

EXHIBIT 5 NOLDER MANUFACTURING COMPANY

ELECTRIC MOTOR DIVISION

Estimated Additional Equipment Requirements and Savings
with Daily Rate of 1,200 Units, Plant #1

Machine	Total Cost*	Earliest Delivery Date‡	Anticipated Yearly Savings
(2) 6″ x 30″ Landis Grinders†	$ 28,000	Feb. 20	$ 1,005
Thread Roller	3,750	Jan. 10	3,410
Dennison Die Cast Machine	15,800	Jan. 3	4,250
(2) 100 Ton Minster Presses†	40,200	Mar. 15	5,600
(2) 75 Ton Minster Presses†	31,400	Feb. 20	3,010
Stator Rivet Press†	7,800	Feb. 1	4,200
Continuous Anneal Oven	72,000	April 20	8,100
Sundstrand Automatic Lathe	48,500	April 19	15,080
National Seam Welder	30,500	May 5	None
Scarf Machine	10,500	Feb. 1	9,500
Gisholt Balancing Machine	7,205	Jan. 10	None
Total Cost	$295,655	Total Anticipated Savings	$54,155

* Including cost of shipping and direct installation costs, but excludes any consideration of production volume which might be lost because of interruptions to normal operations while new machines were being installed.

† Indicates predicted improvement in quality in comparison to comparable units already in use by the Division.

‡ All dates are in the forthcoming calendar year.

some of the new equipment would be superior to that employed, it was believed that certain production economies, quality improvements, or both, would be realized on that portion of production to be achieved on the new machines. Estimates of these savings appear in Exhibit 5. The total floor space necessary for additional pieces of equipment, and for the work areas surrounding them, was estimated at 18,000 square feet.

Alternative #1: Construction of Additional Plant Space

As to the possibility of expanding through the construction of additional plant space, the report submitted the proposed layout shown in Exhibit 6. This represented Plant #1 as it would appear after the construction of an additional 32,000 square feet—16,000 square feet of space at each end of the existing plant land already owned by the Division. The expansion at the southern end of the building would be used for raw stock storage. This would permit the areas currently allocated to these purposes to be freed to receive the necessary new manufacturing equipment. The 16,000 square feet of additional space constructed on the north end of the present building would become the site of packing and shipping operations and also be used for the storage of finished goods. Those areas of Plant #1 that were devoted to these functions could then be used for stator inserting operations, final assembly, testing, and inspection.

Since the necessary additional equipment would require only 18,000 of the proposed 32,000 square feet of new plant area, it was believed that adequate new space would be available for the additional inventories of raw materials, work-in-process, completed subassemblies, and finished goods needed to support an average daily volume of 1,200 units. With this new construction it was estimated that the plant actually might be able to process as many as 1,350 units per day (average) if still additional manufacturing equipment were acquired at some later date.

Plans for the proposed additions had been discussed with several building contractors, and construction costs had been established at approximately a quarter of a million dollars. The various items covered, together with cost estimates, are shown in Exhibit 7. Several of the contractors had given assurances that the project could be completed within four months after the necessary structural steel had been received at the site. A tentative commitment had been made by a major steel supplier to make such deliveries in no more than 90 days after receipt of a firm purchase contract.

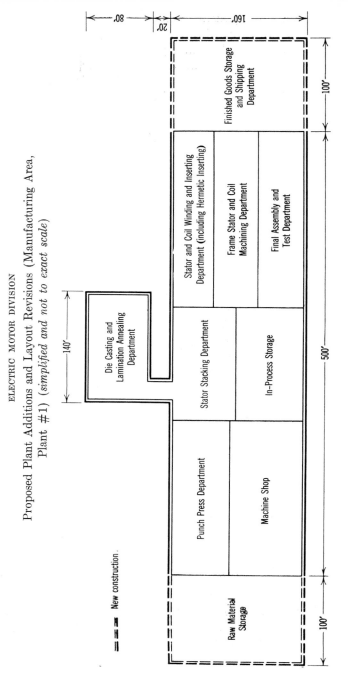

EXHIBIT 6   NOLDER MANUFACTURING COMPANY

ELECTRIC MOTOR DIVISION

Proposed Plant Additions and Layout Revisions (Manufacturing Area, Plant #1) (*simplified and not to exact scale*)

EXHIBIT 7   Nolder Manufacturing Company

ELECTRIC MOTOR DIVISION

Expansion of Factory—32,000 square feet

General Contract	$150,000
Heating	20,000
Ventilation and Exhaust System	8,000
Sprinkler System	13,000
Install Lights	3,000
Install Fence	2,000
Landscaping	3,000
Painting Laboratory and Material	4,000
Floodlights	1,000
Fire Extinguishers	2,000
Parking Lot	5,000
Office Partitions	3,000
Rest Room Partitions	1,000
Plumbing Toilet Facilities	10,000
Light Fixtures and Ducts	12,000
Material—Fence	5,000
Rough Grade	3,000
Survey	500
	$245,500

It appeared that the new plant areas could be ready for use within roughly seven months. Within this same period, deliveries could be made on all necessary new equipment.

The newly constructed space was expected to have a productive life of at least 50 years. For tax purposes, construction costs would be depreciated in equal installments over that period. Annual overhead costs in Plant #1, other than depreciation, amounted at that time to approximately $2.14 per square foot. At the existing levels of production, about 80 per cent of this rate was attributable to variable overhead costs. Were the new space constructed and volume expanded to 1,200 units per day, total manufacturing overhead, other than depreciation on plant and equipment, was expected to increase by approximately $59,000 annually. This would include the salary or wage costs for the additional indirect laborers, inspectors, supervisors, clerks, and related personnel needed at the new volume of production.

The best judgment of the authors of the report was that when new plant area and equipment were available, the required rearrangements of the existing areas of Plant #1 probably could be accomplished in

EXHIBIT 8 NOLDER MANUFACTURING COMPANY

ELECTRIC MOTOR DIVISION

Proposed Conveyor Installations by Plant Area

Plant Area	Length of Conveyors
OVERHEAD CONVEYORS	
Main Frame Assembly	725'
Stator Iron Fabrication	210'
Main Frame Fabrication	180'
Casting	330'
Machine Shop (Area A)	340'
Rotor Shaft Fabrication	145'
Rotor Shaft Storage	130'
Frame Stator and Coil Fabrication	225'
Stator and Coil Fabrication	590'
Inspect to Dip and Bake	115'
Final Assembly Feeder	435'
End Frame and Frame Stator and Coil Bank	790'
Lamination Fabrication	415'
Coil Winding	310'
Frame Stator and Coil Bake	280'
Casting Bake	380'
Machine Shop (Area B)	85'
Total Overhead Conveyors	5,685'
SURFACE CONVEYORS	
Final Assembly Pallet	165'
Final Assembly and Raw Stock Pallet	155'
Inserting Belt A	90'
Inserting Belt B	90'
Hermetic Inserting	50'
Lamination Belt	65'
Final Assembly Roller	400'
Hermetic Working Roller	100'
Hermetic Packing Roller	150'
Shaft Line Skate	230'
Hermetic Connecting Roller	35'
Fractional Connecting Roller	70'
Oscillating Scrap Conveyor	210'
Total Surface Conveyors	1,810'
TOTAL CONVEYORS	7,495'

a single weekend. Move costs would be slight, consisting largely of overtime wages for personnel carrying out the physical relocation of equipment. Note also was made that production processes would be essentially unchanged in the expanded plant. The same operations, processes, and control procedures would continue to be employed as before, only on a larger scale.

Alternative #2: Adding Conveyors to Existing Plant

The staff investigations discovered that the installation of a conveyor system in the existing areas of Plant #1 would require approximately 5,700 lineal feet of overhead conveyors and 1,800 of surface conveyors. The individual requirements of various plant areas are shown in Exhibit 8. All of the equipment, available through a local manufacturer, would be of a type assembled by bolting rather than welding.

Components would be transported on the overhead conveyors by the use of either single or multipronged hooks capable of directly carrying one or more items, or one or more trays on which items had been placed. Photographs of several types of hooks likely to be used, ob-

EXHIBIT 9   NOLDER MANUFACTURING COMPANY

VIEWS OF OVERHEAD CONVEYORS, HOOKS, AND TRAYS

tained from the conveyor manufacturer, are shown as Exhibit 9. Findings of the prior study of conveyors had convinced the Division personnel that the hooks would not damage the parts in transit, and that safety devices would minimize any physical risk to plant personnel.

Since more than three-fourths of the conveyors would move in overhead areas, considerable amounts of floor space required for storage

EXHIBIT 9 (*Continued*)   NOLDER MANUFACTURING COMPANY

and materials handling could be released for other uses. For example, about 6,000 square feet of space now was used for temporary in-process storage of basic motor subassemblies. With the contemplated increase in production, the space needed for this purpose was expected to increase to approximately 8,000 square feet. If, instead, these components were transported overhead, this floor-space requirement would cease to exist. The overhead conveyors themselves would provide the necessary temporary storage space, as well as accomplishing the transportation of the parts.   In most instances, the conveyors could be deployed to provide such "storage-in-transit" for the maximum number of units normally in process between any two manufacturing operations at an anticipated volume of 1,200 motors per day.

From careful investigation, the Assistant Division Manager and his associates concluded that total floor-space savings from all such sources

EXHIBIT 9 *(Continued)*   NOLDER MANUFACTURING COMPANY

would approximate 24,000 square feet.   This would be enough to permit installation of the necessary new manufacturing equipment in the existing areas of Plant #1, and still free 6,000 square feet of floor space for the additional raw material storage, finished goods inventory, and similar needs to arise from increased volume.

The purchase and installation of the proposed conveyor system would require an investment of approximately $183,000.

Overhead Conveyor Units, Hooks, and Related Equipment	$ 72,800
Surface Conveyor Units, Hooks, and Related Equipment	34,250
Construction of Dispatch Deck	4,200
Safety Devices	29,750
Installation of all Units and Devices	25,175
	$166,175
Contingencies (10%)	16,618
TOTAL	$182,793

Installation would take three months and could be begun at any time on a few weeks' notice to the manufacturer, whose home offices were only a few blocks from Plant #1. During this period, normal production at the rate of 900 motors per day theoretically could be maintained, but probably with difficulty. Realistically, it seemed likely that the equivalent of at least several weeks' production might be lost during the installation. The work would be carried out by the Division's own personnel, assisted by specialists from the conveyor manufacturer.

The productive life of the line conveyor units was estimated at 20 years and they could be depreciated over this period. The conveyor hooks and bearings, which represented approximately two-thirds of the initial equipment cost, however, probably would have to be depreciated and replaced in about ten years. Other annual maintenance and operating expenses were estimated at $1,000.

The survey also indicated that in addition to freeing space, the conveyors might give rise to various production economies through the elimination of certain personnel engaged in materials handling. Under the arrangement then in effect, for example, the plant's manufacturing operations required the services of three material handlers at a total wage cost of $10,800, and two fork-lift truck operators at a total annual wage cost of $8,500. If conveyors were introduced to accomplish the major share of materials handling, it might be possible to operate with only one handler and one fork-lift operator, even at the new volume rate. If, on the other hand, the alternative of expanding the plant were adopted, one additional man probably would have to be added in each of these job categories. Gasoline fork-lifts represent an investment of about $7,000 each, have an operating life of about five years, and generate annual maintenance and operating expenses of about $500 apiece exclusive of the wages of the operator.

Under existing conditions, it also was necessary to have four men dispatching goods into final assembly at a total wage cost of approxi-

NOLDER MANUFACTURING COMPANY 297

mately $17,000 per year. If the plant were expanded to achieve the new volume rate, one additional dispatcher might be required. Initially, however, the enlarged plant would continue to operate only with four dispatchers in the belief that this might prove adequate. On the other hand, if conveyors were to be introduced, only a single dispatcher was likely to be required, even at the increased volume of production.

As envisaged by the supporters of the conveyor plan, this single dispatcher would serve as the "nerve-center" for the entire operation. He would be located at a "dispatch deck" situated on a mezzanine 15 feet above the floor of the plant. Here would converge the conveyors from the three separate production lines—end frames, rotor and shaft assembly, and frame stator and coil assembly—as well as the conveyor going to the final assembly department. Relying on data from the production control schedules and parts lists, the dispatcher would remove the proper components from each of the three production-line conveyors, "match" them together, and place them on one of the three-pronged hooks on the assembly line conveyor. En route from the dispatcher station to the final assembly department, this conveyor would pass through a stockroom where any necessary purchased parts, such as bearings, condensers, or miscellaneous hardware items, and stocked subassemblies required for the particular motor being assembled, also would be placed on the hook. In this manner, when the conveyor reached the final assembly department, all of the components necessary for a motor would be together on the same hook, ready for assembly.

In the assembly department there would be two lines, one arranged so that a single operator would perform all assembly operations on each motor. On the second line, for larger orders, assembly would be performed progressively by several operators. The first operator would remove all of the parts from the conveyor and perform those operations for which he was responsible. The partially assembled unit and all remaining units would then be transported on a gravity conveyor to each of the remaining stages of assembly.

The report also advanced the view that since the conveyors, in many cases, would reduce the amount of operator time spent in handling and moving materials, they would result in improvements in the plant's over-all direct labor productivity. In the short time which had been available to prepare the report, it had not been possible to make careful studies of how significant these productivity increases would be. Exact data on this subject would require individual examination of each of the approximately 9,000 different operations upon which standard methods had been determined and standard piece-rates set. A rough estimate had been advanced by the Methods Department,[8] however, that for the plant as a whole, use of conveyors might permit the development of new methods for perhaps a third of the operations. As a further "guesstimate" it was suggested that the new methods, on the average, might be 3 per cent more productive than those in use.

As scheduled, at 9:00 o'clock on the morning of August 21, the key Divisional personnel assembled in Mr. Austin's office.

AUSTIN:	I know these last two weeks have been a long, hard pull for
(Division	all of you. I appreciate the all-out way you've tackled this
Manager)	thing. I've studied your analysis of both possibilities.
	You've done a good job. Now we have to reach a decision.
	Somebody start us off. Where should we come out on this?

---

[8] This group consisted of five men and reported to the Chief Process Engineer.

The Prince Company—Defense Division (I)

In December 1950, the Defense Division of the Prince Company received a $20.5 million contract from the Air Force for approximately 1,000 sets of a highly complex, new electro-mechanical device for aircraft control. Delivery of the first units was scheduled for January 1952. The new contract, coupled with the increased demand for the Division's regular line of products,[1] resulted in a drastic increase in Division activity throughout 1951, with sales rising from the 1950 level of $10 million to $20 million, and employment growing from 1,305 to 2,249 persons. During this same period a new plant was built for the Division, and a new, temporary organization was established to handle preproduction work on the government contract. Furthermore, steps were taken to prepare for an additional step-up in volume in 1952 when sales were expected to reach $58 million.

By the end of 1951 the Division management was able to report: "From an over-all viewpoint 1951 has been a successful year. . . . We are looking ahead with confidence that in 1952 we will be even more successful in attaining the desired sales goal and in improving the profit margin."

COMPANY AND DEFENSE DIVISION BACKGROUND

Prince Company, with headquarters in Southern California, employed approximately 25,000 persons in its several installations throughout the country, and was a recognized leader in the manufacture of electrical equipment. The company's sales and earnings had grown steadily over the years. During the Second World War, Prince engineers had developed a variety of electro-mechanical products of a

---

[1] Hereafter referred to as "regular products."

precise and complex nature for the Air Force. After the war the company's Defense Division, located in the headquarters city, had continued to produce the same general lines of defense products, but at a much reduced level.

As defense demand picked up in 1948 and 1949, the Division found its volume increasing substantially. In mid-1949, Henry Ellicott, age 43, was employed as the Division's Director of Manufacturing, replacing the former Production Manager who wished to return to a staff position. Mr. Ellicott brought to the company a successful background of production management experience in large volume manufacture of light electrical and precision equipment.

In late 1949 the company purchased a modern, one-story factory building of 100,000 square feet, located in another part of the city, for use as the new site of the Defense Division's manufacturing facilities. Machines, assembly equipment, and desks were moved from the corporation headquarters area over a weekend. The Division's factory employees were members of a CIO union and continued to retain city-wide seniority with employees in other Prince plants after the move. In 1950, construction of an office building for the Division's engineering and sales personnel was begun on a tract adjacent to the new plant facilities.

In 1950, the Division's volume reached $10 million in comparison with the $6 million volume achieved in 1949. Although faced with many difficult engineering and production problems on new devices being introduced, it seemed evident to company personnel that during 1950 significant over-all progress was being made in the Division's productivity and in the development of an effective management team.

NEGOTIATIONS ON THE B-D/9G1 CONTRACT

In the fall of 1950, several months after the outbreak of the Korean War, C. B. Locke, President of Prince, received a call from an Air Force General urgently requesting that the Prince Defense Division accept a contract from the Air Force to act as a second source on a vitally needed item of military equipment. The primary source was one of Prince's chief competitors in the same product area—the G. T. McAlpin Company. The equipment consisted of a recently designed, complex, electronic-mechanical device comprised of two major products referred to as the B-D and 9G1. This unit was not yet in production but had been designated by the Air Force for use on its latest aircraft. As a result of the step-up in production schedules for military aircraft occasioned by the War, the devices were needed in quantities which were unusually large for equipment of such complexity. The Air Force therefore had serious doubts that one company could produce the necessary volume in the time allowed, and felt that a back-up contractor would be a mandatory safeguard on so essential an item.

Mr. Locke discussed the Air Force request with W. A. Spalding, Vice President in charge of the Defense Division. Mr. Spalding, in turn, explored the matter with his entire staff. Out of these various conferences the decision was reached to decline the contract. In addition to being reluctant to manufacture a competitor's equipment under a licensing arrangement, the Prince personnel felt that the expansion of their Defense Division had been extremely rapid during the past three years. This growth had already generated many perplexing problems in producing defense equipment of Prince's own design, and it therefore seemed doubtful that the Division was ready to take on a difficult additional assignment that in and of itself would require at least doubling present monthly output within two years. This would be in addition to the major increases of volume in the Division's own military products which the Sales Department was forecasting for this same period (Exhibit 1).

This decision was relayed to the Air Force. At this point, due to the critical urgency of the project, the military brought considerable pressure to bear, urging that in the interest of national security Prince reconsider. A Facilities Contract for supplying machine tools was promised, along with a five-year amortization of new building construction costs. Finally, after further deliberations, Prince felt reluctantly compelled to accept the contract and notified the Air Force of this decision.

Contractual negotiations were begun immediately, culminating in Prince's execution of a licensing agreement with the McAlpin Company on November 10, 1950, and a letter contract with the United States Government, preliminary to a definitive contract, on December 22, 1950.

The licensing agreement specified that the following items were to be furnished to Prince by the McAlpin firm:

1. Three sets of prints of all parts
2. Parts lists
3. Purchasing sources
4. Machine-loading data
5. Tool vendor data
6. Inspection specifications
7. Processing cards
8. Tool drawings

EXHIBIT 1 THE PRINCE COMPANY—DEFENSE DIVISION (I)

SALES, BACKLOGS, AND MANUFACTURING AUTHORIZATIONS

In Thousands of Dollars

	Regular Products				BD/9G1				Totals—All Products			
	Sales				Sales				Sales			
1951	Planned for 1952	Actual	Backlog	Mfg. Authorizations	Planned for 1952	Actual	Backlog	Mfg. Authorizations	Planned for 1952	Actual	Backlog	Mfg. Authorizations
Jan.	—	$1,373	$20,463	N.A.	—	—	$ 2,000	N.A.	—	$1,373	$22,463	$16,928
Feb.	—	1,352	20,684	—	—	—	2,000	—	—	1,352	22,684	20,309
Mar.	—	1,140	21,368	—	—	—	3,250	—	—	1,140	24,618	26,890
Apr.	—	961	23,047	—	—	—	3,250	—	—	961	26,297	28,684
May	—	1,678	24,575	—	—	—	3,250	—	—	1,678	27,825	29,153
June	—	1,735	26,358	—	—	—	3,250	—	—	1,735	29,608	37,082
July	—	1,192	31,083	—	—	—	3,250	—	—	1,192	34,333	42,717
Aug.	—	2,211	34,838	$29,400	—	—	14,706	$15,300	—	2,211	49,544	44,700
Sept.	—	1,870	33,103	29,100	—	—	14,706	19,300	—	1,870	47,719	48,400
Oct.	—	2,789	28,192	25,000	—	—	14,706	19,300	—	2,789	42,898	44,300
Nov.	—	2,237	29,335	26,900	—	—	14,706	19,300	—	2,237	44,042	46,200
Dec.	—	3,021	29,932	27,000	—	—	22,479	19,300	—	3,021	52,412	46,300
1952												
Jan.	$2,500				—				$2,500			
Feb.	2,700				—				2,700			
Mar.	2,800				$ 300				3,100			
Apr.	2,900				600				3,500			
May	3,100				1,100				4,200			
June	3,000				2,000				5,000			
July	3,000				2,800				5,800			
Aug.	3,300				2,900				6,200			
Sept.	3,500				2,500				6,000			
Oct.	3,900				2,600				6,500			
Nov.	4,000				2,600				6,600			
Dec.	4,000				2,700				6,700			

NOTE: Actual data recorded through January 1, 1952. Backlog and Manufacturing Authorization data are as of end of month shown. Manufacturing Authorizations were defined as work which had been released to the shop to build, either due to receipt of orders or in advance of expected orders, expressed in dollars of billing represented.

9. Design engineering data
10. Engineering test data
11. Test equipment drawings
12. Engineering specifications
13. Field service data

These items were to be delivered to Prince during the months of January and February 1951.

In the letter of transmittal accompanying the letter contract, the Defense Division's Vice President, Mr. Spalding, made the following statement to the Air Force:

We note that the delivery schedule calls for initial deliveries in December of 1951. During the various meetings which we held with representatives of the Air Force, we pointed out that based on the meager information on hand at that time, it was felt that initial deliveries could not be made until eighteen (18) months after the issuance of the contract. We have not as yet received all the prints from McAlpin and latest information indicates we apparently will not . . . until January 15, 1951. In the light of our original estimates on the magnitude of this job, and the fact that we will not receive all of the prints until the date mentioned, we feel that the delivery schedule appearing in the contract is highly unrealistic. Since we will not have sufficient information to enable us to propose definitely in terms of prices and delivery schedules for some time, we assume that the question of delivery schedules can again be considered at the time of the issuance of the definitive contract.

As Mr. Spalding requested, the matter of delivery schedules was further reviewed. The compromise delivery schedule agreed upon in the definitive contract signed May 14, 1951, was as follows:

Number of Units

1952	B-D	9G1
January	5	—
February	10	—
March	20	—
April	40	10
May	60	25
June	80	65
July	100	100
August	120	150
September	150	170
October	150	200
November	150	250
December	51	52
Total	936	1,022

ORGANIZING FOR THE B-D/9G1 PROGRAM

Preliminary cost estimates indicated that the sales volume represented by the 1952 schedule of B-D and 9G1 deliveries amounted to approximately $20.5 million. This total was about the same as the anticipated 1951 sales volume in the Division's regular line of defense products. Further, orders on regular products were being received at an ever-increasing rate. For example, 1952 requirements of regular items were expected to be at least $30 million.

Faced with the likely necessity of producing in 1952 at a total rate well in excess of $50 million compared to the 1950 output of $10 million, company and Division management officials made the following decisions in late 1950:

1. To begin construction at the earliest possible date on a 100,000 square-foot addition to the recently acquired Defense Division plant. The new facility would be located adjacent to the present 100,000 square-foot plant and to the office building which was nearing completion.
2. To place orders as soon as possible for approximately 235 machine tools, the majority of which would be purchased under a Government Facilities Contract and thus become government property.
3. To organize a temporary Special Projects Group to handle the pre-production planning, scheduling, processing, tooling, and hiring for the B-D and 9G1. This Group was to be under the direction of E. M. DuMoulin, who would be transferred to the Division from his present post as Manufacturing Vice President of a successful Prince subsidiary purchased after the Second World War. In this new assignment, Mr. DuMoulin was to have the title of Special Projects Manager, and would report to Defense Division Vice President Spalding.
4. It was contemplated that the Special Projects Group would be moved to the new plant when the building was completed in late 1951 at which time it would be integrated promptly into the Defense Division's regular manufacturing organization under Mr. Ellicott. Mr. DuMoulin would then be given another assignment outside of the Division.
5. Because the Division's present production engineering staff was already swamped with the problems connected with new regular products, it was decided to employ two contract engineering firms to handle the processing, tool design, and tool procurement for the B-D and the 9G1. This arrangement would leave the regular Defense

Division personnel relatively free to concentrate on their own pressing problems of meeting customer requirements and increasing production volume on regular products during the preproduction period on the B-D and 9G1 contract.

Since no space was available in the present Division building, 5,000 square feet of office space in a Prince warehouse in another part of the city were assigned to Mr. DuMoulin and his B-D/9G1 Special Projects Group. Mr. DuMoulin, who had moved his family to California a few weeks earlier, hired several key personnel late in 1950 and the project was launched in January 1951.

Philip Burgess, a management consultant long employed by Prince top management, made this comment in a report to the Division Operations Manager, Lewis Trane, on January 31, 1951: "The present rate

EXHIBIT 2   The Prince Company—Defense Division (I)

SPECIAL PROJECTS PERSONNEL (Partial List)
Early 1951

Name	Function	Background	Reports to
Donald Mixon	Production Manager	15 years general manufacturing experience. Recently in farm implements industry.	DuMoulin
Melvin Irwin	Chief Engineer	20 years engineering design and development. Had once worked for The Prince Company before.	DuMoulin
Edward Mellon	Liaison between The Prince Company and G. T. McAlpin Co.	20 years inspection and manufacturing supervision at The Prince Company.	DuMoulin
Dick Garvin	Production Control Manager	10 years production control and manufacturing experience in three other companies.	Mixon
Logan Becker	Chief Methods Engineer	8 years industrial engineering at The Prince Company in another division.	Mixon
L. Nordquist	Liaison with contract engineering, companies re tools	10 years industrial engineering at The Prince Company.	Becker
R. Booer	Liaison with contract engineering, companies re tools	5 years industrial engineering at The Prince Company.	Becker
C. Cushman	Tooling Coordinator	10 years production control at The Prince Company.	Garvin

of [Division] operation is $16 million per year. Plans were laid (recently) to increase this manufacturing rate. The matter of billing in 1951 relies upon two factors:

1. Compressing present schedules to accomplish rate.
2. Projecting sales trends into current rate. (That is, releasing manufacturing authorizations in advance of orders.)"

The newly formed group of B-D/9G1 project supervisors moved rapidly to hire a small staff of technical, production control, and factory supervisory personnel for the Special Project Group. Key appointments are shown in Exhibit 2.

PREPRODUCTION EFFORTS ON THE B-D/9G1

Located in a separate building, under a new supervisory group, and with an impressive job to do, the Special Projects Group quickly developed what seemed to be an excellent team spirit. In the opinion of some company personnel, however, Mr. DuMoulin and his top subordinates seemed mildly critical of the regular Defense Division operations and procedures, and to feel sure that the Special Projects Group could demonstrate superior performance. They also apparently felt that with proper organization and tighter control they could avoid much of the confusion which often attended regular Defense Division operations. Donald Mixon, Production Manager, and Dick Garvin, Production Control Manager, for example, developed certain new production control and assembly-line techniques for the special group, and proposed that these also be adopted in the regular Division. They discussed this possibility enthusiastically with the regular products Production Control Manager and many of his staff. Although the special group personnel believed they were tactful and modest in their suggestions, no changes were forthcoming in the Division's regular procedures.

From the outset it was apparent that the preproduction phase of the B-D/9G1 contract was a task of major magnitude. The parts list for the two devices called for approximately 1,500 items, all of which would require special tooling or outside purchase.

An early phase of the job involved collecting, sorting, and verifying engineering drawings, specifications, tool drawings, process and methods sheets, parts lists, and test data from the McAlpin Company. As early as January 1951, it was evident that the delivery of this basic material from McAlpin would not be completed on the schedule specified in the licensing agreement. Checks indicated much missing material, and it was not until early in June that all of the prints were finally received. Much telephoning and other liaison expediting between McAlpin and Prince was carried on during this period. It became clear that one of the causes of the delay was that the B-D/9G1 devices were really still in semidesign status and not ready for production release. A few devices had been manufactured by McAlpin but final qualification testing had not been completed. It was necessary, nevertheless, for the Prince organization to accept the prints and engineering data available and begin preproduction processing.

The two engineering firms retained by Prince to handle the tooling requirements were selected on the basis of recommendation from the McAlpin Company. Contracts were drawn up and 35 outside contract engineers arrived to begin the work for the Defense Division on the first working day in April. An excerpt from an annual report of one of the Prince production engineering supervisors comments on this development as follows:

The 35 outside tool engineers now arrived on the scene to commence tool designing and processing—only a few days after the two Prince engineers had been transferred to the project and before [they] had an opportunity to screen out the inactive and obsolete prints or even those prints which were not specified on the bill of material for the various devices. As it was necessary that the outside engineers be put to work, they were immediately assigned parts prints on which to commence tooling, in the hopes that the part or assembly for which they were tooling would appear on the final released parts lists. During this time, the Prince engineers were being rushed in an attempt to work with these outside engineers, answer their questions, and check parts lists to be certain of the parts and assemblies which composed each device. In order to keep pace with this quantity of tooling, keep the process engineers busy, and handle other factors, it was not possible for the Prince engineers to evaluate completely the various parts and assemblies from a design, manufacturing, and performance standpoint.

Thus with all tooling and processing engineers [being] outside contractors, and with only two Prince engineers and one Prince inspector on the project [being] familiar with Prince Defense Division procedures, practices, processes, and related matters, . . . there was a considerable departure from Prince standard practices and thus confusion when the project [later] was integrated with the Division's regular plant operation.

The general policy adopted at this time was to tool to the McAlpin prints since McAlpin, as the prime contractor, had design responsibility. Any engineering changes which appeared advisable to the Prince personnel had to be approved on a prior basis by McAlpin. In running down errors, such as dimensions which were obviously incorrect or missing, it was not unusual to discover that McAlpin had already made the changes in question but that their paper work procedures had not yet "ground-out" the ECO (Engineering Change Order) by which Prince would be notified of the change.

Design transition resulted in a continuing flood of ECO's to the Prince organization during 1951 and 1952. By September 1, 1951, 4,349 ECO's had been received, and the cumulative total had risen to approximately 7,800 by August 1, 1952. By the latter date, however, the rate of ECO's began to drop significantly. Prince personnel estimated that each ECO required, on the average, about 14 hours of paper work, exclusive of the engineering time itself. Even more troublesome, however, was the fact that as a result of these changes, approximately 70 per cent of the tooling originally prepared by the Division later had to be scrapped, and about 25 per cent of the original test instrumentation had to be redesigned.

Throughout 1951 the Division's design engineers and the contract engineers submitted many suggested design changes to McAlpin. In addition, they incorporated numerous improvements in the processes and equipment which did not affect the functioning of the devices— and therefore could be incorporated unilaterally. In the midst of this constant change, numerous decisions also were reached regarding processes, and tools were designed, ordered, and expedited to completion by the contract engineers. Tool designs furnished by McAlpin proved to be of only moderate aid because of differences in the machinery, equipment, and manufacturing practices of the two companies.

During this same period, specifications on purchased parts had to be sent out to vendors for quotes, a vendor selected, and orders placed. Final decisions on machine tools to be bought under the Facilities Contract were also required. The selection of machine tools was coordinated through the regular manufacturing group under Mr. Ellicott. Furthermore, assembly processes and lines had to be planned, crewing and training plans developed, test instrumentation designed and ordered, raw material requirements determined and ordered, and many items expedited. In terms of complexity, lead-times, and manufacturing precision, the B-D/9G1 were similar to some of the more intricate units manufactured by the Defense Division for its regular product line.

By the end of 1951, the Division's Production Manager, Mr. Mixon, in a report to top management, listed the following accomplishments of the Special Projects Group:

1. 6,008 special tools, dies, fixtures, gauges, and test equipment for the B-D/9G1, representing a cost of $1,958,085, have been placed on order;

2. 3,427 of these items, representing a cost of $870,197, have been delivered;

3. 763 items of purchased parts have been placed on order; } Representing a total

4. 406 items of raw material have been placed on order; } commitment of

5. 298 items of supply have been placed on order; } $1,740,481

6. 141 items of permanent subcontract on order;

7. All but four of the required raw material items, 12 of the purchased parts, and 140 of the tools were on order by November 1,1951. These remaining items were ordered during November and December.

During August 1951, work on the new building was completed, and by the end of the month the Special Projects Group had moved into the new facilities. At that time, the group's own staff numbered 76 employees, and 60 contract engineers were also still employed on a full-time basis. The contract engineers were gradually released during 1952 as the tooling problems became less numerous, thus permitting the remaining B-D/9G1 processing and tooling load to be handled by the Division's regular Production Engineering staff personnel.

Once the Special Projects Group was established in its new location, its organizational integration into the regular Division was begun. As the first step in this process, Mr. Mixon, although retaining over-all coordinating responsibility for B-D/9G1 production, began to report to Mr. Ellicott. Similarly, over the next few months, the men who had been in charge of production control, engineering, production engineering, tooling, and assembly in the B-D/9G1 Special Projects Group continued to perform these duties, but were placed under direct organizational control of the Division supervisors regularly responsible for each of these functions. The production organization, after these changes were completed in December 1951, is shown as Exhibit 3. During this period the newly acquired machine tools were integrated, both physically and organizationally, into the regular shop facility. Assembly and subassembly areas for the B-D and 9G1 units, however, were set up as a physically separate area in the new building and were not integrated with the assembly operations performed on regular products.

In January 1952, in accordance with previous plans, the head of the Special Projects Group, Mr. DuMoulin, was transferred out of the Defense Division. His new position was that of Assistant to the Corporate Vice President of Manufacturing and his office was moved to the corporate headquarters building on the other side of the city. At

EXHIBIT 3 THE PRINCE COMPANY—DEFENSE DIVISION

PRODUCTION ORGANIZATION

December 1951

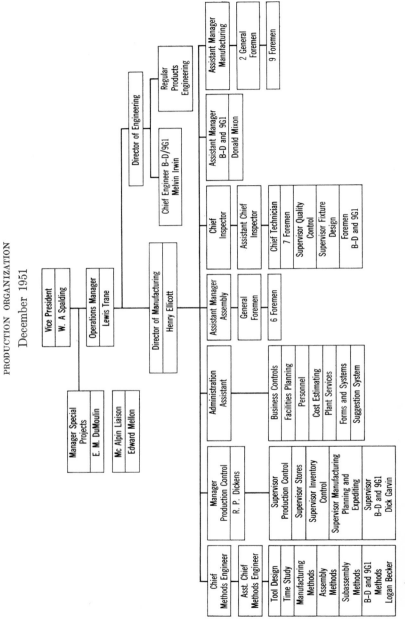

SOURCE: Company records.

that time, Edward Mellon, who was in charge of B-D/9G1 liaison with the McAlpin Company, began to report to Mr. Mixon.

PROSPECTS FOR THE FUTURE

In spite of the mass of accomplishments attained, and the obstacles overcome, it gradually became apparent in the latter half of 1951 that the January 1952, B-D/9G1 delivery commitment probably could not be met. The first formal communication of this more pessimistic estimate was contained in a bi-monthly report from Mr. DuMoulin to Mr. Spalding dated September 11, 1951. The previous report is excerpted for contrast:

August 29, 1951. In summarizing [the Special Products Group's] status at the present time there are several things which make us optimistic. . . . We are looking forward to the conclusion of the 'critical items study'[2] which we trust will provide a basis for developing activities on the last stages of preproduction work and expediting things which appear to be bottlenecks.

September 11, 1951. The 'critical items study' . . . has produced some very significant information. The report of September 7th covers the specific detail; however, we wish to mention at this time that by applying normal processing times and procurement times, there is no component that can be delivered in accordance with the shipping schedule in the definitive contract. Even on the smallest number of items short to build any one component, there are three separate items that are not available in time. The principal component, namely, the amplifier, has 86 items short for January shipment.

A report submitted by Mr. Mixon in October 1951, further stated:

Tool delivery is slowing down due to the fact that the tool shops are rapidly reaching a saturation point. However, we are doing everything possible to expedite delivery. . . . It is impossible to forecast the value of purchase items to be received in November and December due to the falldown and failure of vendors to ship when promised or required. Our inability to secure delivery of raw materials has been [imposing] and is continuing to impose a serious handicap and may delay our established production schedule. . . .

At this time the McAlpin Company had begun to make some deliveries on its B-D/9G1 contract. Prince attempted therefore to secure parts from McAlpin, or McAlpin's subcontractors, with which to begin subassemblies and final assemblies to meet its own January, 1952 requirements. Requests were made covering 111 parts. McAlpin agreed to supply small quantities of 50 of these from its own plant, and to allow its vendors to furnish 33 additional items. On the 28 remain-

---

[2] A project assigned to an outside consulting firm.

ing parts, however, due to its own critical shortage McAlpin was unable to supply aid to Prince either directly or through its subcontractors.

In an October 28, 1951 report to Mr. Trane, Mr. Burgess, the management consultant, wrote:

I do not feel that Production has done the job it is capable of doing in 1951. While it has met its planned billing for 1951, it has been at too high a cost and with too much effort. Furthermore, I do not feel that the groundwork for 1952 is yet properly laid, nor the things done which might have been done. I will list below some of the problems of falldown which exist:

1. Production control;
2. A definitely sustained program covering the ratio of subcontracting versus the total machine shop load;
3. Continuous lack of proper information on the ratio of overauthorizations required in relation to:
    (a) the amount of billing planned within the lead times involved, and
    (b) what is planned for 1952;
4. Continued operation during all of 1951 on a short list basis;
5. Failure to provide sufficient information in time, and with a proper program, in regard to the matter of new tools and replacement tools;
6. Tendency to oversimplify the job required on B-D/9G1 and to accept the reports from DuMoulin and Mixon without examination.

THE 1951 YEAR-END REPORT

For the regular defense products 1951 proved to be a successful year of growth (Exhibit 1).[3] Sales rose from a first-quarter average of $1,300,000 per month to nearly $2,700,000 per month in the last quarter. Total personnel grew from 1,305 to 2,249, including an increase in supervisory personnel from 85 to 119. Many new products were introduced in all lines, and the sales goal of $20 million was achieved by the end of December. For these reasons, within the Division's top management, a spirit of over-all optimism still prevailed at the end of the year, notwithstanding the growing indications of difficulty with the B-D/9G1 contract. The following excerpts from the 1951 year-end report of Mr. Ellicott, the Division's Director of Manufacturing, to top management summarized his views at that time.

The planned program for an output of $20 million, double that of 1950, is an assured accomplishment. During the year the pattern of operation shifted from one of a job shop to a quantity-production type of manufacture. This involved changes in processing and the redesign and procurement of new tooling on a number of the established lines in production. Considerable improvement in business controls was realized with the objective directed

---

[3] See p. 302.

EXHIBIT 4   THE PRINCE COMPANY—DEFENSE DIVISION (I)

ACTUAL AND PLANNED INVENTORY AND PERSONNEL LEVELS

| | INVENTORY AT COST (millions of dollars) | | DIRECT LABOR CREW—Number of People | | | |
| | | | Manufacturing | | Assembly | |
Month Ending	Actual	Planned*	Actual	Planned*	Actual	Planned*
August 1951	$ 7.9	—	372	—	520	—
September	8.4	—	385	—	571	—
October	8.6	—	383	—	582	—
November	9.1	—	376	—	616	—
December	10.2	—	304	—	575	—
January 1952		$10		400		750
February		10.5		450		750
March		11.5		500		800
April		12.5		550		950
May		13.5		600		1,050
June		14.5		650		1,200
July		17.5		700		1,300

* Plans made in late 1951.

NOTE: Inventory and Direct Labor Crew totals include regular products and B-D/9G1 personnel.

toward the accomplishment of the planned program.   A long-range program of improvement in operator efficiency was instigated to establish basic standards and improved measurement of performance.   An intensified effort has been developed toward the establishment of better scheduling, more accurate lead times, the analysis of operational sequences, improved plant layout, better methods, etc., all directed toward a more efficient flow of parts to and in assembly.   The results are very encouraging and continued improvement is expected.

From an over-all standpoint, 1951 has been a successful year for the Defense Division with the main objectives achieved and our relationships with customers considerably improved.

We are looking ahead with confidence that in 1952 we will be even more successful in attaining the desired sales goal and in improving the profit margin.

In this same report, Mr. Ellicott recorded his organization's forecast of the levels anticipated for various phases of the production operations, as shown in Exhibits 4 and 5.

EXHIBIT 5   THE PRINCE COMPANY—DEFENSE DIVISION (I)

PARTS MANUFACTURING

Actual and Planned Machine and Subcontracting Loads and Output
Expressed in Thousands of Standard Hours

	On Order at End of Month			Output During Month			Requirements Based on Production Plan of Dec. 1951		
	In Plant	Sub-contract	Total	In Plant	Sub-contract	Total	In Plant	Sub-contract	Total
September 1951	82.0	75.9	157.9	23.0	17.0	40.0	—	—	—
October	102.2	70.6	172.8	19.0	14.3	33.3	—	—	—
November	90.0	77.3	167.3	18.6	9.0	27.6	—	—	—
December	96.3	95.4	191.7	25.5	15.6	41.1	—	—	—
January 1952							21	23	44
February							24	34	58
March							29	43	72
April							35	49	84
May							37	52	89
June							43	47	90
July							46	45	91

The Prince Company—Defense Division (II)

In August 1952, top management personnel of The Prince Company were appraising the critical production situation existing in their Defense Division. In spite of a steadily increasing order backlog which had grown from $22 million to $92 million in the past 18 months, the Division's monthly volume of shipments had averaged only $2.2 million during 1952, and no upward trend was in evidence (Exhibit 1). Of the total backlog, $45 million represented two new types of aircraft control devices known as the B-D and the 9G1. Both products were of a competitor's design which Prince was manufacturing on a second source basis for the Air Force. Difficulties experienced in producing both these items had prevented deliveries beyond token amounts, creating a serious deficit in the contract schedule.

This failure to increase production volume and meet delivery requirements had resulted in considerable pressure on the Division's management from the military, from aircraft manufacturers, and from Prince's top management group. The critical nature of the military problem was reflected in new planes being parked outside the aircraft companies' plants as long as three months awaiting Prince equipment so they could be completed, tested, and sent into action in Korea. Air Force Generals and high-ranking Defense Department officials had visited the Division factory increasingly during 1952, and, together with Prince's top management, urgently attempted to offer suggestions and to stimulate improved performance. Early in August, after the Division's shipments had remained on a relatively level plateau for many months, Division and corporate officers were reviewing the situation to determine what remedies might be effected.

RESULTS IN EARLY 1952

From the beginning of 1952 the many carefully laid production plans and goals of the Division encountered increasing difficulties

315

EXHIBIT 1   THE PRINCE COMPANY—DEFENSE DIVISION (II)

SALES, BACKLOGS, AND MANUFACTURING AUTHORIZATIONS

In Thousands of Dollars

	Regular Products				BD/9G1				Totals—All Products			
	Sales				Sales				Sales			
1951	Planned for 1952	Actual	Backlog	Mfg. Authorizations	Planned for 1952	Actual	Backlog	Mfg. Authorizations	Planned for 1952	Actual	Backlog	Mfg. Authorizations
Jan.	—	$1,373	$20,463	N.A.	—	—	$ 2,000	N.A.	—	$1,373	$22,463	$16,928
Feb.	—	1,352	20,684	—	—	—	2,000	—	—	1,352	22,684	20,309
Mar.	—	1,140	21,368	—	—	—	3,250	—	—	1,140	24,618	26,890
Apr.	—	961	23,047	—	—	—	3,250	—	—	961	26,297	28,684
May	—	1,678	24,575	—	—	—	3,250	—	—	1,678	27,825	29,153
June	—	1,735	26,358	—	—	—	3,250	—	—	1,735	29,608	37,082
July	—	1,192	31,083	—	—	—	3,250	—	—	1,192	34,333	42,717
Aug.	—	2,211	34,838	$29,400	—	—	14,706	$15,300	—	2,211	49,544	44,700
Sept.	—	1,870	33,103	29,100	—	—	14,706	19,300	—	1,870	47,719	48,400
Oct.	—	2,789	28,192	25,000	—	—	14,706	19,300	—	2,789	42,898	44,300
Nov.	—	2,237	29,335	26,900	—	—	14,706	19,300	—	2,237	44,042	46,200
Dec.	—	3,021	29,932	27,000	—	—	22,479	19,300	—	3,021	52,412	46,300
1952												
Jan.	$2,500	1,911	30,000	27,400	—	—	22,479	19,300	$2,500	1,911	52,477	46,700
Feb.	2,700	1,640	32,888	29,000	—	—	22,479	19,300	2,700	1,640	55,367	48,300
Mar.	2,800	2,013	31,047	31,800	$ 300	—	22,479	24,500	3,100	2,013	53,526	55,300
Apr.	2,900	3,021	31,155	36,200	600	$3	22,479	29,800	3,500	3,024	53,634	66,000
May	3,100	2,544	34,792	34,800	1,100	4	22,477	29,800	4,200	2,548	57,270	64,600
June	3,000	2,393	39,940	35,700	2,000	—	22,475	29,800	5,000	2,393	62,416	65,500
July	3,000	1,476	46,082	42,100	2,800	9	45,484	39,400	5,800	1,485	91,568	81,500
Aug.	3,300	N.A.	N.A.	N.A.	2,900	N.A.	N.A.	N.A.	6,200	N.A.	N.A.	N.A.
Sept.	3,500	—	—	—	2,500	—	—	—	6,000	—	—	—
Oct.	3,900	—	—	—	2,600	—	—	—	6,000	—	—	—
Nov.	4,000	—	—	—	2,600	—	—	—	6,600	—	—	—
Dec.	4,000	—	—	—	2,700	—	—	—	6,700	—	—	—

NOTE: Planned sales are shown for entire year 1952. Actual data recorded through August 1, 1952. Backlog and Manufacturing Authorization data are as of end of month shown. See footnote, p. 321, for definition of Manufacturing Authorizations.

EXHIBIT 2   THE PRINCE COMPANY—DEFENSE DIVISION (II)

PARTS MANUFACTURING

Actual and Planned Machine and Subcontracting Loads and Output
Expressed in Thousands of Standard Hours

	On Order at End of Month			Output During Month			Requirements Based on Production Plan of Dec. 1951		
	In Plant	Sub-contract	Total	In Plant	Sub-contract	Total	In Plant	Sub-contract	Total
September 1951	82.0	75.9	157.9	23.0	17.0	40.0	—	—	—
October	102.2	70.6	172.8	19.0	14.3	33.3	—	—	—
November	90.0	77.3	167.3	18.6	9.0	27.6	—	—	—
December	96.3	95.4	191.7	25.5	15.6	41.1	—	—	—
January 1952	109.5	88.4	197.9	29.4	11.4	40.8	21	23	44
February	130.2	95.1	225.3	17.8	15.4	33.2	24	34	58
March	156.6	92.9	249.5	23.9	20.7	44.6	29	43	72
April	159.5	91.7	251.2	33.5	22.7	56.2	35	49	84
May	162.5	54.7	217.2	26.9	14.9	41.8	37	52	89
June	170.1	67.6	237.7	35.3	18.5	53.8	43	47	90
July	174.8	68.0	242.8	20.5	16.3	36.8	46	45	91

EXHIBIT 3   THE PRINCE COMPANY—DEFENSE DIVISION (II)

ACTUAL AND PLANNED INVENTORY AND PERSONNEL LEVELS
August 1951–July 1952

| | INVENTORY AT COST (millions of dollars) | | DIRECT LABOR CREW—Number of People | | | |
| | | | Manufacturing | | Assembly | |
Month Ending	Actual	Planned*	Actual	Planned*	Actual	Planned*
August 1951	$ 7.9	—	372	—	520	—
September	8.4	—	385	—	571	—
October	8.6	—	383	—	582	—
November	9.1	—	376	—	616	—
December	10.2	—	304	—	575	—
January 1952	9.9	$10	327	400	564	750
February	10.7	10.5	374	450	530	750
March	11.3	11.5	375	500	505	800
April	12.0	12.5	391	550	513	950
May	12.6	13.5	418	600	497	1,050
June	13.3	14.5	450	650	578	1,200
July	14.1	17.5	478	700	628	1,300

* Plans made in late 1951.

NOTE: Inventory and Direct Labor Crew totals include regular products and B-D/9G1 personnel.

(Exhibits 2 and 3). Not only did the contemplated production of the B-D and 9G1 continue to remain bottlenecked, but the output of the Division's regular line of defense products did not experience the anticipated rate of growth. Production of these items during the first eight months of 1952 in fact remained at roughly the same rate as the last eight months of 1951. This stalemate was further highlighted by a $24 million increase in the order backlog of regular products during the same period. Among the Division personnel, the spirit of exhilaration and confidence which attended the closing months of 1951 gradually became one of concern, confusion, and even personal discord as increasingly frantic efforts were employed in many directions to break the plant log jam.

EVOLUTION OF THE CRISIS

Results for January 1952, had not caused particular alarm, although the shop and subcontracted parts output of 40,800 standard machine hours was below the estimated requirement of 44,000 standard hours.

The $2,400,000 volume in stock (of which $1,911,434 was shipped) was also slightly below the $2,481,000 goal.

By the end of February, however, it was clear that the plant was well off the desired pace. Parts output, direct labor, inventory, and sales build-ups were all behind the schedules established in December, notwithstanding the increasing backlogs and machine loads. The monthly "Progress Report," published by the staff of Henry Ellicott and distributed after his review and editing to the top supervisory organization of the Division, stated:

. . . there are indications of trouble in our total program. The source of the trouble seems to lie in the lack of tools. With 54,000 hours available to run in the shop,[1] twice that amount was held for lack of tools, some material shortages, and orders with due dates that are too advanced. Tools being repaired or rebuilt for current devices are creating part of this condition, as well as new tool manufacturing or rework. Although tool receipts increased in February, no results will be noticed in manufacturing until late March or April.

The tooling for the B-D/9G1 was giving particular trouble. Parts would be run in a tool-tryout section before tools were released to the shop. In this tryout operation it was frequently discovered that tools did not fit the machines and accessories available, or that the parts they produced were out of tolerance. Many of these problems appeared to be caused by the fact that most of the consultant engineers who were retained to design the tools had backgrounds in only the automotive industry, and had no thorough knowledge of Prince manufacturing practices, machines, or accessories. The result was a continual deluge of expedited tool tryouts, rework, and modifications. In view of the tooling uncertainties, many shop orders could not be scheduled on the machines. The list of short parts needed by assembly lines, therefore, grew from a level of 363 items in March, to 616 by the end of July.

Short parts were traced and expedited by production coordinators from the Production Control Department. With each of the coordinators placing pressure on the Shop Planning Group (a section of Production Control) and on the shop foremen to schedule and run the particular parts he was expediting, previously established starting dates, due dates, optimum order quantities, and machine loading became academic. Set-ups were torn down after only a few critical parts were run in order to make room for other critical parts.

---

[1] That is, the parts-fabrication areas of the Division's manufacturing operations.

As the months progressed, these conditions frequently led to sharp disagreements within the organization. The Assistant Manager in Charge of Manufacturing, who reported to Mr. Ellicott, felt that the Planning Group was wreaking havoc in his shop, and he concluded that it would be more logical if the Planning Group reported to him rather than to the Production Control Manager, who also reported to Mr. Ellicott. Mr. Ellicott agreed, and upon several occasions discussed this possibility with the Production Control Manager. The latter was so intensely hostile to this suggestion, however, that Mr. Ellicott did not finally introduce the change until early in August, 1952. The previous April, however, as a compromise, he authorized the Assistant Manager of Manufacturing to establish his own eight-man group to handle parts expediting. Henceforth, the coordinators transmitted their short parts lists to the expediters and received promises from them as to the completion of the parts. The B-D/9G1 coordinators, under Dick Garvin, also worked through the newly formed parts expediting group.

As early as March it had become evident that the B-D/9G1 promises made late in 1951 were no longer valid. Monthly output continued on the $2 million plateau, and both the Air Force and corporate top management showed increasingly intense concern over the situation. On March 27, Prince's President, C. B. Locke, called a meeting in Mr. Ellicott's office with Division Vice President Spalding, Mr. Ellicott, and members of Mr. Ellicott's staff. In this meeting Mr. Locke asked why the Defense Division was well behind build-up schedules, and what was being done about it. He emphasized that the Division's production rate had not increased for six months and that its costs were "10 per cent out of line."

Mr. Ellicott replied by reviewing some of the problems being faced, emphasizing the technical difficulties experienced on many parts and devices. He also stressed that "the first three months of production on every device seemed to hit the factory on a crash-program basis," due to customer requirements. Mr. Locke pointed out that these were normal aspects of the defense contracting business. Mr. Locke left the impression that he was understanding and sympathetic with the Division's problems, but made clear his insistence that the plant "must improve the production and cost picture." He also expressed with finality his conviction that work in process inventory was seriously out of line, and asked why it could not be held at a level equal to "three months' billings." This ratio had been the Division's normal experience for many years in its regular line of defense products.

CORRECTIVE ACTION UNDERTAKEN

In early April, Mr. Ellicott ordered a temporary freeze on hiring of direct labor in manufacturing, authorized reductions in assembly crews, and recalled into the plant considerable work that had been assigned to subcontractors. These moves were made partly as a result of Mr. Locke's visit. A further reason was a curious phenomenon that had begun to be evident in the shop, namely, a lack of work for operators to perform even though there were some $55 million in Manufacturing Authorizations[2] outstanding. The steps taken in April were intended to reduce costs, raise work loads and efficiencies, and hold down inventories.

An excerpt from the Division's April Progress Report highlighted the question now being asked throughout the company, "Why the shortage of work when there is such an enormous backlog?"

By analysis of our $55 million of Manufacturing Authorizations the following facts became evident:

1. Items representing $33 million of the total $55 million are in our [work in process] inventory [but require] completion of [additional] work to make it salable.
2. Of the remaining $22 million we have (a) $7 million subcontract hours on order but not yet in inventory, (b) approximately $3 million in the order-writing stage, (c) approximately $2 million in first operational parts not yet in inventory, (d) $8 million in shop orders held for short materials, tools, or advanced due dates. Forty per cent of [item (d)] is held up by lack of tools. On this estimated basis, $2 million is not accounted for.
3. The present incoming order rate provides a flow of work for the shop and for our subcontractors approximately equal to their present output.

The basic conclusions arrived at from this analysis are:

1. We will not be able to improve the shop or subcontracting situation in terms of total load until we can release the thousands of hours [of work] held for tools, materials, or advanced due dates.
2. The incoming order rate, or equivalent (advance) authorizations, must be continued.
3. We must increase inventory turnover so as to utilize the $33 million of potential sales already in inventory. To do this, we must supply critical parts and [achieve] better balanced inventories. . . .

---

[2] See Exhibit 1. Manufacturing Authorizations represented work which the factory had been authorized to manufacture, either because of a receipt of customer orders or because of a decision to manufacture for inventory in anticipation of future orders. For control purposes the Manufacturing Authorizations were referred to in terms of the dollar billings their sales would generate.

Two-to-four-hour daily meetings were held in the Division to review the status of short parts and critical tools. The coordinators concerned reported to the Production Control Manager in the presence of Mr. Ellicott and most of his staff. Ten to twenty people therefore were present at these sessions. Through this direct contact, Mr. Ellicott and his key personnel believed they were able to achieve an intimate feel of the problems and to play an active role in their solution. As the short list continued to lengthen, these meetings occupied more and more time, and the management group found it consistently necessary to work late into the evenings and on most weekends.

TECHNICAL PROBLEMS

As a few complete sets of parts for the B-D and 9G1 became available and assembly operations were begun, a host of new problems became evident. These involved technical difficulties such as the malfunctioning of subassemblies, or the failure of the assembly to meet performance specifications. Some typical examples were:

1. The final requirements of one component called out for a small and continuous movement of an indicating pointer. One of the problems encountered on the first units assembled was "shudder," that is, the pointer moved in a jerky and oscillatory motion. An extensive engineering program, therefore, was initiated to analyze and remove the cause of this malfunction. Experimental units were built holding to a minimum all clearances on bearings, end plays, and so on, to see if by tightening down these requirements the shudder could be eliminated. When units manufactured to these tight specifications were subjected to simulated environmental tests, almost half of them still displayed shudder. Experimental redesigned parts, such as new pinions and gears, then were built, assembled, and tested. The final result was that the design of the pinion had to be changed to a helical configuration to eliminate the stepping action which caused shudder.

2. A die-cast aluminum housing had specifications calling for very tight tolerances for parallelism and flatness between the bottom and center flange surfaces. The initial tooling would not produce parts to specification. After complete retooling, parts still could not be produced to specification. An engineering program, therefore, was initiated to improve the producibility of the part while still meeting its functional requirements. Sample devices had to be built and

tested before permission could be obtained from McAlpin to change the prints.

3. The design of a capacitor housing did not allow sufficient space to accommodate the capacitors and the associated wires. When the fragile capacitor leads were soldered to the AN Connector leads and crammed into the capacitor housing, a great number of "opens" and "shorts" resulted. After many repeated failures the capacitor housing was redesigned by Prince engineers to allow more room. This change necessitated new tooling for a die-cast housing and corresponding revisions in existing manufacturing tools.

4. The specifications for a motor generator were so tight that it was finally necessary to stack laminations in such a way that the metal grain direction in each lamination was parallel to those in every other lamination. Further difficulties were met in encapsulating the laminations, winding and molding the stators, and in final calibrations. Prince engineers considered the design marginal and believed it to be the main cause for a rejection rate which never was reduced below 80 per cent.

CONDITIONS IN SUMMER OF 1952

These and dozens of other problems had to be isolated, analyzed, and overcome—one by one—as the summer wore on. During this period the Air Force was constantly advised of push-outs in delivery promises, and the deliveries of a few scattered components did not relieve their critical supply problem. By the end of June the B-D was 215 sets delinquent and the 9G1, 100. Because of the lack of certainty in regard to the solution of problems, Mr. Ellicott and his staff pushed the schedule and promises further ahead each month, forecasting that the factory would achieve even higher rates four to six months hence and thus would make up output deficits and get back on schedule. The estimate of 1952 dollar billing was reduced from $58,952,000 in December, 1951 to $57 million in February, 1952, $53 million in April, and $40 million in June.

The regular factory shutdown for vacations reduced July output to $1,485,761, and by late that month frenetic efforts in the plant rose to the highest pitch thus far. The monthly shop load for July was 174,800 standard hours, a new peak. Of this total, 31,000 hours were delinquent, 143,800 were due in the current and subsequent months. The short parts list rose to 616 items, yet output still showed no signs of increasing.

Competition for shop time between the B-D/9G1 coordinators, most of whom were relatively new in the organization, and the regular coordinators increasingly proved to be the source of ill feelings. Tension between the Production Control Supervisor and the Assistant Manager of Manufacturing was magnified by the decision to move the planning function into Manufacturing. The inspection staff was under pressure from the plant management to reduce its own departmental costs and maintain quality, but received constant criticism for rejections which crippled output.

On July 31 Mr. Ellicott called a staff meeting in which he described a new assembly technique which he wanted installed immediately. The plan, which caught the staff by surprise, was designed to increase operator efficiency and line flow by making the assembly lines flexible. Instead of maintaining bench set-ups for each product on a continual basis, with perhaps four to six operators producing about 25 units of a specific device per month, Mr. Ellicott proposed henceforth to produce the 25 units in a single week through use of a line requiring 15 or 16 operators. The line would then be switched to another device. Parts would be accumulated between runs, and the run would be started only after parts were available. Mr. Ellicott gave directions for those concerned to prepare for this changeover with the utmost speed, and left most of those attending the meeting with the impression that he wanted action on this proposal, not extended discussion regarding it.

Excerpts from the "Progress Report" of August 1 indicated the emergence of a somewhat different analysis of the Division's problem:

From October 1951, until March 1952, the work placed in the shop by manufacturing authorization has been 50 per cent too low to support the build-up rate called for in our goals. A chart of "production-to-stock" versus additional authorizations received, shows a definite parallel. When the authorizations received dropped from October to March, and total authorizations stopped climbing, three or four months thereafter the production rate showed a corresponding pattern.

The facts support this conclusion: working off a backlog of orders is insufficient to support a continuing production rate increase. It is essential that orders flow into the shop, supplying work pressure from the first operations all the way through to final assembly. The backlog of work has been insufficient to keep up the rate of work in all operations because our long lead times stretch the total supply of work too thin. Additional manufacturing authorizations therefore are needed now.

RECOMMENDATIONS BY MANAGEMENT CONSULTANT

Throughout 1951 and 1952, Division executives, including Mr. Ellicott and his staff, had been counseled by Philip Burgess, a management consultant who for roughly the past five years had been retained for frequent consulting assignments relating to the manufacturing operations of various Prince Divisions.   Mr. Burgess had written many reports to top management covering the Defense Division production crisis, the latest being dated August 12, 1952.   (Excerpts are contained in Appendix A.)   In his current work for the Defense Division, Mr. Burgess reported to Mr. Lewis Trane, the Operations Manager.   Mr. Burgess had worked very closely with the manufacturing staff for several years, but had never had a close working relationship with Mr. Ellicott, Director of Manufacturing.

Regarding the current situation, Mr. Burgess suggested that schedules should be "compressed" at once.   He proposed that this be accomplished by taking all of the shop orders anticipated for the next four months and authorizing the shop to start them during the next six weeks.   He further indicated that he believed it necessary for the Division to release to the shop approximately $24 million of regular defense products devices in advance of receipt of customers' orders. To accomplish this he recommended that the most likely orders for devices already in production should be listed, in order of the probability of their ultimate receipt from customers, up to a $24 million total.   These orders should then be added to the factory schedules in accordance with forecasts of when customers might want delivery. This procedure was clearly risky on defense items, but Mr. Burgess indicated that he was convinced that it was necessary to allow the factory to cut lead times, build up "rate" in the plant, increase billings, and carry along the more difficult production items with the increased flow of operations.

Mr. Ellicott and many of his staff, gravely concerned by the fact that the shop already was falling behind on the existing schedule,[3] seriously questioned the wisdom of adding more work loads by releasing advance manufacturing authorizations.   They further doubted whether it made good sense to compress schedules as Mr. Burgess recommended.

In a memo supporting Mr. Burgess' proposals, however, a member of the Division's production staff presented the following reasoning in favor of the schedule compression:

The shop is falling behind schedule even though output remains constant and total work on order increases.   Therefore, it may seem illogical to place even more work in the shop.   However, the plan to compress schedules is based on the premise that by releasing more work to the shop, more output will result, even though delinquency may arise.   The plan is to compress

---

[3] Delinquent hours had risen from 39,200 hours to 45,500 in August and the short sheet simultaneously hit a new peak of 786 items.

schedules of (*a*) as many of our devices as possible, and (*b*) 18 months of scheduled work into 12 months for a second group of devices. The result is schedule rates of $6 million to $8 million a month, or a maximum increase of 30 per cent of current monthly schedules. However, it is estimated that compression in combination with (the recent) new authorizations will result in doubling total work load (177,700 standard hours would be increased to 350,000 standard hours).

One of the basic purposes of this plan is to jam the pipeline to the point of overflow, resulting in sufficient parts output to achieve the dollar billings we currently need ($5 million to $6 million). This flood of work will result in: (1) more subcontracting, (2) larger runs on fewer parts in our shop, and (3) many problems which must be solved regarding tools, gages, inspection methods, and so forth, brought about by getting increased subcontracting. Proper scheduling of all parts, as well as adding load, are necessary to insure placing prime attention on critical parts, and not merely increasing the schedules on parts comparatively simple to manufacture.

Mr. Ellicott discussed the proposed additional authorizations and compression with his Production Control Manager, R. P. Dickens, who expressed serious concern about the prudence of the move, saying, "This proposal could result in an inventory of $20 million to $30 million . . . the plant could find itself out of work in four to five months [and faced] with a tremendous layoff." An alternative approach which appeared logical to Mr. Dickens was a renewed effort to isolate and resolve the various bottlenecks, starting with a tool survey and proceeding—item by item—through each part, subassembly, and final assembly, until all technical problems and shortages finally were overcome.

Defense Division management personnel were joined with top corporate officials in their concern over the crisis in Defense Division production. The Prince Company reputation for production dependability was being damaged, and sales and profits for the year were far below expectations. In agreement that decisive steps should be taken immediately to improve the situation, the top management group was carefully reviewing Mr. Burgess' recommendations as well as the alternative course of action proposed by Mr. Dickens. They were also attempting to determine if there were still other approaches which held promise of improving the situation.

Supplement A. The Prince Company—Defense Division (II)

Excerpts from August 12, 1952, Report of Philip Burgess, Management Consultant

It should be clearly understood that preplanning in the Defense Division is entirely different from that in any other [Prince] Division, the essential difference being in the incompleted engineering segments in the various devices which cannot be crystallized until certain parts or components are . . . in actual production.

. . . the matter of compression becomes an urgent one. Compression is the reduction of lead time by pushing manufacturing schedules forward and the utmost of skill and planning must be used if such a program is to be successful.

Rate must be accomplished before billing can follow.

Manufacturing releases were not sufficient [to fulfill the Division's] plan. . . . Management action should have been taken. The manufacturing releases, with ten months lead time, starting with February, 1950, began with $15 million. [The issuance of releases] went up steadily through October 1951 [reaching a total of] $42 million, but manufacturing releases leveled off for the next five months . . . which meant, of course, that the corresponding five months of billing would suffer ten months later . . . unless it was possible, by compression of the due dates, to increase the billing rate.

To date, all of the overauthorizations which have been provided have been followed up by actual orders.

Serious consideration should be given immediately to additional overauthorizations in an amount of $24 million at billing value . . . to accomplish both the increased rate and the reduction of backlog.

I had considerable experience with the B-D/9G1 project somewhat over a year ago when I investigated the entire project and reported that the findings of the Group . . . were entirely unrealistic and based upon premises which turned out to be incorrect. The premises were that the drawings as received from McAlpin would be acceptable and could be converted readily into shop drawings for parts which would be acceptable . . . when assembled into devices. Certainly nothing could be further from the truth. . . .

Furthermore, during this current visit I found the B-D/9G1 project . . . interfering with regular production . . . and that any progress on the project was so delinquent as to have a serious effect on regular defense billing and profits.

Except for a most serious faulty appraisal of the load involved, the actual work done by DuMoulin was done exceptionally well, as was the later work by Mixon.

I feel, as do many others, that the B-D/9G1 project was integrated into the [Division's] regular operating group on too quick a basis for its fully successful outcome, but on the other side of the matter, there were good reasons for doing so; namely the fact that many of the regular operating group recognized the completely unrealistic promises which were being made, due to the newness of the B-D/9G1 organization. Furthermore, it is most unfortunate that the B-D/9G1 Group [tried] very seriously to change familiar Prince systems and methods to the detriment of everyone involved. As an example, DuMoulin employed a firm of outside consultants to set up an entirely . . . different production control system. . . . [This move] is still having a serious effect on the system being used in the remainder of the Division, and . . . has held back many of the improvements which [otherwise] could have been made.

. . . on the B-D/9G1—certain items were released far in advance . . . of requirement, or far in advance of the releases of other parts still waiting to be engineered. This not only makes for excessive inventory but also later creates serious situations on the assembly lines and on the short sheet.

It is my opinion that the present inventory is approximately $6 million short of what is required to liquidate the planned billing schedule.

I feel that Henry Ellicott has made three major mistakes in: (1) not properly analyzing his crew requirements against planned load, (2) not properly preplanning methods and tools requirements against load, and (3) trying to change Prince systems to [make them] conform *not* to his requirements, but to the falldown which occurred on the first two items mentioned.

The Kroger Company

Early in November 1957, Mr. R. J. Enersen, Manager of the Processed Foods Division of the Kroger Company, a large midwestern retail grocery chain, returned to his office after a lengthy meeting with the company President, Mr. Joseph Hall. On this occasion, as several times before, the two men had discussed the possibility of organizational decentralization of the Division's large, multiproduct food processing plant in Cincinnati.

In the discussion just concluded, Mr. Hall advised Mr. Enersen that he had become convinced that the proposed decentralization had considerable theoretical appeal and that if successfully implemented, it would offer important advantages.[1] His final approval of the recommendation hung only upon Mr. Enersen's development of a convincing, detailed plan of action demonstrating how the decentralization of the processing plant could be made into a workable concept and how its introduction could be executed successfully.

Prior consideration of the question of implementation had led Mr. Enersen to conclude that there would be tactical, and perhaps even psychological, advantages to making an organizational change of this magnitude coincide with the start of a calendar year. He therefore told Mr. Hall he would begin work immediately on detailed proposals so that if they received Mr. Hall's final approval, the new organizational arrangements could become effective the following January 1. Mr. Hall concurred.

---

[1] Mr. Hall was known to be a staunch advocate of the decentralization of management authority and responsibility. Under his leadership, the Kroger Company had recently introduced a considerable measure of management decentralization into the operation of its chain of more than 1,400 retail food stores. These had been organized into 23 regional Divisions, each under a Divisional Vice President in whom was placed broad independent authority and responsibility for the activities of the units under his control.

EXHIBIT 1 THE KROGER COMPANY

JURISDICTION AND RESPONSIBILITIES OF THE BRAND POLICY BOARD

The jurisdiction and responsibilities of the Brand Policy Board shall be:

1. To have and exercise the sole power of determining the specific products which shall be sold under all private brands.
2. To determine the private brands which shall be used for such products.
3. To formulate and define concepts of usage for all private brands used by the company. Such definitions may include, as the Board may desire:
    a. Statements of the general quality level of products to be sold under each brand.
    b. Statements of the relationship of each brand to other brands.
    c. Statements of the family of products on which the brand is authorized to be used.
    d. Any other restrictions or limitations which the Board may place on the use of the brand.
4. To approve or disapprove the proposed standards and specifications of quality for all products packed under Kroger brand, as submitted to it by the Quality Control Committee.
5. To have and exercise general supervisory authority over the Quality Control Committee and any other committees which the Board may establish to implement its purpose.

The selection and approval of packages and labels and the details thereof are the responsibility of the Brand Policy Board.

The membership of the board shall consist of the President, the Vice President of Merchandising, and the Vice President of Law, Labor Relations, and Public Relations.

BACKGROUND

The Processed Foods Division currently employed approximately 1,800 persons and produced more than 30 major types of food items. These were sold, under the company's brand name or other private labels, in the 1,421 Kroger supermarkets. No items were manufactured for sale to other chains, however, or to other types of retail or wholesale outlets. The Division's output represented about 7 per cent of the chain's total retail sales of more than $1.5 billion per year.

Under company policy, the Processed Foods Division was free to propose the manufacture of any food product that it believed satisfied Kroger's quality standards and could be sold to the company's retail stores at a reasonable profit. Such proposals were submitted to Kroger's Brand Policy Board whose decisions were based, in part, on the recommendations of a Quality Control Committee which reported to it (Exhibits 1 and 2).

EXHIBIT 2 THE KROGER COMPANY

JURISDICTION AND RESPONSIBILITIES OF THE QUALITY CONTROL COMMITTEE

The jurisdiction and responsibilities of the Quality Control Committee shall be:

1. To formulate and approve standards and specifications of quality for all items packed under private brands, other than the Kroger brand, within the patterns and concepts of quality established by the Brand Policy Board for such private brands.
2. To formulate proposed standards and specifications of quality for all products packed under the Kroger brand, within the patterns and concepts of quality established by the Brand Policy Board for the Kroger brand, and to submit such standards and specifications to the Brand Policy Board for approval.

The membership of the committee shall consist of: The Director of the Kroger Food Foundation (a research and testing group of the company), the Director of Grocery Purchasing, and either the Manager of the Processed Foods Division or the Manager of the Baked Foods Division, depending on the product under consideration.

The prevailing philosophy within the organization was that private label products could exist and thrive only when the retailing operation elected to merchandise them willingly, without the "push" of extensive promotional and advertising programs typically required with regularly branded merchandise. Consistent with this belief, and with the decentralization of authority and responsibility for retail operations, the management of each of Kroger's 23 retail Divisions was free to agree, or to refuse, to stock any of the products of the Processed Foods Division. The Division therefore competed in price and quality with independent food manufacturers for shelf space in the Kroger retail stores.

The Division's present organization is shown in Exhibit 3. Its largest single unit, employing about 1,400 of the total Divisional work force, was the Cincinnati processing plant. The major items in the plant's product line are shown in Exhibit 4. Most of these products were manufactured in a variety of brands, flavors, sizes, and package types. Although relatively few changes were made from year to year in the basic products manufactured, numerous and frequent changes occurred in the brands, varieties, and packaging, in response to the intensely competitive conditions and the aggressive, imaginative merchandising techniques in the food industry.

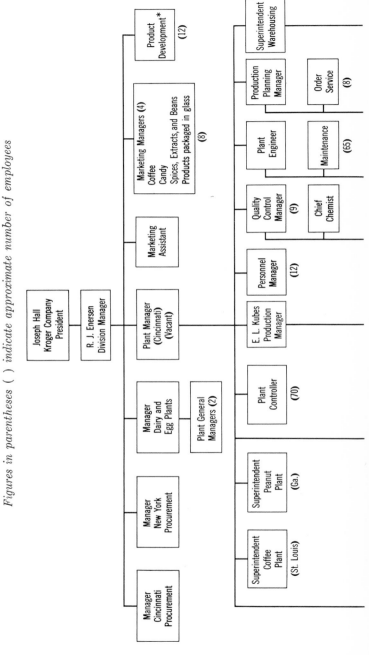

EXHIBIT 3 THE KROGER COMPANY

ORGANIZATION CHART

Processed Foods Division, Fall 1957

Figures in parentheses ( ) indicate approximate number of employees

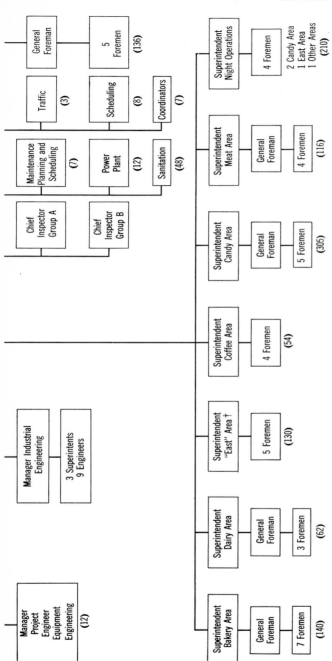

* Development of new varieties, blends, recipes, private brands, etc., a developmental rather than a research function. The selection of new product projects was especially influenced by action of competitors and national food manufacturers, as well as by retail division requests.
† Responsible for processing of all products not otherwise listed as under other superintendents.

EXHIBIT 4 THE KROGER COMPANY

CURRENT LIST OF BASIC PRODUCTS PRODUCED IN THE
CINCINNATI PLANT OF THE PROCESSED FOODS DIVISION

	Approximate Number of Direct Labor Employees Each Shift	Number Shifts	Present Processing Area*
Bacon	14	1	6
Beans (canned)*	10	2	6
Beef Stew*	12	1	6
Bread	30	2	1
Buns	4	2	1
Cake	20	1	1
Candy (hard, soft, chocolate-covered, bulk and fancy)	225	1	5
Cheese	4	1	2
Chili	12	1	6
Coffee (various brands and blends)	16	2	4
Cottage Cheese	4	1	2
Doughnuts	4	1	1
Extract	6	1	3
Fruitcake	8	1	1
Gelatin	6	2	3
Ice Cream	6	1	2
Instant Coffee	8	3	4
Jelly	21	1	3
Marshmallows	8	2	5
Meat (canned, processed lunch meats)	40	1	6
Milk (fresh)	35	1	2
Olives	38	1	3
Peanut Butter	12	2	3
Peanuts (salted)	6	2	3
Preserves	24	2	3
Puddings	6	1	3
Rolls	10	2	1
Salad Dressing	10	2	3
Salted Nuts	6	2	3
Sandwich Spreads	10	2	3
Sausages	40	1	6
Spices	10	2	3
Syrup	20	2	3
Tea (bags and boxes)	18	2	4
Wieners	10	1	6

* (1) Bakery, (2) Dairy, (3) East, (4) Coffee, (5) Candy, (6) Meat.

THE ORIGINS AND NATURE OF
MR. ENERSEN'S RECOMMENDATIONS

With the steady growth in both the size and complexity of operations in the Cincinnati plant, Mr. Enersen had become increasingly convinced that major organizational changes were necessary. This reflected his belief that regardless of the competence of the individuals involved, he and his staff never could manage the Division and its multitudinous product line with full effectiveness under the present arrangements. The fact that the plant managership was vacant[2] at the moment also strengthened Mr. Enersen's belief that this might be an ideal time to decentralize the plant organization. This conviction led to his recommendation to Mr. Hall.

The new organization Mr. Enersen envisioned would entail somewhere between four and seven organizationally independent product groups. These units would continue to operate in the existing factory buildings and might share certain centralized service departments and functions. Each group, however, would be under the control of its own General Manager—an executive who would be given complete authority and responsibility for group operations. As Mr. Enersen saw it, the General Manager of a group would be, in almost all respects, in the position of an executive running his own independent business.

In considering Mr. Hall's request for a specific plan of action describing how the plant could operate on a decentralized basis, Mr. Enersen first considered the existing physical facilities and the manufacturing processes required by the various product lines.

MANUFACTURING PROCESSES AND FACILITIES

The plant consisted of three buildings located in one general area interconnected by covered bridges and walk ways to create essentially a single unit. The floor space in the buildings was in excess of one million square feet. In addition, there were two small buildings located several blocks away which were used as a garage and a salvage

---

[2] The former Plant Manager had resigned five months before after having joined the company only the previous January to take the place of a man who had to be relieved of this post because of illness. The most recent Plant Manager had never moved his family to Cincinnati and his resignation was due to a number of personal problems which required him to return to the community in which he formerly resided.

area. Processing, storage operations, and different product manufacturing areas were wholly interspersed in the main building. For example, manufacturing facilities, in-process storage facilities, or both, for seven different products were located on the fourth floor. A listing of the current locations of product areas is shown in Exhibit 5. Office areas were principally on the fifth floor, where an extensive IBM tabulating installation used for accounting also was located. Laboratory facilities for product development and quality control were housed on the sixth floor.

EXHIBIT 5 THE KROGER COMPANY

LOCATIONS OF MAIN PRODUCT PROCESSING AREAS AND FUNCTIONS

Floor	Product Process or Function
Basement	Spice, general storage, coffee storage
	Dairy storage
	Truck storage, meat processing
1st floor	Shipping department, bakery, truck docks and railroad siding
	Storage and ice cream hardening, milk, cheese, and ice cream packaging, meat distribution, bakery shipping
	Bakery
	Power plant and refrigeration machinery
2nd floor	Maintenance shops, bean department, marshmallow packaging, coffee packaging, starch reclaiming, coffee bag department and coffee storage, flour bins and bread wrapping
	Liquid sugar tanks and general storage, milk and cheese, dairy refrigerant compressors
	Sausage manufacturing and wiener packaging, smokehouse, instant coffee packaging
3rd floor	Gelatin, candy processing and packaging, storage, bread storage
	Storage, spices, tea, olives, extract
	Boilers and condensers for power plant, meat canning, instant coffee
4th floor	Candy manufacturing, peanut department, salad dressing, coffee roasting, peanut butter, storage, cake bakery, bakery mixing room
	Kitchen, cafeteria, locker rooms, spice manufacture; Personnel Department
5th floor	Offices and laboratories
	Preserves, laundry, storage, tea-blending
	Storage for instant coffee
6th floor	Kroger Food Foundation offices and laboratories
	Instant coffee processing

SOURCE: Company plant layouts.

The variety of products manufactured, combined with the large expanse of floor space, resulted in a complex, heterogeneous manufacturing environment. Essentially the plant's operations consisted of numerous relatively independent steps including processing—that is, mixing, grinding, cooking, and similar activities—packaging, and storage operations. Few machines or processing lines required more than ten employees to work together, and more often a team of two to six workers was needed at any given stage of the process. The work did not demand unusual skill for the most part and about 65 per cent of the employees were women. All workers were paid on a straight hourly basis. Operators would be shifted about within general product areas whenever machines were down for changeovers, or when the schedules required variations in output rates. This was not true of equipment, however. Coffee roasting facilities, for example, were not used interchangeably with the equipment employed for peanut roasting.

The processes ranged from single operations, such as the bottling of fluids, to complex ones, such as the manufacturing of instant coffee which required very precise temperature and humidity controls and continuous operation of intricate equipment. A fairly representative process, that employed in producing various soft candies, was as follows:

A mixture of sugar, water, corn syrup, flavoring, and related ingredients, was stirred and cooked in a steam-jacketed kettle until the correct temperature was reached. This usually required about 60 minutes. The mixture was then pumped about 50 feet through a one and one half inch pipe and poured into a trough on the top of a *candy mogul*. This was a machine which automatically prepared trays of starch molds, filled the molds with the liquid candy, and stacked the filled trays for removal to a curing room. There the candy hardened or "cured" for about 12 hours until it reached the proper consistency. The full tray was then returned to the processing area and again fed into the mogul. The mogul emptied the candy and starch onto a vibrating screen. The starch fell through openings in the screen and thus was available for re-use in subsequent machine cycles. The pieces of candy were vibrated off the screen onto a moving belt which conveyed them to the packaging room, or to the chocolate coating department. The empty tray was refilled automatically with starch, into which mold shapes were pressed by descending prongs. Liquid candy was poured into the molds, thus starting another process cycle.

Each mogul was tended by two men. One fed the trays of cured and soft candy into the machine, and also removed them from the conveyor. The other operator was responsible for the feeding of the candy solution. This required him to make machine adjustments to assure that the proper amount was poured into each mold, and to be responsible for cleaning the pipe, the hopper, and the fill-mechanism between batches. Each machine could manufacture gumdrops, marshmallows, butterscotch kisses, candy corn, caramels, and similar candy products at an average rate of about 1,300 lbs. per hour. To switch from one variety of candy to another required approximately one-hour changeover. In a typical shift the output of cured candy averaged about 8,500 pounds per machine.

The plant operated three moguls, each of which was about 30 years old and required a space of approximately 30 x 15 feet. Candy production was scheduled by the plant-wide Planning Department which specified the quantity, sequence, and frequency of the various batches to be run.

Mr. Enersen believed that with few exceptions the plant's processes were not exceptionally intricate or time-consuming when compared with those employed in many other industries. He was aware, nevertheless, that a large amount of expensive and complex machinery, such as the candy moguls, had to be employed in all phases of the operations, from the handling of raw materials to the packaging of finished products.

OTHER CHARACTERISTICS OF THE EXISTING SYSTEM

In thinking further about the operating difficulties under the existing organizational pattern and about various decentralization phases on which Mr. Hall might wish specific assurances, Mr. Enersen considered the following matters:

1. Although the Cincinnati manufacturing operations had been moderately profitable, cost control consistently had been difficult. Currently, a considerable portion of total plant overhead was allocated to specific products on a somewhat arbitrary basis. Many of the various production supervisors therefore apparently felt they had no direct control over many of these charges and thus had little incentive to attempt to reduce them. Costs of equipment maintenance, sanitation, and quality control were cases in point.

2. Scheduling and planning the numerous processes and the flow of products through the various plant areas were cumbersome and time-consuming. Even after they were determined by the central Planning Department, schedules often became meaningless because of delays caused by rush jobs, machine breakdowns, or other disruptions. Unforeseen occurrences of this type also frequently made it impossible for the Maintenance Department to execute machine set-up changes which had been requested by various superintendents or foremen in the operating areas. In such situations, the maintenance orders had to be rewritten, the work rescheduled, and the personnel either reassigned or left temporarily idle. Such occurrences took place almost daily.

3. Coordination between the centralized Marketing Managers, who provided liaison between the factory and the retail Divisions, and the factory's Product Development, Quality Control, and various operating Departments was often inadequate. This often created an unduly slow factory response to customer complaints, or to new marketing opportunities.

4. Mr. Enersen himself, as well as the Plant Manager, the Production Manager, and all of the superintendents were confronted continually with a seemingly unending stream of operating decisions. The other supervisory and staff personnel also appeared to be under considerable continuing pressure. Almost all of these individuals regularly found it necessary to put in more than a normal working day to execute their various duties. These conditions were accompanied by frequent indications of feelings of personal frustration on the part of many. There were also more than a few evidences of personal irritation and dissatisfaction.

5. Many of the staff departments, such as Production Planning, Product Development, Quality Control, Industrial Engineering, and Plant Engineering, often appeared to be at odds with the operating personnel. In some cases it seemed to Mr. Enersen that the existing state of affairs prompted people often to be more concerned with their own departmental interests and conveniences than with the over-all profitability of the plant.

In short, Mr. Enersen felt that the present plant organization required too many individuals to spread their efforts over too many problems and to attempt to be experts in too many divergent products and processes. Although conceding that there was no escaping the necessity of manufacturing a wide variety of products under one roof, he could see no reason why the work could not be organized on a more manageable basis.

To push his thinking further on the assignment he had just received from Mr. Hall, Mr. Enersen jotted down a series of notes and comments relative to the possible move toward decentralization, and the decisions it would require. The resulting outline was as follows:

1. *Selection of Product Areas*
   a. Some products (bakery, candy, meat, dairy, and coffee) appear to be "naturals" for independent "product group" organization.
   b. Probably one to three more groups will be required to include all products, and still form manageable units. The specific make-up of these groupings will have to be determined.
   c. In establishing other product groups I must consider similarity of manufacturing processes, and of retailing characteristics. Note: Many products that are similar from a retail viewpoint (like eggs, milk, cheese) require substantially different plant processes. How can this be resolved?
2. *Organization of Marketing Function*
   a. We need close liaison between the plant and the retail stores to increase Division sales and satisfy retail needs and opportunities.
   b. We probably should have a Marketing Manager, plus appropriate staff, for each product group.
   c. Question: Should a Marketing Manager's functions include any or all of:
      Product development (see No. 3 below)?
      Sales projections—long term, short term, or both?
      Production scheduling?
      Customer service—correspondence, order servicing, and related activities?
      Design of packages?
      Other?
3. *Product Development*—to whom should this function report and what responsibilities should it assume?
   a. Should the product development function be a part of marketing—or a separate function reporting to the General Manager of product group—or should it report directly to the Division Manager?
   b. What type of work should product development personnel be doing?

    c. What type of personnel should be in charge of product development—sales-oriented people, or production-oriented people, or what?

    d. How can we best tie the functions of this group into those of the Brand Policy Board?

4. *Accounting*

    a. If the General Manager of each product group is to be wholly responsible for profits of his own unit, should he have his own Controller to provide whatever cost records and controls the Manager believes he requires? Or should top management decide this for him?

    b. Would a centralized accounting staff be more economical— would it permit use of more sophisticated techniques and the assignment of higher caliber personnel?

    c. How far can or should we go in making the General Manager of each group responsible only for costs that are directly controllable through his own group's efforts?

5. *Quality Control*

    a. Should we retain the present centralized quality control group since this is an increasingly technical activity involving statistical applications? Should the function be kept independent of operating groups to insure top quality?

    b. Or, alternatively, if a General Manager of a product group is really to act as a separate and independent executive, shouldn't he have responsibility for quality as well as for cost?

6. *Plant and Equipment Maintenance*

    a. The centralized Maintenance Department currently performs the following functions:

        Sanitation (cleaning of building and equipment).

        Repairs of equipment (in response to breakdowns or malfunctions)

        Periodic major overhauls of process and packing equipment.

        Building changes and moves requiring painting, relocation of equipment, carpentry, electrical work, pipefitting, and other craft skills.

        Making set-ups, changeovers, and adjustments on nearly all processing and packaging equipment. (This is a continuing, daily function of major importance to productivity.)

        Operating the boiler plant and refrigeration machinery.

        Supervising the plant guard force.

        Screening equipment, replacements, or additions suggested by foremen, superintendents, and industrial engineers.

Making analyses and recommendations to top management in the form of appropriation requests for all equipment purchases.

b. Possible advantages of retaining a centralized maintenance staff reporting to the Division Manager would be:

Reduction in costs and improvements in quality of maintenance due to use of expert personnel and modern procedures.

Greater flexibility.

Less duplication of effort.

Conformity with the fact that some functions (such as running the power plant) serve all plant activities.

c. Possible advantages of decentralizing these functions under product groups would be:

Specialization of maintenance personnel by product area would permit these individuals to achieve greater familiarity with the machines and people involved.

It would create clearer responsibility for maintenance productivity and cost control; blame for poor operating performance of equipment could not be shifted back and forth between the operating and maintenance groups.

7. *Industrial Engineering*

a. Functions of the present centralized I.E. group are:

Methods analysis.

Materials handling.

Processing operations study.

b. This department now reports to the Plant Manager.

c. Where should responsibility for these functions be located in a decentralized operation?

8. *Planning, Scheduling, Purchasing*

a. Functions of the present centralized department are:

Determining production schedules.

Developing one-year load-schedule forecasts from market information.

Traffic-routing and scheduling the dispatching of 1,400–2,000 truck orders per week.

Purchasing all food materials and other needs (except coffee).

Order handling and customer service.

b. Alternatives to be considered:

Should we divide these functions among product groups for closer control?

Or should we continue in centralized posture to achieve economies in buying and staffing and to achieve better coordination?

Another alternative—decentralize one or more of these functions and keep others centralized? If so, which functions should fall into what category?

9. *Warehousing and Shipping*—any advantages in decentralizing?

10. *Personnel—Labor Relations*

a. Plant deals with eight different unions (Teamsters, Machinists, Food and Confectionery Workers, Meat Cutters, Bakers, Firemen and Oilers, Dairy Workers, Bakery Auxiliary). If we decentralize, how shall we coordinate the handling of personnel matters by group foremen and superintendents?

b. If we decentralize, should each product group hire its own work force, keep its own personnel records, have labor relations and training specialists? The processes and skills required, as well as unions involved, might differ considerably between product groups.

11. *People—Staffing—Costs of Supervision*

a. We will probably need at least a 10 per cent increase in the number of foremen if we decentralize.

b. Would decentralization demand higher management and supervisory skills, or lower?

c. If greater management skill will be required, what will it cost? Will we need special training or hiring efforts? We probably already have a nucleus of trainable candidates among our present employees. How long can we "live" until we train these men to handle bigger jobs? Will costly mistakes be likely to occur? Any way to prevent or minimize this danger?

d. How much "voice" should each product group General Manager be given in selecting his own staff? Are we likely to encounter a "battle royal" over who gets the "best" subordinates and staff personnel? Is this avoidable? If so, how?

12. *Changes in Plant Layout and Allocation of Space*

a. Should all operations under a General Manager's jurisdiction be located in the same physical area? If so, how much will it cost to achieve this? How much delay and confusion will this entail?

b. What office moves will be required? Who—where?

13. *Plan of Action Required*

a. It is imperative that I develop answers to each topic noted above.

b. Will this require me to hold discussions with key people to insure good decisions?   Can such an approach be reconciled with the time pressures involved?   Would extensive discussions just "stir" people up?   With so many people personally involved, can I talk to some without talking to all?

c. How should I announce and explain the organizational changes being made?   When?

d. Timing.   When should various changes take place?   Physical moves and building alterations (if any)?   Sequence?   How long should be allowed for an interim period in which General Managers and their staffs prepare for changes?

NOTE: *Hold to January 1 deadline for official start of operations under the new organization if at all possible!*

As Mr. Enersen finished this outline, he realized that he had not defined all of the problems and decisions facing him.   He also was aware that for the most part he had been writing questions, rather than answers, and that very little time existed in which to work out the numerous details.   Nevertheless, he was confident that none of the problems surrounding decentralization were insoluble and that if they were resolved wisely, the resulting organization could be a great deal more effective than the present one.   The fact that he had Mr. Hall's support for the general concept of decentralization was reassuring to Mr. Enersen.   He realized, however, that final approval of his proposal, as well as its ultimate success in operation, would depend in large part on the care and thoroughness with which he resolved the various questions facing him and planned a detailed course of action.

PART 3. FOREIGN PRODUCTION

OPERATIONS

California Farm Implement Turk Fabrikasi

On an afternoon late in November, 1959, Louis deSalle, Co-Director of California Farm Implement Turk Fabrikasi (CFIT) in Istanbul, walked through the company's machine shop. To his irritation, only four of the 110 machines actually were producing parts. Thirty-five workers were employed in the machine shop and as Mr. deSalle looked around the area, he noted that they were engaged in such tasks as cleaning their machines, counting parts, carrying them to other machines, waiting for tools at the tool crib, going and coming from the washrooms, and talking together.

Mr. deSalle also discovered with annoyance that the General Foreman, Mustafa Kap, and the Superintendent, Kamil Gomenc, were in the former's office discussing various ways of machining a new job. Both seemed genuinely surprised to learn that only four of the shop's machines were running, and explained that they had been occupied with the new job and "checking timecards, job tickets, and other essentials." Mr. deSalle reminded them through Kamil Bey,[1] who spoke English, that he had given repeated instructions that at least one of them should be on the floor of the plant at all times to keep production moving. Kamil Bey agreed and said they tried to follow these orders, but were so busy with paperwork and other managerial duties that it was difficult to do so. Mr. deSalle warned, "Nothing is more important than keeping the machines going," and left the office.

Mr. deSalle immediately went upstairs to the large office he shared with Fikret Somer, the other Co-Director, to whom he related the incident, stressing his exasperation with the fact that the superintendent and the foreman were almost never out in the shop supervising the

---

[1] "Bey" is a title of courtesy used after a first name.

men and their jobs. "They give me a thousand excuses every time, and promise to do better, but they seem to gravitate right back to the office," he said. "They don't like to criticize the workers or make them change anything they're doing. They feel, somehow, that the job of a manager is performed in an office." Mr. deSalle added that the increasing work load now confronting the plant gave the whole matter of productivity, cost, and better supervision a new importance. He suggested that he and Mr. Somer should call their department heads together and "really lay down the law."

Mr. Somer agreed and had their secretary call a meeting of the following men to begin a half-hour later:

Haluk Timcer	— Manager of Sales, Purchasing, and Production Control
Lacen Onur	— Manager of Accounting
Fevsi Balkir	— Manager of Tool Design, Processing, Toolroom and Tool Crib
Nahit Kanat	— Personnel Manager
Hamdi Goknil	— Manager of Engineering and Production
Kamil Gomenc	— Manager of Methods and Time Study, and Shop Superintendent

Mr. Somer told the group Mr. deSalle was very unhappy about the work pace and supervision in the plant and that he himself was equally concerned. Speaking mainly in Turkish, he openly criticized the managers for allowing wasted time and sloppy practices. He reminded them that only two days before all had discussed with several visiting professors from Europe and America the need for cutting costs in order to bring in more outside subcontracting work and to complete with foreign-made tractors. Mr. deSalle, who understood a little Turkish, felt that Fikret Bey was not "pulling any punches."

The managers' reactions reflected concern and respect, but made it clear that they felt Mr. deSalle and Mr. Somer were "putting too much pressure" on them. They said they were doing their best, were working hard, and requested that the "continual pressure" on them be decreased. Mr. Somer explained that such pressure was necessary for the plant to succeed, that it had lost money for four years, and that now that the level of activity was increasing they must work together as a team for the one goal of maximum productivity. The men agreed but again pointed out the many problems each of them faced.

The meeting lasted two hours. Although no problems were specifically solved, the Co-Directors felt that this sort of discussion

was good for their subordinates.   Mr. deSalle observed that during
the following week either Kamil Bey or his foreman always was on
the floor of the plant.   But he predicted, "I'll have to be after them
again now any day."

COMPANY HISTORY

Mr. Somer and Mr. deSalle had been appointed Co-Directors of
CFIT in July, 1959, having been members of the management group
since February and March, 1955, respectively.   Since its founding, in
1954, the company had been headed by four different Managing
Directors:

George Oakes	August 1954	— December 1956
Wilbur Fields	January 1957	— July 1958
A. P. Nixon	August 1958	— February 1959
Mahmut Sur	March 1959	— June 1959

Before being assigned to Turkey, the first three of these men had
been employees of the California Farm Implement Company (CFI),
holders of 30 per cent of the stock of CFIT.   Mr. Oakes was recalled
to the United States to become Vice President and Treasurer of the
parent company.   Mr. Fields, on his recall, worked on special assignments in the firm's U.S. assembly plant.   Mr. Nixon died in Turkey
at the age of 55, and was replaced by Mahmut Sur, a Turk who had
been on CFIT's Board of Directors since its founding and who also
held a position as Technical Advisor to Mechanical and Chemical
Industries (MKEK), a nationalized industry group.   Mahmut Sur
was replaced by Mr. Somer and Mr. deSalle after three months, but
remained a member of the Board.   In undertaking their assignment
the new Co-Directors assumed responsibilities for an organization
which had encountered difficulties and financial losses during 3½ years
of its 4½-year existence.

The history of CFIT dated back to 1953.   At that time, faced with
falling export sales, CFI had assigned Charles Boche and Edwin
Piper, General Sales Manager and Export Manager, to travel through
Europe and the Middle East to analyze the foreign sales situation.
During their visit to Turkey, both Mr. Boche and Mr. Piper were
impressed with the potential market that apparently existed there.
After some effort they found a man they believed to be a good prospect
for a CFI distributorship and negotiated a distribution arrangement
with him.   It subsequently developed, however, that the distributor
was unable to obtain an import permit from the Turkish Government.

This failure reflected the facts that Turkey's foreign exchange problem was becoming acute at the time, and that the country already was faced with critical problems in providing repair parts and servicing for the 25 different types of tractor already being imported.

Several months later a representative of the Turkish Government visited CFI and suggested that the company assemble tractors in Turkey. As the matter was discussed, CFI officials became convinced that this proposition appeared more attractive than others as a means of building up the company's foreign business. This was reinforced by the possibility of gaining an exclusive right to manufacture tractors in Turkey, since none of CFI's competitors was then willing to undertake a Turkish manufacturing operation.

The President of CFI, Payton Moore, appointed a four-man team headed by George Oakes, then Assistant Controller of CFI, to go to Turkey. Mr. Moore expressed his interest in the venture with the following comments:

> Our company and the farm machinery industry as a whole are confronted by problems, such as falling sales, excessive inventories, shortage of cash— plenty of things to keep us busy with our domestic operations. . . . The most attractive part of the Turkish proposal is the opportunity it gives us immediately to ship to Turkey goods produced in our U.S. manufacturing operations, a large portion of which we now already have in stock. Were it not for this immediate outlet for sales, we would not consider just going into Turkey and starting an agricultural manufacturing plant from the ground up.[2]

The four-man team left for Istanbul early in February, 1954, and proceeded to negotiate a management contract and the necessary corporate and financial arrangements with representatives of the Turkish Government. In return for tractor designs, patents, and "know-how," CFI received a 30 per cent ownership interest in the new enterprise. Other owners were as follows:

---

[2] This quote, and other information relating to the original negotiations and arrangements, was furnished by a U.S. university faculty member who was in Turkey at the time and who followed these developments closely.

	Ownership Share
Mechanical and Chemical Industries	30%*
Agricultural Supply Bureau	10 *
Cotton Cooperative	10
Agricultural Bank	5 *
Antalya Cotton Cooperative	5
Fig Cooperative	3
Raisin Cooperative	3
Miscellaneous	4
	70%

* Institutions of the Turkish Government.

As part of the arrangement, a 125,000 square-foot plant built by the Turkish government in 1945 to manufacture aircraft engines became the property of CFIT. The plant contained 110 general purpose and 12 special purpose machine tools for making pistons. Most of these facilities were less than ten years old and in good condition.

The management contract was signed in August, 1954, and a letter of credit for tractor parts was obtained the following October 28th. According to the agreement, CFI would bill tractor parts to the new company at the regular distributor price and would receive a royalty of 3 per cent based on the factory selling price of all tractors produced by CFIT. The Turkish company could buy parts anywhere, but was obliged to produce a CFI tractor.

The production program for the first year of operations called for building 1,000 model PKY tractors and 2,750 units of various farm implements with parts obtained entirely from the United States. In the second year, 2,000 model PKY tractors were to be produced, with 30 to 40 per cent of the required parts being manufactured in Turkey, along with a proportionate increase in implement production. The agreements also specified a gradual increase in the percentage of parts to be manufactured locally, the total to reach "75 to 100 per cent of those parts manufactured in our U.S. plants" in three years.

Shortly thereafter, Mr. Oakes, who had been appointed Managing Director of the new company, requested his California superiors to select and transfer men to Turkey to handle seven basic CFIT production functions. The following appointees were assigned to join Mr. Oakes:

Lawrence Dowlin — Production Manager
William Kite — Engineering Liaison

Louis deSalle   — Processing Engineer
James Nordquist — Time Study Engineer
Donald Haglin   — Quality Control and Inspection
William Johnson — Assembly Superintendent
Donald Buckler — Production Control Supervisor

A. P. Nixon was placed in charge of sales and was made Assistant Managing Director.

The newly assigned men had all been performing similar work in CFI's California plant, and were selected by the California management for the Turkish assignment on the basis of general job knowledge and current availability. The men and their wives were briefed on Turkey by a six-page memorandum which covered the country's geography, climate, and history. Accompanied by wives and families, they all moved to Turkey in the late winter of 1955, two months after being notified of their transfer.

For all the newly assigned personnel and their wives, most of whom had never traveled abroad, the new location provided innumerable shocks and surprises. The women, especially, were upset by the lack of familiar household items (milk, cleansing tissue, frozen foods, soft toilet paper, canned vegetables, coffee, and the like), by the need for boiling all drinking water, the poor sanitary conditions, the lack of television, intermittent electricity and water supplies, and "substandard American schools." The living quarters obtained were considerably less comfortable and pleasant than those they had enjoyed in America; they missed their relatives and friends; the language barrier and unfamiliar geography made simple shopping chores complicated and time-consuming; the meat obtainable was of an "inferior quality."

All these problems—and more—combined with the original shock and distaste for the location due to the poorly maintained and dingy aspect of the buildings, the new smells, and the strange often unkempt appearance of the residents, resulted in a long and unhappy period of adjustment. Repeatedly during the first six months one of the men would return to his flat at the end of the day to find his wife in tears, homesick, lonely, and filled with a genuine disgust and loathing of their new location.

By the end of the first year, most of the families had acquired a servant, and established access to supplies from the United States and "the women's lives became somewhat more normal. We began to live again." The Americans in Istanbul tended to live together in a few colonies dubbed "Little America," for they believed the Turks living nearby seemed to resent their higher standard of living. They therefore felt more comfortable in American neighborhoods. With frequent informal social get-togethers for bridge and mutual discussion of their problems as expatriates, they managed to make life tolerable.

There was a great deal to do during the first six months. The factory CFIT took over had been operated by MKEK during the preceding three years, making spare parts for the textile and automotive industries. Operations had been reduced gradually to make way for the new enterprise. From a peak employment of 300, employees had been reassigned one by one to other MKEK plants. The plant manager, Hamdi Goknil, however, was hired by Mr. Oakes to assist Mr. Dowlin. Hamdi Bey promptly re-employed 35 of his former force, offering them about 20 per cent more pay than they had received from MKEK. This group, including the foremen of maintenance, assembly, machine shop, toolroom, and inspection, comprised a nucleus around which additional employees were engaged. The 35 also included machine operators, set-up men, maintenance men, and guards. MKEK then objected to this hiring away of its personnel, whereupon Mr. Oakes agreed to cease employing additional members of the plant's former workforce.

Simultaneously a wage survey was made of the Istanbul area. Wage levels adopted by CFIT were set at 120 per cent of community averages for similar work to provide an incentive to attract specially skilled workers. Using newspaper advertisements which stressed the pay rate, no Saturday work, 56 hours' pay for 44 hours' work,[3] and the advancement opportunities offered by a new enterprise, Hamdi Bey and his foremen by June, 1955, had recruited with relatively little difficulty an original work group of 95 hourly and 50 salaried employees—and promptly initiated production work.

The production plans depended on obtaining foreign exchange allocations of $8 to $10 million annually for parts, machinery, and equipment during the first five years of operations. This amount was agreed to and guaranteed by the Turkish Government. Under this agreement "CFIT would require $275,000 worth of parts and $25,000 worth of equipment each month. By the end of the 36th month, the monthly expenditure would be about $150,000 for parts and about $150,000 for equipment."

A faculty member of a United States university who was in Istanbul at the time, and who followed these developments closely, provided these comments:

---

[3] Fifty-six hours' pay for 48 hours' work was typical in Turkey.

The exchange availability proved to be far short of these requirements and CFI's management felt it could not afford on its own to invest enough to 'prime the pump.' Of the $3.6 million initially promised for the import of components, CFIT received only $2.7 million. After May, 1955, even before production work began, monthly allocations of foreign exchange ceased and foreign exchange was obtained only irregularly. The May allocation was not received until June; further allocations were acquired in March, 1956, September, 1956, and March, 1957. Total foreign exchange received for imported parts during the fiscal year from November 1, 1954 to October 31, 1955 was $2,787,000; for the period from November 1, 1955 to October 31, 1956, $621,000; since October 31, 1956, CFIT has received an additional $542,000 in foreign exchange. Apart from these amounts, CFIT received during the 1955–1956 fiscal year $379,000 in foreign exchange for the purchase and import of machinery and equipment, plus an additional $90,000 in the prior fiscal year.

EFFECTS OF FOREIGN EXCHANGE CRISIS

Parts made available in 1954–55 before the Turkish foreign exchange crisis became acute enabled CFIT to produce 1,208 tractors by April, 1956. But as the foreign exchange shortage prevented the company from receiving any additional tractor parts after June, 1955, production became intermittent, and upon completion of the 1,208 tractors the assembly line was shut down altogether.

The shortage of foreign exchange in Turkey during the years following 1954 was a serious national problem brought on by a variety of causes which in the end analysis added up to the fact that the country was attempting to import capital and consumer goods in excess of exports. Rigid import controls were imposed by the government in 1955, and the CFIT officials were unable to obtain dollars, in spite of many and varied attempts to convince the government that new tractors were essential for increasing agricultural production and exports. Nonetheless, despite the dwindling production volume in the second half of 1955, CFIT made a profit for the year.

It was impossible to forecast when foreign exchange would be released to CFIT but Mr. Oakes and his associates hoped from day to day that their efforts would meet with success. Late in 1956, the company finally obtained a million-dollar allocation. Since the allocation held valid for only three months and the parts had to be ordered from California, it proved impossible for CFI to make deliveries within the specified time. Nonetheless, decisions had to be made concerning use of the CFIT plant and employees. As tractor activity diminished, employees were put to work improving the plant; construction, repair, revisions to the layout, painting, and similar chores. A major layoff was considered but rejected for these reasons:

(1) Under Turkish law employees terminated without due cause—inefficiency, incompetence, habitual absence or tardiness, drunkenness, stealing, and so on—had to receive severance pay according to the following schedule:

Months of employment	Weeks of severance pay
0– 6 months	0
6–12	2
12–18	4
18–36	6
over 36	8

During the latter half of 1955 and 1956 when the layoffs were under consideration, severance pay would have averaged 2–4 weeks per employee. If the entire plant were closed and all employees laid off, the law required that only one-half of one week's pay be given to each employee. CFIT management rejected this alternative lest innumerable key skilled workers be lost to other companies by the time the plant reopened.

(2) It was feared that CFIT's reputation as an employer would be irreparably damaged by a severe layoff. This concern was reinforced by the United States firm's ownership in the company. Mr. Oakes believed that the prevalent opinion among the Turkish working population was that a company had the moral duty to provide continuous employment for its employees, and one frequently heard statements to the effect that companies in the United States treated their employees like machines, discarding them when not needed. Hence, Mr. Oakes felt CFIT's reputation was particularly vulnerable to criticism.

(3) Turkish Government approval was required for a layoff of 20 per cent or more of a labor force. Since the company was 45 per cent government-owned it was felt that political pressures probably would not permit the Labor Ministry to authorize a major layoff.

(4) Only about one-fifth of the company's costs of doing business through the third quarter of 1955 were for personnel, both direct and indirect.

(5) The company's financial position was strong.

(6) The lack of foreign exchange was not expected to be of long duration, especially for a tractor plant in which the government had a substantial ownership interest.

For these reasons only minor layoffs were made, as follows:

Date	No. Laid Off	Jobs Affected	Recalled
9/16/55	9	assembly workers	9 on 10/17/55
1/24/56	2	assembly workers	2 on 4/17/56
2/9/56	8	assembly workers	8 on 4/17/56
8/22/56	4	2 stores, 2 maintenance	—
9/28/56	8	3 office, 4 maintenance, 1 driver	1 on 3/18/57
10/1/56	1	driver	1 on 10/31/56
11/17/56	1	office	—
8/19/57	12	3 maintenance, 2 stores, 3 welders	3 on 1/12/58

Notwithstanding attempts to keep employees gainfully occupied, there was a letdown in effort and spirit throughout the plant after September, 1955. By and large there was a tendency both in the office and in the shop to stretch out assignments, drag out the lunch hour, and spend more time cleaning up and in other nonproductive pursuits. Actually, accounting and personnel people had been kept reasonably busy with normal problems. Engineering and tooling staffs also continued to work on methods of processing parts that in the future would be manufactured by CFIT rather than imported from the United States. Similarly, sales office employees were occupied supplying spare parts and servicing tractors in the field. Thus, the problem of keeping people on their toes had been most serious in the factory.

To the seven Americans in the factory area, this period was especially frustrating. Accustomed to the high pressure activity of meeting schedules and achieving high production rates in California, they now found themselves engaging in extended card games at lunch, tea, and coffee breaks; undertaking increased outside community and recreation interests; and being continually irritated at their inability to obtain parts and build tractors. With this sense of frustration, the adverse reactions felt by most of them over living far from home in unfamiliar and trying surroundings deepened into an intensely critical and sarcastic attitude. With no familiar work to do, the majority tended to belittle the entire CFIT operation and everything Turkish and it became increasingly difficult for management to infuse enthusiasm into its key personnel.

Subcontracting and New Products

Gradually, during 1956 and 1957, CFIT began to seek new types of orders to produce income and provide employment. The manufacture of certain spare parts was initiated, textile machinery parts were made for government textile plants, and a TL[4] 600,000 contract was negotiated with the Turkish Highway Department for the manufacture of 125 road packers and 125 "sheeps-foot" rollers used in highway construction. In September, 1956, the Turkish Minister of State Enterprise strongly urged that CFIT accept an order for the complete manufacture of textile machinery. Mr. Oakes, however, felt that too much work of this sort would change the nature of the entire enterprise and make it difficult to return to the building of tractors when foreign exchange became available. He therefore declined the order.

In this period some progress was made toward increasing the Turkish content of the CFI tractor. Whereas the first tractors had been entirely U.S. built, by the middle of 1956 the company had developed local manufacture to the point at which it represented about one-third of the tractor's weight, and about 23 per cent of its value. Progress in this direction had been slowed, however, by the difficulty of developing local subcontracting sources because of the lack of production continuity and the inability to plan and commit ahead due to the uncertain availability of foreign exchange for U.S. parts. For the same reasons, the development of European sources of supplies for such items as tires, fuel pumps, and ignition and electrical parts was hampered. It was considered impossible to order in advance any European parts for eventual assembly with U.S. parts, since supplies of the latter depended entirely on the availability of foreign exchange.

In 1956 CFIT produced and sold 150 disc harrows, employing a design supplied by the California plant but making the entire implement in Turkey with the exception of the discs. In 1957 the CFIT Engineering Department designed an agricultural pulverizer, a machine for breaking up clods. Four hundred and fifty pulverizers were built and sold in 1957 and 1958.

Sporadic efforts to bring in subcontracting work to fill up the shop continued. For example, in early 1957, following the recall of Mr.

---

[4] TL is the symbol for a Turkish lira (or "pound"), the basic monetary unit of the country. From CFIT's inception until August, 1958, the exchange rate was approximately 3TL to $1.00 US. After August, 1958, the rate was changed to 9TL to $1.00 US.

Oakes to assume increased responsibilities at CFI, Sales Manager Nixon, Chief Engineer Kite, Process Engineer deSalle, and several of the other Department heads visited plants all over Turkey to solicit machine shop work. Shortly afterwards, Wilbur Fields from CFI was appointed Managing Director of CFIT. He discouraged this subcontracting effort, saying, "I do not want to run a variety store." Mr. Fields felt quite strongly that CFIT was in the tractor business, had built its reputation and skills on such products, and should stick to that line.

Under Mr. Nixon's leadership, from July, 1958 until February, 1959, a more aggressive policy was pursued in regard to subcontracting and new products. Initial engineering design work was begun on a stalk mulcher for cotton, a six horsepower gasoline engine, and a centrifugal pump for irrigation. Private, government, and NATO manufacturers and contractors were solicited in early 1959 in a further effort to increase plant work loads.

The limited availability of foreign exchange, combined with the efforts toward developing new products and obtaining subcontract work, produced annual sales totals as follows:

1955	TL	11,377,000	
1956		4,291,000	
1957		4,296,000	
1958		2,490,000	
1959		813,000	(6 months)
		1,673,000	(11 months)

Personnel levels during this period were:

Number of Employees, Month Ending

	March		June		September		December	
	Hourly	Salaried	Hourly	Salaried	Hourly	Salaried	Hourly	Salaried
1955	39	22	95	50	79	53	93	64
1956	85	73	118	74	106	77	120	76
1957	140	79	158	82	131	78	120	75
1958	113	71	106	62	114	63	136	68
1959	163	64	160	63	169	57	—	—

From the inception of the plant through June 30, 1959, the plant's product mix was as follows:

Tractors	TL	18,342,000
Repair parts and production parts for textile looms		1,900,000
Road compactors		1,000,000

Sheeps-foot roller	720,000
Sheet metal and plate steel products (window frames, roof ventilators, motor bases, oil tanks, and related items)	500,000
Disc harrow	375,000
Soil pulverizers	370,000
Tractors spare parts	50,000
Repair work for oil drilling companies	10,000

In early 1957, Mr. Johnson, Mr. Buckley, and Mr. Nordquist were transferred back to CFI, there being no further requirement for their services in Turkey. Mr. Johnson was made a general foreman in the CFI tractor plant, Mr. Buckley left the company and opened a restaurant in San Francisco, and Mr. Nordquist resumed work as a methods man in the tractor assembly operation. Mr. Dowlin retired to Idaho and bought a farm. In early 1958 Mr. Kite was made Chief Engineer for a major farm implement manufacturer in the United States.

Thus, after the first quarter of 1958, Mr. deSalle and Mr. Nixon were the only Americans remaining in the management of CFIT. Mr. Nixon's death in March of 1959 left Mr. deSalle the sole survivor of the group of Americans originally assigned to CFI's Turkish operation.

BACKGROUND OF MR. deSALLE

Louis deSalle was 39 when he was first assigned to Turkey. He was born in Canada, the son of a wheat farmer, and had five brothers and three sisters. The family had moved to the United States when he was nine and he spent the remainder of his boyhood on farms in North Dakota and South Dakota. When Louis was 14 his father died and the family moved to Great Falls, where he attended high school. In 1939, at the age of 23, he went to work for a pump manufacturer as a plumber's assistant and blacksmith, working 16 to 20 hours a day during the years prior to the Second World War when the shop was loaded with defense work. In 1941, lacking citizenship papers, he was forced to leave the defense business, and was employed by the California Farm Implement Company. After starting in the tool room he became foreman of a machine shop operation and was so employed throughout the war years. In 1946 he was appointed a process engineer with responsibility for determining the methods of manufacture of new parts for tractors and implements and for laying out the process and tooling requirements.

About this time Mr. deSalle began to take extension and night courses which he felt would be valuable to him in his work. Between 1946 and 1954 he completed the following courses:

Tool design	University of California
Methods and time study	University of California
General machine shop	University of California
Plastics	University of California
Job instruction training	University of California
Foremanship	LaSalle Extension Training
General management	LaSalle Extension Training

During this period he built his own house, doing 85 per cent of the work himself with the help of a brother.

Mr. deSalle and his wife married in 1943 and in 1959 their family consisted of a son, age 15, and a daughter, age 8. The two children had made a good adjustment in Turkey, attending schools operated by the U.S. Government for military personnel. In the fall of 1959 the deSalles sent their boy back to the United States to attend a military academy because he had not found the school in Turkey challenging.

During their first six months abroad Mr. and Mrs. deSalle had shared the general feeling of distaste for their surroundings. After Mrs. deSalle obtained a responsible position in the financial office of a local U.S. Government agency and they moved to an American neighborhood, they began to enjoy life more.

Mr. deSalle and Mr. Kite had been particularly good friends. After Mr. Kite's resignation from CFIT in late 1958, and the death of Mr. Nixon in March, 1959, Mr. deSalle found himself missing the companionship of Americans with similar backgrounds and interests. He liked his Turkish associates at the plant, and got along well with them at work, but found that nothing took the place of good friends of American origin.

After Mr. Nixon's death Mr. deSalle reported to Mr. Sur, the new managing director. Although his duties remained the same, namely, processing and general over-all responsibility for the manufacturing area, Mr. deSalle found working under Mr. Sur difficult. In June, feeling somewhat alone and believing his usefulness at CFIT gradually decreasing, he offered his resignation to the Board of Directors and prepared to return to the United States.

Shortly thereafter, Mr. deSalle received a phone call from the assistant to one of the highest officials in the Turkish Government, requesting him to come to his office. Mr. deSalle was urged to reconsider his resignation from CFIT, the government representative stating most emphatically that Mr. deSalle's services had been of exceptional value to Turkey in the past and were still urgently needed. He was further told that Mr. Sur was being relieved of his directorship of CFIT and that if Mr. deSalle would agree to remain in Turkey, he and Fikret Somer would be named Co-Directors of the concern. Mr. deSalle explained that one of the reasons he had decided to leave was the lack of effective government support for CFIT. The government official promised that tangible support, in the form of foreign exchange allocations, would be forthcoming shortly. Mr. deSalle requested time to consider his decision.

Mr. deSalle and his family returned to the United States for a vacation. While there, Mr. deSalle decided to return to Turkey and accept the CFIT Co-Directorship for a year or two. An important factor in his decision was the fact that he liked and had confidence in Mr. Somer and was certain that with effective management, CFIT again could become a profitable company.

BACKGROUND OF FIKRET SOMER

The other new Co-Director, Fikret Somer, had been in charge of the foundry for CFIT from early 1955 until April, 1959, when he was made Assistant Managing Director under Mahmut Sur. Somer, 44, had been educated at the Berlin Technical Institute, where he had earned a Master's degree in physics and metallurgy in 1940. Between 1940 and 1949 he had served in the Turkish Army, first in the Ordnance Department and later as an industrial advisor to the Supreme Defense Council. In 1950 he was sent by the Army to the University of Michigan for further technical training. In 1953 he was recalled to Turkey by the Army but resigned in 1954 to work for MKEK. His job there was connected with forgings, powder metallurgy, and munitions, but he felt confined by the government organization and joined CFIT early in 1955.

In addition to his service in the Turkish Army, Fikret Bey had taught Engineering Materials at the Technical Training College and had written four books on this subject. Since 1956 he had been associated with the Middle East Technical University, helping found the institution, and teaching in and later heading its Mechanical Engineering Department. Since April, 1959, he had also been serving as Acting President of the University until a full-time President could be appointed. These duties usually required 30 to 40 per cent of his time.

ACTIVITIES OF THE NEW CO-DIRECTORS

The appointment of Mr. deSalle and Mr. Somer was greeted with apparent enthusiasm by the rest of the CFIT staff. Mr. deSalle believed this reflected not only the fact that their predecessor had not been popular, but also that the employees were pleased that a Turk would share the top responsibility with an American, rather than having another full-time American manager.

Moving into the elegantly furnished office of the Managing Director, they both worked for the most part at the same large table. They usually spent at least half of each day in the office, and from the beginning worked well together. They were careful to keep each other constantly informed, and consulted with each other before taking any major action.

One of their early steps proved unpopular. This was an order that one of their signatures had to be on every purchase order, salary change, financial statement, check, or personnel requisition. In short, any paper committing the company in any way was to be signed by either Mr. Somer or Mr. deSalle. The supervisors objected, feeling this did not show them respect. The new Co-Directors believed this control was necessary, however, and would help them to learn the state of the business quickly.

Mr. Somer and Mr. deSalle did not start out their administration with specific plans beyond the general aim of improving the profit picture as best they could. They both felt that the company should be more aggressive in seeking subcontracting work to increase shop loads. They also believed that the six HP motor and irrigation pump then in the design stage should be developed and placed in production as quickly as possible. To increase the availability of shop work they authorized, with the Board of Directors' sanction, the manufacturing of a second set of 1,000 of those tractor parts that had been processed and tooled for production in Turkey.

Fortunately, about the time of their appointment (July, 1959) the foreign exchange situation began to improve as a result of governmental stabilization and control measures that had been instituted the previous August. The new Co-Directors applied to the government for dollars with which to procure parts and were granted sufficient exchange to obtain an irrevocable letter of credit for $390,000, enough for 211 sets of parts. These parts were ordered from California in August, financed in Turkish lira by the Zurat (Agricultural) Bank on a short-term loan basis. Delivery was expected to start in late November, 1959. Two hundred and fifty additional sets of parts were placed on order in September, 1959 for delivery the following January.

SITUATION IN NOVEMBER 1959

Over-All Outlook

With the apparent easing of the exchange situation and the indication that tractor parts would be available for midwinter assembly, in the judgment of the Co-Directors the future of CFIT looked better in November, 1959, than at any time since 1955. The increased activity in the production area in preparation for the renewal of tractor production was supplemented by work on new products, the second set of 1,000 tractor parts, and the gradually increasing volume of subcontracting work achieved by more active selling efforts. Mr. deSalle and Mr. Somer felt that the renewed activity improved supervisory morale and strengthened confidence in the future of the company. Their own state of mind was far from placid, however, for the combination of events seemed to bring to a head simultaneously many different problems and needs for decisions, action, and improvements.

As new Managing Directors they both felt considerable pressure to get the plant on a profitable basis as rapidly as possible. Not only were the two men naturally anxious for success in the eyes of their employees and associates, but the company also had been increasingly criticized by government ministers for its financial losses. "Even Parliament has criticized CFIT," said Mr. Somer, adding, "I have an especially strong motivation for success, for if you are successful the news goes around very fast. All Turkey will know it."

At the same time both Co-Directors expressed a "need to learn from every direction" and the necessity for tightening up performance in the supervisory group (the CFIT organization and personnel list is shown in Exhibit 1). "Our people are accustomed to move slowly," Mr. de-Salle commented. "The foremen are lax, and there is much looseness in the plant due to a low work load for three years. We are fighting against this." But the new Directors were reluctant to move too fast, for as Mr. Somer expressed it, "Louis and I came from among these people before we were promoted, and for that reason we can't be too unpleasant right away. We must go at it slowly." Mr. deSalle corroborated, "You can't force cooperation here. They wouldn't talk to you." With these feelings, Mr. Somer and Mr. deSalle faced their problems in November, 1959.

EXHIBIT 1 CALIFORNIA FARM IMPLEMENT TURK A.S.

ORGANIZATION CHART—NOVEMBER 1959

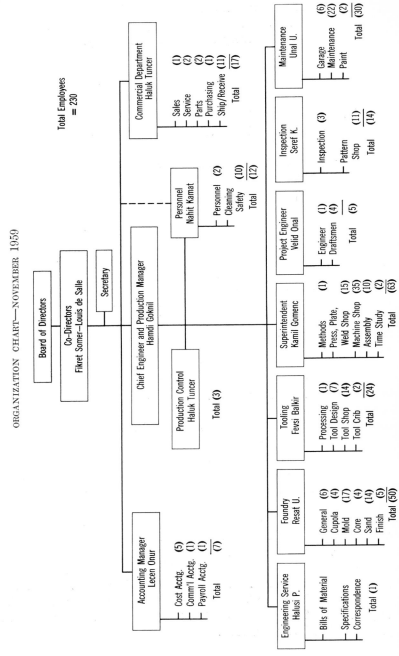

Training

In reactivating the assembly line Mr. deSalle was concerned about training assembly workers in advance of the receipt of parts so that the first 50 units could be assembled and sold as quickly as possible. Avoidance of delay seemed of particular importance because the financing of future parts supplies from the United States depended on the cash resulting from sales of the first tractors assembled. Working capital was severely depleted after four years of losses, and the company had already been extended maximum credit by the Agricultural Bank to finance orders for the first 450 sets of parts. In early November, 1959, Mr. deSalle therefore authorized the assembly foreman, Osman, to hire and begin training nine men who would be group leaders on the assembly line.

In the early years of CFIT, U.S. supervisors had found that training the Turkish workers was usually not difficult. Although most of the workers had no background of mechanical work experience, they were eager to learn and generally mastered the use of tools very quickly. Language was a problem, though, for it was difficult for an American to be sure that the Turk really understood instructions. Very anxious to please, the Turks tended to say, "I know," before they really did know. Mr. deSalle recalled one occasion when a Turk said, "I know, I know," and grabbed the wrench from Mr. Johnson's hand and proceeded to turn a nut the wrong way at full tilt.

It was essential that an American instructor thoroughly understand the work himself and be able to perform it surely and rapidly in front of the Turks, for although the latter were anxious to learn from the Americans, at the same time they were easily "disimpressed" if the American made a mistake or was temporarily stumped. Sometimes an experienced Turk would "test" a newly arrived American by purposely assembling parts incorrectly to see if the American "knew his stuff."

Training in 1959 promised to be somewhat more of a problem than in 1955 because the work now would include engine assembly, whereas the engines had previously been imported complete. Further, the original tractor assembly line had been set up as an almost exact replica of the line used in the California plant and the assembly superintendent from California, Mr. Johnson, had been in Turkey to train the men. Now the training for engine assembly would have to be done by deSalle and Osman, the latter having only plant maintenance experience.

Approximately twice as many men, per tractor produced, were required to run the assembly line in Turkey as in California. Mr.

deSalle felt that, although the Turkish workers had less of a tendency to "goof off" than American workers, they needed more continuous supervision. They were stopped more easily by technical and mechanical problems, perhaps because of lack of experience. Unless watched closely, a man would sometimes lose a whole morning over a broken tool or a poor set-up. The pace tended to be relatively even, however. To Mr. deSalle this reflected the fact that the typical Turkish worker tended to work slowly and steadily, whereas his American counterpart tended to work "in bursts" performing sometimes at maximum output, especially in the morning, and then coasting after gaining assurance of achieving at least minimum production for the day. He felt that the Turkish worker often lacked know-how and practical judgment, citing the example of a machinist who spent nearly his entire time continually removing a "rats' nest" of unbroken chips from a lathe operation instead of mounting a simple chipbreaker on the machine. Similarly, he believed that the Turks rarely measured anything and that their set-ups and quality levels had to be under constant surveillance.

Mr. deSalle left day-to-day training of the new men to Osman, but observed their progress while making his daily rounds of the plant. Osman's training method seemed to be to have the trainees watch him assemble and dismantle several engines and tractors left over from the 1956 production runs and then try their own hands at the job. Mr. deSalle felt this was a wasteful and inefficient approach to training, and wondered whether the new employees would be ready in time. Once when he asked Osman, "If you aren't ready to produce when the first 50 sets of parts get here, who will 'get' it?" the foreman, who could understand some English, replied with a grin, "I will." However, Mr. deSalle saw little point in requesting the Personnel Department to instruct Osman in training methods. Nahit Kamat, the Personnel Manager, had repeatedly declared that he had little experience in, or knowledge of, technical things, and had shown no initiative in participating in training efforts throughout the company.

Make or Buy Decisions

The decision to assemble engines reflected the company's desire to increase the Turkish content of the tractor in order to lessen the cost of parts and assembly, reduce its foreign exchange requirements, and increase CFIT plant work loads. In 1956, as noted, parts manufactured in Turkey represented 23 per cent of the value and 33 per cent of the weight of a CFIT tractor. By 1959 these percentages had been raised to 37 per cent of value and 41 per cent of weight, with

CFIT's own operations accounting for 225 of the 800 parts, excluding nuts, bolts, and hardware. In addition, approximately 40 parts were purchased from non-American sources. All these developments reduced the cost of parts formerly purchased from CFI's California plant by $300 per tractor. The parts manufactured by CFIT were largely sheet metal parts, machined castings, or lathe products. Purchased parts included nuts and bolts, electrical cables, paint, front wheels, copper alloy castings, batteries, forgings, bearings, oil sales, and rubber products such as hoses and the steering wheel, but not tires.

Final decisions about local manufacture were solely Mr. deSalle's province. Hamdi Bey and Fessi Bey supplied him, however, with estimates of the processes needed and the times required for manufacturing each part in the Istanbul plant. These estimates were then translated into costs by the Accounting Department,[5] compared with California prices, and a recommendation was made to Mr. deSalle. If the part could be made for the same cost as it could be purchased from CFI—or less—Mr. deSalle almost invariably authorized its manufacture in Turkey.

Mr. deSalle kept a large board indicating all parts and their sources. The board identified those parts that had been approved for Turkish manufacture and the order in which their manufacture was to be shifted to CFIT. Hamdi Bey was always delighted to move a part from the California list to the CFIT parts-roster, but was often overeager and occasionally unrealistic in scheduling such moves. In late October, 1959, for instance, Hamdi Bey recommended that CFIT make the front-axle pedestal, a large machined casting, on the next 250 units instead of procuring these items from CFI. Mr. deSalle explained it would take at least six months to obtain the necessary tools and patterns alone, making it impossible to complete the parts in time for February and March assembly as required. "Hamdi had not thought of this," Mr. deSalle remarked. "To a Turk, nothing is impossible."

Local Suppliers

From the very start, local procurement had been a major problem to CFIT. In 1956, Messrs. Kite, deSalle, Somer, and Hamdi Bey had made an exhaustive survey of Turkish suppliers to ascertain parts which might be obtained locally. No previous study had been undertaken because of lack of time and the availability of foreign exchange

---

[5] The Accounting Department used an overhead rate of 900 per cent of direct labor costs and amortized the tooling over 1,000 parts.

for off-shore purchases. After the survey, however, the **Purchasing** Department under Haluk Timcer's management had attempted spasmodically to enlarge the list of possible sources of procurement.

Even so, locating Turkish suppliers was a difficult and time-consuming job. Vendors did almost no advertising and little active sales work because they were hard pressed to meet demand, much less to seek out additional business. The Union of Chambers of Commerce had compiled an address book listing products and sources, but Haluk Bey had been unable to find a copy printed more recently than 1955. Nor was he able to obtain much help from the Government in locating procurement sources. Most vendors were found by accident or word of mouth; thorough surveys were slow and costly.

Indeed, the whole procurement function was time-consuming. Not only was travel and telephone communication difficult when not impossible, but vendors, once located, also inclined toward independence. Delivery schedules often were unreliable and quality inadequate. Furthermore, prices were subject often to upward changes between deliveries.

Steel suppliers were a particular problem. Only relatively low-grade steel was produced locally and better grades had to be procured from Germany or the United States. Rolled steel products of Turkish origin were often so bent or uneven as to be unusable. Perishable tools were another major source of difficulty. Drills, taps, reamers, cutters, wrenches, saw blades, and similar tools had to be bought in Europe or in the United States. But because of the foreign exchange problems these purchases had to be planned long in advance, and the usage of such tools had to be forecast carefully. Mr. deSalle found, moreover, that his Turkish supervisors in the shops had insufficient experience to anticipate needs, and concluded after many "crises" that he would be wise to do much of the ordering personally.

In 1955, CFIT bought $50,000 worth of tools and husbanded them carefully over the succeeding three years. Efforts to conserve them were threatened constantly by misuse; for example, the workers often ground tools incorrectly, drastically curtailing their life. In March, 1959 the company obtained a much needed allocation of $20,000 from the ICA[6] for perishable tools, but by November none had been delivered. Such orders had to be advertised in the *United States Small Business Journal* with three bids procured before orders could be placed. The company consequently had to deal with vendors individually instead of placing a single, consolidated order with one

---

[6] International Cooperation Administration.

wholesaler. The resulting delay proved even more vexing than the vast amounts of paperwork concerned so that by November, 1959, CFIT was reduced to making its own vitally necessary tools. Similarly, in setting up its foundry, the company had been forced by a lack of supply sources to make its own roller conveyors, hoists, and casting carts.

Mr. deSalle instructed Haluk Bey to search constantly for opportunities to buy tools and regularly to visit shops where they could be bought. However, Haluk Bey's lack of time and technical knowledge restricted his efforts and achievements markedly. His Department's one buyer, he explained, did only just what he was told. Said Haluk Bey: "He is able to purchase only routine things, and I must devote much of my time to purchasing. It takes time and experience to get to know the various manufacturers' representatives and learn who does what in Turkey. I've just hired a secretary and this eventually will help us to develop a better system."

The Purchasing Department kept stock cards on supplies on hand and endeavored to maintain a one-month supply of easily procured items. It stocked scarcer items in whatever quantities were available, regardless of cost or usage. Total in-plant inventory, excluding spare parts, averaged about TL 4,900,000 in 1959.[7] End-of-year inventories for previous years had been:

1958	TL	3,992,000
1957		2,303,000
1956		1,724,000
1955		663,000

To cut the costs of tractor parts further, Mr. deSalle planned to step up the amount and scope of European purchasing. In the fall of 1959, for instance, he decided to purchase diesel fuel injection pumps in England and excluded them from the first 450 sets of tractor parts ordered from the United States. On the second set of 100 parts he also excluded starters and generators from the American order, purchasing them instead from English sources. Through another decision, tires were to be obtained in the future from English suppliers at savings of $20 per tractor. Mr. deSalle also checked sources for gears in Germany and seriously contemplated the purchase of completely assembled engines from a British manufacturer. This would save $536 over engines procured from America ($973 versus $437).

---

[7] Official rate of exchange in 1959 was nine Turkish lira to the U.S. dollar.

A representative of the British manufacturer had visited the Istanbul plant and his proposal had been attractive concerning performance, delivery, and price. Mr. deSalle expected to begin relying on this supplier early in 1960.

Production Control

The establishment of supply sources in Europe and Turkey created for Mr. deSalle increasingly complex problems of achieving a continuous flow of parts and a reasonable balance of inventories. For example, the English fuel injection pumps had been promised for November to dovetail with the arrival of tractor parts from California, but had not been received by late in the month. The English concern advised that the pumps would not be shipped until the first of February because of a steel shortage for which the American steel strike and its impact on the British market were blamed. The delay in delivery meant that CFIT tractors would have to be built and their engines tested and adjusted by using the few pumps on hand, with the British injection pumps installed later. More seriously, the delay would hold up shipments, sales, and cash receipts until late February, critically affecting CFIT's ability to finance orders for additional parts.

The Board of Directors' authorization of a total of 2,000 sets of Turkish-built parts to be manufactured during slack periods, together with the gradual shifting of parts sources from California to Turkey, created control problems far more complex than those encountered in 1955 when operations had consisted mainly of assembling dismantled tractors. The parts lists had to be kept up to date as to source, and accurate records had to be maintained to avoid duplicate ordering or, even worse, parts shortages because of failure to order at all. The problem was further complicated by the long lead times on shipments from the United States and by the need to provide tooling and allow sufficient process times—including some safety factor—on the parts being made for the first time in Turkey.

The lead times on American parts were lengthened by the months required to obtain an import permit, foreign exchange, Turkish lira financing, and letters of credit. Consequently, once an order was in process, additions or deletions were virtually impossible. Generally, the California factory needed three months' time to produce a part. Shipping and customs' clearance took another two. The temptation to substitute cheaper parts from Turkish and European sources in the long period between placing and receiving an American order was strong, and CFIT officials sometimes succumbed to it. This caused considerable criticism from the parent company, as well as necessitating intricate paperwork and heavy quantities of correspondence.

Mr. deSalle found it necessary, as we noted before, to make most of the basic production decisions himself. He did, of course, rely heavily on the Production Control group and the Engineering Department for requirements, paperwork, and expediting. Such reliance left him uneasy since none of his Turkish colleagues seemed to him to have developed skills in looking ahead and anticipating problems.

The assembly of 50 plows was a case in point. In 1955 and 1956 CFIT had assembled plows from American parts. When this work was suspended during the foreign exchange crisis, 50 sets of parts were still on hand, lacking only a few essential items to permit completion of 50 additional plows. As dollars became available again in 1959 these 50 sets of parts were taken out of inventory, the missing parts were ordered from California, and the factory was instructed to assemble 50 plows immediately upon receipt of the California shipment. When the new parts arrived, and after several days' delay in getting out the parts and laying them out on the floor preparatory to assembly,[8] it was discovered that six parts believed to be in the Turkish inventory actually were not—they had been overlooked somehow in checking the inventory. Hence the plows still could not be assembled! Haluk Bey, whose department was responsible for such checks, conceded his stores men did not understand the importance of an annual inventory and had no useful method for conducting one. Similar errors were frequently discovered, and Haluk readily admitted that his men must improve their performance in this area.

A haunting fear planted in Mr. deSalle's mind by such experiences prompted him to say, "I shudder to think of what we may run into when we try to assemble the first 50 tractors. If six parts were missing from a plow, what will we find missing on a tractor? Especially after three and one-half years and some 200 odd changes in the sources of parts. And the parts we're running here for the first 1,000 sets aren't even complete yet."

As further documentation of his concern he cited three parts which he had personally discovered to be short and which had not even

---

[8] This situation furnished another source of concern to deSalle in regard to training, for Osman had apparently done no planning or organizing as to just how to set up an efficient method for assembling the plows. For several days the six men seemed to stand around, shifting the parts about and tentatively bolting a few together while the others watched. The general foremen and superintendent apparently paid no attention to this inaction, and deSalle found it necessary to "needle" them repeatedly before progress was made.

been started into production by November. He had been expediting these personally because the Turks just didn't seem to get very excited or concerned. As one put it, "Why worry about a few parts that are short, because the big shipment from California isn't even here yet." These parts were a timing gear, an accessory gear, and a side cover for the motor. The first two items had been delayed because a poor set-up had broken the drive gears on the machine tool used in their fabrication. After fruitlessly attempting to get these gears from the U.S. machine tool manufacturer and being hampered by paperwork and exchange problems, Mr. deSalle had found some gears in the plant junkyard which could be adapted to the machine tool. (He visited the junkyard regularly and often found valuable items which could be repaired for use in the plant.) The engine side cover had been delayed due to engineering changes necessitated by the change to the English fuel injection pump.

There was no formal consolidated manufacturing or assembly schedule in the plant, due to the previously low level of activity, the continual delays and uncertainties in the foreign exchange and parts supply picture, and the lack of trained manpower to perform the scheduling function. Available jobs simply had been performed as soon, and as quickly, as circumstances permitted. Time and due dates had not been an essential factor other than on a very few subcontract jobs. Mr. deSalle felt that the reason for this was that "hardly anyone delivers on time in Turkey." He cited several instances in which a customer had not even inquired about jobs on which CFIT was already a year late on delivery. One large manufacturer for whom they had made machinery parts for three years had yet to complete its first machine. Since other suppliers were so late, and the problems in supply and quality were so prevalent, CFIT was seldom expedited by a customer, being relatively prompt by comparison. But now that they were starting in to assemble tractors and other new products of their own design, the matter of time and close scheduling appeared to Mr. deSalle and his management group to be of increasing importance.

Lecen Bey, the Chief Accountant, stated that during the period of uncertainty over foreign exchange he had given up any attempt at budgeting. Now he was about to attempt once again to set up budgetary controls, but needed a basic 1960 manufacturing program in order to do so. Mr. deSalle and Mr. Somer stated that "with so many projects in the air at once, they too felt the need for some sort of schedule, or at least a 'task list.'" Hamdi Bey stated that for Engineering, Tooling, and Shop Planning, an over-all picture of work to be done would be most useful, but that the continuing uncertainty regarding what could be accomplished made such scheduling a very difficult job.

Haluk Bey listed the lack of a specific program as one of the major weaknesses in the plant operation. But he felt that it was hazardous and even foolish to adopt complex scheduling procedures which probably would then have to be changed weekly. He cited as a major problem in scheduling the lack of formal layouts, with processing lists and standards on each part. Similarly, few standards or estimates were available on set-up times, scrap losses, or lead times. A further current difficulty was the frequency of machine shutdowns while missing perishable tools were fabricated or repaired.

Haluk Bey freely admitted that a great deal of work needed to be done in the production control area and that lack of experienced personnel was hampering his efforts. He pointed out that his prior experience had been in personnel work, and that Mr. Buckler had seemed uninterested and unable to either teach or explain what was needed for a good production control system. In 1955 and 1956, when the work was almost entirely the assembly of a few products, the production control job had, of course, been simpler. Mr. Buckler had simply installed the exact assembly control system in use in CFI's California plant, including identical forms and procedures. Haluk had been unable to obtain much in the way of explanation of these. Hence his knowledge and understanding of control had come primarily from textbooks. His only experience using complex controls took the form of a machine loading control he had set up in 1957 for a large order of textile parts. This had proven effective, he believed.

In his department he had an assistant who handled production control and the stores function and did a good job "as far as he went." The production control work was limited at present to issuing shop orders and material and supply requisitions. Haluk was concerned about the future in regard to production control and had recently talked to Somer Bey about the need for more people. He felt that he had not yet convinced Mr. Somer of the importance of this work, especially in the face of the reluctance of the Co-Directors to add overhead while the plant was still losing money.

Liaison with **CFI**

A further difficulty in forward planning was the problem of obtaining firm delivery commitments from the California plant. CFI executives, realizing the difficulty and uncertainty in obtaining import allocation and foreign and local currency in Turkey, insisted that before the

California plant begin work on CFIT parts, it have an official order, on an official order form, signed by Mr. deSalle and Mr. Somer; a New York bank guarantee of payment of dollars; a Zurat Bank guarantee of the lira required; and an official Turkish document showing that the dollars required for the imports had been allocated.

Mr. deSalle and Mr. Somer agreed that these requirements would be desirable but complained that it was impossible to obtain the Zurat Bank guarantee until the import permit was in hand, and that this permit was good only for three months. Since the California plant's lead times exceeded three months, it was imperative therefore that its production work be started prior to actual receipt of the import allocation, accepting CFIT's assurance that the allocation was to be granted later. Having been through the experience of making parts which CFIT was then unable to import, CFI insisted instead that before the California plant started manufacture, and provide a delivery promise, an irrevocable letter of credit had to be furnished the New York bank for the dollars involved. Thus CFI could receive payment for the parts even if CFIT was unable to import them.

It was virtually impossible for CFIT to meet this condition, for it meant that with the existing lead times, the U.S. parts for the 2,000 tractors planned for 1960 production would have had to be financed almost a year in advance. Not only was the money not available, but even had CFIT been able to borrow this amount, the interest rate of about 12 per cent per annum seemed exorbitantly expensive.

Correspondence[9] on this problem had been going on since August, 1959, but nothing had been resolved. As a result of this difficulty CFI had not yet given a delivery promise on the second order of parts, the 250 sets that were to follow the 200 sets promised for November. It now appeared to Mr. deSalle that even if the question of financial guarantees were "solved tomorrow," these items could not possibly be received in Turkey before April or May, 1960.

Such a delay would, of course, result in further intermittent production at CFIT. To provide badly needed working capital Mr. deSalle and Mr. Somer stated that it was imperative that the first 200 units be built and sold as rapidly as possible. This would require CFIT almost immediately to hire 25 more people for assembly work, but with the probability of there being no work for them to do between March, when the 200 units would be completed, and April or May, at the earliest.

---

[9] An exchange of letters between California and Turkey usually took about three weeks.

Another continuing problem was that the CFIT's plant was now producing CFI's model OEP tractor which was no longer in production in the United States. This fact related, in part, to the two major changes in management that had occurred in CFI since 1954. As an informed observer noted:

These changes had an impact on the Turkish operations. In November, 1955, an outside group had bought a controlling interest in [CFI's] voting stock, and a new management came in at that date headed by Richard Rideout, who became Chairman of the Board. Mr. Moore, former Chairman, was retained as President. The principal reason for the management shake-up was a financial crisis, one cause of which was CFI's failure to keep its products up-to-date technically and the consequent sales drop-off, both in the domestic and export markets. Also, because the company had not been assembling or manufacturing on any scale abroad, it had been losing out particularly on exports. Under the new management, the development of an entire new line was launched.

Subsequent to these organizational changes in the U.S. company, a tractor decision was made to shift CFI's tractor manufacture from model PKY to model OEP, a more modern appearing vehicle. When CFI stopped production on the PKY model it therefore sent CFIT a large shipment of unordered parts. The net result was that in November, 1959, CFIT had a majority, but not all, of the parts needed to manufacture 165 PKY tractors. By this time, however, the PKY model was considered obsolete in Turkey and Mr. deSalle believed that any units CFIT assembled would be difficult, if not impossible, to sell.

In 1958 a new management, headed by Jack Hazar, replaced the Rideout management at CFI and made still further changes in tractor models. By now, however, CFIT had made considerable progress on tooling up for the model OEP tractor and elected to continue to produce it indefinitely. Thus CFI's concern over manufacturing parts for CFIT in advance of firm "guaranteed" orders was partly in recognition that it had no other outlet for model OEP parts.

Operating Costs

Mr. Somer and Mr. deSalle both felt that high production costs were one of their chief problems, and were united in their determination to effect savings. As discussed before, they felt it was necessary to increase sales and production volume, but they also expressed dissatisfaction in their current costs and productivity. Mr. Somer said, "Our productivity is poor. It should be at least 50 per cent better. When we have a problem in the plant, workers leave their jobs and swarm around like bees. The engineers and supervision should get things better organized and under control. Our people are accustomed to move slowly. The foundry personnel's work habits, however, are not so bad since they've had a better work load."

One of CFIT's supervisors, asked for his opinion on the productivity problems, replied, "Fikret Bey feels we are not cost conscious enough. But we don't have enough mass production to get costs down. Our plant's performance, in terms of the time taken for a given job, compares well with other Turkish shops. But the overhead and burden take our prices and costs up too far." Until recently CFIT had used its actual burden rate of 1,500 per cent in pricing its bids, but even at 900 per cent, its bids were frequently too high.

Price competition had become far more severe in the tractor market in 1959 when import restrictions had eased. The CFIT tractor sold for TL 33,000, in comparison to models of the following competitors:

Leading British competitor	TL	28,500 with hydraulic accessories[10]
2nd ranking British competitor		26,000 excluding hydraulic accessories
Leading Italian competitor		32,000 with hydraulic accessories
German competitor		30,000 excluding hydraulic accessories
Russian competitor		18,000 with hydraulic accessories

The CFIT supervisory group believed that as the only tractor company producing in Turkey their concern had the best reputation for availability of repair parts and service. They also believed CFIT's reputation for quality was superior to that of their competition because their products were identified as coming from the United States.

The money shortage in Turkey made credit an important sales factor. Farmers purchasing CFIT tractors often could obtain credit through the Zurat Agricultural Bank and, in 1958, lack of funds forced the Zurat to extend credit only to purchasers of CFIT tractors. This provided a fortunate marketing advantage to the company. Credit was expected to ease, however, in 1960, and it therefore was not anticipated that the CFIT advantage would be permanent. In any case, Mr. deSalle and Mr. Somer were convinced that it was imperative

---

[10] Priced by CFIT at TL 4,000 extra.

to reduce the price of their tractor and that, clearly, costs had to be cut in order to turn a profit.

In an application made in June, 1959, to the Export-Import Bank for a working-capital loan, CFIT quoted its tractor costs and selling price as follows:

Imported parts at Port of Embarkation (P.O.E.)	TL	17,150
Turkish freight, customs, taxes, and insurance		3,250
Component parts manufactured in and/or purchased from Turkey		3,500
Assembly, paint, and test		4,500
Total cost		28,400
Gross profit		4,600
Sales price		33,000

Accounting

CFIT's Accounting Department was managed by Lecen Onur, 30, a graduate of the University of Ankara School of Political Science, with a major in Finance, Accounting, and Economics. He had joined CFIT as Chief Cost Accountant after five years of work with the government in Ankara, the last two years in a government manufacturing plant. The former Accounting Manager had left CFIT in August, 1959, to join the Middle Eastern Technical University as Controller. As Lecen Bey put it, "Everybody [in CFIT] was looking for other jobs, for the financial results and condition of the company were poor and its future looked uncertain." "Now," he added, "the situation looks better."

In the present accounting organization, Lecen Bey managed six employees:[11] two timekeepers, one clerk, one payroll accountant, one financial accountant, one cost accountant. He felt that his group was overloaded, pointing out that until August, 1959, there had been two more men in the department. While he was not looking for additional personnel now, he said that finding cost accountants was a real problem because "cost accounting is so little used in Turkey. No other company in the city uses cost accounting. My cost accounting knowledge has come entirely from books and U.S. correspondence school courses."

The Accounting Department published five reports on a regular monthly basis: (1) Profit and Loss, (2) Balance Sheet, (3) Mechanical

---

[11] Five of the Accounting Department personnel were men, and one (the cost accountant) was a woman.

Production Overhead Statement, (4) Foundry Overhead Statement, (5) Analysis of General Administrative and Sales Expenses. These reports and the entire accounting system had been developed by Mr. Oakes in 1955 and had been virtually unchanged since that time.

The cashier (payroll accountant) prepared a daily cash report and the timekeeper sent out each day what Lecen Bey called "variation reports." These were tickets that showed the actual time spent on a job, or operation, compared to the estimated, or standard, time established by the Time-Study Section. Variation tickets were prepared on those jobs on which the actual time was more than 10 per cent over the standard. Anywhere from 6 to 15 variation tickets were prepared each day, with two copies sent to the Accounting Department, and the original sent to the Process and Tool Department. Lecen Bey did not want to publish an over-all variation summary or shop performance report, for he felt that his timekeeper was badly overloaded. Lecen Bey himself spoke to the shop supervision if any variation ticket looked particularly poor. He attempted to spend more than an hour in the shop, engineering, or tooling area each day, but was so busy that he often found it difficult to get away from his office.

Mr. Somer and Mr. deSalle both expressed concern that accounting and figure work were not their personal fortes. Mr. deSalle said, "We don't use Lecen Bey's reports as much as we should. We need to learn to do this." But Mr. Somer said he felt that CFIT's accounting personnel were "almost pure accounting people. They need a broader view of our operations and a better picture of the financial situation in Turkey." He pointed out that some time ago he had asked for an analysis of CFIT operations and a report on the over-all Turkish fiscal position, but that he had received nothing. "They only keep records and can't give us good advice. We need a good, simple financial report."

Examples of the monthly reports follow.

Profit and Loss Report*

		Oct. 1959	Nov. 1959	Year to Date	
Sales	TL	8	101†	TL	285
Cost of Sales		6	85		242
Overhead Gain (or loss)		2	4		3
Factory Margin		4	20		46
General, Administrative, and Sales Expense		13	10		134
Interest and Other Income		—	—		10
Other Expenses		3	—		10
Profit before Amortization		(12)	10		(88)
Amortization Expenses‡		16	16		182
Provision for Profit Sharing		0	0		0
Provision for Income Tax		0	0		0
Net Profit	TL	(28)	(6)	TL	(270)

* Figures disguised by application of a uniform factor. The same factor was applied to the following four accounting reports.

† November sales included a very large sale of spare parts to the Zurat Bank which accounted for 85 per cent of sales for the month. These parts were procured from California and sold at a markup of 25 per cent over cost.

‡ CFIT stock awarded to CFI for patents, engineering, and technical services was being written off over a 10-year period, accounting for 52 per cent of amortization. Depreciation on buildings, and on machines and equipment, accounts for the balance of 16 per cent and 32 per cent, respectively.

CFIT BALANCE SHEET*

	December 31, 1958		November 30, 1959	
ASSETS				
Cash	TL	84	TL	27
Bonds		0		29
Accounts Receivable		169		141
Inventory in Transit	0		28	
In Plant	113		704	
Work in Process	509		282	
Letters of Credit	0		732	
Finished Goods	168		0	
Repair Parts	0		253	
Total Inventory		790		1,999
Total Current Assets		1,043		2,196
Patents and Trade Marks (net)		592		508
Fixed Assets—Land		84		84
Buildings, Machines, and				
Equipment (net)		1,110		985
Uncompleted Assets		0		56
Prepaid Expenses		28		57
TOTAL ASSETS	TL	2,857	TL	3,880
LIABILITIES				
Accounts Payable	TL	28	TL	56
Accruals		29		29
Short-Term Bank Loans		264		1,601
Total Current Liabilities		321		1,686
Capital Shares		3,370		3,298
Earnings to Date		(834)		(1,104)
TOTAL LIABILITIES	TL	2,857	TL	3,880

* Figures disguised by application of a uniform factor. The same factor was applied to the following three accounting reports.

CFIT   Mechanical Overhead Statement*

Direct Labor	September 1959	1959 to Date
Standard Direct Labor	TL 12	TL 97
Nonstandard Products Direct Labor	20	93
Total Direct Labor	32	190
Miscellaneous Labor for Tools and Capital Expenses	11	102
Direct Department Expense—Material	20	240
Labor	42	396
Service	14	116
Indirect Department Expense—Material	19	302
Labor	105	1,158
Services	18	215
Amortization	190	1,743
Total Expenses	408	4,170
Ratio Expenses to Direct Labor	12.7 to 1	22.0 to 1
Less Overhead Applied to Standard Direct Labor	112	877
Less Overhead Applied to Nonstandard Direct Labor	161	830
Less Overhead Applied to Miscellaneous Direct Labor	33	305
Total Applied Overhead	306	2,012
Overhead Gain or Loss	(102)	(2,158)

---

* Figures disguised by application of a uniform factor.   The same factor was applied to the following two accounting reports.

CFIT   FOUNDRY OVERHEAD STATEMENT*

Direct Labor	September 1959
Standard Direct Labor	TL 13
Nonstandard Products Labor	1
Miscellaneous Labor	—
Expenses	
Material	105
Labor	32
Service	31
Amortization	3
(a) Total Expenses	171
(b) Standard Cost per 1,000 kg. Poured	180
(c) Applied Overhead Based on Direct Labor	85
(d) Overhead Gain (or Loss)	94

NOTE: $[d = b - a + c]$.

---

* Figures disguised by application of a uniform factor. The same factor was applied to the following accounting reports.

CFIT   GENERAL ADMINISTRATIVE AND SALES EXPENSE ANALYSIS*

	September 1959	Year to Date
Salaries	TL 7.8	TL 81.9
Materials and Supplies	.3	3.2
Utilities	—	2.4
Telephone, Telegraph, and Postage	.5	3.6
Travel	.6	12.0
Taxes, Legal Fees	.8	9.6
Insurance	.8	9.5
Personnel Insurance	.4	4.0
Advertising	.1	1.2
Other	.3	6.2
	11.6	133.6

---

* Figures disguised by application of a uniform factor.

These reports were given to the Co-Directors about the 17th of every month. In addition, the mechanical overhead statement was transmitted to Hamdi Bey and the foundry statement to Cengis Bey, the Foundry Manager. Lecen Bey received relatively few questions or comments on these reports for, in his opinion, they were rather routine and familiar to the two men receiving them.

Lecen Bey also kept a report of the invoices outstanding. It was necessary to send an accountant out twice a week to make the rounds of customers to "chase down and collect" accounts receivable. This was a common practice in Turkey. In late November, 40 invoices were outstanding. During 1959, Total Accounts Receivable had been averaging about the equivalent of five months of sales.

Recent Cost Reduction Efforts

Both the Co-Directors, as noted earlier, had been concerned about the cost picture and soon after their appointment in July resolved that concrete steps should be taken to reduce the overhead. After much soul-searching, they decided to request ten salaried employees to resign. The selection was based on an evaluation of which individuals represented the highest salaries, the least ability, and the lowest contributions to CFIT's operations. The employees chosen included the Chief Accountant, the Plant Engineer, Assistant Production Manager, Purchasing Agent, Commercial Manager, and five salaried personnel— both men and women—at lower organizational levels. Mr. deSalle and Mr. Somer met personally for discussions with each of the ten, pointing out that by agreeing to resign each would aid both himself and CFIT: individual employment records would not show that each had been discharged, and the company would be obligated to grant termination pay.

Within the organization, reaction to the ten layoffs was mixed. Mr. deSalle and Mr. Somer believed they saw evidence of an immediate improvement in effort and discipline. Hamdi Bey said he believed this was "the right kind of layoff to make. The organization was top-heavy. The earlier layoffs we made were big mistakes—we laid off at the bottom, people with low salaries. This saved but little money and yet hurt morale badly. And then we often had to recall some of those we had laid off, demonstrating weakness in top management planning."

There was evidence that most others in the organization saw any type of layoff as almost immoral, violating the employees' trust and devotion to the company. Since there was no unemployment compensation in Turkey, the supervisors felt particularly sympathetic to those laid off. Mr. deSalle said that in the earlier layoffs, more often than not, the supervisor faced with notifying employees would call in and report himself sick on the appointed day. One supervisor repeatedly refused to inform a subordinate that his services were no longer required, until finally Mr. deSalle told him that his own employment would be terminated if he refused to perform this supervisory responsibility. Some supervisors said they did not sleep for a week before and after any type of layoff or firing, so strongly did they hate to face a friend and give him the bad news.

Plant Engineering

Mr. deSalle often felt that the production tooling and processing work did not properly take costs into account. Jobs tended to be either undertooled or overtooled. For example, he discovered that after the shop had been asked to manufacture replacement parts for the six parts[12] missing on the 50 plows, elaborate tooling and processing were being prepared. This tooling would have doubled the cost and tripled the time delay before the plows could be assembled and sold.

During his daily trips through the shop Mr. deSalle frequently found examples of impractical processing or tooling. To make a simple part with two holes at right angles, a precise drill jig had been prepared, instead of using a boring bar on a turret lathe. On a large lot job run in a drill press, Mr. deSalle personally developed a tooling set-up in an hour and a half that cut the time per unit from $2\frac{1}{2}$ minutes to 55 seconds. "The Turks love to work out elaborate tooling, always going 'by the book.' They don't seem to have the practical judgment necessary to make good processing decisions," Mr. deSalle commented.

Another incident of this type occurred when, through an American friend, Mr. deSalle secured an order to recut interval threads on oil drilling pipes. These pipes were 30 to 40 feet long and weighed three tons each. The Turks worked out on paper what Mr. deSalle described as "an involved, big, fancy cutting rig which would have taken three months to tool, cost 50,000 lira, and probably would not have been accurate anyway." Mr. deSalle then developed an alternate system using two large lathes, one chucking the pipe on the outside and turning it, while the other chucked it internally and cut the thread, its lead mechanism being driven by the turning of the pipe.

---

[12] See p. 371.

Plant Supervision

Mr. deSalle's other main concern in the shop was that supervision tended to be lax, tender-hearted, and influenced by friendship. Personal relationships seemed to him to be especially influential between immediate levels of supervision. The Turkish department heads, for example, tended to become friends with their next lower level supervisors or professional people, and this process was repeated on down the line. Personal loyalties became extremely strong. At salary review time department heads rated all their people with superlatives. Anytime Mr. deSalle would not approve a substantial increase, the department head usually would become quite upset, pleading the merits of the individual at length. Not infrequently a supervisor would even offer to accept a cut in his own salary in order to give a larger increase to a subordinate. When this was denied, the typical reaction was deep and quiet hurt, accompanied by an obvious reluctance to inform the subordinate of an increase his supervisor regarded as too small.

For these reasons Mr. deSalle felt it necessary to keep an eye on shop operations at all times. He was irritated by repeated instances of orders which were not followed, but instead neglected or simply forgotten. Again and again on his trips through the shop he made suggestions, requests, or specific orders, only to discover several weeks later that nothing had been done. "The Turks are friendly and respectful," he said, "and always promise full cooperation and early action—but often nothing happens. Fikret Bey and I are starting a new system now. When we give an assignment, we fill out a slip of paper and keep a carbon. Then the men will know we are going to follow up. As it is now, they just forget it, or put it off, especially if the job is at all disagreeable."

As mentioned at the outset, Kamil Bey, the Superintendent, who had an engineering degree and had worked two years in the California plant, and his General Foreman seemed to gravitate toward the office and paperwork and leave the operators to themselves. For example, after Mr. deSalle had located in the junkyard some gears needed to put a broken machine tool back in operation, he had given them to Kamil Bey for reboring. A day later he observed, to his horror, that a young apprentice performing the boring operation had already removed too much material. It appeared that the precious gears were ruined.[13] He felt this was a typical example of poor supervision, over-

---

[13] They were later salvaged by use of a sleeve insert.

delegation, and impractical judgment, and that it demonstrated why he had to spend so much time on the floor.

Part of the trouble, he felt, was simply lack of experience. "Our supervisors often don't know what to do next," he said. "They hate to give a definite 'yes' or 'no,' and they are so individualistic and so rank and status conscious that there are lots of petty disagreements and hurt feelings. What we need are better supervisors. Our present supervisors are weak, but we can't hire any better ones. It is a problem of getting technical knowledge, practical judgment, and backbone. We can't seem to get all three."

New Products

The shop supervision and cost pictures were becoming further muddied by the new products being developed for production and sales in 1960. The principal products being designed, fabricated, and tested in the fall of 1959 were:

1. 3-inch Irrigation Pump—Prototype and Tooling completed
2. 6 HP Gasoline Motor—Prototype scheduled for completion by 12/31/59
3. Universal Type Tool Bar for Mounting Agricultural Implements
4. Rod Weeder
5. Field Cultivator
6. Garden Cultivator
7. Cotton Planter
8. Heat Treat Ovens for Highway Department
9. Window Frames, Louvres, Ventilators for 250 Gasoline Stations
10. Concrete Mixer
11. Rotary Hoe
12. Plow Packer
13. Straw Chopper

Other than the pump, motor, rotary hoe, and straw chopper, all of these products at the moment were only in the design stage. The pump was successfully tested in late November in a new hydraulics testing room built in the plant. Five hundred and fifty units were on order, and parts production was to get under way in December. The pump consisted of about 25 parts, of which all were made by CFIT except for bearings procured from Italy. The pump would sell for about TL 600 and sales of TL 700,000 were forecast for 1960, 150 units being scheduled for January delivery.

The motor, designed in Turkey, appeared comparable to typical U.S. models. Hamdi Bey had promised Mr. deSalle that the first protype would be running by the end of the year. Messrs. deSalle and Somer estimated the market at 5,000 per year, and forecast sales income of TL 7,000,000 for 1960. Production was scheduled to start in the second quarter of the year. In November, 1959, a great deal remained to be done before a prototype could be assembled. The crankshaft, pistons, and connecting rods had not been started. In fact, Mr. deSalle felt sure that the entire program was lagging.

After the pump and motor, the next products scheduled to be developed and produced were the rotary hoe and the straw chopper. Four hundred hoes were on order at a price of TL 1,500 each with production required in February. The design was essentially CFIT in origin. The straw chopper implement mulched straw very fine to furnish an edible animal food. One thousand were on order at TL 1,000 each with production also scheduled for February.

The Engineering and Tooling Departments had no regular system for scheduling or estimating the completion of development programs. Mr. deSalle kept after Hamdi Bey to give him specific estimates of dates when the necessary parts for the prototypes would be ready. Hamdi Bey, in turn, delegated the problem to Fevsi Bey in the Tooling Department. With tractor implement, engine, and pump parts to be tooled simultaneously, Fevsi Bey considered this request a major problem. "Hamdi Bey," he said, "has asked me to tell him when the tool design and tooling will be completed on the tractor, engine, and pump parts. This is a hard problem, for it is difficult to make such estimates, especially in a tool room. Which parts do we do first? Shall we take them in numerical order? I need to keep all my people busy, yet all the men can't do the same kind of work. And then there are definite steps on each tool, each of which needs to be phased in the proper order. And the machine tools in the toolroom get to be bottlenecks, too. It is very complicated and mixed up. The request is reasonable, but I do not know how to proceed."

Mr. deSalle recognized that the problem of scheduling and following all these parts was not under control. He feared that the end-result would be a delay in initial production of the new products which were badly needed to increase shop loads, balance out assembly work with intermittent tractor production, and provide billings. Delays meant increased development costs as well as further reductions in available working capital.

Mr. deSalle felt he should keep an eye on the type of tooling being planned and its delivery. One day in November, walking through the toolroom, he noticed the usual crowd of five to six workers and engineers gathered about a tool inspection surface plate. Edging in, he found the debate was over the proper approach to checking a gauge being manufactured for use in inspecting a tractor part. One man casually mentioned that he was not even sure the gauge was needed. It developed that the gauge was indeed not necessary, since the part it was to inspect was being eliminated due to a change in the mounting of the new English fuel pump. Mr. deSalle immediately ordered all work stopped on the instrument, but by that time it was almost completed.

While this example was not unusual, even more frequent were problems centering on the design of tooling, both in regard to tolerance requirements and labor savings. The usual tendency was to design tooling that was overly precise and expensive in regard to tolerances, and unimaginative in regard to potential direct labor savings.

The 6 HP engine was the first truly complex new product engineered by CFIT and Mr. deSalle felt somewhat pessimistic about the number of "bugs" that would probably have to be worked out before it could be produced and sold. The Engineering Department was, in a sense, unproven. It had made mistakes on simpler products which suggested the possibility of future delays on this more complex undertaking. For example, in assembling a large valve for a dam it was found that the holes for fastening the valve assembly to the dam had been omitted; the wrong reference point had been used in fixing dimensions, creating a buildup of tolerances so that parts did not fit together; furthermore, the prints did not call for matching one face of a casting, so that when bolted on, the bearings did not line up properly.

Outside Subcontracting Work

New products were sold by Mr. Somer, Mr. deSalle, and Haluk Bey to the Agricultural Bank and various distributors. There was no regular sales organization as such since, until recently, there had been few products to offer and the tractors and implements had been in such demand that they were allocated by the government.

Subcontracting work for the plant was obtained in gradually increasing volume under the Co-Directors' policy of aggressively seeking such work. Seven sales agents had been appointed in various parts of Turkey. These men, paid on a commission basis, devoted a part of their time to CFIT and the remainder to jobs with other companies, to university teaching, or to other occupations. Orders were sent in for factory quotes by these agents, who typically set the final price bid to be given the customer after receiving the CFIT figures, the difference being their commission. The sales agents had been asked to seek orders for individual parts rather than for assemblies or subassemblies, since some of the work obtained to date in the latter categories was judged to be relatively unrelated to the tractor business. No outside tooling work had ever been accepted.

Mr. deSalle himself set final prices on subcontracting jobs, often feeling that the estimates given him by his subordinates were much too high. He tried to take into account the customer's expectations of price, as well as the approximate shop time required. He personally negotiated prices with some of the larger firms, especially U.S.-owned companies. Mr. deSalle felt that it was difficult to get assurance of high quality work in Turkey, and hence, CFIT would and did charge a reasonable premium for the consistent quality expected of a U.S.-managed company.

By November, 1959, Messrs. Somer and deSalle no longer were pushing hard for subcontracting work because they were concerned that once work began on the tractors and other new CFIT products, the shop would have trouble handling additional orders. No backlog or machine load data was available, but it seemed clear that the highest priority should be given to their own products rather than subcontracted parts.

As mentioned earlier, the supervisory group was unsure as to the proper burden or overhead rate to use in bidding on subcontracting work. The rate of 900 per cent had been selected recently by Mr. deSalle as more competitive than either the rate of 1,500 per cent used in the past year, or the actual rate of 2,200 per cent which included amortization expenses. Nevertheless, Lecen Bey and Haluk Bey felt that many jobs were still being lost due to price.

Personnel Administration

From the start, Wage and Salary Administration had been troublesome for CFIT managers. Part of the difficulty lay in coping with a "galloping inflation" imposed on a growing organization struggling against financial losses. Another source of problems was the fact that inequities had been permitted to creep into the wage structure during the first three years through a piecemeal approach to wage and salary increases. Men on the same assignment often received widely varying pay, and workers' complaints on this topic had become more and more numerous.

There was no union, and it was not necessary for CFIT to bargain collectively with its workforce. But almost from the start of operations, elected representatives of the hourly workers pressed for wage increases as the cost of living advanced. Every six months the Personnel Manager made a survey of community wage levels. General wage increases of about 10 per cent had been made in November, 1957, June, 1958, and January, 1959. In November, 1959, the workers' representatives again were pressing for another increase and Mr. deSalle felt that CFIT's wage levels had fallen somewhat behind the community's. But in their efforts to hold the line on costs and prices, Messrs. deSalle and Somer were reluctant to give another general increase at this time. The supervisory organization, however, pressed the subject repeatedly. "We are getting much less than we could on the outside," one said. "I was better off in 1954 at 40 per cent of my present salary than I am now," complained another, pointing out that at all salary levels new employees were being brought in at higher rates than present employees were being paid.

There was no formal supervisory job and pay structure but at Mr. deSalle's suggestion, a system had been developed in late 1958 for the hourly workers. A committee of the Personnel Manager, Assistant Production Manager, and Commercial Manager developed a system of job grades, salary ranges, and a merit rating system. Mr. deSalle guided the group closely and the system was accepted and installed January 1, 1959.

Several hourly grades were established and the various jobs were assigned to these grades by using rankings from U.S. textbooks, checked out for reasonableness by the Turkish supervisors. These grades, ranges, and examples of jobs included, were as follows:

Grade		Min.	Max.	Jobs
1	TL/hr.	0.80	1.00	(Not Used)
2		1.03	1.42	Helpers, Ordinary Assemblers, Janitors
3		1.34	1.85	Milling Mach. C, Arc Welder B, Pattern Maker C, General Maintenance
4		1.65	2.28	Lathe Operator C, Bench Work
5		1.96	2.71	Guider B, Arc Welder A, Drill Press, Painter A
6		2.29	3.13	Lathe Operator B, Milling Operator A, Welder A
7		2.60	3.56	Set-up, Lead Man, Pattern Maker A, Tool Inspector

At the time of the installation of the new system, those men who were too low were given raises but those who were too high were not cut. Group meetings were held to explain the system to the workers and their representatives. No serious complaints were received.

The new system included a merit rating plan. A new worker was brought in at the bottom of the appropriate grade. At the end of six months he was automatically given a raise of approximately 10 per cent. After 12 months the merit rating system was applied and his supervisor rated the man in quality, quantity, attitude, cooperation, dependability, and job knowledge. There were five degrees of performance for each of the five above ratings, each with a short description. For example, under job knowledge was listed:

1st degree—Very poor job knowledge, requires constant supervision
2nd degree—Limited job knowledge, requires frequent supervision
3rd degree—Average job knowledge, requires normal supervision
4th degree—Good job knowledge, requires little supervision
5th degree—Excellent job knowledge, requires minimum supervision, can start job himself.

Each degree for each job provided a certain number of points and if the worker received enough points he was given an increase. Two merit increases brought the man to the top of the range. For example, in the 4th grade the sequence was:

Start	TL	1.65 (min.)
Automatically raised after six months to		1.86
1st merit increase to		2.07
2nd merit increase to		2.28 (top)

The exact number of points necessary to gain the first increase was lower than that for the second. These criteria, as well as the formula for point assignments, were not revealed to the supervisors, however, but instead were applied by the Personnel Manager. The reason for this was simply, as Nahit Bey put it, "We are trying to train the supervisors to be strict. They tend to be easy and want to give a raise to every man. Everyone wants to help the workers. They need it. But we try to train our supervisory people to be tough-minded by having meetings, and, well, just by training them. That's the only way." If a man did not receive an increase after a merit rating he was reviewed again in six months. Otherwise the interval for review was twelve months.

There was no regular system of increases for salaried people. They were usually reviewed annually, at the end of the year, and most had received an increase every year.

Some typical monthly salaries were as follows:

Department heads	2,000–3,100	TL/month
Foremen	1,100–1,900	

Engineers	1,700–2,200
Accountants	1,700–2,200
Tool Designers	600–1,200
Draftsmen	600–1,200
Clerical Workers	600– 800

Mr. deSalle had some doubts as to whether his Personnel Manager himself was as tough-minded as he should be. For example, instead of positively turning down the workers' representatives' request for a 45-minute (instead of 30) lunch period, Nahit Bey had brought the question to Mr. deSalle. Similarly, when assigned the job of screening men for assembly lead hand positions, he had referred the candidates to Mr. deSalle. He seemed easily cowed by government officials who occasionally visited the plant, insisting that the company must provide showers, air conditioning, and similar benefits. Mr. deSalle felt that Nahit Bey tended to direct upstairs many decisions that could have been better settled in the Personnel Manager's office. "He hates to say 'No' all by himself," Mr. deSalle concluded.

Plant Expansion Plans

While preparing for immediate increases in activity throughout the plant in terms of new products and tractors, Mr. Somer and Mr. deSalle were also looking ahead to late 1960 and beyond. Basing their plans on producing 2,500 tractors in 1960 and 5,000 in 1961 (including manufacture of 50 per cent of the parts by value) plus sales of pumps, motors, implements, and other new products as discussed above, the new Co-Directors foresaw the need for additional foundry and machine tool capacity.

An estimated $3,861,000 would be required to build a mechanized foundry with a 35-ton daily capacity, adding to the building, and providing about 125 additional machine tools. These plans were felt to be necessary in order to cast large pieces and manufacture the entire tractor to the same extent as California (50 per cent by value), while increasing the volume of their own products. These plans had been approved by the Board of Directors in mid-1959 and an application for the necessary funds ($2,750,000) for purchased items was made to the Development Loan Fund in Washington, D.C. The Turkish Government had approved this application.

In November the negotiations for this loan were at a standstill pending the firming up of production and financial expectations for 1960. The next step was for CFIT to indicate in specific terms, using reliable financial projections, exactly how this loan was to be repaid.

The lack of production promises from California still prevented an accurate forecast of the earnings and schedule picture for 1960. Mr. Somer and Mr. deSalle hoped to begin the plant expansion in the spring of 1960 but recognized that it might take somewhat longer to obtain the DLF loan.

Organization and Administration

At the meeting with the visiting college professors, Mr. deSalle had pointed out to the group that the present organization was less than perfect because, in an effort to economize, a number of the supervisors were undertaking double and triple assignments, assignments which at least on theoretical grounds should probably be separated. He illustrated this by the facts that production and engineering were under one head, that tool design and tool-making were under one person, and that the shop superintendent was in charge of time study as well. He felt that one advantage of such combined assignments was that it lessened the chance that supervisors could make excuses or blame each other for fall-downs. On the other hand, he was concerned because there were no effective balances of power and control, for example, between the shop and time study.

In his daily work with the men in the organization Mr. deSalle liked to be direct and frank. When he saw something wrong in the factory he called the immediate supervisors over and demonstrated what should be done and why. He seldom lost his temper but did not hesitate to show displeasure. "I can even swear at them in English and feel better myself without their being offended!" Most of the shop supervisory people could understand a little English and they seemed to be eager to learn and take directions from Mr. deSalle. He often spent four or five hours a day in the shop area, going from job to job, making decisions and changes on estimates, set-ups, tools, assembly processes and layouts, and so on.

Privately he commented, "I like the Turks and they seem to like me O.K. They sure are impractical though, and even the trade school graduates are only beginners by American standards. The new man just out of the trade school is only 20 per cent as efficient as a U.S. apprentice. After three years they have partially caught up but are still about 25 per cent behind. I've only had one really good mechanic here, in all these years. A man who can visualize the process, be cost conscious, and set up an entire job right is almost nonexistent. Our general foreman, Mustafa Kap, is typical. He has fifteen years of experience, was sent to England once for a year of training, and also to Germany for a year. But he is not good at teaching or training his men. He does not anticipate problems. He is much too easy on his people—on the merit ratings he rated every single person up near the top.

"The really good Turks have three or four irons in the fire and don't give their time and effort fully to any one company. I had to fire one of the few good plant men I've had here because of this.

"I'd like to have another American around here. In this job you need someone you can talk to and relax with. And the problem I have, of course, is that by the time I was appointed to this job there was no one here to draw knowledge from. For instance, if I'd come over originally as General Manager, I'd have had U.S. specialists here who would have helped me to learn fast in any areas I needed help in. As it is now, I have to learn by myself anything I didn't already know when I took the job."

By a natural choice of interests, Mr. deSalle concentrated on engineering and production, while Somer Bey spent the majority of his available time on finance, sales, and government relations. This latter area was demanding, particularly in regard to import permits, allocations of foreign exchange, and relationships with the Board of Directors. Somer Bey expressed full confidence and admiration of Mr. deSalle. "I hope he will stay in Turkey permanently. [Mr. deSalle openly spoke of returning to the U.S. within a year or two, as soon as the company was doing well.] I like his flexibility and his humbleness. We agree on things. He gets along well with people and understands Turks. He does not like to spend his time in the office, especially at meetings. The other Americans? We had some funny people around here. They did not work hard and they let the whole workforce deteriorate. We inherited this."

Somer Bey went on, "A manager must be in a position to make his men work harder. His job is not to be in his office all the whole day. He must get out and listen. A manager must have ten times as many ears as tongues. Hard work, sacrifice, and devotion on the part of the manager is necessary to set an example. The top man must place the organization and results over and above friendship. He must make people happy with pride and satisfaction of accomplishment. Money alone is not an essential factor."

The Co-Directors held a general meeting of department heads about every two weeks, but not on a regular schedule. They kept up-to-date by daily informal discussions with the department heads and talked with each other about problems on which each was working. Both felt free to give orders in any area, and their subordinates discussed problems with either one if the other was out of the plant. Very few written memoranda were used within the plant.

Hamdi Bey and Haluk Bey were outspoken and frank in regard to their feelings on the operation of the plant, past and present. Hamdi Bey, for example, felt considerable pride in his organization and their accomplishments. Of his general foreman, he said, "A first-class man. Technically he is very good. He holds U.S. patents on milling machine fixtures. He is good at supervision of his people and does not accept mistakes from other departments." In regard to inspection, he said, "Our inspection foreman is a trade school graduate with 24 years of experience. He is very good. He worked a year in Germany and is a first-class man. He's particularly good technically, for he was once a chief tool designer. He has three inspectors who check the first parts off a set-up and then check parts at intervals. No, we do not keep any figures on scrap or rework, but the inspectors do bring to our attention any causes of trouble which they observe. Our inspection is keen and prompt and we have had no complaints so far on any of our products. Any problems have always been the fault of the drawings from California.

"The assembly shop foreman, Osman, is not a trade school graduate. He is good and friendly with his people. The men like him and work well with him. He treats well his men and more or less pushes them in a gentle way. He was very successful recently in assembling 50 plows in less than three weeks in spite of missing parts which delayed him."

Of his tool shop foreman he reported, "Kenan is a first-class foreman. He knows his stuff. He is accurate and precise. He is a good supervisor. He is soft with his men, but with his softness he takes care of his business. Tool makers are highly skilled. You can't shout at them. They are like artists."

The press shop foreman, he said, was "a good boss—serious with his men and insists on action."

He called the wood shop foreman "a first-class man. Thirty-five years experience. When there is continuous work they do a good job."

The maintenance foreman was, he said, "a first-class maintenance man. His men work hard."

In an informal meeting in his office with Haluk Bey and Mr. deSalle late in December, 1959, Hamdi Bey discussed the past years. He had been in charge of the plant for MKEK before the CFIT organization took it over. At that time he was hired as Assistant to the Production Manager, Mr. Dowlin. "This [new position] wasn't hard for me at all. I felt that the plant was like my child and I wanted to see it produce efficiently for the benefit of the country. And I was also glad for a chance to learn from Americans. We felt we could learn from them and wanted to, if allowed to be partners. But I was disappointed in how they went at it. They had no idea of Turks or Turkey when they arrived. Back in the U.S. the executives gave their men write-ups of all CFIT procedures and forms and told them to set it up in Turkey the same way. They did not have a real understanding of what they were doing—they just copied California operations. Then the Americans did not really train the Turks and turn over responsibility to them, except for Mr. Kite and Mr. deSalle. The Americans isolated themselves with other Americans both at work and socially, with their own neighborhoods and parties. They didn't even use our knowledge of the government and officials in dealing with them. The Americans here did not know how to make anything in a factory except tractors. We asked for know-how and they gave us know-nothing. We Turks are not fools. We could have helped but we were not consulted or used. We have good experience and are capable engineers. And, as managers, we would have been better than the Americans."

Haluk Bey agreed and added, "We Turks are more adaptable than Americans. They feel there is only one way to do a job. The Americans should have come here being prepared to adapt to and learn from the Turks, ready to learn and discuss and appreciate our thinking and not get upset if we worked differently. Then they would have gotten along and done better. One man even tried to change the way Turkish people go to the toilet. CFIT was a test case of U.S. business in Turkey and its success would have made a big difference. But the idea has lost much prestige here. The whole trouble was the underrating of the Turkish personnel."

Hamdi Bey went on, "We have no organization at present. It needs to be restudied and reorganized. But we have made great accomplishments in CFIT in the last six months. We have good cooperation and spirit starting at the very top. Team work has been formed. Before, every department was a different company. Now we consult with each other. There is an increase in morale in the workers, too. And we are getting close to making a profit."

Mr. deSalle, who had been present during this discussion, concluded, "November should be our first profitable month in four years. The year 1960 looks like the year when we can make CFIT successful and profitable. If we don't make it this year, we're through."

Osaka Sharin Seizo K.K.

Osaka Sharin Seizo K.K. is an independent supplier of wheels and rear-axle casings to the Japanese automobile industry. In 1960, annual sales were almost ¥1,000 million,[1] about equally divided between wheels and axle casings. Average employment during the year was about 225 workers. During 1960, the company produced over 330,000 wheels, of which 95 per cent were small wheels for passenger cars at an average price of ¥1,370 and 5 per cent were large truck wheels at an average price of ¥5,800 each. The company also produced 171,000 axle casings during the year, at an average price of ¥2,790 each.

In the late 1950's, the company's growth had been very rapid. Between 1956 and 1961 sales volume had doubled. Total assets, fixed assets, and capital had also doubled during this period. Balance sheets, operating statements, and other operating figures are contained in Exhibits 1 to 4.

The profitable company had achieved expansion largely through reinvestment of earnings. In 1961, only 5 per cent of its total invested capital represented long-term debt and company policy discouraged debt of any kind. However, in order to meet the requirements of increased business and to reduce manufacturing costs, Yoshitaro Senda, President of the Osaka Sharin Seizo K.K., was considering whether to undertake a plant modernization program. The plan under consideration involved expenditures of ¥12 million for a new oil-actuated stamping press to speed up the formation of large axle casings and ¥68 million for a new plant to house all operations on the small casings after initial press work.

---

[1] Three hundred and sixty yen are equal to one U.S. dollar.

This case was prepared by Professors Ichiro Kataoka and Stanley S. Miller for Keio Business School, Keio University, Tokyo, as a basis for class discussion.

EXHIBIT 1 OSAKA SHARIN SEIZO K.K.

BALANCE SHEETS 1955–1961

(as of Sept. 30 each year)   (in millions of Yen)

	(30) 1955 9/30	(31) 1956 9/30	(32) 1957 9/30	(33) 1958 9/30	(34) 1959 9/30	(35) 1960 9/30	(36)* 1961 3/31
CURRENT ASSETS	198.1	294.0	337.9	332.2	370.8	513.1	626.2
Deposits and Cash	34.8	43.4	46.2	65.6	59.0	74.1	122.6
Bills Receivable	8.5	39.3	64.1	49.3	67.6	65.5	165.2
Accounts Receivable	115.9	127.8	143.0	153.8	163.0	258.6	241.6
Other	38.9	84.5	84.6	63.5	81.2	114.9	96.8
FIXED ASSETS	65.0	64.6	74.2	89.5	94.6	139.6	142.8
Building	13.3	13.8	14.0	14.1	19.2	25.1	30.1
Machinery	32.2	29.6	31.9	51.7	48.5	56.6	73.0
Wheels and Tools for Transportation	1.9	1.8	1.2	.7	1.9	3.3	2.3
Tools and Parts	.3	.3	6.3	5.2	5.6	6.0	6.7
Land	17.0	17.0	17.0	16.0	16.0	16.0	16.0
Suspense Account for Construction	—	2.0	3.7	1.6	3.5	24.7	6.0
Investment	.3	—	—	—	—	8.0	8.5
TOTAL	263.2	358.7	412.1	421.7	465.4	652.7	769.0
CURRENT LIABILITIES	79.7	126.0	112.5	89.1	96.3	240.0	236.6
Accounts Payable	58.6	69.8	90.0	76.9	83.1	127.6	134.5
Short-Term Debts	20.0	20.0	20.0	10.0	10.0	25.0	20.0
Other	1.1	36.2	2.5	2.2	3.2	88.0	82.1
FIXED LIABILITIES	—	—	—	—	—	5.0	15.3
Long-Term Debts	—	—	—	—	—	—	10.0
Deposit Guarantee	—	—	—	—	—	.5	.5
Retirement Fund	—	—	—	—	—	4.5	4.8
Capital	50.0	75.0	120.0	120.0	120.0	150.0	225.0
Capital Surplus	41.3	27.9	20.4	20.2	20.0	15.3	15.7
Earned Surplus	88.0	120.4	155.5	179.7	212.8	242.5	276.5
TOTAL	263.2	358.7	412.1	421.7	465.4	652.7	769.0

NOTE: Three hundred and sixty yen equal one U.S. dollar.

* Year of Showa, Japanese calendar.

EXHIBIT 2 OSAKA SHARIN SEIZO K.K.

PROFIT AND LOSS STATEMENTS, 1955–1961

(6 months periods) (in millions of Yen)

Period Endings	1955		1956		1957		1958		1959		1960		1961
	3/31	9/30	3/31	9/30	3/31	9/30	3/31	9/30	3/31	9/30	3/31	9/30	3/31
Net Sales	157.3	141.3	163.5	219.9	317.3	256.3	260.3	229.5	227.4	266.7	390.8	476.0	510.9
Other Income	.2	.8	2.6	.5	7.0	2.5	5.0	6.8	1.3	2.3	1.4	8.1	10.7
Total	157.5	142.1	166.1	220.4	324.3	258.8	265.3	236.3	228.7	269.0	392.2	484.1	521.6
Cost of Sales	101.5	95.9	114.3	161.2	246.8	193.0	196.0	168.7	163.8	190.0	290.5	323.4	374.6
Overhead	9.7	9.3	9.5	12.2	12.2	12.8	14.6	15.1	13.9	17.4	21.3	28.0	32.1
Other Expenses	7.2	8.2	9.2	6.8	8.6	10.0	13.0	13.0	8.5	11.5	11.3	86.9	66.0
Profit	39.1	28.6	33.0	40.2	56.6	43.0	41.6	39.6	42.6	50.0	69.0	45.7	49.0
Major Application of Profit													
Reserve for Profit	4.0	3.0	3.0	3.0	4.0	3.0	3.0	3.0	3.0	3.0	3.0	3.0	3.0
Reserve for Tax	21.0	11.0	15.0	19.0	28.0	15.0	16.0	17.0	18.5	23.0	37.0	—	—
Dividend	6.3	6.3	6.3	7.8	8.6	9.8	12.0	10.8	10.8	10.8	11.3	13.5	15.2
Executive Bonus	1.1	1.1	1.1	1.2	1.2	1.2	1.2	1.2	1.2	1.5	1.5	1.5	1.8
Retirement Fund	1.0	1.0	1.0	1.0	1.0	1.0	1.0	—	—	—	—	—	—
Special Reserve	6.0	6.0	7.0	8.0	14.0	13.0	9.0	5.0	7.0	10.0	15.0	24.0	26.0
Reserve for Dividend	—	—	—	—	—	—	—	2.0	2.0	2.0	2.0	3.0	3.0
Total	39.4	28.4	33.4	40.2	56.8	43.0	42.2	39.6	42.5	50.3	69.8	45.0	49.0

EXHIBIT 3A Osaka Sharin Seizo K.K.

SALES AND PRODUCTION BY PRODUCT LINE

	Output (in thousands of units)			Sales (in millions of Yen)		
Year	Small Wheels	Large Wheels	Casings	Small Wheels	Large Wheels	Casings
1955b	45.4	8.4	6.1	115.1	26.4	21.6
1956a	50.9	20.1	5.8	129.3	66.0	21.3
1956b	60.0	25.9	10.5	177.1	86.9	45.2
1957a	42.2	11.9	14.5	132.4	51.3	63.6
1957b	44.9	7.9	25.2	120.9	39.7	94.7
1958a	41.7	11.0	15.2	108.5	56.2	57.2
1958b	51.2	10.3	17.5	119.5	48.5	54.3
1959a	58.1	10.6	30.7	113.7	53.2	98.1
1959b	69.5	9.6	62.6	158.8	44.0	185.3
1960a	146.3	7.9	81.0	200.8	45.8	225.9
1960b 1961a	—180—		90.0	—250—		260.0

a = April 1 to September 30.
b = October 1 to March 31.

EXHIBIT 3B Work Force

Workers	1958a	1958b	1959a	1959b
Office (Men)	10	10	9	9
Office (Women)	6	6	8	8
Engineers	5	6	6	7
Plant Workers	116	115	128	151
Total	137	137	151	175

EXHIBIT 3C 1960 Work Status

Workers	No.	Average Age	Years Employed	Month Wages (Yen)
PERMANENT				
Office Men	23	36.8	5.7	42,325
Office Women	9	27.3	4.8	15,090
Plant Men	77	38.8	7.4	48,202
Total	109	35.5	6.9	44,228
TEMPORARY				
Men	93	32.3	—	13,657
Women	29	38.2	—	8,800
Total	122	33.7	—	12,500

EXHIBIT 4 Osaka Sharin Seizo K.K.

COMPARATIVE FINANCIAL DATA
(in millions of Yen)

1. OSAKA SHARIN

Year	Sales	Fixed Assets	Debt	Capital	Profit
1955	298	65	0	179	68
1956	383	65	0	222	73
1957	573	74	0	295	100
1958	489	89	0	319	82
1959	594	95	0	353	93
1960	876	140	0	408	112

2. SHARIN KOGYO K.K.

Sales	Fixed Assets	Debt	Capital	Profit
998	434	56	250	82
—	—	—	—	—
—	—	—	—	—
—	—	—	—	—
1,835	1,047	76	1,150	241
2,730	1,126	76	1,223	283

3. PRESS KOGYO

Year	Sales	Fixed Assets	Debt	Capital	Profit
1955	—	—	—	—	—
1956	—	—	—	—	—
1957	—	—	—	—	—
1958	2,337	735	252	1,035	140
1959	2,517	1,129	283	1,275	162
1960	3,858	1,724	489	1,356	209

4. ZENKOKU JIDOSHA

Sales	Fixed Assets	Debt	Capital	Profit
—	—	—	—	—
—	3,233	560	4,171	—
18,647	4,005	750	4,423	874
16,745	5,082	1,450	5,759	1,004
22,038	7,924	5,270	8,523	1,745
45,068	14,904	9,759	14,492	3,879

5. AOYAMA

Year	Sales	Fixed Assets	Debt	Capital	Profit
1955	14,199	5,641	1,861	6,700	972
1956	21,403	6,410	2,200	8,034	1,688
1957	39,193	9,735	2,257	11,199	3,199
1958	36,931	11,012	3,815	14,136	2,494
1959	45,469	10,779	4,914	15,972	4,024
1960	68,072	13,795	8,887	18,753	6,318

6. MUSASHINO

Sales	Fixed Assets	Debt	Capital	Profit
—	—	—	—	—
31,677	5,197	1,297	9,083	2,950
53,129	8,403	1,833	11,142	4,777
51,241	11,302	2,977	15,848	4,580
71,205	16,184	4,574	18,866	7,192
—	—	—	—	—

7. KAWAGUCHI

Year	Sales	Fixed Assets	Debt	Capital	Profit
1955	—	—	—	—	—
1956	—	—	—	—	—
1957	—	2,322	818	3,523	—
1958	—	2,656	917	4,472	—
1959	21,327	2,919	1,093	6,322	1,730
1960	32,711	5,235	1,987	10,540	2,758

8. SANSHIN

Sales	Fixed Assets	Debt	Capital	Profit
—	—	—	—	—
2,557	342	0	775	125
—	405	0	844	—
5,228	426	0	941	272
6,107	644	60	1,293	379
—	—	—	—	—

HISTORY OF THE COMPANY

The original manufacturing company was organized in 1919 by Mr. Senda's father. Its principal products during the 1920's and 1930's were fabricated metal parts for office and factory buildings. The company used its stamping presses, machine tools, and welding and grinding tools to cut, shape, and weld metal parts for various kinds of metal structures desired by the building contractors whom it serviced.

In 1935 the company added the manufacture of wheels for the automobile industry, most of which were heavy, large-sized wheels for trucks. The wheel business required more stamping presses and welding machines and the product was more standard than those of the metal-fabricating business. However, every attempt was made to adapt existing machines and equipment to the new business in order to avoid the heavy capital costs usually incurred by mass production factories.

The company merged with the Sharin Kogyo K.K. of Tokyo in 1939, to form a single large enterprise for the manufacture of wheels. Although profits were combined, the two enterprises remained largely independent in their actual operations. The Osaka Division continued to manage its own affairs under the supervision of the Senda family, with many of its customers located in the region south and west of Tokyo, where the company had established its reputation.

In March, 1953, the two companies separated again and Mr. Senda became the President of the independent company for which he had previously been responsible as Divisional Manager. In 1961 Mr. Senda personally owned 49,554 shares of common stock of the new company, Osaka Sharin Zeizo K.K., and was its largest single shareholder. There were 450,000 common shares outstanding, at a par value of ¥500 each.

When Osaka Sharin Seizo became independent in 1953, it obtained the Zenkoku Jidosha K.K. as its special customer for wheels. The Zenkoku company was an important manufacturer of small three-wheeled trucks, and this market was expanding. By about 1958 there was a trend toward small four-wheeled trucks, which increased the demand for wheels.

Osaka Sharin began to make rear-axle casings for Zenkoku Jidosha in 1957. They were made in a large size for the big trucks and in a small size for the smaller three- and four-wheeled trucks. At first, Osaka Sharin merely pressed the two halves of the casings and welded them together. After 1959, the company obtained orders that required additional work on the small casings. This additional work involved the attaching of small parts, the machining of ends and center section on lathes, and the drilling of holes in the center plate in order to complete the casing for final assembly in the automobile plant.

In 1959 the Zenkoku Jidosha K.K. began making automobiles that used the same small axle as in its small trucks; demand for small casings increased further. Although the axle casings had accounted for only 14 per cent of the Osaka Sharin company's total sales in the first half of 1957, it had expanded to 51 per cent by the first half of 1961. Of the Osaka Sharin company's total sales in 1961, 85 per cent went to Zenkoku Jidosha, 10 per cent to Kawaguchi Jidosha, and 2.5 per cent each to Sanshin and Meiji.

Only 10 per cent of the company's products were sold through agents. These were for the replacement of automobile parts. None of the casings was sold through agents. Most of the product was thus sold through original equipment contacts and delivered directly to the automobile assembly plants. The prices for products were determined largely by the automobile companies, and negotiations were allowed only in case of an increase in the price of steel. Each automobile company issued a general production plan four or five months in advance and a more detailed one a month in advance. Only 30 per cent of the price was paid in cash. The remaining 70 per cent was in promissory notes.

In 1961 the prospect of the approaching trade liberalization agreement promised to bring lower-priced foreign automobiles into Japan under reduced tariffs. It was therefore necessary to make major cost reductions throughout the Japanese automobile industry despite the gradual increases in the price of steel. Mr. Senda was considering the possibility of issuing 270,000 new stock shares as a means of obtaining the capital necessary to undertake plant modernization programs. In addition, he was interested in obtaining increased sales from other companies in order to reduce the dependence on Zenkoku Jidosha from 85 per cent to 50 per cent of his company's sales. Actually, he was about to sign a contract with Kawaguchi Jidosha that would increase the sale of casings to it by one or two thousand units per month by October.

EXISTING MANUFACTURING OPERATIONS IN 1961

In 1961 the plant facilities of the Osaka Sharin Seizo consisted of 12 main buildings averaging from 300 to 650 square meters each, plus some smaller sheds and outbuildings (Exhibit 5). Four of the largest buildings, of 650 square meters each, and two others totaling 680 square meters, were used for wheel production. These buildings were adjacent to each other and allowed for movement of materials directly from building to building. The buildings used to make rear-axle casings consisted of three units of 550 square meters each and one irregular U-shaped unit of about 950 square meters at a separate location across the street. In addition, there was a machine shop and a painting plant which serviced both wheels and casings, and a two-story office building for executive offices and accounting and other departments. The major manufacturing operations used in the plant centered around pressing and welding.

In order to cut and form identical metal shapes, stamping presses were used extensively. A stamping press contains two halves of a die which are closed together upon a metal sheet. The upper half of the die is brought down by electric motor power to cut or shape the metal sheet lying on the lower die. The operator inserts the metal sheet, actuates the press, and removes the shaped piece.

The welding together of metal pieces may be accomplished manually with a hand welder or in an automatic welding machine. The welding machines are quite expensive, however, and are feasible only for very long production runs of identical parts.

Although the manufacture of wheels and casings are similar in that they both require presses to stamp sheet metal into special shapes, welding and grinding tools to join the shapes together, and cleaning and painting ovens to finish them, there are many differences in the actual production facilities for the two products.

Manufacture of Wheels

In the manufacturing of wheels, a large number of presses are required to roll the metal strips into rims, shape the disks, and press the completed wheels into proper shape. The large truck wheels require heavy presses to shape the broad gauge metal used. In 1956, truck wheels had accounted for 23 per cent of the wheel output, and the company therefore had many large presses available, although the truck wheels had since declined to 5 per cent of the total wheel

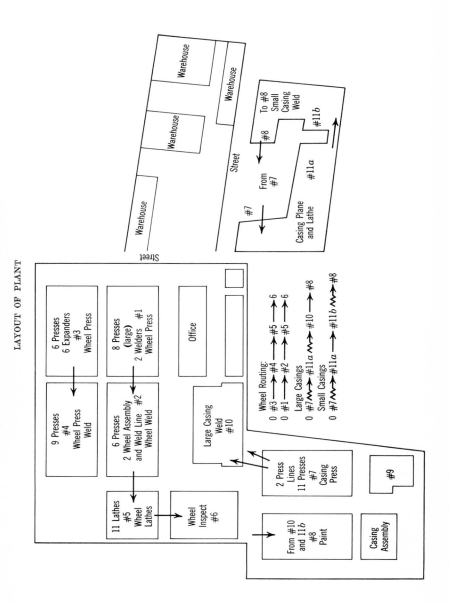

EXHIBIT 5 OSAKA SHARIN SEIZO K.K.

LAYOUT OF PLANT

production. About 70 presses of various kinds were used in wheel production, in addition to about 10 welding machines. The wheel shapes were stacked by each press and welding machine in large numbers, so that the machine could proceed at its own pace without waiting for material to be brought over. However, some presses were linked together by roller conveyors so that the output of one machine could be fed directly to the next. Fork trucks and hand trucks were used to bring material to the presses, but a conveyor had been installed for small wheels in the final stages of painting and inspection.

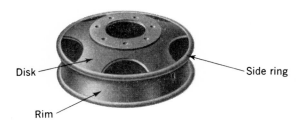

Disk — Side ring

Rim

The operations sequence used in the manufacture of wheels is presented in Exhibit 6 and photographs of the operation appear in Exhibit 7. Side rings were used only for truck wheels. Automobile wheels were manufactured by welding rims and disks together.

The rims were made from metal strips which were passed between two heavy rolls to curl them into a circular shape (Exhibit 7). The two ends were then cut straight, brought together, and welded in a large automatic welding machine. Next the circular rim was deburred, ground smooth, and made truly round in expansion presses and stamping presses. Finally, a hole was cut for the tube valve and the rim was marked and inspected.

The inside disk was made of heavier gauge metal than the rim and required small size, but heavier presses. The disk blank was cut round and pressed several times to obtain its shape before the valve hole was cut and the result was inspected. The disk was then pressed into the rim, aligned, and riveted together. The completed wheel was brought to the painting booths and moved through them on overhead hook conveyors.

Since the annual output of wheels was quite high, the Osaka Sharin company had found it useful to install certain kinds of equipment to speed up the process and reduce hand labor. For example, several automatic welding machines were used to weld the ends of the rims and side rings together into a circle, and a hook conveyor carried the

EXHIBIT 6   OSAKA SHARIN SEIZO K.K.

OPERATION SEQUENCE: WHEELS

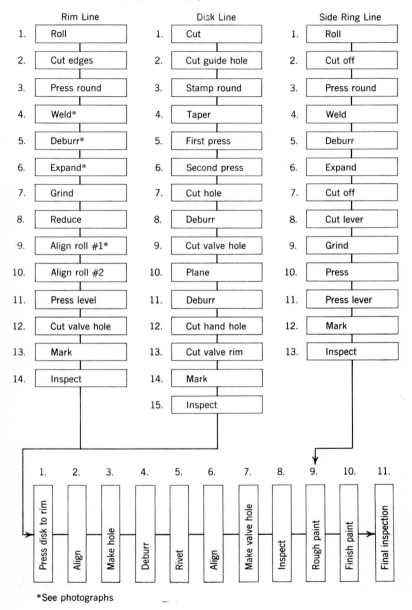

	Rim Line		Disk Line		Side Ring Line
1.	Roll	1.	Cut	1.	Roll
2.	Cut edges	2.	Cut guide hole	2.	Cut off
3.	Press round	3.	Stamp round	3.	Press round
4.	Weld*	4.	Taper	4.	Weld
5.	Deburr*	5.	First press	5.	Deburr
6.	Expand*	6.	Second press	6.	Expand
7.	Grind	7.	Cut hole	7.	Cut off
8.	Reduce	8.	Deburr	8.	Cut lever
9.	Align roll #1*	9.	Cut valve hole	9.	Grind
10.	Align roll #2	10.	Plane	10.	Press
11.	Press level	11.	Deburr	11.	Press lever
12.	Cut valve hole	12.	Cut hand hole	12.	Mark
13.	Mark	13.	Cut valve rim	13.	Inspect
14.	Inspect	14.	Mark		
		15.	Inspect		

1. Press disk to rim
2. Align
3. Make hole
4. Deburr
5. Rivet
6. Align
7. Make valve hole
8. Inspect
9. Rough paint
10. Finish paint
11. Final inspection

*See photographs

EXHIBIT 7 Osaka Sharin Seizo K.K.

PHOTOGRAPHS OF WHEEL OPERATIONS

Photographs 1 and 2: Rolling the Rims

The strips of metal to the right of Photograph 1 are being fed into the rolling press. Photograph 2 is a close-up of a rolling press showing the metal strip being curled into a circle by the turning roll.

EXHIBIT 7 *(Continued)* OSAKA SHARIN SEIZO K.K.

Photograph 3: Welding the Rims

The sparks of flame coming from the machine in the background are caused by the automatic welding of the two ends of the rim to make a complete circle. The machine in the foreground is taking the burr off the seam made by the weld.

Photograph 4: Aligning the Rims

The presses at the left are used to expand and shape the welded rim into a true circle. The Production Manager is standing to the right.

assembled wheels through the paint booth. Fifty-seven workers executed direct labor operations in the manufacture of wheels.

Manufacture of Casings

In the manufacture of casings fewer presses are required, but more welding, grinding, machining, and alignment is necessary to assemble the entire axle casing. At the time more hand labor was used. About ten presses were needed to shape the two halves of the axle casing into "U" forms with a deep bend in the middle to hold the differential gears of the automobile. Before the two halves could be welded together to form a cylinder, however, the edges to be welded had to be machined smooth by a planer. These edges were fairly long and required much hand welding to be joined together. A triangular metal section was also welded into the place where the two halves met at the center disk. Much spot welding and hand grinding were necessary to smooth the welded surfaces. A round cap was then attached to the middle on one side, a disk to the other, and various brackets were welded to the ends and the cylinder surfaces. Both the ends and the disk surface had to be machined smooth on lathes, and ten holes had to be tapped in the surface of the disk. Furthermore, the whole axle casing had to be aligned and tested before final cleaning and painting. As a result of these processes, the manufacture of casings was dominated by assembly operations, whereas wheel production was dominated by the stamping presses. The wheels required capital investment in heavy presses and large welding machines; the casings could be made on simpler machines, but required more workers to weld, grind, assemble, machine, and align the products.

The operations sequence used in the manufacture of casings is shown in Exhibit 8 and photographs of the operations are to be seen in Exhibits 9, 10, and 11. Operations 1 to 10 were carried out in Building 7 where the casing presses were located. Then the casings were moved across the street to Building 11a where the edges were planed smooth so that the two halves could be welded together. The small casings were welded and aligned and parts were attached in Building 11b and then the ends and center were machined smooth on lathes in Building 11a. Next the small casings were brought across the street again to Building 8 where they were painted. The edges of the large casings were planed smooth in Building 11a, then welded and aligned in Building 10, and painted in Building 8. The large casings, unlike the small casings, did not require parts to be attached and were not machined smooth on lathes after having been welded into cylinder shape.

EXHIBIT 8 Osaka Sharin Seizo K.K.

OPERATION SEQUENCE: REAR AXLE CASING

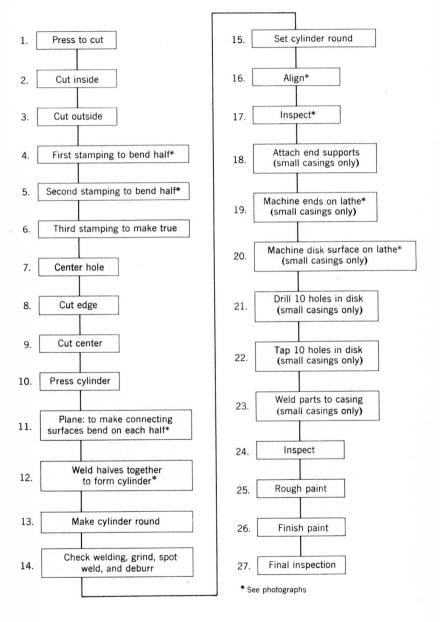

1. Press to cut

2. Cut inside

3. Cut outside

4. First stamping to bend half*

5. Second stamping to bend half*

6. Third stamping to make true

7. Center hole

8. Cut edge

9. Cut center

10. Press cylinder

11. Plane: to make connecting surfaces bend on each half*

12. Weld halves together to form cylinder*

13. Make cylinder round

14. Check welding, grind, spot weld, and deburr

15. Set cylinder round

16. Align*

17. Inspect*

18. Attach end supports (small casings only)

19. Machine ends on lathe* (small casings only)

20. Machine disk surface on lathe* (small casings only)

21. Drill 10 holes in disk (small casings only)

22. Tap 10 holes in disk (small casings only)

23. Weld parts to casing (small casings only)

24. Inspect

25. Rough paint

26. Finish paint

27. Final inspection

* See photographs

EXHIBIT 9   OSAKA SHARIN SEIZO K.K.

PHOTOGRAPHS OF CASING OPERATIONS

Photographs 1 and 2: Pressing the Casing Halves

The straight strip of metal can be seen in Photograph 1 before the top half of the die comes down to press it into the shape of a half casing. The finished halves can be seen stacked in front of the press in Photograph 2.

EXHIBIT 9 (*Continued*)   OSAKA SHARIN SEIZO K.K.

Photographs 3 and 4: Planing the Casing Halves

The edges of the casing halves must be planed smooth to allow a smooth weld to be made when joining them together into a tube.   In Photograph 3, the operator is adjusting the casing halves in the fixture.   In Photograph 4 the cutting tool is smoothing the edges.

EXHIBIT 10   OSAKA SHARIN SEIZO K.K.

PHOTOGRAPHS OF CASING OPERATIONS

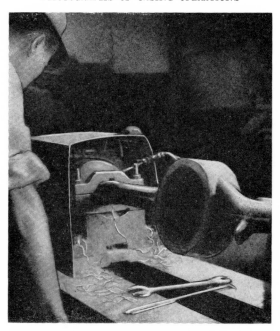

Photographs 1 and 2: The End Lathe

The welded casings must be machined smooth on ends and center disk surface. The ends are machined on the lathe shown here being set up by the operator.

EXHIBIT 10 (*Continued*) OSAKA SHARIN SEIZO K.K.

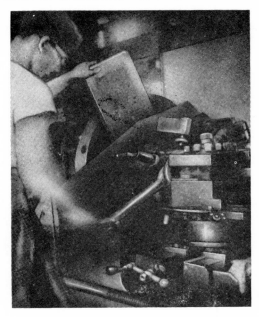

Photographs 3 and 4: The Disk Surface Lathe

A larger lathe is needed to hold the casing across the bed as it turns to enable the cutting tool to smooth the surface of the center disk.

EXHIBIT 11 Osaka Sharin Seizo K.K.

PHOTOGRAPHS OF CASING OPERATIONS

Photographs 1 and 2: Welding and Grinding

The worker in Photograph 1 is using an arc welder to join together the halves of the casing and insert a triangular piece of steel near the center disk. The worker in Photograph 2 is using an electric-driven hand grinder to smooth out the joint made by the weld.

EXHIBIT 11 (*Continued*)   OSAKA SHARIN SEIZO K.K.

Photographs 3 and 4: Alignment and Inspection

The worker in Photograph 3 is correcting a slight curvature of the casing shaft. The workers in Photograph 4 are measuring and aligning the casings before they have been machined on the lathes.

Because of the long edges that had to be joined together to make a casing cylinder and the small parts that had to be attached, there was much need for planing, lathe work, and hand welding in the manufacture of casings. Eighty-two workers were engaged in the direct labor of making casings, not including those assigned to carry parts between plant buildings. As the volume of orders increased, there were times when the work piled up near the two end-lathes and at the painting booths.

When axles had first been made by Osaka Sharin, it was not difficult to adapt the existing plant and equipment to make them. Existing wheel presses were used by inserting new dies in them to make the casings; existing lathes and planers were used to machine the surface joints, the disk surface, and the end plates; existing painting facilities were used jointly with the wheels, and a variety of simple hand tools were used to weld, grind, buff, and align the assembly. However, the increase in unit volume began to make the original adaptation of production facilities appear obsolescent.

GENERAL PLANS

Mr. Senda was pleased by the continual growth of the company and its sound financial position. He was also pleased by the close association with Zenkoku Jidosha, but wished to increase orders for axle casings from other companies in order to avoid, as we have noted, excessive dependence on any one customer. He therefore sought increased orders from Sanshin and other companies. As a result of these orders, and the continuing growth of Zenkoku Jidosha, the production plans for 1962 called for 15,000 small and 10,000 large casings per month, compared to the 11,000 small and 10,000 large casings being produced per month in 1961.

These market expansion plans raised the question of capital investment to increase plant output and reduce production costs. Mr. Senda believed that about 10 per cent of the direct labor cost of making casings was due to the need to move them back and forth between buildings. In order to reduce such transfer costs, a new building would have to be built, at a cost of about ¥20,000 per square meter, using existing land in the plant area. A high speed painting oven would cost ¥5 million, and semiautomatic welding presses ¥15 million. A new stamping press to speed up the bending of large casings would cost ¥12 million. A machine to weld the disk and cap to the small casings would cost ¥10 million. A new end-lathe would cost less than ¥3 million.

Mr. Senda had to decide how much modernization the company should undertake. The present buildings and machinery and tools were valued on the balance sheet at ¥112 million in March, 1961.

As he saw it, there were four main courses:

1. Make no major investment in plant modernization, but allocate larger amounts for maintenance and repair. This would avoid wasteful spending, avoid the need for any debt, and maintain a conservative equipment program in view of the heavy dependence on one customer.
2. Make major investments in the small and large casing operations. These could vary between ¥80 million and ¥200 million, depending on whether fully automatic welding machines were acquired.
3. Make major investments in the wheel operations to establish a full conveyor system in the plant and obtain faster presses.
4. Build a new plant in a different location, in order to obtain the efficiencies of modern facilities for welding, painting, and inspection. This would cost about ¥1,000 million.

EXISTING SMALL CASING OPERATIONS

The existing operations to make small axle casings had recently been analyzed by a young engineer. He made time studies of each of the 56 operations in the six main processes involved in the manufacture of small axle casings. His analysis of these operations is included in Exhibit 12. The following is a summary of his findings:

"The times in the chart," he reported, "represent the period in which one operation is completed. In planing to level the edges, 58 seconds stands for the time required to machine one casing, that is, two halves. Even taking this fact into consideration, the process takes too much time. Welding the temporary body assembly and the final body welding takes much more than the 65.2 seconds average time for assembly; but actually the workers get much assistance from others in nearby positions, which enables them to keep up most of the time.

"In studying these processes, I felt strongly the necessity of determining standard times for the processes. There are too many individual differences in welding. These differences are not caused by differences in the capacity of the worker, but rather in the care with which he performs the work. Quality standards should therefore be determined. It is necessary to purchase a new machine for the end-lathe operation to eliminate a bottleneck.

EXHIBIT 12 Osaka Sharin Seizo K.K.

TIME-STUDY ANALYSIS OF SMALL CASINGS PROCESS

Process	Time (in seconds)	No. of Workers	No. of Machines Used	Comments
PRESS				
1. Cut	23	2	1	
2. Press to shape	36	2	1	Transport from 2–3 by
3. Remove burr	30	1	1	roller conveyor
4. Cut breather hole	7	1	1	
5. Cut drain hole	7.5		1	Transport to next process—by truck
PLANING				
1. Level edges	58	1	1	Processes 1 and 2 are the
2. Level edges	69.5	2	1	same operation done by
3. In plate weld	37		1	different machines
WELDING ASSEMBLY				
1. Temporary breather assembly	12	1	1	
2. Temporary body assembly	240	2	1	
3. Weld rear patch	61	1	1	
4. Weld body	93	1	1	4-main weld
5. Weld body	270	3	3	Welding the rest
6. Grind	113	2	2	
7. Press carrier surface	42	1	1	
8. Weld breather and drain	75	1	1	
9. Temporary cap set	45	1	1	
10. Weld cap	69	1	1	
11. Wire buff	30	1	1	
12. Complete grind	58	1	1	
13. Adjust edges	66	2	1	
Total for Setting Parts	1,442	28	24	Outside Order
ALIGNMENT				
1. Correct warp	23.6	2	2	1 and 2 differ
2. Correct warp	13.8	2	2	
3. Deburr	55	4	4	3, 4, and 5 differ
4. Deburr	249.0	8		
5. Deburr	34	2	2	
6. Adjust sides	77	2	2	
7. Adjust base height	69.8	2	2	
8. Dewarp	20.8	2	2	
9. Check warp	31.6	2	2	9, 10, and 11 jobs di-
10. Adjust breather hole	12	2		vided among 3 people
11. Check measure	7	2		without any clear spe-
12. Pounding	49.3	2		cialization among them

EXHIBIT 12 (*Continued*)   Osaka Sharin Seizo K.K.

TIME-STUDY ANALYSIS OF SMALL CASINGS PROCESS

Process	Time (in seconds)	No. of Workers	No. of Machines Used	Comments
MACHINING				
1. End lathe	142	2	2	
2. Lathe cutting	321.5	7	7	
3. Hole cutting ⎫ 4. Surface ⎬	37.5	1	1	
5. Cutting	109.1	3	3	
6. Return drain	97.5	2	2	
7. Drain hole clean and check	32	2	2	
8. Oil	10	1	1	
9. Hub set	36.2	1	1	
10. Weld hub	35	1	1	
11. Weld support plate	34.8	1	1	
12. Deburr	52.0	2	2	
INSPECTION				
1. Warp in welded hub ⎫ 2. Screw and angle ⎬ 3. Holder height ⎭	63.1	1		
4. Height of carrier surface, etc.	88.7	1		
TOTAL	3,144.3	85	56	
(not including paint and transport)				

Process	Operations	Workers	Purpose	Total Time (in seconds)	Average Time per Worker
1. Press	5	7	To stamp the halves of the casings into tube shape.	103.5	14.8
2. Planing	3	3	To machine the surfaces of the casings in preparation for welding them together.	164.5	54.8
3. Assembly	13	18	To weld and grind the two halves of the casings together; to weld and grind all other parts assembled to the casing.	1,174.0	65.2
4. Alignment	12	32	To make the casing straight and line up in accordance with quality requirements.	642.9	20.1
5. Machining	12	23	To machine edge on end-lathe, and machine and tap holes in center plate.	970.7	42.2
6. Inspection	11	2	To clean, paint, and inspect finished casing.	88.7	44.4
Total	56	85		3,144.3	36.9

EXHIBIT 13   OSAKA SHARIN SEIZO K.K.

LOCATION OF CASING PLANTS

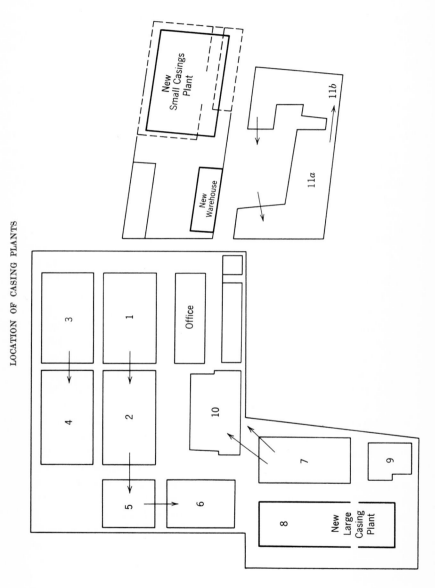

"Materials movement is not considered sufficiently in this plant. Conveyors should be investigated. I estimate that an additional 93.7 seconds is required to transport parts between plants. The plants should be arranged with some system. Nobody has a specific time allowance, so workers are concentrating on whatever process happens to be the bottleneck. People are still *using* machines at this plant; the situation should be reversed."

Mr. Senda found this analysis interesting and useful. However, he believed that the time taken in transporting material between buildings was closer to 320 seconds than to 93 seconds per piece, and he believed that much of the improvement could be achieved by building a single new plant for small casings, using roller conveyors, systematic welding methods, and a high-speed painting oven. The modernization plan called for the expenditure of ¥68 million for such a plant.

PROPOSED SMALL CASINGS PLANT

If the new project were approved, a new casings plant would be built in the warehouse area across the street from the main plant buildings and near the existing casing assembly area (Exhibit 13). The new plant would be 45½ meters by 28 meters, or 1,274 square meters in area, and cost ¥25 million. This cost, however, would also include removal of the present buildings and construction of a small warehouse, and also a dining hall for the workers.

The layout for the new casing plant is shown in Exhibit 14. It would include all operations subsequent to the initial press work, which was to remain in Building 7. These operations were planing, welding, assembly, alignment, machining, inspection, and painting. The new building was designed to obtain a systematic straight-line flow of work, using roller conveyors which would carry the casings to the planers, then from the planers between two lines of workers who would pick up the casings, work on them at their position, and return them to the line. These operations included the 25 operations of welding assembly and alignment that had to be done between the planing and the lathe work. Of these operations, 21 were to be carried out in two positions, one on each side of the line, so that each man could spend twice the cycle time by working on every other casing. Two other operations—grinding and chipping—were to be carried out in four positions each, two on each side of the line, so that each man could spend four times the cycle time on each casing. Most of the

EXHIBIT 14   Osaka

EXISTING LAYOUT,

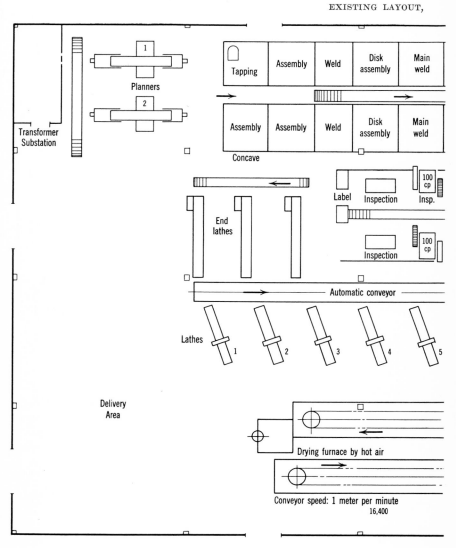

Sharin Seizo K.K.

Large Casings Plant

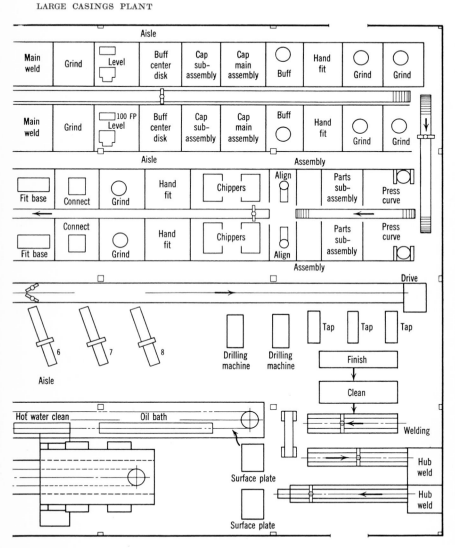

EXHIBIT 15 Osaka

PROPOSED LAYOUT,

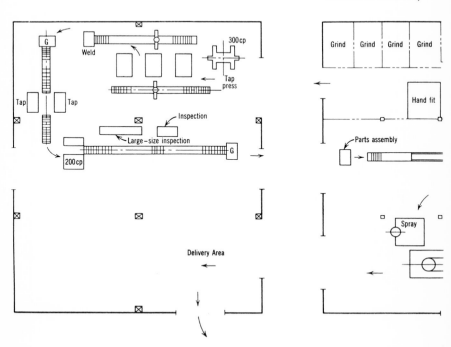

supporting work tools, such as welding tanks and electric motors for the grinders, were to be located *above* the work area so that the worker could pull down the hand tool from above and have adequate work area while still staying close to the conveyor.

In addition to the conveyor and an additional planer, the major items of capital equipment were to be a new painting oven and some semiautomatic welding machines. The new painting facilities included a booth to clean the casings, spray booths, and a force-air oven to dry the paint quickly. Hook conveyors would carry the casings through these facilities at one meter per minute, with the hooks spaced three-quarters of a meter apart. The total cost to install conveyors and paint ovens would be about ¥15 million.

Mr. Senda would have liked to install fully automatic welding presses. However, the price of such equipment was over ¥170 million and he considered this too high for the unit volume involved. He

SHARIN SEIZO K.K.

LARGE CASINGS PLANT

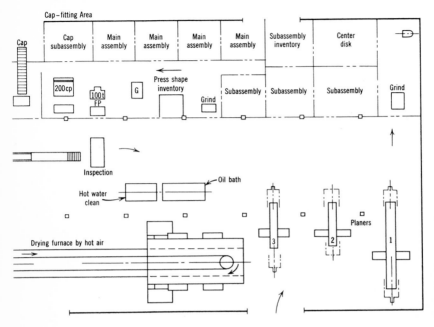

therefore planned to install semiautomatic welding equipment at a total cost of ¥28 million, including the electric lines needed to supply current for the building.

The new plant would contain about 80 workers and would be operated on about a 45-second cycle. Meanwhile, the large casings would be moved into Building 8, which had an area of nearly 1,000 square meters and would be operated on about a 70-second cycle. Since the large casings did not need to be machined on the lathes or have small parts attached to them, less machinery would be needed; the existing paint booth could be used, and new types of special conveyors would not be needed. The new layout of the large casing plant is shown in Exhibit 15.

Approximately 60 per cent of the workers were permanent employees, earning an average of ¥48,200 per month and 40 per cent were temporary, earning an average of ¥12,500 per month.